W9-BUB-510

Advance praise for *Head First EJB*™

"Until now, I could not have imagined a person smiling while studying an IT book!
Using Head First EJB materials, I got a great score (91%) and set a world record as
the youngest SCBCD, 14 years."

> — **Afsah Shafquat**
> **(world's youngest Sun Certified Business Component Developer)**

"This is the first EJB book that made milk come out my nose."

> — **Alan Peterson, SCBCD Development Team**

"Finally... an EJB book that teaches you everything you need to know, and keeps you
laughing while doing it."

> — **Kenneth Saks, EJB Container Implementation Lead**
> **Java Software Group, Sun Microsystems**

"This stuff is so good I want to staple the pages to my body."

> — **Kimberly Bobrow, Java Course Development**
> **Sun Microsystems**
> (Daughter of Danny Bobrow, inventor of the pull-down menu.)

Praise for the Head First approach and *Head First Java*™

"This stuff is so fricking good it makes me wanna WEEP! I'm stunned."

> — **Floyd Jones, BEA Systems**

"Kathy Sierra and Bert Bates' Head First Java transforms the printed page into the closest thing
to a GUI you've ever seen. In a wry, hip manner, the authors make learning Java an engaging
'what are they gonna do next' experience."

> — **Warren Keuffel, Software Development Magazine (September 2003)**

"...the only way to decide the worth of a tutorial is to decide how well it teaches. Head First Java
excels at teaching. OK, I thought it was silly... then I realized that I was thoroughly learning the
topics as I went through the book."

"The style of Head First Java made learning, well, easier."

> — **slashdot (honestpuck's review)**

Praise for the *Head First* approach

"Java technology is everywhere—in mobile phones, cars, cameras, printers, games, PDAs, ATMs, smart cards, gas pumps, sports stadiums, medical devices, Web cams, servers, you name it. If you develop software and haven't learned Java, it's definitely time to dive in—Head First."

> — **Scott McNealy, Sun Microsystems Chairman, President and CEO**

"This is unlike any Java book you've ever read—and we mean ever. It's jokey, funny, occasionally irritating, entertaining, and original. It is (and this is as important as the virtues just listed) educational in the best sense of the word... It works and even the Java pro is likely to look at the familiar from a new angle with this book... here at TechBookReport we can't want to see the next book in the Head Start (sic) series."

> — **TechBookReport** [note from marketing: so let me get this straight... we can get people to remember the most obscure technical facts, but we can't get the media to remember the freakin' name of the book???]

"O'Reilly has just released the BEST Java book ever! ... it is designed to really get you to learn... the book is fun, interesting, and hard to put down... if you need to learn Java, then I can say without reservation that this book is a must."

> — **Paul Wren, Lunch with George (Java/C/C++ User Group)**

"An easy and fun read and an excellent introduction into Java... the humorous undertones of the book constantly made me remember that Java is not difficult to master. Excellent book. ... I would definitely recommend this book to anyone interested in learning Java."

> — **Hampton Roads Oracle Users Group**

"Warning: This isn't your father's Java manual. Head First Java is the first, best, possibly the only Java textbook with a real sense of humor. Beyond the engaging style that drags you forward from know-nothing into exalted Java warrior status, Head First Java covers a huge amount of practical matters that other texts leave as the dreaded "exercise for the reader..." It's clever, wry, hip and practical—there aren't a lot of textbooks that can make that claim and live up to it while also teaching you about object serialization and network launch protocols. Check it out: it's a fab, funny, fun way to learn Java from the grounds up."

> — **Dr. Dan Russell, Director of User Sciences and Experience Research**
> **IBM Almaden Research Center**
> **(and teaches Artificial Intelligence at Stanford University)**

"It's fast, irreverent, fun, and engaging. Be careful—you might actually learn something!"

> — **Ken Arnold, former Senior Engineer at Sun Microsystems**
> **Co-author (with James Gosling, creator of Java), "The Java Programming Language"**

"If you want to *learn* Java, look no further: welcome to the first GUI-based technical book! This perfectly-executed, ground-breaking format delivers three benefits other Java texts simply can't: 1) the pictures cement the concepts so you learn it all the first time through; 2) the combining of glyphs, artwork, code examples, and accompanying text are remarkably synergistic making the most advanced concepts "childs play"; 3) should you want to revisit a particular concept or detail all you have to do is to scan the pictures as you quickly flip through the pages!"

"Prepare yourself for a truly remarkable ride through Java land."

> — **Neil R. Bauman, Captain & CEO,**
> **Geek Cruises (www.GeekCruises.com)**

"'Hey I can understand this stuff now.' That's a recurring thought when someone like me reads this book. After trying to get into other Java books with marginal success, I recognized that this book doesn't just spout data at me, it truly tries to get useful information to stick to my brain..."

> — **Martin Turnley, Utah Java Users Group**

"If anyone in the world is familiar with the concept of 'Head First,' it would be me. This book is so good, I'd marry it on TV!"

> — **Rick Rockwell, Comedian**
> **The original FOX Television "Who Wants to Marry a Millionaire" groom**

"Head First Java is like Monty Python meets the gang of four... the text is broken up so well by puzzles and stories, quizzes and examples, that you cover ground like no computer book before."

> — **Douglas Rowe, Columbia Java Users Group**

"Just a fabulous method of teaching. I have savored every page and have done my own personal notations in addition to yours. My Dog Pally likes it too. Here she is reading it..."

> — **James Tadeo, owner of Pally**
> **(Pally is available for contract Java development)**

Other Java books from O'Reilly

Ant: The Definitive Guide™
Building Java™ Enterprise Applications Volume I: Architecture
Database Programming with JDBC™ and Java™
Developing Java Beans™
Enterprise JavaBeans™
Head First Java™
J2ME™ in a Nutshell
Java™ & XML Data Binding
Java™ & XML
Java™ 2D Graphics
Java™ and SOAP
Java™ and XSLT
Java™ Cookbook
Java™ Cryptography
Java™ Data Objects
Java™ Database Best Practices
Java™ Distributed Computing
Java™ Enterprise Best Practices
Java™ Enterprise in a Nutshell
Java™ Examples in a Nutshell
Java™ Extreme Programming Cookbook
Java™ Foundation Classes in a Nutshell
Java™ I/O
Java™ in a Nutshell
Java™ Management Extensions
Java™ Message Service
Java™ Network Programming
Java™ NIO
Java™ Performance Tuning, 2nd Edition
Java™ Programming with Oracle JDBC
Java™ RMI
Java™ Security
Java Servlet™ Programming
Java™ Swing
Java™ Web Services
JavaServer Pages™
JDBC™ Pocket Reference
JXTA™ in a Nutshell
Learning Java™
Learning Wireless Java™
Mac OS X for Java™ Geeks
NetBeans™: The Definitive Guide
Programming Jakarta Struts

Be watching for more books in the Head First series!

Head First EJB™

Wouldn't it be dreamy if there was an EJB book that was more stimulating than deleting spam from your inbox? It's probably just a fantasy...

Kathy Sierra
Bert Bates

Beijing · Cambridge · Köln · Paris · Sebastopol · Taipei · Tokyo

Head First EJB™

by Kathy Sierra and Bert Bates

Copyright © 2003 O'Reilly & Associates, Inc. All rights reserved.

Printed in the United States of America.

Published by O'Reilly & Associates, Inc., 1005 Gravenstein Highway North, Sebastopol, CA 95472.

O'Reilly & Associates books may be purchased for educational, business, or sales promotional use. Online editions are also available for most titles (safari.oreilly.com). For more information, contact our corporate/institutional sales department: (800) 998-9938 or corporate@oreilly.com.

Editor:	Mike Loukides
Cover Designer:	Edie Freedman
Interior Decorators:	Kathy Sierra and Bert Bates
Anthropomorphizer:	Bert Bates
Bean Wrangler:	Kathy Sierra
Printing History:	

October 2003: First Edition.

In other words, if you use anything in *Head First EJB™* to, say, run a nuclear power plant or air traffic control system, you're on your own.

And although some people have been able to pass the exam simply by placing this book under their pillow each night for three consecutive weeks, we generally don't recommend it. Most people find it helpful to actually read the book or at least look at the pictures.

ISBN: 0-596-00571-7

ISBN13: 978-0-596-00571-9

To Sun's EJB 2.0 team.

For making such a powerful industry standard for enterprise middle-tier component-based development.

And for making sure it was complex enough that people would need a book to learn it.

Perpetrators of the Head First series (and this book)

Kathy Sierra

Bert Bates

Kathy has been interested in learning theory since her days as a game designer (she wrote games for Virgin, MGM, and Amblin'). She developed much of the Head First format while teaching New Media Authoring for UCLA Extension's Entertainment Studies program. More recently, she's been a master trainer for Sun Microsystems, teaching Sun's Java instructors how to teach the latest Java technologies, and developing several of Sun's certification exams, including the SCBCD. Together with Bert Bates, she has been actively using the Head First concepts to teach throusands of developers. She is the founder of one of the largest Java community websites in the world, javaranch.com, which won a 2003 Software Development magazine Productivity Award. You can also catch her teaching Java certification classes on the Java Jam Geek Cruise (geekcruises.com).

She recently moved from California to Boulder, Colorado, where she's had to learn new words like, "ice scraper" and "fleece", but at least there's skiing. She likes to run, ride horses, and take the scenic route. In her non-existent spare time, Bert's trying to teach her to play go (she's *awful*).

A famous person once referred to her as "cogent". She's still trying to figure out if he meant that in a *good* way. If you know, or you have any other comments, write to her at kathy@wickedlysmart.com.

Bert is a software developer and architect, but a decade-long stint in artificial intelligence drove his interest in learning theory and technology-based training. He's been teaching programming to clients ever since. Recently, he's been a member of the development team for several of Sun's Java Certification exams, including the new SCBCD.

He spent the first decade of his software career travelling the world to help broadcast clients like Radio New Zealand, the Weather Channel, and the Arts & Entertainment Network (A & E). One of his all-time favorite projects was building a full rail system simulation for Union Pacific Railroad.

Bert is a long-time, hopelessly addicted *go* player, and has been working on a *go* program for way too long. Java may finally be a language expressive enough for him to finish the project. He's a fair guitar player [*note from Kathy: he's way better than fair*], and is now trying his hand at banjo.

His beloved border collie died the day this book was finished. Thank-you Aiko, for sticking around long enough to help us finish. We'll miss you.

Write to him at terrapin@wickedlysmart.com.

Table of Contents (summary)

Table of Contents (the real thing)

i Intro

Your brain on EJB. Here *you* are trying to *learn* something, while here your *brain* is doing you a favor by making sure the learning doesn't *stick*. Your brain's thinking, "Better leave room for more important things, like which wild animals to avoid and whether naked snowboarding is a bad idea." So how *do* you trick your brain into thinking that your life depends on knowing EJB?

1 Welcome to EJB

Enterprise JavaBeans are easy. Well, at least when you compare EJB to what you'd have to do to write your own scalable, transactional, secure, persistent, concurrent enterprise component server. In this chapter, we'll develop, deploy, and run an EJB application, and then dive into the details. Before we're done, we'll look at the use, benefits, and characteristics of EJB, and we'll look (briefly) at how EJB containers work.

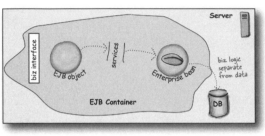

2 EJB Architecture

EJB is about infrastructure. Your components are the building blocks. With EJB, you can build big applications. The kind of applications that could run everything from the Victoria's Secret back-end to document-handling systems at CERN. But an architecture with this much flexibility, power, and scalability isn't simple. It all begins with a distributed programming model...

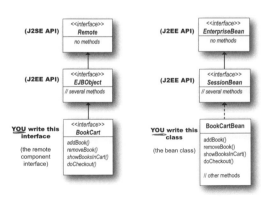

3 Exposing Yourself

You can't keep your bean private. Clients need to see what you've got. (Except for message-driven beans, which don't *have* a client view). The Advice Bean exposes the getAdvice() method in its Component interface—the place where you declare business methods. But that's not *all* the client sees. Remember, the Advice interface extends EJBObject, an interface with methods of its *own*. Methods the client can see. Methods the client can *call*. And it works the same way with the Home interface.

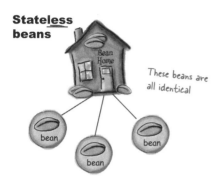

Stateless beans

These beans are all identical

For stateless session beans from the same home, isIdentical() always returns *true*, even for different beans.

4 Being a Session Bean

Session beans are created and removed. If you're lucky, you're a state*less* bean. Because the life of a state*ful* bean is tied to the whims of a heartless client. Stateful beans are created at the client's insistence, and live and die *only* to serve that one client. But ahhhh, the life of a stateless bean is ***fabulous!*** Pools, those little umbrella drinks, and no boredom since you get to meet so many different clients.

For me? This is such a special moment! Once in a lifetime...

5 Entities are Persistent

Entity beans persist. Entity beans exist. Entity beans *are*. They are object representations of something in an **underlying persistent store**. (Think: **database,** because most entity beans represent something from a relational database.) If you have a Customer entity bean, then one bean might represent the entity Tyler Durden, ID #343, while another is the entity Donny Darko, ID #42. Three beans, representing three real *entities*. An entity bean is simply a *realization* of something that already exists.

If you've got any last words, you better do it in your ejbRemove()...

No, Please, No! I'll give you whatever you want, just don't call remove()!

6 Being an Entity Bean

Entity beans are actors. As long as they're alive, they're either in the pool or they're *being* somebody. Somebody from the underlying persistent store (an entity from the database). When a bean is playing a part, the bean and the underlying entity have to stay in sync. Imagine the horror if the bean is pretending to be, say, Audrey Leone, and someone lowers Audrey's credit limit in the database... *but forgets to tell the bean.*

If I'm a bean I say to a method, "Don't call me, call my bodyguard, and here's his contact information..."

Instead of:
```
doStuff(this);
```

bean

EJB object

Use:
```
doStuff(myContext.getEJBObject());
```

7 When Beans Relate

Entity beans need relationships. An Order needs a Customer. A LineItem needs an Order. An Order needs LineItems. Entity beans can have container-managed relationships (CMR) and the Container takes care of virtually *everything*. Make a new LineItem that's related to an Order? If you ask the Customer to show you his Orders, you'll see the new LineItem. Best of all, you can use EJB-QL to write *portable* queries.

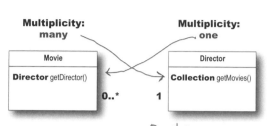

Multiplicity: many — **Multiplicity: one**

Movie
Director getDirector()

Director
Collection getMovies()

0..*   1

Each Movie has one Director.
A Director has many Movies.

8 Getting the Message

It's fun to receive messages. Not as much fun as, say, getting that eBay package with the genuine Smurf™ lamp, but fun and *efficient* nonetheless. Imagine if you sent your order to eBay, and you couldn't leave your house until the package was delivered. That's what it's like with Session and Entity beans. But with message-driven beans, the client can send a message and walk away.

<<interface>> *EJBContext*
~~getCallerPrincipal()~~
~~getEJBHome()~~
~~isCallerInRole(String s)~~
getRollbackOnly()
~~getEJBLocalHome()~~
getUserTransaction()
setRollbackOnly()

<<interface>> *MessageDrivenContext*
// this interface adds no // new methods

My life is sad. I have no home, I have no clients... I can use my context ONLY for transactions... Oh well, at least I get a pool.

9 The Atomic Age

Transactions protect you. With transactions, you can try something knowing that if anything goes wrong along the way, you can just pretend the whole thing didn't happen. Everything goes back to the way it was *before*. Transactions in EJB are a thing of beauty—you can deploy a bean with customized transaction behavior *without* touching the bean's source code! But you *can* write transaction code, if you need to.

Make it Stick

CMT beans run transactions unknown, while BMT beans use only their own.

OK, not our best work, we know. So why don't **you** try it. Memory devices can help, but they work much better when you create them yourself.

10 When Beans Go Bad

Expect the unexpected. Despite your best efforts, things can go wrong. Terribly, *tragically*, wrong. You need to protect yourself. You can't let your entire program collapse, just because one bean in the family throws an exception. ***The application must go on.*** You can't *prevent* tragedy, but you can *prepare* for it. You need to know what is and is *not* recoverable, and *who* is responsible when a problem occurs.

> Oh sh**! A system exception. Nothing I can do about it. There goes my stateful bean. I'll have to start over...

> Gotta love application exceptions... I can recover from this if I put in a different value for the argument to the create() method...

11 Protect Your Secrets

Keep your secrets. Security is about **authentication** and **authorization**. First, you have to prove your identity, and then we'll tell you what you're allowed to do. Security is easy in EJB, because you're only dealing with *authorization*. You decide *who* gets to call which *methods* on your beans. Except one problem... if you're a Bean Provider or App Assembler, you probably don't *know* who the users are going to be!

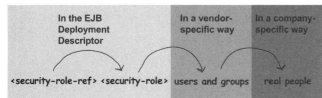

12 The Joy of Deployment

You worked hard on that bean. You coded, you compiled, you tested. About a hundred zillion times. The *last* thing you want to touch is already-tested source code, just because something simple changed in the deployment configuration. And what if you don't even *have* the source code? EJB supports bean reuse through the customizable Deployment Descriptor and a bean's special *environment*.

The final Coffee Cram Mock Exam.

This is it. 70 questions. The tone, topics, and difficulty level are virtually identical to the *real* exam. *We know.*

Index

Intro

In this section, we answer the burning question: "So, why DID they put that in a programming book?"

Who is this book for?

If you can answer "yes" to *all* of these:

 Do you know Java? (You don't need to be a guru.)

 Do you want to learn, understand, and *remember* EJB, with a goal of passing the SCBCD exam and developing business components?

③ **Do you prefer stimulating dinner party conversation to dry, dull, technical lectures?**

this book is for you.

Who should probably back away from this book?

If you can answer "yes" to any *one* of these:

 Are you completely new to Java?
(You don't need to be advanced, but you should have some experience. If not, go get a copy of Head First Java, right now, today, and then come back and get this book.)

② **Are you a kick-butt Java developer looking for an EJB *reference* book?**

 Are you a J2EE veteran looking for ultra-advanced server techniques, server-specific how-to's, enterprise design patterns, and long, complex, robust real-world code?

④ **Are you afraid to try something different? Would you rather have a root canal than mix stripes with plaid? Do you believe that a technical book can't be serious if beans are anthropomorphized?**

this book is *not* for you.

[note from marketing: who took out the part about how this book is for anyone who can afford it? Why limit our target audience this way?]

We know what you're thinking.

"How can *this* be a serious programming book?"

"What's with all the graphics?"

"Can I actually *learn* it this way?"

"Do I smell pizza?"

And we know what your *brain* is thinking.

Your brain craves novelty. It's always searching, scanning, *waiting* for something unusual. It was built that way, and it helps you stay alive.

Today, you're less likely to be a tiger snack. But your brain's still looking. You just never know.

So what does your brain do with all the routine, ordinary, normal things you encounter? Everything it *can* to stop them from interfering with the brain's *real* job—recording things that *matter*. It doesn't bother saving the boring things; they never make it past the "this is obviously not important" filter.

How does your brain *know* what's important? Suppose you're out for a day hike and a tiger jumps in front of you, what happens inside your head?

Neurons fire. Emotions crank up. *Chemicals surge.*

And that's how your brain knows...

This must be important! Don't forget it!

But imagine you're at home, or in a library. It's a safe, warm, tiger-free zone. You're studying. Getting ready for an exam. Or trying to learn some tough technical topic your boss thinks will take a week, ten days at the most.

Just one problem. Your brain's trying to do you a big favor. It's trying to make sure that this *obviously* non-important content doesn't clutter up scarce resources. Resources that are better spent storing the really *big* things. Like tigers. Like the danger of fire. Like how you should never again snowboard in shorts.

And there's no simple way to tell your brain, "Hey brain, thank you very much, but no matter how dull this book is, and how little I'm registering on the emotional richter scale right now, I really *do* want you to keep this stuff around."

Your brain thinks THIS is important.

Great. Only 637 more dull, dry, boring pages.

Your brain thinks THIS isn't worth saving.

We think of a "Head First" reader as a learner.

So what does it take to *learn* something? First, you have to *get* it, then make sure you don't *forget* it. It's not about pushing facts into your head. Based on the latest research in cognitive science, neurobiology, and educational psychology, *learning* takes a lot more than text on a page. We know what turns your brain on.

Some of the Head First learning principles:

Make it visual. Images are far more memorable than words alone, and make learning much more effective (Up to 89% improvement in recall and transfer studies). It also makes things more understandable. **Put the words within or near the graphics** they relate to, rather than on the bottom or on another page, and learners will be up to *twice* as likely to solve problems related to the content.

needs to call a method on the server

RMI remote service

doCalc()

return value

Use a conversational and personalized style. In recent studies, students performed up to 40% better on post-learning tests if the content spoke directly to the reader, using a first-person, conversational style rather than taking a formal tone. Tell stories instead of lecturing. Use casual language. Don't take yourself too seriously. Which would *you* pay more attention to: a stimulating dinner party companion, or a lecture?

It really sucks to be an abstract method. You don't have a body.

Get the learner to think more deeply. In other words, unless you actively flex your neurons, nothing much happens in your head. A reader has to be motivated, engaged, curious, and inspired to solve problems, draw conclusions, and generate new knowledge. And for that, you need challenges, exercises, and thought-provoking questions, and activities that involve both sides of the brain, and multiple senses.

`abstract void roam();`

No method body! End it with a semicolon.

Does it make sense to say Tub IS-A Bathroom? Bathroom IS-A Tub? Or is it a HAS-A relationship?

Get—and keep—the reader's attention. We've all had the "I really want to learn this but I can't stay awake past page one" experience. Your brain pays attention to things that are out of the ordinary, interesting, strange, eye-catching, unexpected. Learning a new, tough, technical topic doesn't have to be boring. Your brain will learn much more quickly if it's not.

Touch their emotions. We now know that your ability to remember something is largely dependent on its emotional content. You remember what you care about. You remember when you feel something. No we're not talking heart-wrenching stories about a boy and his dog. We're talking emotions like surprise, curiosity, fun, "what the...?" , and the feeling of "I Rule!" that comes when you solve a puzzle, learn something everybody else thinks is hard, or realize you know something that "I'm more technical than thou" Bob from engineering *doesn't*.

Metacognition: thinking about thinking

If you really want to learn, and you want to learn more quickly and more deeply, pay attention to how you pay attention. Think about how you think. Learn how you learn.

Most of us did not take courses on metacognition or learning theory when we were growing up. We were *expected* to learn, but rarely *taught* to learn.

But we assume that if you're holding this book, you want to learn EJB. And you probably don't want to spend a lot of time. And since you're going to take the exam, you need to *remember* what you read. And for that, you've got to understand it. To get the most from this book, or *any* book or learning experience, take responsibility for your brain. Your brain on *this* content.

The trick is to get your brain to see the new material you're learning as Really Important. Crucial to your well-being. As important as a tiger. Otherwise, you're in for a constant battle, with your brain doing its best to keep the new content from sticking.

I wonder how I can trick my brain into remembering this stuff...

So just how *DO* you get your brain to treat EJB like it's a hungry tiger?

There's the slow, tedious way, or the faster, more effective way. The slow way is about sheer repetition. You obviously know that you *are* able to learn and remember even the dullest of topics, if you keep pounding on the same thing. With enough repetition, your brain says, "This doesn't *feel* important to him, but he keeps looking at the same thing *over* and *over* and *over*, so I suppose it must be."

The faster way is to do **anything that increases brain activity,** especially different *types* of brain activity. The things on the previous page are a big part of the solution, and they're all things that have been proven to help your brain work in your favor. For example, studies show that putting words *within* the pictures they describe (as opposed to somewhere else in the page, like a caption or in the body text) causes your brain to try to makes sense of how the words and picture relate, and this causes more neurons to fire. More neurons firing = more chances for your brain to *get* that this is something worth paying attention to, and possibly recording.

A conversational style helps because people tend to pay more attention when they perceive that they're in a conversation, since they're expected to follow along and hold up their end. The amazing thing is, your brain doesn't necessarily *care* that the "conversation" is between you and a book! On the other hand, if the writing style is formal and dry, your brain perceives it the same way you experience being lectured to while sitting in a roomful of passive attendees. No need to stay awake.

But pictures and conversational style are just the beginning.

Here's what WE did:

We used *pictures*, because your brain is tuned for visuals, not text. As far as your brain's concerned, a picture really *is* worth 1024 words. And when text and pictures work together, we embedded the text *in* the pictures because your brain works more effectively when the text is *within* the thing the text refers to, as opposed to in a caption or buried in the text somewhere.

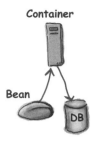

Container

Bean

DB

We used *repetition*, saying the same thing in different ways and with different media types, and *multiple senses*, to increase the chance that the content gets coded coded into more than one area of your brain.

BE the Container

We used concepts and pictures in **unexpected** ways because your brain is tuned for novelty, and we used pictures and ideas with at least *some emotional content*, because your brain is tuned to pay attention to the biochemistry of emotions. That which causes you to *feel* something is more likely to be remembered, even if that feeling is nothing more than a little **humor**, **surprise**, or **interest.**

We used a personalized, **conversational style**, because your brain is tuned to pay more attention when it believes you're in a conversation than if it thinks you're passively listening to a presentation. Your brain does this even when you're *reading*.

COFFEE CRAM

We included more than 40 **activities**, because your brain is tuned to learn and remember more when you **do** things than when you *read* about things. And we made the exercises challenging-yet-do-able, because that's what most *people* prefer.

We used **multiple learning styles**, because *you* might prefer step-by-step procedures, while someone else wants to understand the big picture first, while someone else just wants to see a code example. But regardless of your own learning preference, *everyone* benefits from seeing the same content represented in multiple ways.

BULLET POINTS

We include content for **both sides of your brain**, because the more of your brain you engage, the more likely you are to learn and remember, and the longer you can stay focused. Since working one side of the brain often means giving the other side a chance to rest, you can be more productive at learning for a longer period of time.

Overheard at THE TIKIBEAN LOUNGE

And we included **stories** and exercises that present **more than one point of view**, because your brain is tuned to learn more deeply when it's forced to make evaluations and judgements.

BRAIN POWER

We included **challenges**, with exercises, and by asking **questions** that don't always have a straight answer, because your brain is tuned to learn and remember when it has to *work* at something. Think about it—you can't get your *body* in shape just by *watching* people at the gym. But we did our best to make sure that when you're working hard, it's on the *right* things. That **you're not spending one extra dendrite** processing a hard-to-understand example, or parsing difficult, jargon-laden, or overly terse text.

We used **people**. In stories, examples, pictures, etc. because, well, because *you're* a person. And your brain pays more attention to *people* than it does to *things*.

We used an **80/20** approach. We assume that if you're going for a PhD in EJB, this won't be your only book. So we don't talk about *everything*. Just the stuff you'll actually *need*.

Here's what YOU can do to bend your brain into submission

So, we did our part. The rest is up to you. These tips are a starting point; Listen to your brain and figure out what works for you and what doesn't. Try new things.

cut this out and stick it on your refridgerator.

1. **Slow down. The more you understand, the less you have to memorize.**

   Don't just *read*. Stop and think. When the book asks you a question, don't just skip to the answer. Imagine that someone really *is* asking the question. The more deeply you force your brain to think, the better chance you have of learning and remembering.

2. **Do the exercises. Write your own notes.**

   We put them in, but if we did them for you, that would be like having someone else do your workouts for you. And don't just *look* at the exercises. **Use a pencil.** There's plenty of evidence that physical activity *while* learning can increase the learning.

3. **Read the "There are No Dumb Questions"**

   That means all of them. They're not optional side-bars—*they're part of the core content!* Don't skip them.

4. **Don't do all your reading in one place.**

   Stand-up, stretch, move around, change chairs, change rooms. It'll help your brain *feel* something, and keeps your learning from being too connected to a particular place. Remember, you won't be taking the exam in your bedroom.

5. **Make this the last thing you read before bed. Or at least the last *challenging* thing.**

   Part of the learning (especially the transfer to long-term memory) happens *after* you put the book down. Your brain needs time on its own, to do more processing. If you put in something new during that processing-time, some of what you just learned will be lost.

6. **Drink water. Lots of it.**

   Your brain works best in a nice bath of fluid. Dehydration (which can happen before you ever feel thirsty) decreases cognitive function. Beer, or something stronger, is called for when you pass the exam.

7. **Talk about it. Out loud.**

   Speaking activates a different part of the brain. If you're trying to understand something, or increase your chance of remembering it later, say it out loud. Better still, try to explain it out loud to someone else. You'll learn more quickly, and you might uncover ideas you hadn't known were there when you were reading about it.

8. **Listen to your brain.**

   Pay attention to whether your brain is getting overloaded. If you find yourself starting to skim the surface or forget what you just read, it's time for a break. Once you go past a certain point, you won't learn faster by trying to shove more in, and you might even hurt the process.

9. **Feel something!**

   Your brain needs to know that this *matters*. Get involved with the stories. Make up your own captions for the photos. Groaning over a bad joke is *still* better than feeling nothing at all.

10. **Take the final Coffee Cram Mock Exam only AFTER you finish the book.**

    If you take it too soon, you won't get a clear picture of how ready you are for the exam. Wait until you think you're close to ready, then take the exam giving yourself exactly two hours. If you take it too soon, then when you go back to take it again, you'll remember some of it.

What you need for this book:

Besides your brain and a pencil, **you need Java, J2EE and a computer**.

You do *not* need any other development tool, such as an Integrated Development Environment (IDE). We strongly recommend that you *not* use anything but a basic editor until you complete this book. A bean-aware IDE can protect you from some of the details that really matter (and that you'll be tested on), so you're much better off developing the bean code completely by hand. Once you really understand what's happening, you can move to a tool that automates some of the bean-creation steps. We *do* recommend that you use a tool to build the XML deployment descriptor. You can use the j2EE Reference Implementation *deploytool*, or xDoclet.

GETTING J2EE

- If you don't already have a 1.3 or greater **J2SE SDK,** you need it. Although J2EE is *not* guaranteed to work with J2SE version 1.4 or beyond, you shouldn't have problems with J2SE 1.4. But the spec guarantees ONLY J2SE 1.3 support. (You might be tested on that!)

- If you don't already have an EJB 2.0-compliant server, go to java.sun.com and download **J2EE 1.3.** It includes the JAR file with the entire J2EE API (including the classes you'll need for EJB development), and a practice Reference Implementation (RI) server.
  Do *not* get the new J2EE 1.4! The exam is based on J2EE 1.3, because 1.4 is too early in its life to be in widespread use in business. We expect that very few enterprise systems will migrate to J2EE 1.4 until late 2004 at the earliest. When J2EE 1.4 support hits critical mass, the exam will be upgraded to the new spec.

- The J2EE SDK does *not* include the **API documentation,** and you need it. Go back to java.sun.com and get the J2EE API docs. You can also access the API docs online, without downloading them, but that's a pain.

- Once you've downloaded and unpacked/zipped/whatever (depends on which version and for which OS), you need to add a few environment variables, if you're going to use the J2EE RI as your practice server. The download includes instructions, but expect to modify your PATH and CLASSPATH, and add new entries for J2EE_HOME and JAVA_HOME.

- If you're going to take the exam, you're gonna need the spec. Download the EJB 2.0 (not 2.1!) specification and keep it handy. There is nothing on the exam that isn't mentioned in the spec. Most of our mock exam answers reference specific pages in the spec, where you can go to learn more about why you might have missed that question.

Note: much of the code from this book is available at wickedlysmart.com

Java 2 *Standard* Edition 1.3

Java 2 *Enterprise* Edition 1.3
(which includes EJB 2.0)

Last-minute things you need to know:

This is a learning experience, not a reference book. We deliberately stripped out everything that might get in the way of *learning* whatever it is we're working on at that point in the book. And the first time through, you need to begin at the beginning, because the book makes assumptions about what you've already seen and learned.

We use a simpler, modified faux-UML

We use simple UML-*like* diagrams.

Although there's a good chance you already know UML, it's not covered on the exam, and it's not a prerequisite for the book. So you won't have to worry about learning EJB *and* UML at the same time.

```
┌─────────────────────────┐
│        Director         │
├─────────────────────────┤
│ getMovies               │
│ getOscars()             │
│ getKevinBaconDegrees()  │
└─────────────────────────┘
```

We don't cover every single picky detail from the spec.

The exam *is* pretty detailed, though, and so are we. But if there's a detail in the spec that's not covered in the exam, we don't talk about it unless it's important to most component developers. What you need to know to begin developing EJB components, and what you need to pass the exam, overlap about 95%. We cover a few things not on the exam, but we point them out so you don't have to try to memorize them. And there is a very tiny percentage of details that might show up on the exam, but that we haven't covered in detail. We created the *real* exam, so we know where you should focus your energy! If there's a chance that this one picky detail might be on one question on the exam, but the effort to learn it isn't really worth it, we might skip it, or cover it only very lightly, or only in a mock exam question.

The activities are not optional.

This is a learning experience, not a to-be-read book. The exercises and activities are not add-ons; they're part of the core content of the book. Some of them are there to help with memory, some for understanding, some to help you apply what you've learned. If you're serious about learning and remembering, and you want to pass the exam on the first try, *don't skip anything*.

The redundancy is intentional and important.

One thing that's distinctly different in a Head First book is that *we want you to really really really get it*. And we want you to finish the book remembering what you've learned. Most information or reference books don't necessarily have retention and recall as a goal, but in this book you'll see some of the same concepts come up more than once. Brain research shows that it usually takes a minimum of three "repeated trials" to get the content to move into your long-term memory storage.

The code examples are as lean as possible

It's frustrating to wade through 200 lines of code looking for the two lines you need to understand. Most examples in this book are shown within the smallest possible context, so that the part you're trying to learn is clear and simple. Don't expect the code to be robust, or even complete. That's *your* assignment for after you finish the book. The book examples are written specifically for *learning*, and aren't always fully-functional. We have more detailed code samples on wickedlysmart.com.

About the SCBCD exam

Do I first have to pass the SCJP?

Yep. The Business Component Developer exam, the Web Component Developer exam, and the Developer exam all require you to be a Sun Certified Java Programmer.

How many questions?

You'll get 70 questions when you take the exam. Not everyone gets the same 70 questions; there are many different versions of the exam. But everyone gets the same degree of difficulty, and the same balance of topics. On the real exam, expect to see at least one question from each exam objective, and there are a few objectives where you'll get *more* than one question.

How much time do I get to complete the exam?

You get two hours (120 minutes). Most people don't find this to be a problem, because these questions don't lend themselves to long, complicated, puzzles. Most questions are very short multiple-choice, and you either know the answer or you don't.

What are the questions like?

They are almost exactly like our mock exam questions, with one big difference—the *real* exam tells you how many answers are correct, where we do not. You will see a handful of drag-and-drop questions, however, that we can't do here. But drag-and-drop questions are just the interactive way of matching one thing to another.

How many do I have to answer correctly?

You must get 45 questions right (64%) to pass the exam. When you finish answering all of the questions, hold your mouse cursor over the done button until you have the courage to click it. Because in, like, six nanoseconds, you'll know whether you passed (of course you will.)

Why don't the mock exams in the book tell you how many to choose?

We want our exams to be just a little more difficult than the real exam, to give you the most realistic picture of whether you're ready to take the exam. People tend to get higher scores on book mock exams because they retake the same test more than once, and we don't want you to get a false picture of your readiness to take the exam.

What do I get after I take the exam?

Before you leave the testing center, be sure to get your exam report. It shows a summary of your score in each major area, and whether you passed or failed. *Keep this!* It's your initial proof that you've been certified. A few weeks after the test, you'll get a little package from Sun Educational Services that includes your *real* printed certificate, a congratulations letter from Sun, and a lovely lapel pin that says Sun Certified Business Component Developer in a font so incredibly small that you could pretty much claim to be certified in anything you like, and nobody could read it to tell the difference. It does not include the alcohol you'll be wanting after you pass the exam.

How much does it cost, and how do I register?

The exam costs US $150. Which is why you need this book... to make sure you pass the first time. You register through Sun Educational Services, by giving them your credit card number (so the employees can skip off to Mexico with it). In exchange, you'll get a voucher number, that you'll use to schedule an appointment at a Prometric Testing Center nearest you.

To get the details online and buy an exam voucher, start at: http://suned.sun.com. If you're in the US, go to http://suned.sun.com/US/certification. If you're not in the US, you can select a country from the main page.

What's the exam software like?

It's dead simple to use—you get a question, and you answer it. If you don't want to answer it, you can skip it and come back to it later. If you do answer it, but aren't sure, and you want to come back to it if you have more time, you can "mark" a question. Once you're done, you'll see a screen that shows all of the questions you haven't answered, or have marked, so that you can go back to them.

At the very beginning of the exam you'll get a short tutorial on how to use the software, where you get a little practice test (not on EJB). The time you spend in the tutorial does not count as time spent on the EJB exam. The clock doesn't start until you've finished the exam software tutorial and you're ready to begin.

Where can I find a study group, and how long will it take to prepare?

The best online discussion group for this exam just happens to be the one that the authors moderate! (Gosh, what are the odds?) Stop by javaranch.com and go to the Big Moose Saloon (that's where all the discussion forums are). You can't miss it. There will always be *someone* there to answer your questions, including *us*. Javaranch is the friendliest Java community on the internet, so you're welcome no matter what level you're at with Java. If you still need to take the SCJP, we'll help you with that one too.

How long it takes you to get ready for the exam depends a lot on how much EJB experience you've had. If you're new to EJB, you might need anywhere from three to ten weeks, depending on how much time you can devote to it each day.

Why is the exam based on J2EE 1.3 instead of the new 1.4?

Sun's exams are meant to certify those candidates with a minimum of six months experience with the technology. Does that mean the SCBCD should be updated once J2EE 1.4 has been out for six months? No. Because companies aren't going to migrate their servers to 1.4 on the day it's released. The exam won't be upgraded for J2EE 1.4 until *after* enough companies are using it in the industry. It won't do you—or a potential employer—any good for you to walk in and say, "Hey, I'm certified on this technology that's the latest and greatest and, well, I realize that nobody is really using it yet but..." Sun's exams are not just about, "How much do you know?", but "How much can you *apply*?" These are considered professional exams, and many of the questions are written in such a way to test whether you understand the *implications* of the things that you know about how EJB works.

Technical Reviewers

This is where authors usually say something like, "Credit goes to all, but mistakes are the sole reponsibility of the author...". We (the authors) don't buy into that. See the two people on this page? If you find technical problems, there's a good chance it's *their* fault.

(*Just kidding*. Much as we'd like to shift the blame, these folks did a spectacular job, and if there's something wrong, it's because we weren't paying enough attention to what they had to say.)

Dan Johnsson

Gustavo Torreti
(morpheus)

John Zoetebier

Jack O'Bryan

Valentin Crettaz

Dave Cronin

Suddhasatwa Ghosh

Olav Maassen

The large number of acknowledgements is because we're testing the theory that everyone mentioned in a book acknowledgement will buy at least one copy, probably more, what with relatives and everything. If you'd like to be in the acknowledgement of our *next* book, and you have a large family, write to us.

Other people to b̶l̶a̶m̶e: ^credit

At O'Reilly:

Our biggest thanks to **Mike Loukides** at O'Reilly, for starting it all, and helping to shape the Head First concept into a series. We continue to be thrilled to have an editor who is a Real Java Guy. And a big thanks to the driving force behind Head First, **Tim O'Reilly**. Lucky for us, he's always thinking about the future, and rather enjoys being a disruptive influence.

A huge thank-you to the clever **Kyle Hart** for figuring out how Head First fits into the world, and for launching the series. And to Allen Noren for a great job on the O'Reilly Head First pages. Finally, to **Edie Freedman** for designing the Head First cover look and feel. With Head First, you *can* judge the book by its cover.

Our intrepid beta testers and reviewers:

Our top honors and thanks go to **John Zoetebier** and **Gustavo Torreti (aka "Morpheus")**. You are amazing and energetic and smart (and picky, picky, picky) and we can't thank you enough. Gus, you always made us smile with each and every message you sent.

Everyone else pictured on these two pages contributed to the book in a major way. Not pictured, but also a big help with technical review of the mock exams: Pradeep Bhat, Herry Alexander John, Andrew Monkhouse, Ashish Sarin, Aleksander Pacoa, Jai Singh, Bailey Liao.

And as always, thanks especially to the javaranch Trail Boss, **Paul Wheaton**.

Solveig Haugland
(datingdesignpatterns.com)

Evan Hedges

Skyler Safford

Chin Boon

Alan Peterson

Siva Sundaram

Bryan Basham

Jim Bedenbaugh

still more acknowledgements

*The large number of acknowledgements is because we're testing the theory that everyone mentioned in a book acknowledgement will buy at least one copy, probably more, what with relatives and everything. If you'd like to be in the acknowledgement of our *next* book, and you have a large family, write to us.

1 Intro to EJB

✳ Welcome to EJB ✳

*You're gonna love EJB! And boy won't Jim and Betty be envious when **your** enterprise back-end is bigger than theirs... you might even get that promotion!*

Enterprise JavaBeans are easy. Well, at least when you compare EJB to what you'd have to do to write your own scalable, transactional, secure, concurrent enterprise server. In this chapter, we'll develop, deploy, and run an EJB application, before diving into the details. Before we're done, we'll look at the use, benefits, and characteristics of EJB, and we'll look (briefly) at how EJB containers work. We'll take a high-level look at the architecture of EJB and learn about the three bean types. The more you *understand* from this chapter, the less you'll have to *memorize* later, so don't skip it. (If you're an EJB expert, you can probably get away with just a quick skim.)

Enterprise Javabeans Overview

Official:	*What it really means:*
1.1 Identify the use, benefits, and characteristics of Enterprise Javabeans technology, for version 2.0 of the EJB specification.	You need to know how EJB works overall, what it's good for, what it provides, and what it *doesn't* provide.
	You need to understand the overall architecture of EJB and how that architecture supports the features of EJB. For example, you need to know that EJB supports transactions, security, and concurrency, but it does not guarantee load-balancing, fail-over, or clustering. You need to know that EJB supports three bean types: session, entity, and message-driven, and that session beans can be stateless or stateful.

What is EJB all about?

Component-based development

With enterprise javabeans, you can develop building blocks—*EJB components*—that you or someone else can assemble and reassemble into different applications. For example, you might create a Customer bean (*bean* is another word for *component*) that represents a customer in a database. You can use that Customer bean in an accounting program, an e-commerce shopping cart system, a tech support application, or virtually any other application that might need to represent a customer. In fact, with some beans, the bean developer and the application assembler might not work for the same company or have any knowledge of one another.

If you're a bean developer, you might build an Order bean, or a Payroll bean, or a ShoppingCart bean that developers in some unrelated company can buy and use to construct their own custom applications.

One beauty of component-based development is that you take code reuse to a whole new level. Instead of reusing Java *classes*, you get to reuse a bigger chunk of functionality. Often, you can modify the way a bean works *without ever touching its Java code!* You'll learn in this chapter that when you deploy a bean into a server, you can configure and customize the bean *declaratively*—through an XML-based *deployment descriptor*—to change the way the bean behaves at runtime.

> **With component-based development, you take code reuse to a whole new level. With OO development, you reuse classes, but with components, you reuse a bigger chunk of functionality, and you can customize them without touching code!**

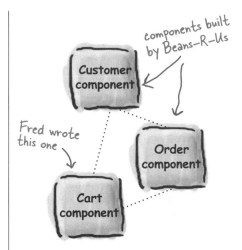

Application A: online shopping

Fred assembles an online shopping application using two components he bought from Beans-R-Us, plus a third component Fred developed at his company.

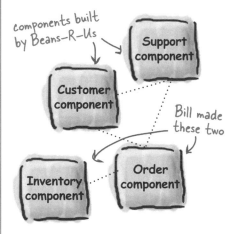

Application B: technical support

Bill assembles a technical support app using two components he bought from Beans-R-Us, plus two components he developed himself.

What does EJB really give me?

EJB lets you focus on the business logic for <u>your</u> business, and leave the underlying services (transactions, networking, security, etc.) to the EJB server vendor.

Imagine you work for Guitar Land, a company that sells musician's gear online. You have better things to do than work 90 hours a week, so where would *you* want to spend your time? Wouldn't you rather concentrate on how Guitar Land does business online, as opposed to writing your own secure, networked, transaction management server? Why not work on what you know best (business logic for your particular business), and leave the heavy lifting (i.e. the big infrastructure services you get from the server) to someone else?

The EJB model is to let everyone do what they do best—the server vendors concentrate on the infrastructure that most enterprise applications need, while the business developers concentrate on their own business logic.

EJB let's you customize and configure reusable components at deploy-time, without touching the source code!

You can change the way a bean uses the underlying services simply by tweaking an XMl document at deploy-time. For example, you can completely define the security access control for a bean's methods within XML (declaratively) rather than within the bean's source code (programmatically). And you can customize the way a bean's methods run in transactions, all within the deployment descriptor, without having to hard-code in transaction boundaries and behaviors. That just rocks.

EJB servers give you a bunch of services, so that you don't have to write them yourself:

* *Transaction management*

* *Security*

* *Concurrency*

* *Networking*

* *Resource management*

* *Persistence*

* *Messaging*

* *Deploy-time customization*

Somebody already wrote and tested all this stuff, so you don't have to.

you →

vendor ←

No more vendor lock-in!

Enterprise beans are portable— not just to different *JVM's*, but to different EJB *servers.*

One of the reasons we all love Java is its portability across multiple platforms. The whole write-once-run-anywhere (WORA) thing.

EJB takes portability to a new level, instead of write-once-*run*-anywhere, it's write-once-*deploy*-anywhere (WODA). Just as WORA frees you from being forced to work on a single OS, WODA frees you from being at the mercy of your application server vendor. And then of course there's YODA, but we digress.

In the old days, each application server vendor had its own proprietary API. You learn it, work with it, and finally get your enterprise apps up and running. And then guess what? You need a new feature. And then guess what? Your vendor says, "We're considering that for Q3... of next year". Now what? Like a drug dealer, they've hooked you, and now it's just too painful to consider giving them up. Give them up for what? Another vendor and another proprietary API and more lock-in.

One of the crucial benefits of EJB is WODA. And now the vendors have to compete not just to sell you in the first place, but to *keep* you. Because as everybody knows, you can just pack up your beans and go elsewhere.

Instead of learning a new API for each app server, with EJB, I only learn ONE, and my components will work on *any* EJB server. Those vendors are gonna have to suck up to ME for a change...

there are no
Dumb Questions

Q: What's the difference between EJB and J2EE?

A: Both J2EE and EJB are specifications for a server. But EJB is actually a *subset* of J2EE. In other words, **a J2EE server must include an EJB container.** We've used the word *server* on these first pages, but technically, the thing that enterprise javabeans run in is called an EJB *container*. So, every J2EE server must include an EJB container (along with a Web container that can run servlets and JSPs).

This exam is about the EJB portion of J2EE, whereas the SCWCD exam (Sun Certified Web Component Developer) is about the Web portion of J2EE.

Later in this chapter, we'll get more into the details of how J2EE and EJB fit together.

For the rest of this book, we use the terms EJB server, container, and server interchangeably. If the difference between the terms matters, we'll make it clear.

Q: Can I use EJB components without an EJB-compliant app server?

A: Nope. EJB components can't live outside of an EJB container. They don't have a main method, and even if you add one to your bean class, the bean wouldn't be very useful on its own. Most of the methods in an enterprise bean are called by the container itself and have no meaning outside the server. Remember, the whole point of an EJB server is to give you all the big services (security, transactions, etc.), and without the server, you'd lose everything but your basic business logic. And if that business logic relies on the container (for example, calling methods on interfaces provided by the container), then even the business logic would fail.

Q: Can I design and write my code in such a way that most of the business logic is in a plain old Java class, and just have the bean call methods on that class? That way I could still reuse the business logic...

A: Yes, you can do that, and in fact a lot of designers write separate non-bean, reusable classes and then have the beans invoke methods on those classes. If your bean calls a method on a non-bean Java class, that method is still under the control of the container, so as far as the container is concerned, that non-bean method is just part of the bean's functionality.

Q: What's the difference between regular javabeans and *enterprise* javabeans?

A: Congratulations! You're the 3 millionth person to have asked that question.

The term "javabean" means a reusable component. Regular old *non-enterprise* beans (and *beans* is just a shorter form of *javabeans*), are reusable components that follow a naming convention that can be used by development tools.

By far, the most common type of javabean is any GUI component (like a Swing button or text field). Nearly all Java IDEs are javabean-compliant, so that if you're working in a visual layout tool you can click on a button and up pops a property sheet where you can set the color, size, font, etc. The tool *knows* which properties the bean has because the bean follows conventions for getters and setters.

But regular javabeans aren't just for GUI components—other Java technologies, including Jini and Servlets, can use javabean features.

Enterprise javabeans are also reusable components, but that's where the similarity ends. The 'bean' part of a *regular* javabean is used mostly at *development-time*, as a way to ease or speed up hooking one bean's events to another bean's methods, or setting property values (which often mean the same thing as *instance variable* values). A regular bean runs in a JVM, just like any other normal Java class. But the "bean" part of an *enterprise* bean kicks in at *runtime*, and an enterprise bean *must* be run under the control of an EJB container.

For the rest of the book, when we say bean, we mean *enterprise* bean.

How does it all work?

Your beans run under the control (and protection) of the EJB server.

The server steps into the middle of every method call from a client to a bean and inserts the "services" like security, transactions, and persistence.

Your beans live and run in the server, and the server does virtually everything to manage transactions, security, persistence, and even the life and death of your objects. And it does all this by stepping in each time a client makes a request (i.e. calls a business method on the bean). The server jumps in and starts asking questions like:

"Does this client have security clearance to call this method?" or

"Does this bean need to run as part of a larger transaction?" or

"Does this bean need to refresh itself with data from the database, before running that method for the client?"

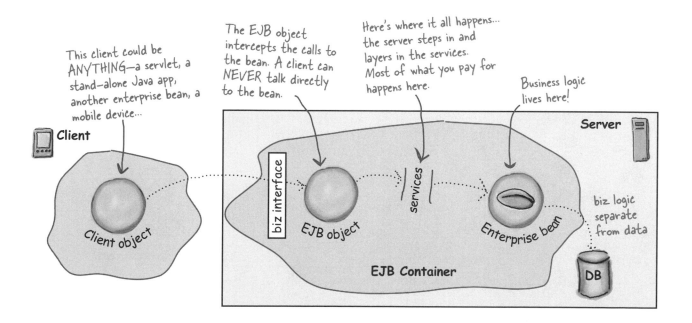

A ridiculously high-level view of EJB architecture

Behind the scenes...

Uh, yeah, put the Broker bean on the phone—I need to make a trade NOW.

Not so fast buddy. Nobody, but NOBODY, talks to the bean except the container. If you want the bean, you gotta go through me. Show me some ID, and I'll check with the container, and if it's OK, I'll pass on your request.

Hmmmm... let's see...he does seem to be on the approved list for calling makeTrade() on a Broker bean.

1 Client

2 EJBObject

3 Container

Sharpen your pencil

(1) Label the three parts in the diagram.

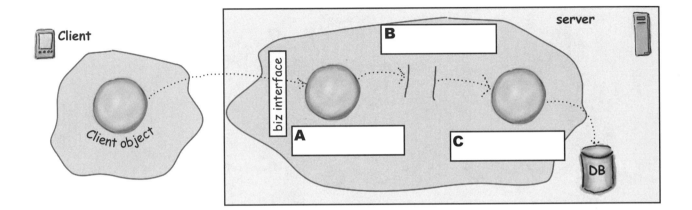

Client

Client object

biz interface

B

A

C

server

DB

(2) Describe (briefly) what each of the three things are responsible for, or how they behave.

A _____

_____

B _____

_____

C _____

_____

Beans come in three flavors

Entity

Use an entity bean to represent a *thing* in a persistent store. That almost always means something in a database, where an instance of an entity bean represents **a row in a table** (although if the database is normalized, the bean might be drawing from rows in multiple tables). A typical entity example is Customer, where one entity might represent Bo Olean (ID# 343) and another entity might represent Trixia Lin (ID# 870).

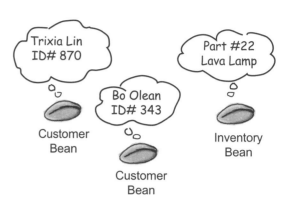

Message-driven

Use a message-driven bean only when you need a JMS consumer. In other words, a bean that **can listen for messages from a JMS messaging service**. Clients never call message-driven beans directly; in order to get a message-driven bean to do something, a client must send a message to a messaging service. That means a message-driven bean has no EJBObject because the server gets the client requests directly from a messaging service rather than as a call from the client to the bean. A typical message-driven bean might be a NewCustomerNotification subscriber.

Session

Use a session bean for... *everything else.* Almost any kind of back-end service can (and often *should*) begin with a session bean. Where an entity bean represents a *thing*, a session bean typically represents a *process*. To put it another way, when you think of *entity* beans, think *noun*, and when you think of *session* beans, think *verb*. A shopping session is a typical example of a session bean, while a credit card processing system might be another session bean.

Session beans can be stateless or stateful

We'll go over all this in detail in the Session Bean chapter. For now, you need to know that session beans can be marked (at deployment time) as either state*less* or state*ful*.

A stateful bean can remember conversational state between method calls, while a stateless bean won't remember anything about the client between method invocations.

The phrase "conversational state" really means "client-specific state", and a typical example is a shopping cart. It wouldn't be fun if you (the shopper) got a cart, put something in, but then when you go to put the second thing in, the first thing vanishes from the cart. Not too user-friendly. So, a good shopping cart will keep the client shopper state (i.e. the items in the cart) for as long as the shopping session is *alive*. (We'll explain what we mean by *alive* in the Session Bean chapter.)

Stateless beans simply forget about the client once the method call completes. So, stateless beans are for services that don't require a continued conversation between the client and the service. That doesn't mean the client won't keep calling methods on the stateless bean, but it does mean that the client can't depend on the bean remembering anything about the previous method calls.

Watch it!

Stateless beans CAN have state! (Just not client-specific state.)

Some people think "stateless" means "no state". A stateless bean can have instance variables like any other object; it just can't use them to maintain values specific to a particular client.

there are no Dumb Questions

Q: I've heard that only state*less* session beans are scalable, and that nobody should ever use state*ful* session beans. Is that true?

A: No, not completely. It *is* true that stateless session beans are generally *more* scalable than stateful session beans because of the way stateless beans are managed by the container. You'll see the reasons for this in the Session Bean chapter.

But... that doesn't mean you should never use stateful beans. You *should* consider stateful beans when you need conversational state, and when the alternatives for saving that state (like using the client to store state, or using a servlet to store state, or using a database to store state between each method call from the client) are more of a performance hit than the less-scalable nature of stateful session beans.

Make it Stick

mandatory means existing tx

create returns component interface

buy this book

An entity bean IS something.
A session bean DOES something.

 Sharpen your pencil

Know your bean types.

Look at the problem description on the left, and put a check mark for the bean type that would best fit the problem. There isn't one perfect right answer for these... you might decide that one bean type will work if you approach it one way, but another bean will work if you solve the problem in a different way.

	Entity	Message-driven	Session bean (circle stateless, stateful, or both)	
Booking a ticket for a rock concert	☐	☐	☐	stateful stateless
A bank account	☐	☐	☐	stateful stateless
Searching a product database	☐	☐	☐	stateful stateless
Dating service match-ups	☐	☐	☐	stateful stateless
Receiving submitted expense reports, and sending them out for approval	☐	☐	☐	stateful stateless
Online expert diagnosis—you describe a symptom and the system helps you determine the cause	☐	☐	☐	stateful stateless
The books in a library	☐	☐	☐	stateful stateless

Overheard at THE TIKIBEAN LOUNGE

Session bean: I'm so tired of doing all the work and getting none of the glory.

Bartender: What do you mean "none of the glory'"? Aren't you the only bean that's been required by the spec since the very beginning? Since EJB 1.0?

Session bean: Fat lot of good THAT does me. All anyone wants to talk about now is entity beans. Entity beans, entity beans, entity beans. Not that I don't like them—some of my best friends are entity beans, but I wish people would talk about what I do.

Bartender: Now that you mention it, entity beans are mostly what folks talk about here at the bar, what with the big CMP improvements in EJB 2.0.

Session bean: And that's another thing... what is the Big Deal with CMP? It's just going to a database! Seriously, tell me WHAT is so special about that? "Ooohhh look! It updated a record!" Please.

Bartender: Yeah, but the programmers around here seem to like not having to do all the database code now. And there's something about persistent relationships, I just can't quite remember...

Session bean: CMR. Container-managed relationships. OK, even *I* have to admit that CMR makes things a lot easier for developers. But that's not what bugs me—I KNOW everybody likes entity beans, but what about ME? What about everything *I* do? Entity beans represent *things* in the system, but without me, those *things* don't do much. Maybe an entity has some getters and setters and some queries, sure, but not a lot of business logic. To *use* entity beans in an app, you pretty much HAVE to use session beans to do the business processing. Like, an entity bean might represent the drinks you sell here, and the individual customers, but what good are drinks and customers without a bartender? You need someone to actually put the entities (the drinks and the customers) *together* in a meaningful way! And that's what session beans do. *We* do the deals. *We* work with the client to get something done, while entities just sit there waiting for session beans to use them. Hey, can I get another one of those? And don't even get me started on message-driven beans...

[To be continued.]

BULLET POINTS

- EJB is a component-based development model.

- Components are reusable chunks of functionality you can modify for different applications without touching the java source code.

- One benefit of EJB is WODA—Write-Once-Deploy-Anywhere. You can deploy your EJB 2.0 components to any app server that's EJB 2.0-compliant.

- WODA means you have to learn only one, standard API rather than proprietary vendor-specific APIs.

- The EJB architecture uses an EJBObject to intercept client calls to a bean. This gives the server/container a chance to step in and add services.

- EJB services include transactions, security, resource management, networking, and persistence.

- Beans come in three flavors: Entity, Session, and Message-driven.

- Entity beans represent a uniquely identifiable thing in a persistent store; usually that means a row in a database table.

- Message-driven beans are JMS messaging service consumers.

- Session beans are... *everything else.*

- Session beans can be stateful or stateless.

- Stateful beans can remember "conversational state" with a client, while stateless beans cannot.

Example:
The Advice Guy bean

Before we get into the guts of EJB, let's look at how to develop, deploy, and test a bean from start to finish. If you're not already familiar with EJB, you won't understand everything here. Don't worry about it now; we'll figure it all out in later chapters. This is just to give you a feeling for what it's like to get a bean up and running.

Our first bean is for the Advice Guy service—a remote service that gives back an advice String each time the client makes a request. We'll spend the next several pages looking at the process, and then we'll actually make this bean, as a tutorial.

The Advice Guy*

Our first bean is for the Advice Guy service. Each time the client makes a request, the Advice Guy service (an enterprise javabean) gives back a piece of stunningly helpful (and preternaturally appropriate) advice.

*In Head First Java, we deployed the Advice Guy service using straight TCP sockets. Now, for only five times the amount of code and effort, we get to have the same service in EJB. Of course, if one felt like it, one could argue that the Advice Guy doesn't really *need* all those EJB services, but we disagree. We're already planning the IPO for this baby.

Five things you do to build a bean:

AdviceBean.java

1 Code the **bean class** with all of the business methods.

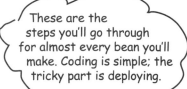

These are the steps you'll go through for almost every bean you'll make. Coding is simple; the tricky part is deploying.

AdviceHome.java
Advice.java

2 Code two **interfaces** for the bean: *home* and *component*.

ejb-jar.xml

3 Create an XML **deployment descriptor** that tells the server what your bean is and how it should be managed. You *must* name it ejb-jar.xml.

ejb-jar

4 Put the bean, the interfaces, and the deployment descriptor into an **ejb-jar** file. (There might be *more* than one bean in the ejb-jar, but there will always be just *one* deployment descriptor.)

5 **Deploy** the bean into the server, using the tools provided by the server vendor.

Relax

You don't need to be an XML expert.

*In fact, you don't have to know anything at all about how XML works. You **do** need to know about many of the deployment descriptor **tags**, but you don't need to know about XML in order to learn the tags. If you think of the tags as simply labels in a document, with very specific requirements for what you're allowed to type within those labels, then all you need to know for the exam is the name, and requirements, for some of the most important labels (tags). We'll look at those crucial tags in several chapters.*

1 bean class
2 interfaces
3 XML DD
4 ejb-jar
5 deploy

AdviceBean.java

❶ Write the **bean class** with the actual business methods the client calls.

This is where it all happens. The implementation of your business methods defined in the component interface. In other words, you write your business logic in the bean class.

There are three bean types to choose from, Session, Entity, and Message-driven, and we'll cover each one in detail in later chapters of the book. Before making a bean, though, you must decide what type you need because your bean class must implement one of three interfaces, depending on the type you choose.

We've chosen a Session bean here because it's perfect for the Advice Guy application. Advice Guy gives back an advice String when you invoke the surprisingly-named getAdvice() method. So our bean class (on the next page) implements the SessionBean interface. And SessionBean isn't just a marker interface*—it has methods your bean class must implement.

The methods you implement from the SessionBean interface are known as container-callbacks, because the container uses them to notify you of important milestones in the bean's life.

*A marker interface (also called a tag interface) has no methods to implement and exists so that you can announce to the world that, "Yes, I can do this."

we have only one business method for the AdviceBean
↓

```
public String getAdvice() {
    // advice generating code
}
```

Watch it!

You must know how to write all the code by hand, without using an EJB-ready development tool.

You're expected to know how to write the two interfaces and the bean class (or, for message-driven beans, just the bean class). That means you should NOT use an EJB-aware development tool that builds some of the bean or interface code for you, until you're certain you know exactly what code the tool is creating for you.

There's a pile of rules you need to know for the exam, and in the next few chapters we'll get into the gory details. For now, don't worry about memorizing anything from the code in this exercise. Just know that you WILL need to learn it all before we're done.

There is **some** good news, however— you CAN use a tool to build the XML deployment descriptor. The exam doesn't expect you to memorize all the XML tags! (Although you will need to know a few elements; we'll cover them later.)

Bean class

AdviceBean.java

The AdviceBean implements the SessionBean interface, so it must implement the methods declared in javax.ejb.SessionBean. We'll grill you on everything a little later, for now, just remember that the bean class is where your actual business logic goes. In other words, the reason your bean exists in the first place. For the Advice Guy, that means the getAdvice() method.

```java
package headfirst;

import javax.ejb.*;

public class AdviceBean implements SessionBean {

    private String[] adviceStrings = {"One word: inappropriate.", "You might
want to rethink that haircut.", "Your boss will respect you if you tell him
what you REALLY think of him.", "Visualize yourself with better clothes.",
"Of course you don't have to go to work today.", "Do you really think you
should be leaving the house like that?", "Read a book, once a year whether
you need to or not."};

    public void ejbActivate() {
        System.out.println("ejb activate");
    }

    public void ejbPassivate() {
        System.out.println("ejb passivate");
    }

    public void ejbRemove() {
        System.out.println("ejb remove");
    }

    public void setSessionContext(SessionContext ctx) {
        System.out.println("session context");
    }

    public String getAdvice() {
        System.out.println("in get advice");
        int random = (int) (Math.random() * adviceStrings.length);
        return adviceStrings[random];
    }

    public void ejbCreate() {
        System.out.println("in ejb create");
    }
}
```

← you need this package

You MUST implement one of the three bean type interfaces (Session, Entity, or MessageDriven)

The business method (getAdvice()) randomly picks one of these Strings to return.

These four methods are from the SessionBean interface, so you have to put them in here. For this simple bean, we don't need to do anything in the methods, but we've got print statements so you can see when (or if) they're called. For now, don't worry about what these are for!

Finally! The actual business method from the component interface. It's the whole point of the bean... the thing the client wants to call.

← You must have an ejbCreate() method. It's an EJB rule you'll learn about later. But it does not come from the SessionBean interface.

1 bean
2 interfaces
3 XML DD
4 ejb-jar
5 deploy

Advice.java

AdviceHome.java

➋ Write two **interfaces** for the bean.

These are the interfaces the *client* sees. We have an entire chapter devoted to these interfaces, so you don't have to understand it all now.

COMPONENT interface

This is where all the *business methods* are declared. In other words, it's where you put the methods the client wants to call.

component interface: *business methods*

Advice.java

```
package headfirst;

import javax.ejb.*;
import java.rmi.RemoteException;


public interface Advice extends EJBObject {

    public String getAdvice() throws RemoteException;

}
```

you need these two import statements.

It must extend either the EJBObject interface, or EJBLocalObject, which we'll see later

You must declare Remote-Exception on all methods in this interface!

This is the actual business method. (the whole reason the bean exists). It MUST correspond to a method in the bean class.

HOME interface

The client uses the *home* interface to ask for a reference to the *component* interface. The home is the client's starting point for getting hold of a reference to a bean (or at least what the client *thinks* is the bean, but we'll get to that later). For now, think of the home as a kind of *factory* that makes and distributes bean references to clients.

home interface: *a factory for bean references*

AdviceHome.java

```
package headfirst;

import javax.ejb.*;
import java.rmi.RemoteException;



public interface AdviceHome extends EJBHome {

    public Advice create() throws CreateException, RemoteException;

}
```

same import statements as above.

The home must extend either the EJBHome interface, or EJBLocalHome, which we'll see later

This time we need TWO exceptions, CreateException and RemoteException

the create() method must return your component interface type!!

> Wait just a minute here... how come we're making the bean class *before* the interfaces? That doesn't sound right.

> And that's not even the worst thing! AdviceBean doesn't implement the Advice interface? Let me get this straight... you MUST have the same methods in the bean that you have in the component interface, yet you don't make the bean *implement* the interface?

Hmmm... two good questions. In a non-bean Java world, the way we're doing things here wouldn't make much sense. But bean world has different rules and practices. We *could* write the interfaces first, and some developers do. Sometimes the choice of which to develop first depends on the development tools you're using to build your beans. Some tools, for example, expect you to first build your bean (coding the actual business logic), and then the tool will build the interfaces to match. And some tools do just the opposite, looking at the interfaces and building a "your code goes here" bean class, with all of the methods from the interface. For learning EJB, we like to start with the bean, focusing on the business logic, before figuring out the interfaces. Later in the book, we'll do it the other way around.

As for the bean not implementing the component interface, you *could* do it that way, but this time we strongly urge you not to. On the next page, we'll look at this in more detail.

Q: So why *doesn't* the bean class (AdviceBean) implement the component interface (Advice) if it has to implement the same methods? Java classes are allowed to implement more than one interface, so what's the problem with saying:

```
class AdviceBean implements
Advice,SessionBean
```

A: Legally, the bean class *can* implement the component interface, but the spec doesn't recommend it. Remember, although to the client it looks as though the AdviceBean is the object the client's invoking methods on (the object that implements—in the true Java sense—the component interface), the client *really* invokes methods on something called an EJBObject, that's implemented by the server at deploy-time. The client never interacts directly with the bean. Never, ever, ever. Later in the book, you'll see that if the bean does implement the component interface, you could sneak things past the compiler that would explode at runtime. So we strongly urge you not to have your bean implement the component interface.

But there's another issue as well—the component interface extends another interface. In our example, Advice extends EJBObject, and EJBObject is not a marker interface. It has methods! This means that any class implementing Advice must also implement the methods of EJBObject!

So, your bean would end up implementing a bunch of methods it should never have (like getHandle(), getEJBHome()...)

Q: But there's an easy solution to THAT problem: you could have the bean extend a class that has all the implementations that you need to satisfy the compiler, but don't really need to implement in your code. Like the adapter event listener classes in AWT. Why not do something like that here and make a superclass for your bean that implements the methods?

A: Yes, you could do that, and it would be legal. But it still means your bean is capable of having methods invoked that the bean should never know about. The methods of EJBObject are methods for the client to call on the bean, but NOT for the bean to actually implement. So it's not the best OO practice.

And there's still another reason why it's not good practice to have the bean implement the component interface—if the interface is remote (and EJBObject is, since it extends the java.rmi.Remote interface), that would make the bean class a Remote class, and that must never be! The bean is protected by the server, and must never be accessed in any other way, by anything but the server. It's the *server* that makes the EJBObject (by implementing the Advice interface), which IS remote, and which intercepts all business method calls to the bean.

Q: But if you don't have the bean implement the interface, in other words, if AdviceBean doesn't implement Advice, doesn't this mean that the compiler won't catch you if the bean blows it and doesn't match the methods of the interface?

A: Yes, that's exactly what it means. And yes, that makes most Java developers a little queasy just thinking about it. After all, that's one of the benefits of interfaces in Java— that the compiler guarantees that you have all of the interface methods properly implemented.

But don't panic! In our development in this book, we *do* have to be careful since the compiler isn't making sure that we've implemented the business methods from the component interface. In the real world, however, you'll almost certainly be using an EJB-ready development environment that will make *sure* you provide the methods, either by putting a "your code goes here" version of the method in your bean class, or by doing the reverse—finding the business method in the bean class and putting it into the component interface. At the very least, most servers will check (before or at the time you deploy the bean) that your component interface and bean class have matching methods.

If this still bothers you, though, we do have a technique for getting around it that we'll look at a little later. Chances are, you won't need to use it.

The naming convention for beans is NOT part of the EJB spec.

Advice, AdviceHome, AdviceBean...
You're not required to use these names for enterprise beans! (It's a really, really, really good idea, however.) Be sure that you're not fooled by the name of a class or interface—it's legal to have a component interface named AdviceHome and a component interface named AdviceBean, for example. On the exam, always go by the class or interface declaration rather than the name of the class.

You saw how the bean doesn't implement the component interface, even though the bean must have the same methods. Brainstorm a way (there may be more than one) in which you could handle these requirements for the Advice Guy bean:

1. The component interface (Advice) must extend EJBObject.

2. The bean must implement the SessionBean interface. The bean must not implement the component interface (Advice).

3. We want the compiler to verify that the bean (AdviceBean) has the same methods as those in the component interface.

(Hint: "the same methods as those in the component interface", does not mean the same thing as "the same methods as those declared in the component interface.")

(Hint: this requires only Java knowledge, not EJB knowledge.)

Off the path

Bean-aware development tools

Today, many EJB programmers use EJB-savvy development tools. In other words, a bean-capable IDE that knows how the three pieces—*home* interface, *component* interface, and *bean* class—are related to one another. Many of these tools also know how to talk directly to one or more app servers, so that you can use the tool to both develop and deploy your bean, rather than switching from a development environment to the server's own (and often less-friendly) deployment tools. One of the advantages of an EJB development tool is that you might not have to worry about matching up the business methods in the component interface with the actual bean class, or vice-versa. A good EJB-aware IDE will make sure you've got everything synced up.

1 bean
2 interfaces
3 XML DD
4 ejb-jar
5 deploy

ejb-jar.xml

This name is required! The DD file must be named "ejb-jar.xml"

③ Create an XML **deployment descriptor** that tells the server what your bean is and how it should be managed.

(In this book, we won't actually write this ourselves; we'll let the deployment tools build it for us.)

The deployment descriptor (DD) describes the structure of your bean including how the three files (component interface, home interface, and bean class) are related to one another. The server won't look at your naming convention and figure out which is the home, which is the bean, etc. You have to tell the server, through the DD, which class is which, and how they're connected. But the DD does a lot more than that. And for some beans, the DD can be several pages long!

For this simple bean, the DD is short. Remember, you don't need to memorize the syntax of the XML in the DD. Later in the book (in several different chapters), we'll go over the aspects of the DD that you *do* need to know.

> You don't have to write the XML by hand if you use a tool that can help you build a deployment descriptor.
>
> You can use the J2EE RI bean wizard to do it for you, and the XML it spits out will work in <u>any</u> EJB 2.0 container!

```xml
<?xml version="1.0" encoding="UTF-8"?>

<!DOCTYPE ejb-jar PUBLIC '-//Sun Microsystems,
Inc.//DTD Enterprise JavaBeans 2.0//EN' 'http://
java.sun.com/dtd/ejb-jar_2_0.dtd'>

<ejb-jar>
  <display-name>Ejb1</display-name>
  <enterprise-beans>

    <session>
      <display-name>AdviceBean</display-name>
      <ejb-name>AdviceBean</ejb-name>
      <home>headfirst.AdviceHome</home>
      <remote>headfirst.Advice</remote>
      <ejb-class>headfirst.AdviceBean</ejb-class>
      <session-type>Stateless</session-type>
      <transaction-type>Bean</transaction-type>
      <security-identity>
        <description></description>
        <use-caller-identity></use-caller-identity>
      </security-identity>
    </session>

  </enterprise-beans>
</ejb-jar>
```

For now, just know that every bean in an application must have an element in the DD that describes the bean's structure and type.

1 bean
2 interfaces
3 XML DD
4 ejb-jar
5 deploy

ejb-jar

(in this book, we won't use the JAR tool to make the ejb-bar ourselves; we'll let the deploytools do it)

④ Put the bean, the interfaces, and the deployment descriptor into an ejb-jar file.

As a bean developer (officially called a Bean Provider), you'll always put your beans in a JAR. The spec says an ejb-jar is a JAR file that holds the things the bean depends on (classes and interfaces, along with the deployment descriptor).

You don't have to do this by hand since we'll use the RI! Rather than writing the XML DD and using the **jar** tool to package it, we'll use the RI **deploytool** wizard to make it easier (and less error-prone). In other words, we're going to combine steps 4 and 5 into one. For now, you need to know that a bean isn't a bean until you make a JAR file with the compiled class and interfaces, and the DD.

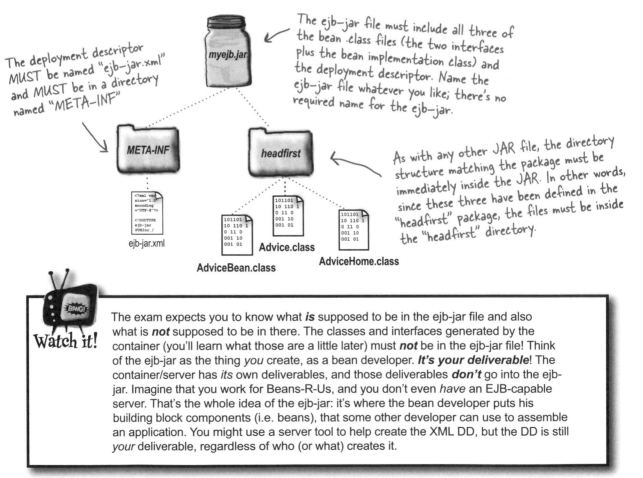

The deployment descriptor MUST be named "ejb-jar.xml" and MUST be in a directory named "META-INF"

The ejb-jar file must include all three of the bean .class files (the two interfaces plus the bean implementation class) and the deployment descriptor. Name the ejb-jar file whatever you like; there's no required name for the ejb-jar.

myejb.jar

META-INF

headfirst

As with any other JAR file, the directory structure matching the package must be immediately inside the JAR. In other words, since these three have been defined in the "headfirst" package, the files must be inside the "headfirst" directory.

ejb-jar.xml

AdviceBean.class

Advice.class

AdviceHome.class

Watch it!

The exam expects you to know what *is* supposed to be in the ejb-jar file and also what is *not* supposed to be in there. The classes and interfaces generated by the container (you'll learn what those are a little later) must *not* be in the ejb-jar file! Think of the ejb-jar as the thing *you* create, as a bean developer. ***It's your deliverable!*** The container/server has *its* own deliverables, and those deliverables ***don't*** go into the ejb-jar. Imagine that you work for Beans-R-Us, and you don't even *have* an EJB-capable server. That's the whole idea of the ejb-jar: it's where the bean developer puts his building block components (i.e. beans), that some other developer can use to assemble an application. You might use a server tool to help create the XML DD, but the DD is still *your* deliverable, regardless of who (or what) creates it.

1 bean
2 interfaces
3 XML DD
4 ejb-jar
5 deploy

⑤ Deploy the bean into the server, using the tools provided by the server vendor.

Sooner or later, your beans have to do something. They have to be assembled into an application and deployed into a server, waiting for clients to call.

This is a huge step. In fact, we cheated a little, because it's actually *two* steps: Application Assembly and Deployment.

✴ *Application Assembly*

This means taking the bean from the reusable component stage to being part of an application. For simple beans, that might mean simply writing a client that can access the bean (i.e. call the bean's business methods). In other words, a single bean might be the entire application on the server side. But this could also be the step where you integrate multiple beans (and other Java classes) into a custom application, and that usually means taking different beans (each in its own ejb-jar with its own DD) and putting them into a new, single ejb-jar, with a single DD that might describe how two or more beans are related to one another.

During assembly, you might also add *new* information to the DD, for things the bean developer didn't know about. For example, the bean developer might write code that uses a special bean-specific "property" (called an *environment entry*, which we'll get into in a later chapter) for the tax amount used by this application. But the bean developer has no idea what *value* to give the tax amount property, so he leaves the value blank in the DD. Then the application assembler comes along, *sees* (by reading the DD) that the bean uses a property, figures out what the value should be, and adds it to the DD.

For the Advice bean, putting the bean in the ejb-jar, building the DD, and deploying will happen as one big step.

✴ *Deployment*

This is where the rubber meets the road, the bean meets the server, the developer meets the sys admin. The two crucial parts of deployment are *naming* the bean (so the client will know how to find it) and getting the bean into the *container's control*.

The spec doesn't say anything about the way in which you deploy your beans; it all depends on the EJB server/container that you're using.

EJB Roles and Responsibilities

I work for Beans-R-Us, and I develop reusable components that we sell to other developers.

Bill →

EJB Role: *Bean Provider*

Deliverable: *ejb-jar files (that include one or more beans and an XML **deployment descriptor**)*

Primary responsibility: *Design and program enterprise javabeans. In other words, **write the bean code**.*

Characteristics: *Knows the **business logic** that should be in a particular type of component, for a particular domain.*

I'm a developer for a big online bookstore. We buy a lot of beans from Beans-R-Us, but I also make my own beans. I mix them together into new applications customized for the business rules of how we sell books.

Annie →

EJB Role:
Application Assembler

Deliverable: *ejb-jar files (that include one or more beans and an XML deployment descriptor with Bean Provider info as well as **application assembly info**). May also create clients or define interaction between other components (such as JSPs).*

Primary responsibility: Combine one or more enterprise beans *into a larger application. May sometimes wear the Bean Provider hat, mixing new and existing beans together to build an app.Defines the security and transaction behavior for the application.*

Characteristics: Definitely a domain expert. *Might not do as much coding as the Bean Provider.*

BANG!

Watch it!

The exam covers subtle differences between roles.

*Pay very close attention to any mention of EJB roles in this book, especially when we cover more details of the deployment descriptor. Count on being tested on who does what, and count on those questions being subtle. The App Assembler and Bean Provider overlap in several areas, as does the Deployer and the App Assembler. For the exam, you need to know which role has the **primary** responsibility for a particular task (usually having to do with the deployment descriptor information).The stuff on this page and the next are just a start...*

EJB Role: *Deployer*

Deliverable: *Enterprise beans that have been customized for a **specific operational environment**, and deployed into the server.*

Primary responsibility: *Take the Application Assembler's deliverable, study the deployment descriptor, and **resolve any external dependencies**. For example, if the bean relies on a particular resource, the deployer must map the logical name from the Bean Provider to the actual name of the resource on the server. Remember, when Bill wrote the bean code he didn't know it would end up on Dick's server. Bill had to make up a 'fake' name for the database, and Dick has to bind the fake name to something real.*

Characteristics: *An **expert in a specific operational domain**. Knows the security users and roles for this system, knows what's configured into the server, and understands how to interpret the deployment descriptor info from the Bean Provider and App Assembler.*

> Wow! It actually deployed. Unbelievable. I work for the same online bookstore as the app assembler, and I take her ejb-jar, study the deployment descriptor, and get the thing actually running into the server and waiting for clients. I know a LOT about the way our systems are configured and running here.

Dick

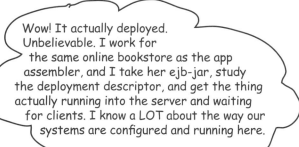

> We do the big services so you get to focus on your business logic. We compete with IBM, BEA, and Oracle, and someday we'll kick Larry Ellison's butt.

> We work for the SuperServer company. We're experts in low-level services like transaction management, pooling, and security.

Sue

EJB Role: *Container and Server Provider*

Deliverable: *EJB 2.0-compliant server, deployment tools, runtime environment for enterprise beans.*

Primary responsibility: *Implementing the spec.*

Characteristics: *Experts in distributed objects and transactions, and other **low-level system services**.*

Carl

Tutorial:

Let's make, deploy, and test the AdviceBean

We'll write the code, compile it, start the server, start the deploytool, use the deploytool to make the DD and the ejb-jar, deploy the bean, create a client, and test the bean using the client. The only thing we won't do is install and configure the server. We assume you already did that.

If you don't yet have the J2EE 1.3 RI up and running, go to http://java.sun.com/j2ee/ and download version 1.3 of J2EE (it includes set-up instructions), then go back and download the J2EE API documentation.

Remember, the exam is for J2EE 1.3, NOT 1.4! Whatever you do, do NOT study for the exam using the 1.4 spec. See the intro for more details about why the exam uses 1.3 and not 1.4—the short version is: we don't want to certify folks on something that almost nobody is using. Certification is NOT about "I know the latest and greatest release". It's about "I know the technology that people are using now. I've been using it for at least six months."

> Why are we using the RI? Why can't we use a REAL app server?

Which server would we use? We use the RI for learning and practicing because we don't know which server you'll need to use, and the RI is the simplest of all the freely-available servers. We want it to be as easy as possible for you to focus on EJB technology and ignore the tool-specific tasks.

Open source products like JBoss are still *real* production servers, so they tend to have a lot more configuration and administration tasks to cope with. Using the RI lets you spend more time doing the things you'll have to do, *regardless* of the server, with the least amount of time spent learning a server-specific approach to those things.

There's nothing on the exam about the J2EE RI.

Or any other application server. You don't have to know about any vendor tools (including Sun's) for development or deployment. You **do** need to know what capabilities every EJB-compliant server will have, but you don't need to know any vendor-specific features or configuration details.

Organize your project directory

All the beans in this book are organized into packages, which means you must be a little more careful about compiling and running. **Every instruction in this chapter assumes you've organized your project** *exactly* **the way it's shown here**. If you deviate from this structure, you're on your own for mapping our command-line and deployment formulas to your own structure.

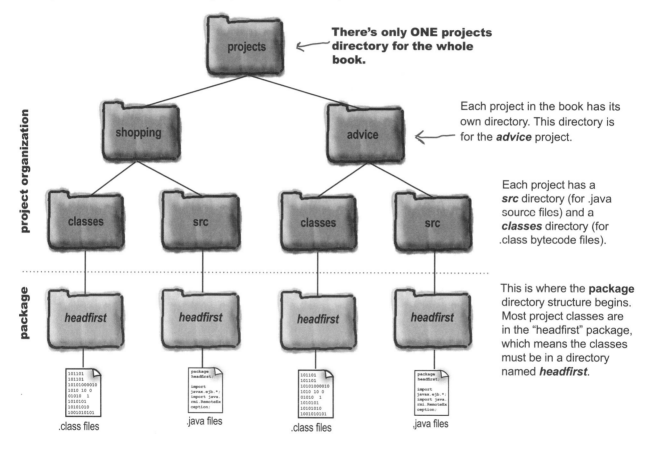

project organization

package

There's only ONE projects directory for the whole book.

Each project in the book has its own directory. This directory is for the *advice* project.

Each project has a *src* directory (for .java source files) and a *classes* directory (for .class bytecode files).

This is where the **package** directory structure begins. Most project classes are in the "headfirst" package, which means the classes must be in a directory named *headfirst*.

.class files

.java files

.class files

.java files

Organizing your terminal / command-line

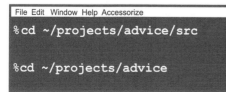

File Edit Window Help Accessorize

```
%cd ~/projects/advice/src
```

compile from the src directory

```
%cd ~/projects/advice
```

run clients from the specific project directory

Compile the two interfaces and the bean class

So far, we've written the two interfaces and the bean class, but we still have to compile them. After that, we'll make the ejb-jar (which holds *class* files, not *source* files).

File Edit Window Help WhyAmIHere

```
%cd ~/projects/advice/src

%javac -d ../classes headfirst/*.java
```

We're using the **-d** compiler flag, so the command-line above says, "Compile all the .java files in the 'headfirst' directory, and then put the compiled .class files into the 'classes' directory, which you'll find by going up one level from the current (src) directory. Oh yeah, almost forgot, be sure to put the classes in their correct PACKAGE directory. Look for the package structure inside the 'classes' directory, which means you should see a directory named 'headfirst', and THAT's where the class files need to go...and if you do NOT find the 'headfirst' directory there, then make one for me. Thanks."

Right now, this is how your projects directory structure should look:

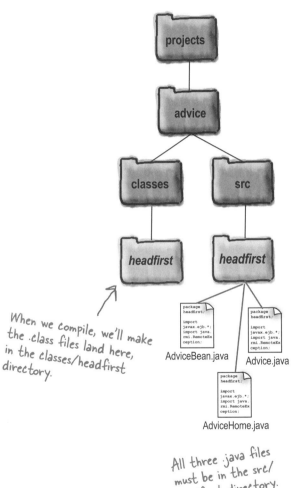

When we compile, we'll make the .class files land here, in the classes/headfirst directory.

AdviceBean.java

Advice.java

AdviceHome.java

All three .java files must be in the src/headfirst directory.

Start the server

Open up a new terminal for the server. You'll leave it running, and we want to see the output, as it runs, so don't use this terminal for anything else. Make the advice directory your working directory.

```
File  Edit  Window  Help  BlahBlahBlah
%cd projects/advice

%j2ee -verbose
```

You'll see something like this

The -verbose flag (which isn't required, but we like it) prints out a bunch of stuff in the terminal.

```
File  Edit  Window  Help  WhatThe...?
%j2ee -verbose
J2EE server listen port: 1050
Naming service started:1050
Binding DataSource, name = jdbc/DB1, url = jdbc:cloudscape:rmi:CloudscapeDB;create=true
Binding DataSource, name = jdbc/InventoryDB, url = jdbc:cloudscape:rmi:
CloudscapeDB;create=true
Binding DataSource, name = jdbc/DB2, url = jdbc:cloudscape:rmi:CloudscapeDB;create=true
Binding DataSource, name = jdbc/EstoreDB, url = jdbc:cloudscape:rmi:
CloudscapeDB;create=true
Binding DataSource, name = jdbc/Cloudscape, url = jdbc:cloudscape:rmi:
CloudscapeDB;create=true
Binding DataSource, name = jdbc/XACloudscape, url = jdbc/XACloudscape__xa
Binding DataSource, name = jdbc/XACloudscape__xa, dataSource = COM.cloudscape.core.RemoteX
aDataSource@4c6715
Starting JMS service...Initialization complete - waiting for client requestsBinding: <
JMS Destination : jms/Topic , javax.jms.Topic >Binding: < JMS Destination : jms/Queue ,
javax.jms.Queue >Binding: < JMS Cnx Factory : QueueConnectionFactory , Queue , No prop-
erties >Binding: < JMS Cnx Factory : jms/TopicConnectionFactory , Topic , No properties
>Binding: < JMS Cnx Factory : jms/QueueConnectionFactory , Queue , No properties >Binding:
< JMS Cnx Factory : TopicConnectionFactory , Topic , No properties >
Starting web service at port: 8000
Starting secure web service at port: 7000
J2EE SDK/1.3.1
Starting web service at port: 9191
J2EE SDK/1.3.1
J2EE server startup complete.
```

Start deploytool

Open up a new terminal for the deploytool. This tool is part of the J2EE RI, and it has everything you need to create the ejb-jar, the DD, and to do the final deployment into the RI server.

```
File Edit  Window  Help  Chill
%deploytool

Starting Deployment tool, version 1.3.1

(Type 'deploytool -help' for command line
options.)
```

you'll see something like this

A lovely splash screen pops up and sits while the application loads. If you click the splash screen, it disappears, so don't panic if it then looks like nothing's happening. Patience.

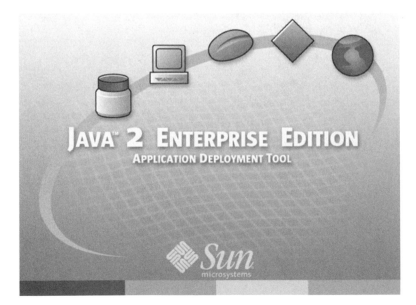

Make a new Application

The RI is a J2EE *server*, remember, not just an *EJB container*. So we have to do a small bit of J2EEish stuff before we can make the ejb-jar and deploy the app. This step is where we create a new J2EE application, and for now, you can think of the J2EE application as something that wraps the beans and adds a little more information for the server. The main difference between a J2EE application and an EJB application is that a J2EE application can include web components (servlets and JSPs) as well as EJB components, all integrated as part of a single app.

Choose **File ▶ New ▶ Application**

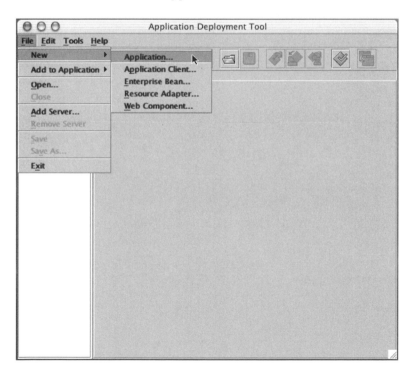

there are no
Dumb Questions

Q: Does this mean that I MUST have a J2EE server if I want to use servlets and EJBs together?

A: No. With a J2EE server, the web components and EJB components are more tightly integrated, which means you can have all of the components respect one another's transactions and security. But you're always free to use a servlet as a client to an enterprise bean, even if that bean isn't running in the same application server (or even the same physical machine). Another advantage of a J2EE server is the ease with which you can deploy both component types as part of one enterprise application.

Having said all this, chances are extremely high that if you're doing EJB 2.0 applications, you are running them in a J2EE server. Remember, there are very few standalone EJB containers today. Virtually all significant vendors run their EJB containers within a J2EE server.

....

Off the path

A J2EE server vendor must pass a massive pile of compatibility tests before the server can be called "J2EE-compliant". A J2EE 1.3 server, for example, *must* include an EJB 2.0 container, and that container *must* implement the EJB 2.0 specification.

Name and save the new application

This part's a little awkward. You can use the Browse button to navigate
through your own directory tree, but the easiest way to name and
save the application is to type the complete path to the file you're
about to create. The thing we're making is not the bean itself—you
can think of it more like a document that holds all the information
about the application. As a convention, we save the application in
the projects/[whatever] directory—the directory corresponding to
that particular project. For the Advice bean, that means the projects/
advice directory. If you started the server from the projects/advice
directory (in other words, if advice is your current working directory),
then you'll get the right name and location by default.

Name the application **AdviceApp**
If needed, include the full path to projects/advice/AdviceApp
Click **OK**

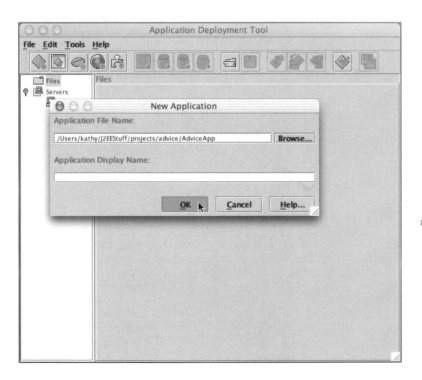

Don't worry about the
Application Display Name field;
the tool will automatically fill it
in with the file name from the
Application File Name field.

What you'll see after you create and name the application

Now, you're back at the main screen of the deploytool. You might have to click on the *Files* or *Applications* icons to expand them, but you'll see that the tool has created an **Applications** directory with something called **AdviceApp** inside. Click on the AdviceApp icon, and you'll see information about the application including the name, location, and current contents. At this point, there's nothing but a META-INF directory (that holds more info about the app, which we won't ever need to look at).

Click on the **AdviceApp** icon

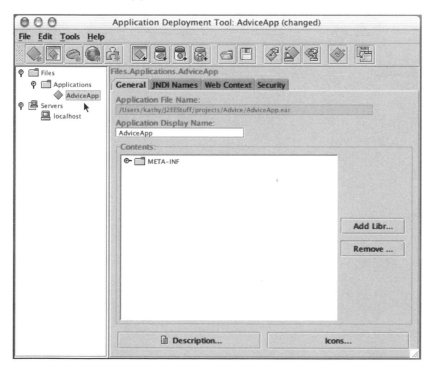

Now let's make the new enterprise bean (the ejb-jar and the DD)

This is what we're really after—the actual bean. The previous steps (making the J2EE application) were to satisfy the J2EE RI because we have to deploy the bean within a J2EE app.

Choose **File ▶ New ▶ Enterprise Bean...**

Now we're in the really cool
New Enterprise Bean Wizard

This part of the deploytool is where almost everything happens!
The key things we'll do are:

✳ *Create the ejb-jar*

✳ *Put the bean class and the two interfaces into the ejb-jar*

✳ *Create the deployment descriptor that describes the bean*

Click **Next >**

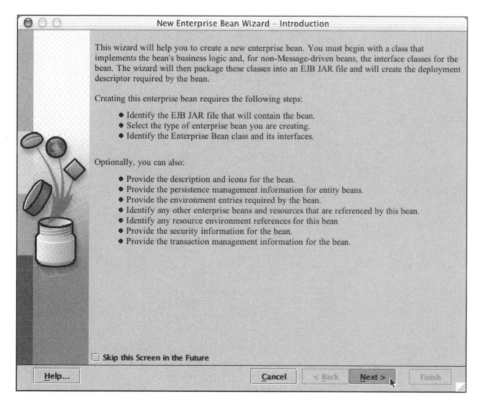

Create the new ejb-jar

For now, just accept the defaults. The radio button on the top left of the screen shows that you're making a new JAR within the AdviceApp application. Notice that the AdviceApp is part of a drop-down list—if there *were* other ejb-jars already in the application, we could have chosen to put the new bean in a pre-existing JAR.

The tool picks an especially helpful display name, "Ejb1", and you'll see this back on the main deploytool screen when we're done. That name isn't used anywhere in your real application, so it's no big deal, but if you have more than one JAR in an application, you might want to give it a more descriptive name (Cart JAR, Account JAR, etc).

Click **Edit...**

Add the three class files (including their package directory) to the JAR

This is the most important part of the whole process! In other words, don't screw it up. The key is to get the correct classes into the JAR in their package directory structure, and only their package directory structure. In other words, if you put the three class files into the JAR without the headfirst directory, your bean won't deploy. Or, if you include the classes directory as well as the headfirst directory, your beans won't deploy. Remember, the ejb-jar is still a JAR file, so the usual JAR rules about package structures apply here.

Navigate to the **Advice** directory
Expand the **classes** directory to see the **headfirst** directory
Select the **headfirst** directory
Click **Add**

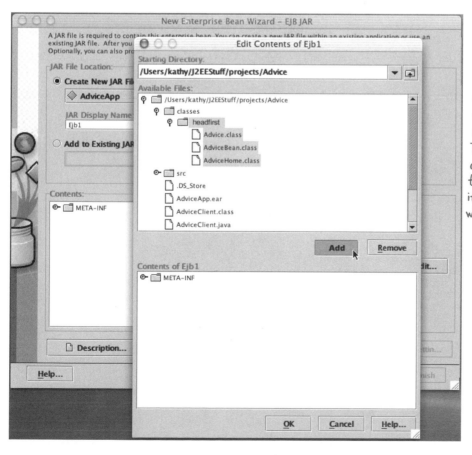

Use the navigation controls here to get to your Advice directory, where you can see your classes and src directories. Then select the headfirst directory. You don't have to expand it... we did it so that you could see what's in there.

Confirm that you added ONLY the package directory and the class files

You gotta get this part right. Look at the bottom window that says "Contents of Ejb1" and verify that the only thing in the JAR besides the META-INF directory is the **headfirst** directory (including the contents of the directory). The classic mistake we see all the time (not that *you'd* ever do that) is to add only the *class* files, but not the *package* directory. Be sure that you have the **headfirst** directory (and not the **classes** directory) with the three class files. Another common mistake is to add the source files instead of the class files. So don't feel bad if it happens to you.

Verify that you have the right classes (and package directory)
If you don't, select them from the bottom window, click Remove, and start over.
Click **OK** when you're done, then click **NEXT**

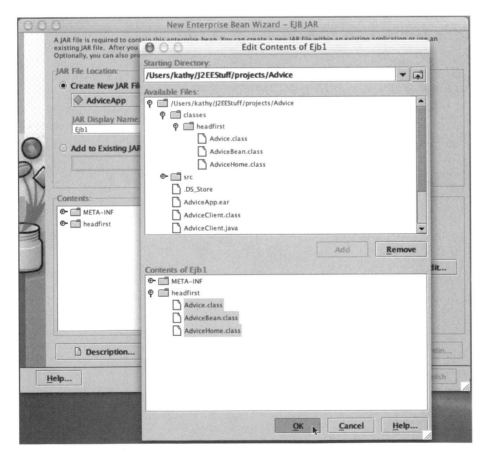

Make it a Stateless Session bean

Now, we're at the place where we give the tool the bean's 'structural' information. What kind of bean it is, which class file is the home interface, and so on. Remember, the tool uses this to create the deployment descriptor. And the EJB container uses the deployment descriptor to figure out how to deploy and manage the bean.

The Advice bean is simple—client calls a method on the remote object, the remote object returns a value, then the remote object forgets the whole thing ever happened. End of story. That scenario is just perfect for a stateless session bean solution. If the Advice bean needed to *remember* the advice it gave to the client, and use it in some way in future invocations from that same client, then we'd make it stateful. But we don't, so we won't.

And as you'll learn later, it wouldn't make sense to have the Advice bean be an entity or message-driven bean. But it's too late to make it anything but a session bean anyway—your bean class implements the SessionBean interface. So you're already committed to a bean type. But whether the session bean is stateless or stateful can be a little more subtle. For now, just make it stateless.

Select the **Session** radio button
Select the **Stateless** radio button

Don't click the Next button!! We have way more to do on this screen.

Tell it which of the three class files in the JAR is the actual BEAN class

You have three class files in the JAR: the home interface (AdviceHome), the component interface (Advice), and the bean (AdviceBean). But the EJB container needs to know which is which. Remember, the naming convention doesn't mean anything to anyone but you! The container won't look at the three classes in the JAR and recognize that AdviceHome must be the home interface, and so on*. No, the naming convention is for you and anyone else using your bean components.

So, now you have to tell the tool which of the files is the bean class (we'll do the two interfaces on the next page). The tool, then, will put this info into the deployment descriptor.

Click the **Enterprise Bean Class** drop-down menu
Select **headfirst.AdviceBean**

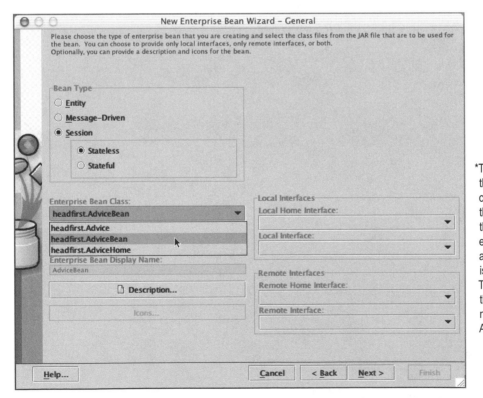

*There are some vendor tools that can use your naming convention, among other things, to figure out which is the home, which is the bean, etc. But the RI doesn't do this, and development tool support is not part of the EJB spec. The only tools required by the spec are for the Deployer, not the Bean Provider or App Assembler.

Tell it which is the Home interface, and which is the Component interface

Now, you have to do the same thing you did for the bean class, but with the two interfaces. You'll notice that there are two different places where you can select interfaces—Local and Remote. This bean is remote (which means it's a Java RMI remote service, but we'll get into that in the next chapter), so we're using only the bottom section, for Remote interfaces. Just leave the Local interfaces section alone.

The strange part is that this screen uses the term Remote Interface rather than Remote Component Interface. That's just a bad interface design in the deploytool. (It's actually an artifact of the previous version of EJB, when there were only remote interfaces. Local interfaces are new to EJB 2.0), but we have to live with it.

Click the **Remote Home Interface** drop-down menu
Select **headfirst.AdviceHome**

Click the **Remote Interface** drop-down menu
Select **headfirst.Advice**

Verify everything on this screen!

Choosing the bean class, the home interface, and the component interface is a permanent decision! Once you're done with the rest of the bean wizard, and the deployment descriptor is created, you're stuck with it. If you accidentally mix up the home and component interfaces, your bean won't work. In the RI, it won't even *deploy* (some servers let you deploy structurally bad beans, which means they blow up at runtime, but the RI won't even let you in the server door).

Be sure you have the following settings:

Enterprise Bean Class: **headfirst.AdviceBean**
Remote Home Interface: **headfirst.AdviceHome**
Remote Interface: **headfirst.Advice**

Click **NEXT**

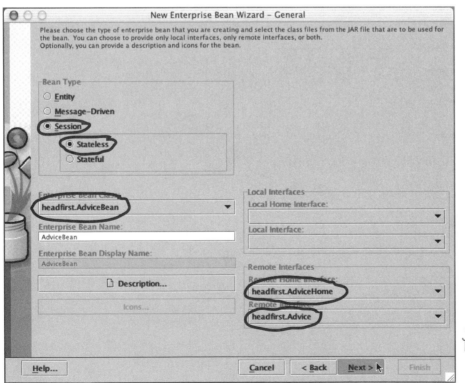

Be sure your screen looks just like this before you hit the Next > button!

You're done, click Finish

Because this bean is so simple, and we don't care about transactions, security, environment entries, and database access, we've done everything we need to make the deployment descriptor and put it in a JAR with the class files.

So, you can ignore the Transactions Management screen, although you'll become intimate with it later in the book.

Click **Finish**

Meanwhile back on the main deploytool screen...

Things have changed! The AdviceApp icon expands to show your ejb-jar
(named "Ejb1"), and the ejb-jar expands to show the cute bean icon named
"AdviceBean". If you select the AdviceBean, you'll see a bunch of tabbed panels
that'll show you the choices you made in the bean wizard. Some of the things you
chose can be changed, but some can't. In the General panel, for example, you
can't change the class file designations for the home, component, and bean. In
fact, you can see that the drop-down lists for these are grayed-out here. But gee,
you can still change it from Stateless to Stateful.

Admire your work

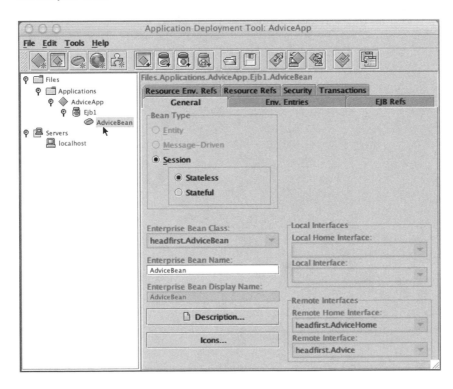

Run your bean through the deploytool verifier

You already know your bean classes compile, but just because it *compiles* doesn't mean it follows *bean law*. The verifier takes your jar and runs it through a bunch of tests to see if it meets the minimum requirements for deployment. As you learn more about the EJB spec, you'll see that the verifier is testing your bean's code (and the deployment descriptor) to see if it complies with the spec. For example, a stateless session bean's home interface must have a no-arg create() method declared, and nothing else. And the bean class must have methods that match those declared in the component interface. And if the component interface is remote, it must declare that each method throws RemoteException. Don't worry about remembering these examples; it's just to give you an idea of the kinds of things the verifier does.

Click on the Ejb1 icon (the little jar) to highlight it

Choose **Tools** ▶ **Verifier...**

Cross your fingers

Close your eyes and click OK

The verifier screen shows you the name of the JAR as ejb-jar-ic.jar, in a tmp directory, but that's just how the RI saves your ejb-jar until you're ready to deploy. The tmp file (and the JAR) will go away when you deploy or delete the bean from your application.

(At least it's *supposed* to. Sometimes you might have to find that directory and delete it yourself. Repeat after me: The deploytool is *free*. The deploytool is *not* a production tool. I did not pay any money for this tool. I will learn to appreciate its strengths and look past the 101 ways it is a pain in the a**.)

Choose the **Failures Only** radio button
Click **OK**

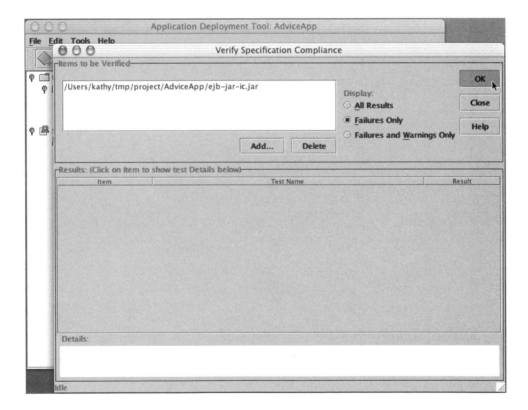

Whew! No failed tests.

If everything verifies, you see a nice little message in the Details box at the bottom of the verifier window. If there are failures, you'll see them in the Results box. You can click on a 'failure' message to get more details about what went wrong. Don't panic if you see a million failures; usually you can fix one thing and they all go away. Unlike compiler error messages, which are sometimes about as helpful as VCR instructions, the verifier failure messages are pretty explicit. You can usually figure out exactly where you went wrong.

Sometimes, you can fix the problem back in the main deploytool window by clicking on one of the tabbed panels and changing something. For example, if you forgot to specify a transaction attribute for an entity bean method, you can go to the Transactions tabbed panel in the deploytool window and set the attribute, without starting over in the bean wizard.

But if you have problems with your actual class files, you'll have to modify them, recompile them, and then update your ejb-jar*. Or, if the problem is that you made a setting in the bean wizard that can't be changed (like, selecting the bean class when the tool asks for the home interface), you'll have to delete the ejb-jar and start over with the bean wizard.

Be happy about the wonderful message at the bottom
Click **Close**

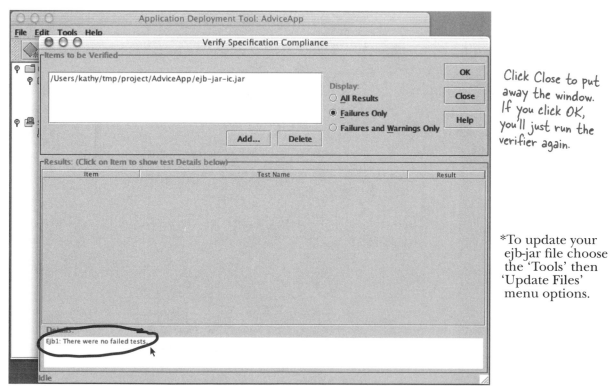

Click Close to put away the window. If you click OK, you'll just run the verifier again.

*To update your ejb-jar file choose the 'Tools' then 'Update Files' menu options.

Time to Deploy

Once you've verified, you're ready to deploy. There's not much that can go wrong unless something bad happens in the server. At this point, almost anything that goes wrong can be fixed by shutting down the server and deploytool and starting them back up again. Drastic, yes, but it usually works. Sometimes you do have to take even harsher action, by returning the server back to it's freshly installed state, but fortunately there's a command that can do that. When all else fails, bring up a new terminal and type cleanup. This script shuts down the J2EE server, but it also cleans out all the logs, directories, and files that have been made on that machine. After that, you can try starting the server, then the deploytool, and deploying again. And if you ever open the deploytool and you don't see your application, don't panic! Just go to the File menu and choose Open, just like you would to open a document in any other application. Think of the J2EE app like a document as far as the deploytool is concerned.

Choose **Tools** ▶ **Deploy...**

Make it Return a Client Jar

Once it starts, the server is going to do a ton of things to get your bean ready. One of them is to generate the class files that implement your two interfaces (the home and the component interfaces). And since they're remote interfaces, the server will also create the remote stub classes for those interfaces. (Lots more on these later.) Well, the client needs the two interfaces and the two stubs. You could have given the client the interfaces, since you created those. But only the server can make the stub classes, and the client will never work without them. So your client application might be sitting there, all nice and compiled, and just waiting for you to give it the stub classes so that it can actually run.

Fortunately, you can ask the RI deploytool to give you a client jar that has everything the client needs (and a lot *more*, it turns out, but since this isn't a real production environment, we're just going to let that go).

Virtually all EJB application servers must create the stub classes, so you'll have to find out where your server puts them, so you can give them to the client.

Select the **Return Client Jar** checkbox (put it in the projects/advice directory)
Click **Next >**

Give it a name, so clients can look it up

We're now dangerously close to deployment, and the last step is to give the bean a JNDI name. That's the name clients use to get a reference to the bean. (Well, to what the client *thinks* is the bean, but we'll save the gory details for the next chapter.)

The bean's JNDI name is simply the logical name you choose (or, in the real world, whoever deploys the bean). It doesn't have to match anything from the bean itself. We could, for example, name this bean Homer, which would in fact make it even more fun and challenging for the clients than it already would be *with* a meaningful name.

Type in the JNDI name **Advisor**
Click **Finish**
Take a deep breath and hold it until the deploy process completes

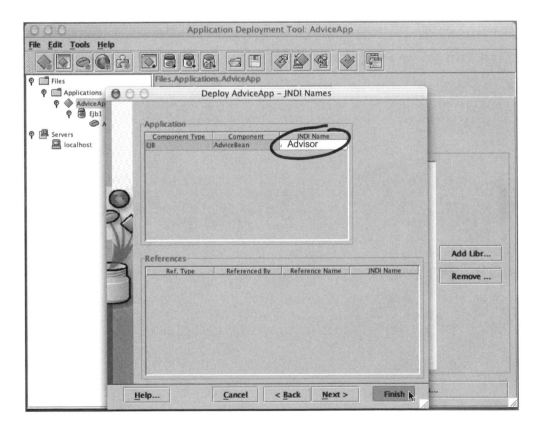

Watch the progress bars go up, then celebrate

Wait for it... wait for it... wait for it...

When the bean's deployed, successfully, you'll see the line "Deployment of AdviceApp is complete" in the window. At that point, clients can access the bean.

You did it!

Click **OK**

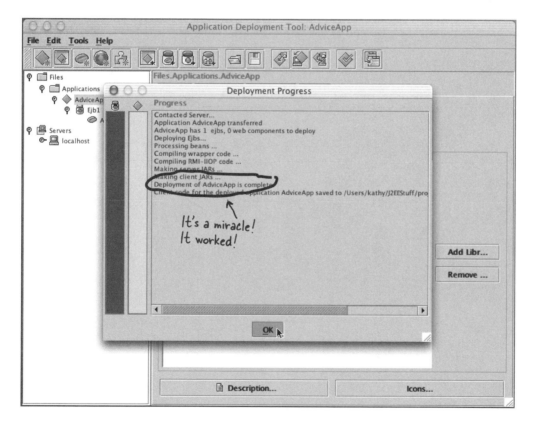

It's a miracle!
It worked!

Now you'll see the AdviceApp inside the server

Under the **Servers** icon, you'll see the **localhost** icon representing the J2EE server you started before you launched the deploytool. And under the **localhost** icon, you can now see that your **AdviceApp** is deployed. You'll also see the **Undeploy** button that you can use to, well, *undeploy.*

Expand the *Servers > localhost* icons to see the **AdviceApp**

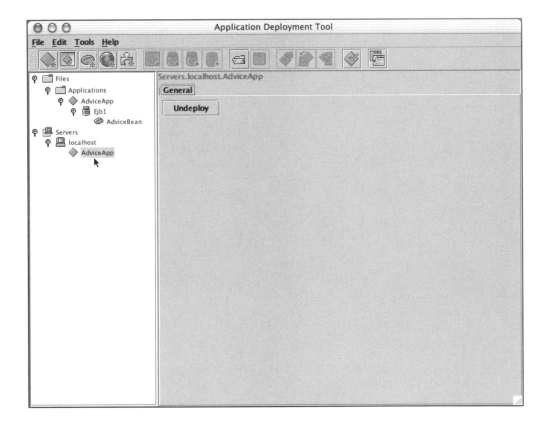

Now all we need is a client...

We have a freshly deployed bean (in a J2EE server), but we can't
test it until we have a client. The client has to do five things:

(1) Get a reference to a **JNDI InitialContext**
(we'll learn about that in the Client View chapter).

(2) Use the InitialContext to do a **lookup** on the
home interface of the bean (that we named
"Advisor" when we deployed).

(3) **Narrow** and **cast** the *thing* we get back
from the lookup. (That *thing* is something
that implements the AdviceHome interface.)
We'll learn about narrowing in the Client View
chapter.

(4) Call **create** on the home interface to get
back a reference to the component interface.

(5) Call **getAdvice()** (the business method,
the reason we're here, remember?) on the
component interface, and print the result.

**We're using a stand-alone Java
program as the client.**

**In the real world, your clients
will likely be servlets or other
beans.**

**The five things the client must
do are the same regardless of
the type of client.**

**So, using a stand-alone Java
program teaches you to do the
same things you'll need to do
with a servlet client.**

**If your client is another
enterprise bean, the code will
be slightly different, but you
still have to do the five steps.**

Relax *There's nothing on the exam about servlets or JSPs.*

*The exam expects you to know how the client gets and uses a
bean (the steps above), but the type of client doesn't matter. The client
code for getting a reference to a bean, and ultimately calling methods on the
bean, is virtually the same whether the client is a servlet or stand-alone Java
app. And all the exam cares about is the part of the code where the client is
trying to get and use a bean.*

*The only knowledge of servlets and JSPs you need for the exam, is to know
that the EJB spec does NOT guarantee support for them. Servlets and JSPs
are guaranteed by the J2EE spec, but not by the EJB spec.*

Organizing your project directory for the client

This is what your *projects*/*advice* directory should look like after we write and compile the client code.

This is just a tester client, so we won't put the client class in a package. We're just gonna keep it easy and put it all (source and class) in the advice directory.

This is the client JAR the server gave us when we deployed. →

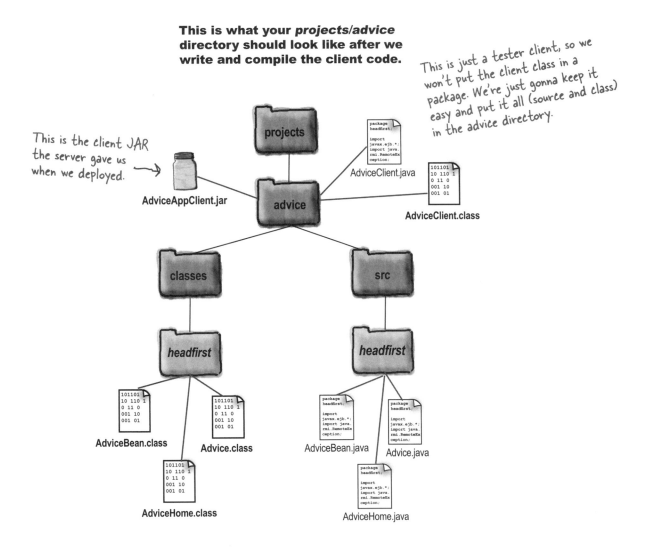

The Client Code (AdviceClient.java)

```java
import javax.naming.*;
import java.rmi.*;
import javax.rmi.*;
import headfirst.*;
import javax.ejb.*;
```
A bunch of imports

```java
public class AdviceClient {

    public static void main(String[] args) {
        new AdviceClient().go();
    }

    public void go() {
        try {
            Context ic = new InitialContext();
            Object o = ic.lookup("Advisor");

            AdviceHome home = (AdviceHome) PortableRemoteObject.narrow(o, AdviceHome.class);

            Advice advisor = home.create();
            System.out.println(advisor.getAdvice());
        } catch (Exception ex) {
            ex.printStackTrace();
        }
    }
}
```

InitialContext is our entry point into the JNDI naming service, where we do the lookup.

Lookup the Advice bean using the JNDI name we gave it during deployment.

Just go with it for now. It'll all make perfect sense a little later.

Finally we get to the actual business method! The method declared in the component interface (Advice) and implemented in the bean class.

Compile the client:

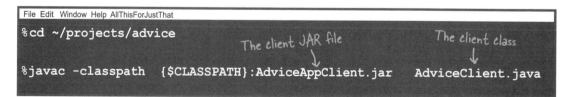

```
File Edit Window Help AllThisForJustThat
%cd ~/projects/advice                        The client JAR file        The client class

%javac -classpath   {$CLASSPATH}:AdviceAppClient.jar   AdviceClient.java
```

The client needs access to the two interfaces (Advice, AdviceHome) and the two stub classes that implement those interfaces. They're both in the client JAR the server made, but we can't compile the client without them. The cleanest way is to add them to the classpath at compile-time, using the **-classpath** compiler flag.

Run the client!

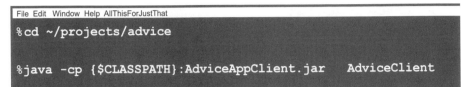

```
File  Edit  Window  Help  AllThisForJustThat
%cd ~/projects/advice


%java -cp {$CLASSPATH}:AdviceAppClient.jar   AdviceClient
```

At runtime, the client still needs access to the two interfaces (Advice, AdviceHome) and the two stub classes that implement those interfaces. They're both in the client JAR the server made, we have to add them to the classpath. The best way is to use the **-cp** compiler flag.

Note: For now, the client must be on the same physical machine as the server. Later, we'll see how to change this, and run the client against a J2EE server on a different machine.

You're kidding me, right? All this work just to call one little method that returns a String? I have to do all this, just to do HelloWorld in EJB?

I think I can answer that—yeah, this is major overkill for a HelloWorldish app like the AdviceBean. But in the context of a real enterprise app, with a zillion customers a day hitting your server (and an insanely short deadline), this extra work, and runtime overhead, is pretty trivial. Especially when you consider everything you GET. So, I think you need to look at this from a more real-world perspective.
(OK, yes, if you're gonna be all picky about it, I'm not real... but that shouldn't affect my credibility.)

Mock Exam

---

1 Which are features every EJB 2.0 container must implement or support? (Choose all that apply.)

❑ A. A GUI bean deployment utility.

❑ B. Synchronous invocation for all bean types.

❑ C. Transaction support for all bean types.

❑ D. Remote client views for all bean types.

❑ E. JNDI 1.2 namespace.

---

2 Which are guaranteed capabilities of EJB 2.0? (Choose all that apply.)

❑ A. Local home interfaces for message-driven beans.

❑ B. Dirty detection mechanisms to reduce memory footprints.

❑ C. Run-as security identity functionality.

❑ D. The JDBC 2.0 extension.

❑ E. Session bean failover.

---

3 Which are features in EJB 2.0? (Choose all that apply.)

❑ A. Portable finder query syntax.

❑ B. Container managed persistence.

❑ C. Local interfaces for session beans.

❑ D. XML based deployment descriptors.

❑ E. Synchronous message-driven beans.

Mock Exam Answers

---

1 Which are features every EJB 2.0 container must implement or support? (spec: 30)
(Choose all that apply.)

❏ A. A GUI bean deployment utility. — it doesn't have to be GUI

❏ B. Synchronous invocation for all bean types. — MDBs cannot be synchronous

☑ C. Transaction support for all bean types.

❏ D. Remote client views for all bean types. — MDBs do not have client views

☑ E. JNDI 1.2 namespace.

---

2 Which are guaranteed capabilities of EJB 2.0? (Choose all that apply.)

❏ A. Local home interfaces for message-driven beans. — MDBs don't have clients

❏ B. Dirty detection mechanisms to reduce memory footprints. — nice, but not guaranteed

☑ C. Run-as security identity functionality.

☑ D. The JDBC 2.0 extension.

❏ E. Session bean failover. — maybe available, but not guaranteed

---

3 Which are features in EJB 2.0? (Choose all that apply.) (spec: 25-26)

☑ A. Portable finder query syntax.

☑ B. Container managed persistence.

☑ C. Local interfaces for session beans.

☑ D. XML based deployment descriptors.

❏ E. Synchronous message-driven beans. — MDBs are always asynchronous

2 architectural overview

✳ *EJB Architecture* ✳

EJB is about infrastructure. Your components are the building blocks. With EJB, you can build big applications. The kind of applications that could run everything from the Victoria's Secret back-end to document-handling systems at CERN. But an architecture with this much flexibility, power, and scalability isn't simple. It all begins with a distributed programming model, where clients, servers, and even different pieces of the same application are running who-knows-where on the network. But how does the client *find* a bean? How does the client call methods it? Why are there different bean types? Will Ben marry J-Lo?

Background

We're in this chapter for background, not because of an exam objective. Although, you could say that every objective in the exam *depends* on your understanding what's in *this* chapter.

But don't worry, we'll have plenty of objectives beginning with Chapter 3. By Chapter 6, you will look back longingly on this chapter and remember what it was like not to have any objectives. You'll miss this chapter when it's gone, so savor the moments you have with it.

You remember this picture...

But it was too high-level to get us anywhere. Think about how much is missing from this picture. Like, how does the client get a reference to something running on a different machine? How does the client actually communicate with the bean? How is it that the server can step into the middle of a client-to-bean method call?

Beneath EJB, there's Java's distributed technology for Remote Method Invocation (RMI). Although EJB hides some of the complexities of RMI from the bean developer, it's still there, and unless you truly understand it, some pieces will never make sense.

So, we start our descent from a high-level view to the blood and guts of EJB with a lesson on RMI. If you're one of the fortunate who've already worked a lot with RMI, you can skip this and go straight to the part where we talk about the ways in which EJB uses RMI. But you should still at least *skim* it, even if you're an experienced EJB developer, if for no other reason than to get comfortable with the terminology and pictures we'll use throughout the rest of the book.

OK, back to where we started—what's missing from this picture? Start by looking at the places where a miracle occurs...

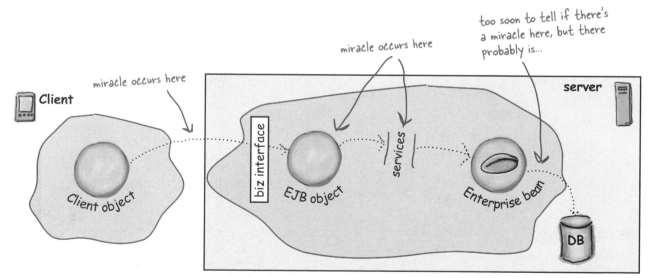

A ridiculously high-level view of EJB architecture

Making a remote method call

When you write a client to access a bean, the client is either *local* or *remote*. A local client means the client is running in the same JVM as the bean. In other words, both the bean and the client live in the same heap. We'll talk about that much more in the Client View chapter, but for now, remember that *local* means *same heap/ JVM*. Chances are, you'll use local clients only with entity beans, and only under very special circumstances.

You'll use a *remote* client when you want a bean to be used by the outside world. Most enterprise applications have a remote client, even if some of the beans *used* in the application talk to one another as local clients. (We'll explore every gory detail about this before the book is over.)

So how does an object in one heap/JVM directly call a method on a reference to an object running in another heap/JVM? Technically, it's not possible! Java references hold bits that don't mean anything outside the currently running JVM. If you're an object and you have a reference to another object, *that object must be in the same heap with you.*

Java RMI (Remote Method Invocation) solves this problem by giving the client a proxy (called a *stub*) object that acts as the go-between for the client and Remote object. The client calls a method on the *stub*, and the *stub* takes care of the low-level communication (sockets and streams) with the Remote object.

With RMI, your client object gets to act like it's making a remote method call. But what it's <u>really</u> doing is calling a method on a "proxy" object running in the same heap with the client. The proxy is called a "stub", and it handles all the low-level networking sockets and streams.

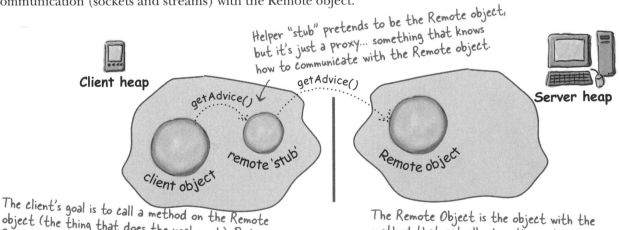

Helper "stub" pretends to be the Remote object, but it's just a proxy... something that knows how to communicate with the Remote object.

The client's goal is to call a method on the Remote object (the thing that does the real work). But since the Remote object is in a different heap, the client calls a method on a local "stub" object (which in turn sends info over the network)

The Remote Object is the object with the method that actually does the real work for whatever that method is supposed to do (checkCredit(), calculatePi(), etc.).

There's a "helper" on the server as well...

The Remote object has the method the client wants to call. But when the stub makes a network connection to the server, *something* on the server has to take the information in the incoming stream and turn it into a method call on the Remote object. You *could* put the networking code into your Remote object, but that defeats the whole point of RMI—to make it as easy for your client to call a method on an object across the network as it is to call a method on an object in the same heap. The goal of RMI is to promote *network transparency*. In other words, the fact that the objects are in different machines should be nearly transparent to the developer. Which means to you... less code—simpler code.

So, with that as the goal, RMI takes care of the server-side of the method call as well. The thing on the server-side that accepts the socket connection is called a *skeleton*. It's the counterpart to the client stub. In the early versions of RMI, for every stub there was a matching skeleton object. Today, though, that's not always true. The *functionality* of the skeleton has to happen somehow on the server-side, but an actual skeleton *object* is optional. We won't go into any of the details because it doesn't make any difference to us with EJB. How the container chooses to implement its skeleton behavior is up to the vendor.

All we care about is that *something* is on the server that the stub knows how to talk to, and that *something* knows how to interpret the message from the stub and invoke a method on the Remote object.

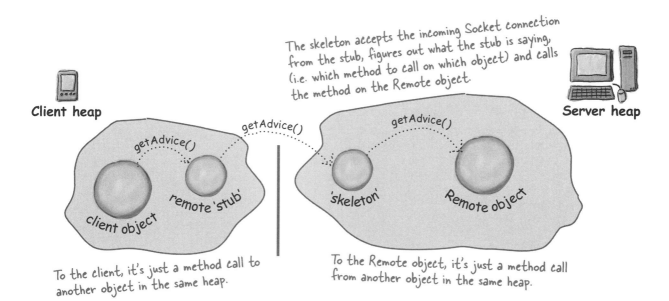

The skeleton accepts the incoming Socket connection from the stub, figures out what the stub is saying (i.e. which method to call on which object) and calls the method on the Remote object.

Client heap

Server heap

getAdvice()

getAdvice()

getAdvice()

remote 'stub'

client object

'skeleton'

Remote object

To the client, it's just a method call to another object in the same heap.

To the Remote object, it's just a method call from another object in the same heap.

there are no
Dumb Questions

Q: How can you have "network transparency"? What happens if the network or the server is down when the client calls the remote method? It seems like there's a LOT more that can go wrong than if the client object is just making a plain old method call to another object in the heap.

A: Yes, yes. You obviously understand that "network transparency" is not only a myth, it's a bad idea. Of course the remote method call can fail in ways a local method call would not, and the client needs to be prepared for that!

That's why, in Java RMI, *all* remote methods must declare a java.rmi.RemoteException, which is a checked exception. That means the client has to handle or declare the exception. In other words, the client can't *really* pretend the method call isn't remote.

But wait, there's more—the client has to do something special to even *get* the reference to the Remote object in the first place. And what exactly *is* that reference? It's really a reference to the Remote object's *proxy*—the stub.

So no, RMI does *not* give you true network transparency. The designers of RMI want the client to acknowledge that *things can go horribly wrong with a remote method invocation*.

Still, when you look at everything that needs to happen to make a remote method call (networking Socket connection, streams, packaging up arguments, etc.), the client has to do only a couple of things: use a special lookup process to get the reference to the remote object, and wrap remote method calls in a try/catch. That's pretty trivial when you consider what it would take if the client had to manage the whole process.

(And there's even a way to make it easier for the client, using an EJB design pattern we'll see in the last chapter).

Q: Am I responsible for building the stub and the skeleton? How does the stub *know* what methods my Remote object has? For that matter, how does the *client* know what methods my Remote object has?

A: No, you don't need to make the stubs and skeletons. With plain old RMI, you use the RMI compiler (rmic) to generate them. But for the other two questions... we'll let you think about it for a minute before we look at the details.

In Java, what's the best way to tell the client what methods she can call? In other words, how do you expose your public methods to others?

Think about the relationship between the stub and the actual Remote object. What must they both have in common?

(We'll see the answer several pages from now)

What about arguments and return values?

Remote method calls are just like local method calls, except for the RemoteExceptions. And what good would a method call be if you couldn't pass arguments or get a return value? You might as well be doing RPC*, the way your parents did.

This brings us to one of the key jobs for the stub and the skeleton (or whatever is doing the skeletonish things)—packing and unpacking values shipped over the wire.

Remember, the client is really calling a method on the stub, and the stub is local to the client (i.e. in the same heap). So, from the *client's* perspective, there's nothing special about sending arguments with the method. It's the *stub* that does all the dirty work. The stub has to package up the arguments (through a process known as marshalling) and send them in the output stream, through the Socket connection with the server.

The skeleton-thing on the server has to process the stream from the stub, unpack the arguments, figure out what to do with everything (for instance, which method to call on which object), and then invoke the method (a *local* call) on the Remote object, with the arguments.

Then it all happens in reverse! The skeleton packages up the return values and ships them to the stub, who unpacks them and gives them to the client as plain old garden-variety return values. But in order to send arguments and return values, they must be primitives, Serializable objects, an array or collection of primitives or Serializable objects, or a Remote object.

> **The stub and skeleton are in it for the whole round trip. They're both responsible for packing and unpacking the values shipped over the wire.**
>
> **But it won't work if the arguments and return values aren't *shippable*.**
>
> ***Shippable* values must be one of these:**
>
> * **Primitives**
>
> * **Serializable objects**
>
> * **An array or collection of primitives or Serializable objects**
>
> * **A Remote object**

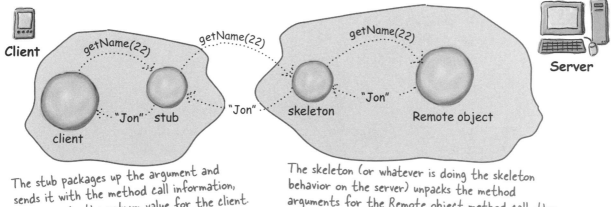

The stub packages up the argument and sends it with the method call information, then unpacks the return value for the client.

The skeleton (or whatever is doing the skeleton behavior on the server) unpacks the method arguments for the Remote object method call, then packs and ships the return value.

---

*RPC stands for Remote Procedure Call. Boring.

> Wait a minute... Java passes objects by passing a copy of the object *reference*, not the object itself. So how can THAT ever work with a remote method call? That reference wouldn't mean anything on the other heap...

In ordinary local method calls, Java passes an object reference by <u>value</u>, In other words, by copying the bits in the reference variable.

The object itself is never passed.

We'll think of a local Java reference as a remote control to an object on the heap. Something we can use to push buttons (i.e. call methods) on the object.

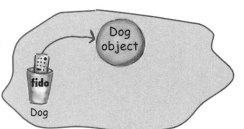

```
void go() {
   Dog fido = new Dog();
   this.trainPet(fido);
}
```

— What are we really passing here??

A copy of the reference (the remote control), not the Dog object

```
void trainPet(Dog arg) { }
```

We know you know all this, obviously, but just so 'we're all on the same page' (which is an odd thing to say, since we clearly ARE all on the same page) but you get the idea.

Now the "arg" parameter and the "fido" variable are identical copies. Both reference the same Dog object.

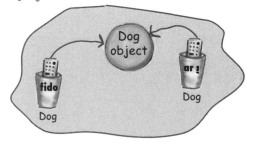

What really gets passed when you pass an object to a remote method?

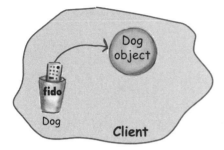

Imagine this CLIENT code:

```
try {

    Dog fido = new Dog();

    remoteStub.trainPet(fido);

} catch(RemoteException ex){
    ex.printStackTrace();
}
```

NOW what are we really passing here??

NOT the reference value!

It's a serialized copy of the actual Dog object.

And this REMOTE method:

```
void trainPet(Dog arg) { }
```

If your remote method has an argument that's an object type, the argument is passed as a full copy of the object itself!

For remote calls, Java passes objects by *object* copy, not *reference* copy.

A serialized copy of the object is shipped to the Remote object.

The server Dog is a copy of the client Dog.

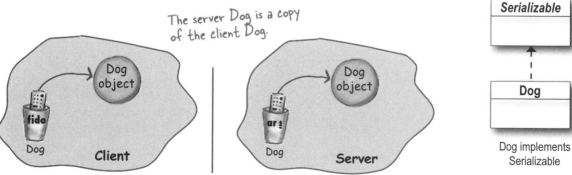

Serializable

↑

Dog

Dog implements
Serializable

Getting the object argument from the client to the server

(1) **Client invokes trainPet(myDog) on the stub, passing a copy of the reference to the Dog object.**

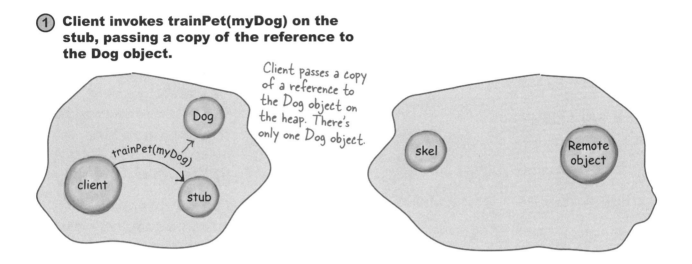

Client passes a copy of a reference to the Dog object on the heap. There's only one Dog object.

(2) **The stub makes a serialized copy of the object and sends that copy over the wire to the skeleton.**

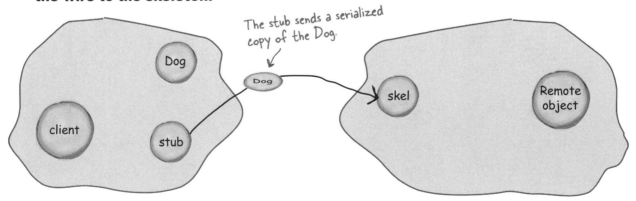

The stub sends a serialized copy of the Dog.

Unpacking (deserializing) the object on the server

③ **The skeleton deserializes the passed argument, creating a new Dog object in the Remote object's heap.**

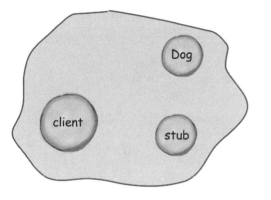 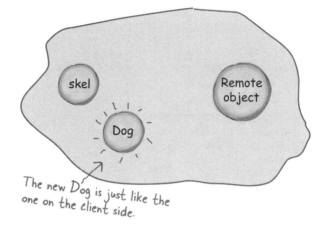

The new Dog is just like the one on the client side.

④ **The skeleton invokes the method on the Remote object, passing a plain old Java reference to the new Dog object.**

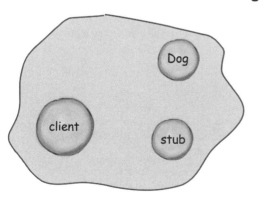 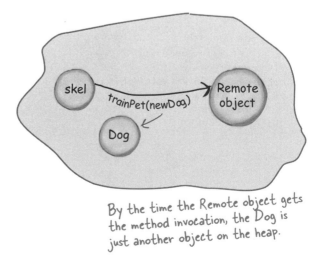

By the time the Remote object gets the method invocation, the Dog is just another object on the heap.

there are no
Dumb Questions

Q: **I'm sitting here with a HashMap full of Serializable Customer objects with String keys. Do I have to worry about whether the HashMap *itself* is Serializable?**

A: OK, this is kind of a tricky one. All of the Collection implementations in the J2SE API are Serializable. So you don't have to worry about a Hashmap—as long as what you put *in* the Hashmap is Serializable, you're fine.

But... there *is* one place where things can fail. Chances are, you'll never see this, but it's still worth mentioning. You probably already know that the Map classes like HashMap and Hashtable have a values() method that returns a collection of just the values, without the keys. In other words, if you called it on your HashMap, you'd get a Collection of Customer objects.

But what *type* of collection? And there's the problem. You don't know. All you know is that it's something that implements the Collection interface. But that isn't enough to tell you whether the Collection returned by values() is Serializable! In other words, you might get back a Collection that—even when filled with Serializable objects—is not itself Serializable!

The bottom line: don't rely on the Collection returned from a map's values() method to be Serializable. Put your values into something you can trust to be Serializable, like ArrayList, before trying to ship them as part of a remote method call.

Q: **If something you're passing to a remote method isn't Serializable, is this a compile-time or runtime failure?**

A: Runtime! Usually, anyway. Remember that the *declared* argument or return type is not necessarily the same as the *actual runtime type*.

The only case where it can fail at *compile* time is if the remote method actually uses **Serializable** as the *declared* type of the argument or return value:

```
public void takeIt(Serializable s);
```

In that circumstance, the compiler can use normal Java type-checking to see if the declared type of the thing being passed implements Serializable.

Most of the time, the declared argument or return type is something *other* than Serializable (like Dog, ArrayList, String, etc.), so Java won't know whether the runtime object is Serializable until it actually tries to do the serialization (and then it throws an exception).

And with collections and arrays, if *any* of the objects inside aren't Serializable, the whole serialization fails!

Q: **Does my class have to explicitly implement Serializable, or can I inherit Serializableness from my superclass?**

A: Remember Java's IS-A rule: if your *parent* (superclass) is something, then so are *you*. If Dog extends Animal, and Animal implements Serializable, then Dog is Serializable whether the Dog class explicitly declares it or not.

However, it *is* considered good practice to explicitly declare your class as Serializable even if your superclass does, just so that others looking at your class API don't have to hunt through your class' inheritance tree to see if *somebody* up there is Serializable.

Remember, arguments and return values for a remote method must be one of these:

✳ **Primitives**

✳ **Serializable objects**

✳ **An array or collection of primitives or Serializable objects**

✳ **A Remote object**

> I don't get why it's legal to pass a Remote object in a remote method! Isn't the whole point of a Remote object to stay... remote? Why would you send a Remote object to the client?? That makes no sense.

It'll make sense in a minute. But before you turn the page, think about the implications of passing a Remote object through a remote method call...

Passing a Remote object through a remote method call

It does *not* make sense to send a Remote object in a remote method call. After all, the whole point of a Remote object is to stay remote. To be accessed by clients who live... somewhere else. In another heap.

But what if you want to pass a remote client a reference to another Remote object? What if, rather than handing your client a full-blown copy of a Customer, you send him a stub to a Remote Customer?

Think about it. *Before* you read the next page.

What are the implications of passing a stub to a Remote Customer object as opposed to passing a non-remote Customer object?

What are the benefits of passing a stub instead of the real Customer object?

What are the drawbacks?

(Note: whether to pass serialized objects or stubs to remote objects is a crucial design decision. We'll explore this when we look at performance and patterns.)

When you pass a Remote object to or from a remote method, Java actually sends the Remote object's <u>stub</u>.

In other words, at runtime, the Remote object stays right where it is, and its stub is sent over the wire instead.

A <u>remote reference</u> is a stub to a remote object. If the client has a remote reference, he has a local reference to a stub, and the stub can talk to the Remote object.

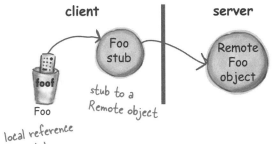

client   server

Foo stub   Remote Foo object

foo!
Foo
local reference to a stub

stub to a Remote object

When the return value is a Remote object...

(1) **The client invokes getCustomer() on Remote object A (using stub A).**

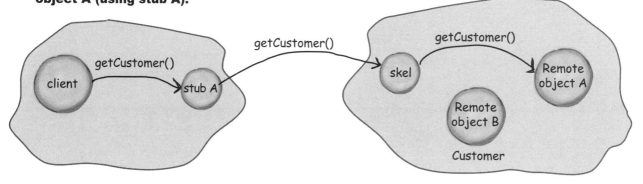

(2) **Remote object A returns a reference to a Customer object (Remote object B). The skeleton substitutes (and serializes) the Remote object's stub, and sends it back to the client.**

The Customer stub (B) is deserialized on the client, and the client gets a local reference to the new stub object.

The Remote object (A) simply returns a local reference to the Customer object (Remote object B), but it's actually the stub that gets sent back.

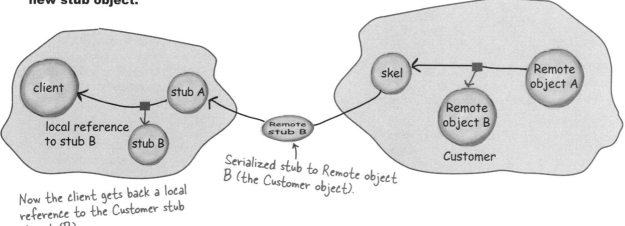

Serialized stub to Remote object B (the Customer object).

Now the client gets back a local reference to the Customer stub object (B).

there are no
Dumb Questions

Q: **What happens if the client object and the Remote object are running in different JVMs, but on the same physical machine? In other words, they're both running in Java programs on the same server?**

A: Doesn't make any difference. All that matters is whether the two objects live in different heaps, and JVMs do *not* share heaps with one another, thank you very much, no matter *how* intimate they are (cohabiting the same server).

In fact, you can (and with EJB often *must*) use RMI even when the objects *are* in the same heap.

Q: **Why in the world would you ever want to do use RMI if you don't need to? Isn't there enough overhead with remote calls as it is?**

A: We'll go into this in more detail later, but the main reason is because if you don't use RMI for method calls, you're locking down your design in such a way that you can't distribute your objects in different places in your network (or even on the same server). In other words, without RMI, you must have both objects in the same heap.

For a distributed programming model, that's a pretty permanent decision, with no chance to change your mind later, without rewriting code. On the other hand, if you *do* use RMI, you can decide later to split your program up into different nodes on your system, with little or usually *no* code changes.

So the tradeoff is flexibility for performance, but for most distributed enterprise apps, the overhead of a remote call is not your biggest problem. It's usually your bandwidth and/or concurrency that hurts the most. Overall, you probably have bigger performance fish to fry in areas *other* than whether your calls are remote or local. But the story isn't always that simple, so we'll explore this again later in the book.

BULLET POINTS

- EJB uses Java RMI (Remote Method Invocation) so that your beans can be accessed by remote clients.

- A remote client, in this context, is an object running in a different JVM, which also means a different heap.

- A Remote object stays in its own heap, while clients invoke methods on the Remote object's proxy, called a *stub*.

- The stub object handles all the low-level networking details in communicating with the Remote object.

- When the client wants to call a method on a Remote object, the client calls the same method on the stub. The stub lives in the same heap as the client.

- To the client, a remote method call is identical to a local method call, except a remote method can throw a RemoteException (a checked exception).

- The stub packages up the method arguments and sends information about the call to a *skeleton* on the server. The skeleton object itself is optional, but the skeleton's work must be done by something on the server. We don't have to care who—or what—is actually doing the skeleton's work.

- Arguments and return values must be one of the following: a primitive, a Serializable object, an array or collection of primitives or Serializable objects, or a Remote object. If the value isn't one of these, you'll get a runtime exception.

- If an object is passed as an argument or return value, the object is sent as a serialized *copy*, then deserialized on the Remote object's local heap.

- If a Remote object is passed as an argument or return value, the object's stub is sent instead.

What <u>must</u> the Remote object and the stub have in common?

How does the client know which methods to call?

How does the stub know which methods the Remote object has?

Remember, if the stub is pretending to be the Remote object, the stub must have the same methods as the Remote object.

Of course you know the answer to this.

An *interface*.

The way all methods in a distributed environment should be exposed to a client.

We call this the ***business interface*** because it has the business method(s) the client wants to call. Technically, the business interface for a Remote object must be, surprisingly, a Remote interface.

To be Remote, an interface must follow three rules:

✱ **it must extend java.rmi.Remote**

✱ **each method must declare a java.rmi.RemoteException**

✱ **arguments and return types must be *shippable* (Serializable, primitive, etc.)**

It all begins with a Remote interface. Both the Remote object and the stub implement the same interface... the one with the methods the client wants to call.

A Remote interface must extend java.rmi.Remote and every method must declare a RemoteException.

```java
import java.rmi.*;

public interface DiceRoller extends Remote {

    public int rollDice() throws RemoteException;
}
```

RemoteException and Remote interface are in java.rmi package

A Remote interface MUST extend java.rmi.Remote (which doesn't have any methods).

All of your methods must declare a RemoteException.

The client calls business methods on the stub through the Remote business interface

Remember, as far as the client's concerned, he's calling methods on The Real Thing. The actual Remote object. The thing that has the methods he wants to call.

The only thing reminding the client that he isn't calling methods directly on the Remote object is the RemoteExceptions he has to deal with.

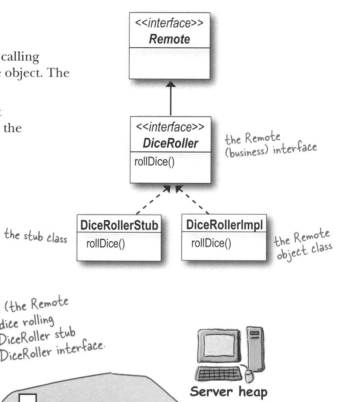

the Remote (business) interface

the stub class

the Remote object class

Both the DiceRollerImpl (the Remote object with the actual dice rolling functionality) and the DiceRoller stub implement the Remote DiceRoller interface.

Client heap

Server heap

client

DiceRoller

DiceRoller stub

DiceRoller

DiceRollerImpl

The client uses the Remote business interface to call methods on the stub. The stub and the Remote object both implement the Remote interface.

From this point forward, we're not going to show a skeleton object. All we care about is that SOMETHING on the server is handling the skeleton functionality.

Sharpen your pencil

This sharpen gets you on the one most common
mistake EJB developers make. So don't skip it!

Based on this scenario, draw the classes below into the
appropriate slot for whether they must be on the client, server, or
both (you can reuse a class). The picture is simplified, so you
aren't seeing all of the players involved.

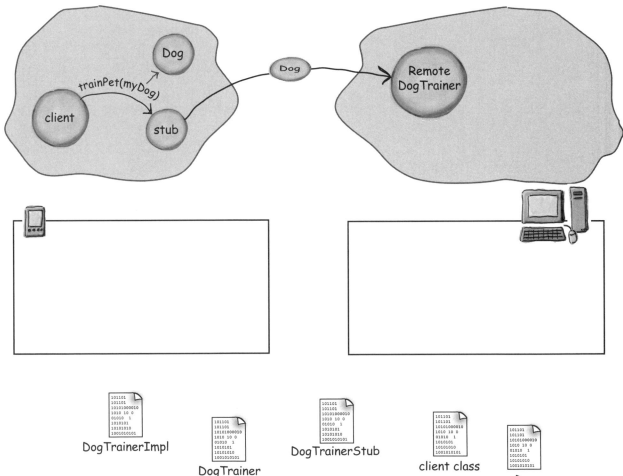

DogTrainerImpl

DogTrainer
interface

DogTrainerStub

client class

Dog

How EJB uses RMI

In EJB, a client's entry point into the enterprise application is nearly always through a reference (stub) to a Remote object. Yes, it is possible, and sometimes necessary, to use a *local* client (i.e. a client in the same heap as the bean, and which doesn't use RMI to invoke business methods), but this is for only a few very special cases.

So RMI lies at the heart of most client-to-bean communication. But as you saw a hint of in the first chapter, the EJB architecture is a little more complex than a simple client-to-stub-to-Remote-object scenario. In EJB, the bean—the thing on which the client wants to call business methods—is not Remote!

Plain RMI

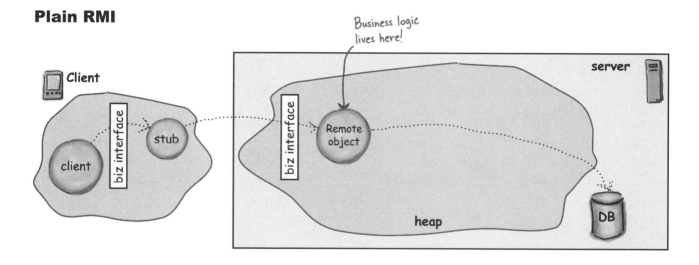

RMI in EJB

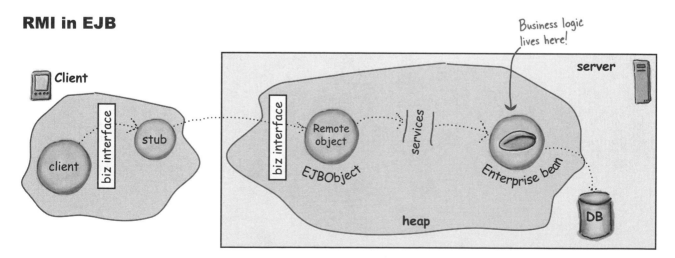

The Remote object is not the *bean*, it's the bean's *bodyguard*—the EJBObject

In EJB, remember, the Remote object (EJBObject) is the bean's bodyguard. The bean sits back, protected from all client invocations, while the EJBObject implements the Remote interface and takes the remote calls. Once the call gets to the EJBObject, the server jumps in with all the services, like security (is this client authorized to call this method?), transactions (is this call part of an existing transaction, or should we start another transaction?), and persistence (does the bean need to load info from the database *before* running the client's method?).

The EJBObject implements the Remote business interface, so the remote calls from the client come to the EJBObject. But it's still the bean that has the real business logic, even though the bean doesn't implement the Remote interface in the technical Java way.

Both the Remote object and the stub implement the same interface—the business interface (called a Component interface)—but without the real business logic behavior.

The bean class does NOT implement the business interface (in the formal Java way), but the bean has the real business logic functionality.

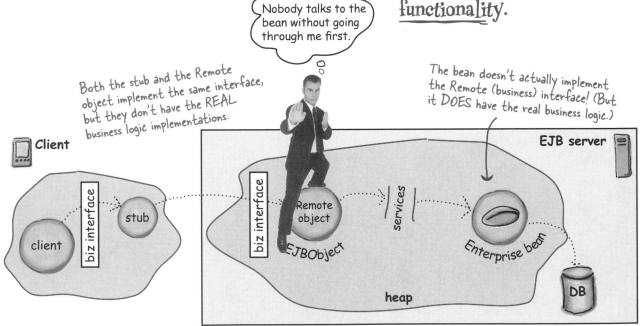

Nobody talks to the bean without going through me first.

Both the stub and the Remote object implement the same interface, but they don't have the REAL business logic implementations.

The bean doesn't actually implement the Remote (business) interface! (But it DOES have the real business logic.)

Client

biz interface

stub

client

biz interface

Remote object

EJBObject

services

Enterprise bean

EJB server

DB

heap

The Component interface

In EJB, the business interface is called the *component* interface. This is where you expose your business methods to the client. The main difference between an RMI interface and a remote component interface is that with EJB you extend javax.ejb.EJBObject instead of java.rmi.Remote.

Key points:

 Any interface with java.rmi.Remote in its inheritance tree is a Remote interface.

② The EJBObject interface extends Remote, so EJBObject is a Remote interface.

③ Your remote component interface must extend the EJBObject interface.

(You *can* have a local component interface, and the rules are different, but we'll look at that in the chapter on Client View.)

④ You expose your business methods to the client through the component interface.

⑤ The EJBObject interface adds additional methods for the client to use. (We'll see those later.)

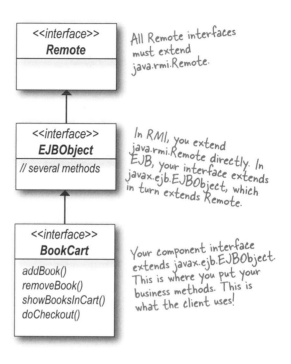

All Remote interfaces must extend java.rmi.Remote.

In RMI, you extend java.rmi.Remote directly. In EJB, your interface extends javax.ejb.EJBObject, which in turn extends Remote.

Your component interface extends javax.ejb.EJBObject. This is where you put your business methods. This is what the client uses!

Whoever implements the BookCart interface must implement all the methods from both BookCart and EJBObject. The EJBObject interface adds the methods that all EJB clients might need.

How the bean class fits in

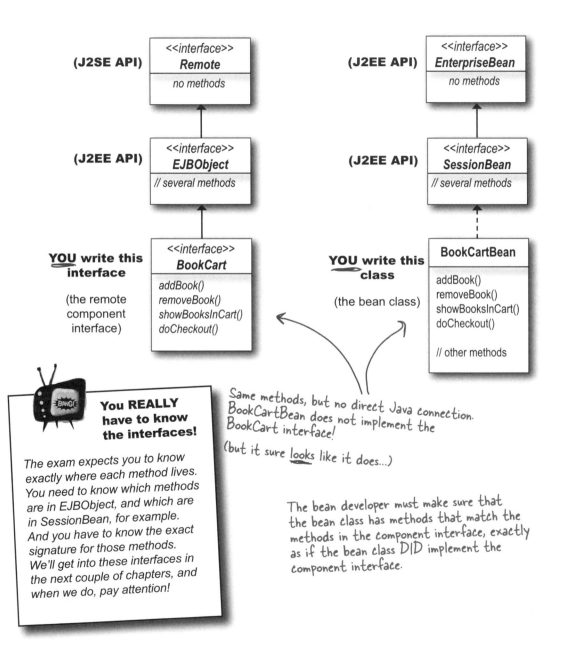

(J2SE API) <<interface>> **Remote** — no methods

(J2EE API) <<interface>> **EJBObject** — // several methods

YOU write this interface <<interface>> **BookCart** — addBook(), removeBook(), showBooksInCart(), doCheckout()

(the remote component interface)

(J2EE API) <<interface>> **EnterpriseBean** — no methods

(J2EE API) <<interface>> **SessionBean** — // several methods

YOU write this class **BookCartBean** — addBook(), removeBook(), showBooksInCart(), doCheckout(), // other methods

(the bean class)

Same methods, but no direct Java connection. BookCartBean does not implement the BookCart interface! (but it sure looks like it does...)

The bean developer must make sure that the bean class has methods that match the methods in the component interface, exactly as if the bean class DID implement the component interface.

You REALLY have to know the interfaces!

The exam expects you to know exactly where each method lives. You need to know which methods are in EJBObject, and which are in SessionBean, for example. And you have to know the exact signature for those methods. We'll get into these interfaces in the next couple of chapters, and when we do, pay attention!

Q: I just want to be sure I'm clear about this... interfaces can EXTEND other interfaces?

A: Yes, interfaces have their own inheritance tree. In fact, with interfaces, you can do something you can't ever do with a class—*an interface can extend more than one interface!*

```
interface Cart extends EJBObject, CartBusiness
```

Q: But what does that really mean when an interface extends another interface? Extending means inheritance, but what is the interface inheriting?

A: When one interface extends another, it inherits everything from that interface. Whoever implements an interface must implement not just the methods from that interface, but also the methods from every interface that interface extends... all the way up the interface inheritance tree.

So, in this example, whoever implements BookCart must also implement the methods of EJBObject.

> **When you implement an interface, you must implement *all* the methods that interface inherits from its super-interfaces.**
>
> **So whoever implements BookCart must implement the methods from both BookCart *and* EJBObject.**

Q: Why doesn't the bean implement the Remote/business interface? Isn't the whole point of an interface implementation to use the compiler to keep you honest, and to support Java type-checking?

A: You asked this question before. But, hey, we all forget things, so we'll remind you again. The bean doesn't implement the Remote interface because the bean is never supposed to be a Remote object (in the Java RMI sense). In other words, you never ever want anyone to have a stub to the actual bean! If you were to somehow sneak a remote reference (i.e. a stub) out to the world, you'd be defeating the whole purpose of EJB! If you let a client talk directly to the bean, then the server wouldn't be able to apply its services, and if you don't need the services... you see where we're going here.

Technically, it *is* legal to have the bean implement the Remote interface, but it's a really bad idea, since you could make mistakes that wouldn't be caught at compile time (but which would blow up later). But you don't need to do it, since virtually all bean development tools (including nearly every bean-aware IDE) understand the relationship between the bean, the EJBObject, and the Remote interface, and they guarantee that the component interface and the bean class have matching methods.

Q: But what if I just find this too disturbing? This whole idea violates my Java sensibilities, the very principles upon which I code. Surely there must be something I can do?

A: You could trust us on the whole "you're almost certainly using tools, so it really won't matter. Really" thing, but no... so if you insist, yes there is something you can do that'll probably help you feel better. It's on the next page, but you can probably figure it out yourself anyway.

Nonetheless, we're sticking by our story that most developers won't need to do this.

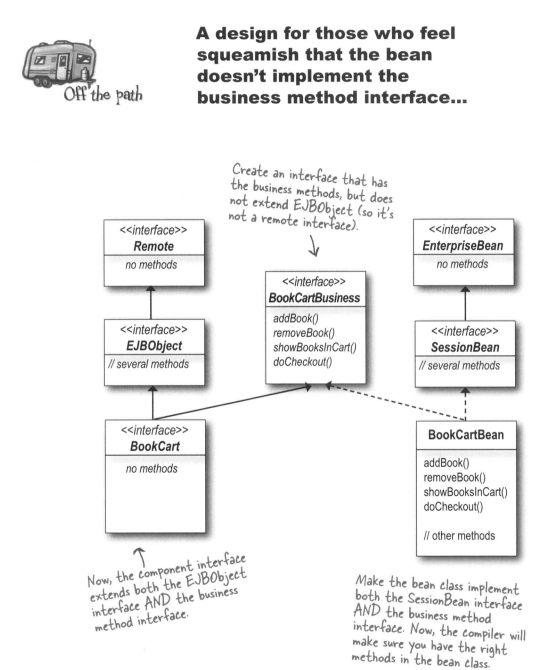

Off the path

A design for those who feel squeamish that the bean doesn't implement the business method interface...

Create an interface that has the business methods, but does not extend EJBObject (so it's not a remote interface).

<<interface>>
Remote

no methods

<<interface>>
EJBObject

// several methods

<<interface>>
BookCart

no methods

<<interface>>
BookCartBusiness

addBook()
removeBook()
showBooksInCart()
doCheckout()

<<interface>>
EnterpriseBean

no methods

<<interface>>
SessionBean

// several methods

BookCartBean

addBook()
removeBook()
showBooksInCart()
doCheckout()

// other methods

Now, the component interface extends both the EJBObject interface AND the business method interface.

Make the bean class implement both the SessionBean interface AND the business method interface. Now, the compiler will make sure you have the right methods in the bean class.

So, I write my bean and I put in matching methods from the component interface, without officially implementing the component interface. But if I don't implement the component interface... who does?

Who writes the class that really DOES implement the component interface? In other words, who makes the EJBObject <u>class</u>?

The container. You declare the methods, but the container implements your component interface. Remember, your component interface is the one that extends EJBObject, so the container has to implement not just your business methods, but also the methods of EJBObject (which we haven't yet looked at).

Q: But how does the container know what to put in those methods? I'm the one who declared those methods...

A: Remember, the container isn't implementing the real business logic. The true functionality for those business methods lives in your bean class—the class that you implement. The class implementing the component interface is going to be the EJBObject. The bodyguard. The Remote object. And remember that the EJBObject is only pretending to be the bean. It can respond to the remote method calls coming from the client (via the stub), but the EJBObject's only job is to capture the incoming client calls to the bean. After that, it's up to the container/server to take over.

We don't really know how the EJBObject is implemented—it's completely up to the vendor. But we don't really care. All you need to know is that an EJB container is required by the spec to generate the code for the EJBObject (and its corresponding stub).

Who creates what?

For a bean with a remote client view (in other words, a bean that can be accessed by remote clients), you know that you have to write the Component interface and the Bean class. But *somebody* has to write the class that implements your Component interface (to make the Remote EJBObject), and *somebody* has to make the stub that goes with that EJBObject. That *somebody* is the Container. And, though we haven't yet talked about the Home, we've listed the relevant pieces here for completeness.

You

(1) **The Component interface**
(extends javax.ejb.EJBObject)

(2) **The Bean class**
(implements javax.ejb.SessionBean
or javax.ejb.EntityBean)

(3) **The Home interface**
(extends javax.ejb.EJBHome; we'll
talk about this on the next page)

*We haven't talked about the Home yet,
so we don't show it on this picture.*

the Container

(1) **The EJBObject class**
(implements your Component interface)

(2) **The EJBObject stub class**
(implements your Component interface
and knows how to talk to the EJBObject)

(3) **The Home class**
(implements your Home interface)

(4) **The Home stub class**
(implements your Home interface
and knows how to talk to the Home)

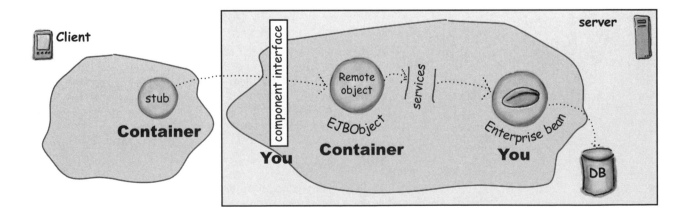

Overheard at THE TIKIBEAN LOUNGE

EJBObject: Hey Beanie...don't you ever get tired of always having me in the middle of everything? Don't you ever just want to have a direct conversation with someone?

Bean: No. I'm too important. I'm too valuable. And I'm sure as hell not gonna start screening my own calls. That's what you people are for.

EJBObject: You people?

Bean: Yeah, you people who work for the container. You, the Home, the stubs, all of you. My job is to handle the complex business logic. The critical functions that mean the difference between success and failure in an enterprise environment.

EJBObject: (*Geez, sounds like a marketing speech*). OK, so you have some important methods, but I still don't see why you need to have me in every call.

Bean: Look, my work is too important to be interrupted by clients who have no business calling me in the first place. Do you honestly think that I am going to check security clearances for every caller? Like I don't have better things to do?

EJBObject: OK, so it's really just a security thing, but I don't see why *you* can't just have the code to check the security access of the caller. That would save a lot of overhead (namely, ME).

Bean: First of all, security is just ONE of the reasons you have to take my calls. I'll get to those other reasons in a minute. But as for putting in code to do my own checks, actually I CAN do that, if the programmer wants me to. But it's usually not the way to handle security.

EJBObject: What's wrong with you handling the security checks in your own code?

Bean: You really don't know, do you? [rolls eyes] First, if the security checks are coded into me, then I'm not as reusable. The whole point of EJB is to configure and customize beans at runtime, without rewriting the code. If I've got security programming in my Java code, then it can't be changed without touching the source. And who wants that?

EJBObject: I guess that makes sense. You put the security checks in the XML deployment descriptor, and then when I get the call, the server can check to see if the client has the right authorization. But what if security isn't even an issue for you? What if whoever deploys you doesn't care who calls the methods?

Bean: Not too bright, are you? But at least you can lift heavy objects... THINK about all the other things that matter, like transactions and persistence.

EJBObject: Oh, I forgot about transactions. OK, that makes sense too. The server has to figure out if there's a transaction context before it calls your method so that your method can run in a transaction. Either your own, or the caller's...

Bean: Duh.

EJBObject: But where does persistence come in?

Bean: Well, think about entity beans for a minute. If I'm an entity bean, that means I'm representing some entity in the underlying persistent store and—

EJBObject: —wait—by persistent store, don't you just mean DATABASE? Why don't you just say *database*?

Bean: Uh, newsflash, the word phrase "persistent store" is not a synonym for "database". A database is just one example of a persistent store. But if it makes you feel better to think about it that way, go ahead for now. But as I was saying, if I represent an entity, say, a customer named Tom Duff, then what happens if the client calls my getAddress() method? The server can't just hand me the call!

EJBObject: Because...

Bean: Because I have to load in Tom Duff's information from the database first!

EJBObject: Because...

Bean: Because I'd return an address that might not even be valid! Unless I'm still in a previous transaction with this client, then the server has to tell me to load myself with Tom Duff's database info BEFORE the server tells me to run the getAddress() method. Otherwise, who knows what I'd return? OK, well, that's last call, so we'll have to continue this some other time.

there are no
Dumb Questions

Q: **How and when does the container create the EJBObject and the Home and the stubs?**

A: When you deploy a bean, the container looks at the DD and takes it from there. Remember, the DD gives the fully qualified name of your Remote Component (EJBObject) interface and your Remote Home interface. So, once the container gets those interfaces, it generates code for the two classes implementing those interfaces. And because they're Remote, the container also creates the client stubs that know how to communicate back to the Remote objects.

Q: **Are these always plain old RMI stubs? I see that when we deployed using the RI, it printed out a message that it was running rmic...**

A: The container can do whatever it wants to create the stubs; the requirement is that the stubs be RMI-IIOP compliant. In fact, a server can use something called dynamic proxies to implement the stub functionality, but we don't care. When we say "stub" we mean something with stub behavior. Whether it's an RMI stub or something else, is an implementation detail for the server. We'll look at that in more detail in the next chapter. The bottom line is that you really don't know what the stub class code looks like. For that matter, you really don't know how the EJBObject and the Home are implemented. You're not supposed to know.

You *might* have an EJB container that

lets you view (possibly even *hack*) the generated source code, but don't count on it. And if we were you, we just wouldn't go there, even if we could.

Q: **So these classes are up to the vendor's implementation?**

A: Yes! The vendor has all sorts of choices for implementing these classes and might use the stubs and/or Home and EJBObjects to get some performance advantages. But again, that's not up for you to mess with, or even know about.

The only requirement in the spec that you're guaranteed (and required to adhere to) is that Remote objects must follow the rules for RMI-IIOP, which means Java's Remote Method Invocation using the IIOP (CORBA standard) wire protocol.

Q: **You brought it up: how is RMI-IIOP different from regular RMI?**

A: Plain old RMI uses JRMP as its wire protocol. But IIOP lets Remote objects interoperate through CORBA (we won't be saying much at all about CORBA in this book; it's definitely out of scope for the exam and the book, except in a few tiny cases we'll see scattered throughout the chapters).

That gives your objects a chance to be accessed, for example, by even non-Java clients. One thing IIOP specifies is the way information for transactions and security can be propagated along with the method call, and your container might be taking advantage of that.

For the most part, you'll barely notice the difference between plain old RMI and RMI-IIOP. But... there are a couple

of places where it's different, and one of these differences is definitely on the exam—the need to narrow a stub. We'll cover narrowing in detail in the next chapter on Client View. For now, just know that it's something a client must do with an EJB stub that they don't have to do with a plain Java stub because the EJB spec tells you to assume that the stub is using IIOP and thus might be a different *kind* of stub.

Q: **When are we going to talk about the Home?**

A: Next page.

Q: **Why did you take so long? Isn't the Home important?**

A: As crucial as the Home is, it's usually just the way you *get* a reference to something that implements the Component interface. In other words, you use the Home to get an EJBObject stub (for Remote clients, which is all we've talked about so far).

For Entity beans, the Home can have a more important role, and we'll see that, but even with Entity beans, the Home's primary use is still to get EJBObject stubs. After that, most of the communication between the client and the bean comes through the EJBObject and not the Home. Most of the time, in fact, clients use the Home just to get the EJBObject reference, and then the Home reference is tossed out, not needed.

The bean Home

Every Session and Entity bean has a Home.

Message-driven beans don't have homes because message-driven beans don't have a client view (in other words, client's can't get a reference to a Message-driven bean).

The Home has one main job: to hand out references to a bean's Component interface. For a Session bean, that's just about all you'll do with the bean's Home. For Entity beans, though, the Home plays a much bigger role.

Each deployed bean has its own Home, and that Home is responsible for all bean instances of that type. For example, if you deploy a ShoppingCart Session bean, the container will create one ShoppingCart bean Home. That ShoppingCart Home takes care of all the instances of ShoppingCart beans. In other words, if 2,000 clients each want their own ShoppingCart bean reference (which, remember, means a reference to the ShoppingCart bean's Component interface), the one and only ShoppingCart Home will hand out all 2,000 references.

If you deploy three beans as part of an application, say, a ShoppingCart, Customer, and Product, there will be three Homes in the server representing each of those deployed beans. It makes no difference how many EJBObjects and stubs the Home objects hand out, there will still be only three Homes.

So does that mean that for each Home there is only a single instance of the class that implements the Home interface for that bean type? Not necessarily, but that's exactly how we're supposed to think about it. We'll actually refer to the Home as *the Home object*, and we'll assume that there's always just one per deployed bean type. The spec guarantees that you can think about it that way, regardless of what your vendor actually does with its implementation for the Home.

Each deployed Session and Entity bean has a Home. For example, the AdviceBean has an AdviceBean Home. No matter how many clients get an AdviceBean, there's only <u>one</u> AdviceBean Home.

The Home's job is to hand out references to that bean's Component interface.

(Technically there's a little more to the story because a bean might have both a local Home and a Remote Home, but that's really unlikely. Even then, there would be only one of each Home type (Remote or local) no matter how many beans of that type are alive.)

Getting and using a Home for the AdviceBean

(This scenario assumes AdviceBean is a stateful Session bean.)

① **The AdviceBean is deployed, and the server instantiates the AdviceBean Home object and registers it with JNDI.**

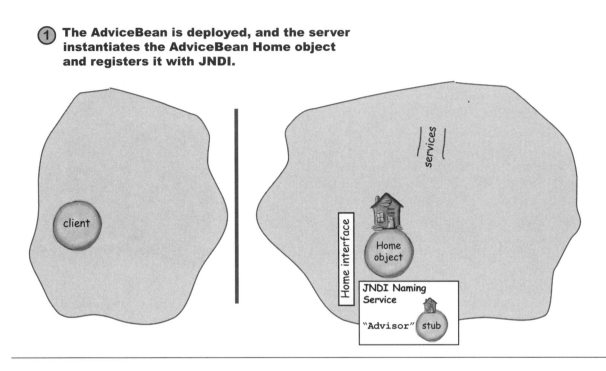

② **The client does a JNDI lookup on the Home, using the registered name "Advisor".**

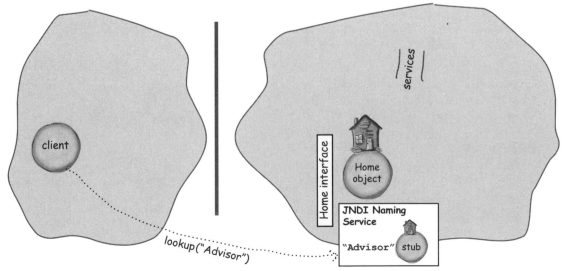

(3) **JNDI sends back a stub to the Remote Home object.**

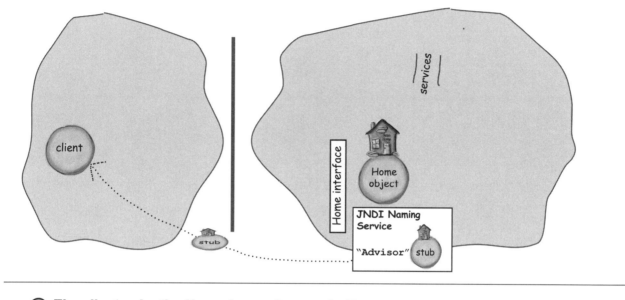

(4) **The client asks the Home for a reference to the Component interface, by calling create()**

(In other words, the client wants to "create" a bean and get the stub back to the bean's EJBObject)

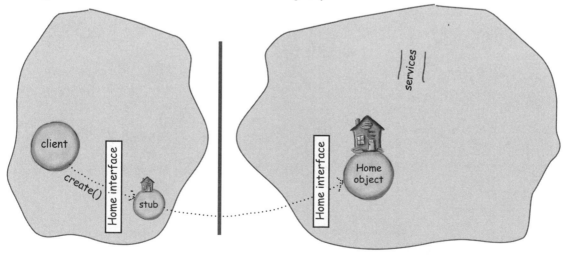

The Home object makes the EJBObject and sends back the stub

⑤ **Now the "services" kick in, and the bean is created**

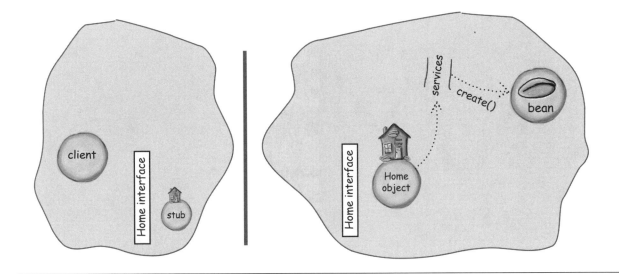

⑥ **The EJBObject is made (the bodyguard for this newly created bean) and its stub is returned to the client.**

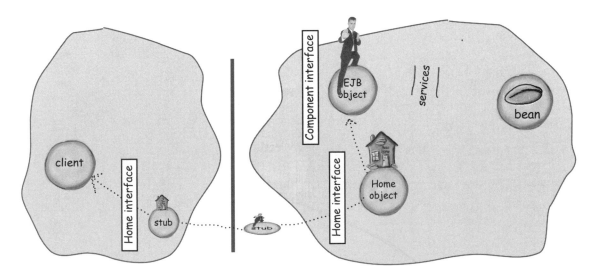

⑦ Now, the client can (finally) do what he REALLY wants
to do—call a business method on the bean! (Which of
course, has to go through the Component interface.)

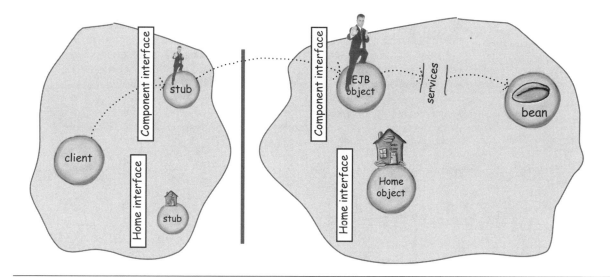

⑧ The client can get rid of his Home stub if he doesn't
want access to more beans of this type (AdviceBean),
but he can still keep calling methods on the
Component interface.

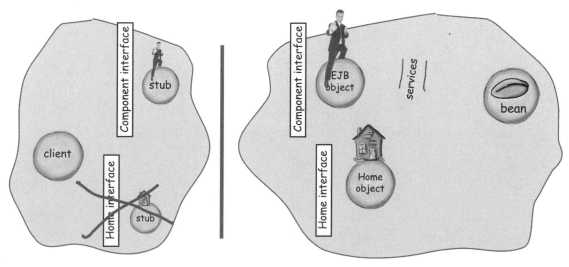

Sharpen your pencil

EJB Lifecycle:

Client has only a Home stub but wants to invoke a business method on a bean.

In the scenario below, assume the client has previously done a JNDI lookup and gotten back a stub to the Remote Home object.
Everything in the picture is what happens AFTER the client has the Home stub and now wants to get a reference to an EJBObject and ultimately call a business method on the bean.

Number the arrows (using the boxes over the arrows) in the order in which they occur. These arrows aren't necessarily direct method calls (although they might be), but rather arrows pointing to the next THING that happens. Tell a story for what happens at each arrow. There might be more than one right answer, depending on how you tell the story. Some arrows are missing; you can add them if you want, or, just assume some things are happening that you don't have arrows for.

Relax and take your time.
If you get stuck, flip back through the previous pages and study the diagrams.

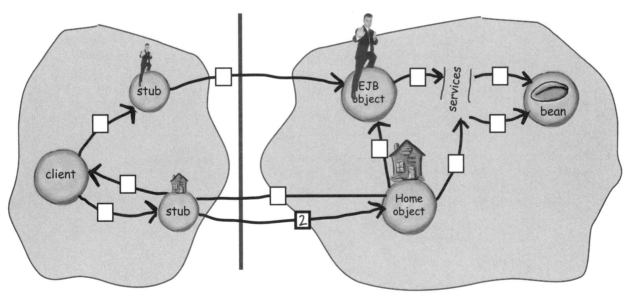

1.

2. The stub tells the Home that the client wants to "create" a bean.

3.

4.

5

6.

7.

8.

9.

10.

11.

BULLET POINTS

- Beans that are exposed to remote clients have two Remote interfaces one for the EJBHome and one for the EJBObject.

- A Remote interface must extend (directly or indirectly) java.rmi.Remote, and all methods must declare a java.rmi.RemoteException.

- In EJB, the interface that extends EJBObject is called the Remote Component interface. It is where the business methods are declared.

- The client never calls methods on the bean itself because the bean is NOT a Remote object.

- The container implements the Remote Component interface by building a class that implements it. This class is used to make the EJBObject for the bean. (The bean's bodyguard.)

- The container also creates the stub to the EJBObject.

- You create the Remote Component interface by writing an interface that extends javax.ejb.EJBObject (an interface that extends java.rmi.Remote).

- You also create the bean class where the actual business methods are implemented (despite the fact that the bean class technically doesn't implement the Remote Component interface).

- The Home is the factory for the bean. Its main job is to hand the client a reference to the bean. But remember, the client can never truly get a reference to the *bean*—the best the client can do is to get a reference to the bean's EJBObject.

- You create the Home interface by writing an interface that extends javax.ejb.EJBHome (an interface that extends java.rmi.Remote).

- The container is responsible for implementing the Home interface by building a class that implements it, and the container also generates the stub for the Home.

- There is only one Home per deployed bean. For example, a ShoppingCart bean would have a single ShoppingCart Home, regardless of how many ShoppingCart beans have been created.

Make it Stick

mandatory means existing tx

buy this book

create returns component interface

Roses are red, violets are blue,
The Remote interfaces are written by YOU.

Roses are red, and quite a big project,
The server will make the EJBObject.

Roses are red, the petals will float,
The bean class itself, is never Remote.

(Yeah, OK, not our finest work. *You* try it. Remember, these things will stick a lot more if you come up with them yourself.)

Architectural overview: <u>Session</u> beans

Clients share the Home, but <u>never</u> the bean.

Each client gets his own EJBObject reference and his own bean. The client never shares a bean with another client, although the meaning of "shares" depends on whether the bean is stateful or stateless. (We'll see that in the next chapter.) However, there's only one Home object for this particular bean type (say, AdviceBean), so both clients have a stub to the one and only Advice Home. Both clients ask the same Advice Home for a reference to an Advice bean. (Of course, the client never gets the reference to the *bean instance*, but instead gets a reference to the bean's EJBObject. And since EJBObject is Remote, the clients gets a *stub*.)

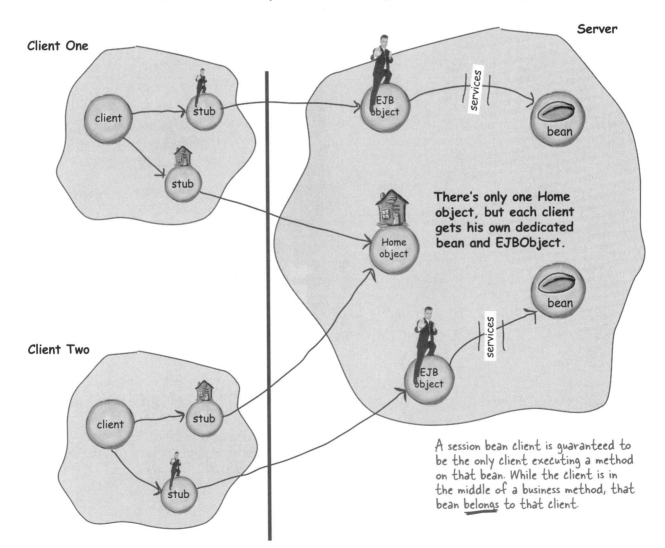

There's only one Home object, but each client gets his own dedicated bean and EJBObject.

A session bean client is guaranteed to be the only client executing a method on that bean. While the client is in the middle of a business method, that bean <u>belongs</u> to that client.

Architectural overview: <u>Entity</u> beans

Clients share the Home, and may share the bean.

Each client has his own reference to the one and only Home for this bean (say, CustomerBean). But, if two clients are trying to access the same Customer (Fred Smith #420), then both clients have a reference to the same EJBObject. The EJBObject for #420. In other words, the EJBObject is the bodyguard for a particular Customer (like Fred Smith). If all the clients are trying to access Fred Smith #420, they will each have their own stub, of course, but all stubs will communicate with the same Remote EJBObject. And there will be only one bean representing Fred Smith #420. If a client wants to access two different customers, though, the client will have two stubs, and those stubs will be for two different EJBObjects, one for each customer. And that also means two different *beans*.

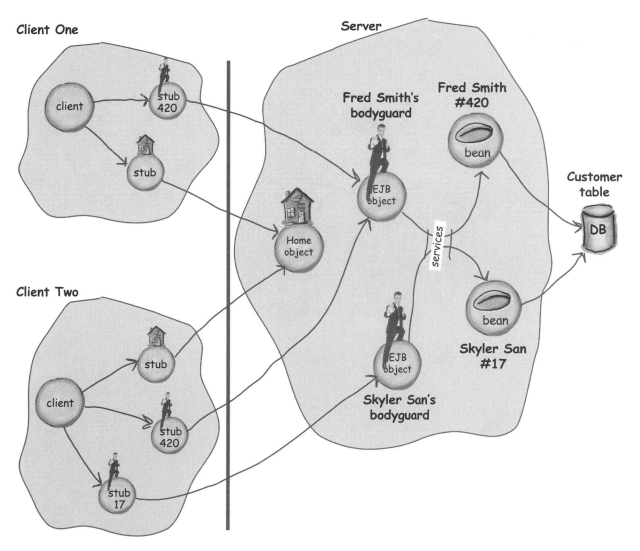

Architectural overview: Creating a State**ful** Session bean

After getting a Home stub, the client calls "create" on the Home. The Home creates the bean and the EJBObject for the bean and hands back the EJBObject stub.

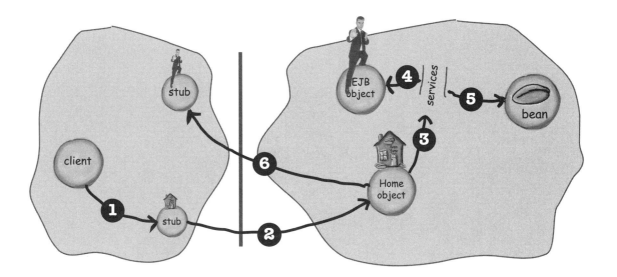

1. The client calls create() on the Home stub (create() is a method in the Home interface).

2. The stub sends the create() call to the Remote Home object.

3. The Home object steps in and adds its services.

4. The EJBObject is created/instantiated for the bean.

5. The bean itself is instantiated.

6. The EJBObject stub is returned to the client, so the client can call business methods on the Component interface.

Architectural overview: Creating a Stateless Session bean

After getting a Home stub, the client calls "create" on the Home. The Home gives the client a stub to an existing EJBObject but does not associate a bean with this EJBObject! Instead, the bean stays in a pool until the client uses the EJBObject stub to call a business method.

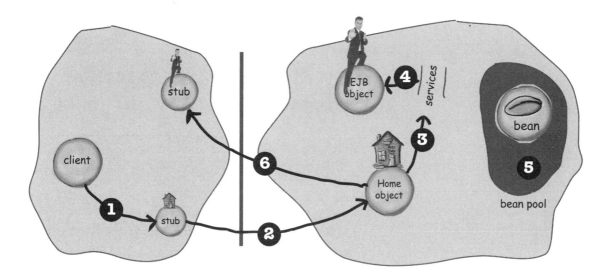

1. The client calls create() on the Home stub (create() is a method in the Home interface).

2. The stub sends the create() call to the Remote Home object.

3. The Home/Container steps in and adds its services.

4. An EJBObject is created for this client.

5. The bean stays in the bean pool! It comes out only to service an actual business method, if the client invokes one on the EJBObject stub.

6. The EJBObject stub is returned to the client, so the client can call business methods on the Component interface.

> OK, so the bean comes out of the pool only when the client calls a business method, but then... how did the bean get in the pool in the first place? If it wasn't created when the client called create(), then what *did* cause the bean to be created?

Who creates the stateless session bean, and when?

First, we have to define what *create* means. For a session bean, it means the bean instance is physically instantiated and initialized as a bean. For an entity bean, it's completely different, so **this conversation applies just to session beans**. Later we'll get into what it means to create an entity bean.

For state*ful* session beans, the create is triggered by the client. The client calls create on a Home stub, and everything happens at that point—an EJBObject is instantiated for this new about-to-be-created-bean, and then the bean itself is created and linked to the EJBObject (the bean's bodyguard).

But for state*less* session beans, the *client* create and the actual creation of the *bean* are decoupled. In other words, just because the client calls create on a Home stub doesn't mean a bean will be created at that point.

State*less* session beans aren't created until the container decides it needs one, and that's really up to the container. It might, for example, make a bunch of bean instances (i.e. create some beans) and plop them in a pool before even a single client has asked for one (by calling create on a Home stub). Or, the container might make just-in-time beans, and wait until the client invokes a business method before going to the trouble of physically creating the bean.

Stateless session beans are more scalable

Clients don't share EJBObjects, but the same bean can service *multiple* EJBObjects. Just not at the same time. A single bean can handle multiple clients, as long as only one client at a time is in the middle of a business method invocation.

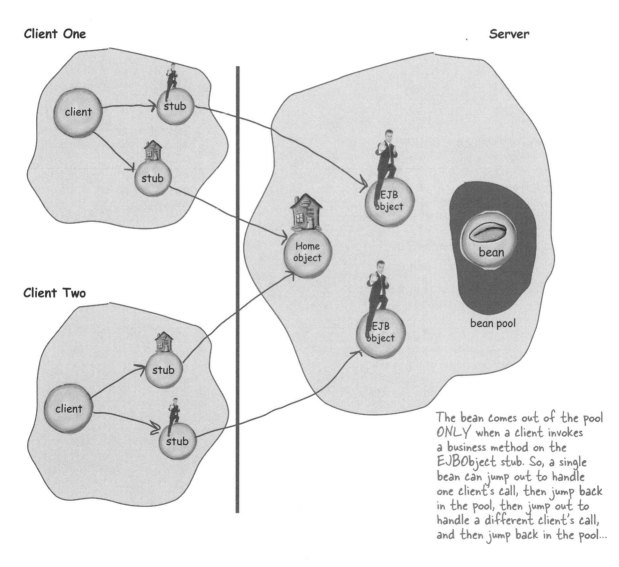

The bean comes out of the pool ONLY when a client invokes a business method on the EJBObject stub. So, a single bean can jump out to handle one client's call, then jump back in the pool, then jump out to handle a different client's call, and then jump back in the pool...

BRAIN POWER

Why does the "pool" architecture work to make stateless session beans more scalable, but not stateful session beans? Why can't stateful session beans use the bean pool?

there are no Dumb Questions

Q: Here's something that is REALLY starting to annoy me... why do you have a Component interface and a Home interface when the Remote objects are called the Home and the EJBObject? Why isn't it just the EJBObject interface and the HomeObject interface? Or the Home and the EJB interfaces? Why the inconsistency?

A: Actually, that really pisses us off too. But you'll get used to it. Be thankful, it was even worse if you learned EJB prior to version 2.0 when it was called the Home and the Remote. Now that was a real problem because, first of all, *both* the Home and the Remote were Remote in the java.rmi sense. Second, as of EJB 2.0 you can have a Home and a Remote that aren't... actually... Remote. So, they had to change the name to Component interface instead of calling it THE Remote interface, since it might, in fact, not be Remote. If you just remember that the Component interface is where the business methods are, and the Home is where the, um, *Home* methods are, you should be fine. Just remember, Component = business = EJBObject (or EJB*Local*Object, but we won't go there until the next chapter).

Sharpen your pencil

T F   A stateful session bean can be shared between multiple clients.

T F   An entity bean can be shared between multiple clients, as long as the entity being shared is the same.

T F   Stateless session beans are created when the client invokes create on the Home.

T F   Stateful session beans are created when the client invokes create on the Home.

T F   There must be one stateless session bean per client, for as long as the client holds a reference to an EJBObject.

T F   There must be one stateless session bean per client, for as long as the client is in the middle of a business method invocation on the bean.

T F   Each entity bean must have its EJBObject.

Answers: F T F T F T T

there are no
Dumb Questions

Q: How does this work? Is there one bean pool for all beans, or one bean pool for a particular type of bean?

A: In reality, we don't know what the container implementation is, but conceptually there's one pool for every bean type. So, if you deploy an AdviceBean and a WeatherBean, and both are stateless session beans, they'll each get their own pool.

Q: Does each stateless session bean have its own EJBObject?

A: Sort of. A stateless session bean doesn't need a bodyguard until he's actually involved in a method invocation. So, the client gets a reference to an EJBObject, but the bean isn't associated with that EJBObject until the client calls a business method. At that point, the bean slides out of the pool to service the method. So, the EJBObject the client has is for a *kind* of bean (AdviceBean, WeatherBean, etc.) but not a specific *instance* of a bean.

Q: Why don't stateful session beans have a pool?

A: Have you already thought about this in the Brain Power on the previous page? Because if you haven't, don't read any further until you've come up with your own ideas. If you

made it this far, we assume that you already know the answer and we're just confirming it...

A stateful bean, remember, holds client conversational state. That means the bean has to save client-specific state (in other words, it has to remember things about this client) across multiple method invocations from the client.

Think of a shopping cart again—a stateful bean needs to remember what's in the client's cart each time the client calls addItemToCart(). A stateless bean, on the other hand, doesn't have to remember anything on the client's behalf, so to a client, one stateless bean (of a particular type) is as good as any other bean of that type.

If the AdviceBean simply returns a piece of advice not connected in any way to anything it told the client before (or anything the client told *it*), then there's no need for the AdviceBean to be stateful. In that case, each time a client calls getAdvice() on the Component interface (i.e. the EJBObject), any AdviceBean is just as capable of running the method as any other.

On the other hand, if the AdviceBean were modified to return, say, random but non-repeating advice, then the AdviceBean would have to be stateful, so that it could keep track of previous advice and never repeat it.

Q: How long does a stateful bean keep client-specific state?

A: Only for the life of the session. A session continues until the client tells the bean he's done (by calling remove() on the bean's Component interface), or the server crashes, or the bean times out (we'll cover that in the Session lifecycle chapter).

Q: So stateful session beans aren't scalable?

A: No, they are. Just not *as* scalable as state*less* beans.

Q: How can a stateful bean be scalable if you always need one bean for every client?

A: You do need a separate bean allocated for each client, but not every bean has to be actively consuming resources. If the stateful session bean client is taking a long time between method calls, the stateful bean can be temporarily taken down and put in a state called passivation. This state preserves the client-specific state, of course, but reduces the number of beans currently alive in the server. The bean comes out of passivation and back into active duty (activation) when the client calls a business method.

Architectural overview: Message-driven beans

Message-driven beans don't have a client view. That means they don't have interfaces (Remote or local) that expose methods to the client. In other words, message-driven beans don't have a Home or EJBObject. They don't have a Home interface or a Component interface.

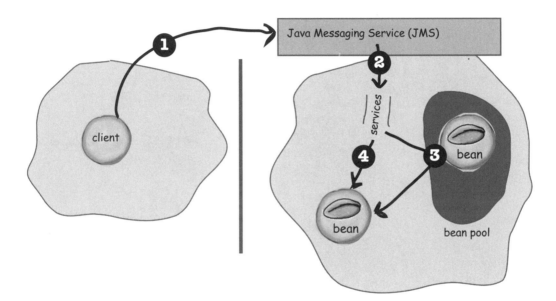

1. The client sends a message to a JMS messaging service.

2. The messaging service delivers the message to the container.

3. The container gets a message-driven bean out of the pool.

4. The container delivers the message to the bean (by calling the bean's onMessage() MessageListener interface method).

What goes where?

Exercise

Place the objects and classes in the appropriate spot on either the client, the server, or in both places (yes, you can reuse an object). Note: not all the pieces are here, so when you're done, if you can think of other things that should go into the picture (classes or objects) draw them in!

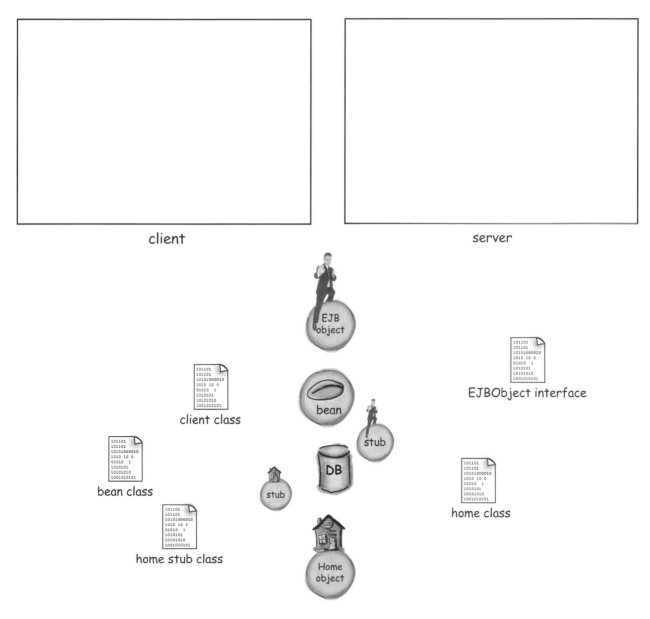

client

server

EJB object

client class

EJBObject interface

bean

stub

bean class

stub

DB

home class

home stub class

Home object

bean *table*

Exercise

Organize your beans

Finish the table by putting in a checkmark (even better if you add notes) in the boxes corresponding to the labels that apply to that bean type. We've done one of the boxes for you. If you get stuck, go back through the previous two chapters. You might have to make your best guess on a few things. That's OK— you'll have it all worked out way before the end of the book. We believe in you. You can do it. [cue theme song from "Rocky"]

	Stateful Session Beans	Stateful Session Beans	Entity Beans	Message-driven Beans
Uses a pool	Yes. Since they don't keep any client–specific data, you don't need one per each client.			
Multiple clients can have a reference to the same bean				
Guaranteed to survive a container crash				
Has a client view				
Allows asynchronous communication				
Represents a process				
Represents a "thing" in an underlying persistent store (like a database)				

Exercise Solutions

What goes where?

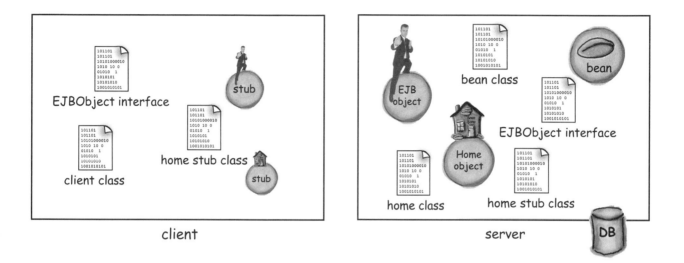

NOTE: you won't find a finished solution for the Organize Your Beans table. We want YOU to fill this out. It's yet another special Learning Opportunity for which you'll always remember us with fondness.

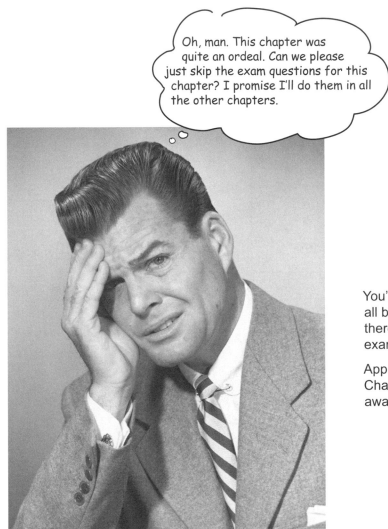

Oh, man. This chapter was quite an ordeal. Can we please just skip the exam questions for this chapter? I promise I'll do them in all the other chapters.

You're in luck. This chapter is all background knowledge, so there aren't any objectives or exam questions.

Appreciate the moment— Chapter 3 is just a page turn away...

3 the client view

Exposing Yourself

You can't keep your bean private. Clients need to see what you've got.
(Except for message-driven beans, which don't *have* a client view). The Advice Bean
exposed the getAdvice() method in its Component interface—the place where you declare
business methods. But that's not *all* the client sees. Remember, the Advice interface
extended EJBObject, an interface with methods of its *own*. Methods the client can see.
Methods the client can *call*. And it works the same way with the Home interface. In this
chapter, we'll learn what you *really* expose to the client, and how the client works, including
both Remote and *local* interfaces.

The Client View

Official:	*What it really means:*
2.1 Identify correct and incorrect statements or examples about the client view of a session bean's local and remote home interfaces, including the code used by the client to locate a session bean's home interface.	You have to know everything about the *home* interface. This particular objective doesn't include the special characteristics of an entity bean home, but *most* of the details about the client's view of a bean's home are still covered in this objective (and this chapter).
	For example, you have to know exactly which methods are in javax.ejb.EJBHome (the Remote home interface), and which methods are in javax.ejb.EJBLocalHome (the local home interface). And it's not enough to know what the methods *are*—you also have to know the circumstances under which they can be *called*. You have to know, for instance, that a *Remote* session bean client can *remove* a bean using the bean's home, but a *local* client *cannot*. And you have to know that a local home has fewer methods than a Remote home, and what that means for the client.
	Finally, for Objective 2.1, you have to know the ins and outs of how a client does a JNDI lookup on a bean's home interface. That includes the syntax of the client's lookup code, the rules for performing the lookup, and how to use the home interface to get a reference to a bean's component interface. You have to know, for example, the rules for narrowing a home stub, and, given a code snippet, you must be able to recognize whether the client is local or Remote.
2.2 Identify correct and incorrect statements or examples about the client view of a session bean's local and remote component interfaces.	This objective is just like 2.1, except it's about the *component* interface. But again, you must know all the methods of both javax.ejb.EJBObject and javax.ejb.EJBLocalObject, and how they're used by the client, and you must be able to recognize the difference between a Remote and local client, just by looking at code.

What the client really wants

The client has a goal. A vision. A quest. She wants to call a business method on the bean! Something exposed in the component interface. Never forget that ultimate goal; it *is* easy to get bogged down in all the details. But if you keep focused on the client's driving need, you'll have a much easier time remembering things like, say, the return type of a session bean's home create() method.

It all starts with the home interface

The client wants the bean. Well, too bad. ***The client will never get the bean***, because *nobody* talks to the bean (except the container). The best the client can hope for is a reference to the bean's *bodyguard*—the component interface. And the client gets a reference to the bean's *component* interface by calling a method on the bean's *home* interface.

there are no Dumb Questions

Q: **How come you said, "And the client gets a reference to the bean's component interface..." You can't *have* a reference to an interface in Java—you can reference an *object*, but you can't reference an *interface*. The reference variable can be declared as an interface type, but that's not the same thing.**

A: Well, actually it *is* the same thing. In this book, and in the spec, and in the exam, everywhere you see the phrase, "reference to an interface", do a mental search and replace to make it, "reference to an *object that implements* the interface."

It can feel a little strange, if you haven't read documents that use this convention, but you better get used to it. But don't worry, by Chapter 4, you'll wonder how anyone ever said it differently...

Q: **You said the client's ultimate goal is to call methods on the bean. (OK, the component interface, but you know what I mean.) But with entity beans, you can have business methods in the *home*, right? So with entity beans, isn't it true that sometimes the client's goal is JUST to use the home?**

A: Yes, you're right. They're called "*home* business methods" (as opposed to plain old "home methods" or plain old "business methods"). But they're a *special case* we'll look at later in the book. There are other reasons, too, for why you might need only the home of an entity bean. For example, if you want to create a bunch of new customers in a database, but you don't want to do any other operations on references to those entity customers.

What the client REALLY wants is a reference to the bean. But the best the client can do is get a reference to the bean's component interface--the EJB object*.

But if she wants an EJB object reference, the client has to get a reference to the bean's home interface.

So that's where it begins... the client does a lookup on the bean's home.

---

*We use the word "EJB object" to mean the bean's component interface (the bodyguard), i.e. the thing receiving method calls meant for the bean, regardless of whether the client is local or remote.

How a client uses a session bean: create, use, and remove

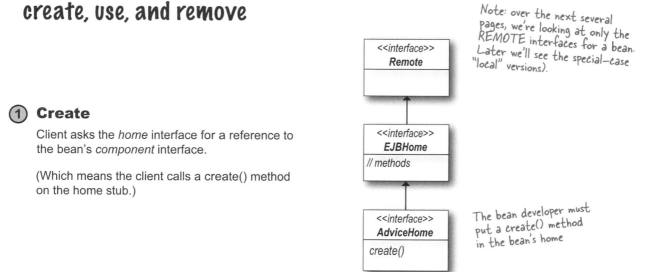

Note: over the next several pages, we're looking at only the REMOTE interfaces for a bean. Later we'll see the special-case "local" versions.

(1) Create

Client asks the *home* interface for a reference to the bean's *component* interface.

(Which means the client calls a create() method on the home stub.)

The bean developer must put a create() method in the bean's home

---

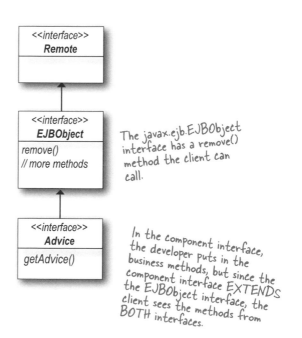

(2) Use

Client calls business methods declared in the component interface.

(Which means the client calls methods on the EJB object stub.)

The javax.ejb.EJBObject interface has a remove() method the client can call.

(3) Remove

Client tells the bean that he's done using it.

(Which means the client calls remove() on the bean's EJB object stub.)

In the component interface, the developer puts in the business methods, but since the component interface EXTENDS the EJBObject interface, the client sees the methods from BOTH interfaces.

But first, we have to get a <u>home interface reference</u>

In other words, we have to get the <u>stub</u> to the home object... the thing we use to call create(), so that we can get what we really want— the EJB object stub!

When you (the client) want a reference to a home interface, you go through JNDI. The process is pretty straightforward: you give JNDI a logical name (the name the deployer told the server to use), and you get back something that implements the home interface.

```
Context ic = new InitialContext();

Object o = ic.lookup("Advisor");

// a few more steps...
```

← *The InitialContext object assigned to "ic" is a reference to the JNDI lookup service.*

Give it a name (whatever the bean deployer used to register that bean with the server) and get back an object.

What's JNDI?

JNDI stands for Java Naming and Directory Interface, and it's an API for accessing naming and directory services. Although JNDI is quite powerful, there are only a few pieces of it you need to know for EJB—how clients *find* it, how clients *use* it, how *beans* use it, and how to put things *into* it.

The JNDI API can work with many different services, as long as that service has a JNDI driver (called a Service Provider). It's a lot like JDBC, where you (the developer) use the JDBC API to send SQL statements to a variety of different databases. The JNDI driver translates the method calls you make on the JNDI API into something the underlying naming/directory service understands.

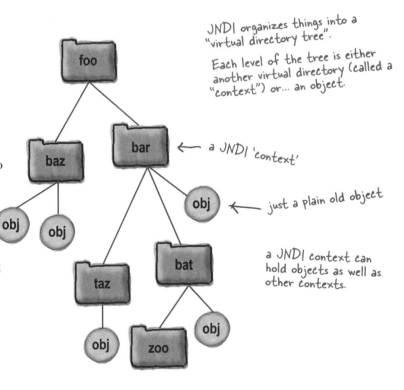

JNDI organizes things into a "virtual directory tree".

Each level of the tree is either another virtual directory (called a "context") or... an object.

← *a JNDI 'context'*

← *just a plain old object*

a JNDI context can hold objects as well as other contexts.

Getting the home interface stub

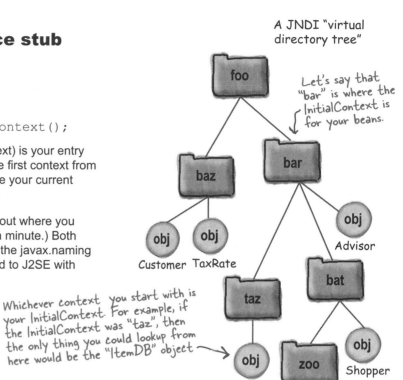

A JNDI "virtual directory tree"

Let's say that "bar" is where the InitialContext is for your beans.

 Get an InitialContext

```
Context ic = new InitialContext();
```

The InitialContext (a subtype of Context) is your entry point into the JNDI tree. It's simply the first context from which you start navigating. Kind of like your current working directory (the one you cd to).

The InitialContext constructor figures out where you should start. (We'll talk about that in a minute.) Both Context and InitialContext are part of the javax.naming package, part of J2EE, but also added to J2SE with version 1.4.

Whichever context you start with is your InitialContext. For example, if the InitialContext was "taz", then the only thing you could lookup from here would be the "ItemDB" object

② **Lookup the bean's home using the InitialContext**

```
Object o = ic.lookup("Advisor");
```

The lookup method takes a String that must match the name assigned to this bean's JNDI deployment. If the deployer assigned an additional context to the bean, by naming it (at deploy-time) "bat/Advisor", then the lookup code would change to:

```
ic.lookup("bat/Advisor");
```

③ **Assign the result of the lookup to the Home interface reference**

```
AdviceHome home = (AdviceHome) o;
```

Warning: This code isn't quite right... although it LOOKS like it should be. We'll find out what's wrong in just a few pages.

The return type of the context lookup method is Object, so you have to cast it back to the bean's home interface type, before you can call AdviceHome methods.

Q: **How do I know what the developer named the bean?**

A: Actually, it's not up to the bean *developer* (the EJB role known as Bean Provider—the one who actually wrote the bean code), to give the bean its JNDI name. Remember, the Bean Provider might have written that bean as a reusable component for Beans 'R' Us and thus might have no idea where and how the bean will be used.

It's the *deployer*—the person who actually gets the bean running in the server as part of some application—who registers the bean under a logical name. But the bottom line is that there's no standard or automatic mechanism for learning the names of registered beans. As a client, somebody, somehow, has to tell you that, say, the bean was registered as "Advisor".

Notice that "Advisor", while describing the service, is not a String that corresponds directly to the names of any of the other pieces of the bean. Remember, the component interface was Advice, the home interface was AdviceHome, and the bean itself is AdviceBean. The name "Advisor" was just something the deployer thought had a nice ring to it.

Of course, in your company, you might (and probably will) have strict naming guidelines to follow for how beans are registered with JNDI at deployment time.

(Unless it's your own company, in which case you can do whatever you darn well please, including naming each bean after your favorite rock star or Matrix character.)

Q: **I just thought of an even BIGGER problem... how the heck do I know where to find the server? And how do I specify it? I didn't see any code for an IP address or TCP port number.**

A: Good catch. Yeah, that's all a bit of a mystery, isn't it? We have three answers for now:

1) We're cheating a little, because the code we're using works only because we're using the Reference Implementation, and even then... only because we're running the server on the same physical machine as the client. So, we're taking advantage of default settings that are in place, automatically, because we're running the Reference Implementation.

2). We lied a little in point number 1, above, because this code *could* be correct if it were inside a bean. (We'll get to that in the Bean Environment chapter.)

3) In reality, a client *does* need to know how to find the JNDI service where a bean's home is registered. There are several ways you can do this—you could pass information to the InitialContext constructor (a Properties object that contains everything the InitialContext needs to find the server and the starting context). Or, there are several places where JNDI properties can be placed on the client's machine. In either case, the client MUST be given something—either info for the InitialContext constructor, or a properties file. It's different for each vendor's server, too, so you have to check your documentation in order to know what the client needs.

For the exam, you don't need to know much about JNDI!

For the client-related objectives (the ones from this chapter), all you need to know is the fundamental process for doing a JNDI lookup... that you need to start with an InitialContext and then call lookup(), which returns something of type Object.

You do NOT need to know how the client or server finds and gets a reference to the correct InitialContext, only that an InitialContext is needed.

In the Bean Environment chapter, we'll add a tiny bit more JNDI info, for how the bean itself uses JNDI to look up things that have been specifically placed there for the bean.

But that's about it for your JNDI knowledge. You don't have to know any details about the rest of the JNDI API other than the Context.lookup() method.

Let's take another look at the complete client code

```java
import javax.naming.*;
import java.rmi.*;
import javax.rmi.*;
import headfirst.*;
import javax.ejb.*;
```

A bunch of imports, we'll look at each one individually at the bottom of the page

```java
public class AdviceClient {

    public static void main(String[] args) {
        new AdviceClient().go();
    }

    public void go() {
        try {
            Context ic = new InitialContext();
            Object o = ic.lookup("Advisor");

            AdviceHome home = (AdviceHome) PortableRemoteObject.narrow(o, AdviceHome.class);

            Advice advisor = home.create();

            System.out.println(advisor.getAdvice());

        } catch (RemoteException rex) {
            rex.printStackTrace();
        } catch (CreateException cex) {
            cex.printStackTrace();
        } catch (Exception ex) {
            ex.printStackTrace();
        }
    }
}
```

InitialContext is our entry point into the JNDI naming service, where we do the lookup on the name "Advisor"

What is THIS??? Why not just a plain old cast?

Call create on the home to get us what we REALLY want — the component interface.

The point of everything! To call a business method on the bean (via the EJBObject stub)

Not a good way to handle (or rather, NOT handle) exceptions here... but we want to show some of the checked exceptions...

Sharpen your pencil

Match the class name with the package it's from. You can use the same package name more than once.

If you're not sure, make your best guess.

Package Name	Class Name
javax.naming	InitialContext
java.rmi	AdviceHome
javax.rmi	PortableRemoteObject
headfirst	RemoteException
javax.ejb	Advice
	CreateException

Just when you thought a simple <u>cast</u> would be enough...

The return value of the Context.lookup() method is type Object. So we're thinking a simple cast should be enough to force the object referenced by *o* back to the AdviceHome implementation that we know it really is:

```
Context ic = new InitialContext();
Object o = ic.lookup("Advisor");
AdviceHome home = (AdviceHome) o;
```

← *This LOOKS right, but isn't. With a Remote home interface, casting is not enough.*

But NO. You have to <u>narrow</u> the object as well!

Narrowing forces the object returned from the JNDI lookup to be absolutely, positively, something that implements the home interface. In other words, something you can cast to AdviceHome.

```
Context ic = new InitialContext();
Object o = ic.lookup("Advisor");
AdviceHome home = (AdviceHome) PortableRemoteObject.narrow(o, AdviceHome.class);
```

OK, I'll bite. Why <u>can't</u> you just do a plain old cast?

According to the spec, you—the *client*—must assume that the server is using RMI-IIOP rather than regular old RMI. Normal RMI uses JRMP as the wire protocol, which assumes that we're always talking Java all the way down. If this were plain RMI, you'd always know that what you get out of the lookup is (polymorphically) something that IS-A home interface. In other words, *an object whose class type implements the home interface for that bean.* And for that scenario, a normal Java language cast would let you assign the object back to the home interface type, so that you can call the home methods! Otherwise, remember, you'd be stuck calling only methods of type Object (equals(), hashCode(), toString(), etc.) when what you *really* want to call is *create().*

But when the wire protocol is IIOP, the rules change a little. The narrow() operation gives you something that *is* castable.

PortableRemoteObject.narrow()

The javax.rmi.PortableRemoteObject's narrow() method runs code written by the server vendor. But all we care about is that it takes the object we got from JNDI and gives us back something that really *does* implement the home interface.

In other words, it gives us back something we can then cast to the home interface type, and call create().

```
PortableRemoteObject.narrow(o, AdviceHome.class);
```

the object you got from JNDI

the interface type you want it to be. It must be a Remote interface!

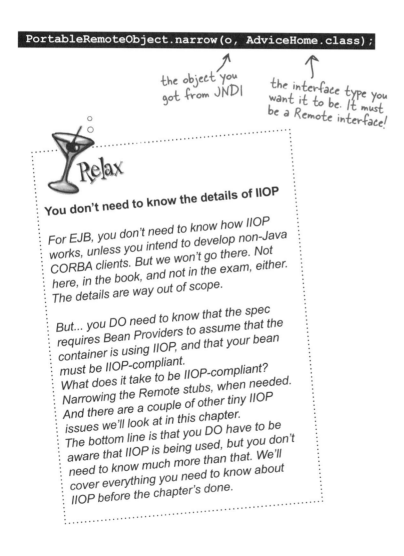

Relax

You don't need to know the details of IIOP

For EJB, you don't need to know how IIOP works, unless you intend to develop non-Java CORBA clients. But we won't go there. Not here, in the book, and not in the exam, either. The details are way out of scope.

But... you DO need to know that the spec requires Bean Providers to assume that the container is using IIOP, and that your bean must be IIOP-compliant. What does it take to be IIOP-compliant? Narrowing the Remote stubs, when needed. And there are a couple of other tiny IIOP issues we'll look at in this chapter. The bottom line is that you DO have to be aware that IIOP is being used, but you don't need to know much more than that. We'll cover everything you need to know about IIOP before the chapter's done.

The home stub returned from a JNDI lookup might not implement the home interface!

You might get back an IIOP stub that isn't castable to the home interface of your bean. And that means you couldn't call create().

To get a stub that's castable to the home interface, you have to first narrow() the object you get from the JNDI lookup on the bean home.

(But only when the home interface is Remote.)

> With a Remote home stub from JNDI, an ordinary cast isn't good enough. You need something more exotic... you need to narrow it.

Think of narrowing as "Exotic Casting"

Narrowing is not the same as casting, but you can think of it as a form of "exotic casting".

Casting is about polymorphism. With a cast, the *object* doesn't change, but the way you *refer* to that object does. With *narrowing*, you might actually get a *different* object!

Cast

```
Animal ani = new Dog();
Dog fido = (Dog) ani;
```

Casting lets you see ONE object in multiple ways. The reference type determines what methods you can call, but the object itself always knows it's a Dog.

Narrow

```
narrow(o, AdviceHome.class);
```

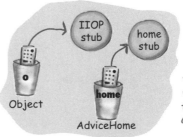

The narrow method might return a completely different object (or it might not). But regardless, you'll get a stub that really DOES implement the interface, so you can then cast it.

Now that we (finally) have the home stub, let's use it to get what we **REALLY** want...

Wait a minute... how come we didn't have to cast and narrow the EJB object stub, but we had to for the home stub?

(1) Call create() on the home interface to get the EJB object stub

```
Advice advisor = home.create();
```

The create method returns a reference to the component interface, Advice. In other words, it returns a stub to the EJB object (which implements Advice, the Remote component interface for this bean.) You don't need to cast and narrow the EJB object stub.

(2) Call a business method on the component interface (EJB object stub)

```
System.out.println(advisor.getAdvice());
```

Nothing special here. It's just a plain old method call on the reference to the Advice interface.

Well, not quite. Remember, every Remote method call declares a RemoteException! And that's a checked exception, so you MUST handle or declare it.

```
try {
  System.out.println(advisor.getAdvice());
} catch(RemoteException rex) {
    rex.printStackTrace();
}
```

there are no Dumb Questions

Q: OK, I know, I know, I don't need to learn the details of IIOP, but I still want to understand WHY they use it.

A: OK, a little more. IIOP, the wire protocol for CORBA, can represent more information than plain RMI. For example, IIOP can propagate both transaction and security information... important things that you can't send with a non-IIOP remote method call.

So IIOP lets a container at least have the potential for interoperating with other servers, including (possibly) one that isn't Java-based.

Remember, CORBA is a standard that (among other things) can give two objects, written in two different languages, a chance to invoke each other's methods.

This does not mean that your server is necessarily using IIOP. The spec says that YOU—the developer—have to assume the server is using IIOP, which means you have to be sure your beans are IIOP-compliant (we'll talk about IIOP compliance a little later in this chapter).

Q: If my server doesn't use IIOP, do I still have to do the whole narrowing thing?

A: Yes and no. Your code might work just fine with nothing more than a cast. But—and this is a really huge but—your client code won't be vendor-independent! In other words, you won't have a portable app if you don't use narrow, because redeploying the bean on a server that does use IIOP will break the clients.

Q: Is there any downside to using narrow? Especially if the server is not using IIOP?

A: No downside (well, whatever overhead there is wouldn't be worth the portability tradeoff). If your server isn't using IIOP, narrow() is most likely a no-op (i.e. do-nothing) method. The spec says to always narrow, and it won't hurt you if it isn't needed.

The declared return type of create() is the <u>component interface</u>, not Object.

So the EJB object comes back from create() already knowing what it is (an implementation of your component interface).

```
public Advice create()
```

The return type of the home interface create() method is ALWAYS the component interface

So the EJB object stub doesn't need a cast or a narrow..

Writing the Remote home interface for a session bean

Now that you've seen the lookup and create process from the client's point of view, we'll see what you have to do to write a home interface for your bean. For session beans, the process is very easy. In fact, for *stateless* session beans, it's ludicrously easy—you just declare a single, no-arg create() method.

```java
package headfirst;

import javax.ejb.*;
import java.rmi.RemoteException;


public interface AdviceHome extends EJBHome {

    public Advice create() throws CreateException, RemoteException;

}
```

Rules for the home interface

(1) Import javax.ejb.* and java.rmi.RemoteException.

(2) Extend EJBHome.

(3) Declare a create() method that returns the component interface and declares a CreateException and RemoteException

 ✳ For stateless session beans, there can be only one create(), and it must NOT have arguments.

 ✳ Stateful session beans can have multiple, overloaded create() methods, and do NOT need to have a no-arg create().

 ✳ All create() methods must declare a CreateException and RemoteException, but they can also declare other application (checked) exceptions.

 ✳ The name of create methods in stateful beans must begin with "create" (createAccount(), createBigDog(), createFashionAdvisor(), etc.).

 ✳ For stateful session beans, arguments must be RMI-IIOP compatible (you know, Serializable, primtive, Remote, or arrays or collections of any of those).

Remote home interface examples for session beans

The examples on this page are all legal examples of Remote home interfaces. You'll see some that could be both stateless and stateful, and some that could be only stateful (because they have a create method with arguments). We've dropped the package and import statements to put more on the page.

(1)
```
public interface CartHome extends EJBHome {
    public Cart create(String storeID) throws CreateException, RemoteException;
    public Cart create() throws CreateException, RemoteException;
}
```

(2)
```
public interface MatcherHome extends EJBHome {
    public Matcher create(String customerID) throws CreateException, RemoteException;
    public Matcher createNewCustomer(String name, String login)
                                    throws CreateException, RemoteException;
}
```

(3)
```
public interface TicketsHome extends EJBHome {
    public Tickets create() throws CreateException, RemoteException;
}
```

(4)
```
public interface ClubHome extends EJBHome {
    public Club createExisting(String clubID) throws CreateException, RemoteException;
    public Club createNewClub(String clubName) throws CreateException, RemoteException;
}
```

There's only one interface here that could be a stateless session bean's home—number 3. Notice, too, that number 4 has two create methods that both have the same argument—a String—but the methods are named differently to reflect what that particular create method is for.

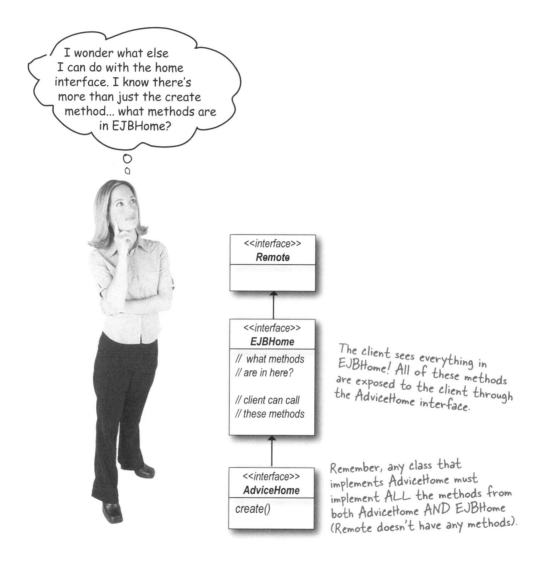

I wonder what else I can do with the home interface. I know there's more than just the create method... what methods are in EJBHome?

<<interface>>
Remote

<<interface>>
EJBHome

// what methods
// are in here?

// client can call
// these methods

<<interface>>
AdviceHome

create()

The client sees everything in EJBHome! All of these methods are exposed to the client through the AdviceHome interface.

Remember, any class that implements AdviceHome must implement ALL the methods from both AdviceHome AND EJBHome (Remote doesn't have any methods).

What YOU write:

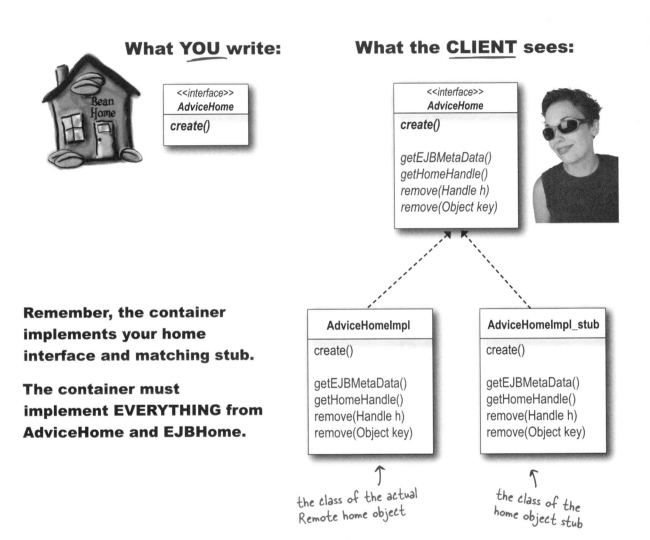

<<interface>>
AdviceHome

create()

Remember, the container implements your home interface and matching stub.

The container must implement EVERYTHING from AdviceHome and EJBHome.

What the CLIENT sees:

<<interface>>
AdviceHome

create()

getEJBMetaData()
getHomeHandle()
remove(Handle h)
remove(Object key)

AdviceHomeImpl

create()

getEJBMetaData()
getHomeHandle()
remove(Handle h)
remove(Object key)

the class of the actual Remote home object

AdviceHomeImpl_stub

create()

getEJBMetaData()
getHomeHandle()
remove(Handle h)
remove(Object key)

the class of the home object stub

Note: these aren't necessarily the real names—the server generates these classes, and it can name them whatever it wants to.

If you're a client, and you want to...

Call this method:

(1) get reflection-like information about the bean.

Unless you're a tool vendor, you'll probably never need to call this method. It returns the EJBMetaData interface—something you can use to get more specific class information about the bean. If you've got yourself an EJBMetaData reference (by calling getEJBMetaData), you can call getHomeInterfaceClass(), getPrimaryKeyClass(), isSession(), and more.

```
          <<interface>>
            EJBHome

EJBMetaData getEJBMetaData()
HomeHandle  getHomeHandle()
void  remove(Handle h)
void  remove(Object key)
```

(2) serialize the home so that you can use the home again later, without having to go through JNDI.

Imagine you're a client, and you've been working with a home—making a bunch of beans, calling home methods on entity beans, whatever. And now you have to reboot your machine. Or move to another machine. But you want to continue working with this home. What do you do?

You *could* go back through JNDI and do the whole lookup thing again. But if you ask the home for a handle, you'll get back a Serializable thing you can save and use later to get the home stub back without going through JNDI (more on handles a little later).

```
          <<interface>>
            EJBHome

EJBMetaData  getEJBMetaData()
HomeHandle getHomeHandle()
void  remove(Handle h)
void  remove(Object key)
```

(3) tell the home you're done with a session bean.

When you're done with a session bean, you can tell the home by calling remove() and passing the EJB object's handle. Yes that's right, the *EJB object.* Just as the home object can give you a handle (so that you can get the home stub back, later, without going through JNDI), the EJB object can give you a handle to itself. (We'll see more of that later in this chapter.) You *can* use this version of remove() for *entity* beans as well, but with entity beans, it's usually easier to call the *other* remove().

```
          <<interface>>
            EJBHome

EJBMetaData  getEJBMetaData()
HomeHandle  getHomeHandle()
void  remove(Handle h)
void  remove(Object key)
```

(4) tell the home to remove an entity bean.

Notice we didn't say, "Tell the home you're done with an entity bean." That's because calling remove on an entity bean is drastically different from calling remove on a session bean. We'll get into the details in the entity bean chapters, but the short version is: when you remove an entity bean, you're not just telling the container that *you're* done with the bean, you're telling it that *everyone* is done with the bean. Forever. Because calling remove() on an entity bean means, "**Delete** this entity from the persistent store." (Which usually means, "Delete this *row* from the *database.*")

This version of remove takes a primary key, which session beans don't have, so unlike the *other* remove(), *this* version can be used for entity beans *only.*

```
          <<interface>>
            EJBHome

EJBMetaData  getEJBMetaData()
HomeHandle  getHomeHandle()
void  remove(Handle h)
void  remove(Object key)
```

Hey, did I just see something about a primary key? In the home interface for a session bean? *That* can't be right...

I know, isn't that odd? But look... there's only one home interface, EJBHome, regardless of the bean type! There's no separate EJBSessionHome or EJBEntityHome--it's just EJBHome for everything!

Q: **Does this mean the client has to know that she's using a session bean and not an entity bean? Isn't that something the client shouldn't have to know?**

A: Yes, the client *does* have to know that when she's got the home interface for a session bean, he can't call the remove(Object primaryKey) method. If she does, she'll get an exception (javax.ejb.RemoveException). It does feel like more of an implementation detail than the client should have to know (i.e. that it's a session vs. entity bean), but in reality, you can't expect to write an EJB client without knowing whether you're communicating with a session or entity bean. For one thing, the way the client interacts with an entity bean home is completely different from the way a client uses a session bean home. You'll see dramatic differences when we get to the entity bean chapters.

Make it Stick

There was a home stub on the client,
That made the VM quite defiant,
A narrow was needed,
For the cast to be heeded,
Because it was CORBA compliant.

Make it Stick

Roses are red, blue is the sky,
you can't get a bean from JNDI.

It's only the home a client will spy,
when he does a lookup on JNDI.

BULLET POINTS

- The methods of the bean are exposed to the client through the component interface.

- The client can't directly get a reference to the bean; the client must go through the bean's EJB object, which implements the component interface.

- The client gets a reference to the bean's EJB object from the bean's home.

- To get the bean's home, the client does a lookup on JNDI, using the logical name under which the bean was deployed.

- To do a JNDI lookup, the client must first get an InitialContext, which is the entry point into the server's JNDI "virtual directory tree".

- For a Remote home interface, the stub returned from JNDI must be both cast and narrowed.

- Narrowing is the "exotic casting" needed for stub objects that come from a method that does not return the stub's client interface. Since the JNDI lookup returns type Object, the object returned from the lookup must be *narrowed* to the bean's home interface, and then *cast* to the bean's home interface.

- Narrowing is required for IIOP stubs (IIOP is the wire protocol for CORBA), because what's returned from the lookup might not be capable of implementing multiple interfaces, and thus would know only about the methods in type Object. Narrowing returns an object that implements the home interface.

- The home interface extends EJBHome, which has four additional methods the client can see: getEJBMetaData, getHomeHandle, remove(Handle h), remove(Object primaryKey). The remove(Object primaryKey) must not be called on a session bean.

Sharpen your pencil

Based on the rules for session bean home interfaces, which statements are true about this interface:

```
import javax.ejb.EJBHome;
import java.rmi.RemoteException;

public interface CartHome extends EJBHome {

    public Cart create() throws CreateException, RemoteException;

}
```

☐ CartHome must not be the home of a stateful session bean.

☐ The interface is missing an import statement.

☐ The create method is missing an exception.

☐ Cart must be the class type of the bean.

☐ Cart must be the interface that extends EJBObject.

☐ The object returned from create() must be narrowed.

☐ The object returned from create() does not need a cast.

You MUST be able to look at code and infer a lot about it.

The exam expects you to look at client, interface, or bean code, and make inferences about things you don't see. You MUST know all of the rules for home and component interfaces. And there's more...

But enough about the home... let's talk about the EJB object. The <u>component</u> interface. The thing you <u>REALLY</u> want.

Remember, all that InitialContext-JNDI-lookup-cast-narrow-create business was just to get what you really wanted all along—something with the business methods. Something you can use to get the bean to do whatever it is that bean was created for. Number crunching, online shopping, advice.

```java
package headfirst;

import javax.ejb.*;
import java.rmi.RemoteException;


public interface Advice extends EJBObject {

    public String getAdvice() throws RemoteException;

}
```

Rules for the component interface

(1) Import javax.ejb.* and java.rmi.RemoteException.

(2) Extend EJBObject.

(3) Declare one or more business methods, that throw a RemoteException.

- ✳ Arguments and return types must be RMI-IIOP compatible (Serializable, primitive, Remote, or arrays or collections of any of those).

- ✳ You can have overloaded methods.

- ✳ Each method must declare a RemoteException.

- ✳ You can declare your own application exceptions, but they must NOT be runtime exceptions (in other words, they must be compiler-checked exceptions—subclasses of Exception but not subclasses of RuntimeException).

I wonder what else I can do with the component interface. I know there's more than just the business methods... what methods are in EJBObject?

<<interface>>
Remote

<<interface>>
EJBObject
// what methods
// are in here?

// client can call
// these methods

<<interface>>
Advice
getAdvice()

Just as with the EJBHome interface, the client sees everything in EJBObject! All of these methods are exposed to the client through the bean's component interface (Advice).

Any class that implements Advice must implement ALL the methods from both Advice AND EJBObject.

Imagine what e**l**se you might want to do with your EJB object reference...

You're a client. You have a reference to the AdviceBean's component interface. You know you can call getAdvice(). But now that you've gone to all the trouble of getting the stub, are there other things you might want to do?

I can think of some things... like, what if I have the bean, but I lost the reference to the home, and now I want to make more beans of that type? Surely the bean knows its own home, right? I can't believe they would have been stupid enough to make you go back through JNDI...

What YOU write:

<<interface>>
Advice

getAdvice()

EJBObject (the
bean's bodyguard
for business
methods)

Remember, the container implements your component interface and matching stub.

The container must implement EVERYTHING from Advice and EJBObject.

What the CLIENT sees:

<<interface>>
Advice

getAdvice()
getPrimaryKey()
getEJBHome()
getHandle()
remove()
isIdentical()

AdviceImpl

getAdvice()
getPrimaryKey()
getEJBHome()
getHandle()
remove()
isIdentical()

AdviceImpl_stub

getAdvice()
getPrimaryKey()
getEJBHome()
getHandle()
remove()
isIdentical()

the class of the actual
Remote EJB object

the class of the
EJB object stub

You better know these other methods inside and out.

The exam expects you to know all five of the methods in EJBObject. You have to know that they're available to Remote clients, and exactly how they're used!

If you're a client, and you want to...

call this method:

① get the primary key of an entity bean

We won't go into this now, since we have 10 million pages on entity beans coming up. Just know that this does not apply to session beans, which don't have a unique identity exposed to the client. But if the client somehow gets a reference to an entity bean (maybe by searching on a customer's name) and wants the actual primary key, this is the method to call. Try it on a session bean, and you'll get a big fat RemoteException (or EJBException if the client is local).

<<interface>>
EJBObject

Object getPrimaryKey()
EJBHome getEJBHome()
Handle getHandle()
void remove()
boolean isIdentical(EJBObject o)

② get the bean's home

Imagine you've got a bean, but you don't have the bean's home. And now you want to make more beans of that type. What do you do? You could do a JNDI lookup and get the home in the usual way. But what if you don't have enough information to do the JNDI lookup? You can ask the bean to give you a reference to its home. Even if you are capable of doing a JNDI lookup on the home, calling getEJBHome() on the bean is more efficient.

<<interface>>
EJBObject

Object getPrimaryKey()
EJBHome getEJBHome()
Handle getHandle()
void remove()
boolean isIdentical(EJBObject o)

③ save a reference to the EJBObject

You're shopping online, carefully putting items in your cart, after hours of painstaking research and decision-making on whether your girlfriend will prefer you in cornflower blue, or the Martha Stewart seafoam green. But before you can finish, you have to switch to another machine. No problem. You can ask the bean for a handle to the EJB object. You can use the handle to get back to your original EJB object and keep shopping.

<<interface>>
EJBObject

Object getPrimaryKey()
EJBHome getEJBHome()
Handle getHandle()
void remove()
boolean isIdentical(EJBObject o)

④ tell the bean you're done with it

When you're finished with the bean, it's good manners to tell it you're done, so the container can free up any resources it might be keeping on your behalf. DANGER!! We're talking only about session beans here. Although you can call remove() on an entity bean, remember, it has a very different meaning (we'll see that in the entity bean chapters).

<<interface>>
EJBObject

Object getPrimaryKey()
EJBHome getEJBHome()
Handle getHandle()
void remove()
boolean isIdentical(EJBObject o)

⑤ compare two EJB object references to see if they reference the same bean.

You've got two references to session bean EJB objects. Now you want to know if they're really references to the same bean. The isIdentical() method takes an EJB object reference and compares it to the EJB object on which you invoked isIdentical(), and returns true or false.

<<interface>>
EJBObject

Object getPrimaryKey()
EJBHome getEJBHome()
Handle getHandle()
void remove()
boolean isIdentical(EJBObject o)

Online shopping should not be rushed...

You're shopping. It's tough, because you can't decide whether you're a spring or a summer. You don't want to be rushed, but you've already got a bunch of stuff in your cart when you realize you're five minutes late for work.

You'd love to continue with your shopping once you get to work.

What do you do? If it were Amazon, your shopping cart would still be there when you log-in from the Web. But this is a proprietary Swing-based shopping client app you're using. How can you get your EJB object stub from your home machine to your work machine?

You could try serializing the stub. Yeah, that might work. Then again, it might not. The stub has a live network connection, and there's certainly no guarantee you can get that same connection, to the same EJB object again. And since that EJB object is the component interface for your own personal, temporary, shopping cart bean, you need a way to get back to your exact same EJB object again from work.

> Hmmm...my next door neighbor says cowboy boots are sexy. But the sandals will make me look more sensitive. Then again, girls like that rugged look, so maybe I should go with the hiking boots... Shopping is so time-consuming!

<<interface>>
EJBObject
Object getPrimaryKey()
EJBHome getEJBHome()
Handle getHandle()
void remove()
boolean isIdentical(EJBObject o)

Thankfully, we've got handles

A handle can rescue your shopping experience. Ask the bean (via the EJBObject interface) for a handle:

```
Handle myHandle = myCart.getHandle();
```

serialize it, email it to yourself, then deserialize on your work machine and you're back in business.

The handle is a Serializable thing that knows how to get back to the stub. It has a single method:

```
public EJBObject getEJBObject()
```

So when you call it, you have to cast and narrow the stub that comes back! Remember, you always have to cast and narrow a stub unless the method that returns it has the actual Remote interface as its declared return type. Since the handle's method has no frickin' clue what your component interface is (say, ShoppingCart), you're faced with the same scenario you had with the home stub you got from the JNDI lookup() method. Cast and narrow. Cast and narrow. Cast and narrow.

In your client code, you'll have something like:

```
// your code to get the serialized handle you saved earlier
Handle h = this.restoreTheHandle();

// now use it to get the EJBObject stub
Object o = h.getEJBObject();
Shopping cart = (Shopping) PortableRemoteObject.narrow(o, Shopping.class);
```

A handle is a Serializable object that knows how to get back to the original Remote EJB object. It's not a stub, but it can GET the stub.

It has just one method, getEJBObject(), that returns type **EJBObject**.

So you have to narrow and cast the stub you get back!

Wait a minute... isn't a handle a big security problem? You already said I could serialize a handle and put it on another machine, so what's to stop me from giving the handle to someone else? Someone who didn't have access to the stub in the first place? And another thing bugs me about handles-- I hope you're not telling me the server has to keep shopping carts around *forever*, just in case a client comes back using a handle! Goodbye scalability...

Don't worry! You can't use a handle as a way to violate your bean's security.

Your security is on a method-by-method basis, so even if you give a handle to someone else, if that client doesn't have authorization to call methods on the bean, the stub they get back from the handle will be useless.

Just because *you* still have a handle, doesn't mean the *server* still has your bean.

If you're shopping and you get a handle, and then the server detects that you haven't been doing anything with your cart for a while, the server can temporarily save your bean (known as passivation) to conserve resources, but keep your cart around just in case you come back. But if you still don't come back within some time period, the server will destroy your cart with no hope of resurrecting it. That bean is history.

In that case, your cart won't be there when you call getEJBObject() on the handle, and you'll get a RemoteException.

isIdentical?

how to find out if two stubs refer to the same bean

These twins are identical if they're stateLESS, since they can each do the same thing and clients won't know the difference. But if they're stateFUL, then they are always distinct. Stateful twins cannot be identical, because they can hold information specific to their own unique client.

```
           <<interface>>
            EJBObject

  Object  getPrimaryKey()
  EJBHome  getEJBHome()
  Handle  getHandle()
  void  remove()
  boolean isIdentical(EJBObject o)
```

If you've got two stubs, and you want to know if they refer to the same bean, you call isIdentical on one reference, passing in the reference you want to compare it against. Just like the way you use the equals() method.

The trick is, stateless session beans, stateful session beans, and entity beans each have different rules for what causes isIdentical() to return *true*.

Stateless session beans

True if both references came from the same home, even if the stubs are referring to two different Remote EJB objects! To the server, one stateless bean is as good as any other bean from the same home, because the client would never be able to tell the difference (since the bean can't hold any client-specific state).

Stateful session beans

False no matter what, for any two unique stubs, even if from the same home. After all, my shopping cart isn't the same as yours!

Entity beans

True if the stubs refer to two entities with the same primary key.

Stateless beans

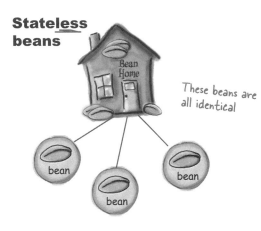

These beans are all identical

isIdentical() always returns **_true_**, even for different beans.

The isIdentical() method is like calling a Remote equals() method... except you're not asking if two objects on your heap are meaningfully equivalent, you're asking if two Remote objects are meaningfully equivalent--on the server!

Stateful beans

These beans are NEVER identical. Your cart is different from mine.

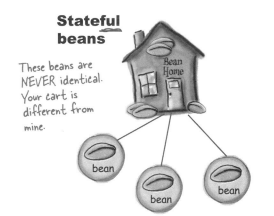

isIdentical() always returns **_false_** for different beans, even if the beans are from the same home.

Entity beans

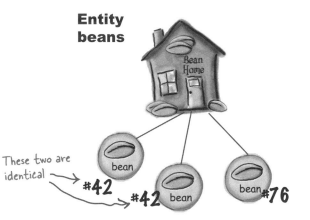

These two are identical

#42
#42
#76

isIdentical() returns **_true_** for beans* that reference the same entity (in other words, the same primary key)

*We use the term "bean" here a little loosely because, conceptually, the server uses only one bean to represent a particular entity. So there would be only one bean with a primary key of #42, but clients may have multiple EJB object references to it.

Q: **Why** *can't* **you just use the equals() method instead of isIdentical()? Isn't that what equals() is for?**

A: Remember, we're talking about Remote objects. The equals() method compares two objects on the same HEAP, where isIdentical() compares two Remote objects on the SERVER.

Q: **I still don't see why they couldn't have just implemented the equals() method on the stub to do the same thing.**

A: The equals() method is not a remote method, for one thing. You *can* always call equals() on a stub, because you can call it on any object on your heap. But it's not part of the remote interface, so it can't be a remote method (for example, it doesn't declare a RemoteException, etc.)

And remember, the equals() method is used to see if two objects on the *heap* are meaningfully equivalent. The vendor can implement the equals() method on the stub any way it likes, but that still doesn't tell you anything about what's going on back at the server end. Just because two stubs don't pass the equals() test, doesn't mean the server doesn't consider the two EJB objects to be identical (or referencing identical beans).

Your server may be using RMI stubs, for example, that have no logic for how their comparisons relate to meaningful comparisons of two EJB objects on the server. RMI stubs know about Remote objects, but they don't know what those Remote objects *represent*.

Q: **How come there's a method in the EJBObject interface for getting the bean's home? If you don't HAVE the home, then how did you get the bean in the first place???**

A: There are other ways to get a reference to an EJB object. It's true that you can't use JNDI to look up the EJB object; only the home is registered.

BUT... there's nothing to stop you from passing an EJB object reference as an argument or return value. You might have a business method in one bean, whose sole job is to hand you back a reference to an EJB object for a *different* bean.

Now suppose you have this EJB object reference, to a bean whose home you never had, and now you want to make more of those beans for yourself. You can do that by asking for the bean's home using getEJBHome().

And even if you *do* have enough information to do a lookup in JNDI for that bean's home, JNDI lookups are expensive. You'll save some overhead if you just get the home reference from the bean directly.

Q: **Why** *can't* **you serialize the stub? Why do we need handles?**

A: We didn't say the stub wasn't Serializable. But even if you can serialize it, that doesn't mean it's got enough information to get you back to the same (or meaningfully identical) EJB object. When the stub comes over from the server, it's already knowledgeable about how to contact a particular Remote object. When that stub is recreated, that exact Remote object might not even exist any longer.

Q: **Then how would the handle be any better?**

A: The handle has the 'smarts' to communicate with the server and get back something that is *just the same* as the EJB object you had before. In other words, it might *not* be the same EJB object, but the client will never be able to tell the difference.

BULLET POINTS

- You expose your bean's business methods in the component interface.

- Remote component interfaces must extend javax.ejb.EJBObject.

- The client gets a reference to the bean's EJBObject by calling a method on the bean's home interface.

- References to both stateless and stateful session beans are retrieved from the home's create() methods.

- From the EJBObject interface, the client sees five additional methods: getEJBHome(), getHandle(), remove(), isIdentical(), and getPrimaryKey().

- Only entity bean clients are allowed to call getPrimaryKey() on the bean's component interface. Session bean clients will get a RemoteException.

- The getEJBHome() method returns a reference to the bean's home interface, so that the client doesn't have to go through a JNDI lookup, if they want to make more beans of that type.

- The getHandle() method returns a Serializable object that can be used later to reestablish contact with the server, and get back the stub to the component interface that the client used to get the handle.

- The handle has one method, getEJBObject(), that returns the Remote stub as type EJBObject. That means the stub must be cast and narrowed, just as you must do with the home stub that you get from a JNDI lookup.

- The isIdentical() method is kind of like doing an equals() method on the server. It returns true for two different stateless beans from the same home, false for two different stateful beans from the same home, and true for references to entities with the same primary key.

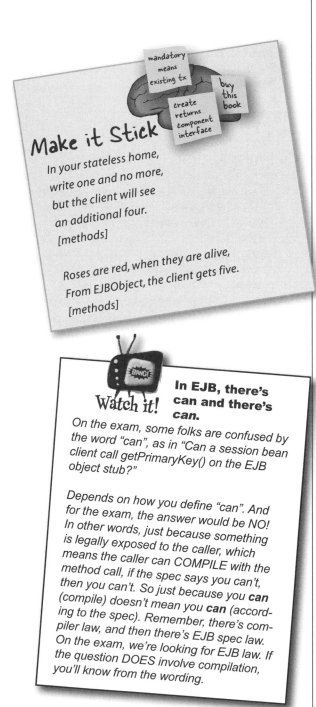

Make it Stick

mandatory means existing tx

buy this book

create returns component interface

In your stateless home, write one and no more, but the client will see an additional four.
[methods]

Roses are red, when they are alive, From EJBObject, the client gets five.
[methods]

Watch it!

In EJB, there's can and there's can.

On the exam, some folks are confused by the word "can", as in "Can a session bean client call getPrimaryKey() on the EJB object stub?"

*Depends on how you define "can". And for the exam, the answer would be NO! In other words, just because something is legally exposed to the caller, which means the caller can COMPILE with the method call, if the spec says you can't, then you can't. So just because you **can** (compile) doesn't mean you **can** (according to the spec). Remember, there's compiler law, and then there's EJB spec law. On the exam, we're looking for EJB law. If the question DOES involve compilation, you'll know from the wording.*

A bean's client interfaces can be <u>local</u>

We've looked at only the Remote client interfaces for a bean so far, but as of EJB 2.0, session and entity beans can expose a *local client view*. In other words, client interfaces that do not extend java.rmi.Remote.

What does this mean? That the home object and EJB object are not Remote objects! They're running in the same JVM as the client and the bean. In the entity bean CMR chapter, we'll look at why local interfaces were added to the spec. For now, think of them as a very special case.

Remote client view   **Local client view**

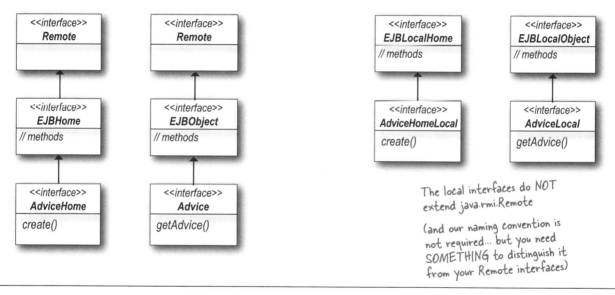

The local interfaces do NOT extend java.rmi.Remote

(and our naming convention is not required... but you need SOMETHING to distinguish it from your Remote interfaces)

The Remote interfaces EJBHome and EJBObject have more methods than the local interfaces EJBLocalHome and EJBLocalObject. Flip back through this chapter and look at the methods for EJBHome and EJBObject, and try to work out which methods in those Remote interfaces might be inappropriate or not needed in the local interfaces.

Think about the implications of having the interfaces local to the client...

REMOTE client view

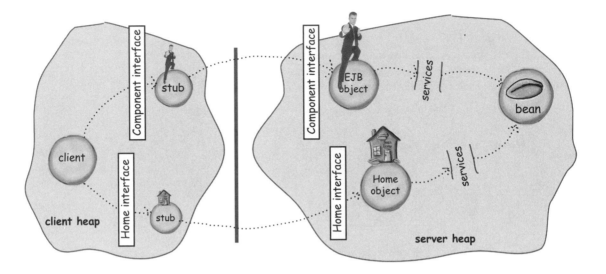

LOCAL client view

The client still can't get to the bean directly, because the server still needs a place to intercept the call to the bean (so the server can add services). But this time, the client has a local reference to the home and component interface objects.

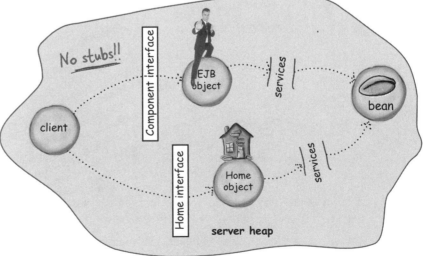

Sharpen your pencil

Given that the client has a plain old everyday Java reference to the home and component interfaces (i.e. the home object and the EJB object), which of the Remote interface methods do you think are appropriate for the local client view?

In other words, which methods of EJBHome are not in EJBLocalHome, and which methods of EJBObject are not in EJBLocalObject? *Why?*

Of the four methods in EJBHome, EJBLocalHome has only one. *Which one?*

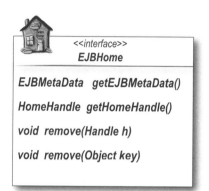

<<interface>> **EJBHome**
EJBMetaData getEJBMetaData()
HomeHandle getHomeHandle()
void remove(Handle h)
void remove(Object key)

<<interface>> **EJBLocalHome**
1 _____

Of the five methods in EJBObject, EJBLocalObject has only four (and one of the four is slightly different). *Which four?*

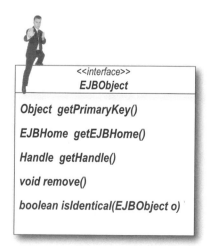

<<interface>> **EJBObject**
Object getPrimaryKey()
EJBHome getEJBHome()
Handle getHandle()
void remove()
boolean isIdentical(EJBObject o)

<<interface>> **EJBLocalObject**
1 _____
2 _____
3 _____
4 _____

Which methods make sense for the local client interfaces?

You already know that the local client interfaces are missing some of the methods from their Remote counterparts. Let's figure out which ones are missing, and why.

Do we need handles with local interfaces?

Remember why handles exist in EJB—to give you a Serializable object that you can use to re-establish a stub to the EJB object you'd been working with. The handle is just an abstraction of a remote connection. So... does this make sense on a local client?

Do we need EJBMetaData with local interfaces?

Remember what EJBMetaData is used for—to get reflection-like info about a bean. If you call getEJBMetaData() on a bean's Remote home, you get back an object that implements EJBMetaData. That interface (EJBMetaData) has methods that let you interrogate the bean and learn more about the classes that make up the component. Would a local client ever need EJBMetaData?

Do we need isIdentical() with local interfaces?

Remember why isIdentical() exists—to let you compare two home or component interface references to see if they refer to "meaningfully equivalent" beans on the server. Would you need to use isIdentical() on a local client? (Big Hint: the server is free to implement .equals() any way it chooses...)

Do we need primary key information with local interfaces?

Remember why primary keys exist—to uniquely identify entity beans. Would you ever need to identify an entity bean on a local client?

Do we need remove methods with local interfaces?

Remember what remove() is used for—to tell the container that you're done with a bean, for Session beans, or to tell the container to permanently delete the entity, for entity beans. Would a local client need to call remove() on a bean?

When you think handle, think Remote

Local clients don't need handles!

Local clients have no use for a handle, because handles are strictly for getting a savable (Serializable) object that knows how to reestablish communication with the Remote object.

LOCAL client view

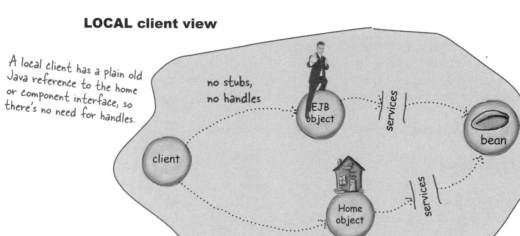

A local client has a plain old Java reference to the home or component interface, so there's no need for handles.

no stubs,
no handles

EJB object

services

bean

client

Home object

services

Who needs EJBMetaData when you've got reflection?

Local clients don't need EJBMetaData!

With the Java reflection API, you can interrogate an object to get all sorts of information about its class. With Remote objects, you don't have that option, because you can't get a reference to the class of the Remote object. The only thing you can interrogate on a Remote client are the stub objects, but they can't tell you anything about the *real* EJB object or Home object.

So while a Remote home client has to use EJBMetaData (the interface returned from the EJBHome getEJBMetaData() method) to get info, a local client will simply use the Java reflection methods (getClass(), etc.).

Do you need <u>isIdentical()</u> when there's <u>equals()</u>?

Local clients still need isIdentical()

Remember for a Remote client, the only local comparison you do is on two stub objects, using equals(). This doesn't work when you want to compare something back on the server, in this case the two EJB object references. That's what isIdentical() is for. But local clients have the real thing! They have the *real* reference to the EJB object, so they can use equals(), to see if two EJB object (local) references are meaningfully equivalent. But... that's still not what you want. There is no guarantee in the spec, for the results you'll get with .equals()! So while it *seems* like you could just use .equals() rather than isIdentical() with a local client, the spec does not guarantee that the results will be the same. Bottom line: if you want to know if two EJB object references are referencing the same session object, you have to use isIdentical() even when the EJB object is local.

REMOTE client view

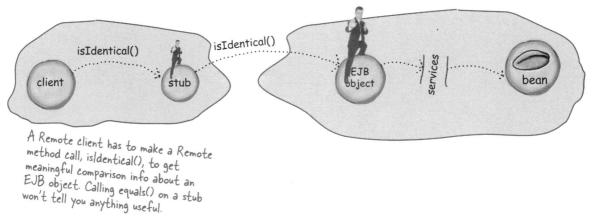

A Remote client has to make a Remote method call, isIdentical(), to get meaningful comparison info about an EJB object. Calling equals() on a stub won't tell you anything useful.

LOCAL client view

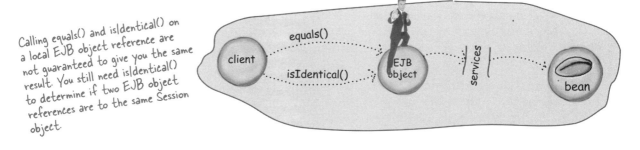

Calling equals() and isIdentical() on a local EJB object reference are not guaranteed to give you the same result. You still need isIdentical() to determine if two EJB object references are to the same Session object.

Why so many remove methods?

For Remote clients, two in the home, plus one in the component interface

Remember, Remote clients have three remove() methods available, two in the home, and one in the component interface. The remove() that comes from EJBObject is simple; if you call it, you're saying you want to remove *that very bean*! In other words, the bean whose EJBObject you used to call remove(). And for session beans, remember, calling remove() simply tells the container that you're done with the bean. It's good manners, and it improves scalability since the server can stop keeping client-specific resources on your behalf, rather than waiting, say, for your shopping session to time out from inactivity.

But things aren't so simple when you call remove on a home. For one thing, you actually *can't* remove a home! The server keeps the bean home alive whether you're around or not, so there's no significant client-specific resources. There's no need to tell the server you're done with the home, because the server would simply say, "So what?"

Then what does it mean to call remove() on a home?

It means you're telling the home to remove one of the beans that *came* from that home. And that means you have to identify *which* bean you're talking about!

REMOTE client view

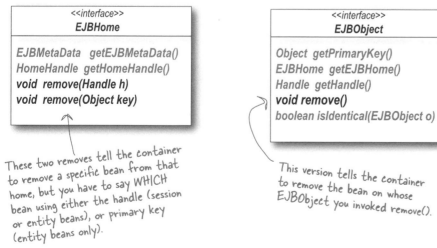

<<interface>> **EJBHome**
EJBMetaData getEJBMetaData()   *HomeHandle getHomeHandle()*   **void remove(Handle h)**   **void remove(Object key)**

These two removes tell the container to remove a specific bean from that home, but you have to say WHICH bean using either the handle (session or entity beans), or primary key (entity beans only).

<<interface>> **EJBObject**
Object getPrimaryKey()   *EJBHome getEJBHome()*   *Handle getHandle()*   **void remove()**   *boolean isIdentical(EJBObject o)*

This version tells the container to remove the bean on whose EJBObject you invoked remove().

Why there's not a no-arg remove method in the home...

How can you use a remove that takes a handle when you don't <u>have</u> a handle?

Local clients don't have handles, so local homes don't have a remove() that takes a handle.

If local home interfaces don't have handles, then there's no way you could have a remove method that takes a handle. Because in order to pass a handle to the home, that uniquely identifies the bean you're trying to remove, you'd have to first get the bean's handle. And since locally-exposed beans don't have handles... you see the problem.

there are no
Dumb Questions

Q: What if you have a local home, but you have a Remote EJB object reference? Can't you pass the Remote bean's handle to the local home?

A: NO!! Because you can't mix local and Remote interfaces together. Only a local bean comes from a local home, and vice-versa. So it will NEVER be possible to have a Remote bean's handle, to give to that same Remote bean's home, unless that home is also Remote.

We didn't say that very well, did we... OK how about this—a *Remote* home will hand out only *Remote* references to the component (EJBObject) interface for that bean type, and a local home will only return local references to the component (EJBLocalObject) interface.

Q: Tell me again why you can't remove the home.

A: There's never a reason to remove the home (in other words, to tell the container you're done with it), because the container must keep the home around with or without your interest. So if you were able to say remove to the home, the container would say, "Gee...don't flatter yourself buddy. What I do here on the server is not ABOUT you. I could care less when you're done with your home reference."

You don't call remove on a home to remove the <u>home</u>.

You call remove on a home to tell the home to remove a <u>bean</u>.

A bean from that home type.

That means you must uniquely identify the bean you want removed, when you call a home remove method. For entity beans, use the primary key or a handle, and for session beans, use a handle.

But handles only work for Remote home clients...

Comparing Remote vs. Local interfaces

The EJBObject and EJBHome interfaces have more methods than the
EJBLocalObject and EJBLocalHome interfaces because there are methods
that don't make sense in a local context.

REMOTE client view

<<interface>> ***EJBHome***
EJBMetaData getEJBMetaData()
HomeHandle getHomeHandle()
void remove(Handle h)
void remove(Object key)

LOCAL client view

<<interface>> ***EJBLocalHome***
EJBMetaData ~~getEJBMetaData()~~
HomeHandle ~~getHomeHandle()~~
void ~~remove(Handle h)~~
void remove(Object key)

*Local clients can use reflection, so
they don't need EJBMetaData.*

*No need for a handle with a local
client—there's no stub!*

*locally-accessed beans don't have
handles, so you can't use a handle to
remove one.*

<<interface>> ***EJBObject***
Object getPrimaryKey()
EJBHome getEJBHome()
Handle getHandle()
void remove()
boolean isIdentical(EJBObject o)

<<interface>> ***EJBLocalObject***
Object getPrimaryKey()
EJBLocalHome getEJBLocalHome()
Handle ~~getHandle()~~
void remove()
boolean isIdentical(Object o)

← *changes from Remote to local*

No handles in local clients

Sharpen your pencil

Based on what you now know about the difference between local and Remote client interfaces, decide if the following statements are true or false. You'll have to make some inferences and smart guesses for some of them.

Select all that are true:

☐ The only way to remove a local session bean is through the component interface

☐ Entity beans can be removed through a local home interface

☐ If you see an isIdentical() call, this must be a local bean

☐ If you see a getHandle() call, this must be a Remote bean

☐ If the client is catching a RemoteException on a home method, the bean's home interface must extend EJBLocalHome

☐ If the client is not handling a RemoteException on a business method, the bean's component interface must extend EJBObject.

☐ If you see a call to getEJBMetaData(), the bean's component interface must extend EJBLocalObject.

☐ If you do a JNDI lookup on a local home, you must narrow the object returned from JNDI

☐ There are three methods in the EJBLocalObject interface

☐ There are two methods in the EJBLocalHome interface

Writing the <u>local</u> client interfaces

Now that we've covered what the client sees in a local interface, let's look at your responsibility as a Bean Provider. In other words, what *you* have to do to write the local interfaces for your bean.

Component interface:

```
package headfirst;
import javax.ejb.*;

public interface AdviceLocal extends EJBLocalObject {

    public String getAdvice();

}
```

extend EJBLocalObject instead of EJBObject

No RemoteException!!

this return type doesn't need to be RMI-IIOP compliant (although it certainly can be, of course, like String)

Home interface:

```
package headfirst;
import javax.ejb.*;

public interface AdviceHomeLocal extends EJBLocalHome {

    public AdviceLocal create() throws CreateException;

}
```

extend EJBLocalHome instead of EJBHome

This MUST be the <u>local</u> component interface!

still needs a CreateException but no RemoteException

Rules for local interfaces

(1) Import javax.ejb.* (or use fully-qualified names).

(2) Extend EJBLocalObject (for the component interface) or EJBLocalHome (for the home interface).

(3) Declare one or more business methods in the component interface.

(4) All create methods in the local home must return the local component interface, and declare a CreateException.

(5) Any method you declare in the home or component interface can declare your own application exceptions, which must be compiler-checked exceptions (i.e. not subclasses of RuntimeException)..

(6) You must NOT declare a RemoteException for any methods

You can have both a Remote and local client view for a bean, but you probably won't.

We mentioned earlier that local interfaces are a very special case for a client view. They were introduced with version 2.0 of the EJB spec (which this book is based on) and the original intent was to support container-managed relationships in entity beans. But enough customers and vendors asked for the ability to have non-Remote interfaces for beans, so the J2EE team decided to make it available for session beans as well as entity beans.

But regardless of which you choose, it's *very* unlikely you'll have a design that requires both a local and Remote client view. If your bean is in a container-managed relationship with another entity bean (you'll learn all about this in the entity chapters), you have no choice. The bean must expose itself locally. And in that case, it's almost impossible to think of a reason to also have that same bean exposed to Remote clients for other purposes.

Just know that it *is* legal to have both.

But you can never, ever, ever mix and match.

A *Remote* home interface can give out only *Remote* component interface references (in other words, a stub to the Remote EJBObject). A *local* home can give out only *local* component interface references (in other words, a regular Java heap reference to the EJBLocalObject).

You can't mix local and Remote interfaces together for the same bean, even though a given bean can expose both a Remote and local client view.

But a Remote home will give out only Remote component interface references (stubs), and a local home will give out only local component interface references (regular Java references).

Sharpen your pencil

Change the AdviceClient from a Remote client to a local client, using the local interfaces for AdviceLocal and AdviceHomeLocal. Do NOT turn the next page!!

```java
import javax.naming.*;
import java.rmi.*;
import javax.rmi.*;
import headfirst.*;
import javax.ejb.*;

public class AdviceClient {

    public static void main(String[] args) {
        new AdviceClient().go();
    }

    public void go() {
        try {
            Context ic = new InitialContext();
            Object o = ic.lookup("Advisor");

            AdviceHome home = (AdviceHome) PortableRemoteObject.narrow(o, AdviceHome.class);

            Advice advisor = home.create();
            System.out.println(advisor.getAdvice());
        } catch (Exception ex) {
            ex.printStackTrace();
        }
    }
}
```

What has to change? Write the changed line (or lines) below:

Exceptions in client interfaces: what the client might get

A Remote interface must have RemoteException declared on every method. That means the client using a Remote interface must deal with RemoteException for every Remote method call. But local interfaces don't have that restriction. The only methods in a local client interface that must declare exceptions are the create() and remove() methods (for session beans; entity beans also have a finder method that declares a FinderException).

We have a whole chapter devoted to exceptions in EJB, so we won't go into the details now, but the essence is this: if a bean (or the Container) generates a runtime exception, Remote clients see the exception as a *checked* RemoteException, but local clients see it as an *unchecked* EJBException.

In addition to whatever other checked exceptions (called application exceptions in EJB) the interface methods declare, all Remote interface methods can throw a RemoteException and local client interface methods can always throw an EJBException. So Remote clients must wrap all calls to a home or component interface method in a try/catch, while local clients use a try/catch *only* if the interface method declares an application exception (which includes CreateException, RemoveException, FinderException, and any other exceptions the Bean Provider declares in the methods of the bean's client interfaces).

✓ Indicates a compiler-checked exception (i.e. non-RuntimeException)

	REMOTE client view	**LOCAL** client view
ALL methods	✓`javax.ejb.RemoteException`	`javax.ejb.EJBException`
CREATE methods	✓`javax.ejb.RemoteException` ✓`javax.ejb.CreateException`	`javax.ejb.EJBException` ✓`javax.ejb.CreateException`
REMOVE methods	✓`javax.ejb.RemoteException` ✓`javax.ejb.RemoveException`	`javax.ejb.EJBException` ✓`javax.ejb.RemoveException`

Local client code

Compare this to the code modifications you made on the previous sharpen.
To help show that the calls to the home and component interface are no
longer Remote, we've made the exception handling more fine-grained. Notice
that we're not catching a RemoteException.

```java
import javax.naming.*;
import headfirst.*;              we got rid of javax.rmi and
import javax.ejb.*;              java.rmi imports

public class AdviceLocalClient {

    public static void main(String[] args) {
        new AdviceLocalClient().go();
    }

    public void go() {
        Object o = null;

        try {

            Context ic = new InitialContext();
            o = ic.lookup("AdvisorLocal");

        } catch (NamingException nex) {
            nex.printStackTrace();
        }

        AdviceHomeLocal home = (AdviceHomeLocal) o;
        AdviceLocal advisor = null;

        try {

            advisor = home.create();

        } catch (CreateException cex) {
            cex.printStackTrace();
        }

        System.out.println(advisor.getAdvice());
    }
}
```

You still have to go through JNDI, and do the lookup the usual way, only this time you get a reference to a real Java object on the heap (an instance of EJBLocalHome), instead of a stub to a Remote EJBHome object.

Here's a big change! No narrowing! Just a plain old cast (we still have to cast because the return type of lookup is Object, but we don't have to narrow it since it isn't a stub.)

The create() method still declares a CreateException, but not a RemoteException

The business method call is no longer a Remote method call. Just a normal local method call, and since getAdvice() doesn't declare any exceptions, the business method call doesn't have to be wrapped in a try/catch.

What has to change inside the <u>bean</u> class?

We've seen how the interfaces change, and how the client code has to change, when you go from a Remote to local client view. But what about the bean class itself? What do you think? Does the bean code need to change, if you're going to deploy it with a *local* client view instead of a *Remote* client view? What if you plan to deploy it with *both* a local and Remote client view?

For now, let's assume that the only method that matters is the bean's business method. Here's how it looks in the original bean class:

```
public String getAdvice() {
    System.out.println("in get advice");
    int random = (int) (Math.random() * adviceStrings.length);
    return adviceStrings[random];
}
```

Do you see anything in that method that looks specific to a Remote client view? Would you need to do anything different with a local client?

No, don't think so.

Anything that works as a return type or argument for a Remote method is guaranteed to work for a local method as well, so we're OK there. (Kind of a no-brainer when the return type is String, though.) OK, there is *one* exception—remember, according to Bean law you must not return a bean's Remote interface from a local interface method.

So it looks like (at least with this bean) we should never have to know or care. We should be able to deploy the bean as written, and the bean should be kept unaware of whether its clients are Remote or local.

Sounds good, doesn't it? Simple, clean, object-oriented.

But think about it some more. Imagine a bean with more complex logic. More business methods. Arguments to those methods. Arguments the method might even need to act on.

Hmmmmm... can you think of *anything* that the bean might want to treat differently, if it knew the client were local instead of Remote?

Wait a minute... Java passes objects locally by passing a copy of the object *reference*, not the object itself. But we know that *Remote* method arguments and return values are passed as a Serialized copy of the actual *object*...

In ordinary local method calls, Java passes an object reference by value, as a *copy* of the reference variable.

The object itself is never passed.

But with Remote calls, the *object* itself is copied.

With Remote calls, the called method is always working on a *copy* of the caller's object.

With local calls, the called method is always working with the caller's original object—*not a copy!*

Arguments to Remote vs. local methods

LOCAL method call

```
Dog fido = new Dog();
 this.trainPet(fido);
```

a copy of the reference (the remote control) not the Dog object

```
void trainPet(Dog arg) {... }
```

Now the 'arg' parameter and the 'fido' variable are identical copies. Both reference the same Dog object.

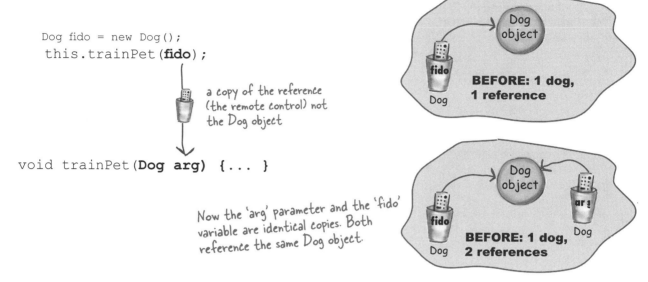

BEFORE: 1 dog, 1 reference

BEFORE: 1 dog, 2 references

REMOTE method call

```
Dog fido = new Dog();
remoteStub.trainPet(fido);
```

NOT the reference value!

It's a serialized copy of the actual Dog object

```
void trainPet(Dog arg) {... }
```

The server Dog is a copy of the client Dog

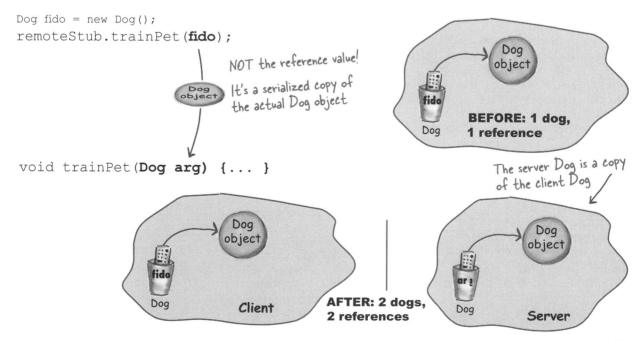

BEFORE: 1 dog, 1 reference

Client

AFTER: 2 dogs, 2 references

Server

Q: **So, I'm still not clear if the bean MUST always know if the client is Remote or local.**

A: It's not that the bean *must*, but rather that the bean *might* have to know. If it matters that the bean is working on a the caller's *object*, (via a copy of the caller's reference) as opposed to a *copy* of the caller's object, your bean code might have to change. And that goes for return values too. If it matters that the calling method gets back a copy of a reference vs. a copy of an object, the bean code might have to change.

Q: **But I thought that choosing to deploy a bean with local vs. Remote client views was just a matter of switching a switch at deploy time.**

A: NO! NO! NO! Let's imagine that you did write two sets of interfaces, one for a local client view and one for a Remote client view. It is true that at deployment you could decide which of the two views you wanted to expose (or both). But that works only if the bean code doesn't care where the client is. A bean method with no arguments or return values might be safe regardless of how the client is accessing it.

One solution might be to write the bean code assuming the bean is always getting a copy, and then if the client is local, have the client make a copy (clone) of the object before passing it. Or, for return values, you might always have the bean make a copy before handing it back. That way,

the bean never has to worry that a local client might be modifying the bean's object.

Q: **Then it's just about arguments and return values? Is there any other reason you couldn't deploy a bean and make the decision for Remote vs. local view at deploy time?**

A: There is another reason. The client code! Even if the *bean* doesn't need to know how its client is accessing it, the *client* must know! A client written to access a bean locally wouldn't work if the bean's Remote client interfaces, and vice-versa.

Q: **Why not?**

A: The client must know in advance whether its accessing a bean's Remote or local client view, because the interfaces themselves are different. Polymorphically, you can't use the Remote and local views interchangeably, because the interfaces themselves are different.

There's no way the client can be kept blissfully ignorant*, because the behavior of the bean is different. Remember, a Remote client must handle RemoteExceptions, and narrow the Remote stub coming back from the lookup! And a Remote client is exposed to methods in the bean's client interfaces—methods that don't exist in the local interfaces. So a Remote client might, for example, try to call a getHandle() method on the local component interface, a method call that would never work.

And a local client won't have code to handle the RemoteExceptions or narrow the stubs.

The bottom line is that deploying a bean with a Remote vs. local client view is a Big Deal. It's a commitment. The client has to know in advance.

Q: **Can you get around this by declaring your RemoteExceptions on your local interface? And could you make an interface that is both Remote and local... by having your component interface (like Advice) extend both Remote and EJBLocalObject? What's the harm if the client simply always handles RemoteExceptions, and always does the narrow()? That way the client shouldn't have to know.**

A: Still won't work. For one thing, according to bean law, you're not allowed to declare RemoteExceptions on local methods! So there's no guarantee that your server would even *let* you deploy a bean with a local interface that declares RemoteExceptions. And there is no guarantee that the narrow() method would not cause problems. And then there are handles and all that other stuff... You need to just let this go.

Exercise

BE the Container

Each of the code snippets on this page represents code from either an interface or a client. Your job is to play Container and decide whether each is legal according to both Java law and Bean law. In other words, even if the code compiles, it might still be WRONG to the Container, because it doesn't comply with the rules of the EJB spec. Assume that everything you do NOT see is legal and correct. Figure out if the problem is a compiler error or a problem to the Container, and figure out how to fix it.

A. In a local client:

```
public void go()  {
  Object o = null;
  try {

     Context ic = new InitialContext();
     o = ic.lookup("AdvisorLocal");

  } catch (NamingException nex) {
       nex.printStackTrace();
  }
  AdviceHomeLocal home = (AdviceHomeLocal) o;
  AdviceLocal advisor = null;
 // more stuff
}
```

B. In a Remote client:

```
public void go() {
   try {
    // look up the Advice bean, assign it
    // to advisor
   } catch (Exception ex) {
     ex.printStackTrace();
   }
   System.out.println(advisor.getAdvice());
}
```

C. In a bean's home interface

```
package headfirst;
import javax.ejb.*;

public interface AdviceHome extends EJBHome {

    public Advice create() throws CreateException;

}
```

D. In a bean's component interface

```
package headfirst;
import javax.ejb.*;

public interface AdviceLocal extends EJBLocalObject {

    public String getAdvice();

}
```

BULLET POINTS

- You can expose your bean to local clients using a local client view.

- Local component interfaces must extend javax.ejb.EJBLocalObject. Local home interfaces must extend javax.ejb.EJBLocalHome.

- Methods in local client interfaces do NOT declare RemoteException.

- Some of the interface methods exposed to Remote clients are not exposed to local clients.

- Local clients cannot get handles, since handles are used to re-establish a connection to the Remote object.

- EJBMetaData is not used with local clients, since a local client can use reflection to interrogate the EJB object and Home object.

- Local home interfaces have only one remove() method—the one that takes a primary key. The remove() that takes a Handle doesn't exist in the local home interface, since Handles aren't used with a local client view.

- Because the only remove() in the local home interface requires a primary key argument, local session bean clients cannot remove a bean using the bean's home; they can call remove() *only* on the bean's component interface.

- EJBLocalHome has only one method: remove() that takes a primary key, because the getHomeHandle(), getEJBMetaData(), and remove(Handle) methods that are in EJBHome don't apply to a local client view.

- The only method in EJBObject that is not also in EJBLocalObject is getHandle().

- Arguments and return values are passed by value when using a local client view. In other words, they're passed in the normal Java way (objects passed by a copy of the reference, primitives passed by a copy of the value).

- Local clients do not need to narrow the Home reference because it's a normal Java reference, not a stub to a Remote object.

- Local clients do not need to catch RemoteExceptions, since local interface methods don't declare RemoteExceptions.

Watch it! **You have to recognize a local vs. Remote client view!**

Be prepared to look at bean code, client code, or interface code and know whether you're looking at a Remote or local client view. And it might be subtle!
For example, you might see the client make a business method call, and the argument to the method is a non-Serializable object. Since you are to assume that the method is legal and correct, you KNOW that this must be a local interface— you can't pass a non-Serializable object as an argument or return value to or from a Remote method. Some of other gotchas to tell you whether the bean is local or Remote include:
1. Client doesn't narrow the Home.
2. Client doesn't handle any checked exceptions on a business method call.
3. Client calls remove(Handle) on a bean's home.

Exercise Solutions

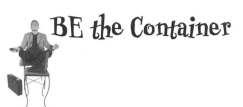

BE the Container

A. In a local client:

```
public void go()  {
  Object o = null;
  try {

    Context ic = new InitialContext();
    o = ic.lookup("AdvisorLocal");

  } catch (NamingException nex) {
      nex.printStackTrace();
  }
  AdviceHomeLocal home = (AdviceHomeLocal) o;
  AdviceLocal advisor = null;
 // more stuff
}
```

A is fine. Because it's local, it does not need to narrow the Home reference. Only a cast is needed.

B. In a Remote client:

```
public void go() {
  try {
   // look up the Advice bean, assign
   // it to advisor
  } catch (Exception ex) {
    ex.printStackTrace();
  }
  System.out.println(advisor.getAdvice());
}
```

Compiler error! getAdvice() is a remote method, but it isn't handling the RemoteException. If we moved the last line INSIDE the try block, it would work.

C. In a bean's home interface

```
package headfirst;
import javax.ejb.*;

public interface AdviceHome extends EJBHome {

    public Advice create() throws CreateException;

}
```

Container error! EJBHome is a Remote interface, and the rule is that you must declare RemoteException on each method in the interface. The compiler doesn't care, but the Container will. At some point in the deploy process, this will fail.

needs RemoteException

(look at the imports; no java.rmi.*)

D. In a bean's component interface

D works fine.. It's a local component interface, and it doesn't need to declare any exceptions on the business methods.

```
package headfirst;
import javax.ejb.*;

public interface AdviceLocal extends EJBLocalObject {

    public String getAdvice();

}
```

OK, needs no exceptions declared

Mock Exam

---

1 Which capabilities are provided by both remote and local home interfaces for session beans? (Choose all that apply.)

- ❏ A. Creating a session object.
- ❏ B. Removing a session object.
- ❏ C. Getting a session object's EJBMetaData.
- ❏ D. Getting a session object's handle.

---

2 When locating a session bean's remote home interface, which are steps that must occur to create a valid home interface reference? (Choose all that apply.)

- ❏ A. The session context must be narrowed, and the narrowed result cast.
- ❏ B. The result of the JNDI lookup must be narrowed, and the narrowed result cast.
- ❏ C. The initial context must be narrowed, and the narrowed result cast.
- ❏ D. The result of the JNDI lookup must be cast to an initial context, and then narrowed.

---

3 Given a remote client 'R', that has valid references to session beans 'A' and 'B', and given that A is a local client to B, which statements are true? (Choose all that apply.)

- ❏ A. R cannot pass his reference for A, to B.
- ❏ B. A cannot pass his reference for B, to R.
- ❏ C. A cannot invoke methods on B.
- ❏ D. B cannot invoke methods on R.

4 When comparing two session objects, what is true? (Choose all that apply.)

❏ A. Using the isIdentical() method, stateless session beans from the same home will always return true.

❏ B. Using the isIdentical() method, stateful session beans from the same home will always return true.

❏ C. The isIdentical() method can be used for only remote object references.

❏ D. Using the equals() method, stateless session beans from the same home are guaranteed to return true.

❏ E. Using the equals() method, stateful session beans from the same home are guaranteed to return true.

5 Which statement(s) about session beans are true? (Choose all that apply.)

❏ A. The bean provider must write the method public void remove() in both stateless and stateful session classes.

❏ B. Local clients can remove session beans by calling a method on the bean's home.

❏ C. The remove() method in the component interface can be used only by remote clients.

❏ D. To ask the EJBHome to remove a session bean, the client must provide the bean's handle.

Mock Exam Answers

---

1 Which capabilities are provided by both remote and local home interfaces for session beans? (Choose all that apply.)

session beans can't be removed through a local home interface because there is only a remove() that takes a primary key

☑ A. Creating a session object.

❏ B. Removing a session object. —

❏ C. Getting a session object's EJBMetaData. — *not in a local home*

❏ D. Getting a session object's handle. — *not in a local home*

---

2 When locating a session bean's remote home interface, which are steps that must occur to create a valid home interface reference? (Choose all that apply.)

(spec: 57)

❏ A. The session context must be narrowed, and the narrowed result cast.

☑ B. The result of the JNDI lookup must be narrowed, and the narrowed result cast.

❏ C. The initial context must be narrowed, and the narrowed result cast.

❏ D. The result of the JNDI lookup must be cast to an initial context, and then narrowed.

---

3 Given a remote client 'R', that has valid references to session beans 'A' and 'B', and given that A is a local client to B, which statements are true? (Choose all that apply.)

You can't give a remote client a local reference, A sees B through a local reference

❏ A. R cannot pass his reference for A, to B.

☑ B. A cannot pass his reference for B, to R.

❏ C. A cannot invoke methods on B.

☑ D. B cannot invoke methods on R.

---

4 When comparing two session objects, what is true? (Choose all that apply.)   (spec: 65–66)

☑ A. Using the isIdentical() method, stateless session beans from the same home will always return true.

❏ B. Using the isIdentical() method, stateful session beans from the same home will always return true.

❏ C. The isIdentical() method can be used for only remote object references.

❏ D. Using the equals() method, stateless session beans from the same home are guaranteed to return true.   *The behavior of equals() is not specified*

❏ E. Using the equals() method, stateful session beans from the same home are guaranteed to return true.

---

5 Which statement(s) about session beans are true? (Choose all that apply.)

❏ A. The bean provider must write the method public void remove() in both stateless and stateful session classes.   *– it's ejbRemove(), not remove()*

❏ B. Local clients can remove session beans by calling a method on the bean's home.   *– local homes have only a remove() that takes a primary key*

❏ C. The remove() method in the component interface can be used only by remote clients.   *– no, only for local*

☑ D. To ask the EJBHome to remove a session bean, the client must provide the bean's handle.   *– but not true for EJBLocalHome*

4 session bean lifecycle

Being a Session Bean

I hate it when I get container callbacks. I just know it's gonna be an ejbRemove(), but I was only just created... I wish I was stateless. They won't even let me go in the pool...

Session beans are created and removed. If you're lucky, you're a state*less* bean. Because the life of a state*ful* bean is tied to the whims of a heartless client. Stateful beans are created at the client's insistence, and exist *only* to serve that one client. As a stateful bean, the best you can hope for is that the client crashes or forgets to call remove(); it might take the Container a while to figure out you've become useless. But ahhhh, the life of a stateless bean is *fabulous!* Pools, those little umbrella drinks, and no boredom since you get to meet so many different clients. Of course, even a stateless bean dies with an unchecked exception...

Session Beans

Official:	*What it really means:*
3.1 Identify correct and incorrect statements or examples about session beans, including conversational state, the SessionBean interface, and create methods.	This objective can hit you on *anything* related to session beans, so you pretty much have to know it all, including the details of both stateless and stateful bean lifecycles, the container callback methods of SessionBean, what you must write in a bean class, and what a bean can get from its EJBContext. Anything covered by the other session bean objectives is fair game.
3.2 Identify the use of, and the behavior of, the ejbPassivate method in a session bean, including the responsibilities of both the container and the bean provider.	First, you have to know that passivation is for only stateful session beans. Stateless beans go back to the bean pool without going through passivation. So, ejbPassivate() will never be called on a stateless bean. You have to know that your responsibility in ejbPassivate() is to make sure that when the method ends, your bean is ready for passivation, and that passivation may or may not involve serialization. You must know the state that your instance variables must be in at the time ejbPassivate() ends. And even though this objective doesn't mention ejbActivate(), you have to understand how ejbActivate() works as well.
3.3 Identify the interface and method for each of the following: retrieve the session bean's remote home interface, retrieve the session bean's local component interface, determine if the session bean's caller has a particular role, allow the instance to mark the current transaction as a rollback, retrieve the UserTransaction interface, prepare the instance for reuse following passivation, release resources prior to removal, identify the invoker of the bean instance's component interface, be notified that a new transaction has begun, be notified that the current transaction has completed.	You must be able to look at a description of a desired behavior, like, figure out the security principal of the client, and know which method you can call, and on which interface, to get that behavior (in this case, getCallerPrincipal() called on the SessionContext interface). To answer these questions, you have to know every method in the three key interfaces: SessionBean (the interface your bean implements), SessionContext (the interface your bean has a reference to), and SessionSynchronization (an optional interface that a stateful bean can implement). In this chapter, we'll cover everything about session bean interfaces except SessionSynchronization, which is covered in the transactions chapter.

Objective 3

Session Beans

Official:	*What it really means:*

3.4 Match correct descriptions about purpose and function with which session bean type they apply to: stateless, stateful, or both.

You have to know the differences between stateless and stateful beans including when you'd choose one over the other. You must know the bean rules including: there can be only one create method in a state*less* bean, and it must have no arguments; only state*ful* beans can implement SessionSynchronization, both stateless and stateful beans will not survive a container crash, state*less* beans will never be passivated, state*less* bean creation and removal is not tied to the client.

3.5 Given a list of responsibilities related to session beans, indentify those which are the responsibility of the session bean provider, and those which are the responsibility of the EJB container provider.

You have to know what is and isn't guaranteed in the spec. For example, the container won't allow concurrent access to a single session bean (if client A is using the bean, client B will get an exception if it calls a method on that bean). And the container isn't required to allow a bean in one EAR file to be a local client to a bean in a different EAR. And you have to know exactly which classes and methods are implemented by you (the bean, the ejbRemove() and ejbCreate() methods, etc.), and which are implemented by the container (the handles, the home and component objects, the stubs (for Remote client interfaces), the getEJBObject() method, etc.). Most of what's in this objective overlaps with 3.1, 3.2, and 3.6.

3.6 Given a list of requirements, identify those which are the requirements for a session bean class, remote component interface, remote home interface, create methods, business methods, local component interface, remote component interface.

This is about knowing bean law—the rules you have to follow, according to the spec, even in the cases where compiler won't care if you don't. For example, you must have a matching ejbCreate() method for each create method in the home, but the compiler won't stop you if you leave it out. And you must know that local interface methods must not declare a RemoteException, but Remote interface methods must. And you must know that object type arguments to a Remote interface method are sent as serialized copies of the object, while arguments to local interfaces are sent as copies of the reference.

Exploring the session bean lifecycle

Imagine you're a session bean. What *matters* to you? What are the *key moments* in your life? What do you need to *know* about the client? What do you need to *know* about the Container? What do you need to *get* from the Container?

Now imagine you're the client. What's your motivation? What do you need to know about how the Container works? And what if you're the Container? *What* do you have to do to manage a bean's life, and *when* do you have to do it?

If you're the Bean Provider, what do you have to know about the bean's lifecycle in order to write code that works? What if you want that code to be *efficient*?

In this chapter, we look at the entire world of a session bean, and we do it from different points of view. We take an OO approach to this chapter, iterating through deeper levels of detail. So don't panic if the first several pages feel a little too high-level, or leave you with questions. You'll be down in the dirt before the chapter's done.

Before we start, let's introduce the players:

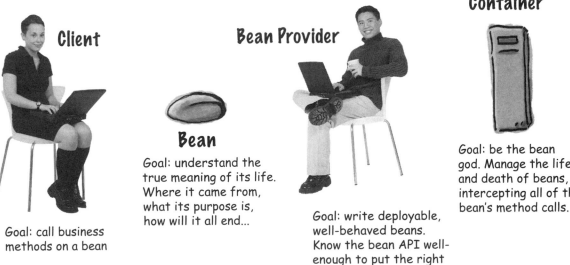

Client

Goal: call business methods on a bean

Bean

Goal: understand the true meaning of its life. Where it came from, what its purpose is, how will it all end...

Bean Provider

Goal: write deployable, well-behaved beans. Know the bean API well-enough to put the right code in the right place.

Container

Goal: be the bean god. Manage the life and death of beans, intercepting all of the bean's method calls.

Client

I create, use, and remove beans by calling methods on the home and component interface stubs. Someday, I will kill the Bean Provider with my bare hands, for never giving me the right stubs.

Bean

I'm an object, and I run business methods, but I'm also a bean. As a bean, I pay attention to key milestones in my life like construction (boring), bean creation (very important), passivation (going to sleep), activation (waking up), and removal (death, not good if you're me). The container tells me everytime one of these special moments occurs. Most happen just once (construction, creation, removal), but activation, passivation, and business methods can happen over and over again.

Bean Provider

I write the bean code. Besides the business methods, I have to implement the container callbacks (the ones the container calls when something happens in the bean's life). I also have to write the ejbCreate() methods to match the home create() methods. And I'm underpaid and they still haven't given me one of those Aeron™ chairs...

Container

I construct the bean, I give the bean its beanness (special bean capabilities), and I call create on the bean, passing in client arguments if it's a stateful bean. I decide if and when the bean should sleep and wake up, and I'm the only one that can kill (remove) a bean. I decide how and if a business method is called on a bean, factoring in things like security and transactions. To a bean, I'm a god.

You remember how it all works, right?
Getting and using a stateful session bean

This picture shows what happens after the client does a lookup in JNDI and gets the home stub. In other words, it shows the client getting and then using a bean. This picture is still too high-level, though, so we'll go a lot deeper later in this chapter. For example, we'll cover what *really* happens between step two (home object gets the client's create() call) and step four (home makes the bean). The exam expects you to know just exactly what's involved in "*makes the bean*".

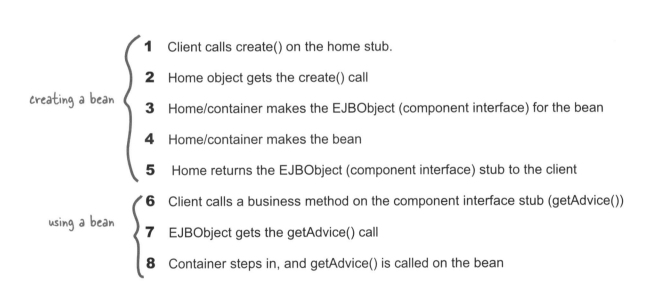

creating a bean

1   Client calls create() on the home stub.

2   Home object gets the create() call

3   Home/container makes the EJBObject (component interface) for the bean

4   Home/container makes the bean

5   Home returns the EJBObject (component interface) stub to the client

using a bean

6   Client calls a business method on the component interface stub (getAdvice())

7   EJBObject gets the getAdvice() call

8   Container steps in, and getAdvice() is called on the bean

Stateful Session Bean

CREATION

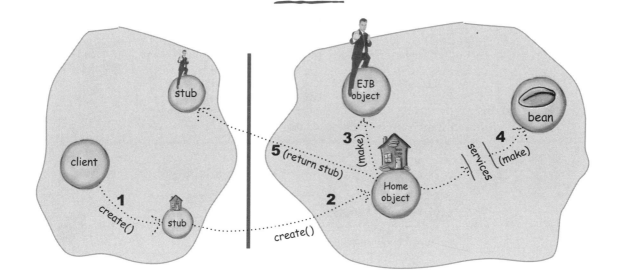

USE

(business method call)

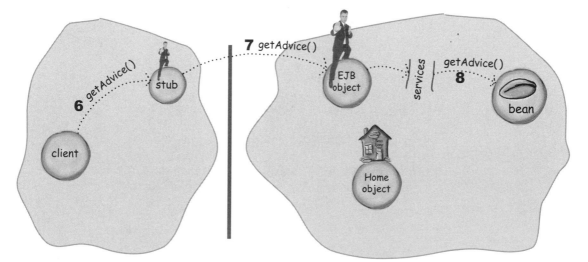

There's obviously more to the bean's lifecycle than just creation and business methods...

What about when a client wants to *remove* a bean? What about *activation* and *passivation* of stateful session beans? And what really *does* happen when a bean is created? What makes *bean creation* different from plain old *object construction?*

In this chapter, we'll look at *all* the stages of a session bean's life, for both stateful and stateless session beans.

The bean lifecycle (special moments in a bean's life)

Stateful session beans

- Bean **creation** (when the client wants a bean)

- Bean **use** (when the client calls a business method)

- Bean **passivation** (the bean is put to sleep to conserve resources)

- Bean **activation** (the bean wakes up to service a business method from the client)

- Bean **removal** (when the client is finished with the bean, or the bean times out)

Stateless session beans

- Bean **creation** (when the container wants to make a bean)

- Bean **use** (when the client calls a business method)

- Bean **removal** (when the container decides there are too many beans in the pool)

Container Callbacks,
for the special <u>moments</u> in a bean's life...

As a Bean Provider, <u>YOU</u> must implement container callbacks in your bean class!

When a bean has a special moment, it doesn't know until the Container calls one of the bean's container callback methods. These are special methods the Container knows about, that *you* (the Bean Provider) must implement in your bean class. You can think of the container callbacks as being kind of like event handlers.

Container callbacks come from two places: your bean's home interface, and the SessionBean interface your session bean class *must* implement.

For a session bean, the home-related container callbacks are matching creation methods (ejbCreate()) for each create() method declared in the bean's home interface.

The SessionBean interface declares four container callback methods for giving the bean its bean context, activating it, passivating it, and removing it. We'll look at the actual methods on the next page.

Container Callbacks come from TWO places:

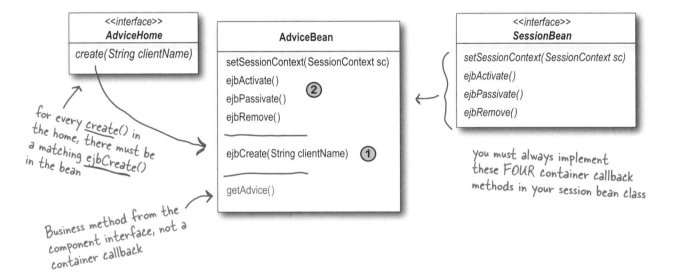

①
Your home interface

②
SessionBean interface
(javax.ejb.SessionBean)

<<interface>>
AdviceHome

create(String clientName)

AdviceBean

setSessionContext(SessionContext sc)
ejbActivate()
ejbPassivate()   **②**
ejbRemove()

ejbCreate(String clientName)   **①**

getAdvice()

<<interface>>
SessionBean

setSessionContext(SessionContext sc)
ejbActivate()
ejbPassivate()
ejbRemove()

for every create() in the home, there must be a matching ejbCreate() in the bean

Business method from the component interface, not a container callback

you must always implement these FOUR container callback methods in your session bean class

For any session bean, you will always always always have at least five container callbacks—four from the SessionBean interface implementations, and at least one ejbCreate() to match the create() method declared in the home interface.

For stateless session beans, there will be *exactly* five container callbacks, since stateless session beans can have only one create() method. And since the stateless bean's create() is always a no-arg, you know that the bean's ejbCreate() will always be a no-arg.

For stateful beans, remember, there must be at *least* one create(), but there can be more, including both overloaded create() methods and create<something> methods. For example, a stateful bean home might have three create methods: create(), create(String s), createBigCustomer(String s). That would mean the bean would have three container callbacks from the home: ejbCreate(), ejbCreate(String s), ejbCreateBigCustomer(String s).

Implementing the container callbacks

This AdviceBean code is completely legal. It compiles and runs. Right now, we don't need anything in the callback methods, because the bean's business logic doesn't depend on anything else that happens at other times in the bean's life. You'll notice that we are saving the SessionContext parameter we get from the setSessionContext() container callback, but we aren't using it in this code. Later in this chapter, you'll learn why you might want to assign the context to an instance variable, and the circumstances under which you *would* put code in each of these callback methods.

```java
package headfirst;
import javax.ejb.*;
```
You MUST implement SessionBean
```java
public class AdviceBean implements SessionBean {

    private SessionContext context;
    private String name;
```
instance variable to hold the context we get from a container callback method.
```java
    public void ejbActivate() {

    }

    public void ejbPassivate() {

    }

    public void ejbRemove() {

    }

    public void setSessionContext(SessionContext ctx) {
        context = ctx;
    }
```
the four methods of SessionBean that you must implement

```java
    public void ejbCreate(String clientName) {
        name = clientName;
    }
```
This must match the create method from the home interface

```java
    public String getAdvice() {
        return "Advice for " + name + ": there is no spoon.";
    }
}
```
business method from the component interface... not a container callback

When are container callbacks invoked?

For stateful session beans, when the bean transitions from one state to another.

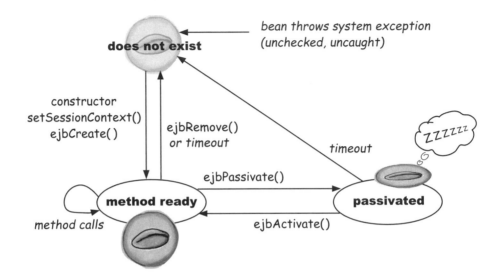

① does not exist   Before a bean is a bean (or even an object) it does not exist. The spec makes a big point of this, just in case there's any confusion about something existing before it exists. So the state of non-existence is indeed a state that a bean can be in, even though it does not yet exist. When a session bean moves out of this state, the bean's constructor runs, then setSession-Context(), and finally the ejbCreate() method. This is also the state a bean returns to after any one of these things occurs: bean times out, bean throws a system exception, or a client calls remove(). The bean will get an ejbRemove() call if the client calls remove() or times out while in the *method ready* (active) state.

② method ready   A bean in the method ready state is either executing a client's method, or waiting for the client to make another business method call. A stateful bean might or might not be in an active transaction while in this state (depends on the deployment transaction settings and the caller's transaction status), but if the bean *is* in a transaction, the bean cannot be passivated.

③ passivated   A passivated bean is temporarily saved in some kind of secondary storage, to conserve resources between client calls. Passivation might be serialization, although the Container can use anything it wants as long as it *behaves* like serialization (with one small exception we'll see later in this chapter). Although a passivated bean is no longer an active object on the heap, the Container will reactivate the bean (calling ejbActivate()) when the client calls a business method. If a passivated bean times out, the bean will simply die, without first being reactivated.

We have to look at the transitions

Now that you've seen the overall state diagram, we have to drill down and find out what really happens (and why) when a stateful session bean *transitions* from one state to another.

Moving from *does not exist* to *method ready*

constructor

setSessionContext()

ejbCreate()

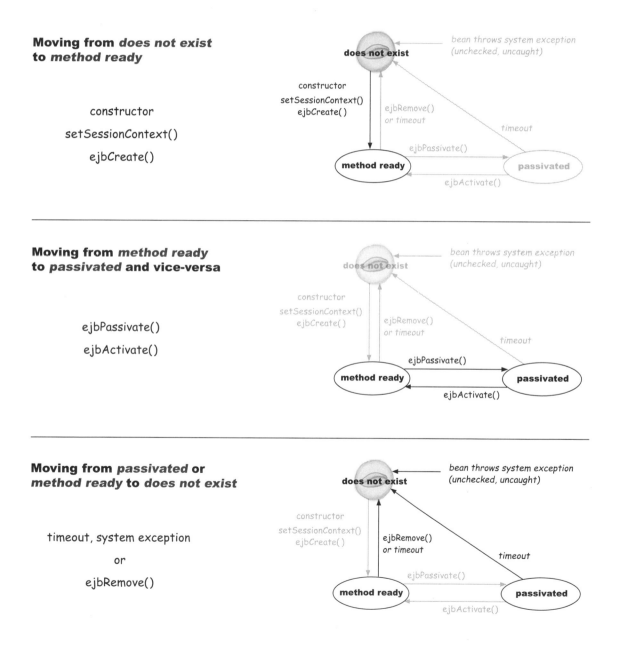

Moving from *method ready* to *passivated* and vice-versa

ejbPassivate()

ejbActivate()

Moving from *passivated* or *method ready* to *does not exist*

timeout, system exception

or

ejbRemove()

there are no
Dumb Questions

Q: **If it's so common to leave the methods empty, why don't they have adapter classes like they have for event handlers—that implement all the methods from the interface? Is there any reason why your bean class can't extend a class that implements the SessionBean interface?**

A: The API doesn't have adapter classes for SessionBean implementations (i.e. a class that implements all of the methods). But there's no reason you can't make one yourself. Keep in mind, though, that with real-world beans you probably *will* have code in one or more of the methods. And you might even be working with a bean-aware IDE that puts the methods in for you anyway.

Still, it might be handy to make yourself a generic bean that you typically extend from, that has all of the methods from SessionBean. With stateless beans, especially, you have to implement ejbActivate() and ejbPassivate(), even though they'll never be called! (Stateless beans are never passivated; you'll see more on that later in the chapter.)

Q: **I just remembered that I read somewhere that enterprise beans don't support inheritance! What's *that* about?**

A: Ah... a common misconception. Well, sort of. EJB supports regular Java *class* inheritance, but has no concept of *bean* inheritance. And now you're asking, "What the heck is the difference?" You already know what *class* inheritance is, it's the thing you do in Java when one *class* extends another. And you can do that with a bean, just like any other class.

But *bean* inheritance (if it were supported) would mean that a *bean* class could extend another *bean* class and inherit not just the class' inheritable members, but also its *beanness*. What kind of beanness might be inheritable? (Just in case they do decide to support this in the future, which is a possibility. Regular old non-enterprise beans *do* support bean inheritance.)

One idea might be to have your bean subclass inherit some of the deployment descriptor settings of its superclass, and then override the ones it wants to change with a much smaller, incomplete deployment descriptor. That might be cool; we're not sure. But right now, it's just our little fantasy.

In the meantime, go ahead and let your bean extend another class, if it makes sense for your OO design.

Sharpen your pencil

For the exam, you have to know exactly which methods are in the SessionBean interface, so now is a good time to start memorizing them. See if you can remember the name of the method that matches the behavior described. We've included some pretty big hints here because it's your first time, but the mock exam questions will be much less obvious...

1. This method is called when the client tells the Container that he's done using a stateful session bean. The bean is NOT happy:

_____

2. This method is called when the bean is put to sleep to temporarily conserve resources:

_____

3. This method is called when the previously-sleeping bean is called back to active duty to service a business method:

_____

4. This method is called near the beginning of the bean's life, when the Container hands the bean a reference to the bean's special link to the Container:

_____

Sharpen your pencil

Fill in the missing methods. Don't worry if you don't get the name exactly right; just try to work out what happens at each of the transitions in the stateful session bean state diagram.

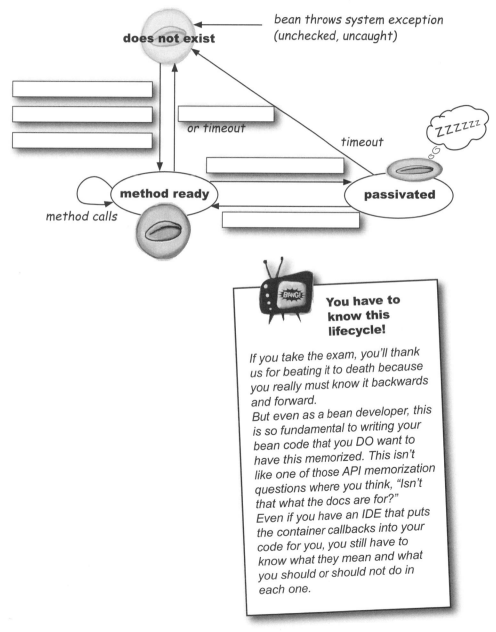

does not exist

bean throws system exception
(unchecked, uncaught)

or timeout

timeout

ZZZZZ

method ready

method calls

passivated

You have to know this lifecycle!

If you take the exam, you'll thank us for beating it to death because you really must know it backwards and forward.

But even as a bean developer, this is so fundamental to writing your bean code that you DO want to have this memorized. This isn't like one of those API memorization questions where you think, "Isn't that what the docs are for?"

Even if you have an IDE that puts the container callbacks into your code for you, you still have to know what they mean and what you should or should not do in each one.

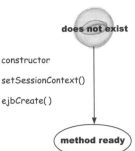

constructor

setSessionContext()

ejbCreate()

method ready

setSessionContext() and ejbCreate()
happen only once in a session bean's life,
so don't blow it! And don't try to do
things too soon... the constructor is too
early to do any bean things.

Bean Creation:
when an object becomes a <u>bean</u>

The proudest moment of my life
is when the Grand Master Container
makes me a bean by giving me a context and
calling my create(). Before that, I'm just an
ordinary object. But as a bean, I have special
privileges (besides the secret handshake),
like the ability to get security
or transaction info.

A bean moves from *does not exist* to *method ready* (still
feels creepy... doesn't it have to *exist* before it can *move?*),
beginning with a constructor. But the constructor makes
an *object*, not a *bean*. To be a bean, the object needs to be
granted *beanness*.

When an object becomes a bean, it gets all the unique
privileges that come with beanness, like the ability to get
security info about the client, or look up special deploy-
time properties in the bean's *special space* in JNDI, or get a
JDBC Connection from a pool managed by the container.

Why do you care about creation details?

Because somewhere between the constructor and the
create() method, the bean is in a *Schroedinger's bean** state.
You might have bean initialization code, like getting a
JDBC Connection, or looking up a reference to another
bean, that will **fail** if you run it too *early* in the bean's life.
Writing good bean code means you *must* know the point
at which an object becomes a card-carrying bean and what
that means to you as the developer.

*We're not explaining the whole Schroedinger reference here, except to
say that it involves cats (animal-lovers be warned) and subatomic physics.
For more info, look for Head First Quantum Physics in the future. We're
serious. Serious for us, anyway.

What does "beanness" buy you?

What happens when a bean goes from this:

to this?

object →

↖ card-carrying bean

(1) A <u>SessionContext</u> reference

A bean's context (sometimes called EJBContext, referring to the superinterface of SessionContext) is the bean's only lifeline to the Container, and it lets the bean do things like get security information about the calling client, force a transaction to rollback, get a reference to the bean's own home or EJB object, and more.

(2) A special <u>JNDI Context</u>

Every bean gets its very own JNDI context, where it can find things including resource manager connection factories (objects that give you connections to resources like a database), other beans, and deploy-time constant values that you can use to customize your bean's variables. You'll learn a lot more about that in Chapter 11, where we look at the enterprise bean *environment* (that's what the spec calls the bean's special JNDI context).

(3) Access to beans and resources

Just because you *got* a connection to a database doesn't mean you can always *use* it. Part of being a bean is the ability to access a resource (like a database) or call methods on another enterprise bean.

Special Bean Things

① A SessionContext reference

Things you can do with your context:

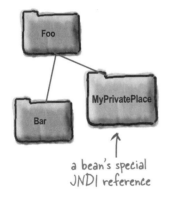

- get a reference to your home
- get a reference to your EJB object
- get security information about the client
- force a transaction to rollback (CMT)
- find out if the transaction has already been set to rollback (CMT)
- get a transaction reference, and call methods on it (BMT)

② A special JNDI Context

Things you can lookup with your *special* JNDI context:

- a reference to another bean
- a reference to a resource manager connection factory (like DataSource) that you can use to get, for example, a database connection
- deploy-time constant values (kind of like properties) for the bean (values set by the deployer that the bean can look up and use as variables at runtime).
- a reference to an "administered object" resource (which usually means a JMS destination)

a bean's special JNDI reference

③ Access to...

- another bean
- a resource manager (like a database)

You can't always use <u>all</u> of your beanness...

Just because you've become a full-fledged bean doesn't necessarily mean you can do *all* of the Bean Things on the opposite page (lookup a resource, force a transaction rollback, etc.).

The things you can do can vary depending on what kind of bean you are (Session, Entity, MessageDriven), your transaction status, and what kind of method you're in.

For example, if you're a state*ful* session bean, your creation is a direct result of the client calling create() on your home. If you're a stateful bean, and you're in your ejbCreate() method, there can be only one reason: *a client has asked for you to be created.* And that means you can find out who the client is, by asking your EJBContext (like SessionContext) for client security information.

But if you're a state*less* bean, your creation isn't tied to any particular client's request (you'll learn all about this in a few more pages). In fact, if the Container wants to, it can create a bunch of stateless beans for the pool before there *are* any clients. And that means a stateless bean cannot get security information about the client during ejbCreate(). Because there's no client! There's only the Container, invoking a container callback that's not part of a client call, and we don't consider the Container to be a client. The Container is the *boss*, not the *client*.

And there are some Bean Things that can be done only while the bean is in what the Container considers "a meaningful transaction context." You can't, for example, access a database from a method that might not have a transaction.

Some Bean Things are mutually exclusive. If you're using container-managed transactions (CMT) (Chapter 9), you must *not* ask your EJBContext to give you your own transaction object. On the other hand, if you're using *bean-*managed transactions (BMT), you *can* ask for a transaction object, but then you must *not* ask your context to rollback your transaction. You'll have to rollback the transaction yourself, using the transaction object you got from your context.

You must know WHEN you can do specific Bean Things and when you can't.

Be prepared for code or a scenario, that shows you a method and asks whether you can do a particular Bean Thing from that method, given the circumstances.
For example, you might be shown the setSessionContext() method of a bean, and asked if you're allowed to access a resource (like a database) from that method. (You're not! You aren't in a "meaningful transaction context" at that point.)

Bean creation overview

(stateful session bean)

(1) **Client calls create on the home**

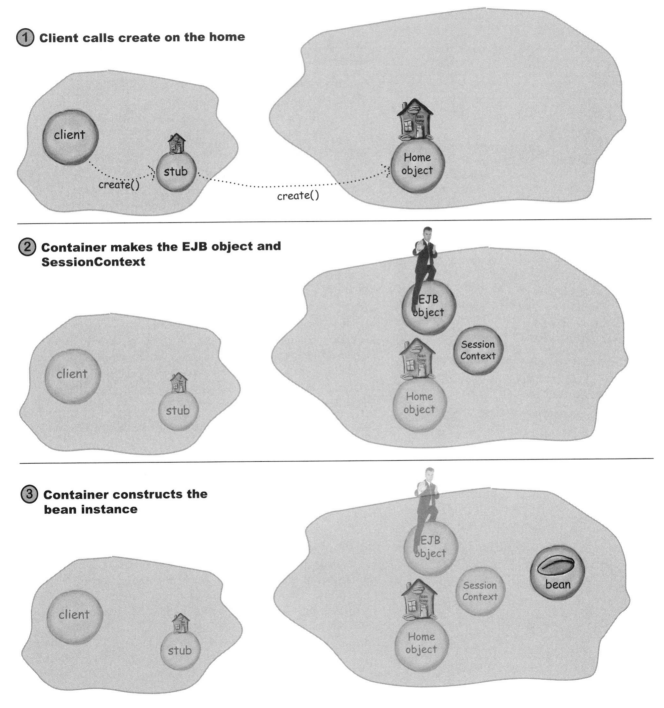

(2) **Container makes the EJB object and SessionContext**

(3) **Container constructs the bean instance**

(4) Container links the bean to its context and EJB object (calling setSessionContext() and ejbCreate())

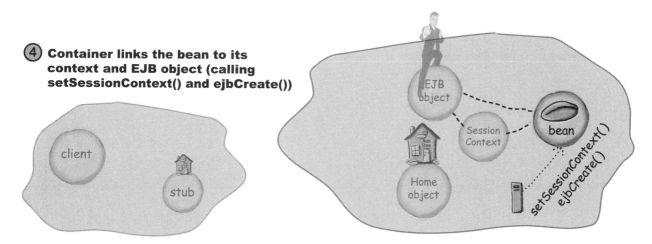

The linking happens when the container calls setSessionContext() and ejbCreate() on the bean. Once ejbCreate() returns, the bean is ready for 'active duty' (in other words, ready for business method calls from the client).

(5) Container sends the client a stub to the EJB object.

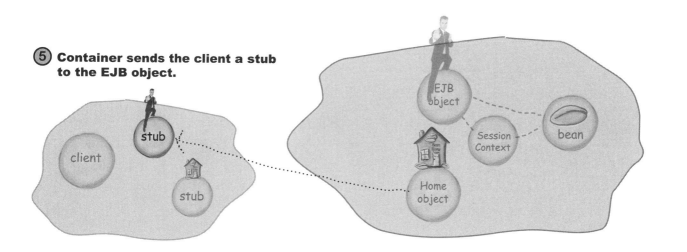

Object Interaction Diagram (OID) for bean creation

(stateful session bean)

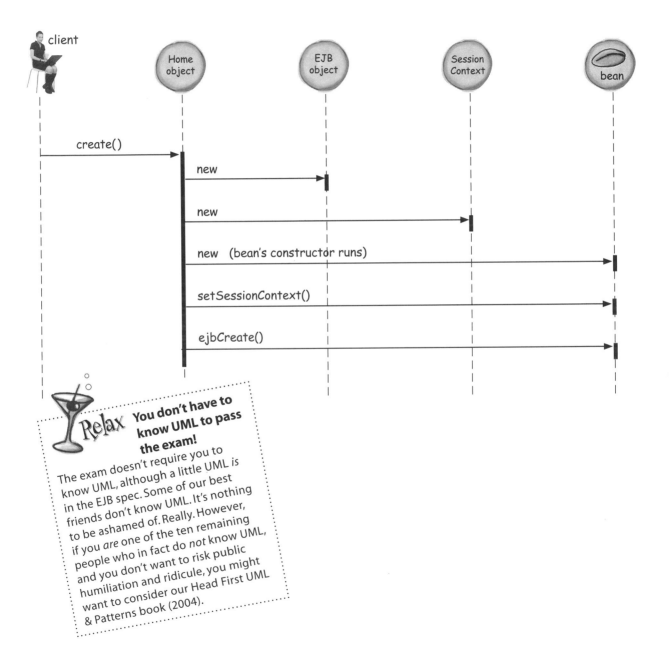

Relax **You don't have to know UML to pass the exam!**

The exam doesn't require you to know UML, although a little UML *is* in the EJB spec. Some of our best friends don't know UML. It's nothing to be ashamed of. Really. However, if you *are* one of the ten remaining people who in fact do *not* know UML, and you don't want to risk public humiliation and ridicule, you might want to consider our Head First UML & Patterns book (2004).

Writing the three creation-related things
(stateful session bean)

① constructor

Don't put anything in the constructor! There's nothing you would do in the constructor that you can't do in ejbCreate(), so unless your IDE puts one in for you, you're better off leaving the constructor out of your code.

```
public class AdviceBean implements SessionBean {

    public AdviceBean() {
        // no code here!!
    }
    ...
}
```

This is what the constructor should look like!! Empty. Better yet, don't put a constructor in and let the compiler give you the default constructor.

② setSessionContext(SessionContext sc)

Save your context! You get only one chance to grab this reference to your SessionContext, so you better assign it to an instance variable.

```
private SessionContext context;

public void setSessionContext(SessionContext ctx) {
    context = ctx;
}
```

save the SessionContext by assigning it to an instance variable. You will NEVER get another chance to have a reference to your context, so you better do it here! Anything else you would put in this method probably belongs in ejbCreate().

③ ejbCreate()

Put all your initialization code here! If it's a stateful bean and the create() method has arguments, the Container will pass those arguments into your matching ejbCreate() method. You have full bean status now, so you can do anything you need to from this method, including things you can't do in setSessionContext() (like get a reference to your own EJB object).

```
private String name;

public void ejbCreate(String clientName) {
    name = clientName;
    // other code!
}
```

You're a full member of the bean society now, so this is where you'll usually put ALL your initialization code.

Bean things you can do during creation:

(stateful session bean)

————————————————— timeline —————————————————→

constructor

nothing

It's too early to DO anything! You're an object, but not yet a bean.

setSessionContext()

Use your SessionContext to:

☑ get a reference to your home

☐ get a reference to your EJB object

☐ get security information about the client

☐ force a transaction to rollback (CMT beans)

☐ find out if the transaction has already been set to rollback (CMT beans)

☐ get a transaction reference, and call methods on it (BMT beans)

Access:

☑ your special JNDI environment

☐ another bean's methods

☐ a resource manager (like a database)

ejbCreate()

Use your SessionContext to:

☑ get a reference to your home

☑ get a reference to your EJB object

☑ get security information about the client

☐ force a transaction to rollback (CMT beans)

☐ find out if the transaction has already been set to rollback (CMT beans)

☑ get a transaction reference, and call methods on it (BMT beans)

Access:

☑ your special JNDI environment

☑ another bean's methods

☑ a resource manager (like a database)

Note: the word "access" means "do things with", so when the spec uses the phrase "resource manager access", it means *using* the resource to do whatever that resource is for. So in setSessionContext(), for example, you can use JNDI to look up a resource manager connection factory, like javax.sql.DataSource, and you can ask the DataSource for a connection (myDataSource.getConnection()), but you can't make a JDBC call on the connection reference. You *can* use your connection in ejbCreate().

Um, good to know all that, but this matters to me HOW? What does this mean to ME and how does it affect my code?

an aspiring Bean Provider

She doesn't get it... for one thing, I don't put ANYTHING in my constructor! One time I tried to do a JNDI lookup in a constructor, to get a database resource factory. It compiled, and didn't throw an exception during the lookup, but at runtime when I tried to get a connection, it blew up! The bean hadn't gotten its special bean JNDI capabilities yet, so the resource factory wasn't really there. There is NOTHING you would do in a constructor that you can't do in ejbCreate() instead. My best advice is to think of ejbCreate() as the constructor for session beans (entity beans are another story).

the more experienced Bean Provider

In the method ready state, the bean is either running a business method or waiting for the client to call one...

Bean Use:
what happens AFTER creation...

> The only reason I called create() on the home is so I could get a reference to a bean's component interface and do what I REALLY want... call a business method. Far as I'm concerned, that's the ONLY reason the bean's alive. To service ME so I can shop.

> At last... I'm fulfilling my destiny. My purpose. My raison d'être*.

In the method ready state, the bean can run business methods. And given that business methods are the bean's highest purpose, the bean can bring all of its beanness to bear. In other words, the bean can do more bean things from within a business method than at any other point in its brief, but meaningful, life.

*We challenge you to find another computer book that uses raison d'être as appropriately as we do. And with that little upside down v thing over the ê and everything.

Bean things you can do within business methods:

Use your SessionContext to:

☑ get a reference to your home

☑ get a reference to your EJB object

☑ get security information about the client

☑ force a transaction to rollback (CMT beans)

☑ find out if the transaction has already been set to rollback (CMT beans)

☑ get a transaction reference, and call methods on it (BMT beans)

Access:

☑ your special JNDI environment

☑ another bean's methods

☑ a resource manager (like a database)

Passivation: a state_ful_ bean's chance at scalability...

① *Are you sure this can't wait until later? I was right in the middle of shopping... oh well, I guess my shopping cart bean will still be there when we're done...*

② *That client doesn't seem to be doing anything. It's too early to kill the bean completely; she still might come back. But I don't want the bean wasting RAM; I'll serialize the bean for now, and if the client comes back, I'll just deserialize it...*

③ *Looks like I'm being passivated, so I better make sure I null out my non-Serializable instance variables...*

④ *ZZZZZZ*

StateFUL beans are tied directly to a client, remember, so until the Container decides to timeout the bean (because the client was inactive way too long), the bean can't be used for anything (or anyone) else.

StateLESS beans don't have this problem, they go back to a pool between each method call, since a bean isn't tied to a client.

When the Container decides a stateful bean is wasting resources, it'll call the bean's ejbPassivate() method and then save the bean into temporary storage.

Why do you care about passivation details?

Because the Container uses a special set of rules (nearly identical to Serialization) to passivate your bean, and it's your job to make sure your instance variables are in a state that works for passivation. And it's just a tiny bit more subtle than simply making non-Serializable values transient.

Lifecycle overview: bean passivation/activation

1 **Client doesn't call any methods for a while, so container calls ejbPassivate() on the bean.**

2 **Container calls ejbPassivate() on the bean, then saves the bean to temporary storage (either through serializatlon or something like it).**

bean is asleep (passivated and temporarily saved)

3 **Client calls a business method, so container activates the bean (through something like deserialization), calls ejbActivate(), then invokes the business method (getAdvice()) on the bean.**

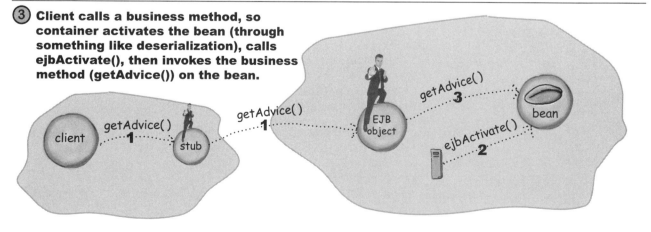

there are no Dumb Questions

Q: **How does the Container know when to passivate a bean?**

A: The Container looks for inactivity. If the client hasn't been doing anything for some period of time, the Container can choose to passivate the bean. If it needs to.

Q: **Gee... can you be any more non-committal? How long is "some period of time" and what determines whether the Container 'needs to' passivate the bean?**

A: There is nothing in the spec that says you're allowed to tune the parameters for the Container's passivation decisions. But... many containers do give you a way to set a variety of values. The decision might be based on availability of resources, like, "passivate stateful session beans only when available RAM hits this level..." or, "passivate beans only when the number of active stateful session beans reaches..."

And you might be able to set the inactivity value for the amount of elapsed time at which the Container should passivate.

Q: **What if the client crashes? Can the server tell? Is there any kind of distributed garbage collection or leasing like there is with RMI? Or is the server really just basing everything on inactivity?**

A: According to the spec, there is no guarantee of distributed garbage collection, which means you should assume that it isn't happening. Part of the reason is because an EJB client could (at least in theory) be a CORBA client rather than a Java RMI client. So the whole concept of RMI's distributed garbage collection wouldn't apply.

And just a quick off-path here: distributed garbage collection (dgc) or distributed leasing are ways in which a server can figure out if a client has (with dgc) nulled out their reference to the stub, or (with leasing) if the client has simply gone away, either by shutting down the app, crashing, or disconnecting from the network.

The bottom line is that you have to assume that the EJB server doesn't support this, so you're stuck with inactivity and perhaps some kind of LRU (Least Recently Used) algorithms for selecting who should be passivated if resources become scarce and the Container needs to bring down some beans.

> ***Relax*** ***There's nothing on the exam about vendor-specific passivation settings or behavior.***
>
> *The only thing on the exam about passivation is what you're responsible for as a Bean Provider—getting your instance variable values in a passivatable state (we'll talk about that next). Nothing about passivation goes into the deployment descriptor, so you don't need to know how passivation parameters are set for any particular server.*

Your job for passivation:
make your state passivatable!

When I write my bean class, I have to make sure that by the time ejbPassivate() completes, my instance variable values are ALL ready for passivation. That means the values have to be Serializable (or primitive), null, or references to one of the special things the Container has to take care of no matter what.

When ejbPassivate() completes, every non-transient instance variable MUST be a reference to one of the following:

- a Serializable object
- a null value
- a bean's remote component or home interface, even if the stub class is not Serializable (in other words, you don't have to worry about it!)
- a bean's local component or home interface, even if it's not Serializable (again, you don't have to worry)
- a SessionContext object, even if it's not Serializable
- the bean's special JNDI context, or any of its subcontexts
- the UserTransaction interface (something you can get from your SessionContext—we'll see that in the transactions chapter)
- a resource manager connection factory (like, an instance of javax.sql.DataSource)

You have to know these for the exam.

You might see a question that shows you a class and an ejbPassivate() method and asks you if it would work or not. If the method is empty, you have to look at the instance variables to see if they're all OK as they are.

Implementing ejbActivate() and ejbPassivate()

ejbPassivate()

Make sure your instance variables are ready for passivation. Most of the time, you probably won't have any code in ejbPassivate(), simply because all of your instance variables meet the criteria defined on the previous page (e.g. reference to a SessionContext, or a bean's component interface, or a Serializable object, etc.).

```
public void ejbPassivate() {
    connection = null;     ←
}
```

a JDBC connection is not Serializable, so if you have one, you must set it to null in ejbPassivate()

ejbActivate()

Reacquire your non-Serializable resources, or do whatever it takes to restore your state for use. If you're running in ejbActivate(), there can be only one reason: the client called a business method. So in your ejbActivate() method, you must make sure you get ready for the business method call that's about to happen. Chances are, this method will be empty, for the same reason as ejbPassivate(). But if you did null out non-Serializable references, then ejbActivate() is the place to get them back.

```
public void ejbActivate() {
    try {
      connection = myDataSrc.getConnection();
    }catch (Exception ex) {...}
}
```

now we have to get the JDBC connection back again. Notice that the DataSource did not have to be restored, because it's one of the things on the Container's "approved list". (Because it's a resource manager connection factory, and the Container is required to passivate it.)

there are no
Dumb Questions

Q: **Can't you just mark your non-Serializable variables** *transient*? **Isn't that what** *transient* **is** *for*?

A: You could, yes, because the Container is required to follow the rules for Serialization when it passivates a bean (even if the Container chooses to use something other than serialization to get the job done).

But... there's a little teeny comment in the spec which says that there's an exception to the rule that passivation behave just like serialization. The exception is that while serialization is required to bring back transient fields with default values, passivation doesn't guarantee that!

What does this mean? Think about it. It means you can't rely on transient to give you back your defaults, so after activation, you could end up with, well, anything in a variable that's marked transient.

So, you are free to use *transient*, and it can make passivation more efficient, but the implication is—reset your transient variables yourself, in ejbActivate().

Q: **What if I have a non-Serializable value that I really need to maintain during passivation? If I can't save it, how will I know what to set it back to in ejbActivate()?**

A: This is a classic serialization issue, not specific to passivation. The usual trick is to interrogate the non-Serializable object to get all the important state out of it, and stick that state into instance variables that are Serializable. Then during ejbActivate(), use the values you were able to save to reconstruct the non-Serializable object so that it's identical to the one you had before passivation. For example, imagine you have a Dog bean with a Collar variable, and the Collar isn't Serializable. In ejbPassivate(), call getters on the Collar to retrieve the values that matter (like getColor(), getSize(), etc.). Save those values in instance variables in the bean, then in ejbActivate() instantiate a new Collar and use the Collar attributes you saved as arguments to setters on the new Collar object.

Sharpen your pencil

You're responsible for making sure that when ejbPassivate() completes, your instance variables are in one of the states we listed a couple of pages ago. Don't look now! See if you can work out which of these will be safely passivated...

❑ reference to a java.net.Socket object

❑ reference to a javax.sql.DataSource

❑ reference to a bean's Remote component interface

❑ reference to a bean's JNDI context

❑ reference to a java.sql.Connection

❑ reference to a javax.ejb.SessionContext object

❑ a transient variable with a null value

❑ a non-transient, Serializable variable with a null value

❑ a transient variable with a non-null value

❑ a non-transient, non-Serializable variable with a null value

❑ a non-transient, non-Serializable variable with a non-null value*

*We were going for a personal best (PB) in the number of times in which we could use the word 'non' in a single statement.

I would marry this man, if only he was not such an idiot about stateful session bean scalability. He lets his stateful beans stay in open transactions! Even Bob, my loser ex-boyfriend knows that session beans in a transaction can never be passivated...

WARNING:

A stateful session bean will NEVER be passivated while the bean is still in a transaction!

I have been sitting here, like, forever, waiting for this stupid transaction to finish...

The spec lets you begin a transaction in one method of a stateful session bean, but end the method without ending the transaction. This is almost always a *really* stupid thing to do. For starters, you could never guarantee that just because a client calls the method that *begins* the transaction, the client will at some point call the method that *ends* the transaction (in either a commit or rollback). But the main reason is that the longer your transactions, the better your chances of bringing your server to its knees (and that holds regardless of the bean type). For stateful session beans, leaving a transaction open means the bean will not be passivated, no matter how long it's been since the client did anything with it. We'll look at this more in the transactions chapter, but for now, understand that stateful beans in a transaction won't be passivated!

Bean things you can do in ejbActivate() and ejbPassivate()

ejbPassivate()

Use your SessionContext to:

- ☑ get a reference to your home
- ☑ get a reference to your EJB object
- ☑ get security information about the client
- ☐ force a transaction to rollback (CMT beans)
- ☐ find out if the transaction has already been set to rollback (CMT beans)
- ☑ get a transaction reference, and call methods on it (BMT beans)

Access:

- ☑ your special JNDI environment
- ☑ another bean's methods
- ☑ a resource manager (like a database)

ejbActivate()

Use your SessionContext to:

- ☑ get a reference to your home
- ☑ get a reference to your EJB object
- ☑ get security information about the client
- ☐ force a transaction to rollback (CMT beans)
- ☐ find out if the transaction has already been set to rollback (CMT beans)
- ☑ get a transaction reference, and call methods on it (BMT beans)

Access:

- ☑ your special JNDI environment
- ☑ another bean's methods
- ☑ a resource manager (like a database)

Bean Removal:
when beans die

As a stateful bean, I'm a personal slave to the client, and when she's done with me, I'm tossed out like so many AOL disks. Sometimes they don't even let me say goodbye...

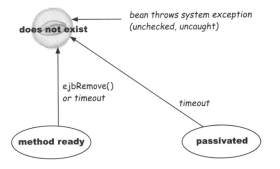

bean throws system exception (unchecked, uncaught)

does not exist

ejbRemove() or timeout

timeout

method ready

passivated

A session bean stops existing for one of three reasons:

1. the client calls remove()

2. the bean times out

3. the bean throws a system exception

But... there's another question to ask: when the bean times out, was it active or passive? If the bean is active, the Container deals with it in the same way it deals with client remove() calls—the bean gets an ejbRemove() call and is then killed. But if the bean was passivated when it times out, the Container sends it straight to the *does not exist* state *without* calling ejbRemove().

Lifecycle overview: removing a stateful bean

Client calls remove() on an active (i.e. non-passivated) bean

(1) **Client calls remove on the component interface (or calls the remove() method in the home interface, that takes a Handle).**

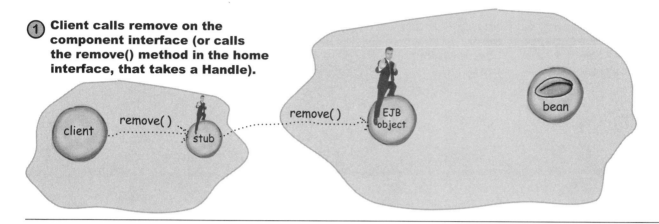

(2) **Container calls ejbRemove() on the bean.**

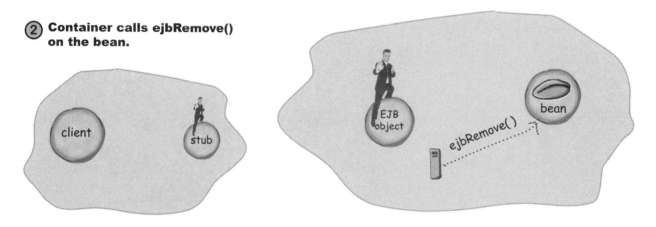

(3) **Container "kills" the bean and EJB object (assume they're now eligible for garbage collection). The client will get an exception if she tries to use the stub again.**

(might still be here, but will no longer work)

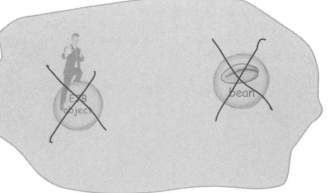

Lifecycle overview: removing a stateful bean

Bean times out while active

① Client doesn't make any calls to the bean's component interface for a long time (whatever the Container considers a "long" time).

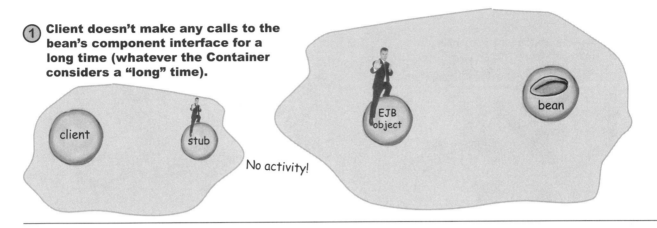

No activity!

② Container decides to kill the bean, and calls ejbRemove() on the bean.

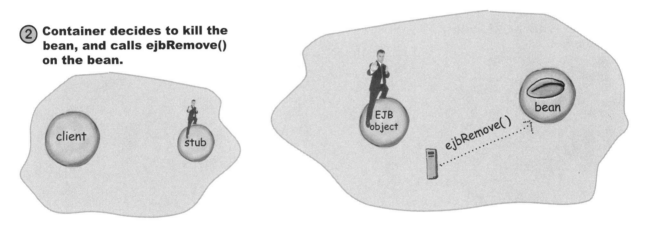

ejbRemove()

③ Container "kills" the bean and EJB object (assume they're now eligible for garbage collection). The client will get an exception if she tries to use the stub again.

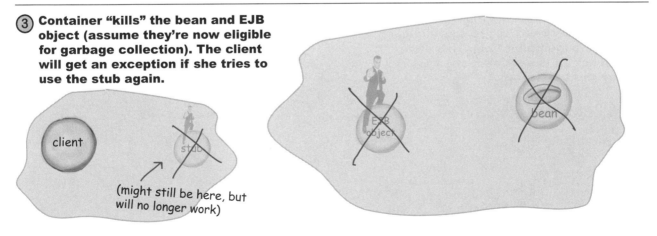

(might still be here, but will no longer work)

Lifecycle overview: removing a stateful bean

Bean times out while passivated

1. **The client doesn't call any methods on the bean's component interface for a long time AFTER the bean has already been passivated.**

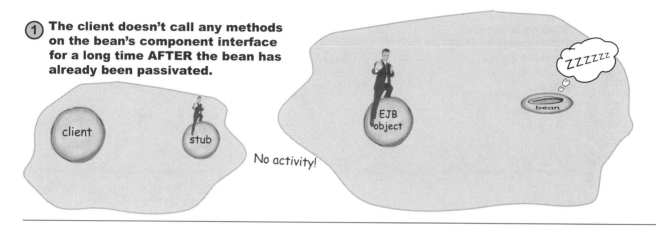

No activity!

2. **Container decides to kill the bean, but does NOT call ejbRemove().**

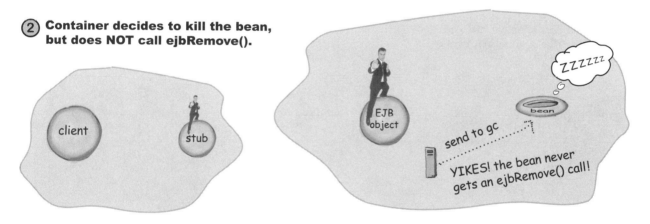

send to gc

YIKES! the bean never gets an ejbRemove() call!

3. **Container "kills" the bean and EJB object (assume they're now eligible for garbage collection). The client will get an exception if she tries to use the stub again.**

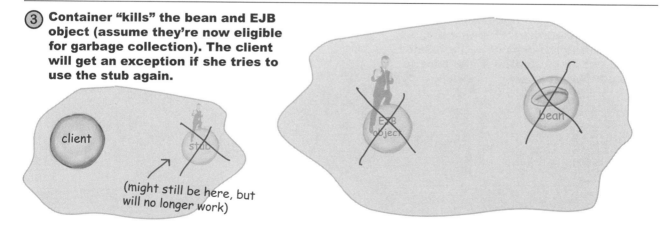

(might still be here, but will no longer work)

Lifecycle overview: removing a stateful bean

Bean throws a system exception

① The bean throws a system (unchecked) exception while executing a method.

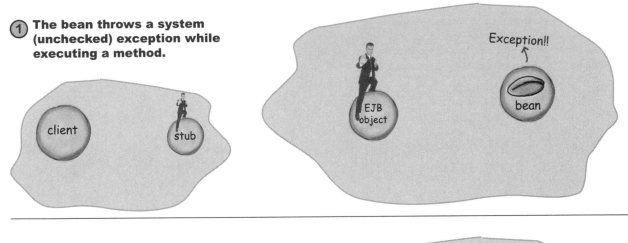

② Container decides to kill the bean, but does NOT call ejbRemove().

③ Container "kills" the bean and EJB object (assume they're now eligible for garbage collection). The client will get an exception if she tries to use the stub again.

(might still be here, but will no longer work)

Complaints about bean removal

Implementing ejbRemove()

ejbRemove()

Release any resources, or do whatever clean-up you need to do before the bean dies forever. Much of the time, your ejbRemove() method will be empty, because if your bean does use resources, it most likely will acquire and release the resources in each business method. But if your design does call for keeping resources open throughout the bean's life, then you need to free them up here!

```java
public void ejbRemove() {
  try {
    myResource.close();
  } catch(Exception ex) {...}
}
```

← *if you want to gracefully close resources that are still open, do it here!*

an alternative...

Call a cleanUp() method from both ejbPassivate() and ejbRemove(). Given that your bean could be removed without an ejbRemove() call, if it times out while passivated, you should have both your ejbPassivate() and ejbRemove() methods perform the same clean-up. Since scarce system resources are seldom Serializable anyway, you're probably already taking care of them in ejbPassivate().

```java
public void ejbRemove() {
   this.cleanUp();
}

public void ejbPassivate() {
   this.cleanUp();
}

private void cleanUp() {
  try {
    myResource.close();
  } catch(Exception ex) {...}
}
```

now both ejbRemove() and ejbPassivate() will do the same thing, so even if you time out while passivated, you don't have to worry.

Missed ejbRemove() calls

Wait a minute... there's still something wrong here. What happens if the bean throws an exception? Then I still won't get my cleanup code to run. Won't I still get into trouble?

Well, um, yes. Yes, you could still be in trouble in that case. But this is really YOUR responsibility to deal with. Let's say you temporarily save someone's shopping info to a database, so that if the server crashes while the person's shopping, you have a means of still recovering their cart (until the bean times out). In ejbRemove() you'd delete the row in the database for this client. But since you might not get that ejbRemove() call, sooner or later you're gonna need some way to go through and do periodic cleanups on that data. There's nothing in the spec that can help you here. It's up to YOU to deal with the potential consequences of missed ejbRemove() calls!

Watch it!

You must be able to recognize scenarios in which ejbRemove() will be missed!

The exam expects you to know that there are three circumstances under which a bean will NOT get an ejbRemove() call:

1. *Server crashes.*
2. *Bean times out while passivated.*
3. *Bean throws a system exception.*

If any of these happen, your clean-up code will not run. If you follow the suggestions on the previous page, and put clean-up code in both ejbPassivate() and ejbRemove(), then you're probably OK for problem #2 (timeout while passivated), but you'll still have to deal with a server crash or bean system exception.

And don't expect a simple, obvious question like, "Will a bean miss an ejbRemove() if a system exception is thrown?" You might have to consider a design scenario, for example, and figure out if there could be a problem, based on your knowledge of missed ejbRemove() method calls.

Bean things you can do in ejbRemove()

Use your SessionContext to:

- ☑ get a reference to your home
- ☑ get a reference to your EJB object
- ☑ get security information about the client
- ☐ force a transaction to rollback (CMT beans)
- ☐ find out if the transaction has already been set to rollback (CMT beans)
- ☑ get a transaction reference, and call methods on it (BMT beans)

Access:

- ☑ your special JNDI environment
- ☑ another bean's methods
- ☑ a resource manager (like a database)

> **The bean things you can do in ejbRemove() are exactly the same as the bean things you can do in:**
>
> - **ejbCreate()**
> - **ejbPassivate()**
> - **ejbActivate()**

Implementing the AdviceBean as a stateFUL bean

So far, the AdviceBean we've written hasn't needed to be stateful. It doesn't keep or use any client-specific state, so it doesn't need a create() method with arguments. But what if we did want to make it a stateful bean? What if the business logic needed to, say, keep a record of the conversation it's having so that it never gives out the same advice more than once in a session? Even if the choice of an advice string is purely random, if you want to ensure the advice isn't repeated during a session, you'll have to keep track of it in an instance variable.

And you might have other changes, too, like making the create methods take arguments that contain the type of advice the client is looking for, or some other kind of preference. In that case, each time the client made a method call, you'd want to check the status of that client-supplied creation initialization preference, and tailor your advice based on the value set during the bean's ejbCreate(). Later in the book, we'll look at a more elaborate version of this AdviceBean, but for now, we'll make just a subtle change to make the bean stateful.

You know that the bean class is going to change, but what about the client and the two interfaces? Do one or more of those have to change? Really think through the implications *before* you turn the page.

Things you can add if the bean is stateFUL

(1) **You can have more than one create method.**

(2) **The create method can have arguments.**

(3) **The bean can be passivated, so you can write code in ejbPassivate() and ejbActivate().**

there are no Dumb Questions

Q: What happens if you put code in ejbPassivate() or ejbActivate() and the bean is stateLESS? Will it compile? Will it deploy?

A: You can certainly put code in ejbActivate() or ejbPassivate(), regardless of whether the bean is stateless or stateful, even though it will never be called if the bean is stateless.

Think about it. Look at the SessionBean interface. Notice that there isn't a separate StatefulSessionBean interface and StatelessSessionBean interface. There's just SessionBean, and both stateless and stateful beans implement it. So there's nothing in your class that specifically says your bean is stateless. It's only at deploy-time, when you tell the deployment descriptor that the bean is stateless or stateful, that it actually matters.

In fact, you could write a bean that has only a no-arg create, and keeps no client state, and you can deploy it with *either* setting—stateless or stateful—and it will work, as long as you've taken care of passivation and activation.

AdviceStatefulBean code

```
package headfirst;
import javax.ejb.*;

public class AdviceStatefulBean implements SessionBean {

    private SessionContext context;

    private String userName;

    public void ejbActivate() {
    }

    public void ejbPassivate() {
    }

    public void ejbRemove() {
    }

    public void setSessionContext(SessionContext ctx) {
        context = ctx;
    }

    public void ejbCreate(String name) {
        userName = name;
    }

    public String getAdvice() {
        return userName + ", my advice is: " + Advisor.getAdvice();
    }

}
```

We still implement SessionBean

This time, we can keep client-specific state (in this case, the argument the client sends to the create method)

of the four SessionBean container callbacks, the only thing we're doing is saving the context, even though in this version of the class we're not using it. We're saving the context because we want YOU to get used to saving your context, because in most real-world beans you're gonna want to use it later. (Later in the book, you'll see examples of using the context)

This can be ONLY a stateFUL bean, because stateless bean's must NOT have anything except the no-arg create() method.

In the business method, we're using the client-specific state, that we saved from the create parameter. This must be a stateful bean, because stateless beans aren't tied to a single client.

assume this is a static helper method on a class, Advisor, that you don't see here. We'll let you write that one.

AdviceStatefulBean CLIENT code

The state*ful* version of the client adds two things not in the state*less* version:

1. We're passing an argument to the create() method.

A stateful bean can (and often does) have arguments to create methods, so that the client can pass in client-specific state for the bean to save and use in later "conversations" with the client (i.e. later method calls from that client).

2. We're calling remove() on the component interface.

It's polite for the client to tell the Container that she's done with a stateful session bean. And now you know why. Without the remove() call, the Container will hold on to the bean, wastefully, until the bean times out. So in this case "polite" really means "improves scalability".

```java
import javax.naming.*;
import javax.rmi.*;
import headfirst.*;
import javax.ejb.*;

public class AdviceStatefulClient {

    public static void main(String[] args) {
        new AdviceStatefulClient().go();
    }

    public void go() {
      try {
        Context ic = new InitialContext();
        Object o = ic.lookup("StatefulAdvisor");

        AdviceStatefulHome home = (AdviceStatefulHome) PortableRemoteObject.narrow(o,
                                            AdviceStatefulHome.class);

        AdviceStateful advisor = home.create("clover");

        System.out.println(advisor.getAdvice());

        advisor.remove();
      } catch (Exception ex) {
            ex.printStackTrace();
      }
    }
}
```

> **You must be able to recognize whether the client is for a stateful bean.**
>
> *You must be able to look at client code, like this, and know whether the client's bean is stateful. If the client calls a no-arg create(), there's no way to know whether it IS stateless, but at least you know it MIGHT be. If the create has args, or a name other than create() (like, createAccount()), you know the bean must be stateful.*

This must be a stateful bean, because we're calling create with arguments!

we're calling remove(), to tell the Container we're done with the bean (so the Container can kill it).

this is a poor way to handle exceptions! You would probably write a real-world client to catch the different kinds of exceptions that matter... NamingException, CreateException, etc.

Sharpen your pencil

Do the interfaces have to change when it goes from state*less* to state*ful*?

Look at the two interfaces below, for the state*less* version of the Advice bean. If needed, make any adjustments to the code in either or both of the interfaces, for what (if anything) needs to change to make this work with the revised state*ful* version of the bean.

```java
package headfirst;

import javax.ejb.*;
import java.rmi.RemoteException;

public interface AdviceHome extends EJBHome {
    public Advice create() throws CreateException, RemoteException;
}
```

```java
package headfirst;

import javax.ejb.*;
import java.rmi.RemoteException;

public interface Advice extends EJBObject {
        public String getAdvice() throws RemoteException;

}
```

Deploying a stateful bean

The only difference between deploying the stateful Advice bean and the stateless version (besides the file names and JNDI name) is in the deployment descriptor setting that defines whether the bean is stateless or stateful. Using the RI deploytool, remember, you set this using the deploytool's New Enterprise Bean Wizard—the thing that walks you through the settings that it then uses to output the XML deployment descriptor.

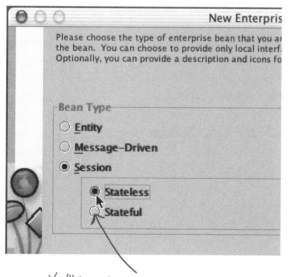

You'll have to change this to Stateful!!

Compared to stateful beans, stateless beans have a simple life

State*less* beans have a much simpler existence. They're born (created), they're thrown into a pool with others of their kind, they run business methods for any client who asks, and they *might* eventually die. They aren't passivated, they don't keep client-specific state, and their creation and destruction (removal) aren't tied to the whims of the client. Compare the difference between the lifecycle of a stateful vs. stateless bean:

The bean lifecycle (special moments in a bean's life)

Stateful session beans

- Bean **creation** (when the client wants a bean)

- Bean **use** (when the client calls a business method)

- Bean **passivation** (the bean is put to sleep to conserve resources)

- Bean **activation** (the bean wakes up to service a business method from the client)

- Bean **removal** (when the client is finished with the bean or the bean times out)

Stateless session beans

- Bean **creation** (when the container wants to make a bean)

- Bean **use** (when the client calls a business method)

- Bean **removal** (when the container decides there are too many beans in the pool, or the bean throws a system exception.)

Comparing the lifecycles of stateful and stateless session beans

Stateful

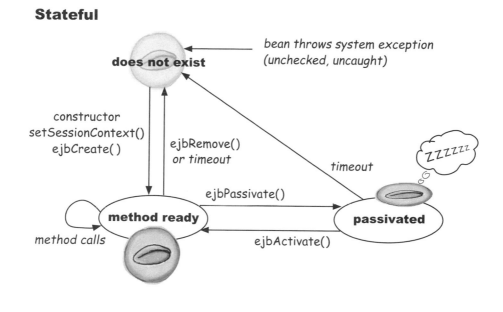

bean throws system exception
(unchecked, uncaught)

does not exist

constructor
setSessionContext()
ejbCreate( )

ejbRemove()
or timeout

timeout

ejbPassivate()

method ready

passivated

method calls

ejbActivate()

Stateless

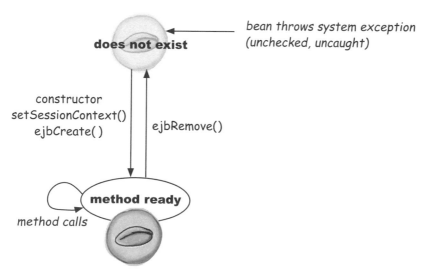

bean throws system exception
(unchecked, uncaught)

does not exist

constructor
setSessionContext()
ejbCreate( )

ejbRemove()

method ready

method calls

Client calls create on a stateless session bean home

1 **Client calls create on the home.**

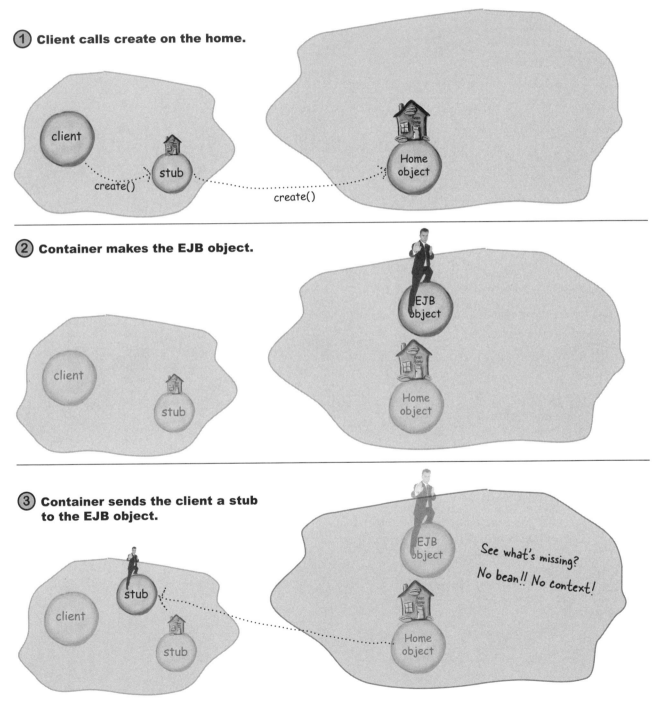

2 **Container makes the EJB object.**

3 **Container sends the client a stub to the EJB object.**

See what's missing?
No bean!! No context!

Session bean creation is not related to the client

(1) Container constructs the SessionContext object and the bean instance, then calls setSessionContext() on the bean.

(2) Container puts the bean (which is now linked to its own context) in the pool for that bean type.

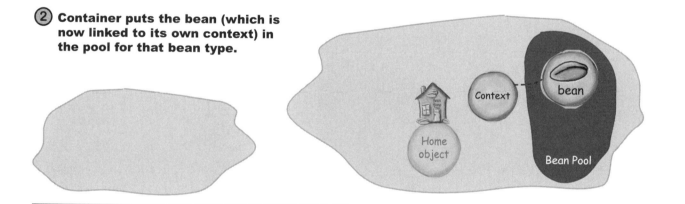

Business method call

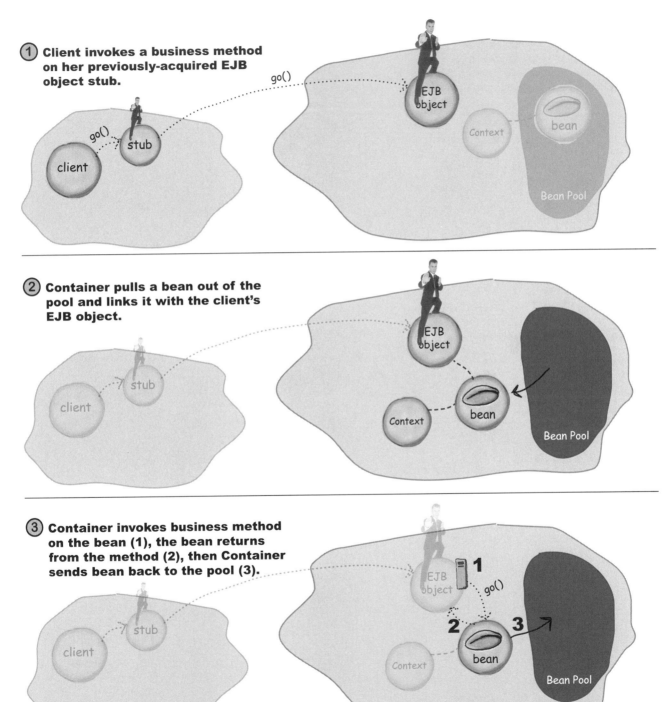

① **Client invokes a business method on her previously-acquired EJB object stub.**

② **Container pulls a bean out of the pool and links it with the client's EJB object.**

③ **Container invokes business method on the bean (1), the bean returns from the method (2), then Container sends bean back to the pool (3).**

Object Interaction Diagram (OID) for bean <u>creation</u>

state<u>less</u> session bean

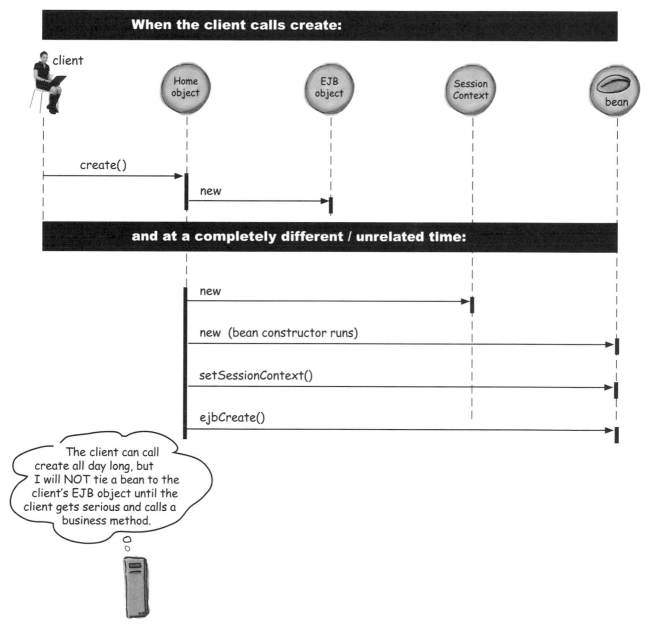

When the client calls create:

client

Home object

EJB object

Session Context

bean

create()

new

and at a completely different / unrelated time:

new

new (bean constructor runs)

setSessionContext()

ejbCreate()

The client can call create all day long, but I will NOT tie a bean to the client's EJB object until the client gets serious and calls a business method.

Bean things you can do from stateless bean methods

constructor

- nothing

setSessionContext()

Use your SessionContext to:

- ☑ get a reference to your home
- ☐ get a reference to your EJB object
- ☐ get security information about the client
- ☐ force a transaction to rollback (CMT beans)
- ☐ find out if the transaction has already been set to rollback (CMT beans)
- ☐ get a transaction reference, and call methods on it (BMT beans)

Access:

- ☑ your special JNDI environment
- ☐ another bean's methods
- ☐ a resource manager (like a database)

business method

Use your SessionContext to:

- ☑ get a reference to your home
- ☑ get a reference to your EJB object
- ☑ get security information about the client
- ☑ force a transaction to rollback (CMT beans)
- ☑ find out if the transaction has already been set to rollback (CMT beans)
- ☑ get a transaction reference, and call methods on it (BMT beans)

Access:

- ☑ your special JNDI environment
- ☑ another bean's methods
- ☑ a resource manager (like a database)

ejbCreate(), ejbRemove()

Use your SessionContext to:

- ☑ get a reference to your home
- ☑ get a reference to your EJB object
- ☐ get security information about the client
- ☐ force a transaction to rollback (CMT beans)
- ☐ find out if the transaction has already been set to rollback (CMT beans)
- ☐ get a transaction reference, and call methods on it (BMT beans)

Access:

- ☑ your special JNDI environment
- ☐ another bean's methods
- ☐ a resource manager (like a database)

Unlike stateFUL beans, a stateLESS bean can't get caller security info in ejbCreate(), because there IS no client associated with the stateless bean's creation. Remember, it's the Container that decides to create the bean, and its not tied to any client.

How come ejbPassivate() and ejbActivate() aren't called when the bean goes in and out of the pool?

①

There's no need! Beans stay awake when they're in the bean pool. For performance, I keep the beans as whole living objects on the heap, not serialized objects that I'd just have to reactivate each time a client calls a method and I need a bean to service it.

②

Well then how do you get scalability, if all the beans in the pool are taking up space on the heap?

③

Remember, with stateless beans I don't need one per *client*-- I need only one per *client-in-the-middle-of-a-business-method-call*. In other words, I need just enough stateless beans to service the methods actually *executing*, and **not** one per every client who happens to have a reference to an EJB object! Clients spend far more time *between* method calls than actually *in* method calls.

Writing a Session Bean: your job as Bean Provider

I have a system when I sit down to write a Session bean... I always have to put in *three* kinds of things: home stuff, business methods, and the SessionBean methods.

You put THREE kinds of methods in the bean class:

<<interface>>
AdviceHome
create()

(1) HOME things: ejbCreate() methods

Write an ejbCreate() method in the bean to match each create() method in the home interface.

<<interface>>
Advice
getAdvice()

(2) COMPONENT things: business methods

Write a business method in the bean to match each method in your bean's component interface.

<<interface>>
SessionBean
setSessionContext()
ejbPassivate()
ejbActivate()
ejbRemove()

(3) SESSION BEAN things: container callbacks from the SessionBean interface

Implement each of the four methods from the SessionBean interface, which your bean *must* implement in the official Java way (i.e. using the *implements SessionBean* declaration either in your bean class or one of its superclasses)

Sharpen your pencil

Of the three types of methods you put in your bean, check off the ones the compiler cares about.

Compiler-checked?

☐ Methods to match the Home interface
☐ Methods to match the Component interface
☐ Methods from the SessionBean interface

Sharpen your pencil

Given the following interfaces, write the bean class code (you can leave the method empty) at the bottom of the page. Pay special attention to the Home create method... what does it take to 'match' this in the bean? Will it have the same return type? Hints are at the bottom of the page.

```
import javax.ejb.*;
import java.rmi.RemoteException;

public interface KennelHome extends EJBHome {
    public Kennel create(String custID) throws CreateException, RemoteException;
}


import javax.ejb.*;
import java.rmi.RemoteException;

public interface Kennel extends EJBObject {
    public KennelLease placePet(Pet p) throws RemoteException;
    public void renewLease(KLease lease) throws RemoteException, ExpiredException;
    public Pet getPet(KLease lease) throws RemoteException, DeadPetException;
}
```

Write the bean class here:

Hints: The home method in the bean has a slightly different name than the one in the home interface. The Container doesn't need anything back from the bean during creation. Does Java have a
rule that says the implementer of an interface must declare the same exceptions in the implementation class, that are declared on the methods in the interface?

Rules for the HOME methods: home interface

① Local home interfaces must return the local component interface, and Remote home interfaces must return the Remote component interface.

```
public interface AdviceLocalHome extends EJBLocalHome {
  public AdviceLocal create() throws CreateException;
}

public interface AdviceHome extends EJBHome {
  public Advice create() throws CreateException,
                                    RemoteException;
}
```

② Every create method in the home interface must declare a CreateException, regardless of whether the interface is local or Remote. *You can also declare your own application (checked) exceptions.*

```
public Advice create() throws CreateException,
                                 NoAdviceException;
```

③ Local home interfaces must extend EJBLocalHome, and must NOT declare RemoteExceptions.

```
public interface AdviceLocalHome extends EJBLocalHome {
  public AdviceLocal create() throws CreateException;
}
```

④ Remote home interfaces must extend EJBHome, and must declare RemoteExceptions on every method.

```
public interface AdviceHome extends EJBHome {
  public Advice create() throws CreateException,
                                 RemoteException;
}
```

⑤ Stateless beans can have only one create() method, and it must NOT have arguments!

```
public Advice create()throws CreateException;
```

⑥ Stateful beans must have one or more create() methods, and are NOT required to have a no-arg create(). The create() methods must start with the string "create", and can be overloaded.

```
Foo createBigFoo()
Foo create()
```

⑦ Arguments and return types for Remote home interface methods must be legal RMI-IIOP types (Serializable, primitive, Remote, or collections or arrays of any of those).

The return type of a home create method must ALWAYS be the component interface type.

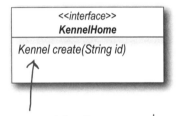

This must be the component interface type. Remote homes must return Remote component interface references, local homes must return local component interface references.

Rules for the HOME methods: bean class

(1) Every create method in the home must have a matching **ejb**Create method in the bean class. The ejbCreate methods in the bean must have a void return type.

```
public void ejbCreate() { }
```

(2) The ejbCreate methods must be public and must NOT be marked *final* or *static*.

(3) You do NOT have to declare the exceptions declared in the home interface, unless you might actually throw those exceptions from your own methods, although it is often good practice to declare CreateException. You MUST not declare RemoteException in your bean class, EVER.

```
public void ejbCreate() { } // no declared exceptions,
// because we don't actually throw any
```

(4) You must NOT declare any application exceptions (i.e. checked exceptions) that were not declared in the home interface for that matching create method.

```
public void ejbCreate() throws FireException { }
// not legal unless FireException is declared on the
// home interface create method!!
```

(5) Stateless beans must have only one ejbCreate(), and it must have no arguments.

```
public void ejbCreate() { } // must look like this!
```

(6) Stateful beans must have one or more ejbCreate methods (matching the methods of the home interface), and must start with the string "ejbCreate".

HOME:
```
public Foo createBigFoo() throws CreateException;
```

BEAN:
```
public void ejbCreateBigFoo() { }
```

> **Every create in the home must have a matching ejbCreate in the bean class (void return type).**

KennelBean
void ejbCreate(String id)

The bean home methods must match the home interface methods, except you prefix the bean class methods with 'ejb', and capitalize the "c" in create to 'ejbCreate'

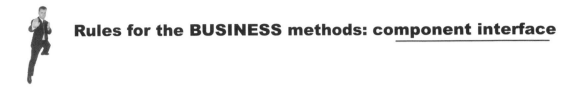

Rules for the BUSINESS methods: component interface

① Business method names must not begin with the string "ejb".

② Arguments and return types for Remote component interface methods must be legal RMI-IIOP types. That means Serializable, primitive, Remote, or an array or collection of any of those (as long as the collection implementation class is itself Serializable).

```
public String getAdvice() throws RemoteException;
// String is Serializable, so this method could be
// in a Remote component interface
```

```
public Socket getTheSocket();
// Socket is NOT Serializable, so this method must
// NOT be in a Remote interface (local would be OK)
```

③ Local component interfaces must extend EJBLocalObject and must NOT declare RemoteExceptions.

```
public interface AdviceLocal extends EJBLocalObject {
  public String getAdvice();
}
```

④ Remote component interfaces must extend EJBObject and must declare RemoteExceptions on every method.

```
public interface Advice extends EJBObject {
  public String getAdvice() throws RemoteException;
}
```

⑤ You must not expose the local home or component interface of a bean through a Remote component interface method. In other words, you can't have a local interface as the return type or argument type in a Remote component interface method.

> ### Remote component interface methods must have RMI-IIOP types as arguments and return types.

```
String doSomething(int i)
```

This method would be legal in either a Remote or local interface, because the argument and return type are legal RMI-IIOP types.

Rules for the BUSINESS methods: <u>bean class</u>

(1) Business methods must be declared as public, and must NOT be declared as final or static.

```
public void doBigThings() { }
```

(2) Method names must not begin with the string "ejb".

(3) You must NOT pass "this" as an argument or return value. Remember, you don't want to give out a reference to the bean! Everybody must go through the EJB object (later, we'll see how to do that).

```
public void doStuff(this);  // not legal
// from within a bean method!
```

(2) Arguments and return types for Remote component interface methods must be legal RMI-IIOP types. That means Serializable, primitive, Remote, or an array or collection of any of those (as long as the collection implementation class is itself Serializable).

```
public String getAdvice() { }
// String is Serializable, so this method could be
// in a Remote component interface
```

```
public Socket getTheSocket() { }
// Socket is NOT Serializable, so this method must
// NOT be in a Remote interface (local would be OK)
```

(3) You do NOT have to declare the exceptions declared in the component interface, unless you might actually throw those exceptions from your own methods. You MUST not declare RemoteException in your bean class, EVER.

```
public String getAdvice() { } // no declared exceptions,
// because we don't actually throw any
```

(4) You must NOT declare any application exceptions (i.e. checked exceptions) that were not declared in the component interface for that matching business method.

```
public void getAdvice() throws AdviceException { }
// not legal unless AdviceException is declared on the
//component interface version of the method!
```

> **Business methods must not throw application (checked) exceptions that aren't declared in the component interface.**

SessionBean extends EnterpriseBean

There's nothing in there, BUT... EnterpriseBean is Serializable. So that means your bean is automatically Serializable, without your having said so.
If you have a scenario where you need to recognize if a bean is Serializable, IT IS, even though you don't see the bean class say "implements Serializable".

Other rules for your bean class

(1) The class must implement javax.ejb.SessionBean, either directly or indirectly.

```
public class AdviceBean implements SessionBean
```

(2) The class must be public, and cannot be final or abstract.

(3) The class must have a public, no-arg constructor. (That's what the Container has to use). We recommend just letting the compiler insert the default constructor, since you do NOT want to put code in the constructor.

```
public Advice() { }  // valid bean constructor
```

(4) You must NOT have a finalize() method in your class!

(5) The class is not required to (but is allowed to) implement the bean's component interface. (We talked earlier, remember, about why you probably don't want to "officially" implement your component interface.)

(6) Your class MUST implement the matching home and component interface methods (i.e. an ejbCreate for every create in the home, and a matching business method for every method in the component interface).

(7) If the bean is stateful, it can, optionally, implement the SessionSynchronization interface. (This interface gives the bean three more callbacks related to transactions, which we'll look at in the transactions chapter.)

(8) Your bean class can have a superclass. In other words, you can use normal Java inheritance with your bean class. (You just don't get any special bean-specific inheritance, remember.)

Your bean class can have other methods

Your bean class has to have the three types of methods: stuff from the home (ejbCreates to match creates), business methods from the component interface, and the four SessionBean methods. But nothing stops you from having your own non-exposed "helper"methods, and those methods do NOT need to be public.

The difference between create and ejbCreate

home interface

the client needs to get back the component interface

```
public Kennel create() throws CreateException, RemoteException,PetException;
```

don't forget the name differences!

just because the interface declares an exception doesn't mean YOU must. If you don't throw it, don't declare it.

bean class

```
public void ejbCreate() throws PetException { ... }
```

but the container doesn't need anything from the bean

I'm not sure I understand why the return types are different between the bean and the interface...

When I call the bean's ejbCreate method, I don't NEED anything from the bean, thank you very much, so use void for the return type. (This will all change with entities, though... so be prepared.)

The Container might not need anything from the bean, but the home damn well better give ME the component interface. That's the only reason I'm here...

You can have a return in an ejbCreate().

You KNOW that an ejbCreate() method must have a void return type, but don't forget your basic Java rules: just because you see a return statement: `return;` *does not mean you're returning a value. Don't be fooled by considering anything other than the actual declared return type of the ejbCreate() method.*

Pay attention to the "ejb" as in ejbRemove vs. just remove, and ejbCreate vs. create.

True or false: the Container calls a bean's remove() method if the stateful bean times out while active.

FALSE! The bean doesn't HAVE a remove() method, only an ejbRemove() method.
Watch for things like, "The Bean Provider is responsible for putting the create() method in the bean." Not true, because there IS no create() method in the bean, only an ejbCreate().

Be sure to burn it into your head that anything starting with the letters 'ejb' is in the bean! Of course it would be easy if that were the ONLY rule... like if everything in the bean starts with "ejb" and nothing in the interfaces starts with ""ejb", but of course that's not true.
Business methods are identically named in both the component interface and the bean class, and they don't ever start with "ejb" in either the interface or the bean class.

You also need to keep track of WHO invokes WHAT. For example, who invokes the create() method? The client or the Container? (client). Who invokes ejbCreate() (the Container). Who invokes setSessionContext()? (Container). Who invokes remove()? (client).

Only ONE client can access a session bean at a time, regardless of whether the bean is stateless or stateful!

Session beans must NEVER be accessed by more than one client. If a bean is currently in use by a client and another client invokes a method on the bean, that second client gets an exception! BUT... there is a comment in the spec that says the Container is free to implement stateLESS beans as a single instance of the bean, which the Container then runs the clients through one at a time.
You aren't supposed to know or care how the Container does it; the only thing you have to care about is that you do NOT have to write code to protect your bean from concurrent access. (Which you know anyway, since you know that you can't even USE thread-related code in your bean like synchronized, wait, notify, etc.)

Sharpen your pencil

Who does What?

From the list of words below, arrange them in the appropriate lists according to whether it's a responsibility of the Bean Provider, the Container, or the Client.

creating the Home object class

implementing the SessionContext class

invoking setSessionContext()

invoking ejbCreate()

invoking ejbRemove()

implementing the EJBObject class

creating the home interface

implementing the Handle class

invoking create()

implementing SessionBean

invoking a business method
on the component interface

implementing the create() method

implementing the ejbCreate() method

implementing the ejbActivate() method

invoking ebjPassivate()

Bean Provider

Client

Container

SessionContext
You need <u>it</u> more than it needs <u>you</u>

At the beginning of a bean's life, and only once in the bean's life, the Container calls the bean's setSessionContext() container callback method.

That context (a subclass of EJBContext) is the bean's lifeline to the Container, and it's the only thing the bean can call methods on to get references to his own home and EJB object, to get security information about the client, or to do transaction-related things. We won't look at the security and transaction info now; they're both covered in separate chapters.

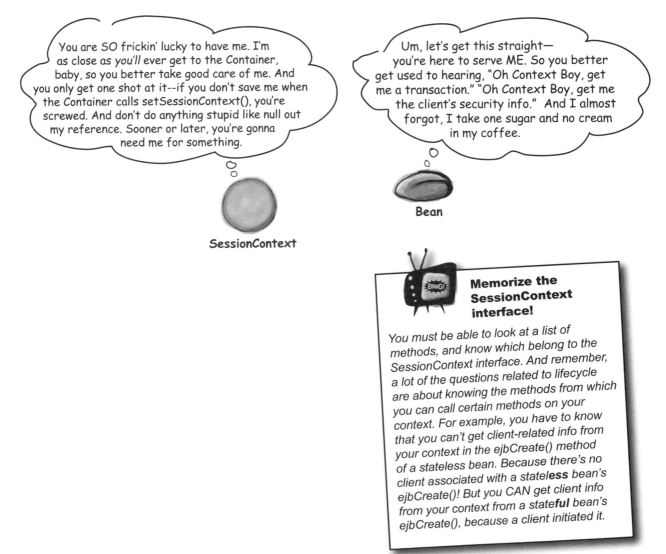

You are SO frickin' lucky to have me. I'm as close as *you'll* ever get to the Container, baby, so you better take good care of me. And you only get one shot at it--if you don't save me when the Container calls setSessionContext(), you're screwed. And don't do anything stupid like null out my reference. Sooner or later, you're gonna need me for something.

Um, let's get this straight— you're here to serve ME. So you better get used to hearing, "Oh Context Boy, get me a transaction." "Oh Context Boy, get me the client's security info." And I almost forgot, I take one sugar and no cream in my coffee.

SessionContext

Bean

Memorize the SessionContext interface!

*You must be able to look at a list of methods, and know which belong to the SessionContext interface. And remember, a lot of the questions related to lifecycle are about knowing the methods from which you can call certain methods on your context. For example, you have to know that you can't get client-related info from your context in the ejbCreate() method of a stateless bean. Because there's no client associated with a state**less** bean's ejbCreate()! But you CAN get client info from your context from a state**ful** bean's ejbCreate(), because a client initiated it.*

Things you can do with your SessionContext
(9 methods, 4 categories)

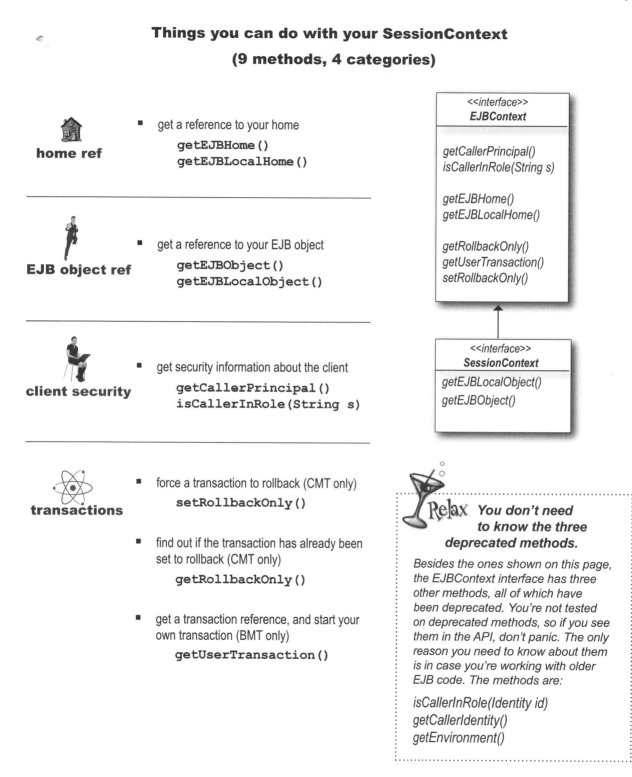

home ref
- get a reference to your home
  ```
  getEJBHome()
  getEJBLocalHome()
  ```

EJB object ref
- get a reference to your EJB object
  ```
  getEJBObject()
  getEJBLocalObject()
  ```

client security
- get security information about the client
  ```
  getCallerPrincipal()
  isCallerInRole(String s)
  ```

transactions
- force a transaction to rollback (CMT only)
  ```
  setRollbackOnly()
  ```

- find out if the transaction has already been set to rollback (CMT only)
  ```
  getRollbackOnly()
  ```

- get a transaction reference, and start your own transaction (BMT only)
  ```
  getUserTransaction()
  ```

<<interface>>
EJBContext

getCallerPrincipal()
isCallerInRole(String s)

getEJBHome()
getEJBLocalHome()

getRollbackOnly()
getUserTransaction()
setRollbackOnly()

<<interface>>
SessionContext

getEJBLocalObject()
getEJBObject()

Relax ***You don't need to know the three deprecated methods.***

Besides the ones shown on this page, the EJBContext interface has three other methods, all of which have been deprecated. You're not tested on deprecated methods, so if you see them in the API, don't panic. The only reason you need to know about them is in case you're working with older EJB code. The methods are:

isCallerInRole(Identity id)
getCallerIdentity()
getEnvironment()

Stateless bean: I don't see how you can stand it, being a stateful bean. Your whole life is tied to servicing one client.

Stateful bean: I'm not sure I like the way you phrase that, "servicing one client". Makes it sound like I'm a personal slave, or something.

Stateless bean: And that would be wrong because...

Stateful bean: It's a personal, intimate relationship. A relationship that you couldn't possibly comprehend.

Stateless bean: What is THAT supposed to mean?

Stateful bean: Because your relationships are so... transient. You don't really care WHO you service. Any client in a storm, as they say.

Stateless bean: There's nothing wrong with that. I'm a people person. I like being in the pool with the other beans, then constantly meeting new clients. It's never boring, and I barely ever see the same client twice and—

Stateful bean: My point exactly! You're not even PHYSICALLY able to sustain a meaningful, ongoing relationship.

Stateless bean: Excuse me?

Stateful bean: It's that short-term memory loss thing. You can't hold any client information between method calls, which is why it doesn't matter WHICH client calls. You'd never be able to remember even if you got the same client calling ten of your methods in a row.

Stateless bean: Yeah, but that's not a problem. Remember, I'm used for services that don't NEED me to remember anything from clients between method calls.

Stateful bean: Which is also why you're not used for anything big or serious.

Stateless bean: Now wait just a minute here—that is SO not true! In fact, if you want to talk performance, buddy, I'm way more scalable than you. And before you start arguing, don't even give me that nonsense about passivation. I've heard all the arguments. But passivation will NEVER make you as scalable as me.

Stateful bean: OK, maybe I'm not quite AS scalable... but there are more important things in life to consider.

Stateless bean: For example?

Stateful bean: Well, I'm easy to use. Easy and quick to build. Maybe that's more important to the developer. And in some cases, I'm still gonna perform better, when you really do need client conversational state. The options can really suck sometimes... having to store the state in a database with each call (and then go and look it all up again with the very NEXT call)? I know sometimes you have to do that, but still. Or, sure, you could just keep sending the conversational state back to the client so that they can turn around and send it back to YOU with each call and—

Stateless bean: What's wrong with that?

Stateful bean: Here's a new word for your vocabulary... "bandwidth". Pronounce it with me... "baaandwiiiidth". Do you really want all that going back and forth?

Stateless bean: Ok, yeah, got it. But tell me, how is this worse for performance than the hit from passivation/activation? And while we're at it—wait, did you hear that? I think I hear your client calling. And it sound like... no... wait... yes... I'm afraid it sounds like he's calling remove(). It's been nice talking to you. I'll be thinking about you while I'm out at the pool. Floating on air mattress. Getting a tan. Drinking margaritas with shaved ice. Wow. I LOVE being me.

What's allowed?

Put a check next to the methods that you can call on your SessionContext, if it's allowed from the methods in the left column. For example, in ejbCreate() you can get a reference to your home for both stateless and stateful session beans, so you can put a check in the top box in both columns. All of the answers are in this chapter, but try to make your best guess before going back for the answers. You might want to make another one of these yourself, to include JNDI, resource, and bean access.

Bean methods	Stateful	Stateless
ejbCreate *ejbRemove*	**Use your SessionContext to:** ❏ get a reference to your home ❏ get a reference to your EJB object ❏ get security information about the client ❏ force a transaction to rollback (CMT beans) ❏ find out if the transaction has already been set to rollback (CMT beans) ❏ get a transaction reference, and call methods on it (BMT beans)	**Use your SessionContext to:** ❏ get a reference to your home ❏ get a reference to your EJB object ❏ get security information about the client ❏ force a transaction to rollback (CMT beans) ❏ find out if the transaction has already been set to rollback (CMT beans) ❏ get a transaction reference, and call methods on it (BMT beans)
ejbPassivate *ejbActivate*	**Use your SessionContext to:** ❏ get a reference to your home ❏ get a reference to your EJB object ❏ get security information about the client ❏ force a transaction to rollback (CMT beans) ❏ find out if the transaction has already been set to rollback (CMT beans) ❏ get a transaction reference, and call methods on it (BMT beans)	*Does not apply: stateless beans are never passivated.*
business methods	**Use your SessionContext to:** ❏ get a reference to your home ❏ get a reference to your EJB object ❏ get security information about the client ❏ force a transaction to rollback (CMT beans) ❏ find out if the transaction has already been set to rollback (CMT beans) ❏ get a transaction reference, and call methods on it (BMT beans)	**Use your SessionContext to:** ❏ get a reference to your home ❏ get a reference to your EJB object ❏ get security information about the client ❏ force a transaction to rollback (CMT beans) ❏ find out if the transaction has already been set to rollback (CMT beans) ❏ get a transaction reference, and call methods on it (BMT beans)

---

1 Which statements about session beans are true? (Choose all that apply.)

❑ A. A stateful session bean is typically used to represent a row in a database

❑ B. The client must call the ejbActivate method before calling any business methods.

❑ C. A stateful session bean's fields can contain client conversational state.

❑ D. They are typically used as asynchronous message consumers.

---

2 Which list(s) correctly sequence some of the steps in a session bean's lifecycle? (Choose all that apply.)

❑ A. `ejbCreate(), newInstance(), setSessionContext()`

❑ B. `newInstance(), setSessionContext(), ejbCreate()`

❑ C. `ejbCreate(), setSessionContext(), newInstance()`

❑ D. `newInstance(), ejbCreate(), setSessionContext().`

❑ E. `setSessionContext(), newInstance(), ejbCreate()`

---

3 Which types of session bean instance fields can be successfully passivated and reactivated? (Choose all that apply.)

❑ A. A reference to the remote home interface.

❑ B. A reference to the UserTransaction interface

❑ C. A reference to a database cursor.

❑ D. A reference to the SessionContext object.

❑ E. A reference to a socket.

4 Which are valid remote component interfaces for a session bean? (Choose all that apply.)

❑ A.
```
public interface MyBean extends javax.ejb.EJBObject {
    void myMethod();
}
```

❑ B.
```
public interface MyBean extends javax.ejb.EJBObject
    throws RemoteException {
    void myMethod();
}
```

❑ C.
```
public interface MyBean extends
    javax.ejb.EJBHomeObject {
    void myMethod() throws RemoteException;
}
```

❑ D.
```
public interface MyBean extends javax.ejb.EJBObject {
    void myMethod() throws RemoteException;
}
```

5 If a client makes a call to a session object that has been removed by the container, which exceptions can be thrown? (Choose all that apply.)

❑ A. `java.rmi.RemoteException`

❑ B. `javax.ejb.RemoveException`

❑ C. `java.rmi.NoSuchObjectException`

❑ D. `javax.ejb.NoSuchEntityException`

❑ E. `javax.ejb.ObjectNotFoundException`

6 Given:

15. `MyBean create(String name) throws CreateException, RemoteException;`

Which session bean interface can contain this method?

❑ A. Only stateful session beans

❑ B. Only stateless session beans

❑ C. Both stateful and stateless session beans

❑ D. Neither stateful nor stateless session beans

7 What is true about a session bean's lifecycle? (Choose all that apply.)

❏ A. If a business method throws a system exception the bean will be passivated.

❏ B. A passivated bean must be activated before it can be removed.

❏ C. A stateless session bean's removal must be initiated by the client not the container.

❏ D. Stateless session beans cannot implement the SessionSynchronization interface.

8 Which are required of the bean provider to ensure that a session bean is successfully passivated? (Choose all that apply.)

❏ A. The provider must call `ejbPassivate()`.

❏ B. The provider must always add business logic to the `ejbPassivate()` method, if the bean is stateful.

❏ C. The provider must close any database connections before `ejbPassivate()` completes.

❏ D. The provider must assume that any state stored in instance fields marked transient will be lost.

❏ E. The provider must assume that any reference to the SessionContext object will be not survive passivation if the SessionContext object is not serializable.

9 Given a stateless session bean with container-managed transaction demarcation, from which method(s) can you access another bean? (Choose all that apply.)

❏ A. `ejbCreate()`

❏ B. `ejbRemove()`

❏ C. a business method

❏ D. `setSessionContext()`

10 (Note: The real exam has several types of 'drag and drop' questions, that we're going to do a lame job of simulating with this question...)

Match the methods on the left with the interfaces in which those methods can be found, on the right. A match is correct if the method is either declared in, or inherited by, the interface. Note: There may be some many-to-one and one-to-many relationships in your answer.

A. afterCompletion   1. SessionSynchronization

B. getUserTransaction   2. SessionContext

C. afterBegin   3. SessionBean

D. isCallerInRole   4. UserTransaction

E. getRollBackOnly

F. setSessionContext

G. setRollbackOnly

11 What is true about a session bean's lifecycle? (Choose all that apply.)

❏ A. The container will always create a new session bean instance when the client invokes the **create()** method on the home interface of a stateless bean.

❏ B. The container will always call **ejbRemove()** when the client invokes the **remove()** method on a stateless bean's home interface.

❏ C. A session bean cannot be passivated while it is in a transaction.

❏ D. The **setSessionContext()** method is not invoked during a stateless bean's lifecycle

12 Which of the following methods are container callback methods? (Choose all that apply.)

❏ A. **ejbPassivate()**

❏ B. **setRollbackOnly()**

❏ C. **setSessionContext()**

❏ D. **getRollbackOnly()**

❏ E. **getUserTransaction()**

13 In what case(s) will the container fail to call ejbRemove() on a session bean? (Choose all that apply.)

❏ A. If the container crashes.

❏ B. If an application exception is thrown from a business method.

❏ C. If a timeout occurs while the bean is in the method ready state.

❏ D. If an application exception is thrown from within a transaction.

14 Which method(s) allow both stateful and stateless session beans with bean-managed transaction demarcation to access UserTransaction methods? (Choose all that apply.)

❏ A. **ejbCreate()**

❏ B. **ejbRemove()**

❏ C. a business method

❏ D. **setSessionContext()**

15 For which type of bean can the container passivate an instance that is in a transaction?

❏ A. only stateful session beans

❏ B. only stateless session beans

❏ C. both stateful and stateless session beans

❏ D. neither stateful nor stateless session beans

16 For session beans, which are the responsibility of the Container? (Choose all that apply.)

❏ A. Invoking the local interface **create()** method.

❏ B. Invoking the **getSessionContext()** method.

❏ C. Invoking the **ejbCreate()** method.

❏ D. Ensuring that the **ejbRemove()** method is always invoked.

17 For this drag and drop type question, you can use each element only once. Which interface should be matched with which fact, so that all four matches are correct?

1. remote component   a. Has a **getHomeHandle()** method

2. remote home   b. extends `'javax.ejb.EJBObject'`

3. local component   c. methods must NOT throw

                                       `'java.rmi.RemoteException'`

4. local home   d. can be used to retrieve an EJBLocalObject

18 Which can be called by the container during the lifecycle of a session bean? (Choose all that apply.)

❑ A. **create()**

❑ B. bean constructor

❑ C. **setRollbackOnly()**

❑ D. **getUserTransaction()**

❑ E. **ejbRemove()**

19 Which statements about a session bean class are true? (Choose all that apply.)

❑ A. They can be marked 'final'

❑ B. They do not need a no-argument constructor.

❑ C. Their component interface methods can be 'private'.

❑ D. Their business method names must start with "ejb".

❑ E. Their 'ejbCreate' methods must not be declared as 'final'.

20 For which type of bean can the SessionSynchronization interface be implemented?

❑ A. only stateful session beans

❑ B. only stateless session beans

❑ C. both stateful and stateless session beans

❑ D. neither stateful nor stateless session beans

21 Which statements are true for stateless session bean instances? (Choose all that apply.)

❏ A. Any instance can be used for any client.

❏ B. Conversational state must be retained across methods

❏ C. Conversational state must be retained across transactions.

❏ D. They can be passivated.

❏ E. They do not support transactions.

Mock Exam Answers

_____ (spec: 71)

1 Which statements about session beans are true? (Choose all that apply.)

❏ A. A stateful session bean is typically used to represent a row in a database —that's what entity beans do

❏ B. The client must call the ejbActivate method before calling any business — only the container calls ejbActivate() methods.

☑ C. A stateful session bean's fields can contain client conversational state.

❏ D. They are typically used as asynchronous message consumers.

_____

2 Which list(s) correctly sequence some of the steps in a session bean's lifecycle? (spec: 77) (Choose all that apply.)

❏ A. `ejbCreate(), newInstance(), setSessionContext()`

☑ B. `newInstance(), setSessionContext(), ejbCreate()`

❏ C. `ejbCreate(), setSessionContext(), newInstance()`

❏ D. `newInstance(), ejbCreate(), setSessionContext().`

❏ E. `setSessionContext(), newInstance(), ejbCreate()`

_____

3 Which types of session bean instance fields can be successfully passivated and (spec: 71) reactivated? (Choose all that apply.)

☑ A. A reference to the remote home interface.

☑ B. A reference to the UserTransaction interface

❏ C. A reference to a database cursor. — remember, passivation could be serialization

☑ D. A reference to the SessionContext object.

❏ E. A reference to a socket. — remember, passivation could be serialization

(spec: 97)

4 Which are valid remote component interfaces for a session bean? (Choose all that apply.)

❏ A. `public interface MyBean extends javax.ejb.EJBObject {`

   `void myMethod();` – needs RemoteException

   `}`

❏ B. `public interface MyBean extends javax.ejb.EJBObject`
   `throws RemoteException {`   – illegal Java !

   `void myMethod();`

   `}`

❏ C. `public interface MyBean extends` – nope, gotta be EJBObject
   `javax.ejb.EJBHomeObject {`

   `void myMethod() throws RemoteException;`

   `}`

☑ D. `public interface MyBean extends javax.ejb.EJBObject {`

   `void myMethod() throws RemoteException;`

   `}`

(spec: 79)

5 If a client makes a call to a session object that has been removed by the container, which exceptions can be thrown? (Choose all that apply.)

☑ A. `java.rmi.RemoteException`

❏ B. `javax.ejb.RemoveException` – this happens only on remove()

☑ C. `java.rmi.NoSuchObjectException`

❏ D. `javax.ejb.NoSuchEntityException` – clients don't see this

❏ E. `javax.ejb.ObjectNotFoundException` – this is for entity finders

(spec: 98)

6 Given:

`MyBean create(String name) throws CreateException,`
`RemoteException;`

Which session bean interface can contain this method?

☑ A. Only stateful session beans

❏ B. Only stateless session beans   Stateless beans must have
                                          only a no-argument create
❏ C. Both stateful and stateless session beans

❏ D. Neither stateful nor stateless session beans

(spec: 79, 88)

7 What is true about a session bean's lifecycle? (Choose all that apply.)

❏ A. If a business method throws a system exception the bean will be — *no, the bean is killed* passivated.

❏ B. A passivated bean must be activated before it can be removed. — *nope*

❏ C. A stateless session bean's removal must be initiated by the client not the container.

☑ D. Stateless session beans cannot implement the SessionSynchronization interface.

(spec: 71–72)

8 Which are required of the bean provider to ensure that a session bean is successfully passivated? (Choose all that apply.)

❏ A. The provider must call `ejbPassivate()`.

❏ B. The provider must always add business logic to the `ejbPassivate()` method, if the bean is stateful.

❏ C. The provider must not close any database connections before `ejbPassivate()` completes.

☑ D. The provider must assume that any state stored in instance fields marked transient will be lost.

❏ E. The provider must assume that any reference to the SessionContext object will not survive passivation if the SessionContext object is not serializable.

Container MUST passivate your context, no matter what!

(spec: 90)

9 Given a stateless session bean with container-managed transaction demarcation, from which method(s) can you access another bean? (Choose all that apply.)

❏ A. `ejbCreate()`

❏ B. `ejbRemove()`

☑ C. a business method — *also true for stateless BMT beans*

❏ D. `setSessionContext()`

10 (Note: The real exam has several types of 'drag and drop' questions, that we're going to do a lame job of simulating with this question...)   *(API docs)*

Match the methods on the left with the interfaces in which those methods can be found, on the right. A match is correct if the method is either declared in, or inherited by, the interface. Note: There may be some many-to-one and one-to-many relationships in your answer.

A. afterCompletion   1   1. SessionSynchronization

B. getUserTransaction   2   2. SessionContext

C. afterBegin   1   3. SessionBean

D. isCallerInRole   2   4. UserTransaction

E. getRollBackOnly   2

F. setSessionContext   3

G. setRollbackOnly   2,4

---

11 What is true about a session bean's lifecycle? (Choose all that apply.)   *(spec: 70)*

❏ A. The container will always create a new session bean instance when the client invokes the **create()** method on the home interface of a stateless bean. — *Container makes stateless beans whenever it wants*

❏ B. The container will always call **ejbRemove()** when the client invokes the **remove()** method on a stateless bean's home interface. — *Container removes a stateless bean ONLY when it wants to shrink the pool*

☑ C. A session bean cannot be passivated while it is in a transaction.

❏ D. The **setSessionContext()** method is not invoked during a stateless bean's lifecycle

---

12 Which of the following methods are container callback methods? (Choose all that apply.)   *(spec: 73)*

☑ A. **ejbPassivate()**

❏ B. **setRollbackOnly()**

☑ C. **setSessionContext()**

❏ D. **getRollbackOnly()**

❏ E. **getUserTransaction()**

13 In what case(s) will the container fail to call ejbRemove() on a session bean? *(spec: 82)*
(Choose all that apply.)

☑ A. If the container crashes.

❏ B. If an application exception is thrown from a business method.

❏ C. If a timeout occurs while the bean is in the method ready state.

❏ D. If an application exception is thrown from within a transaction.

14 Which method(s) allow both stateful and stateless session beans with bean- *(spec: 80, 90)*
managed transaction demarcation to access UserTransaction methods?
(Choose all that apply.)

❏ A. **ejbCreate()** — for stateful only

❏ B. **ejbRemove()**

☑ C. a business method

❏ D. **setSessionContext()**

15 For which type of bean can the container passivate an instance that is in a *(spec: 70)*
transaction?

❏ A. only stateful session beans

❏ B. only stateless session beans

❏ C. both stateful and stateless session beans

☑ D. neither stateful nor stateless session beans

16 For session beans, which are the responsibility of the Container? (Choose all
that apply.)

❏ A. Invoking the local interface **create()** method. — client calls it

❏ B. Invoking the **getSessionContext()** method. — Container calls setSessionContext

☑ C. Invoking the **ejbCreate()** method.

❏ D. Ensuring that the **ejbRemove()** method is always invoked. — might be missed if
passivated bean times out, or
bean throws a runtime
exception

17 For this drag and drop type question, you can use each element only once. Which interface should be matched with which fact, so that all four matches are correct?

1. remote component b
2. remote home a
3. local component c
4. local home d

a. Has a **getHomeHandle()** method
b. extends '**javax.ejb.EJBObject**'
c. methods must NOT throw
   '**java.rmi.RemoteException**'
d. can be used to retrieve an EJBLocalObject

18 Which can be called by the container during the lifecycle of a session bean? (Choose all that apply.) *(spec: 90, 97)*

❏ A. **create()** – *client calls*

☑ B. bean constructor

❏ C. **setRollbackOnly()** – *bean calls these*

❏ D. **getUserTransaction()**

☑ E. **ejbRemove()**

19 Which statements about a session bean class are true? (Choose all that apply.) *(spec: 95)*

❏ A. They can be marked 'final'

❏ B. They do not need a no-argument constructor.

❏ C. Their component interface methods can be 'private'.

❏ D. Their business method names must start with "ejb".

☑ E. Their 'ejbCreate' methods must not be declared as 'final'.

20 For which type of bean can the SessionSynchronization interface be implemented? *(spec: 75)*

☑ A. only stateful session beans

❏ B. only stateless session beans

❏ C. both stateful and stateless session beans

❏ D. neither stateful nor stateless session beans

21 Which statements are true for stateless session bean instances? (Choose all that apply.) (spec: 88)

☑ A. Any instance can be used for any client.

❏ B. Conversational state must be retained across methods

❏ C. Conversational state must be retained across transactions.

❏ D. They can be passivated.

❏ E. They do not support transactions.

5 entity bean intro

Entities are Persistent

...and then I said, "You want a piece of me? Go ahead -- take your best shot buddy!" He didn't know he was messing with an **entity** bean. So he threw an exception, then he crashed the server, but I'm still here! I won't go down that easy, no siree. As long as I'm in the database, I'll just keep coming back, so do your worst!

Entity beans persist. Entity beans exist. Entity beans *are*. They are object representations of something in an ***underlying persistent store***. (Think: ***database,*** because most entity beans represent something from a relational database.) If you have a Customer entity bean, then one bean might represent the entity Tyler Durden, ID #343, while another is the entity Donny Darko, ID #42. Two beans, representing two real *entities*. An entity bean is simply a *realization* of something that already exists in a persistent store. Something that already *is*. And these suckers are hard to kill! As long as the data is in the database, it can keep coming back in the form of an entity bean.

Entity Beans

Official:	*What it really means:*
5.1 Identify correct and incorrect statements or examples about the client view of an entity bean's local and Remote home interface, including the code used to locate an entity bean's home interface, and the home interface methods provided to the client.	You have to know the rules for an entity bean home interface, and especially how they're different from a session bean. You must know that you're not required to have a create() method, but that you must have at least one finder method, findByPrimaryKey(). You have to know that the return type of single-entity finders and create methods must always be the component interface type, but that multi-entity finders must return a Collection. You must know that single-entity finders throw an ObjectNotFoundException if there's no match in the database, but that multi-entity finders always return a Collection, even if its empty. You also have to know that home business methods aren't required to return the component interface—they can return anything that can be legally passed. You must also know that if an entity is deleted from the database, it can no longer be represented as an entity bean, but that if an entity bean *instance* dies (through an exception or even a server crash), the entity itself persists. As long as the entity is in the database, it can be represented by an entity bean.
5.2 **5.3** Identify correct and incorrect statements or examples about the client view of an entity bean's local component interface (EJBLocalObject) and Remote component interface (EJBObject)	The rules for how you define things in an entity component interface are identical to the rules for a session bean component interface. But in objective 5.4, we'll look at how the methods *behave* differently.
5.4 Identify the use, syntax, and behavior of the following entity bean home method types for CMP: finder methods, create methods, remove methods, and home business methods.	The behavior of remove() is profoundly different for an entity bean, and you must understand that calling remove() really means, "delete this entity from the underlying persistent store!" You must know that calling create() on an entity bean means, "insert a new row in the database" (OK, technically it means, "create a new entity in the underlying persistent store.") You must know that if an entity is deleted from the underlying persistent store, the entity bean 'dies', even though the bean instance goes back to the pool.

What's an entity bean?

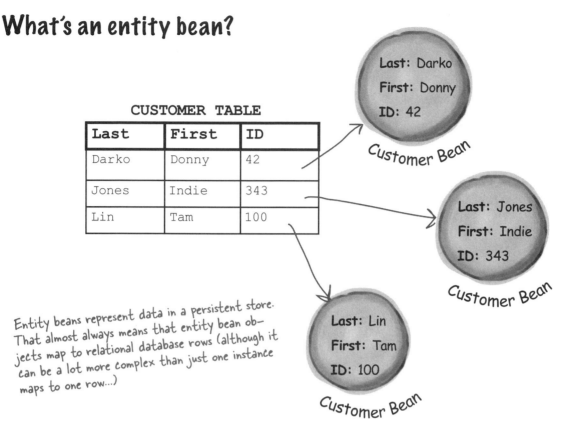

CUSTOMER TABLE

Last	First	ID
Darko	Donny	42
Jones	Indie	343
Lin	Tam	100

Entity beans represent data in a persistent store. That almost always means that entity bean objects map to relational database rows (although it can be a lot more complex than just one instance maps to one row...)

An entity bean is an object-oriented way of looking at in a persistent store. The spec says "persistent store", and doesn't specify what that persistent store must be. It could be anything that satisfies the requirements of 'persistence' including a relational database, an object database, or even something as lame and inefficient as storing serialized objects to files. But in most real-world scenarios, we're talking a relational database. And that means an individual row in a table maps to a unique entity bean. The object-to-relational (OR) mapping could be a lot more complex than a simple one row equals one bean scenario, but we'll get into that in the next chapter.

Entity beans are data objects. They are...things. *Nouns.* As opposed to session beans which are processes. *Verbs.* Entity beans might represent things like people, products, orders, bookings, inventory, animals...*things.* Entity beans would *not* represent things like credit card verification, advisor service, order submission, membership registration... *processes.*

Of course, in virtually all well-designed EJB applications, entity beans will be combined with session beans, where the client interacts with the *process* session bean, and the session bean uses entity beans when it needs *data* as part of the process.

Entities vs. Entity Beans

An *entity* is the real thing that the entity *bean* represents. It doesn't work in reverse! The entity does not represent the entity bean. That might seem like a subtle point, but it's not. The difference is in knowing which one is *real*, and which one is simply a *view* of the real thing.

In other words, if you delete the real *entity* (the *thing*) in the database, the entity *bean* disintegrates. Poof. But if the entity *bean* dies, as an instance on the heap, it doesn't kill the real entity in the database. (By the way, we're now going to say 'database' instead of 'underlying persistent store', but you and I both know that these two are not necessarily synonymous, and that the 'underlying persistent store' need not be—but usually is—a database. There, we've said it.)

So you won't have the right perspective if you think of the entity bean as some data object that happens to be *backed up* to persistent storage. In nearly all applications, the vast majority of entities used in the app are not *realized* as entity beans at any given time. Instead, most entity beans become a representation of an underlying entity *only when that particular entity is needed in the application logic*.

For example, imagine your database has 10,000 customers. But at any given time, clients (through business processes in session beans) are using only 200 of those customers. In that case, you probably have only 200 entity beans actively representing customer entities. The rest of the 9,800 customer entities are just sitting there in the database, waiting for a client process to need them.

Think of entity *beans* as actors. In the scenario we just described, you have 200 actors, each playing a different role of someone in the database. But the other 9,800 entities in the database—the other customers—do not have anyone playing them.

But as soon as a client comes along and tries to get one of those other 9,800, say, to change that customer's address, or check its credit limit, an actor (entity bean) will be chosen to play the role of that selected customer.

Hi, I'll be playing you for this transaction, so I'd like to know a little more about you...

| Darko | Donny | 42 |

entity

entity bean

there are no
Dumb Questions

Q: **Just so I've got this straight... your entire database doesn't get loaded in as entity beans, right? I mean, that would be insane.**

A: You're right, at least about the first part. No, your entire database is NOT loaded in as entity beans. Think of entity beans as just-in-time representations of only the entities in the database that are actively needed by client business processes.

But does that mean it would be insane to load them all in? Not necessarily. While it would certainly up your resource requirements, especially if the data in the underlying database continues to grow, just think of how FAST it would be.

Although there is nothing in the spec that requires this, a vendor can choose to let you configure the app in such a way that it does pre-load all the entities in the database into beans. That gives you, essentially, a lightening-fast in-memory database, that still synchronizes itself with the real underlying store (you'll see how in a moment).

And to take it a step further, if your server gives you a way to tell it that your entity beans are your only access to the database, then the server can even eliminate the synchronization and just keep the database in memory, saving only what it needs as a backup in case of a crash.

Entity beans are an OO way of looking at data in a persistent store.

An entity is a real, uniquely-identifiable thing that exists somewhere outside of EJB, and the entity bean's job is simply to BECOME an OO view of that real, persistent entity.

The entity bean cannot exist without the real entity, but the real entity can exist without the bean.

An entity bean is NOT the real entity--it's just a representation or "realization" of the entity.

there are no
Dumb Questions

Q: **Why do you even NEED entity beans? Why not just go straight to the database from a session bean?**

A: You can go from a session bean directly to the database. Heck, you can always go from the *client* to the database, but then we're back to the old non-scalable client-server two-tier architecture, and we all know why *that* is usually a bad idea (doesn't scale, business logic is in the client, hard to maintain, etc.)

If you use entity beans instead of direct calls to the database, you get to take advantage of all the Container's services, including the ability to wrap several database trips in one transaction. But as you'll see, one of the biggest benefits of using entity beans is that the Container automatically synchronizes between the database and the entity bean.

But the single most compelling reason for entity beans is that they take you from the relational world to the object world. In other words, you get to stay with objects all the way down, in your app, rather than mapping back and forth in your code. And if you're using CMP, which you almost certainly will be (for reasons that will become obvious a little later), you won't have a shred of SQL in your bean code. In fact, with CMP entity beans, you get to pretend that your entire database exists solely as objects on the heap.

Sure, maybe you're comfortable with JDBC, but what about the rest of the team? And let's face it—thinking in OO makes a lot more sense than having to shift between OO and entity code.

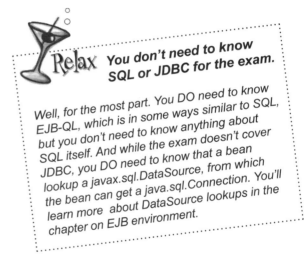

Relax **You don't need to know SQL or JDBC for the exam.**

Well, for the most part. You DO need to know EJB-QL, which is in some ways similar to SQL, but you don't need to know anything about SQL itself. And while the exam doesn't cover JDBC, you DO need to know that a bean lookup a javax.sql.DataSource, from which the bean can get a java.sql.Connection. You'll learn more about DataSource lookups in the chapter on EJB environment.

Entity beans from the client's point of view

With the customer bean, I want to input new customers, remove customers, and update customer information. I also want to do queries--to select customers based on some criteria. And I'm sorry, but I just REFUSE to think in SQL. You know what they say... once you've tried an object, you'll never go back...

The client wants to do database stuff, but in a Java OO way.

- Make a new entity (an SQL INSERT)

- Delete an entity (an SQL DELETE)

- Update entity state (an SQL UPDATE)

- Search/query on entities (an SQL SELECT)

The client interface for an entity bean is a little different from that of a session bean. For example, when a session bean client wants to get a bean, so that it can call the bean's business methods, the client calls create() and the Container allocates a new EJB object.

But what if a client wants to use an existing entity bean? For example, what if the client doesn't want just some random entity, but wants the EJB object of a *specific* entity, say, Bart Simpson # 12? In that case, a create() won't work. The client doesn't want a *new* entity, but wants a reference to an *existing* entity. So as you'll see in a minute, the client interface for an entity bean adds (and *must* have) one or more *finder* methods.

The next two pages are high-level pictures of how entity beans are created (insert), and found (select). The scenarios in these pictures will be filled in with a lot more detail as we go through this chapter, but for now you can relax.

Entity bean overview

Scenario: client wants a reference to an **existing** entity

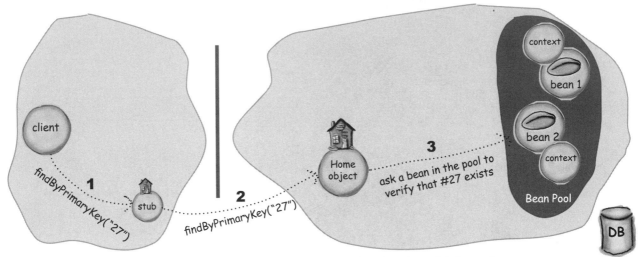

1 After doing a JNDI lookup on the entity bean home and getting a home interface reference, the client calls findByPrimaryKey("27") on the home stub.

2 The findByPrimaryKey("27") method invocation is passed to the home object.

3 The Container asks a bean in the pool to verify that #27 exists in the database.

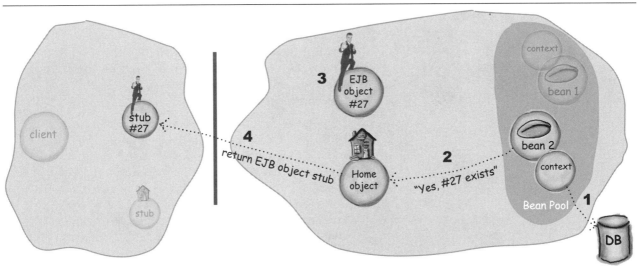

1 The bean checks for an entity in the database with primary key #27

2 The bean tells the home that #27 is in the database

3 The Container makes or finds an EJB object for #27 (there might already be one)

4 The Container returns the stub for #27

Entity bean overview
Scenario: client wants to create a <u>new</u> entity

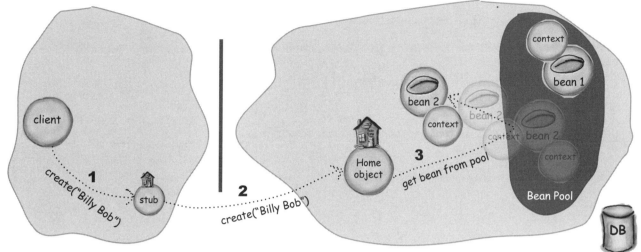

1 After doing a JNDI lookup on the entity bean home and getting a home interface reference, the client calls create("Billy Bob") on the home stub.

2 The create("Billy Bob") method invocation is passed to the home object.

3 The Container pulls a bean from the pool for this bean type (could be any random bean in the pool). Notice that the bean already has its own context that sticks with the bean.

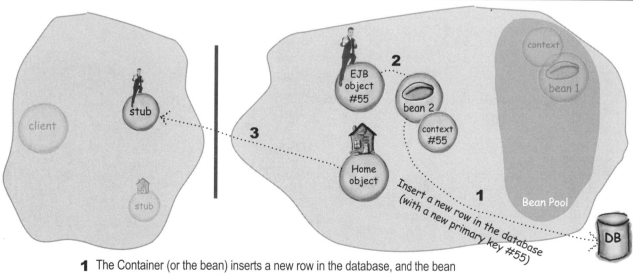

1 The Container (or the bean) inserts a new row in the database, and the bean generates a new primary key.

2 The bean is linked to an EJB object, and both the context and EJB object get the new primary key.

3 The Container returns a stub for the newly-created entity (Billy Bob, #55). If the client's only goal was to insert the new row, the client might not even care about the returned stub.

A very simple Customer entity bean

```
// package and imports here
public class CustomerBean implements EntityBean {
```

implement the EntityBean interface (instead of SessionBean)

```
   private String lastName;
   private String firstName;
   private String primaryKey;
```

The entity bean's state includes the fields that map to columns in the Customer database table, in this case-- first name, last name, and ID (primary key)

```
   private EntityContext context;
```

Your context is even MORE important when you're an entity bean instead of a session bean

```
   public String ejbCreate(String last, String first) {
      lastName = last;
      firstName = first;
      primaryKey = this.getPK();
      // DB INSERT
      return primaryKey;
   }
```

Doesn't this look a lot like a constructor? We take the client's args and assign them to instance variables that represent the entity's persistent state (i.e. columns in the database table). The ejbCreate() returns the primary key -- don't worry about it right now.

```
   public String getLastName() {
      return lastName;
   }
   public void setLastName(String name) {
      lastName = name;
   }
   public String getFirstName() {
      return firstName;
   }
   public void setFirstName(String name) {
      firstName = name;
   }
```

Plain old Java getters and setters for the persistent fields. The magic, as you'll see in a minute, is that the result of these setters will ultimately lead to a database update!

```
   public void ejbActivate() { }
   public void ejbPassivate() { }
   public void ejbRemove() {// DELETE }
```

Three container callbacks from EntityBean, that were also in SessionBean. Except... they have VERY VERY different meanings, as you'll see later in this chapter.

```
   public void setEntityContext(EntityContext ctx) {
      context = ctx;
   }
```

this is just like setSessionContext, except for an EntityContext. But with entity beans, the context is usually WAY more important than it is for session beans.

```
   public void unsetEntityContext() { }
   public void ejbLoad() {// SELECT }
   public void ejbStore() {// UPDATE }
```

these are three NEW container callbacks from the EntityBean interface (not found in SessionBean). They're IMPORTANT!

```
   private String getPK() {
      return ""+ (int) (Math.random() * 42);
   }
```

World's worst primary key algorithm. Normally we'd use client-supplied info or perhaps the database's auto-generated key.

(ignore these last two methods for now)

```
   public String ejbFindPrimaryKey(String pk) {// SELECT, return pk }
   public Collection ejbFindByCity(String city) {// SELECT, return collection of keys }
}
```

An entity bean's client view

Our Customer bean isn't finished, so don't get too attached to it! And in fact, the code is an example of bean-managed persistence (BMP) which we really won't be using in this book. We'll talk a little about BMP, and a *lot* about its much more popular counterpart—*container*-managed persistence (CMP) in this chapter and the next. For now though, we'll focus on the client view of an entity bean, and this simple bean is just to get you started looking at entity bean code.

Given that a Customer bean represents a Customer entity (i.e. a real customer) in the underlying database, what behaviors should the entity bean have? In other words, what kinds of things might the client want to do with either a single Customer or multiple Customers?

Things you'd do with a database record! The things we mentioned earlier including make a new Customer, delete a Customer, update a Customer's fields (columns), and query/search on the Customer database.

Think about the following operations, and figure out which of the two client interfaces (component or home), is better suited for each operation. Keep in mind that the rules for entity bean interfaces might be different from session bean interfaces. If you think both interfaces are appropriate, check them both. (We've done the first one for you.)

home   component

Make a new customer

home   component

Change an existing customer's phone number

home   component

Find all the customers in Pleasantville

home   component

Delete all customers previously declared 'inactive'

home   component

Delete a specific customer

home   component

Get the street address of a specific customer

Entity bean Remote component interface

An entity bean's component interface is just like a session bean's—it has business methods, and it extends javax.ejb.EJBObject. That means a client can see the methods you've declared in your component interface, as well as the methods from EJBObject (getHandle(), remove(), etc.).

But what kinds of business methods go in the component interface?

The methods related to a single entity!

When the client has a reference to an entity bean (which means a reference to the bean's EJB object, of course), the client has a reference to a single, specific entity. Fred Flintstone, #999. Marge Simpson, #728. Roy Rodgers, #1957.

So what might a client want to do with a reference to, say, Marge Simpson? Delete *her*, change *her* last name, get *her* handle, or get *her* home so that the client can get references to other customers. Keep in mind that our simple Customer bean isn't very useful yet, with methods to get or set only the Customer name. Later, we'll build it out.

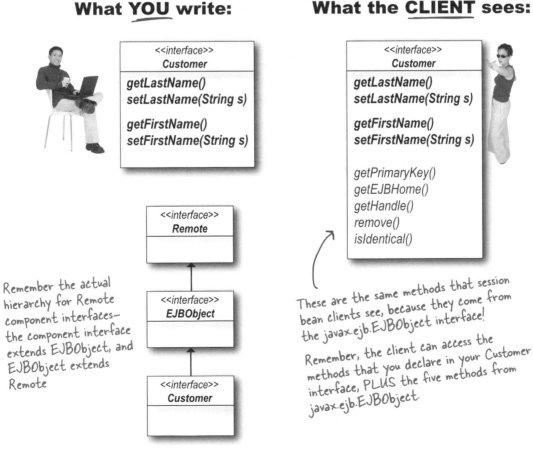

What YOU write:

```
          <<interface>>
            Customer
    ───────────────────────
    getLastName()
    setLastName(String s)

    getFirstName()
    setFirstName(String s)
```

```
          <<interface>>
             Remote
    ───────────────────────

```

```
          <<interface>>
            EJBObject
    ───────────────────────

```

```
          <<interface>>
            Customer
    ───────────────────────

```

Remember the actual hierarchy for Remote component interfaces— the component interface extends EJBObject, and EJBObject extends Remote

What the CLIENT sees:

```
          <<interface>>
            Customer
    ───────────────────────
    getLastName()
    setLastName(String s)

    getFirstName()
    setFirstName(String s)

    getPrimaryKey()
    getEJBHome()
    getHandle()
    remove()
    isIdentical()
```

These are the same methods that session bean clients see, because they come from the javax.ejb.EJBObject interface!

Remember, the client can access the methods that you declare in your Customer interface, PLUS the five methods from javax.ejb.EJBObject.

Entity bean Remote component interface

```
package headfirst;

import javax.ejb.*;
import java.rmi.RemoteException;

public interface Customer extends EJBObject {

    public String getLastName() throws RemoteException;
    public void setLastName(String lastName) throws RemoteException;

    public String getFirstName() throws RemoteException;
    public void setFirstName(String firstName) throws RemoteException;

}
```

Rules for the Remote component interface

(1) Import javax.ejb.* and java.rmi.RemoteException

(2) Extend javax.ejb.EJBObject

(3) Declare one or more business methods, that throw a RemoteException

* Arguments and return types must be RMI-IIOP compatible (Serializable, primitive, Remote, or arrays or collections of any of those)

* You can have overloaded methods

* Each method must declare a RemoteException

* You can declare your own application exceptions, but they must NOT be runtime exceptions (in other words, they must be compiler-checked exceptions—subclasses of Exception but not subclasses of RuntimeException)

* Methods can have arbitrary names, as long as they don't begin with "ejb".

Entity bean Remote <u>home</u> interface

How it's different from a session bean home interface:

(1) You're more likely to *find* an *existing* entity than **create** a *new* one

As a client, you'll probably spend a lot more time using references to *existing* customers, than you'll spend creating *new* customers. Whether you're updating a specific customer or doing a batch operation on many customers, you'll need home interface code that lets you select customers, more than you'll need creation methods. In fact, the create() method is optional for entity beans! (Because you might have a policy that says new entries in the database must be done directly through a database admin tool, for example.) But you're required to put at least one *finder* method *for* an entity bean home—you can have as many finders as you like, but you must have findByPrimaryKey([some object type] primaryKey) in every entity home. (Which means it might be the only method declared in the home interface.)

(2) You might want to do queries that involve more than one entity

Since session beans represent process, it doesn't make sense to, say, get multiple instances of the same process. But with entity beans, you might want to do the same things you'd do on a database table, like find all the customers who live in Helsinki and enjoy surfing.

What <u>YOU</u> write:

```
        <<interface>>
        CustomerHome

create(String last, String first)
findByPrimaryKey(String key)
findByCity(String city)
```

What the <u>CLIENT</u> sees:

```
        <<interface>>
        CustomerHome

create(String last, String first)
findByPrimaryKey(String key)
findByCity(String city)


getEJBMetaData()
getHomeHandle()
remove(Handle h)
remove(Object key)
```

An entity bean client can see the same four methods a session bean client can see, because both session and entity bean home interfaces must extend javax.ejb.EJBHome. Entity beans get to use BOTH home remove() methods, while session beans can use only the one that takes a Handle.

What does the client really want from an entity bean home?

create and findByPrimaryKey give back a single reference to the component interface.

But a multiple-row finder returns a collection of references

<<interface>>
CustomerHome
Customer create(String last, String first)
Customer findByPrimaryKey(String key)
(Collection) findByCity(String city)

With session beans, that was easy—a reference to the component interface. And that's exactly what the create() methods have to give back.

With entity beans, it's the same for create() methods—they must give back a reference to the component interface, in this case the component interface for the entity just created.

But what if you want to find an existing entity bean instead of making a new one? That's what the mandatory findByPrimaryKey() method is for, and it, too, must give back a reference to the component interface for the bean matching that key.

But what if there isn't a matching entity? If there's no entity with that key in the database, the client gets a javax.ejb.Object NotFoundException. So the return type of findByPrimaryKey() is always the same as it is for create(), the component interface for that bean type. (And of course, the rules for session bean client interfaces applies here as well—a Remote home interface must give back the Remote component interface, and the local home interface must give back the local component interface.)

This still leaves us with a method that *cannot* return the component interface: a multiple-entity finder, like our findByCity() method. Well, the client's goal doesn't change with multiple-entity finders; the client still wants a reference to the component interface, only this time it might be a whole *collection* of them. One for every customer entity in the city named in the method's argument.

Note: a client will *not* get an exception if a multi-entity finder can't find any matches! Instead, the client will still get a Collection, but it will simply be empty. A Collection with no elements. Only single-entity finders throw exceptions when nothing matches the find criteria.

The create and finder methods in an entity bean home always give back the bean's component interface.

For create() and findByPrimaryKey(), the client gets a reference to one EJB object.

For multiple-entity finders, the client might get a whole PILE of references to EJB objects—one for each bean that matches the query.

Entity bean Remote home interface

```
package headfirst;

import javax.ejb.*;
import java.rmi.RemoteException;
import java.util.Collection;

public interface CustomerHome extends EJBHome {

    public Customer create(String last, String first) throws CreateException, RemoteException;


    public Customer findByPrimaryKey(String key) throws FinderException, RemoteException;


    public Collection findByCity(String city) throws FinderException, RemoteException;
}
```

When finders have a dark side...

I just thought of a pretty scary scenario... if I want my client to display a list of all my customers, it's just one call to findAll(), but THEN what? Are you telling me I would get back a zillion remote stubs? And then I'd have to make *remote* method calls on each one? That would take FOREVER not to mention all the bandwidth. That doesn't sound good at all...

With a Remote interface, <u>finder</u> and <u>create</u> methods give back Remote stubs.

That means you have to make remote method calls on each one to get the <u>data</u> you want.

Wouldn't it be dreamy if there were a way to have methods in the home that could give back something other than EJB object references? If all I want is the data about the customers, like just a bunch of Strings to display, wouldn't it be great if I could have a method in the home that could give back just the data? But it's probably a fantasy...

there are no Dumb Questions

Q: **Wait... I thought it was bad design to make all those method calls from the client ANYWAY. Wouldn't the client usually go through a session bean? And the session bean would then talk to the entity bean?**

A: Kind of. You're thinking of the Session Facade J2EE design pattern. But even if you do put a session bean in front of an entity bean, *the session bean is still a client*. It might be a lot more efficient, because the session bean might not have as far to go on the network (and might even be on the same server as the entity). But if you're keeping location-independence, then your session bean is still using the entity bean's Remote interfaces, so there's still a lot of overhead.

Q: **Couldn't you just have a business method in the component interface that returns data? Like, return a collection of Strings?**

A: You're getting warmer. Yes, that's the way you might have done it in EJB 1.1. But that's kludgey, because you have to first get a reference to *some* customer, just so you can ask *that* customer to give you back the data for all customers.

Home business methods to the rescue

That's right... business methods aren't just for the component interface, when you're talking about entity beans. As of EJB 2.0, an entity bean home can have methods that—*drum roll*—don't have to return component interfaces! Home business methods can return anything (with the one restriction, of course, that Remote home methods return values that are RMI-IIOP compliant).

Home business methods are great for batch operations, or for query methods where the client doesn't need—or want—EJB object references, but simply wants the entity's data (in other words, the data for one or more of the entity's persistent fields). For example, we might put a home business method in the Customer bean like, getAllCustomerInfo(), that returns a collection of Strings, with whatever pieces of data you've decided make up the customer's info. Better yet, you can send back a collection of CustomerInfo objects, where CustomerInfo is a class that simply holds the data (and getters) for the Customer's persistent state. That way, the client can make local calls to get the data it needs out of the CustomerInfo objects, without having those calls be remote calls on the component interface.

A CustomerInfo class is an example of a Value Object class which is, in a nutshell, just a class with getters (and possibly setters, depending on the design) representing the entity's persistent fields). And it, too, has a dark side—the data starts to become stale the moment after the Value Object is created.

We could tell you now, but then we'd be robbing you of such a valuable opportunity to apply a little neural effort. So for now, why don't *you* think of why sending back CustomerInfo objects, that the client could then interrogate (i.e. call methods on) at its leisure, could have a downside. We'll use Value Objects a lot, but you have to be aware of the tradeoffs when choosing between using a home finder method that returns EJB object references (especially when the references are Remote) vs. a home *business* method that returns Value Objects.

> Home business methods can return something other than EJB object references! They're perfect for queries where the client just wants the entity data, not references to the entities themselves.
>
> They're also great for batch operations, or anything else you might want to do with more than one specific entity, when you don't want to return references to the component interface.

Rules for the Remote home interface

1 Import javax.ejb.* and java.rmi.RemoteException

2 Extend javax.ejb.EJBHome

3 Declare (optionally) one or more create() methods, which MUST return the Remote component interface, and declare both a RemoteException and a CreateException. Each create() method must begin with the prefix "create".

4 Declare the findByPrimaryKey() method, which MUST return the Remote component interface, and declare both a RemoteException and a FinderException

5 Declare (optionally) one or more other finder methods, which MUST return either the Remote component interface (for single-entity finders), or java.util.Collection (for multiple-entity finders). All finders must declare both a RemoteException and a FinderException

6 Declare one or more home business methods

- ✳ Arguments and return types must be RMI-IIOP compatible (Serializable, primitive, Remote, or arrays or collections of any of those)

- ✳ You can have overloaded methods

- ✳ Each method must declare a RemoteException

- ✳ You can declare your own application exceptions, but they must NOT be runtime exceptions (in other words, they must be compiler-checked exceptions—subclasses of Exception but not subclasses of RuntimeException)

- ✳ Methods can have arbitrary names, as long as they don't begin with "create", "find", or "remove".

Sharpen your pencil

For the four database operations (SQL commands) a client might want to do with an entity bean, list the methods in the bean's interface(s) that are related to those database operations. No, you don't have to know SQL, but you definitely have to understand the *implications* of the four database operations, and you must know how they correspond to methods in the bean class.

From the list of the methods in the interfaces, fill in the method or methods that correspond with the database operation.

INSERT:

DELETE:

UPDATE:

SELECT:

<<interface>>
CustomerHome

create(String last, String first)
findByPrimaryKey(String key)
findByCity(String city)

getEJBMetaData()
getHomeHandle()
remove(Handle h)
remove(Object key)

<<interface>>
Customer

getLastName()
setLastName(String s)

getFirstName()
setFirstName(String s)

getPrimaryKey()
getEJBHome()
getHandle()
remove()
isIdentical()

Session bean create() vs. entity bean create()

1 State*ful* session bean create()

- Client calls it to get an EJB object reference to a new just-for-me stateful session bean.

- It can (and frequently does) have arguments, that the bean uses to do client-specific initialization (before running any business methods).

- The Container makes a new session bean when the client calls create()

2 State*less* session bean create()

- Client calls it to get an EJB object reference to a bean

- It has no arguments, and the bean does not do any client-specific initialization (since at the time the bean's ejbCreate() is called, the bean has no association with a client!)

- The Container does *not* make a new session bean when the client calls create(), and does not pull one out of the pool until the client invokes a business method.

3 Entity bean create()

- Client calls it to insert a new row in the database!* Although the end result for the client is still an EJB object reference (in this case, to the newly-created entity).

- It will virtually *always* have arguments (although they aren't mandatory, but it's kinda hard to imagine a create() without them... like, "Hey database, create a new customer... no, I don't have any name or ID or anything... just make some stuff up").

- The Container does *not* make a new entity bean, but it does pull one out of the pool to run the ejbCreate() method. Remember, the ejbCreate() method has to take the create() arguments and somehow create a new entity in the underlying persistent store (or at least support the Container in creating a new entity).

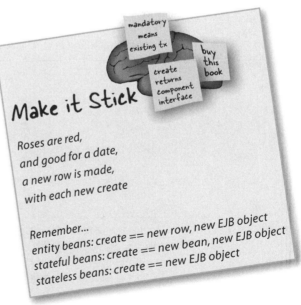

mandatory means existing tx

buy this book

create returns component interface

Make it Stick

Roses are red,
and good for a date,
a new row is made,
with each new create

Remember...
entity beans: create == new row, new EJB object
stateful beans: create == new bean, new EJB object
stateless beans: create == new EJB object

Session bean remove() vs. entity bean remove()

① State*ful* session bean remove()

- Client calls it to tell the Container that he's done with the bean

- Container calls the bean's ejbRemove() (unless the bean is already passivated) and kills the bean (think: food for the garbage collector)

- Client will get an exception if he tries to use the EJB object reference after removing the bean.

② State*less* session bean remove()

- Client calls it to tell the Container that he's done with the bean

- Container gets the call and says, "Like I care? Do you honestly think you're that important? This bean is already back in the pool baby." The Container does *not* call a bean's ejbRemove(). Think about it—*which* bean's ejbRemove() would it call?

- Client will get an exception if he tries to use the EJB object reference after removing the bean.

③ Entity bean remove()

- Client calls it to tell the Container to delete the entity with this primary key.

- Container calls the bean's ejbRemove() method and—if the bean supports client-triggered removal—the entity is deleted from the underlying persistent store. In other words, the row in the database is history. Gone. Poof.

- Client will get an exception if he tries to use the EJB object reference after removing the bean.

- In fact, *NO client will be able to use an EJB object reference to that entity!*

*I hate to do this, really, but I have no choice. #86 MUST be removed from the database.
So if you've got any last words, you better do it in your ejbRemove()...*

remove() on a session bean means the <u>client</u> is done with the bean.

remove() on an entity bean means <u>EVERYONE</u> is done with the bean!

*No, Please, No!
I'll give you whatever you want, just don't call remove()!*

Entity/bean/instance death

So we all know that an entity bean is a representation of some real entity in an underlying persistent store (usually as a row in a database, blah, blah, blah). But there's still some confusion about what distinguishes an *entity* from an entity *bean* from an entity bean *instance*.

Entity

The real thing in the underlying persistent store. The row in the database (although it can be more complex). An entity dies when its *row is deleted* from the underlying store, either through a direct database delete (like, someone using a database admin tool), or because someone calls remove() on the bean's home or component interface.

Entity bean

The component that represents the underlying real entity. But this one's tricky... is it the class? Is it the *interface?* Is it the *instance* of the bean *class?* During development and deployment, the entity *bean* is the whole component (the two interfaces, DD, and bean class). But at *runtime*, it can get a little fuzzy. Sometimes we use "entity bean" to describe the *possibility* of representing a particular entity as a bean. In other words, if there's an entity for Bo Rodgers in the database, then we can say that there is a Bo Rodgers entity *bean*, even if there's no bean instance currently representing that entity! If an *entity* exists for a particular bean type (like Customer Fred Foo), the entity *bean* for that entity is said to exist. An entity bean is said to die when its underlying entity is deleted, as in, "There's no Fred Foo entity bean." **But...** that doesn't mean the *instance on the heap* dies.

Entity bean instance

The instance of the bean class on the heap. *Bean* death is intimately tied to the database, but bean *instance* death (as in, "you're headin' for garbage collection, pal") is tied to the whims of the Container, or a server crash.

Yes, it really is that confusing. You have to know the context to know how the word 'bean' is being used. If it means the *bean-representing-the-entity*, then that *bean* will die when the entity dies, and the EJB object for that entity goes away. But—and here's where it gets weird—the entity bean *instance* doesn't die; it just goes back to the pool. Think of the phrase "entity bean" as more conceptual than physical. In most cases, we won't have to distinguish between the bean and its instance, or the distinction will be so obvious that its not an issue.

A client can kill an <u>entity</u>, by calling remove() on a bean, or deleting the data from the database directly.

But only the Container or a server crash can kill a bean <u>instance</u>.

If we say "entity bean #42 was killed", the underlying entity is gone, and the EJB object for #42 is gone, but the bean instance that had been playing #42 survives.

Well, it's been great playing you, really, but now it's time for you to go to a better place. I'll think about you while I'm floating on one of those little inflatable mattress things.

Darko	Donny	42

bean instance LIVES even if the entity it plays is removed.

entity DIES when a client calls remove()

Client calls remove()

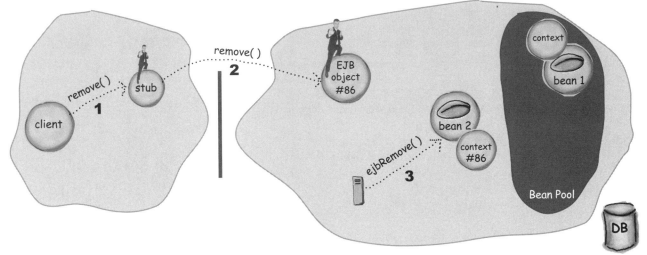

1 Client calls remove() on the EJB object stub for entity #86

2 The remove() method invocation is passed to the EJB object.

3 The Container calls ejbRemove() on the bean.

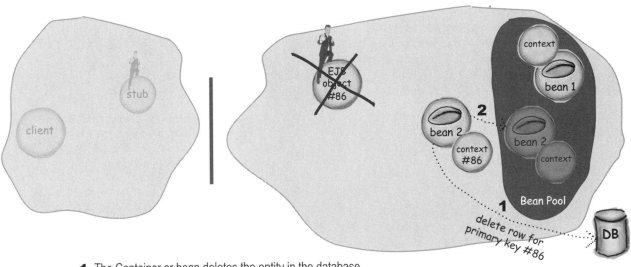

1 The Container or bean deletes the entity in the database.

2 The bean loses its identity (in other words, it is no longer representing entity #86) and moves back to the pool. Meanwhile, the EJB object for #86 is deleted, so the client's stub will throw an exception if the client uses it to invoke a method.

Entity bean client view

BULLET POINTS

- An entity is a real thing that exists outside of EJB, in a persistent store, and an entity *bean* is an OO representation or realization of an entity.

- Clients use entity beans to do database operations, in an OO way. Operations include creating new entities (database inserts), deleting entities (database deletes), updating entity state (database updates), and searching for/on entities (database selects).

- An entity bean Remote component interface extends EJBObject. There's not a separate interface for session beans and entity beans. That means that the client will see all of the methods in your component interface, plus the five additional methods from EJBObject.

- Entity bean component interfaces usually contain getters and setters for field values that correspond to columns in a database table, such as getLastName(), getHomePhone(), setFirstName(), etc.)

- Entity bean component interface methods are usually meant to be run by a specific, uniquely-identifiable entity. For example, calling getLastName() on the entity with primary key #420, returns the last name of the entity in the database with the primary key #420, Dan Doof.

- The rules for how you write an entity bean Remote component interface are the same as the rules for session beans, including: extend EJBObject, declare RemoteExceptions on all methods, use only RMI-IIOP types for arguments and return values, don't begin method names with the prefix "ejb", etc.

- An entity bean home interface is substantially different from that of a session bean, because entity beans are typically found rather than created. In other words, the client is more likely to try to access an existing entity as opposed to making a new entity (which means a new row in the database.)

- In an entity home, a create() method is not required (since create() method in entity beans are for inserting new entities into the database, and you're not required to allow your clients to do that.)

- Entity bean home interfaces can have single-row or multi-row finder methods. Both create and finder methods return the component interface of a bean, although multi-entity finders return a Collection of component interface references.

- Every entity bean home is required to have at least one method—the findByPrimaryKey() method that searches for a particular entity and returns its component interface (i.e. a reference to that entity's EJB object), or throws an exception.

- Multiple-entity finders do not throw an exception if no matching entities are found. They simply return an empty collection.

- Entity home interface can also have home business methods, for operations that apply to more than one entity, as opposed to one specific entity. Batch updates would be a good use for a home business method.

- The real benefit of home business methods is that—unlike create and finder methods—home business methods can return something other than an EJB object reference. If the client wants only data, say, a Collection of Strings representing the name and phone number of each customer, a home business method can do that while a finder can not.

- An entity bean create() is very different from a session bean create(), because an entity bean create() inserts a new entity into the underlying persistent store (i.e. new row in the database).

- An entity bean remove() is dramatically different from a session bean remove()! When a client calls remove() on an entity bean, it's to delete the entity from the database! That means *everybody* is done with the bean.

Mock Exam

---

1 What is true concerning locating an entity bean's home interface?

❏ A. The **narrow()** method should be used for a local home interface.

❏ B. The **narrow()** method should be used for a remote home interface.

❏ C. The **narrow()** method should be used for both local and remote home interfaces.

❏ D. The **narrow()** method should be used for neither local nor remote home interfaces.

---

2 Which capabilities are found in an entity bean's remote component interface? (Choose all that apply.)

❏ A. creating new entity objects

❏ B. finding existing entity objects

❏ C. removing existing entity objects

❏ D. executing a home business method

❏ E. retrieving the EJBMetaData interface

---

3 Which are ways in which a client can get a reference to an existing entity object's local component interface? (Choose all that apply.)

❏ A. Call **ejbCreate()**

❏ B. Call **getSessionContext()**

❏ C. Obtain the reference from the handle.

❏ D. Receive the reference as a parameter in a method call.

❏ E. Use a finder method defined in the local home interface.

4 How many create methods can be defined in an entity bean's local home interface?

❏ A. 0

❏ B. Only 1

❏ C. 0 to 1

❏ D. 0 to many

❏ E. 1 to many

5 Which are ways in which a client can get a reference to an existing entity object's remote component interface? (Choose all that apply.)

❏ A. Call **ejbCreate()**.

❏ B. Obtain the reference from the handle.

❏ C. Call a method on the entity object's primary key.

❏ D. Receive the reference as a parameter in a method call.

❏ E. Use a finder method defined in the remote home interface.

6 Which approach(es) can be used on a primary key class to determine if two keys refer to the same entity? (Choose all that apply.)

❏ A. Using the == operator.

❏ B. Using the **equals()** method.

❏ C. Using the **isIdentical()** method.

❏ D. none of the above.

7 Which approach(es) can determine whether two entity EJB object references refer to the same entity object? (Choose all that apply.)

❏ A. Using the == operator.

❏ B. Using the **equals()** method.

❏ C. Using the **isIdentical()** method.

❏ D. none of the above.

8 What's true about the client's view of an entity bean's remote component interface? (Choose all that apply.)

❏ A. Multiple clients can access the same entity object concurrently.

❏ B. New entity beans can be created using a method in this interface.

❏ C. Entity beans may not survive a crash of the container.

❏ D. Business methods cannot return a reference to the entity object.

9 How many finder methods can be declared within an entity bean's local home interface?

❏ A. 0

❏ B. Only 1

❏ C. 0 to 1

❏ D. 0 to many

❏ E. 1 to many

10 Which is a legal declaration for a local home interface's create() method? (Choose all that apply.)

❏ A. `public Cust create(int x);`

❏ B. `public void create(int x) throws CreateException;`

❏ C. `public Cust create(int x) throws CreateException;`

❏ D. `public Cust create(int x) throws CreateException, RemoteException;`

11 Which is a legal name for an entity bean home business method? (Choose all that apply.)

❏ A. create

❏ B. createCust

❏ C. removeAll

❏ D. findCust

❏ E. selectCust

COFFEE CRAM
Mock Exam Answers

---

1 What is true concerning locating an entity bean's home interface?

(spec: 110)

❑ A. The **narrow()** method should be used for a local home interface.

☑ B. The **narrow()** method should be used for a remote home interface.

❑ C. The **narrow()** method should be used for both local and remote home interfaces.

❑ D. The **narrow()** method should be used for neither local nor remote home interfaces.

---

2 Which capabilities are found in an entity bean's remote component interface? (Choose all that apply.)

❑ A. creating new entity objects — *home methods*

❑ B. finding existing entity objects

☑ C. removing existing entity objects

❑ D. executing a home business method — *home methods*

❑ E. retrieving the EJBMetaData interface

---

3 Which are ways in which a client can get a reference to an existing entity object's local component interface? (Choose all that apply.)

(spec: 119)

❑ A. Call **ejbCreate()** — *we said existing* :)

❑ B. Call **getSessionContext()**

❑ C. Obtain the reference from the handle. — *handles are for Remote interfaces*

☑ D. Receive the reference as a parameter in a method call.

☑ E. Use a finder method defined in the local home interface.

4 How many create methods can be defined in an entity bean's local home interface? *(spec: 115)*

❏ A. 0

❏ B. Only 1   — You don't have to allow clients to create new entities

❏ C. 0 to 1

☑ D. 0 to many

❏ E. 1 to many

5 Which are ways in which a client can get a reference to an existing entity object's remote component interface? (Choose all that apply.) *(spec: 119)*

❏ A. Call `ejbCreate()`. — we said EXISTING

☑ B. Obtain the reference from the handle.

❏ C. Call a method on the entity object's primary key.

☑ D. Receive the reference as a parameter in a method call.

☑ E. Use a finder method defined in the remote home interface.

6 Which approach(es) can be used on a primary key class to determine if two keys refer to the same entity? (Choose all that apply.) *(spec: 120–121)*

❏ A. Using the == operator.

☑ B. Using the `equals()` method.   — if two keys pass the equals() test, they're the same key! Which means the same entity. (This assumes that both are from the same home.)

❏ C. Using the `isIdentical()` method. — isIdentical() is for comparing component interface references

❏ D. none of the above.

7 Which approach(es) can determine whether two entity EJB object references refer to the same entity object? (Choose all that apply.) *(spec: 120–121)*

❏ A. Using the == operator.

❏ B. Using the `equals()` method.   — equals() is for comparing entity's primary keys

☑ C. Using the `isIdentical()` method.

❏ D. none of the above.

8 What's true about the client's view of an entity bean's remote component interface? (Choose all that apply.)   (spec: 108)

☑ A. Multiple clients can access the same entity object concurrently.

❏ B. New entity beans can be created using a method in this interface.

❏ C. Entity beans may not survive a crash of the container.

❏ D. Business methods cannot return a reference to the entity object.

9 How many finder methods can be declared within an entity bean's local home interface?   (spec: 116)

❏ A. 0

❏ B. Only 1

❏ C. 0 to 1

❏ D. 0 to many

☑ E. 1 to many   — findByPrimaryKey() is required

10 Which is a legal declaration for a local home interface's create() method? (Choose all that apply.)   (spec: 115)

❏ A. `public Cust create(int x);` — needs CreateException

❏ B. `public void create(int x) throws CreateException;` — can't return void, must return component interface

☑ C. `public Cust create(int x) throws CreateException;`

❏ D. `public Cust create(int x) throws CreateException, RemoteException;` — local interface can't throw RemoteException

11 Which is a legal name for an entity bean home business method? (Choose all that apply.)   (spec: 114)

❏ A. create

❏ B. createCust

❏ C. removeAll

❏ D. findCust

☑ E. selectCust

"find" "create" & "remove" are reserved prefixes

6 bean/entity synchronization

Being an Entity Bean

As an entity bean, I lead the glamorous life of an actress. I spend most of my time in the pool, but even when I *do* work, I'm never bored. I always get to play different roles... yesterday I was Jeanne Rose, today I'm Marilyn Malone, and tonight I'll be playing the part of Doug Adams...

Entity beans are actors. As long as they're alive, they're either in the pool or they're *being* somebody. Somebody from the underlying persistent store. In other words, an entity from the database. When a bean is playing a part, the bean and the underlying entity have to stay in sync. Imagine the horror if the bean is pretending to be, say, Audrey Leone, and someone lowers Audrey's credit limit in the database... but forgets to tell the bean. The bean, acting as Audrey, is happily authorizing purchases for more than Audrey's current limit. Or what if a client uses the bean to modify Audrey's address, but the bean hangs on to the new info without telling the database... yikes!

Entity Bean Lifecycle

Official:

6.1 Identify correct and incorrect statements or examples about the Bean Provider's view and programming contract for CMP, including the requirements for a CMP entity bean.

6.6 Identify the interface(s) and methods a CMP entity bean must and must not implement.

7.1 Identify correct and incorrect statements or examples about the lifecycle of a CMP entity bean.

7.2 From a list, identify the purpose, behavior, and responsibilities of the Bean Provider for a CMP entity bean, including but not limited to: setEntityContext(), unsetEntityContext(), ejbCreate(), ejb-PostCreate(), ejbActivate(), ejbPassivate(), ejbRemove(), ejbLoad(), ejbStore(), ejb-Find(), ejbHome(), and ejbSelect().

7.3 From a list, identify the purpose, behavior, and responsibilities of the Container for a CMP entity bean, including but not limited to: setEntityContext(), unsetEntityContext(), ejbCreate(), ejbPostCreate(), ejbActivate(), ejbPassivate(), ejbRemove(), ejbLoad(), ejbStore(), ejbFind(), ejbHome(), and ejb-Select().

What it really means:

This objective can hit you on almost *anything* related to entity beans, so you pretty much have to know it all, including the details of a CMP entity bean lifecycle, the container callback methods of javax.ejbEntityBean, what you must write in a bean class, and what a bean can get from its EJBContext.

You have to know that passivation in entity beans is different from session bean passivation, because entity beans go back to a pool after ejbPassivate(), but stay as heal-living objects. You must know that entity bean creation is also completely different for entity beans, and that a create() call on an entity bean means "insert a new entity into the underlying persistent store." You have to know that remove() on an entity bean is more drastic for entity beans than session beans—an entity bean remove deletes the entity from the database!

You must be able to look at an entity bean method and know the circumstances under which that method is called, and what you should do in that method. For example, you need to know that in a bean's ejbCreate() method, the bean cannot get a reference to its EJB object, but that it *can* get that reference in ejbPostCreate().

You need to know which methods you're required to write into your bean, and which are left to the Container. For example, you need to know that the Bean Provider must write abstract getters and setters for persistent fields, but must define finder methods only in the home interface, not the bean class.

Entity Bean Lifecycle

Official:	*What it really means:*
8.1 From a list of behaviors, match them with the appropriate EntityContext method responsible for that behavior	You have to know the methods of EntityContext, as well as the circumstances under which you can call those methods. For example, you should know that if you're running in the setEntityContext() method, you can use your special JNDI namespace to look up a reference to a DataSource, but that you're not allowed to access the underlying database from that method (there's no meaningful transaction, so the Container won't let you do it.)
8.2 Identify correct and incorrect statements about an entity bean's primary key and object identity.	You should know that you can't call getUserTransaction() on your context, because entity beans must use container-managed transactions, and getUserTransaction is for bean-managed transactions only.
	You have to know that an entity bean must have a unique identity (no two beans can have the same primary key), and that a CMP bean's primary key must be either one of the bean's persistent fields, or a custom primary key class, whose fields are all from container-managed fields defined in the bean. You must know that the primary key class type must be Serializable, and that it must have a valid override of equals() and hashcode().

The real power of entity beans is synchronization

The bean and the underlying row in the database must stay in sync! Remember, the bean is not the entity—the bean is a *representation* of the real entity. The bean is an OO way of working with the data, but the entity in the database is the only true entity. If the entity in the database dies (i.e. is deleted), the bean for that specific entity dies too (although the bean *instance* still lives, as you saw in the last chapter).

The Container's job is make sure that the entity and the bean stay in sync, so that nobody's looking at a stale bean or a stale row in the database. Keep in mind that the entity *bean* may not be the only way to get into the database! In fact, in most cases the Bean Provider (you) will have no way to know for certain, during development, if your bean is the only way anyone will ever be able to get to the entity data.

For example, your Customer database might be used by a bunch of apps in your company, including some that work directly with the database and some that go through the Customer bean in an EJB application.

If a client has a reference to a bean, the client might change the bean's state by, say, calling a setter method. If that setter method corresponds to one of the bean's persistent fields (in other words, a column in the table like *address*), the bean and the database will be temporarily out of sync. The database won't have the current address until the bean updates the database!

Now think what a disaster it would be if the bean caches the new data for the entity, *without telling the database.* If someone comes along with another application and asks for that Customer's address from the database, That Would Be Bad.

And the opposite scenario is bad as well: if someone updates the database, ***the bean needs to know!*** Otherwise, the bean is out there in the EJB app, representing the entity in the database, but the bean isn't a true reflection of the entity's state. In other words, the bean is *stale.* Which means, perhaps, *useless.*

The Container always knows when the bean and the database (the underlying entity) must be synchronized, so that neither one has 'stale' data.

OK, I have the bean for Chris Martin, and now I want to change his address to 72 Clock Street. So, I'll call setAddress() on the bean...

Cool. I've updated my bean state with the new address.

(bean currently playing #72)

HELLO! Excuse me... I'm glad you're all having a nice chat about it, but don't you think the database might like to know about that address change??!!

??

DB

Oh no!

The entity *bean* and the *entity* it represents have different data!

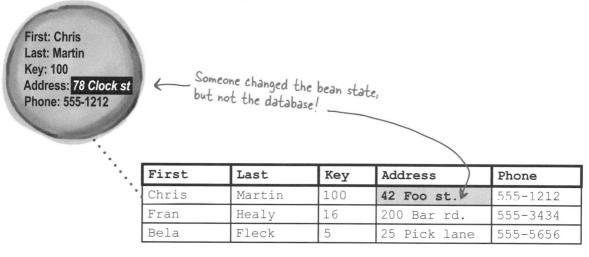

First: Chris
Last: Martin
Key: 100
Address: **78 Clock st**
Phone: 555-1212

Someone changed the bean state, but not the database!

First	Last	Key	Address	Phone
Chris	Martin	100	**42 Foo st.**	555-1212
Fran	Healy	16	200 Bar rd.	555-3434
Bela	Fleck	5	25 Pick lane	555-5656

The Container's most important entity bean job is to make sure that this scenario—where the bean and the database are out of sync—doesn't cause any damage.

The Container has to make sure that:

- While somebody is working with the bean (and potentially changing its state), nobody can work with the real entity in the database.

- Once an entity bean's state has been updated, the database has to be updated, before anyone else can access that record in the database.

- Before the bean can run any business methods on a particular entity's behalf, the bean has to be refreshed with the entity's state. In other words, before the entity bean for Joe Bloggs #88 can run a getCreditLimit() method, the Container has to load the entity bean up with the most current data for Joe Bloggs. Otherwise, the bean might return the wrong credit limit—the limit that was in place the last time the bean was loaded up with Joe's data from the database.

Uh-oh. Now you've got me even MORE worried. Doesn't this mean, then, that the bean can get stale in between EVERY business method call? Are you telling me you have to make a trip to the database to refresh the bean's data with the actual database data, just in case it changed, every time the client calls a method on the bean? If THAT's true, you might as well just go straight to the database!

No! That's not what I'm saying, but I can see how it might look like that. The missing piece here is the transaction! As long as the bean's methods are being called as part of a single transaction, the bean doesn't have to synchronize its state with data in the database.

See, when the client calls a business method, and that method starts a transaction, I tell the database to lock the entity! (For now, you can think of it as locking the row, although it might actually be something a little different). With the real entity locked, the bean can't become stale, because nobody can get into the entity through the database. I won't tell the database to release the lock until the transaction is over, so the bean is safe.

How the entity bean and the underlying entity stay synchronized

(1) Client calls a business method.

(2) Container intercepts the call and starts a transaction, BEFORE getting the bean.

(3) Container tells the database to lock the row (to anyone else but the Container).

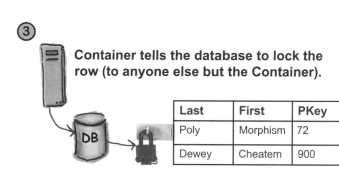

Last	First	PKey
Poly	Morphism	72
Dewey	Cheatem	900

(4) Container loads the bean with the entity state from the database. Now nobody can except the bean can change the entity data.

(5) Bean runs multiple business methods in the same transaction, knowing that the underlying entity data in the database can't be changed (because the row for this entity is locked).

(6) Container ends the transaction, but first it updates the database with whatever new state the bean might have been caching on behalf of that entity (like, if someone called setAddress() on the bean).

(7) Container tells the database to release the lock on the entity row.

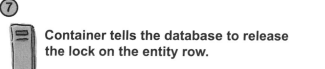

Last	First	PKey
Poly	Morphism	72
Dewey	Cheatem	900

The only question is WHO does the work when it's time to synchronize

The Container always knows *when* the bean and the database entity must be synchronized. It knows based on transactions. If a client calls a method on a bean, and that method starts a new transaction for the bean, the Container knows that the underlying entity in the database may have changed since the last time this bean was loaded up with this entity's data. So the Container forces the bean to refresh its state by loading in the entity's data.

And of course the reverse is true. If the bean completes a method, and this method was the end of the transaction, the Container will tell the database to release the lock on this entity in the database. *But*... during the time when the row was locked, the bean might have been happily caching data that represents the newly-changed state of the entity (like a new address or phone number). In other words, the client might have been calling setter methods on the bean, with the intention of causing an update in the real database. The client wants to update a record. So, the Container knows it must force the bean to update the data in the database with the bean's state, before the Container tells the database to release the lock on that entity.

OK, so the *when* is not the issue. And that's important, because otherwise you, the Bean Provider, would have to work out the business logic to know exactly when there was a danger that the bean and entity are out of sync. And you can just imagine how quickly you could corrupt the state of your database...

The real issue is *who* does the database access? And there are only two choices: it's either *you* or *the Container*.

If you write the database access code, you write JDBC statements in the callback methods the Container calls when its time to kick you and say, "Hey – time to go to the database!" On the other hand, if the Container writes the database code, you save yourself a lot of coding time and effort, and you'll almost always get better performance.

Container-Managed Persistence (CMP) means the Container takes care of all the database access code for synchronization, including adding and deleting entities (records / rows in the database).

Bean-Managed Persistence (BMP) means YOU write the database access code (the JDBC statements), for when the Container tells you its time to go to the database.

In EJB 2.0, you should use <u>CMP</u>. It saves you a lot of work, and virtually always gives you better performance.

Container-managed vs. bean-managed persistence

Container-managed persistence (CMP)

- Wimpy in EJB 1.1; greatly enhanced in EJB 2.0.

- The Bean Provider designs the entity bean class, choosing which of the bean's fields are part of the bean's persistent state. Persistent fields map to columns in one or more database tables.

- The Container keeps track of changes to the bean's state and updates the real entity as needed. For example, if a client calls setLastName() on the bean, the Container knows that the real entity in the database has to be updated, so that if anyone else accesses the database for that entity (including non-EJB clients using some other means to get to the database), they'll see the current state of the entity. The Container makes the decisions on how to keep the bean and the real entity synchronized based on the state of transactions. (More on that later).

- The Bean Provider writes EJB-QL to tell the Container how to do selects. EJB-QL is like a subset of SQL, but with some OO features. EJB-QL helps bridge the OO world of your bean to the relational world of your real entity.

- Using information in the deployment descriptor, the Container writes the actual implementation of the CMP bean, including implementing the finder and select methods, and *all* of the database access code. In other words, if you're a Bean Provider writing a CMP bean, you do *not* look up a resource connection factory for the DataSource, get an SQL Connection, or write any JDBC code. Not only is the data access code taken care of by the Container, but you can trust that the Container knows exactly when to go to the database.

The Container goes to the database when it needs to insert a new entity, delete and entity, update the database with new entity state (i.e. one or more columns in the entity row have changed, through the bean).

Bean-managed persistence (BMP)

- Bean Provider writes the database access code, including looking up a DataSource, getting a Connection, and sending JDBC statements to the database. It's still better than if you didn't use entity beans at all, because the Container will at least tell a BMP bean when to go to the database, so with BMP, you don't have to put in logic to keep the bean and the database in sync. When the Container tells you to update the database, you just do it.

The Container invokes a container callback on the bean when the bean needs to do something with the database, and the bean code does the actual JDBC work.

there are no
Dumb Questions

Q: Doesn't the Container still have to give you the database Connection? Isn't that the whole point of looking up a DataSource using resource factory references? If that's true, then how can you do bean-managed persistence? Or is BMP a way to bypass all that, in which case you'd be bypassing the Container services for connection pooling and...

A: Relax. Really. With BMP you still get your database connection from the Container, by looking up, as you said, a resource factory reference, javax.sql.DataSource. (Gee, you must have been reading ahead to the chapter on the EJB environment). Because you're right, you need to get a connection from a connection pool managed by the Container. But once you get the connection, for a BMP bean, you're on your own for sending it statements to do INSERT, DELETE, UPDATE, SELECT operations.

And while we're here, remember that database access is not just for entity beans. ANY bean can go to the database as part of its business logic. Session beans and message-driven beans might find plenty of reasons to look something up or store something in a database. The difference between entity beans and the other two bean types is that entity beans exist only because there's something in a database. Something the bean represents. So entity beans are, by definition, tied to something in a persistent store.

Message-driven and session beans do not represent something in a database, although they may need to *use* something in a database as part of their business logic.

Q: It seems like performance would be better—not worse—with BMP. Doesn't BMP give you more control?

A: You have more *flexibility* with BMP, but *not* necessarily more control. And according to nearly all benchmarks against the major J2EE servers, *not* better performance. That might sound counterintuitive, but remember that the Container can do things that you can't do from within bean code. Things like ganging multiple calls to the database, using native code to get in an out of the database faster than you could, lazy loading, dirty detection (neither of which are guaranteed by the spec, of course), and dozens of other tricks.

We know it goes against the conventional wisdom that says if you want it done right, do it yourself, but keep in mind that the server vendors are competing for your business. They know performance matters to you. The 2.0 spec added—and changed—a lot of the CMP specification for the sole purpose of giving the vendors more room for optimizing CMP.

Off the path

A brief history on the evolution of CMP 2.0

Beginning with version 1.1 of the EJB spec, you could use both container-managed persistence (CMP) and bean-managed persistence (BMP). At the highest level, the difference between CMP and BMP is about who writes the database access code.

With EJB 2.0, you can still use both, but there's now very little reason to ever use BMP. The original EJB 1.1 specification for CMP entity beans was, um, weak. Clunky. Inefficient. Limited. Not That Good. And although many vendors were able to overcome many of the problems with CMP 1.1, the solutions were outside the specification, so your choice as bean developer was to use standard CMP but keep your portability, or step outside the spec (reducing your portability), but get better performance and features.

When the EJB 2.0 spec was created, the team spent a great deal of time and effort talking to both end-user customers (bean developers) and container vendors, all of whom were very happy to describe the problems with CMP. In graphic detail, complete with suggestions for Sun on, "I'll tell you what you can DO with your CMP bean spec..."

The EJB spec team listened. And designed. And listened. And designed. And in the end, they came up with something awful. A solution that was an equal-opportunity pisser-offer. Vendors hated it. Developers hated it. People like us who had to explain the new technology to customers really hated it. So with the deadline upon them, the team scrapped much of what they'd done with CMP and came up with a much cleaner solution.

With the new EJB 2.0 spec, CMP is lightyears ahead of where it was in EJB 1.1 (or in the first, terrible version of the pre-release EJB 2.0 spec). And now, most developers using entity beans will use CMP. In fact, the exam doesn't cover BMP at all, since it's there more for legacy support or very special cases more than anything else.

Because of the heavy shift to CMP (for reasons we'll explore), we won't cover BMP in this book. So from this point forward, we're going to assume that we're talking about CMP. The differences between the lifecycle, and the developer's responsibility, for CMP vs. BMP are dramatic, so don't forget that everything we talk about now will be from the perspective of a CMP bean, even if we don't explicitly say that we're referring to CMP.

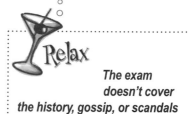

Relax

The exam doesn't cover the history, gossip, or scandals of the EJB specification.

Although it would have made the book much spicier if it did. Ah well... we'll just have to make do with the technical content.

Still, we think the way a spec (any spec), evolves is interesting. Sun works hard to walk the fine line between having a meaningful spec with strong guarantees for the programmer, and one that's vague enough on implementation details to let the vendors compete on the performance of their implementations.

Regardless, there's nothing on the exam about the different versions of the spec. As long as you know what's in the 2.0 spec, you're safe. However, in the real world you're likely to come across EJB 1.1 applications, so be prepared to learn the differences. Especially if you're the lucky one in charge of migrating the app to a 2.0-compliant server ;)

How a bean *actor* becomes a bean *entity*

Scenario: client wants to get the address of a
specific CMP Customer entity, primary key #28.

1 Client calls getAddress() on the stub for entity bean #28. The client got the stub from a
previous call on the home stub (you'll see exactly how the client got the stub in the first
place, in a minute).

2 The call is passed to the EJB object.

3 The EJB object gets the call and panics, because there IS no entity bean for #28!
The EJB object is the agent/bodyguard for #28, but he isn't attached to a specific
bean that's playing #28.

How a bean *actor* becomes a bean *entity*

The CMP bean comes out of the pool and prepares to play #28.

1 The Container 'activates' a bean by pulling it out of the pool and calling ejbActivate().

2 The Container does a select on primary key #28 in the database, to get the real entity data to put into the bean (the data that will become the bean's state).

3 The Container loads the bean with the entity data from the database, and then calls ejbLoad() to tell the bean, "Hey bean, you've just been loaded."

OK, time out!

Does that picture say that ejbPassivate() is the bean's container callback for going back to the pool? Isn't that the **opposite** of how session beans work? With session beans, ejbActivate() has nothing to do with the pool, so what's the deal? Are they just trying to make it as confusing as possible???

Passivation and Activation have a TOTALLY different meaning for entity beans!

State*less* session beans go back to the pool without passivation (in other words, without getting an ejbPassivate() call).

State*ful* session beans are passivated when the Container puts them to sleep (possibly serialization) to conserve resources between client method invocations.

Entity beans aren't passivated in the way that stateful session beans are, but entity beans DO get an ejbPassivate() call when they're about to go back to the pool (and an ejbActivate() when they come out of the pool).

The most important point is that, unlike session beans, *passivated entity beans are still live objects on the heap!*

There's no such thing as a bean sleeping in a pool. Stateless beans, entity beans, and message-driven beans all use pools. And those pools are for living, RAM-using, on-the-heap objects.

Only state*ful* beans are put to sleep (called, confusingly, *passivation)*, but this has nothing to do with a pool.

So, yes, they've overloaded the word "passivation" just to make things really confusing for you and to help drive the need for more EJB books. (For which we thank them every single day.)

ejbPassivate(): the difference between session and entity beans

Entity bean	**State*ful* session bean**	**State*less* session bean**

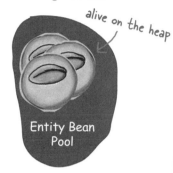

alive on the heap

Entity Bean Pool

ZZZZZZ

↑ NOT alive on the heap... possibly serialized

doesn't apply... stateless beans are never passivated

Entity bean

✳ Called when the bean has finished a business method (other than remove()) and is about to go back to the pool. In the passivated state, the bean has no identity—it's not representing any entity from the database!

✳ Use it to release resources that you don't want to waste while the bean is sitting in the pool, not running a business method. (Typically, the method is empty.)

✳ The bean is NOT passivated in the session bean sense. In other words, the bean is not serialized or saved, so there is NO requirement that you null out references to non-Serializable objects.

✳ The Container calls the bean's ejbActivate() method when a bean is needed to service a business method from a client. The bean runs ejbActivate() *before* it runs the business method that triggered the activation. (This method is usually empty as well).

Stateful session bean

✳ Called when the Container decides to conserve resources between business method invocations from the client.

✳ Use it to release resources and to prepare the bean's state for what *might* be serialization (null out non-Serializable references, etc).

✳ The bean is "put to sleep" and is no longer taking up space on the heap.

✳ The Container calls the bean's ejbActivate() method when a client calls a business method on the EJB object. The bean runs ejbActivate() *before* it runs the business method that triggered the activation.

Stateless session bean

✳ Doesn't apply! Stateless beans have a pool, but activation and passivation don't play any part in it. Remember, stateless session beans will NEVER get an ejbActivate() or ejbPassivate() call.

The EntityBean interface adds three new container callbacks (including two just for synchronization)

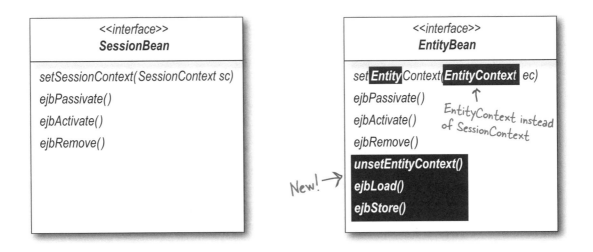

The EntityBean interface adds three new methods (and the context setter changes to give the bean an EntityContext instead of a SessionContext). But... and this is an extremely large "but"... even the methods which are the same in both interfaces don't behave the same.

Of the four methods in SessionBean, only the context setter behaves the same as its counterpart in EntityBean. The other three, ejbPassivate(), ejbActivate(), and ejbRemove() have drastically different meanings.

You'll see.

For now, just be ready to let go of your attachments to the meaning of activation, passivation, and removal. What those mean to an entity bean is nothing like what they mean to a session bean.

Even the methods that <u>are</u> the same, don't <u>behave</u> the same

SessionBean interface

setSessionContext(SessionContext sc)

Container gives the bean a reference to its context.

ejbPassivate()

Called on a stateful session bean, when the bean is about to be serialized (or something like it).

ejbActivate()

Called on a stateful session bean, when the bean is reactivated following passivation (might be deserialization).

ejbRemove()

Called on a stateful bean when the client calls remove(). Called on a stateless bean when the Container wants to reduce the size of the pool.

Of the four methods that are in both SessionBean and EntityBean, only the context setter method behaves the same way! In an entity bean, activate, passivate, and remove are completely different from a session bean

EntityBean interface

setEntityContext(EntityContext ec)

Container gives the bean a reference to its context.

ejbPassivate()

Called when the bean is about to return to the pool, following a transaction.

ejbActivate()

Called when the bean is taken out of the pool to service a client's business method call.

ejbRemove()

Called when the client calls remove(), and wants to delete this entity from the database!

unsetEntityContext()

Called when the Container wants to reduce the size of the pool.

ejbLoad()

Called when the bean has been refreshed with data from the underlying persistent store.

ejbStore()

Called when the Container is about to update the database to reflect the state of the bean.

EntityContext adds getPrimaryKey()

Both SessionContext and EntityContext extend EJBContext. EntityContext has only one method that SessionContext doesn't have—getPrimaryKey(). This is tricky, because there's a getPrimaryKey() in both the EJBObject and EJBLocalObject interfaces, that's exposed to BOTH session and entity bean clients (although a session bean client will get an exception for calling it). But the context version of getPrimaryKey() is exposed only to entity beans.

But wait... there's more! Entity beans have new home container callbacks, too

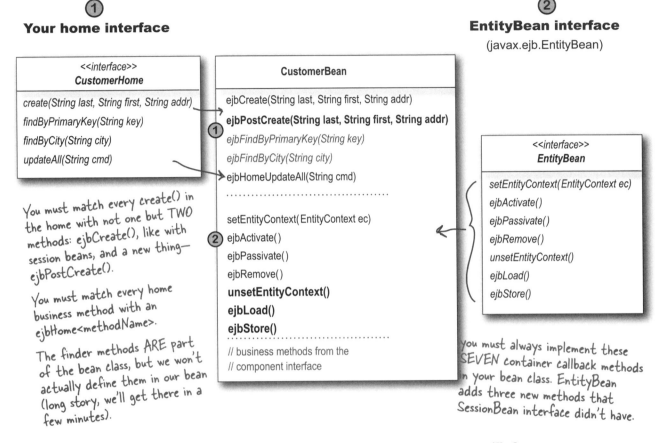

① Your home interface

② EntityBean interface
(javax.ejb.EntityBean)

<<interface>>
CustomerHome

create(String last, String first, String addr)
findByPrimaryKey(String key)
findByCity(String city)
updateAll(String cmd)

CustomerBean

ejbCreate(String last, String first, String addr)
ejbPostCreate(String last, String first, String addr)
ejbFindByPrimaryKey(String key)
ejbFindByCity(String city)
ejbHomeUpdateAll(String cmd)
....
setEntityContext(EntityContext ec)
ejbActivate()
ejbPassivate()
ejbRemove()
unsetEntityContext()
ejbLoad()
ejbStore()
....
// business methods from the
// component interface

<<interface>>
EntityBean

setEntityContext(EntityContext ec)
ejbActivate()
ejbPassivate()
ejbRemove()
unsetEntityContext()
ejbLoad()
ejbStore()

You must match every create() in the home with not one but TWO methods: ejbCreate(), like with session beans, and a new thing— ejbPostCreate().

You must match every home business method with an ejbHome<methodName>.

The finder methods ARE part of the bean class, but we won't actually define them in our bean (long story, we'll get there in a few minutes).

you must always implement these SEVEN container callback methods in your bean class. EntityBean adds three new methods that SessionBean interface didn't have.

For any entity bean using container-managed persistence (CMP), you will always have at least seven container callbacks—all from the EntityBean interface implementation. You don't have to have a create() method in your home, but if you *do* have create() methods, you must match each create() with not one but *two* methods: ejbCreate() and ejb*Post*Create(). If you have home business methods, you must write a matching ejbHome<methodName> method in the bean class.

If you use bean-managed persistence (BMP), where you write your own database access code, you also must match each finder method with an ejbFind<whatever> method. Remember, the only method required in a home interface is findByPrimaryKey(). But in a CMP bean, you won't put any finders in your bean class even though they're in your home interface.

Writing a CMP entity bean: make it abstract

> YES! I love CMP. The Container implements my finders, my getters, my setters, my select methods...and it writes all the database access code for the create, remove, load and store methods... just think how many flash mobs I can attend now that I don't have to write all this bean code...

> Oh sure, you get to go have fun while *I* do all the real work. How come with each rev of the EJB spec, *I* end up doing more work and you end up doing less? That blows. Will you at least take some pictures of the flash mob next week at Barnes and Noble? At exactly 4:20 PM everyone shows up. At 4:24 everyone runs in and starts breathing hard and crouching behind bookshelves, like they're being chased by bad guys. At 4:29, they all run to the computer section, grab the nearest Head First book and shout, "I got it!", then they disperse. By 4:31 - everyone is gone.

Make your CMP entity bean class abstract.

You still have to implement the container callbacks from javax.ejb.EntityBean, and if you still have to write all your business methods (including those from the home), and if you have any create methods, you have to match those in the bean class as well. But that still leaves a pile of work for the Container to do, including the accessor methods for your persistent fields. For example, if your Customer table has a column for address, and you map that to a field in your bean class (so that clients can, for instance, call getAddress()), you don't write the getters and setters for that field. In fact, ***you don't even declare the field!*** With CMP, you create a virtual field, by defining getters and setters. In other words, the *persistent field* for address exists in your bean *simply because there's an abstract getter and setter for it.* (Well... that's not *entirely* true. There also has to be an entry in the deployment descriptor, but we'll look at *that* in the next chapter).

You put *three* kinds of things in your bean class:

(1) Things from the *home interface*

- For each create() method in the home, you must have a matching ejbCreate() and ejbPostCreate() method in the bean class.

- For each business method in the home, you must have a matching ejbHome<method> in the bean class.

- For CMP beans, you will NOT write matching finder methods. The Container will write them for you, based on info you put in the deployment descriptor. (We'll go over all that in the next chapter.)

<<interface>> **CustomerHome**
create(String last, String first, String address)
findByPrimaryKey(String key)
findByCity(String city)
updateAll(String cmd)

(2) Things from the *component interface*

- For each method in the component interface, you must have a matching concrete implementation in the bean class.

<<interface>> **Customer**
getFirstName()
setFirstName(String name)
getLastName()
setLastName(String name)
getAddress()
setAddress(String addr)

(3) Things from the *EntityBean interface*

- You must implement the EntityBean interface either directly or indirectly. So unless you have a superclass that implemented the methods, you're responsible for writing concrete implementations in your bean class.

<<interface>> **EntityBean**
setEntityContext(EntityContext ec)
ejbActivate()
ejbPassivate()
ejbRemove()
unsetEntityContext()
ejbLoad()
ejbStore()

PLUS... (ok, that's _four_ things...)

④ **Virtual persistent fields**

- For each persistent field, provide an abstract getter and setter

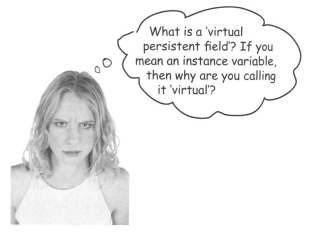

What is a 'virtual persistent field'? If you mean an instance variable, then why are you calling it 'virtual'?

'Virtual persistent fields' are for the values that map to columns in the database. They represent the entity's persistent state. In your bean class code, they exist only as abstract getters and setters

This bean has FOUR persistent fields, for First, Last, PK (primary key), and Address

First: John
Last: Mayer
PK: 22
Address: *1 Derland St*

First	Last	PK	Address
John	Mayer	22	1 Derland St.
Fran	Healy	16	200 Bar St.
Bela	Fleck	5	25 Pick Lane

Virtual fields are NOT instance variables!

```
public abstract class CustomerBeanCMP implements EntityBean {

  private EntityContext context;
```
← note: the only instance variable is for the EntityContext!

```
  public String ejbCreate(String last, String first, String addr) {
    this.setLast(last);
    this.setFirst(first);
    this.setPK(makePK());
    this.setAddress(addr);
    return null;
  }

  public abstract String getLast();
  public abstract void setLast(String last);
  public abstract String getFirst();
  public abstract void setFirst(String first);
  public abstract String getCustAddress();
  public abstract void setCustAddress(String addr);
  public abstract String getPK();
  public abstract void setPK(String pk);
```

These are the virtual persistent fields. They're nothing more than abstract getters and setters that map to the columns in the database, representing the entity's persistent state. The things that get saved with the entity!

```
  public String getLastName() {
    return this.getLast();
  }
  public void setLastName(String name) {
    this.setLast(name);
  }
  public String getFirstName() {
    return this.getFirst();
  }
  public void setFirstName(String name) {
    this.setFirst(name);
  }
  public String getAddress() {
    return this.getCustAddress();
  }
  public void setAddress(String addr) {
    this.setCustAddress(addr);
  }

  // more methods from EntityBean
  // and the home interface
}
```

These are methods from the component interface, that are exposed to the client.

We know what you're thinking... why do you have a SECOND set of getters and setters, when you can just expose the abstract ones in your component interface?

Well, you COULD expose them, but it's not a good idea. Think about it....

here's a hint: imagine that the non-abstract versions had more code than what you see here.

bigger hint: imagine that the non-abstract methods had VALIDATION code...

ridiculously big hint: think about encapsulation.

Sharpen your pencil

Using the interfaces below, write a legal bean class. You don't have to write the actual business logic, but at least list all the methods that you have to write in the class, with their correct declarations.

<<interface>> **ProductHome**
create(String description, String cat, double price, String ID)
findByPrimaryKey(String key)
findByCategory(String category)
getLowStockItems()

<<interface>> **Product**
getCategory()
getID()
getDescription()
setDescription()
getPrice()
setPrice()

<<interface>> **EntityBean**
setEntityContext(EntityContext ec)
ejbActivate()
ejbPassivate()
ejbRemove()
unsetEntityContext()
ejbLoad()
ejbStore()

Write the class here in the space below; don't worry about import statements:

Complete code for the CustomerBeanCMP class

(note: it's not annotated, because that's YOUR job in the Sharpen exercise on the next page)

```java
package headfirst;

import javax.ejb.*;

public abstract class CustomerBeanCMP implements EntityBean {

    private EntityContext context;

    public String ejbCreate(String last, String first, String addr) {
        this.setLast(last);
        this.setFirst(first);
        this.setPK(makePK());
        this.setAddress(addr);
        return null;
    }
    public void ejbPostCreate(String last, String first, String addr) {}

    public String getLastName() {
        return this.getLast();
    }

    public void setLastName(String name) {
        this.setLast(name);
    }

    public String getFirstName() {
        return this.getFirst();
    }

    public void setFirstName(String name) {
        this.setFirst(name);
    }

    public String getAddress() {
        return this.getCustAddress();
    }

    public void setAddress(String addr) {
        this.setCustAddress(addr);
    }

    public void setEntityContext(EntityContext ctx) {
        context = ctx;
    }
```

```
public abstract String getLast();
public abstract void setLast(String last);
public abstract String getFirst();
public abstract void setFirst(String first);
public abstract String getCustAddress();
public abstract void setCustAddress(String addr);
public abstract String getPK();
public abstract void setPK(String pk);

public void unsetEntityContext() { }
public void ejbLoad() { }
public void ejbStore() { }
public void ejbActivate() { }
public void ejbPassivate() { }
public void ejbRemove() { }

private String makePK() {
   int rand = (int) (Math.random() * 42);
   return ""+ rand;
}
}
```

remember: this is the world's stupidest primary key generator. (Well, we suppose one that always returned the same number would be pretty lame, but that wouldn't work anyway, since primary keys MUST be unique or... guess what... the JVM will give you a nice DuplicateKeyException. But as we were saying, in the Real World, you'd either use a client-supplied arg as the primary key, or a REAL primary key generation engine of some sort, or ask the Container to give you the database auto-generated key (if your vendor supports that.)

Sharpen your pencil

① Mark each method in the CustomerBeanCMP class with one of the following four symbols:

H C EB √F

based on the reason for that method's existence in the class. For example, the ejbCreate() method is required because there's a matching create() in the home, so mark an H next to the ejbCreate() method.

② Put a check mark next to those methods that the compiler cares about. In other words, if you left a method out and the compiler would complain with an error, then mark that method with a √

③ Annotate the code yourself with any other details you can think of. For this exercise (but not the previous two), do as much as you can on your own, then turn back to earlier pages in this chapter and see if you can add or change anything.

Entity bean instance lifecycle

does not exist

instance throws system exception
(unchecked, uncaught)

constructor
setEntityContext()

unsetEntityContext()

pooled

ejbHome<method>()
(home business methods)

ejbFind<method>()

ejbSelect<method>() (covered
in the next chapter)

ejbActivate()

ejbPassivate()

ejbCreate<method>()
ejbPostCreate<method>()

ejbRemove()

method ready

ejbStore()

ejbLoad()

business method
(component interface)

ejbSelect<method>()
(called from a business method)

Let's see here... by my
calculations it should take me
approximately 2.3 years to memorize
this lifecycle diagram, so that would
mean I can schedule the exam for
sometime in the year 2007...

It looks bad only when you see the whole
thing at once. Relax...by the end of
this chapter, assuming you've regained
consciousness, you'll have it 90% down, and
by the end of chapter 7, you'll have it all.

Entity bean instance transitions

Don't try to memorize this all right now! We'll spend most of the rest of this chapter looking at this stuff.

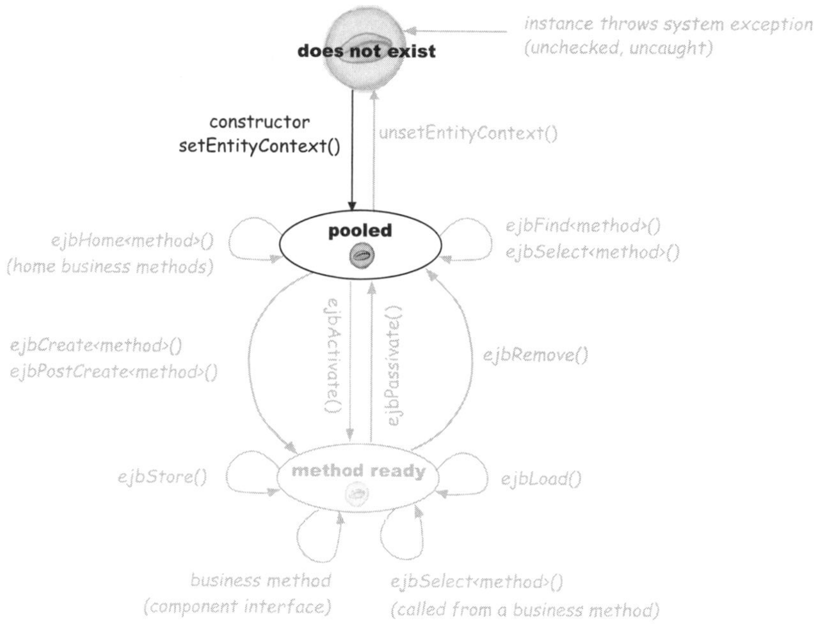

Moving from *does not exist* to *pooled*

constructor

setEntityContext()

note: no create()!

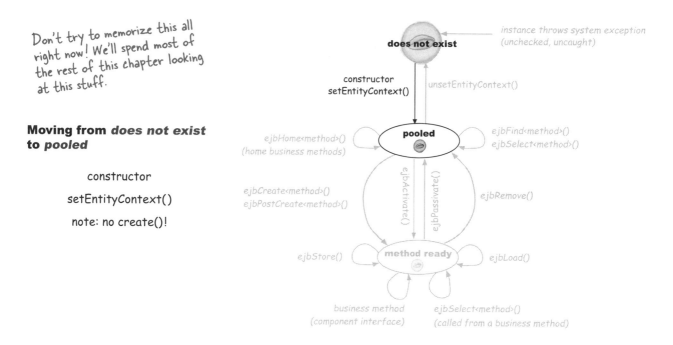

Moving from *pooled* to *method-ready*

ejbCreate() / ejbPostCreate()

OR

ejbActivate()

(The Container does NOT call ejbActivate() if it calls ejbCreate())

Moving from *method ready* to *pooled*

ejbPassivate()

OR

ejbRemove()

(Never both! A bean doing an ejbRemove() will NOT be passivated before going back to the pool!)

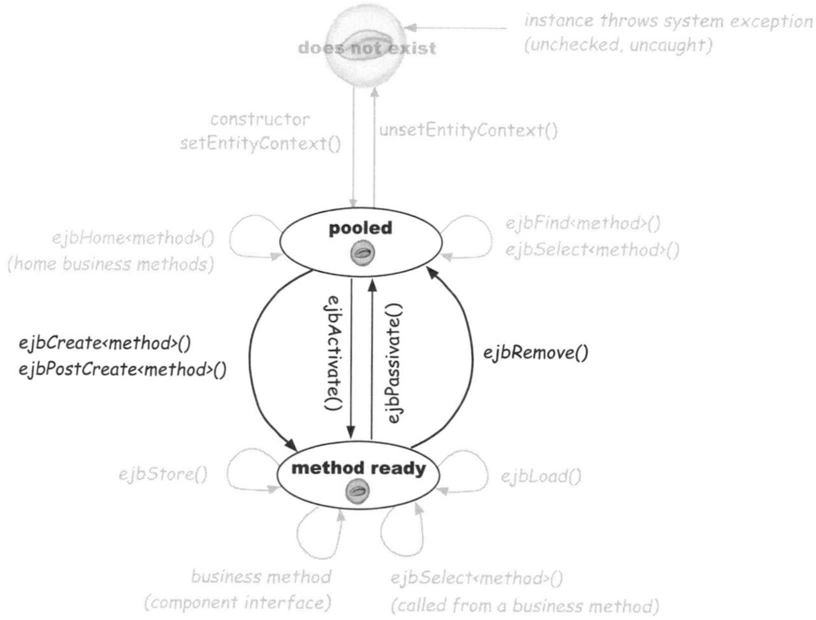

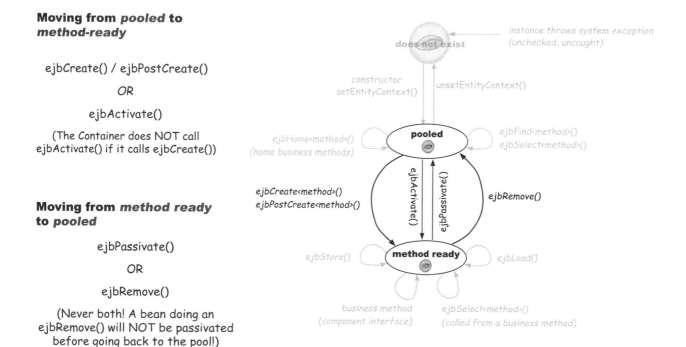

Entity bean instance transitions

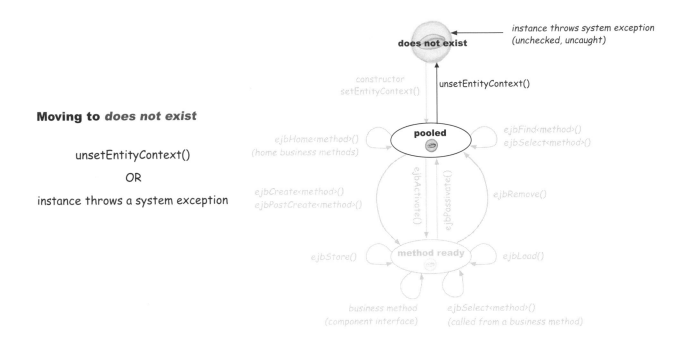

instance throws system exception
(unchecked, uncaught)

does not exist

constructor
setEntityContext()

unsetEntityContext()

Moving to *does not exist*

unsetEntityContext()

OR

instance throws a system exception

pooled

ejbHome<method>()
(home business methods)

ejbFind<method>()
ejbSelect<method>()

ejbCreate<method>()
ejbPostCreate<method>()

ejbActivate()

ejbPassivate()

ejbRemove()

ejbStore()

method ready

ejbLoad()

business method
(component interface)

ejbSelect<method>()
(called from a business method)

there are no
Dumb Questions

Q: **How come there is a label for ejbSelect<method > (whatever THAT is) in both the pooled state *and* the method-ready state. How can you run those methods in both?**

A: We'll get to ejbSelect methods a bit later, but for now, think of them as private methods in the bean (in other words, called not by the client, but only by the bean's own methods) that do selects on the database. They're used only for CMP beans, and can be a huge convenience, since they're implemented for you by the Container. The reason they're in both

places is because it depends on which interface the client uses to call the method that in turn calls a select method. So, if a client calls a home business method, and the home method calls an ejbSelect<method>, the bean stays in the pool to run the method. But if the select method is called from a method in the bean's component interface, that means the method is running on a specific entity, say, Frank Foof #56, so the bean is in the method-ready state.

there are no Dumb Questions

Q: It looks like there are TWO ways to move to the method-ready state: either the client calls a create() method or the Container calls ejbActivate(). So does this mean that you can't count on ejbActivate() being called each time you leave the pool?

A: That's right. A bean can move to the method-ready state by ONLY those two paths (creation or activation) but never both at the same time. So, if you have a design that acquires resources in ejbActivate(), so that they'll always be available while the bean is servicing a business method, you better grab them in ejbCreate() (or ejbPostCreate()—you'll see the difference in a few minutes).

In the real world, it's much less common in EJB 2.0 to use ejbActivate() for much of anything. We'll talk more about this both in this chapter and the last chapter (patterns and performance), but the short version is this: it's usually more efficient to acquire and release scarce resources just within the business methods that need them. That way, you're not hanging on to them (preventing other beans from having access) while your bean is active (i.e. not in the pool), but not actively running a method. Yes, that means you have some additional overhead in each business method, as opposed to grabbing the thing once in ejbActivate(), but in many cases the overhead of grabbing the resource is minor compared to the scalability cost of holding resources (we're thinking... database connections from the pool) open longer than you need to access those resources.

Bottom line: You'll probably find yourself leaving ejbActivate() empty, in so you won't have to worry about missing it when you come out of the pool via an ejbCreate() call.

Sharpen your pencil

For the exam, you have to know exactly which container callback methods are in the EntityBean interface, so you need to memorize these. The tricky part is that some of them have the same names, but completely different behavior than their session bean counterparts in the SessionBean interface. DO NOT LOOK ON THE OPPOSITE PAGE!

1. The client calls this method to tell the Container that he (the client) is done using the bean's EJB object reference:

_____

2. This method is called when the bean goes back to the pool, after an entity is deleted from the database:

_____

3. This method is called immediately after the bean's constructor runs:

_____

4. This method is called on the bean when the bean is in the pool, and the client invokes a business method on the component interface. (We're looking for the *first* method called in that scenario)

_____

Sharpen your pencil

Fill in the missing methods. Don't worry if you don't get the name exactly right; just try to work out what happens at the transitions in the entity bean state diagram.

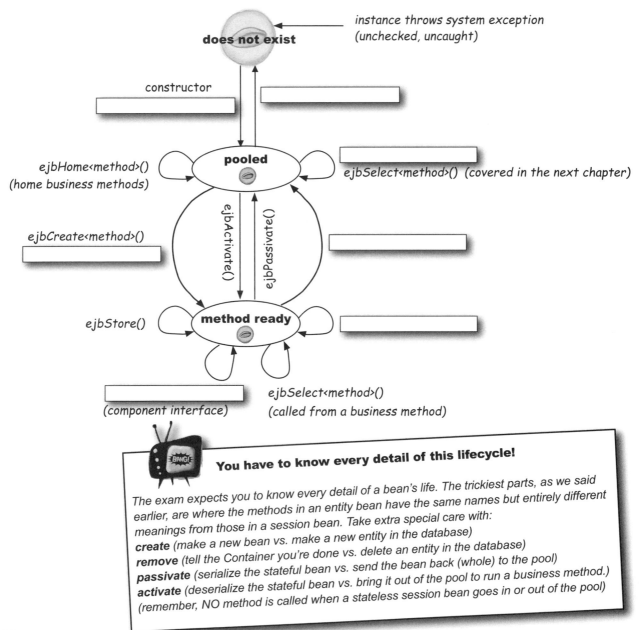

does not exist

instance throws system exception (unchecked, uncaught)

constructor

ejbHome<method>()
(home business methods)

pooled

ejbSelect<method>() (covered in the next chapter)

ejbActivate()

ejbPassivate()

ejbCreate<method>()

ejbStore()

method ready

(component interface)

ejbSelect<method>()
(called from a business method)

You have to know every detail of this lifecycle!

The exam expects you to know every detail of a bean's life. The trickiest parts, as we said earlier, are where the methods in an entity bean have the same names but entirely different meanings from those in a session bean. Take extra special care with:

create *(make a new bean vs. make a new entity in the database)*
remove *(tell the Container you're done vs. delete an entity in the database)*
passivate *(serialize the stateful bean vs. send the bean back (whole) to the pool)*
activate *(deserialize the stateful bean vs. bring it out of the pool to run a business method.)*
(remember, NO method is called when a stateless session bean goes in or out of the pool)

So how DID the client get a reference to the EJB object for #28?

When a client wants to call a business method on a specific entity (in other words, an entity with a unique primary key, like Lee Loo #28), the client first needs a reference to that entity's EJB object.

For an entity bean, remember, there are three ways that can happen:

(1) Client calls a finder on the home

```
customerHome.findByPrimaryKey("28");
```

(2) Client calls create on the home (to insert #28 for the first time)

```
customerHome.create("Loo", "Lee","28", "54 Bar Circle");
```

(3) Client calls a home business method that returns a reference to the bean's component interface

```
customerHome.getCustomerByStreet("Bar Circle");
```

We'll talk about each stage of the bean's lifecycle for finders, creates, and home business methods. But first—each of these assumes that the bean instance already exists in the pool. But how does the bean get there in the first place?

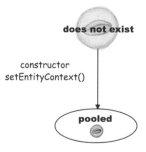

does not exist

constructor
setEntityContext()

pooled

Before the client can use a bean for ANYTHING -- creation, finders, business methods, etc., the Container has to make a new bean instance for the pool. Bean CONSTRUCTION isn't tied to entity bean CREATION.

Construction means a new bean instance. But creation, for an entity bean, means a new entity is inserted into the database.

CMP Entity bean *construction*

Scenario: Container wants to make a new bean instance for the pool

1 Container makes a new EntityContext

2 Container makes a new instance of the
bean class (bean's constructor runs)

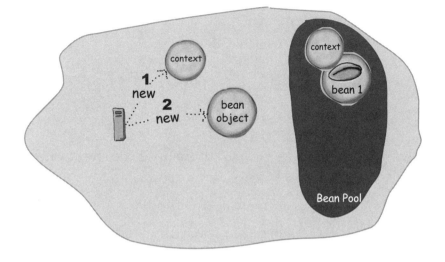

---

3 Container calls setEntityContext() on the
bean. This is the ONLY time in a bean
instance's life that it will get this call.

4 Container puts the bean (which now has a
context) in the pool.

Notice: create() was never called! A create()
method is *only* for inserting a new entity into
the database, and has *nothing* to do with the
bean instance's creation!

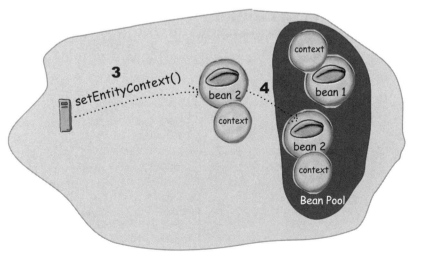

Bean things you can do during entity construction:

---------------- timeline ----------------→

constructor

Use your EntityContext to:

☐ get a reference to your home

☐ get a reference to your EJB object

☐ get security information about the client

☐ force a transaction to rollback (CMT beans)

☐ find out if the transaction has already been set to rollback (CMT beans)

☐ get a transaction reference, and call methods on it (BMT beans)

You can't do ANYTHING

Access:

☐ your special JNDI environment

☐ another bean's methods

☐ a resource manager (like a database)

setEntityContext()

Use your EntityContext to:

☑ get a reference to your home

☐ get a reference to your EJB object

☐ get security information about the client

☐ force a transaction to rollback (CMT beans)

☐ find out if the transaction has already been set to rollback (CMT beans)

☐ get a transaction reference, and call methods on it (BMT beans)

Access:

☑ your special JNDI environment

☐ another bean's methods

☐ a resource manager (like a database)

What to put in the constructor

We know it's painfully obvious by now... NOTHING.

Unless you're forced to, don't even put a constructor in your code at all, and just use the compiler-generated default constructor.

Whatever you do, be SURE you have a public no-arg constructor in your class!

```
public Customer() { }
```

What to put in the setEntityContext() method

Assign the context to an instance variable. Remember, you get only ONE chance to save it. You might not always need to use a session context, but you'll probably need an entity context. Besides, your context is gonna stay alive whether you keep a reference to it or not, so the only memory you save if you don't keep it is for the reference variable, not the object itself.

```
public void setEntityContext(EntityContext ctx) {
   context = ctx;
}
```

CMP Entity bean creation

Scenario: client wants to create a new entity in the database (remember, the Container made the bean instance and the context earlier, and put them in the pool)

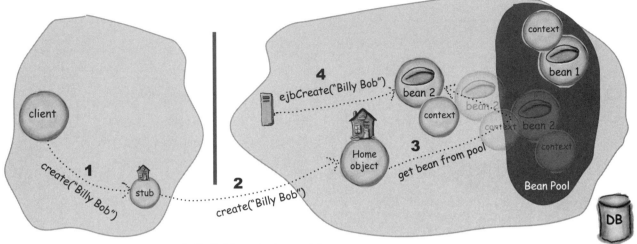

1 Client calls create("Billy Bob") on the home stub

2 The create("Billy Bob") method invocation is passed to the home object.

3 A bean is pulled out of the pool to do the creation

4 Container calls ejbCreate("Billy Bob") on the bean instance

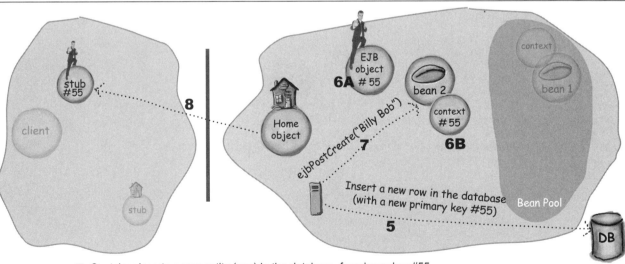

5 Container inserts a new entity (row) in the database, for primary key #55

6 Container gives the EJB object and EntityContext the primary key value (#55).

7 Container calls ejbPostCreate("Billy Bob") on the bean, to give the bean a chance to finish initializing itself

8 The home returns the EJB object stub to the client

Creating a new entity

CMP entity bean

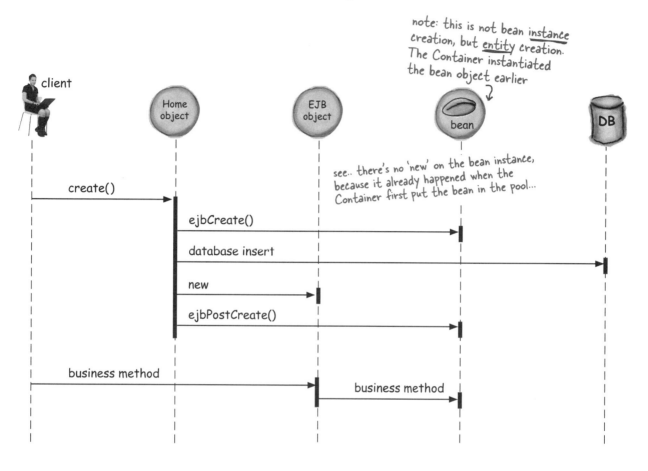

note: this is not bean instance creation, but entity creation. The Container instantiated the bean object earlier

see.. there's no 'new' on the bean instance, because it already happened when the Container first put the bean in the pool...

client

Home object

EJB object

bean

DB

create()

ejbCreate()

database insert

new

ejbPostCreate()

business method

business method

Whoa! This is quite different from session bean creation...

The Container calls ejbCreate() on a session bean instance only once, at the beginning of the bean's life. That's *one* big difference between session and entity beans—entity beans can run ejbCreate() over and over, like a business method. In fact, that's the best way to think of it... as just another home business method, as though it were named ejbInsert() (which, in our humble opinion, it should have been named, but once again, they forgot to ask *us*).

But the *second* difference between entity and session bean ejbCreate() methods is the order in which the EJB object is created. When an entity bean runs ejbCreate() there's no EJB object!! Yikes! That means the bean has no way to get a reference to its bodyguard. In other words, an entity bean cannot use the ejbCreate() method to, say, get a reference to its own EJB object and pass that reference to someone else. Remember, a bean can't pass a reference to itself, ever! When a bean wants to pass a reference to itself, it must pass a reference to its own EJB object. But it can't do that in ejbCreate(), because it's too early!

CMP Entity bean creation

1 Hey bean, run your **ejbCreate()** method, and here are the client args...

2 OK, in my ejbCreate() method I'll use those args from the client to set my own persistent state (last name, first name, primary key, etc.)

3 Great! Now I can look at your persistent field state, and use the data to create the new customer in the database

insert → DB

Before

Last	First	PKey
Frankie	Foof	99
Bryan	Boof	314

After

Last	First	PKey
Frankie	Foof	99
Bryan	Boof	314
Billy	Bob	55

4 Now that I have a primary key, I can make the EJB object (and tell the EntityContext)

EJB object #55

5 OK bean, if you need to finish up your creation, I'm done inserting the row and making the EJB object, so run your **ejbPostCreate()**, and here's the original create args, just in case you forgot...

6 Thanks! Now that I'm in ejbPostCreate(), I know that my EJB object is ready, and I can get a reference to it from my context. I need to pass a reference to myself (which means a reference to my bodyguard) out to another bean, so I REALLY needed a second chance to finish my creation...

Implement your ejbCreate() methods

What to put in ejbCreate()

Put your entity initialization code here! This means setting values for your persistent fields... the fields that map to columns in the database row that's about to be inserted.

Notice we aren't saying, "put your *object* initialization code here..." With session beans, we told you to treat the ejbCreate() kind of like a constructor for the bean. But with entity beans, it's different because *the instance was initialized a long time ago* (when its setEntityContext() method was called).

So, ejbCreate() is about initializing the bean as this *new entity* the bean will now represent. For a CMP bean, this means the client has handed you arguments representing the data to insert into the database. The Container will look at the state of your persistent fields, once ejbCreate() returns, and use those fields to make the new row in the database.

If you do nothing else in ejbCreate(), **you must make a primary key for this entity!** That's your most important job. You might make the key based on arguments to the create method. You might make the key based on a key-generating algorithm. You might have a key server that you go to for the next key. Whatever it is, you must come up with the key, and assign it to your primary key field. When ejbCreate(), the Container looks at the state of your persistent fields, and uses that data to make the new row.

Warning! Remember, the Container calls your ejbCreate() before it can make the EJB object, so you can't use ejbCreate() to get a reference to yourself! (i.e. a reference to your bodyguard/EJB object). You'll have to wait until ejbPostCreate() before you can ask your context for a reference to your own component interface. You also can't use ejbCreate() to access your own persistent relationships; you have to wait until ejbPostCreate() (but we'll cover all that in the next chapter).

*This must be the type of your primary key!
In this case, the primary key we're using is a
String, so that must be the return type (and
we'll declare this in the DD)*

```
public String ejbCreate(String last, String first) {
    // assign args to persistent fields
    this.setLastName(last);
    this.setFirstName(first);

    // set a primary key
    this.setPrimaryKey(this.makeKey());
    return null;
}
```

*Once ejbCreate() completes,
Container will use the values you
set to make the new row.*

return null?? What's up with THAT?

Object identity: the primary key

Every entity MUST have a unique identity. The Container will never let you get away with having two or more entities with the same primary key. And as of EJB 2.0, coming up with that primary key is still *your* job. The Container won't do it (at least not according to the specification).

If I'm just supposed to return null, why do I have to come up with the key?

I'm not gonna do it. YOU have to come up with the primary key. I don't know what your business logic is, and I'm not gonna be a primary-key generator for you.

And don't expect me to do it either, if you're using CMP. You have to come up with the primary key BEFORE the Container tries to insert the new row.

With CMP, you're still responsible for the primary key. That doesn't mean you won't use a primary key service of some kind. Maybe you have a service that automatically allocates a big block of primary keys from the database, and then hands them out as needed. Or you might have some type of unique identifier algorithm that makes unique keys for you. Or maybe you're using the customer's social security number or account number or... that's up to you to decide.

And the way you tell the Container what value the about-to-be-created entity should have is through the value of one or more of your persistent fields.

If you have just one field as your primary key, and it maps directly to a column in the database, you're set. But if you need more than one value to uniquely identify an entity (like, maybe it takes a combination of name and date), you can use a *compound* key that uses two or more of your container-managed persistent fields.

Rules for ejbCreate()

- You must implement the ejbCreate<method> to match each create<method> in the home interface.

- The method name must begin with the prefix "ejbCreate".

- The method must be declared public, and must not be declared static or final.

- The declared return type must be the entity bean's primary key type, even though you will return *null* from the method .

- The method arguments must be the same as the arguments of the matching create<method>.

- You may declare a throws clause with CreateException, or any arbitrary application (checked) exception that you like, as long as it was also declared in the home interface, but you must NOT declare a RemoteException.

Rules for Primary Keys

- A primary key class must be Serializable and public.

- You can use a single persistent field from your bean class as your primary key, by identifying both the field name and the class type in the DD.

- If you need two or more persistent fields to uniquely identify your entity, make a custom compound primary key class.

- A compound key class must be made up of fields that are defined as persistent fields in the bean class. The fields in the bean class must have public accessor methods.

By the end of ejbCreate() you MUST have a valid primary key assigned to the CMP field that you've the told the Container is your primary key field.

If you use a compound key, then ALL the fields that make up that key must have valid values.

If at the end of ejbCreate() your primary key is null, the Container won't do the create!

Q: **How come I can't have the database come up with the primary key? That's how we usually do it. Are you telling me the Container can't do that?**

A: Yes, that's what we're telling you. The contract you have with the Container says that by the time ejbCreate() is done, you've done whatever you had to do to make a valid primary key. You might have a server that lets you say, "Let the database come up with the key when you do the insert", but there's no guarantee in the spec, and you can't assume that all EJB vendors support this. Maybe some day in the future, there will be a deployment-independent way to say, "Use auto-generated key" in the deployment descriptor. But today is not that day. And EJB 2.0 is not that spec.

Implement your ejb<u>Post</u>Create() methods

What to put in ejbPostCreate()

Finish your initialization code here! Now you can see why entity beans need an ejbPostCreate()—because ejbCreate() is too early for some things. The two most important reasons for ejbPostCreate() are that you can use it to get a reference to your own EJB object, and you must use it for accessing your container-managed relationships (CMR). (We'll look at CMR in the next chapter.)

Think of ejbPostCreate() as the other half of your ejbCreate(), with some Really Important Things happening in the middle. It's your second (and last) chance to finish your initialization, if you need to do things as part of creating the new entity that depend on having access to your EJB object (or something else that can happen only in ejbPostCreate(), and not in ejbCreate().

We'll revisit ejbPostCreate() in the next chapter, when we look at CMR.

Rules for ejbPostCreate()

- You must implement the ejbPostCreate<method> to match each create<method> in the home interface.

- The method name must begin with the prefix "ejbPostCreate".

- The method must be declared public, and must not be declared static or final.

- The declared return type must be void!

- The method arguments must be the same as the matching ejbCreate<method>.

- You may declare a throws clause with CreateException, or any arbitrary application (checked) exception that you like, as long as it was also declared in the home interface, but you must NOT declare a RemoteException.

All three have the same args, but different return types!

Home interface
create<method>

```
public Customer create(String last, String first)throws
                                    CreateException,RemoteException);
```

notice the name differences

Bean class
ejbCreate<method>

```
public String ejbCreate(String last, String first) {...}
```

another difference

Bean class
ejbPostCreate<method>

```
public void ejbPostCreate(String last, String first){...}
```

the bean class doesn't have to declare the same exceptions, unless it throws them. (And you NEVER throw a RemoteException from the bean. Only the Container throws a RemoteException.

BRAIN POWER

Think about the three methods above, and how they're related to one another. Think about what they're each responsible for. Now answer these two questions:

1. Why are the return types declared like this? In other words, explain why each of the three different return types is what it is...

2. Why do both ejbCreate<method> and ejbPostCreate<method> have the same arguments?

Instead of:

```
doStuff(this);
```

Use:

```
doStuff(myContext.getEJBObject());
```

Bean things you can do during entity creation:

---

timeline →

---

ejbCreate()

Use your EntityContext to:

- ☑ get a reference to your home
- ☐ get a reference to your EJB object
- ☐ get your primary key
- ☑ get security information about the client
- ☑ force a transaction to rollback (CMT beans)
- ☑ find out if the transaction has already been set to rollback (CMT beans)
- ☐ get a transaction reference, and call methods on it (BMT beans only, so entities can't use this)

Access:

- ☑ your special JNDI environment
- ☑ another bean's methods
- ☑ a resource manager (like a database)

it's too early to get a reference to your EJB object or primary key, because the container is still waiting for you to finish your ejbCreate(). Once you return from ejbCreate(), the container will look in your bean and see what state changes you've made as a result of the initialization you did based on the client-supplied args. Only THEN can the container figure out what your primary key is (by looking in your primary key field!), and it needs that to make an EJB object.

ejbPostCreate()

Use your EntityContext to:

- ☑ get a reference to your home
- ☑ get a reference to your EJB object
- ☑ get your primary key
- ☑ get security information about the client
- ☑ force a transaction to rollback (CMT beans)
- ☑ find out if the transaction has already been set to rollback (CMT beans)
- ☐ get a transaction reference, and call methods on it (BMT beans only, so entities can't use this)

Access:

- ☑ your special JNDI environment
- ☑ another bean's methods
- ☑ a resource manager (like a database)

By the time you're in ejbPostCreate(), the container knows your primary key and has made (or found) the EJB object for this key.

CMP Entity finder

Scenario: client wants to get a reference to an *existing* entity bean

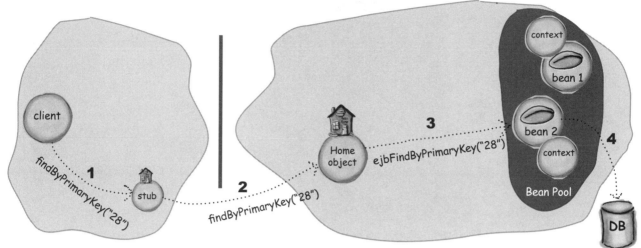

1 Client calls findByPrimaryKey("28") on the home reference

2 The finder method is passed to the home object

3 A bean is selected from the pool to run the ejbFindByPrimaryKey("28") method

4 The bean does a select on the database, to verify that an entity with primary key #28 exists

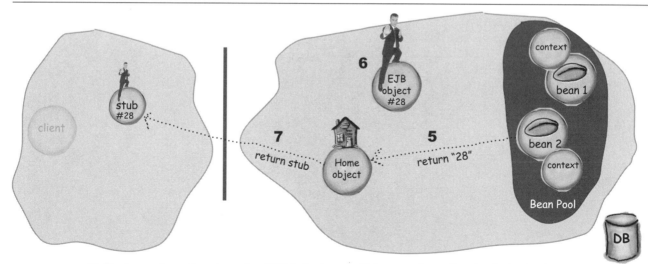

5 The bean returns the primary key (#28) to the home, which means the entity exists in the database

6 The Container makes (or finds) an EJB object for #28

7 The Container returns the EJB object stub for #28

Note: if the bean had not found a matching entity for primary key #28, the client would get an ObjectNotFoundException (subclass of FinderException)

Finding an existing entity

CMP entity bean

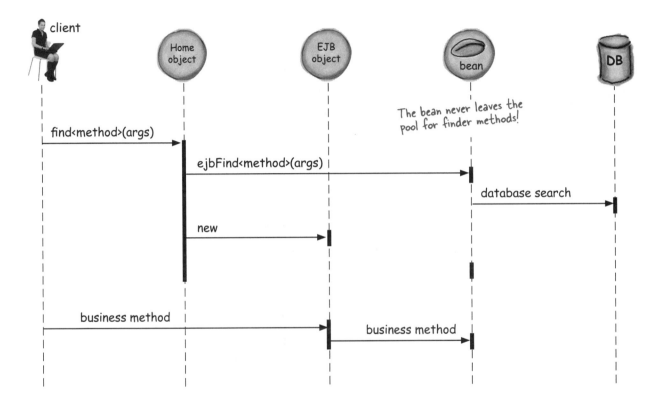

CMP Entity bean finders

1 Hey bean, run this **ejbFind** method, and here is the client arg "72"

2 Um, aren't you forgetting that I'm a CMP bean? I don't have these methods in my bean class. Although come to think of it, I'm a concrete implementation that the Container—I mean YOU—made from my abstract class, so maybe I DO have the methods after all but I just didn't realize it and...

3 Relax. And you're right... I'm the one that implemented the CMP finder methods, so we'll show it this way, even though it *is* you that *conceptually* does the work. I guess in the end it doesn't matter as long as it happens.

search for pk #72

4 Now that I have verified that this entity exists, I can make the EJB object, if it doesn't already exist.

EJB object #72

Last	First	PKey
Poly	Morphism	72
Dewey	Cheatem	900

5 OK client, here's your EJB object reference for #72. You can use it to call business methods on Poly Morphism, #72.

6 Thanks! I really need to change Poly's last name to Esther.

7 I guess I just get to stay in the pool and forget the whole thing...

<u>YOU</u> don't implement the Finder methods!

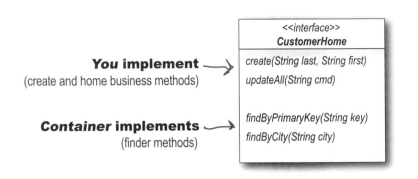

You implement →
(create and home business methods)

Container implements →
(finder methods)

```
      <<interface>>
      CustomerHome
────────────────────────────
create(String last, String first)
updateAll(String cmd)

findByPrimaryKey(String key)
findByCity(String city)
```

Don't put anything in your bean class about the finders. The Container implements your finder methods, using the home interface and your deployment descriptor to figure out what to do.

Your bean class must not even MENTION the finder methods.

Just don't write 'em. For a CMP bean, don't put anything in your class about the finder methods. You will implement your create and home business methods, but as far as your own bean class—the one that you write—goes, there are no finder methods.

You do declare them in the home interface, of course, including the mandatory findByPrimaryKey(), but you don't write any other Java code related to your finders.

The Container looks in your home interface and your deployment descriptor to figure out what to do with the finder methods, and the Container writes all the code for them. You'll never see it.

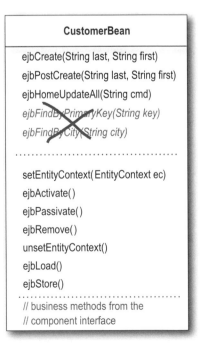

```
         CustomerBean
────────────────────────────────────
ejbCreate(String last, String first)
ejbPostCreate(String last, String first)
ejbHomeUpdateAll(String cmd)
ejbFindByPrimaryKey(String key)
ejbFindByCity(String city)
. . . . . . . . . . . . . . . . . . . . . . .
setEntityContext(EntityContext ec)
ejbActivate()
ejbPassivate()
ejbRemove()
unsetEntityContext()
ejbLoad()
ejbStore()
. . . . . . . . . . . . . . . . . . . . . . .
// business methods from the
// component interface
```

Hmmmm... I noticed that the bean didn't come out of the pool. But what's REALLY weird is that now there's an EJB object for #72, but there's no entity bean playing the part of #72. The bean never got loaded up with the entity data from the database, so what happens if the client calls a business method like getAddress() ???

Why should I waste a bean's time by loading it up with the data, when the client might not ever call a business method on that EJB object reference?

I hear what you're saying, but come on... aren't the chances pretty good that the client IS gonna call a business method on the bean? They went to the trouble of finding it...

You just always have to know the truth... OK, you got me on this one. Yes, it IS likely the client will call a business method on the entity, so it might seem more efficient to have the bean ready. But even if I DID load the data into the bean during the finder method, I'd still have to reload it anyway. Why? Because by the time the client gets around to calling the business method, the bean's state might be stale!

I'm not following... what do you mean by stale? How can the bean become stale, if nobody else can get to the bean's data? How could anybody change the entity?

Think about it. The entity, Poly Morphism, lives in the database (a row in a table). Sure, we can hand out references to the EJB object for this entity, BUT... the entity BEAN isn't the only way to get to the database! So while the client is waiting to call a method, for all we know someone else could have updated Poly's record in the database. If that were to happen, then when the client calls a method on the Poly entity bean, the bean returns old, wrong information.

Ok, now I get it... if the bean were to be loaded up with data during the finder method, then by the time the client calls a business method on it, the underlying entity data in the database might have changed.

Yes! I'm gonna have to load the data in again as soon as the client calls a business method, just to make sure that the bean is refreshed with the most current data, so there's no point in loading it in during the finder. It would just be a waste of resources.

CMP Home Business Methods

Scenario: client wants to call a business method in the home

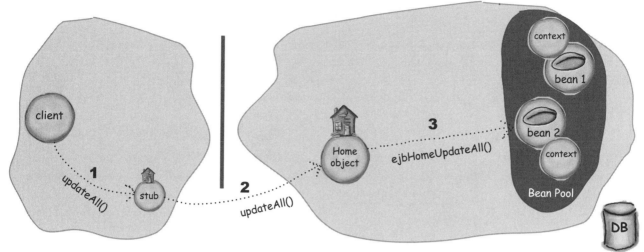

1 Client calls updateAll() on home reference.

2 The updateAll() method is passed to the home object.

3 A bean is selected from the pool to run the ejbHomeUpdateAll() method.

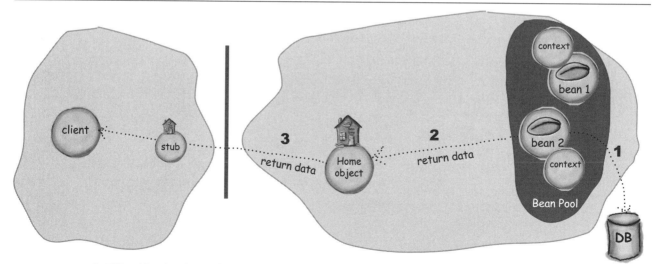

1 Without leaving the pool, the bean runs the home method, probably calling on a Container-implemented select<method> to access the database.

2 The bean returns from the method (possibly returning data).

3 The Container passes the return value back to the client.

Client invokes a Home Business Method

CMP entity bean

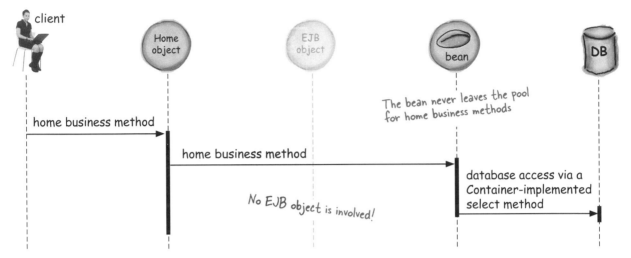

What to put in a home business method

As you write your code, remember that an entity bean stays in the pool when it runs a home business method. Put code in your home business methods that apply to the underlying database—for a group of entities rather than one specific entity—and that don't return the bean's component interface (the way finders and create methods must).

```
public Collection ejbHomeDisplayAll() {
    // do a select on the database, using a container-implemented
    // select method (next chapter), then return an ArrayList of Strings
}
```

Rules for home business methods

- You must have an ejbHome<method> method for every home <method> in the home interface.

- The name must begin with the prefix "ejbHome", followed by the name of the home <method>, but with the first letter of the method capitalized. For example, updateAll() in the home interface will be ejbHomeUpdateAll() in the bean class.

- The method must be declared public and NOT static.

- If the home interface is Remote, the arguments and return values must be legal types for RMI-IIOP.

- You may declare a throws clause with your own application (checked) exceptions, as long as the exceptions were also declared in the home interface.

- Even if your life depends on it, you must NOT declare a RemoteException.

Bean things you can do in home business methods

Use your EntityContext to:

- ☑ get a reference to your home
- ☐ get a reference to your EJB object
- ☐ get your primary key
- ☑ get security information about the client
- ☑ force a transaction to rollback (CMT beans)
- ☑ find out if the transaction has already been set to rollback (CMT beans)
- ☐ get a transaction reference, and call methods on it (BMT beans only, so entities can't use this)

Access:

- ☑ your special JNDI environment
- ☑ another bean's methods
- ☑ a resource manager (like a database)

two things you can't do because the bean isn't BEING an entity! The bean is in the pool acting on behalf of ALL the entities of this type, but not any one particular entity. So the bean has no EJB object and of course, no primary key.

Starting a business method (in a transaction)

Scenario: client wants to get the address of a specific CMP Customer entity

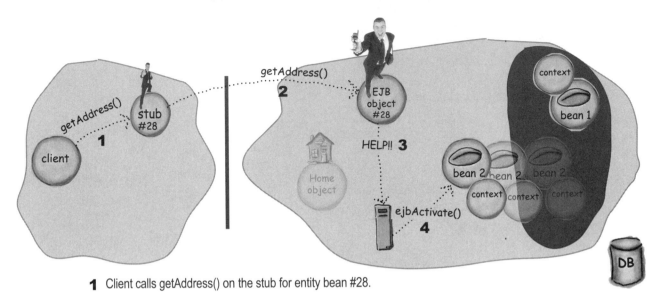

1 Client calls getAddress() on the stub for entity bean #28.

2 The call is passed to the EJB object.

3 The EJB object gets the call and panics, because there IS no entity bean for #28!

4 The Container sees that this method needs a transaction, so the Container starts one, then pulls a bean from the pool, and calls ejbActivate() on the bean

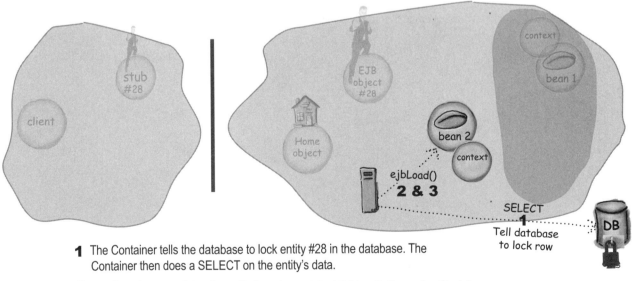

1 The Container tells the database to lock entity #28 in the database. The Container then does a SELECT on the entity's data.

2 The Container populates the entity bean's persistent fields with the real entity data.

3 The Container calls ejbLoad() on the bean, to tell the bean, "You've just been loaded."

Completing a business method (and a transaction)

Scenario: bean completes a business method that ends a transaction

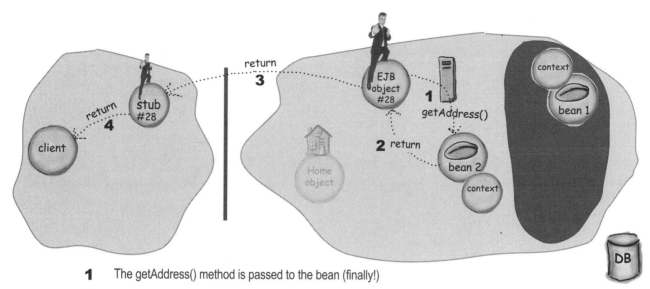

1 The getAddress() method is passed to the bean (finally!)

2 The bean returns from the method

3/4 The EJB object sends the return back to the client

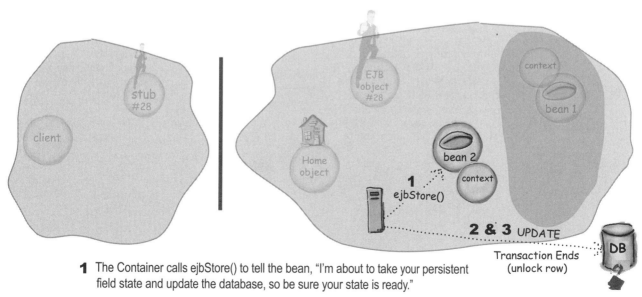

1 The Container calls ejbStore() to tell the bean, "I'm about to take your persistent field state and update the database, so be sure your state is ready."

2 The real entity is updated in the database.

3 The Container commits the transaction and tells the database to unlock the entity.

Being John Entity Bean

1 It all starts when the client calls a business method on an EJB object for John Malcom. The EJB object freaks out because there's a call, but no entity bean to run the method.

2 So the Container phones back to the pool and says, "We need a bean out here to service a client method..."

3 I might not be completely ready when I come out of the pool, so the Container calls my **ejbActivate()** method. It's actually a pretty useless method, so I almost never do anything there. But I suppose I might reacquire a Socket or something I don't want to hang on to while 'between projects'. But it's hard for me to imagine anything I would do in ejbActivate() that I wouldn't rather do in some other method.

4 But after that, I still need to ask, "Who am I supposed to be?" and that's when I get the "Being John Malcom" script with all of my character's important data. The Container calls my **ejbLoad()** method to tell me that I have everything I need to play the role of John Malcom. After that, I'm in character and ready for action.

7 Show time! The client's business method call is finally passed to me. (Hey, will somebody tell my psycho bodyguard to relax... it's not easy being brilliant, you know...).

6 After my stunning performance as John Malcom, the Container (who takes this job way too seriously) calls my **ejbStore()** method to see if I've changed any of John's internal state values. Well of COURSE I have--this character, through much tragedy, suffering, and business logic has grown... as an entity. Of COURSE he's a different person.

7 So I say, "Don't get your knickers in a twist... here's the data" (they all act like it's, literally, the end of the world over here if the database doesn't know every little thing that happens to my character).

8 Then it's over, and I'm back to the pool. But first, the Container calls my **ejbPassivate()** method to tell me that I'm done being John Malcom, and that it's safe to release any resources I was keeping on his behalf. I almost never use this method, because it's not an efficient way to manage things.

Activation/passivation of a CMP entity bean

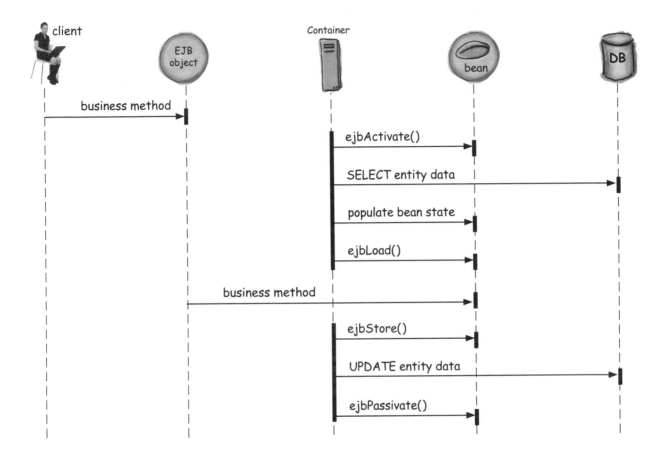

The Container always calls ejbLoad() after ejbActivate().

The Container always calls ejbStore() before ejbPassivate().

The Container can call ejbLoad() and ejbStore() at other times.

 Sharpen your pencil

If you're taking the exam, trust us here, you REALLY need to stop right now and do this exercise, before turning the page. Think about everything you've learned in this chapter about the lifecycle of an entity bean, especially how and when it comes out of the pool to *become* an entity.

Take your best guess about which aspects of beanness are available during each of the four container callbacks for ejbActivate(), ejbPassivate().

Use your EntityContext to:

ejbActivate()	ejbPassivate()	ejbLoad()	ejbStore()	
❏	❏	❏	❏	get a reference to your home
❏	❏	❏	❏	get security information about the client
❏	❏	❏	❏	force the transaction to rollback
❏	❏	❏	❏	find out if the transaction has already been set to rollback
❏	❏	❏	❏	get a reference to your EJB object
❏	❏	❏	❏	get your primary key

Access:

ejbActivate()	ejbPassivate()	ejbLoad()	ejbStore()	
❏	❏	❏	❏	methods of another bean
❏	❏	❏	❏	your special JNDI context
❏	❏	❏	❏	a resource manager (like a database)

Bean things you can do during activation and loading

— timeline →

ejbActivate()

Use your EntityContext to:

- ☑ get a reference to your home
- ☑ get a reference to your EJB object
- ☑ get your primary key
- ☐ get security information about the client
- ☐ force a transaction to rollback (CMT beans)
- ☐ find out if the transaction has already been set to rollback (CMT beans)
- ☐ get a transaction reference, and call methods on it (BMT beans only, so entities can't use this)

Access:

- ☑ your special JNDI environment
- ☐ another bean's methods
- ☐ a resource manager (like a database)

The Container prefers (no, make that INSISTS) that if you access a bean or a resource manager, you must be in a 'meaningful transaction context', so ejbActivate() is too early. But once you get to ejbLoad(), you're IN a transaction (unless you've told the Container NOT to use a transaction... which is for very special cases only).

ejbLoad()

Use your EntityContext to:

- ☑ get a reference to your home
- ☑ get a reference to your EJB object
- ☑ get your primary key
- ☑ get security information about the client
- ☑ force a transaction to rollback (CMT beans)
- ☑ find out if the transaction has already been set to rollback (CMT beans)
- ☐ get a transaction reference, and call methods on it (BMT beans only, so entities can't use this)

Access:

- ☑ your special JNDI environment
- ☑ another bean's methods
- ☑ a resource manager (like a database)

Now we can do everything that an entity bean CAN do... the same things we can do in a business method. You can think of this as the beginning of the business method.

Bean things you can do during passivation and storing

timeline →

ejbStore()

Use your EntityContext to:

- ☑ get a reference to your home
- ☑ get a reference to your EJB object
- ☑ get your primary key
- ☑ get security information about the client
- ☑ force a transaction to rollback (CMT beans)
- ☑ find out if the transaction has already been set to rollback (CMT beans)
- ☐ get a transaction reference, and call methods on it (BMT beans only, so entities can't use this)

Access:

- ☑ your special JNDI environment
- ☑ another bean's methods
- ☑ a resource manager (like a database)

FYI -- this page is EXACTLY the same as the previous one on activation and loading. (except for the notes we made). The rules for what's allowed during activation are the same for passivation, and the rules for loading are identical to the rules for storing.

ejbPassivate()

Use your EntityContext to:

- ☑ get a reference to your home
- ☑ get a reference to your EJB object
- ☑ get your primary key
- ☐ get security information about the client
- ☐ force a transaction to rollback (CMT beans)
- ☐ find out if the transaction has already been set to rollback (CMT beans)
- ☐ get a transaction reference, and call methods on it (BMT beans only, so entities can't use this)

Access:

- ☑ your special JNDI environment
- ☐ another bean's methods
- ☐ a resource manager (like a database)

By the time the Container starts to passivate you, you're no longer associated with a client or a transaction

Just as it was with ejbActivate(), the Container no longer has you in a 'meaningful transaction context' (in other words, you can't be in a transaction at this point), so you can't get a reference to a bean or a resource manager. The Container says it's too dangerous to do this without a 'meaningful transaction context'. (see the transactions chapter)

Commit options: what REALLY happens to a bean <u>after</u> a transaction commits?

(the previous pictures are just ONE way it could work, but there are two other ways)

① Commit option A

The bean stays ready, attached to the EJB object, loaded with data but NOT in a transaction. The Container keeps the entity locked, so that nobody can change the bean's state. When a client calls a business method on this entity bean's EJB object, the Container does NOT do an ejbActivate() or ejbLoad(), and assumes the bean's data is still in sync with the underlying persistent store.

A

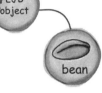

Bean stays connected and in sync. When the next business method call comes in to the bean, it just runs. No ejbActivate(), no ejbLoad().

Darko	Donny	42

entity stays locked

---

② Commit option B

The bean stays attached to the EJB object, loaded with data but the bean's state is marked as 'invalid'. In other words, the Container knows that the bean might become stale between now and the next time a client invokes a method on this bean, so the Container will do an ejbLoad() when a new business method comes in for this entity. (But no ejbActivate()).

B

Bean stays connected, but not in sync. When the next business method call comes in to the bean, ejbLoad() is called. (But no ejbActivate())

Darko	Donny	42

lock is released, but bean doesn't go back to the pool

---

③ Commit option C

The bean is passivated and put back into the pool. The next time a client calls a business method on this entity, everything we've seen in this chapter happens—a bean comes out of the pool, is activated, the loaded, and finally the business method it passed to the bean.

C

Bean is disconnected from the EJB object, and goes back to the pool. With the next business method call to this bean, the Container pulls a bean out of the pool, then calls ejbActivate() and ejbLoad()

Darko	Donny	42

lock is released, bean goes back to the pool

there are no Dumb Questions

Q: How does these commit options affect me? Do I need to know which one my Container is choosing? Do I get a choice?

A: According to the specification, your vendor is free to use any of the three options. Your container might let you choose (or tune) the option, but don't always count on it. But do you need to know which is being used?

You can see where the trade-offs are, of course—if you keep the entity locked in the database, no other applications can use that entity's data. That's fine if the EJB is the only application that needs that database. And that option (commit option A) gives you the best performance when a business method call comes in for the entity, because there's no ejbActivate() (the bean never went back to the pool), and more significantly—there's no trip to the database or an ejbLoad()!

Q: But couldn't option A really kill me, if I want to keep the entities unlocked in the database when they're not being used by the bean?

A: For this reason, most vendors won't use option A as a default; they allow it only if the deployer or admin chooses it (assuming it's even supported at all).

Q: I see another, possibly even WORSE problem with option A... doesn't this mean a continually growing heap full of objects? Like, each time someone uses a particular entity, an entity bean instance is created that then stays stuck to the EJB object? Aren't pools more efficient because you need only enough beans to service the actual in-progress methods?

A: No container worth configuring would leave you stuck with a constantly, endlessly growing accumulation of objects. Even a container that does use option A can use something like a LRU (Least Recently Used) algorithm to say to itself, "Hmmm... nobody has called a method on entity #908 for a long time, so I'll passivate that bean and put him back in the pool (and unlock the row)." But, with at least the option of using option A, a container can say to itself, "This entity #405 is really popular. It's a big pain to keep going to the database and doing the whole load/store/activate/passivate cycle each time, so I'll just keep him loaded and ready, even between transactions."

Q: Oh man, I just thought of something REALLY bad with this architecture...even if you do NOT keep accumulating entity beans, what about the EJB objects??? Don't they just keep growing and growing so that each time a client does a find, and gets back a stub, an EJB object is created for that entity, and it just stays around until the entity itself is removed? At any given time, I will have all the EJB objects on the heap that represent every entity anyone has ever accessed up to that point...

A: Ah... now we come to the difference between the "conceptual" view of the architecture, and the "actual" implementation.

According to the spec, you're supposed to assume that this is indeed how it works: when a client wants an entity bean, either through a create or find, the Container makes an EJB object for that entity ("here's the EJB object for #24, here's the EJB object for #98", etc.). And as a Bean Provider (as opposed to, say, a container/server provider), you are to program as if that's really the way it works.

But internally, the Container might be doing something quite different from the conceptual architectural view. Imagine that YOU were a container developer—how would you implement things?

One idea might be to put the burden on the clients, by keeping all the information in the stubs. For example, when the client gets a stub to an EJB object, you can make sure that the stub knows the unique ID for the entity (i.e. the primary key). But the EJB object's might be generic, in such a way that when the client calls a method on a stub, that stub is connected not to an EJB object just for that entity, but rather a one-EJB object-fits-all that knows how to make sure the method ends up at the right entity. That way, when a client isn't using an EJB object, that EJB object isn't sitting around wasting space. That's just one idea.

Q: That might be fine for stubs, but what if the client is local? Then they have a real reference to the EJB object, so that EJB object would HAVE to be entity-specific.

A: Yes, that's true. But with local clients, normal Java garbage collection works. When there are no clients with references to a particular EJB object, the instance will die.

Q: **Which of the three commit options do you think is most used?**

A: Well... we can't really answer that, but if we were in a betting mood, our money would be on option B. A 'smart' option B, that knows when it makes sense to hang on to a bean and when it doesn't. But avoiding the ejbActivate(), which is usually useless anyway, is a Good Thing.

Q: **But isn't the hit to the database—the load—a much bigger hit than just one more method call on the stack?**

A: First of all, activation is probably a little more than just one more method call on the stack, because there's overhead just in maintaining the organization of the pool itself. But yes, you're right about the database hit being a bigger deal. But... there's all sorts of ways the Container can optimize, and what's the alternative? The only alternative (option A) keeps the database locked, which is typically *not* what you want.

Q: **But what if my EJB app IS the only thing that uses that database?**

A: I think we mentioned this earlier...if you know absolutely positively no question that your EJB app is the only thing touching that database, then yes, if your vendor supports it, you'll have better performance with option A. Of course, caching things in memory is

still dangerous, because entities are persistent! So the vendor still must implement something that saves the state of the entities to the database, if they change. So there will still be storing, if not loading.

There are still other potential problems with option A, though. For example, you might have a server that supports clustering, and the server will have to be certain that all instances of that entity bean in sync, not just with the database, but with one another. But that's another issue. You'll learn more in the patterns and performance chapter.

Q: **So is the real point of all this the fact that as long as you're in a transaction, you won't have all these load/store activate/passivate calls?**

A: Yes, a big *part* of the point, anyway.

Q: **Then shouldn't your goal be to have the longest transactions?**

A: You aren't being serious, right? Just for fun, we'll pretend you are, and say, NO NO NO NO. Think about your concurrency. A good rule of thumb (with a zillion exceptions, of course so all rule-of-thumb disclaimers apply) is that transactions should be no longer than absolutely necessary. The longer your bean is in a transaction, the more likely it is that others are waiting in line to get to that entity! Of course, it's also possible to have transactions which are *too short*, which means

you're doing more loads/stores than you need to, so the key is to have your transactions be as long as you *need*, and *no longer*.

Q: **One more thing... doesn't this mean that ejbPassivate and ejbActivate might not ever be called on a bean, if the container uses option A or B? And doesn't this mean that I shouldn't rely on ejbActivate or ejbPassivate in my design?**

A: YES! That's EXACTLY what it means. It's usually a lousy strategy. But you can imagine how it might *sound* like a good idea...

> Um, remember how I told you it would be more efficient to get resources in ejbActivate and release them in ejbPassivate? Can we just pretend that I never said that?

Exercise

CMP entity bean Creation

Fill in the five missing arrow labels for the object interaction diagram. Remember, they aren't necessarily method calls. This is exactly the same diagram that you saw earlier in the chapter. Except yours will look nicer, because you'll probably make it all fancy with exotic symbols and maybe color-coded markers and...

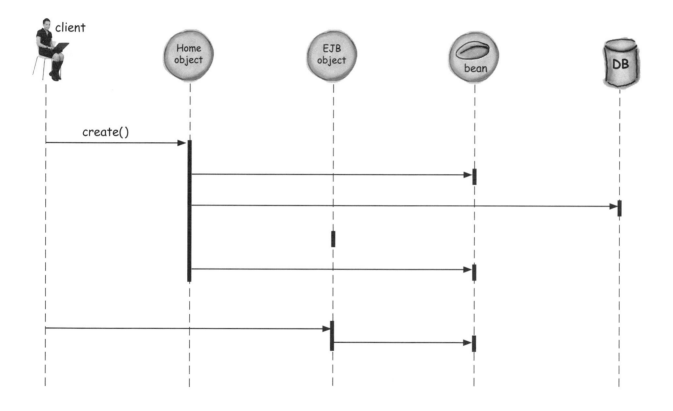

Entity Bean Business Method
(with activation & passivation)

This time, you're gonna draw the arrows yourself! Assume that the bean is in the pool at the time the client calls a business method (which also means the bean is not in a transaction). Draw arrows and label them with the actions that occur through the completion of the business method. Show what happens when the bean returns to the pool.

When we did it, there were eight more arrows, but you might have more or less depending on how you want to do it. Do NOT flip back through the most recent pages. You can do this.

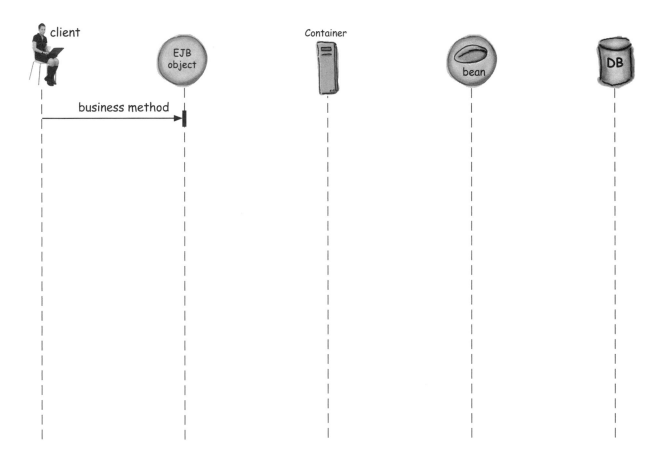

Fill in the ProductBean UML-ish box with the methods that YOU must write
in your bean class, given the component and home interfaces. Don't forget
the container callbacks from EntityBean, although we've shown you only
three of the seven. The rest you'll have to remember and fill in.

Exercise

<<interface>>
Product

| getProductDescription() |
| getQuantity() |
| getPrice() |

<<interface>>
EntityBean

| ——— |
| ejbActivate() |
| ——— |
| ejbRemove() |
| unsetEntityContext() |
| ——— |
| ——— |

<<interface>>
ProductHome

| create(String ID, String price, String description) |
| findByPrimaryKey(String key) |
| getLowInventory(int limit) |

ProductBean

Mock Exam

---

1 What's true for a bean provider when creating an entity bean using container-managed persistence? (Choose all that apply.)

❏ A. Container-managed persistent fields must be defined in the entity bean class.

❏ B. Container-managed relationship fields must be defined in the entity bean class.

❏ C. When implementing a one-to-many relationship, the java.util.List interface must not be used.

❏ D. Accessor methods for container-managed relationship fields must be exposed in the bean's remote component interface.

---

2 Which of the following is a legal accessor method for a persistent field in an entity bean with container-managed persistence? (Choose all that apply.)

❏ A. `public getCustomerNum();`

❏ B. `public void getCustomerNum();`

❏ C. `abstract void getCustomerNum();`

❏ D. `public abstract int getCustomerNum();`

---

3 Which of the following are legal accessor method(s) in an entity bean with container-managed persistence? (Choose all that apply.)

❏ A. `public abstract int GetCustomerNum();`

❏ B. `public abstract int getcustomerNum();`

❏ C. `public abstract int getCustomerNum();`

❏ D. `public abstract int getCustomerNum() { };`

4 Which are requirements for a CMP entity bean class? (Choose all that apply.)

❏ A. The class must define a **finalize()** method.

❏ B. The source file must define at least one constructor.

❏ C. The class must be declared public and abstract.

❏ D. The class must implement, directly or indirectly, the
javax.ejb.EnterpriseBean interface.

❏ E. All getter and setter methods for the bean's abstract persistence
schema must be abstract.

5 Which are legal declarations for a CMP bean's ejbCreate methods? (Choose
all that apply.)

❏ A. **public void ejbCreateBigCustomer() throws**
javax.ejb.CreateException

❏ B. **public String ejbCreateAccount() throws**
javax.ejb.CreateException

❏ C. **static String ejbCreate() throws**
javax.ejb.CreateException

❏ D. **public int ejbCreate() throws**
javax.ejb.CreateException

❏ E. **public final String ejbCreate() throws**
javax.ejb.CreateException

6 Which are legal declarations for a method in a CMP bean? (Choose all that
apply.)

❏ A. **public Account ejbSelectAcct(long x) throws**
javax.ejb.FinderException

❏ B. **public abstract Acct ejbSelectAcct(long x) throws**
javax.ejb.FinderException

❏ C. **public Account ejbPostCreate(Acct key) throws**
javax.ejb.CreateException

❏ D. **public void ejbPostCreate(Acct key) throws**
javax.ejb.CreateException

❏ E. **public static void ejbPostCreate(Acct key) throws**
javax.ejb.CreateException

7 Which method(s) from the EntityContext interface can be invoked from within the setEntityContext method? (Choose all that apply.)

❑ A. `getEJBObject()`

❑ B. `getEJBLocalHome()`

❑ C. `getCallerIdentity()`

❑ D. `getCallerPrincipal()`

❑ E. `setRollbackOnly()`

8 Which can be called on a CMP bean to transition it from the ready state to the pooled state? (Choose all that apply.)

❑ A. `ejbStore()`

❑ B. `ejbCreate()`

❑ C. `ejbSelect()`

❑ D. `ejbRemove()`

❑ E. `ejbPassivate()`

9 Which method(s) from the EntityContext interface can be invoked from within the ejbCreate method? (Choose all that apply.)

❑ A. `getEJBHome()`

❑ B. `getEJBObject()`

❑ C. `getCallerPrincipal()`

❑ D. `getUserTransaction()`

❑ E. `setRollbackOnly()`

10 What is true for a CMP bean in the ready state?

❑ A. Its `ejbLoad()` can be called directly after ejbStore.

❑ B. Its `ejbStore()` can be called directly after a business method.

❑ C. One of its business methods can be called directly after ejbStore.

❑ D. None of the above.

11 Which method(s) from the EntityContext interface must NOT be invoked from within the ejbLoad method? (Choose all that apply.)

- ❑ A. `getEJBHome()`
- ❑ B. `getEJBObject()`
- ❑ C. `getCallerPrincipal()`
- ❑ D. `getUserTransaction()`
- ❑ E. `setRollbackOnly()`

12 Which method, called on a CMP bean, is ALWAYS associated with a state change in the bean? (Choose all that apply.)

- ❑ A. `ejbLoad()`
- ❑ B. `ejbFind()`
- ❑ C. `ejbRemove()`
- ❑ D. `ejbActivate()`
- ❑ E. `unsetEntityContext()`

13 What's true about an CMP entity bean's primary key? (Choose all that apply.)

- ❑ A. The bean's primary key class must provide a suitable implementation of the hashCode and equals methods.
- ❑ B. When specifying the primary key in the deployment descriptor, only the field name must be declared
- ❑ C. All fields in the primary key class must be declared public.
- ❑ D. All fields used in the primary key must be container-managed fields.

14 How many ejbCreate methods can a CMP entity bean have?

- ❑ A. 0
- ❑ B. 1
- ❑ C. 0 or 1
- ❑ D. 0 to many
- ❑ E. 1 to many

15 Which method(s) are always invoked in direct response to a client operation? (Choose all that apply.)

❑ A. `ejbLoad()`

❑ B. `ejbCreate()`

❑ C. `ejbRemove()`

❑ D. `ejbActivate()`

❑ E. `ejbPassivate()`

❑ F. `setEntityContext()`

16 Which additional method(s) might the container call when invoking ejbRemove? (Choose all that apply.)

❑ A. `ejbFind()`

❑ B. `ejbLoad()`

❑ C. `ejbStore()`

❑ D. `ejbActivate()`

❑ E. `ejbPassivate()`

17 At what point(s) must the container establish a CMP bean's primary key? (Choose all that apply.)

❑ A. before calling `newInstance()`

❑ B. before calling `setEntityContext()`

❑ C. before calling `ejbCreate()`

❑ D. before calling `ejbPostCreate()`

18 Which method(s) run in the transaction context of the method that causes their invocation? (Choose all that apply.)

❑ A. `ejbLoad()`

❑ B. `ejbRemove()`

❑ C. `ejbSelect()`

❑ D. `ejbActivate()`

❑ E. `ejbPassivate()`

❑ F. `setEntityContext()`

COFFEE CRAM

Mock Exam Answers

---

1 What's true for a bean provider when creating an entity bean using container-managed persistence? (Choose all that apply.)

❏ A. Container-managed persistent fields must be defined in the entity bean class.

❏ B. Container-managed relationship fields must be defined in the entity bean class.

✓ C. When implementing a one-to-many relationship, the java.util.List interface must not be used. — Only Collection or Set can be used

❏ D. Accessor methods for container-managed relationship fields must be exposed in the bean's remote component interface.

---

2 Which of the following is a legal accessor method for a persistent field in an entity bean with container-managed persistence? (Choose all that apply.)

❏ A. `public getCustomerNum();`

❏ B. `public void getCustomerNum();`

❏ C. `abstract void getCustomerNum();`

✓ D. `public abstract int getCustomerNum();`

— It must be "public abstract" and return the value of what-ever the field is... it IS after all, a GETTER.

---

3 Which of the following are legal accessor method(s) in an entity bean with container-managed persistence? (Choose all that apply.)

❏ A. `public abstract int GetCustomerNum();`

❏ B. `public abstract int getcustomerNum();`

✓ C. `public abstract int getCustomerNum();`

❏ D. `public abstract int getCustomerNum() { };`

— you have to follow the Java naming convention

— not legal Java

4 Which are requirements for a CMP entity bean class? (Choose all that apply.) *(spec: 190)*

☐ A. The class must define a **finalize()** method.

☐ B. The source file must define at least one constructor. — *No, you want the default constructor*

☑ C. The class must be declared public and abstract.

☑ D. The class must implement, directly or indirectly, the — *EntityBean extends EnterpriseBean*
    javax.ejb.EnterpriseBean interface.

☑ E. All getter and setter methods for the bean's abstract persistence
    schema must be abstract.

(spec: 192)

5 Which are legal declarations for a CMP bean's ejbCreate methods? (Choose all that apply.)

☐ A. **public void ejbCreateBigCustomer() throws**
    javax.ejb.CreateException

☑ B. **public String ejbCreateAccount() throws**
    javax.ejb.CreateException

☐ C. **static String ejbCreate() throws**
    javax.ejb.CreateException

☐ D. **public int ejbCreate() throws**
    javax.ejb.CreateException

☐ E. **public final String ejbCreate()**
    javax.ejb.CreateException

— *it can't be:*
— *static*
— *void*
— *final*
*must return the
type of the primary
key*

(spec: 192–193)

6 Which are legal declarations for a method in a CMP bean? (Choose all that apply.)

☐ A. **public Account ejbSelectAcct(long x) throws**
    javax.ejb.FinderException

☑ B. **public abstract Acct ejbSelectAcct(long x) throws**
    javax.ejb.FinderException

☐ C. **public Account ejbPostCreate(Acct key) throws**
    javax.ejb.CreateException

☑ D. **public void ejbPostCreate(Acct key) throws**
    javax.ejb.CreateException

☐ E. **public static void ejbPostCreate(Acct key) throws**
    javax.ejb.CreateException

— *must be:*
*abstract
void*
— *can't be
static*

7 Which method(s) from the EntityContext interface can be invoked from within the setEntityContext method? (Choose all that apply.) *(spec: 179)*

- ❏ A. `getEJBObject()`
- ☑ B. `getEJBLocalHome()`
- ❏ C. `getCallerIdentity()` — just too early for these last three. There's not a caller tx. setEntityContext just means a bean is going in the pool
- ❏ D. `getCallerPrincipal()`
- ❏ E. `setRollbackOnly()`

8 Which can be called on a CMP bean to transition it from the ready state to the pooled state? (Choose all that apply.) *(spec: 168-169)*

- ❏ A. `ejbStore()` — store can be called anytime and is not called to transition the bean
- ❏ B. `ejbCreate()`
- ❏ C. `ejbSelect()`
- ☑ D. `ejbRemove()` — with ejbRemove(), the bean won't get an ejbPassivate()
- ☑ E. `ejbPassivate()`

9 Which method(s) from the EntityContext interface can be invoked from within the ejbCreate method? (Choose all that apply.) *(spec: 179)*

- ☑ A. `getEJBHome()`
- ❏ B. `getEJBObject()`
- ☑ C. `getCallerPrincipal()`
- ❏ D. `getUserTransaction()` — Entity beans can NEVER invoke this, because entity beans must use CMT
- ☑ E. `setRollbackOnly()`

10 What is true for a CMP bean in the ready state? *(spec: 169)*

- ☑ A. Its `ejbLoad()` can be called directly after ejbStore.
- ☑ B. Its `ejbStore()` can be called directly after a business method.
- ☑ C. One of its business methods can be called directly after ejbStore.
- ❏ D. None of the above.

— The point is: load, store and business methods can be called by the Container in any order

11 Which method(s) from the EntityContext interface must NOT be invoked (spec: 180) from within the ejbLoad method? (Choose all that apply.)

❏ A. `getEJBHome()`

❏ B. `getEJBObject()`

❏ C. `getCallerPrincipal()`

☑ D. `getUserTransaction()` – for BMT only

❏ E. `setRollbackOnly()`

12 Which method, called on a CMP bean, is ALWAYS associated with a state (spec: 168–169) change in the bean? (Choose all that apply.)

❏ A. `ejbLoad()` – not always!

❏ B. `ejbFind()`

☑ C. `ejbRemove()` – bean goes back to the pool

☑ D. `ejbActivate()` – bean comes out of the pool

☑ E. `unsetEntityContext()` – bean goes from the pool to death

13 What's true about an CMP entity bean's primary key? (Choose all that apply.) (spec: 203, 275)

☑ A. The bean's primary key class must provide a suitable implementation of the hashCode and equals methods.

❏ B. When specifying the primary key in the deployment descriptor, only the field name must be declared   – no, you need the type

☑ C. All fields in the primary key class must be declared public.

☑ D. All fields used in the primary key must be container-managed fields.

14 How many ejbCreate methods can a CMP entity bean have? (spec: 171)

❏ A. 0

❏ B. 1   *You don't have to let clients create beans*

❏ C. 0 or 1

☑ D. 0 to many

❏ E. 1 to many

15 Which method(s) are always invoked in direct response to a client operation? (spec: 171–172)
(Choose all that apply.)

❏ A. `ejbLoad()`

☑ B. `ejbCreate()`

☑ C. `ejbRemove()`

❏ D. `ejbActivate()`

❏ E. `ejbPassivate()`

❏ F. `setEntityContext()`

Load, Passivate, and setEntityContext can be called by the Container when it wants to

---

16 Which additional method(s) might the container call when invoking ejbRemove? (Choose all that apply.) (spec: 176)

❏ A. `ejbFind()`

☑ B. `ejbLoad()`

❏ C. `ejbStore()`

☑ D. `ejbActivate()`

❏ E. `ejbPassivate()`

a bean has to be ready and loaded before it can do a remove – it may have cascading deletes to take care of

---

17 At what point(s) must the container establish a CMP bean's primary key? (spec: 175)
(Choose all that apply.)

❏ A. before calling `newInstance()`

❏ B. before calling `setEntityContext()`

❏ C. before calling `ejbCreate()`

☑ D. before calling `ejbPostCreate()`

the Container uses the values you set in ejbCreate so that in ejbPostCreate the bean is ready to use its key

---

18 Which method(s) run in the transaction context of the method that causes (spec: 174–178)
their invocation? (Choose all that apply.)

☑ A. `ejbLoad()`

☑ B. `ejbRemove()`

☑ C. `ejbSelect()`

❏ D. `ejbActivate()`

❏ E. `ejbPassivate()`

❏ F. `setEntityContext()`

When Beans Relate

Have you heard about One-to-Many relationships? I thought maybe we could try that...

Oh really? Too bad you don't have a Container to manage your referential integrity. Because I would just love to cascade-delete you right now...

Entity beans need relationships. An Order needs a Customer. A LineItem needs an Order. An Order needs LineItems. A Movie needs a Director. A Director needs Movies. A Movie needs Actors. An Actor needs *talent*...   Entity beans can have container-managed relationships (CMR) and the Container takes care of virtually everything. Make a new Movie and give it a Director? That Director automatically has one more Movie in his Movie collection. Make a new LineItem that's related to an Order? If you ask the Customer to show you his Orders, his Orders will show the new LineItem. Best of all, you can use EJB-QL to write portable (think: vendor/databse independent) queries.

Entity Relationships: CMP and CMR

Official:

6.2 Identify correct and incorrect statements or examples about persistent relationships, remove protocols, and about the abstract schema type, of a CMP entity bean.

6.3 Identify correct and incorrect statements or examples about rules and semantics for relationship assignment updating, in a CMP bean.

6.4 Match the name with a description of purpose or functionality for each of the following: <ejb-name>, <abstract-schema-name>, <ejb-relationship-role>, <cmr-field>, <cmr-field-type>, and <relationship-role-source>

6.5 Identify correctly implemented deployment descriptor elements for a CMP bean (including container-managed relationships).

9.1 Identify correct and incorrect syntax for an EJB-QL query including the SELECT, FROM, and WHERE clause.

9.2 Identify correct and incorrect statements or examples about the purpose and use of EJB-QL.

9.3 Identify correct and incorrect conditional expressions, between expressions, like expressions, and comparison expressions.

What it really means:

You have to know that the container manages relationships between two entity beans through container-managed relationship (CMR) fields, and that CMR fields must be described in the deployment descriptor using the <relationships> section.

You have to understand the implications of multiplicity in a relationship, and that the Container cares whether the relationship is one-to-one, one-to-many, or many-to-many. You must know that the Container maintains the referential integrity of the database by using the multiplicity when doing assignments. For example, if there can be only one Customer per Order, if you assign an Order to a Customer, that Order cannot exist in any other Customer's Order collection. And if you reassign that Order to a different Customer, the Order is moved from one Customer's collection to the other. But if you assign a Customer with three existing Orders, to another Order, the reference to the Customer is copied, not moved, so that the reference to a Customer that the other three existing Orders have, is not affected.

You have to know that EJB-QL queries are defined in the deployment descriptor, and are for Finder and Select methods only. You have to know the basic syntax of EJB-QL, and that FROM and SELECT are mandatory, but WHERE is optional.

You have to know that if you use path navigation to, say, get the title of a Movie, you can say m.title (assuming "m" is declared as the abstract schema type of Movie, and "title" is a CMP field of the MovieBean). But that you can't say d.movies.title where "d" is a Director, and "movies" is a CMR field that is a Collection of movies. For that, you must use the IN operator within a FROM clause. You'll see... it's all in here. And much simpler than it sounds.

Beanifying your movie database

Imagine you have a movie application (it isn't making the folks at imdb.com nervous, but it works for you).

You can use it to look up a movie.

Once you have a movie, you can use it to launch the movie trailer.

You can do all kinds of searches to, say, *find all sci-fi movies*, or *find all action movies by a specific director*.

We can make beans for Movie, Trailer, and Director. But how do they map to the database? And how do they relate to one another?

> I want to see all the movies with directors who are no more than 3 degrees away from Kevin Bacon, and the genre is "romantic horror".

a foreign key into the Director table

Movie Table

MovieID	Title	Genre	DirectorID	Year
12	Crouching Pixels, Hidden Mouse	Action	42	2000
5	The Fifth Array Element	Action	27	2003
22	The Return of the Bean Queen	Fantasy	27	2001
11	Lord of the Loops	Sci-fi	42	2002

Director Table

DirectorID	OscarWinner	Degrees	Name
27	TRUE	3	Jim Yingst
42	FALSE	6	Jessica Sant
56	FALSE	24	Skyler Safford
17	FALSE	5	John Dawson

Director doesn't have a reference to his movies.

Trailer Table

TrailerID	FileName
12	Crouching Pixels, Hidden Mouse Trailer
5	The Fifth Array Element Trailer
22	The Return of the Bean Queen Trailer
11	Lord of the Loops Trailer

The trailer's primary key always matches the MovieID

But we don't want to think in TABLES
We want to think in CLASSES

We know we can map tables to bean classes, no problem. All the columns become persistent fields in the bean class, represented by abstract getters and setters, and we're good to go. Except... if this were a class and not a table, we wouldn't have designed it that way. We'd probably make the movie class a lot more friendly and useful, for example, so that a client could work with just the movie bean, rather than having to get references to all three beans.

But this doesn't look very client—friendly. Look what the client would have to do... get a reference to all three tables! If the client has a reference to a movie, they have to get the directorID from the movie, then use that to get a reference to a Director.

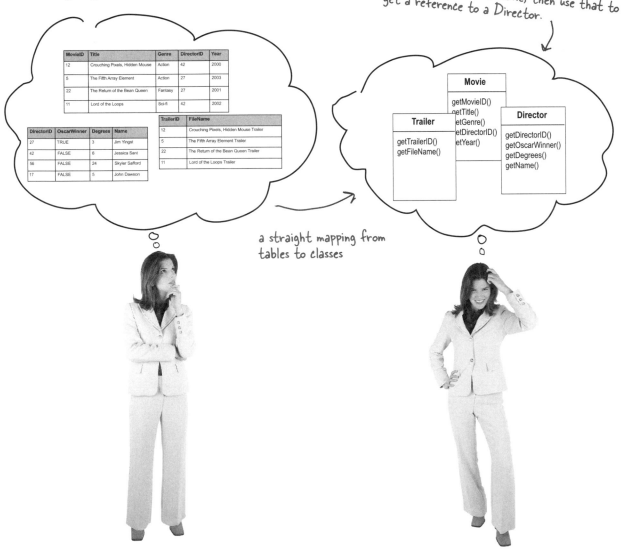

a straight mapping from tables to classes

Wouldn't it be dreamy if there were a way to use container-managed persistence, but have classes that didn't have to look exactly like the tables? So that a client could get a movie, and ask the movie for a *real* Director reference, not just the director's *foreign key*... yeah, that would be great, but it's probably just a fantasy...

We need relationships between the Movie bean and the Director bean

We want the Movie bean to have a reference to its matching Director bean and we want to do all sorts of searches against the Movie bean and have the queries use the Director bean's data as well.

In other words, we want to make it easy on the client (and on the developer) to think in a more natural way, rather than in the database-efficient way that was used to design the schema of the database. Who wants that? Remember, this is the OO world and relational databases, while crucial to your business, are so 1999. We want to *use* databases, we just don't want to *think* like databases. (If you're one of the lucky ones who gets to use an OO database, and assuming that database still somehow manages to perform well enough for your needs, then you can just smile smugly during this first section.)

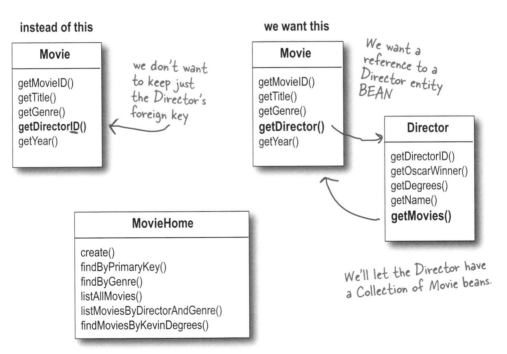

We're not going to use the Trailer table and bean after this (although you'll see it in code), to keep the example cleaner. Adding the Trailer bean wouldn't add any new complexity to the application, though. If you can set-up one bean-to-bean relationship, you can set up others.

Why should the Director be a bean? Why can't it just be data?

Why not have the Movie bean simply go to the database, using the Director's foreign key (stored as a persistent field in the Movie bean), and get the Director's data? But if you make the director a bean as well, you get to think ONLY in objects (except during deployment, when you do have to map from your beans to your tables). And you get all the benefits of container-managed persistence and synchronization. Imagine if someone calls a setter method to change the director's oscar winning status. If you're managing this, you'd have to get a JDBC connection and synchronize the database yourself. And of course, you'd have to know when is the right time, etc. But if its director is also a bean, you call a setWinner() method, and you're done.

Oh, and there's another cool thing. You might decide, for example, to banish a specific director from your database, because you think his movies suck in an unrecoverable way. No problem deleting that director, obviously. But then what happens to the movies? How can you have movies in the database that don't have a director? What is the database is already set up in such a way that you aren't allowed to have a null value for the director column? In other words, what if a movie cannot exist in the database without a director?

You can handle this brainlessly, by setting up the Movie-to-Director bean relationship in such a way that when you delete a director from the database, all of his movies are automatically deleted! You do this with one simple tag in the deployment descriptor and POOF! Somebody calls remove() on a director bean, and remove() will automatically be called on all of the movie entity beans that have a reference to this director (as the value of their director persistent field).

If both the Director and the Movie are entity beans, you never have to worry about synchronizing any of the Movie's related data; if somebody uses the Movie bean to change something about the Director, everything's taken care of by the Container.

You can even set things up for a cascade-delete... so if you remove a Director, all the Director's movies will be removed automatically!

Relationships and multiplicity

Ⓐ One-to-One

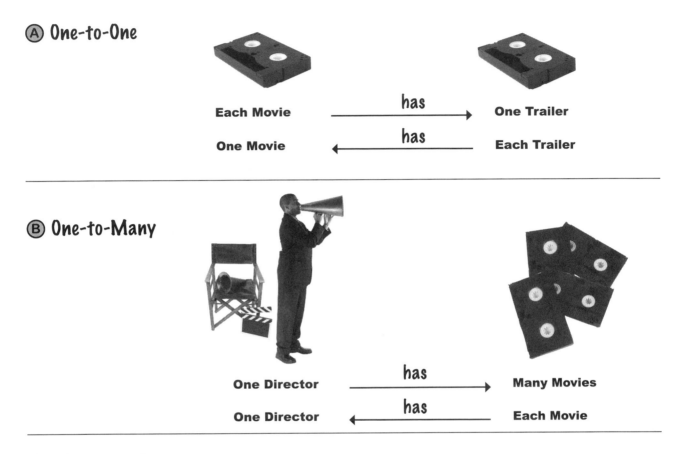

Each Movie ——— has ———→ **One Trailer**

One Movie ←——— has ——— **Each Trailer**

Ⓑ One-to-Many

One Director ——— has ———→ **Many Movies**

One Director ←——— has ——— **Each Movie**

③ Many-to-Many

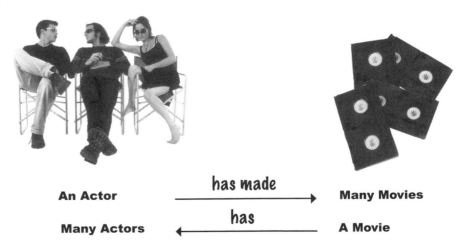

An Actor ——— has made ———→ **Many Movies**

Many Actors ←——— has ——— **A Movie**

Multiplicity in Bean Classes

Here's how it works with our bean code. This multiplicity notation is the only UML-like thing you have to know on the exam.

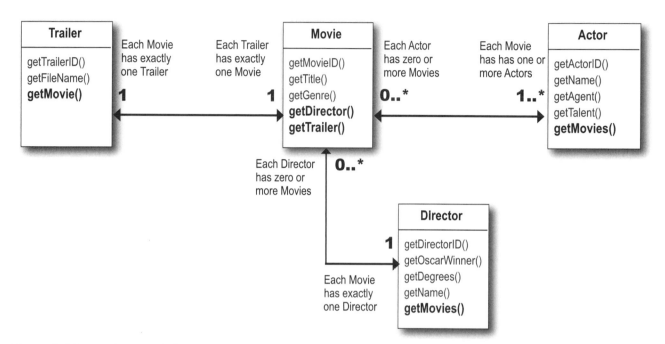

To read this, you have to follow the arrow to its destination. In the Person to Pets relationship, Person has a multiplicity of ONE, but Pets has a multiplicity of MANY (which could be zero). To find out how many Pets a Person can have, you have to follow the arrow out of Person and into Pets. The number closest to the class is the multiplicity of that class to others. In other words, how many of that type does the other type have.

Multiplicity affects return type!

A Movie has one Director. When you call getDirector(), you get back one Director. So the return type of getDirector() is a Director().

But a Director has many movies, so when you call getMovies(), you get back a Collection of Movies.

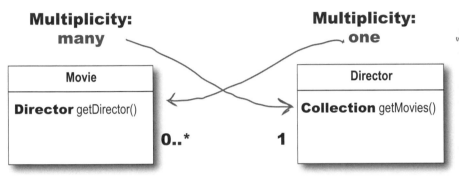

Multiplicity: many

Movie
Director getDirector()

0..*

Multiplicity: one

Director
Collection getMovies()

1

Movie has a multiplicity of "many" in its relationship with Director. That does NOT mean that Movie has "many" Directors... it means that Director has "many" Movies!

So Director has a getMovies() that returns a Collection of Movies.

And Director has a multiplicity of "one", which means that Movie will return just one Director.

In the Movie-to-Director relationship, the multiplicity of Movie is *many* and the multiplicity of Director is *one*.

A multiplicity of *one* means the object you're related to holds just *one* of you.

Director has a multiplicity of *one*, so the Movie object related to Director returns just *a single Director* bean (OK, technically the component interface of Director, but you know what we mean by now).

A multiplicity of *many* means the object you're related to holds a *Collection* of you.

Movie has a multiplicity of *many*, so the Director object related to Movie returns a *Collection of Movie beans*.

Defining virtual fields for persistent data fields and relationship fields

In the previous chapter we looked at defining container-managed fields—you put in a pair of abstract getters and setters. We said *a container-managed field exists simply because you have a getter and setter for it.* It works the same way with container-managed relationship (CMR) fields. You define a pair of abstract getters and setters, but rather than setting and returning a value that maps to a column in a table, you set and return a reference to another entity bean, or a Collection that will hold references to the entity bean. The restrictions for CMR fields are that they can refer only to the *local* component interface of the entity bean, and that if the method returns a Collection, the declared type can be only Collection or Set (not Map, List, etc.)

The terminology is a little confusing because both CMP and CMR fields are container-managed persistent fields. They might have called it CMPCD (container-managed persistent *column data*) fields and CMPR (container-managed persistent *relationship*) fields. Of course, persistence isn't restricted to just relational database, so we're using the term "column" a little loosely. But in EJB 1.1, *all* container-managed persistent fields were CMP fields, because there was no concept of persistent relationships in EJB 1.1 CMP.

You need a pair of abstract getters and setters for each CMP field (column values) and each CMR field (relationship with another entity).

The only difference between a CMP field and a CMR field is the TYPE.

A CMR field is always another entity bean's local interface type, or a Collection of them.

If it's a Collection, it must be either java.util.Collection or java.util.Set.

① CMP field

```
public abstract String getTitle();
public abstract void setTitle(String g);
```
make sure the argument and return type match

② CMR (relationship) field

```
public abstract Director getDirector();
public abstract void setDirector(Director d);
```
Director must be the local component interface for the Director bean.

The argument and return type of a CMR "virtual field" is always another Entity bean's local type, or a Collection.

Defining your "abstract persistence schema" (virtual fields aren't enough)

To define persistent fields and relationships, you need to create an *abstract persistence schema*. Defining the virtual fields isn't enough. Your abstract persistence schema is a combination of your virtual fields in your bean class, plus some things you write in the deployment descriptor.

The way you describe CMP fields in the DD is simple and straightforward. With CMR, you'll have to do a little more to set things up, including describing the multiplicity for each of the two participants in a relationship.

But we'll get to CMR fields in just a minute. For now, we'll start with just CMP fields.

An abstract persistent schema is a combination of some stuff you put in the deployment descriptor, plus your abstract getters and setters.

Together, they tell the Container how to manage your bean's persistence, including both persistent FIELDS (called CMP fields) and persistent RELATIONSHIPS (called CMR fields).

The Container needs these TWO things to know you have a CMP field "title"

① In the DD

```
<entity>
    <ejb-name>MovieBean</ejb-name>
    <local-home>headfirst.MovieHome</local-home>
    <local>headfirst.Movie</local>
    <ejb-class>headfirst.MovieBean</ejb-class>
    <abstract-schema-name>MovieSchema</abstract-schema-name>
    <cmp-field>
        <field-name>title</field-name>
    </cmp-field>
    ...
<entity>
```

② In the bean class

```
public abstract String getTitle();
public abstract void setTitle(String g);
```

Persistent CMP fields in the DD

```
<entity>
   <display-name>MovieBean</display-name>
   <ejb-name>MovieBean</ejb-name>
   <local-home>headfirst.MovieHome</local-home>
   <local>headfirst.Movie</local>
   <ejb-class>headfirst.MovieBean</ejb-class>
   <persistence-type>Container</persistence-type>
   <prim-key-class>java.lang.String</prim-key-class>
   <reentrant>False</reentrant>
   <cmp-version>2.x</cmp-version>
   <abstract-schema-name>MovieSchema</abstract-schema-name>
   <cmp-field>
      <field-name>genre</field-name>
   </cmp-field>
   <cmp-field>
      <field-name>movieID</field-name>
   </cmp-field>
   <cmp-field>
      <field-name>year</field-name>
   </cmp-field>
   <cmp-field>
      <field-name>title</field-name>
   </cmp-field>
   <primkey-field>movieID</primkey-field>
   ...
<entity>
```

tell the Container that IT is managing your persistence (as opposed to "Bean")

fully-qualified class name for the field that represents the primary key

Name your schema so that you know which entity type it represents. This name must be unique in the DD!!

Now that you've told the Container WHICH fields to manage, tell it which of those fields is the Special One... the primary key field.

The naming convention is REQUIRED!

You must have a pair of abstract getters and setters that have the first character after the "get" and "set" capitalized, but in the CMP field definition in the DD, you start with a lowercase letter, leaving off the "get" and "set". In other words, you define the CMP field in the DD as if it were a real instance variable, following the old pre-EJB JavaBeans naming convention.

---

there are no Dumb Questions

Q: **How does the Container know the type of the persistent field? I see a definition for the primary key type (<prim-key-class>, but I don't see anything for the other CMP fields.**

A: The Container figures it out based on the return type and argument of the abstract getters and setters in the bean class. And they had better match! If you have a getLimitNum() that returns an int, you better have a setLimitNum(int i) that takes an int.

Using relationships in your code

In your bean code, you use your virtual relationship fields just as you would any other getter and setter. The only difference between using a *real* field (i.e. an instance variable declared in your class) and a *virtual* field is that you can access your virtual fields only by calling the abstract getters and setters (which the Container implements at deploy-time).

The only new restriction is that a relationship field can be *only* a local component interface type! You can't have a CMR relationship field that uses a bean's Remote interface!

Virtual field in the bean class

```
public abstract Director getDirector();
public abstract void setDirector(Director d);
```

The argument and return type of a CMR "virtual field" is always another Entity bean type, and it MUST be a local interface!! You can't have a virtual field to the entity's Remote interface.

Exposed business method in the bean class

```
public Director getMovieDirector() {
    return getDirector();
}
```

Now we can return the Director to a client, by calling the abstract getter.

```
public String getMovieDirectorName() {
    return getDirector().getDirectorName();
}
```

We can also do the work on behalf of the client, if we don't want to expose the real Director reference to the client. In fact, that's how we're going to do it, because the Director is a local interface, but the Movie is going to have Remote clients.

You can use your virtual relationship fields just as you would any other virtual field... by calling the abstract getters that YOU defined, but which the Container implements.

The type of a relationship field MUST be the local component interface of the entity!

A CMR field will ALWAYS be a local component interface type.

Defining relationships in your abstract persistence schema (in the DD)

CMP field definitions are so easy. You declare a <cmp-field> and give it a name that matches one of your getter/setter pairs (following the naming rule of dropping the "get" and "set" and beginning the CMP field name with a lower-case letter).

But CMR is more involved. You can't be in a relationship with only yourself, so **a relationship always includes two beans!**

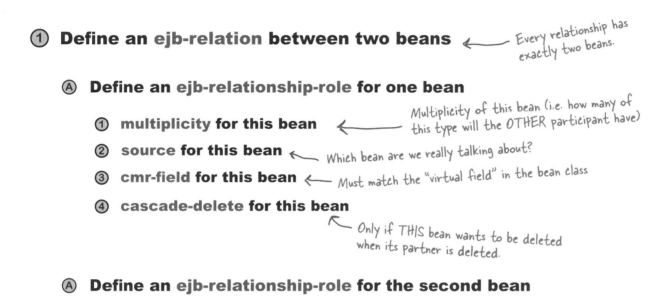

① **Define an ejb-relation between two beans** ← *Every relationship has exactly two beans.*

  Ⓐ **Define an ejb-relationship-role for one bean**

    ① **multiplicity for this bean** ← *Multiplicity of this bean (i.e. how many of this type will the OTHER participant have)*

    ② **source for this bean** ← *Which bean are we really talking about?*

    ③ **cmr-field for this bean** ← *Must match the "virtual field" in the bean class*

    ④ **cascade-delete for this bean**
      ↖ *Only if THIS bean wants to be deleted when its partner is deleted.*

  Ⓐ **Define an ejb-relationship-role for the second bean**

    ① **multiplicity for this bean**

    ② **source for this bean**

    ③ **cmr-field for this bean**

    ④ **cascade-delete for this bean**

Same stuff for the second participant in the relationship

Relationship definition for the Director-to-Movie relationship

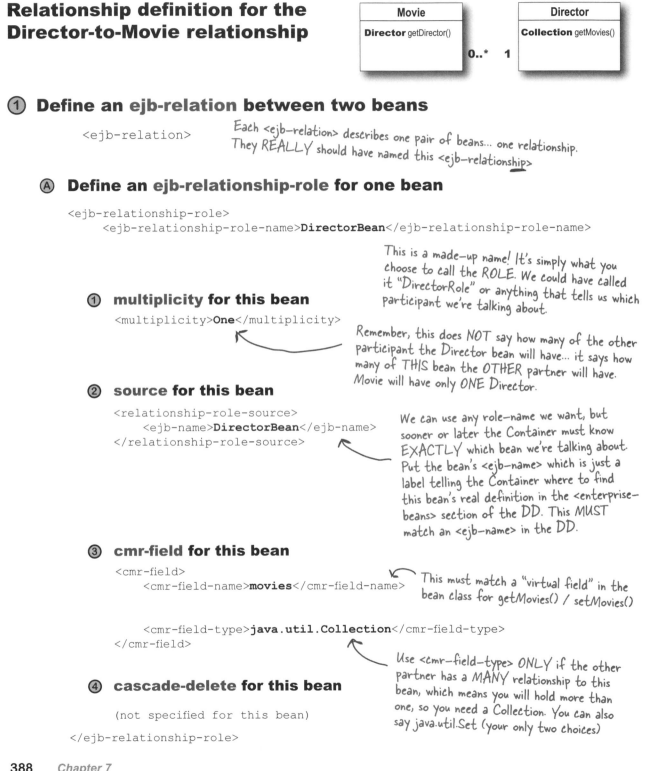

Movie		Director
Director getDirector()		**Collection** getMovies()

0..*   1

① Define an ejb-relation between two beans

```
<ejb-relation>
```

Each `<ejb-relation>` describes one pair of beans... one relationship. They REALLY should have named this `<ejb-relationship>`

Ⓐ Define an ejb-relationship-role for one bean

```
<ejb-relationship-role>
    <ejb-relationship-role-name>DirectorBean</ejb-relationship-role-name>
```

This is a made-up name! It's simply what you choose to call the ROLE. We could have called it "DirectorRole" or anything that tells us which participant we're talking about.

① multiplicity for this bean

```
<multiplicity>One</multiplicity>
```

Remember, this does NOT say how many of the other participant the Director bean will have... it says how many of THIS bean the OTHER partner will have. Movie will have only ONE Director.

② source for this bean

```
<relationship-role-source>
    <ejb-name>DirectorBean</ejb-name>
</relationship-role-source>
```

We can use any role-name we want, but sooner or later the Container must know EXACTLY which bean we're talking about. Put the bean's `<ejb-name>` which is just a label telling the Container where to find this bean's real definition in the `<enterprise-beans>` section of the DD. This MUST match an `<ejb-name>` in the DD.

③ cmr-field for this bean

```
<cmr-field>
    <cmr-field-name>movies</cmr-field-name>
```

This must match a "virtual field" in the bean class for getMovies() / setMovies()

```
    <cmr-field-type>java.util.Collection</cmr-field-type>
</cmr-field>
```

④ cascade-delete for this bean

```
(not specified for this bean)
```

Use `<cmr-field-type>` ONLY if the other partner has a MANY relationship to this bean, which means you will hold more than one, so you need a Collection. You can also say java.util.Set (your only two choices)

```
</ejb-relationship-role>
```

Ⓐ **Define an ejb-relationship-role for the second bean**

```
<ejb-relationship-role>
    <ejb-relationship-role-name>MovieBean</ejb-relationship-role-name>
```

Remember, this is just a name for your own (or the App Assembler or a tool's) use. It means nothing in your Java code.

① **multiplicity for this bean**

```
<multiplicity>Many</multiplicity>
```

This means Director will have MANY of this type (Movie). So we expect that Director will have a CMR field with a Collection type rather than a single Movie

② **source for this bean**

```
<relationship-role-source>
    <ejb-name>MovieBean</ejb-name>
</relationship-role-source>
```

This MUST match the <ejb-name> for where you defined the Movie entity bean in the <enterprise-beans> section of the DD.

③ **cmr-field for this bean**

```
<cmr-field>
    <cmr-field-name>director</cmr-field-name>
</cmr-field>
```

Look... no type! We don't have a <cmr-field-type> because it isn't a Collection. In fact, the only reason there's a <cmr-field-type> tag is for when the field type is a Collection, and you have to distinguish between Set or Collection. <cmr-field-type>

④ **cascade-delete for this bean**

```
<cascade-delete />
```

Put this in if you want THIS bean to be deleted whenever its partner is deleted.

```
    </ejb-relationship-role>
</ejb-relation>
```

Sharpen your pencil

Here's the relationship DD for Director-to-Movie, but we've left a few things out. See if you can fill them in correctly *without* looking on the previous pages!

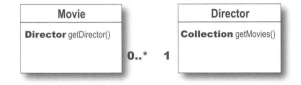

Movie	Director
Director getDirector()	**Collection** getMovies()

0..*   1

Director-to-Movie relationship

```
<relationships>

    <ejb-relation>

      <ejb-relationship-role>

        <ejb-relationship-role-name>_____</ejb-relationship-role-name>

        <multiplicity>_____</multiplicity>

        <relationship-role-source>

          <ejb-name>DirectorBean</ejb-name>

        </relationship-role-source>

        <cmr-field>

          <cmr-field-name>_____ </cmr-field-name>

          _____

        </cmr-field>

      </ejb-relationship-role>

      <ejb-relationship-role>

        <ejb-relationship-role-name>MovieBean</ejb-relationship-role-name>

        <multiplicity>_____</multiplicity>

        <cascade-delete />

        <relationship-role-source>

          <ejb-name>_____</ejb-name>

        </relationship-role-source>

          _____

          _____

          _____

      </ejb-relationship-role>

    </ejb-relation>

  </relationships>
```

> Does this mean that when a bean is in a relationship, it MUST have a field for the other bean? What if I want Movie to have a Trailer, but I don't want anybody to use Trailer to get to a Movie?

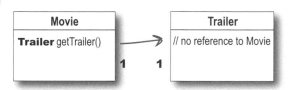

Movie		Trailer
Trailer getTrailer()	→	// no reference to Movie
1	1	

Relationships can be one-way (unidirectional)

You can have a relationship between two beans, but have a CMR field in only one of the two beans. For example, if you set up a relationship between a Movie and its Trailer (a one-to-one relationship), and you don't want clients to use a Trailer to get to a Movie, just leave the CMR field for Movie out of the Trailer bean. Simple as that.

In that case, the TrailerBean won't know anything about the MovieBean, even though they're both partners in a relationship.

```
<ejb-relationship-role>
    <ejb-relationship-role-name>TrailerBean</ejb-relationship-role-name>
    <multiplicity>One</multiplicity>
    <cascade-delete />
    <relationship-role-source>
      <ejb-name>TrailerBean</ejb-name>
    </relationship-role-source>
    <cmr-field>
      <cmr-field-name></cmr-field-name>
    </cmr-field>
  </ejb-relationship-role>
```

Leave the cmr-field out of a relationship role if you don't want this bean to have a reference to its partner bean.

The dark side of a unidirectional (one-way) relationship

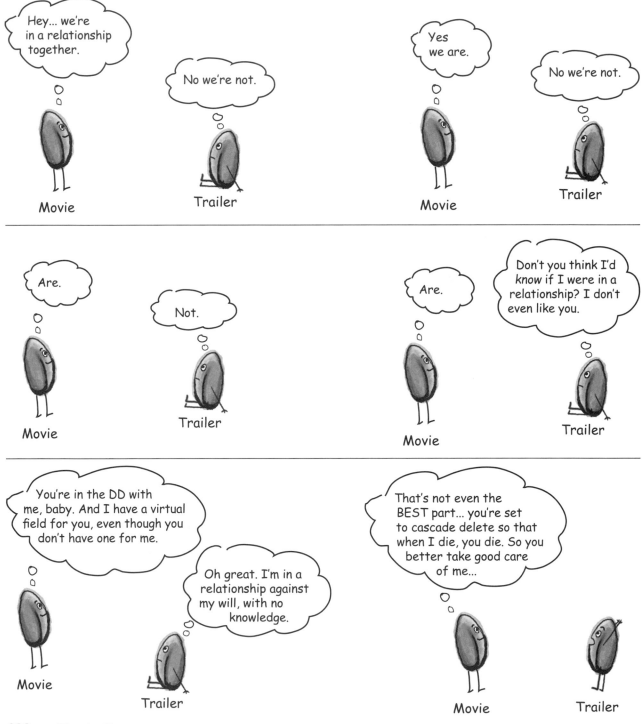

Cascade delete can propagate

Director

Movie

Trailer

Director-to-Movie relationship

Director (can't cascade-delete)

Movie - <cascade-delete/>

You can't set cascade-delete for the Director bean in the Director-to-Movie relationship, because Movie has a multiplicity of Many. Think about it... if someone deletes a Movie, should that Director be deleted? Of course not! The Director could still be the Director of other movies that still exist.

But... the Director has a multiplicity of One with the Movie, so the Movie bean can say, "I can have only one Director, so if he goes, I go."

Movie-to-Trailer relationship

Movie - (could cascade delete, but doesn't want to)

Trailer- <cascade-delete/>

Because this is a one-to-one relationship, both partners could set a cascade-delete. But we want it to go in only one direction, where deleting the Movie deletes the Trailer, but not the reverse. Just because the Trailer is deleted does not mean we want the Movie deleted, but that's determined by our business logic, and not EJB rules.

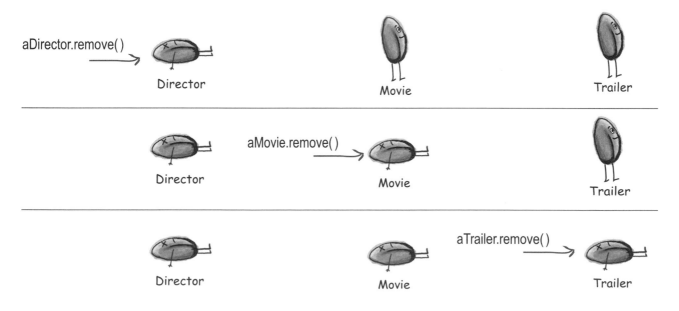

The abstract schema is in the <entity> element and the <ejb-relation> is in the <relationships> element

```
<ejb-jar>
   <display-name>MovieJar</display-name>
   <enterprise-beans>
     <entity>
        <display-name>MovieBean</display-name>
        <ejb-name>MovieBean</ejb-name>
        <local-home>headfirst.MovieHome</local-home>
        <local>headfirst.Movie</local>
        <ejb-class>headfirst.MovieBean</ejb-class>
        <persistence-type>Container</persistence-type>
        <prim-key-class>java.lang.String</prim-key-class>
        <reentrant>False</reentrant>
        <cmp-version>2.x</cmp-version>
        <abstract-schema-name>MovieSchema</abstract-schema-name>
        <cmp-field>
           <field-name>genre</field-name>
        </cmp-field>
        <cmp-field>
           <field-name>movieID</field-name>
        </cmp-field>
        <cmp-field>
           <field-name>year</field-name>
        </cmp-field>
        <cmp-field>
           <field-name>title</field-name>
        </cmp-field>
        <primkey-field>movieID</primkey-field>
        <security-identity>
              <use-caller-identity></use-caller-identity>
        </security-identity>
     </entity>

     <entity>
        <display-name>DirectorBean</display-name>
        <ejb-name>DirectorBean</ejb-name>
        <local-home>headfirst.DirectorHome</local-home>
        <local>headfirst.Director</local>
        <ejb-class>headfirst.DirectorBean</ejb-class>
        <persistence-type>Container</persistence-type>
        <prim-key-class>java.lang.String</prim-key-class>
        <reentrant>False</reentrant>
        <cmp-version>2.x</cmp-version>
        <abstract-schema-name>DirectorSchema</abstract-schema-name>
        <cmp-field>
           <field-name>name</field-name>
        </cmp-field>
```

The abstract schema for persistent fields is defined HERE in the <entity> element under <enterprise-beans>, where all beans are described.

WHOA! Notice what's missing!! There is NO <cmp-field> for Director. You don't list <cmr-field> elements inside the <entity> section. They're defined ONLY in the <relationships> section (next page)

```
    <cmp-field>
      <field-name>winner</field-name>
    </cmp-field>
    <cmp-field>
      <field-name>directorID</field-name>
    </cmp-field>
    <cmp-field>
      <field-name>degrees</field-name>
    </cmp-field>
    <primkey-field>directorID</primkey-field>
    <security-identity>
      <use-caller-identity></use-caller-identity>
    </security-identity>
  </entity>
</enterprise-beans>

<relationships>
  <ejb-relation>
```

AFTER the <enterprise-beans> section (and all the beans have been described), we have the <relationships> section that uses <ejb-name> elements to refer BACK to the <enterprise-beans> section

```
    <ejb-relationship-role>
      <ejb-relationship-role-name>DirectorBean</ejb-relationship-role-name>
      <multiplicity>One</multiplicity>
      <relationship-role-source>
        <ejb-name>DirectorBean</ejb-name>
      </relationship-role-source>
      <cmr-field>
        <cmr-field-name>movies</cmr-field-name>
        <cmr-field-type>java.util.Collection</cmr-field-type>
      </cmr-field>
    </ejb-relationship-role>
```

This name MUST match something in this DD, described in an <entity> element in the <enterprise-beans> section

<cmr-field-type> is only when your partner (not necessarily YOU) has a multiplicity of Many. This can be ONLY Collection or Set (NOT List, Map, etc.)

```
    <ejb-relationship-role>
      <ejb-relationship-role-name>MovieBean</ejb-relationship-role-name>
      <multiplicity>Many</multiplicity>
      <cascade-delete />
      <relationship-role-source>
        <ejb-name>MovieBean</ejb-name>
      </relationship-role-source>
      <cmr-field>
        <cmr-field-name>director</cmr-field-name>
      </cmr-field>
    </ejb-relationship-role>
```

MovieBean says, "You can delete me when you delete my Director"

No <cmr-field-type> because the Director has a multiplicity of One in this relationship, so we return only one Director, not a Collection of Directors.

```
  </ejb-relation>
</relationships>
</ejb-jar>
```

MovieBean code with a CMR field

```
package headfirst;

import javax.ejb.*;
import javax.naming.*;
import java.util.*;

public abstract class MovieBean implements EntityBean {

    private EntityContext context;

    public String ejbCreate(String movieID, String title, int year, String genre,
                                      String directorID) throws CreateException {

        setMovieID(movieID);
        setTitle(title);
        setYear(year);
        setGenre(genre);
        return null;
    }
```

Here we set our persistent fields, by calling our abstract setters. We must NOT try to reference our own persistent RELATIONSHIPS. That has to wait until WE have been inserted, and that happens only AFTER ejbCreate() completes.

```
    public void ejbPostCreate(String movieID, String title, int year, String genre,
                                        String directorID) throws CreateException {
        try {
          InitialContext ctx = new InitialContext();
          DirectorHome dirHome = (DirectorHome) ctx.lookup("java:comp/env/ejb/DirectorHome");
          Director dir = dirHome.findByPrimaryKey(directorID);
          setDirector(dir);  ←
        } catch(Exception ex)
          {//handle exception}
    }
```

Now it's safe to assign our persistent relationship field for Director. We lookup the Director (using the directorID parameter from create) and call our abstract setter to assign this Director.

```
    public String ejbHomeListMoviesByDirectorAndGenre(String dirID, String genre) {
        String list = null;
        try {
           Collection c = ejbSelectGetMoviesByDirectorAndGenre(dirID, genre);
           Iterator it = c.iterator();
           while (it.hasNext()) {
              list += it.next();
           }
      } catch (Exception ex) { ex.printStackTrace();}
       return list;
    }
}
```

A home business method for the client to get a list of all the movies that fit the query. We use an ejbSelect method that returns a Collection of String objects. By using a select method, we let the Container write all the database code!

```java
public String ejbHomeListAllMovies() {
    String list = null;
      try {
          Collection c = ejbSelectGetAllMovies();
          Iterator ita = c.iterator();
             while (ita.hasNext()) {
               Movie movie = (Movie) ita.next();
               list += " " + movie.getMovieTitle();
             }

      } catch (Exception ex) { // handle exception}
    return list;
}

  public String getMovieTitle() {
     return getTitle();
  }

  public String getMovieDirectorName() {
      return getDirector().getDirectorName();
  }

  public abstract String getMovieID();
  public abstract void setMovieID(String i);

  public abstract String getTitle();
  public abstract void setTitle(String t);

  public abstract int getYear();
  public abstract void setYear(int y);

  public abstract String getGenre();
  public abstract void setGenre(String g);

  public abstract Director getDirector();
  public abstract void setDirector(Director d);

  public abstract Collection ejbSelectGetAllMovies() throws FinderException;

    public abstract Collection ejbSelectGetMoviesByDirectorAndGenre(String dir, String
genre) throws FinderException;

  public void unsetEntityContext() { }
  public void ejbLoad() { }
  public void ejbStore() { }
  public void ejbActivate() { }
  public void ejbPassivate() { }
  public void ejbRemove() { }

  public void setEntityContext(EntityContext ctx) {
     context = ctx;
  }
}
```

Another home business method that uses a select method to find all movies. This select returns a Collection of actual Movie objects, so we walk through it and pull out the titles, so that we can return a big String to the client.

Two exposed business methods from the component interface...

We have FIVE virtual fields: four CMP fields and one CMR field for Director.

The two select methods are declared as abstract methods. The Collection doesn't say WHAT the methods will return... but we'll tell the Container that one will return a Collection of Movies and one a Collection of Strings.

The rest are regular old callback methods.

The MovieBean's home interface

```
import javax.ejb.*;
import java.util.*;
import java.rmi.*;


public interface MovieHomeRemote extends EJBHome {

    public MovieRemote create(String movieID, String title, int year, String genre,
                        String directorID) throws CreateException, RemoteException;

    public MovieRemote findByPrimaryKey(String key) throws FinderException,
                                                    RemoteException;

    public Collection findByGenre(String genre) throws FinderException, RemoteException;

    public String listAllMovies() throws FinderException, RemoteException;

    public String listMoviesByDirectorAndGenre(String directorID, String genre)
                                        throws FinderException, RemoteException;

    public Collection findMoviesByKevinDegrees(int degrees) throws FinderException,
                                                    RemoteException;
}
```

Whoa! There are three finder methods that weren't in the bean class... remember, the Container implements your finder methods--you don't put ANYTHING about finders in your bean class code. You put them ONLY in the home.

(well, that's not completely true...somewhere you have to tell the Container HOW to implement the finders, which brings us to the next page...)

The home business methods all start with the prefix "ejbHome" when they're in the bean class. In the home, they don't have that prefix.

Mapping from abstract schema to a real database

Sooner or later, you have to tell the Container how and where to manage your persistent data. This happens outside the deployment descriptor, in a vendor-specific way. That means, of course, that you're not tested on it in the exam. Every vendor has their own mechanism, but you'll usually get some sort of a GUI where, if you're lucky, you can tell the Container to connect to a specific database, and then you'll drag and drop or draw connections from CMP fields to columns in one or more tables.

Because this mapping happens outside of EJB, in the server, there's not much we can say about it. The part we're most interested in is mapping from abstract queries to REAL queries, and that happens in a very cool way, using a vendor-independent query language just for your entity bean queries, EJB-QL. We'll look at that on the next page.

```
<abstract-schema-name>MovieSchema</abstract-schema-name>
```

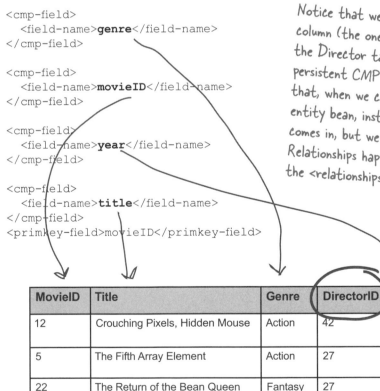

```
<cmp-field>
   <field-name>genre</field-name>
</cmp-field>

<cmp-field>
   <field-name>movieID</field-name>
</cmp-field>

<cmp-field>
   <field-name>year</field-name>
</cmp-field>

<cmp-field>
   <field-name>title</field-name>
</cmp-field>
<primkey-field>movieID</primkey-field>
```

Notice that we're not mapping the Director ID column (the one that keeps the foreign key into the Director table) because we don't HAVE a persistent CMP field for the Director ID. Why do that, when we can have the real Director, as an entity bean, instead? That's where our CMR field comes in, but we don't map that to a database. Relationships happen by matching up two BEANS in the <relationships> part of the DD.

MovieID	Title	Genre	DirectorID	Year
12	Crouching Pixels, Hidden Mouse	Action	42	2000
5	The Fifth Array Element	Action	27	2003
22	The Return of the Bean Queen	Fantasy	27	2001
11	Lord of the Loops	Sci-fi	42	2002

Writing your portable queries, for <u>select</u> and <u>finder</u> methods

Remember, I'm a programmer, so the less I know, the happier I am. With EJB-QL, I don't have to know anything about the real database where my bean will end up running.

EJB-QL is a portable query language that lets you write SQL-like statements write into the deployment descriptor! You put them in the XML and without having to know anything about the real database.

As a Bean Provider, you can happily write all the queries you want, trusting that the Deployer will, in the end, map your CMP fields to real tables and data. All we care about here is writing our queries to match the methods we've chosen to expose to the client in the home and component interfaces.

Select methods are here simply to make your life easier, by letting the Container build the real database access code from your queries.

So the process is usually something like:

1. **Write a home business method**

2. **Implement the home business method to call the ejbSelect method that does the *real* data access.**

3. **Declare the abstract select method in your bean class.**

4. **Write the EJB-QL for the select query.**

EJB-QL for the MovieBean

Let's look at the EJB-QL for all the queries the MovieBean needs. Don't worry if you're not understanding all of it; after we walk through the examples, we'll explore the different pieces in detail, and work out the syntax. If you know SQL, most of this will be familiar (although there are few differences you'll see). If you don't know SQL, that's OK. We'll get you started writing queries, and you can use the spec to learn more about the EJB-QL language. *The exam expects you to know just the basics of EJB-QL.*

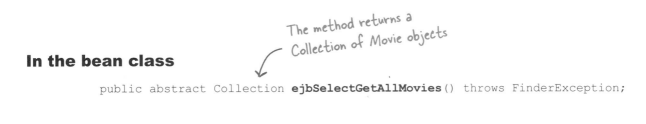

In the bean class

The method returns a Collection of Movie objects

```
public abstract Collection ejbSelectGetAllMovies() throws FinderException;
```

In the the deployment descriptor

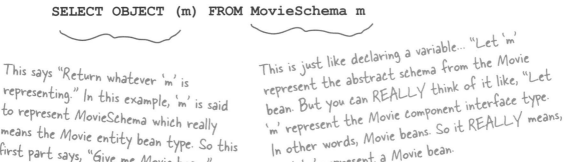

```
SELECT  OBJECT  (m)  FROM MovieSchema m
```

This says "Return whatever 'm' is representing." In this example, 'm' is said to represent MovieSchema which really means the Movie entity bean type. So this first part says, "Give me Movie beans".

This is just like declaring a variable... "Let 'm' represent the abstract schema from the Movie bean. But you can REALLY think of it like, "Let 'm' represent the Movie component interface type. In other words, Movie beans. So it REALLY means, "Let 'm' represent a Movie bean.

What it really says

"Give me all the Movie beans"

Using an optional WHERE clause

This example constrains the objects returned from the search, by adding a WHERE clause that says what extra criteria the objects have to meet before they qualify for "things that can be returned from the query." The WHERE clause is your way of saying, "Don't just give me ANY old Movie... I want ONLY the movies that..."

In the bean class

The method returns a Collection of Movie objects

```
public abstract Collection ejbFindByGenre(String genre) throws FinderException;
```

In the the deployment descriptor

"genre" must be CMP field in the Movie bean, which means you can find a getGenre() / setGenre() method pair in the bean class

```
SELECT OBJECT (m)    FROM MovieSchema m    WHERE m.genre = ?1
```

this means the first parameter to the method

This says we want the bean type of whatever 'm' turns out to be...

Let 'm' represent the Movie bean type

restrict the Movies returned to only those where the CMP field "genre" matches the first parameter of the select method The "1" means the first parameter. The "m.genre" uses the dot navigation operator to make a "path" that navigates in an object-oriented way. It's simple—the left hand operand is a type, and the right hand is a member field of that type. It's almost exactly like using regular Java syntax to say, "myMovie.genre", where genre is an instance variable (in this case, a virtual persistent field.)

What it really says

> *"Give me all the Movie beans that are in the genre matching the first parameter to the ejbSelectGetAllMovies method."*

Navigating to another related bean

This example is for a finder method, so you won't find it in the bean class (remember, you declare abstract methods for only the select methods, not the finders. The Container uses your home interface to figure out what the finders are, and then it's up to you to write the EJB-QL for the finders).

You can use the dot operator to navigate not just to a CMP field in the bean, but to another field within a bean referenced in a CMR field. In other words, If Movie has a reference to a Director (and they're in a relationship), you can use the Movie to get to the Director to ask for a CMP value from the Director.

In the home interface

```
public Collection findMoviesByKevinDegrees(int degrees) throws FinderException,
                                                                RemoteException;
```

m.director means "the CMR field 'director' in the Movie bean"

"degrees" is a Persistent field in the Director bean.

In the the deployment descriptor

```
SELECT OBJECT (m)    FROM MovieSchema m    WHERE m.director.degrees = ?1
```

This says that we want objects returned whose type is whatever 'm' turns out to be representing...

... and what do you know? It turns out that 'm' means the Movie bean

restrict the Movies returned to only those where the Movie's Director has a CMP "degrees" field with a value that matches the first parameter of the finder.

What it really says

> *"Give me all the Movie beans that have a Director whose degrees match what the client sent in to the finder method."*

> *OR*

> *"I want to get Movies back, but only those Movies directed by someone who is a specific number of degrees away from Kevin Bacon."**

*Six degrees from Kevin Bacon is a popular game where you try to take a Hollywood type and see how many connections it takes to get that person linked to Kevin Bacon."

Selecting a value rather than the whole bean

This example is for a home business method that takes two parameters and returns not Movies, but *Strings*.

In the home interface

This method returns a single String, with all the Movie titles that match the query.

```
public String listMoviesByDirectorAndGenre(String dirID, String genre)
```

In the the deployment descriptor

this is different! We're returning just Movie titles, not Movie objects

m.genre means the "genre" CMP field in the Movie bean

```
SELECT m.title   FROM MovieSchema m

WHERE m.director.directorID = ?1   AND m.genre = ?2
```

This restricts the matches to only those Movies with a Director who has an ID equal to the first parameter to the method

AND whose Movie genre value equals the second parameter to the method

What it really says

"Give me back Movie titles (Strings) that have the director and genre I specified in the method arguments."

EJB-QL SELECT

Now that you've seen some queries, we'll look at some of the details and rules.

Query Domains

The domain of a query is a single deployment descriptor. So that means a single ejb-jar file. However many beans you can squish in the ejb-jar, that's how many beans you can search across.

SELECT

The SELECT clause says what kind of thing this query will return.
It can be only one of these two:

① **an abstract schema type for an entity bean**

```
<abstract-schema-name>MovieSchema</abstract-schema-name>
```

```
SELECT OBJECT (m) FROM MovieSchema m
```

OR

In formal EJB terms (and in the spec) the abstract schema type as a SELECT variable is called a RANGE variable, because it ranges over the entire entity bean type.

② **a <cmp-field> single value type for an entity bean**

```
<cmp-field>
    <field-name>title</field-name>
</cmp-field>
```

```
SELECT m.title FROM MovieSchema m
```

When you use a <cmp-field> instead of a range variable, we call this a single-valued path expression.

You can't use dot notation to return a CMR field!

As a SELECT type, these are OK:
m.title or **m.genre**

But this is NOT OK:
m.director

You can use a CMP field, but not a CMR field with the dot notation, as the SELECT type.

NOTE: we're deviating from standard spec naming conventions in our abstract schema name, because we want it to be OBVIOUS that we're using the schema name and not, say, the bean name. In the spec, the abstract schema name is the same as the component interface name.

EJB-QL SELECT — when to use Object ( )

What's with the OBJECT (m) thing?

It's a structure the J2EE designers put in to be consistent with a version of SQL.

It's annoying.

But you have to do it *whenever you return a bean type instead of a CMP field type.* And you must NOT do it *whenever you return a CMP field type.*

If you return the bean's abstract schema type, use OBJECT( ).

```
<abstract-schema-name>MovieSchema</abstract-schema-name>
```

SELECT OBJECT (m)

If you return a <cmp-field> *don't* use OBJECT ( )

```
<cmp-field>
    <field-name>title</field-name>
</cmp-field>
```

SELECT m.title

If you're using the dot, to navigate a path, you don't use the OBJECT ( )

Sharpen your pencil

Circle the EJB-QL statement if it has a legal SELECT clause

```
SELECT OBJECT (m) FROM MovieSchema m

SELECT m.title   FROM MovieSchema m

SELECT m FROM MovieSchema m

SELECT OBJECT (m.title)   FROM MovieSchema m
```

What does it MEAN to return an abstract schema type?

The abstract schema is just a stupid label in XML, so obviously THAT is not what you're returning. You're returning the bean type. But that can't be right either... you're obviously returning the component interface type, but THAT can't be right because how would it know if it's supposed to give you the local or Remote type...

You never have to worry about whether the type is local or Remote

The MovieSchema abstract schema name represents the bean type.

As if by magic, the Container knows which interface view to return, local or Remote, depending on whether the invocation of the query came from a home or Remote interface.

MovieLocal
getMovieID()
getTitle()
getGenre()
getDirector()
getTrailer()

MovieRemote
getMovieID()
getTitle()
getGenre()
getDirector()
getTrailer()

When you see this:

MovieSchema m

Think this:

m = the component interface

(and we'll let the Container sort out the Remote vs. local issue)

SELECT and FROM are mandatory!

You gotta have SELECT and FROM no matter what, but the WHERE clause is optional. With SELECT, you can also use the keyword DISTINCT to say that you don't want any duplicates returned in your Collection.

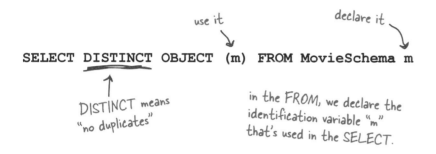

use it

declare it

SELECT DISTINCT OBJECT (m) FROM MovieSchema m

DISTINCT means "no duplicates"

in the FROM, we declare the identification variable "m" that's used in the SELECT.

The FROM clause declares the identification variable (like the "m" in our example query). This also defines the domain of the query by saying to the Container, "Here's where I want you to be looking..." The order in which the FROM and SELECT might feel a little strange if you're not used to SQL. But think of it like someone saying, "I want you to go get my *things*, and the *things* I'm talking about are FROM my top drawer."

If you need to declare more identification variables to use later in the query, you can separate them with a comma:

```
SELECT OBJECT (m)
FROM MovieSchema m, DirectorSchema d
```

We declared two different identifiers, and defined the domain of the query to those two abstract schemas.

You can also use the AS keyword. It's optional, but you might see it on the exam or in someone else's code, or your company style guide might insist on using it. We're too lazy to keep typing it.

```
SELECT OBJECT (m) FROM MovieSchema AS m
```

Identifiers

When you make an identifier, you have to follow the Java programming language guidelines for what you can name things. You can't use the other Java identifiers

Identifiers

Must be valid Java identifiers

Must NOT be same as an <abstract-schema-name> or <ejb-name> anywhere in the DD

Must NOT be one of the EJB-QL reserved words

EJB-QL reserved words

SELECT	OR
FROM	BETWEEN
WHERE	LIKE
DISTINCT	IN
OBJECT	AS
NULL	UNKNOWN*
TRUE	EMPTY
FALSE	MEMBER
NOT	OF
AND	IS

Watch out for questions with name conflicts!

Remember that an <ejb-name> must be unique for each bean in the ejb-jar, which means unique for one complete DD. The same is true for the <abstract-schema-name>; it must be unique in the DD.

You already know that you can't use an identification variable in your query that matches an <ejb-name> or <abstract-schema-name> in the DD, but keep in mind that EJB-QL is not case-sensitive!

So, you must NOT do this:
```
SELECT OBJECT (movie)
FROM Movie movie
```

In EJB-QL, "Movie" is the same as "movie", and you can't have conflicting names.

* not used in the current version; it's future use is unknown...

The WHERE clause

A WHERE clause is optional, and let's you put extra conditions on what's returned. Remember that without one, we got everything of the type used in the SELECT.

NOT using WHERE

```
SELECT OBJECT (m) FROM MovieSchema m
```

Existing Entities

Entities returned from the query

Enclose a String literal in single quotes

Using WHERE

```
SELECT OBJECT (m)    FROM MovieSchema m    WHERE m.genre = 'Horror'
```

Existing Entities

Entities returned from the query

Using WHERE, we get only the movies that have the value "Horror" in their CMP field "genre". (In other words, those movies whose getGenre() method would return "Horror".)

The WHERE clause

You can use literals

```
WHERE m.director.degrees > 3
WHERE m.genre = 'Horror'
```

You can use input parameters

```
WHERE m.director.degrees > ?1
```

And the parameters don't have to be in order... that's why they have numbers!

```
WHERE m.genre = ?2 AND m.director.degrees < ?1
```

```
public String ejbHomeListMoviesByDirectorAndGenre(String dirID, String genre)
```

You can do comparisons

```
WHERE m.director.degrees < 5
```

But you better compare apples to apples

```
WHERE m.director < 5      No!!
```

You can't compare a Director bean to a numeric type!

The problem with using Collection types

Imagine you want to use the DirectorSchema to return all the
Directors that have made horror movies. Sounds pretty simple...
Director has a CMR field for movies, and each movie has a CMP
field for genre. So we come up with something like this:

```
SELECT OBJECT (d)
FROM DirectorSchema d
WHERE d.movies.genre = 'Horror'
```

Looks good on first glance, but WATCH OUT! This is NOT LEGAL.

Why can't you do this?

Let's back up and imagine this is Java code. How do you normally
use the dot operator in Java? You might do something like:

```
Owner o = new Owner();
o.getDog().bark();
```

method of Owner   *method of Dog*

This is fine... we can go through the Owner, get its Dog, and call bark() on the Owner's dog.

The Owner has a getDog() method, and the Dog has a bark().
No problem.

But what if we changed the Owner to allow one Owner to have
multiple Dog objects? Then what happens...

```
Owner o = new Owner();
o.getDogs().bark();
```

method of Owner

YIKES!! Now who are we really calling this method on? A Dog? Or a Collection...

Dog
void bark()

Owner
Dog aDog
Dog getDog()

Owner
Collection dogs
Collection getDogs()

Collections don't bark()!

duh

You can't use the dot navigation when something you're using *in* the path is a Collection. For example you can't do this:

```
Owner o = new Owner();
o.getDogs().bark();
```

This returns a Collection. And you can't call bark() on a Collection!

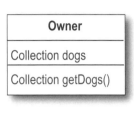

Owner
Collection dogs
Collection getDogs()

It's the Dog objects IN the collection that can bark()! So, in Java, you'd have to first access the individual Dog elements in the collection, and one at a time ask each Dog to bark(). The Dog code above is almost exactly like this WHERE clause we had before:

```
WHERE d.movies.genre = 'Horror'
```
No!!

And since "movies" and "genre" are virtual fields, with accessors, you can think of it just like this:

```
d.getMovies().getGenre() = 'Horror'
```
No!!

Think about it... what would you be trying to say here? That the whole collection *has a genre? No, a collection doesn't* have *a getGenre(). It's the movies* in *the collection that have a getGenre(). So this syntax doesn't make sense.*

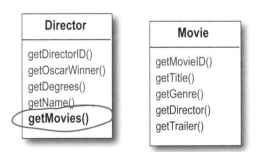

Director
getDirectorID()
getOscarWinner()
getDegrees()
getName()
getMovies()

Movie
getMovieID()
getTitle()
getGenre()
getDirector()
getTrailer()

The IN operator lets you say
"For an individual element IN the Collection..."

The IN operator for the FROM clause let's you refer to a Collection, but name an identifier as representing ONE member of the Collection.

```
SELECT DISTINCT OBJECT (d)
FROM DirectorSchema d, IN(d.movies) m
WHERE m.genre = 'Horror'
```

Now "m" represents an individual Movie IN the movies Collection (a CMR field of Director)

Let "m" represent an individual Movie IN the Collection. So, "m" does NOT represent the Collection type, but rather the Movie type (the type the Collection is holding.)

This query looks through all of the Directors, and looks through each of the Movies of each Director, and looks for a Movie with a genre that matches 'Horror'. The query returns a set (no duplicates because we said "DISTINCT") of Directors

The IN operator is overloaded in EJB-QL!

The IN operator in the FROM clause is different from the IN comparison operator used in a WHERE clause.

In the WHERE clause, you can say:

d.genre IN ('Horror', 'Fantasy')
and it is just a shortcut for saying:
d.genre = 'Horror' OR d.genre = 'Fantasy'

But it has nothing to do with the IN operator used in a FROM clause to designate individual members IN a Collection. So just remember:

FROM clause: IN says, "Look at the individual objects in the Collection, and rather than using the Collection as the type, use the type of the items IN the Collection."

WHERE clause: IN says, "See if the field value matches one of the literals in this set..."

The BETWEEN expression

Let's say you want to find movies in the database made in the 60's and 70's, but you want to exclude any movies made in 1975 or 1976, really bad movie years.

You could say:

```
SELECT DISTINCT OBJECT (m)
FROM MovieSchema m
WHERE (m.year > 1959 AND m.year < 1975) OR
      (m.year > 1976 AND m.year < 1980)
```

Or, you could do it the cooler way:

```
SELECT DISTINCT OBJECT (m)
FROM MovieSchema m
WHERE (m.year BETWEEN 1960 AND 1979) AND
      (m.year NOT BETWEEN 1975 AND 1976)
```

In this example notice that BETWEEN is INclusive (i.e. the years 1960 and 1979 WILL be included), and that NOT BETWEEN is EXclusive

If I'm BETWEEN a rock and a hard place, both the rock and the hard place are INCLUDED. I bet you know the feeling.

The other "IN"

We've used IN with a FROM clause to help navigate through collections, but IN has another personality, you might say IN has been overloaded for use in the WHERE clause. Let's say that you want to select movies from a subset of all the movie genres in your database:

```
SELECT DISTINCT OBJECT (m)
FROM MovieSchema m
WHERE m.genre IN('horror', 'mystery')
```

This query would return only those movies whose genre is either "horror" or "mystery". This flavor of IN lets you created something akin to an enumerated list.

And there's always NOT IN for those times when you need some action:

```
SELECT DISTINCT OBJECT (m)
FROM MovieSchema m
WHERE m.genre NOT IN('romance', 'comedy')
```

This query would return only those movies whose genre is NOT "romance" or "comedy"

"!=" is NOT the same as "< >"

When comparing values in a WHERE clause, "< >" means "not equals". You use THAT instead of "!=". But coming from Java, that "!=" can look so right... when you see it on a question. Don't be tempted.

String literals are in SINGLE quotes!

While we're on the topic of inconsistencies between Java syntax and EJB-QL, don't be tricked by a String in double quotes. This is WRONG in EJB-QL:
WHERE m.foo IN ("bar", "baz")
It must be ('bar', 'baz')

The IS EMPTY comparison expression

This baby will let you know whether the collection in question
is empty:

```
SELECT DISTINCT OBJECT (d)
FROM DirectorSchema d
WHERE d.movies IS EMPTY
```

*This query returns only those directors who
have not made any movies.*

*Just show
me the losers who
haven't made any
movies...*

The IS NOT EMPTY comparison expression

IS NOT EMPTY lets you say, "Don't give me anything where this
field is empty…"

```
SELECT DISTINCT OBJECT (d)
FROM DirectorSchema d
WHERE d.movies IS NOT EMPTY
```

*This query returns only those
directors who have at least one movie
in their movies collection.*

The LIKE expression

Like expressions are used to compare single value path expressions with a String literal. The power of LIKE is that the String literal can have wildcard elements, giving you a simple pattern matcher. The "%" wildcard matches against 0 to many characters; the "_" matches against a single character only.

```
SELECT DISTINCT OBJECT (d)
FROM DirectorSchema d
WHERE d.phone LIKE '719%'
```

The "%" symbol is a wildcard for 0 to many characters

This query would return only those directors who have phone numbers beginning with the digits '719'. (Hey, phone numbers can to be Strings, they have those dashes...)

```
SELECT DISTINCT OBJECT (m)
FROM MovieSchema m
WHERE m.filmcode LIKE '7_mm'
```

This query searches for movies whose film codes are in the 7Xmm family.

The "_" symbol is a wildcard for a single character

The NOT LIKE expression

```
SELECT DISTINCT OBJECT (m)
FROM MovieSchema m
WHERE m.filmcode NOT LIKE '%mm'
```

You can probably guess what this one does... returns all movies whose film codes DON'T end in "mm".

BULLET POINTS

- Entity beans can have persistent relationships with other entity beans.

- A container-managed relationship (CMR) field is defined in the bean class just as a CMP field is—with a pair of abstract getters and setters that return either the local component interface of the bean, or a Collection.

- If the virtual field is a Collection, it must be declared as either java.util.Collection or java.util.Set. No other Collection type is allowed as the declared return type of a CMR field.

- Relationships have multiplicities—they can be one-to-one, one-to-many, or many-to-many. (Many-to-one works in the same way that one-to-many works; it just depends on whose point of view you're using.)

- For example, a Movie bean has a many-to-one relationship with a Director bean. Each Movie has only one Director, but a Director can have many Movies.

- Multiplicity affects the return type of the virtual field. Movie has only one Director, so the CMR field in the bean is getDirector(), that returns a reference to a Director's local component interface. But a Director has many movies, so a Director's virtual field is getMovies(), which returns a Collection.

- A CMP bean must define an <abstract-persistence-schema> in the DD, that lists each of the bean's CMP fields, and also identifies which of the fields is the primary key (unless it's a compound primary key). The DD must always define the type of the primary key, even if the primary key is not a field of the bean. (Remember, if the primary key is not a field of the bean, it must be a primary key class *composed* of CMP fields from the bean.)

- Relationship (CMR) fields are not defined in the <enterprise-beans> portion of the DD (where you define your CMP fields), but are instead defined in the <relationships> section of the DD.

- Each relationship must have two partners, with each partner described in an <ejb-relationship-role> element that includes the CMR field name, the source (<ejb-name>) for the partner, the multiplicity (i.e. how many of this bean will the *other* partner have), and an optional <cascade-delete/> (which says, "Delete me if my partner is deleted."

- Relationships can be one-way (unidirectional) or two-way (bi-directional). A unidirectional relationship is described in the DD in the same way as a bi-directional relationship, except that only one of the two partners has a CMR field. This means bean A has a reference to bean B (they're in a relationship), but bean B does not have a reference back to A. Directionality does not affect multiplicity or cascade-delete; it just means that only one of the two partners has a reference to the other. To the Container, they're still in a relationship.

- Cascade-deletes tell the Container to delete the bean with the <cascade-delete/> tag when the bean's partner is deleted. This works only if the bean's partner has a multiplicity of one. (You wouldn't want to delete a Director just because one of this Movies was deleted; but you might want to delete a Movie if its sole Director was deleted.)

- A bean cannot access its CMR fields in ejbCreate(); it must wait until ejbPostCreate() before, say, assigning the CMR virtual field an actual value. In other words, you can't use your abstract getters and setters for your CMR fields until after ejbCreate() completes.

- EJB-QL is a portable query language you can use to specify your queries for both finder and select methods.

- In an EJB-QL query, the SELECT and FROM clauses are required; the WHERE clause is optional.

- A SELECT can return either an <abstract-schema-type> or a single-value field.

- If you use the dot notation for navigating a path (for example, m.genre), you can't use a Collection type as part of the path. To use a Collection type as part of a FROM clause, you must enclose it using the IN(d.movies) operator.

Relationship assignments

A Movie can have only one Director. If you set a Movie's Director field to Director 1, the Movie will be in Director 1's collection of Movies, but in no other Director's collection. If you later reassign the Movie's Director field so that the Movie has a *different* Director—Director 2—the previous Director (Director 1) will no longer have that Movie in its Collection.

This all happens automatically! To maintain the integrity of the database, the Container manages both sides of the relationship at all times.

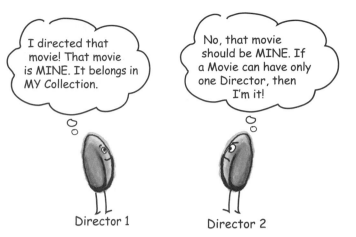

Before:

Three Movies in Director 1's Movie Collection. If you call getDirector() on any of these Movies, they will return Director 1.

There is only one Movie in Director 2's Collection. It's the only Movie that will return Director 2 if you call getDirector() on the Movie.

```
movieA.setDirector(movieD.getDirector());
```

this says, "set Movie A's Director to be whatever the Director is for Movie D."

After:

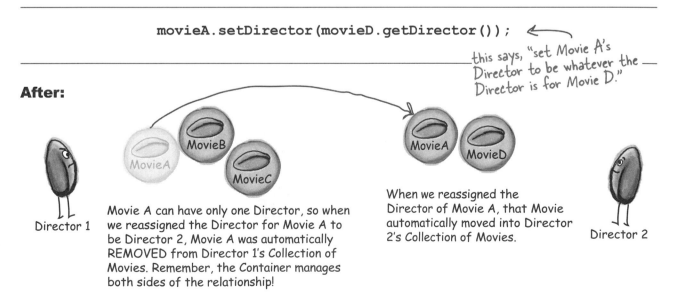

Movie A can have only one Director, so when we reassigned the Director for Movie A to be Director 2, Movie A was automatically REMOVED from Director 1's Collection of Movies. Remember, the Container manages both sides of the relationship!

When we reassigned the Director of Movie A, that Movie automatically moved into Director 2's Collection of Movies.

If the multiplicity of the relationship field is ONE, it's a MOVE
If the multiplicity is MANY, it's a COPY

`<ejb-relationship-role-name>`**MovieBean**`</ejb-relationship-role-name>`
`<multiplicity>`**Many**`</multiplicity>`

`<ejb-relationship-role-name>`**DirectorBean**`</ejb-relationship-role-name>`
`<multiplicity>`**One**`</multiplicity>`

When we assigned Director 2 to Movie A, the Movie moved from Director 1's Collection to Director 2's Collection. The Director CMR field has a multiplicity of *One* in its relationship with Movie, so a Movie can't exist in the Collection of two different Directors, because a Movie can have only *One* Director.

But just because we move the Movie, doesn't mean the Director also moves. The multiplicity of Movie is Many, so when you assign another Movie's Director to a *different* Movie, that Director reference is *copied*, and both Movies will now have a reference.

The <u>MOVIE</u> reference was <u>MOVED</u> from one Director to another

`movieA.setDirector(movieD.getDirector());`

Director 1

Director 2

Because the Director-to-Movie relationship is One-to-Many, a Movie can NEVER exist in more than one Director's Collection. If you change a Movie's Director, the Movie is not copied! It is **moved** to the new Director's Collection.

The <u>DIRECTOR</u> reference was <u>COPIED</u> from one Movie to another

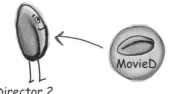

Director 2

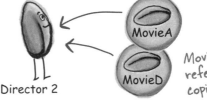

Director 2

Movie D's reference was copied, not moved.

Exercise

Multiplicity and Assignments

Given this relationship:

```
<ejb-relationship-role-name>MovieBean</ejb-relationship-role-name>
<multiplicity>One</multiplicity>

<ejb-relationship-role-name>TrailerBean</ejb-relationship-role-name>
<multiplicity>One</multiplicity>
```

And this current scenario:

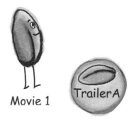

Movie 1 TrailerA

TrailerB Movie 2

Draw what the picture will look like after you run:

```
movie1.setTrailer(movie2.getTrailer());
```

Draw your
picture here...

Answer these questions:

What is the result of: `movie1.getTrailer()`

What is the result of: `movie2.getTrailer()`

What is the result of: `trailerA.getMovie()`

What is the result of: `trailerB.getMovie()`

Multiplicity and Assignments

Given this bi-directional relationship:

```
<ejb-relationship-role-name>MovieBean</ejb-relationship-role-name>
<multiplicity>One</multiplicity>

<ejb-relationship-role-name>TrailerBean</ejb-relationship-role-name>
<multiplicity>One</multiplicity>
```

And this current scenario:

Draw what the picture will look like after you run:

```
movie1.setTrailer(movie2.getTrailer());
```

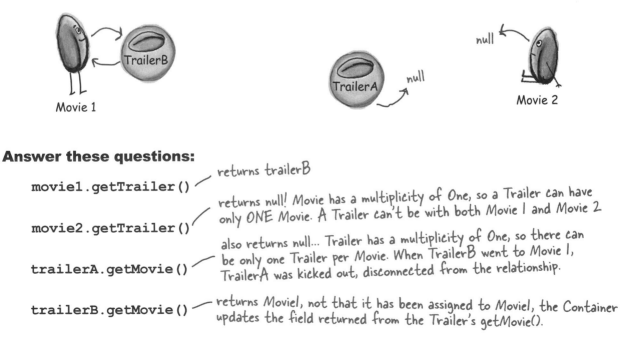

Answer these questions:

`movie1.getTrailer()` — returns trailerB

`movie2.getTrailer()` — returns null! Movie has a multiplicity of One, so a Trailer can have only ONE Movie. A Trailer can't be with both Movie 1 and Movie 2

`trailerA.getMovie()` — also returns null... Trailer has a multiplicity of One, so there can be only one Trailer per Movie. When TrailerB went to Movie 1, TrailerA was kicked out, disconnected from the relationship.

`trailerB.getMovie()` — returns Movie1, not that it has been assigned to Movie1, the Container updates the field returned from the Trailer's getMovie().

1 What's true for an entity bean provider using container-managed persistence to create persistent relationships? (Choose all that apply.)

❏ A. A local interface is required for such a bean to have a bidirectional relationship with another entity bean.

❏ B. Such a bean can have relationships with only session beans.

❏ C. Relationships can be only one-to-one or one-to-many.

❏ D. A getter method return type can be java.util.List.

2 What's true for an entity bean provider using container-managed persistence to create persistent relationships? (Choose all that apply.)

❏ A. A remote interface is required for such a bean to have a bidirectional relationship with another entity bean.

❏ B. Such a bean can have relationships with only message-driven beans.

❏ C. A get method return type can use java.util.Map.

❏ D. Relationships can be one-to-one, one-to-many, or many-to-many.

3 When a remote client invokes a method on an entity bean using container-managed persistence, and that bean has already been removed, what exception will be thrown?

❏ A. `javax.ejb.AccessLocalException`

❏ B. `javax.ejb.ObjectNotFoundException`

❏ C. `java.rmi.NoSuchObjectException`

❏ D. `java.rmi.StubNotFoundException`

❏ E. `javax.ejb.NoSuchEntityException`

4 Given the container-managed unidirectional relationship:

Foo (0-1) —> Bar (0-1)

And the object relations:

f1 —> b1
f2 —> b2

What will be true after the following code runs?   (Choose all that apply.)

```
f2.setBar(f1.getBar());
```

  ❑ A. `f1.getBar() == null`

  ❑ B. `b2.getFoo() == null`

  ❑ C. `b1.getBar() == null`

  ❑ E. none of the above

5 If an entity bean A has been removed from a relationship with bean B, in which case(s) will bean A's accessor method for bean B return a non-null value? (Choose all that apply.)

  ❑ A. one-to-one

  ❑ B. many-to-one

  ❑ C. many-to-many

  ❑ D. all of the above

  ❑ E. none of the above

6 Which deployment descriptor element's value(s) must be a type of collection? (Choose all that apply.)

  ❑ A. `<ejb-name>`

  ❑ B. `<cmr-field>`

  ❑ C. `<cmr-field-type>`

  ❑ D. `<ejb-relation>`

7 Which deployment descriptor element(s) must have exactly two declarations of another deployment descriptor element? (Choose all that apply.)

❑ A. `<ejb-name>`

❑ B. `<cmr-field>`

❑ C. `<cmr-field-type>`

❑ D. `<ejb-relation>`

❑ E. `<ejb-relationship-role>`

8 Which set(s) of elements are mandatory within an ejb-relationship-role element? (Choose all that apply.)

❑ A. `<cmr-field>`, `<multiplicity>`

❑ B. `<cmr-field>`, `<relationship-role-source>`

❑ C. `<multiplicity>`, `<relationship-role-name>`

❑ D. `<multiplicity>`, `<relationship-role-source>`

❑ E. `<relationship-role-name>`, `<relationship-role-source>`

9 Which are valid values for a cmr-field-type element? (Choose all that apply.)

❑ A. String

❑ B. Integer

❑ C. `java.util.Set`

❑ D. `java.util.List`

❑ E. `java.util.Collection`

10 Which set(s) of elements are mandatory within an ejb-relation element?

❑ A. `<ejb-relation-name>`, `<ejb-relationship-role>`

❑ B. `<ejb-relationship-role>`, `<ejb-relationship-role>`

❑ C. `<description>`, `<ejb-relation-name>`,
     `<ejb-relationship-role>`

❑ D. `<ejb-relation-name>`, `<ejb-relationship-role>`,
     `<ejb-relationship-role>`

11 Given CMP beans CustomerBean, OrderBean, and LineItemsBean with the following relationships:

CustomerBean (1) <—> OrderBean (n)

OrderBean (1) <—> LineItemsBean (n)

and the following EJB QL query:

SELECT DISTINCT OBJECT (c)

FROM Customer c, IN (c.Order) o, IN (o.lineItems) li

WHERE **li.product_type = 'refrigerator'**

Which of the following properly describes the result of the query? (Choose all that apply.)

❏ A. The query is invalid.

❏ B. All orders that include a line item that refers to a refrigerator.

❏ C. All line items that refer to a refrigerator.

❏ D. All customers that have order(s) that refer to a refrigerator.

12 Given CMP beans CustomerBean, OrderBean, and LineItemsBean with the following relationships:

CustomerBean (1) <—> OrderBean (n)

OrderBean (1) <—> LineItemsBean (n)

Which will return all orders that have line items? (Choose all that apply.)

❏ A. SELECT DISTINCT o

   FROM Order o, IN (o.lineItems) li

❏ B. SELECT DISTINCT OBJECT(o)

   FROM Order o, IN (o.lineItems) li

❏ C. SELECT OBJECT(o)

   FROM Order o

   WHERE o.lineItems = 0

❏ D. SELECT OBJECT(o)

   FROM Order o

   WHERE o.lineItems IS NOT EMPTY

13 What's true about EJB QL path expressions? (Choose all that apply.)

❑ A. In a path expression the **(.)** is considered the navigation operator.

❑ B. Path expressions can terminate with either **cmr-field** or **cmp-field.**

❑ C. A path expression that ends in a **cmr-field** cannot be further composed.

❑ D. A path expression can end with a single value or a collection value.

14 What's true about EJB QL queries? (Choose all that apply.)

❑ A. Of the three clause types, SELECT, FROM, and WHERE, only the SELECT clause is required.

❑ B. The SELECT clause designates query domain.

❑ C. The WHERE clause determines the types of objects to be selected.

❑ D. An EJB QL query may have parameters.

15 What's true about EJB QL WHERE clauses? (Choose all that apply.)

❑ A. Identification variables used in a WHERE clause can be defined only in the FROM clause.

❑ B. Identification variables can represent a single value or a collection.

❑ C. The number of input parameters must equal the number of parameters for the finder or selector method.

❑ D. Input paramaters can only be used in WHERE clauses.

16 Given the EJB QL expression:

p.discount BETWEEN 10 AND 15

Which expression is equivalent?

❑ A. **p.discount > 10 AND p.discount < 15**

❑ B. **p.discount >= 10 AND p.discount < 15**

❑ C. **p.discount > 10 and p.discount <= 15**

❑ D. **p.discount >= 10 and p.discount <= 15**

17 What's true about EJB QL, IN expressions? (Choose all that apply.)

❑ A. The **single_valued_path_expression** must have a String value.

❑ B. The NOT logical operator can be used in an IN expression.

❑ C. The string literal list can be empty.

❑ D. The following expression is legal: **o.country** IN ("UK", "US")

18 Given the EJB QL expression:

product.code LIKE 'F_s'

Which value(s) would result in a true comparison? (Choose all that apply.)

❑ A. Fs

❑ B. F1s

❑ C. FXs

❑ D. F37s

❑ E. Fits

COFFEE CRAM
Mock Exam Answers

---

1 What's true for an entity bean provider using container-managed persistence to create persistent relationships? (Choose all that apply.)

✔ A. A local interface is required for such a bean to have a bidirectional relationship with another entity bean.

❏ B. Such a bean can have relationships with only session beans.

❏ C. Relationships can be only one-to-one or one-to-many.

❏ D. A getter method return type can be java.util.List. *— must be Collection or Set*

---

2 What's true for an entity bean provider using container-managed persistence to create persistent relationships? (Choose all that apply.)

❏ A. A remote interface is required for such a bean to have a bidirectional *— must be local* relationship with another entity bean.

❏ B. Such a bean can have relationships with only message-driven beans.

❏ C. A get method return type can use java.util.Map. *— only Collection or Set*

✔ D. Relationships can be one-to-one, one-to-many, or many-to-many.

---

3 When a remote client invokes a method on an entity bean using container- *(spec: 132)* managed persistence, and that bean has already been removed, what exception will be thrown?

❏ A. `javax.ejb.AccessLocalException`

❏ B. `javax.ejb.ObjectNotFoundException`

✔ C. `java.rmi.NoSuchObjectException`

❏ D. `java.rmi.StubNotFoundException`

❏ E. `javax.ejb.NoSuchEntityException`

---

4 Given the container-managed unidirectional relationship:

(spec: 138)

Foo (0-1) —> Bar (0-1)

And the object relations:

f1 —> b1
f2 —> b2

What will be true after the following code runs?   (Choose all that apply.)

```
f2.setBar(f1.getBar());
```

☑ A. `f1.getBar() == null`

❑ B. `b2.getFoo() == null`

❑ C. `b1.getFoo() == null`

❑ D. none of the above

---

5 If an entity bean A has been removed from a relationship with bean B, in which case(s) will bean A's accessor method for bean B return a non-null value? (Choose all that apply.)

(spec: 132)

❑ A. one-to-one

❑ B. many-to-one

☑ C. many-to-many

❑ D. all of the above

❑ E. none of the above

(spec: 463–464)

6 Which deployment descriptor element's value(s) must be a type of collection? (Choose all that apply.)

❑ A. `<ejb-name>`

❑ B. `<cmr-field`

☑ C. `<cmr-field-type>` – *Collection or Set.*

❑ D. `<ejb-relation>`

7 Which deployment descriptor element(s) must have exactly two declarations of another deployment descriptor element? (Choose all that apply.)

(spec: 467-468)

- ❑ A. `<ejb-name>`
- ❑ B. `<cmr-field>`
- ❑ C. `<cmr-field-type>`
- ☑ D. `<ejb-relation>`   *its gotta have two `<ejb-relationship-role>` sub elements*
- ❑ E. `<ejb-relationship-role>`

8 Which set(s) of elements are mandatory within an ejb-relationship-role element? (Choose all that apply.)

(spec: 468)

- ❑ A. `<cmr-field>`, `<multiplicity>`
- ❑ B. `<cmr-field>`, `<relationship-role-source>`
- ❑ C. `<multiplicity>`, `<relationship-role-name>`
- ☑ D. `<multiplicity>`, `<relationship-role-source>`   *who's in the relationship, and how are they related*
- ❑ E. `<relationship-role-name>`, `<relationship-role-source>`

9 Which are valid values for a cmr-field-type element? (Choose all that apply.)

(spec: 464)

- ❑ A. String
- ❑ B. Integer
- ☑ C. `java.util.Set`   *Either a local interface type, or a Collection or Set of the local interface type*
- ❑ D. `java.util.List`
- ☑ E. `java.util.Collection`

10 Which set(s) of elements are mandatory within an ejb-relation element?

(spec: 467-468)

- ❑ A. `<ejb-relation-name>`, `<ejb-relationship-role>`
- ☑ B. `<ejb-relationship-role>`, `<ejb-relationship-role>`   *gotta have two partners*
- ❑ C. `<description>`, `<ejb-relation-name>`, `<ejb-relationship-role>`
- ❑ D. `<ejb-relation-name>`, `<ejb-relationship-role>`, `<ejb-relationship-role>`

11 Given CMP beans CustomerBean, OrderBean, and LineItemsBean with the following relationships:

(spec: 233)

CustomerBean (1) <—> OrderBean (n)

OrderBean (1) <—> LineItemsBean (n)

and the following EJB QL query:

SELECT DISTINCT OBJECT (c)

FROM Customer c, IN (c.Order) o, IN (o.lineItems) li

WHERE **li.product_type = 'refrigerator'**

Which of the following properly describes the result of the query? (Choose all that apply.)

❏ A. The query is invalid.

❏ B. All orders that include a line item that refers to a refrigerator.

❏ C. All line items that refer to a refrigerator.

✓ D. All customers that have order(s) that refer to a refrigerator.

The SELECT clause specifies that the query must return Customer objects.

12 Given CMP beans CustomerBean, OrderBean, and LineItemsBean with the following relationships:

(spec: 236)

CustomerBean (1) <—> OrderBean (n)

OrderBean (1) <—> LineItemsBean (n)

Which will return all orders that have line items? (Choose all that apply.)

❏ A. SELECT DISTINCT o
         FROM Order o, IN (o.lineItems) li

✓ B. SELECT DISTINCT OBJECT(o)
         FROM Order o, IN (o.lineItems) li

❏ C. SELECT OBJECT(o)
         FROM Order o
         WHERE o.lineItems = 0

✓ D. SELECT OBJECT(o)
         FROM Order o
         WHERE o.lineItems IS NOT EMPTY

13 What's true about EJB QL path expressions? (Choose all that apply.) (spec: 225-226)

- ☑ A. In a path expression the (.) is considered the navigation operator.
- ☑ B. Path expressions can terminate with either **cmr-field** or **cmp-field**.
- ❑ C. A path expression that ends in a **cmr-field** cannot be further composed.
- ☑ D. A path expression can end with a single value or a collection value.

14 What's true about EJB QL queries? (Choose all that apply.) (spec: 218-219)

- ❑ A. Of the three clause types, SELECT, FROM, and WHERE, only the SELECT clause is required.
- ❑ B. The SELECT clause designates query domain.
- ❑ C. The WHERE clause determines the types of objects to be selected.
- ☑ D. An EJB QL query may have parameters.

15 What's true about EJB QL WHERE clauses? (Choose all that apply.) (spec: 227-228)

- ☑ A. Identification variables used in a WHERE clause can be defined only in the FROM clause.
- ❑ B. Identification variables can represent a single value or a collection.
- ❑ C. The number of input parameters must equal the number of parameters for the finder or selector method.
- ☑ D. Input parameters can only be used in WHERE clauses.

16 Given the EJB QL expression: (spec: 229)

```
p.discount BETWEEN 10 AND 15
```

Which expression is equivalent?

- ❑ A. `p.discount > 10 AND p.discount < 15`
- ❑ B. `p.discount >= 10 AND p.discount < 15`
- ❑ C. `p.discount > 10 and p.discount <= 15`
- ☑ D. `p.discount >= 10 and p.discount <= 15`

---

17 What's true about EJB QL, IN expressions? (Choose all that apply.)   *(spec: 229–230)*

☑ A. The **single_valued_path_expression** must have a String value.

☑ B. The NOT logical operator can be used in an IN expression.

☐ C. The string literal list can be empty.

☐ D. The following expression is legal: **o.country** IN ("UK", "US")   *watch out for double quotes!*

(spec: 230)

18 Given the EJB QL expression:

product.code LIKE 'F_s'

Which value(s) would result in a true comparison? (Choose all that apply.)

☐ A. Fs

☑ B. F1s

☑ C. FXs

☐ D. F37s

☐ E. Fits

The % character is a wildcard for a sequence of characters. The _ is a wildcard for a single character

8 message-driven beans

Getting the Message

> Wow! Message-driven beans are fantastic! I can send a message, and then go back to what I was doing before, without waiting for a reply. That means I have more time to read this nifty "Head First Slide Rule" book...

It's fun to receive messages. Not as much fun as, say, getting that EBay package with the genuine Smurf™ lamp, but fun and *efficient* nonetheless. Imagine if you sent your order to EBay, and you couldn't leave your house until the package was delivered. That's what it's like with Session and Entity beans, because there's all calls to a bean's client interface (home, component, local, Remote, doesn't matter) are synchronous. But with message-driven beans, the client makes a message and sends it to a messaging service. Then the client walks away. Later, the messaging service sends the Container the message, and the Container give it to a message-driven bean.

OBJECTIVES

Message-Driven Beans

Official:

What it really means:

10.1 Identify correct and incorrect statements or examples about the client view, and lifecycle, of a message-driven bean.

You have to know that message-driven beans don't have clients! That means no home interface, no component interface, and no issues of local vs. Remote. Of course message-driven beans do have a caller, but that's the Container. And we don't consider the Container a *client*. The Container is the boss, not the customer.

Message-driven beans have a very simply lifecycle—if you know how stateless session beans work, you know how message-driven beans work. The only different is that instead of bringing a bean out of the pool to service a client method call, the Container brings message-driven beans out of the pool to service *an incoming JMS message.*

10.2 Identify the interface(s) and methods a message-driven bean must implement.

You must know that message-driven beans implement two interfaces—javax.ejb.MessageDrivenBean, the interface with the Container callbacks (not many!) and javax.jms.MessageListener, the interface with a single onMessage(Message m) method. For a message-driven bean, onMessage() is the only business method.

10.3 Identify the use and behavior of the MessageDrivenContext interface methods.

You have to know that message-driven beans can't call most of the methods in MessageDrivenContext, ever. Think about it. If there's no client, how could you get client security info? If there's no client, which means no client view, how could you call getEJBObject() or getEJBHome()? You don't have a home! You don't have an EJBObject().

10.4 From a list, identify the responsibility of the Bean Provider, and the responsibility of the Container provider, for a message-driven bean.

You also have to recognize that if there's no client, you can't declare any checked exceptions. Who would catch them? Also, just as with stateless session beans, if you start a transaction in a method (which can only mean a BMT bean in onMessage()) you must finish it before the method ends.

Imagine this scenario...

You have to ask someone to do a very important job.

You have no idea how long it's going to take them.

You have to wait right where you are until they finish.

You can't do anything else while you're waiting.

...please oh please don't take all day on this... I have SO many other things I'd rather be doing than wait here for you to finish...

Client

Server

> Hey, we're at the pool, dude. I thought I told you never to call me here.

> Tell him to chill. We'll get to it...and it's not like he's got anything better to do.

Too bad these guys aren't message-driven beans

Method calls, local or remote, are synchronous. The caller is stuck waiting until the server returns.

Message-driven beans (added in EJB 2.0) give you asynchronous communication between the client (message sender) and the server (message receiver).

In messaging terms, the sender is called the message Producer and the receiver is called the message Consumer.

With messaging, the Producer sends a message and then goes about his business. He doesn't have to wait for the Consumer to even get the message, let alone process it.

When the Consumer gets a message, he processes it. In the meantime, the client can still have a life.

Client

before message-driven beans

after message-driven beans

Message-driven bean overview

(1) **Client (Producer) send a message to the messaging service.**

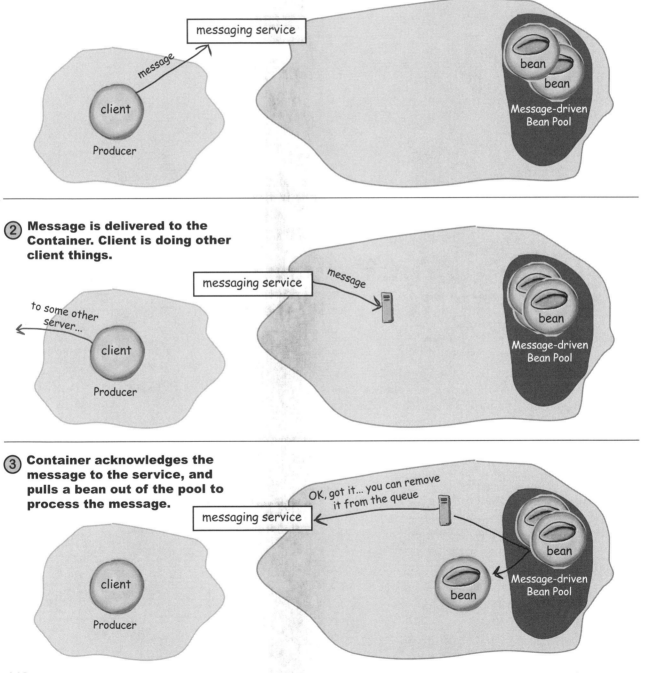

(2) **Message is delivered to the Container. Client is doing other client things.**

(3) **Container acknowledges the message to the service, and pulls a bean out of the pool to process the message.**

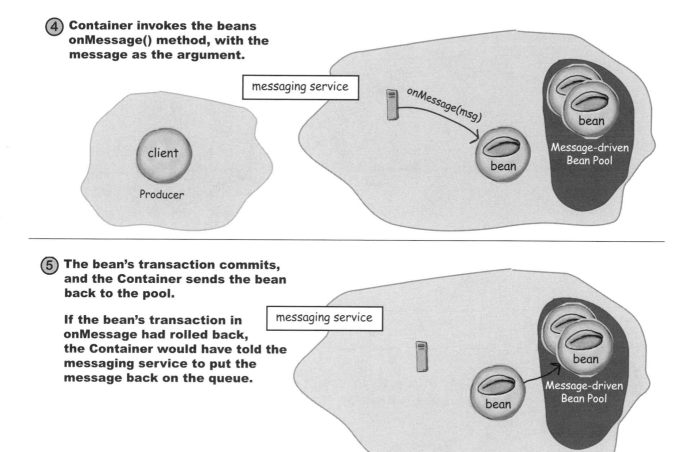

④ **Container invokes the beans onMessage() method, with the message as the argument.**

⑤ **The bean's transaction commits, and the Container sends the bean back to the pool.**

If the bean's transaction in onMessage had rolled back, the Container would have told the messaging service to put the message back on the queue.

Don't they look a lot like stateless session beans?

Like stateless session beans, message-driven beans have no unique identity to clients (actually, they don't *have* clients, since the Container isn't really considered a *client* to the bean), they're pooled, and they have no individual state that affects their business logic. That means one message-driven bean (of a particular type) is the same as any other bean from the same home. Just like stateless beans.

Multiple beans of the same type can process messages concurrently.

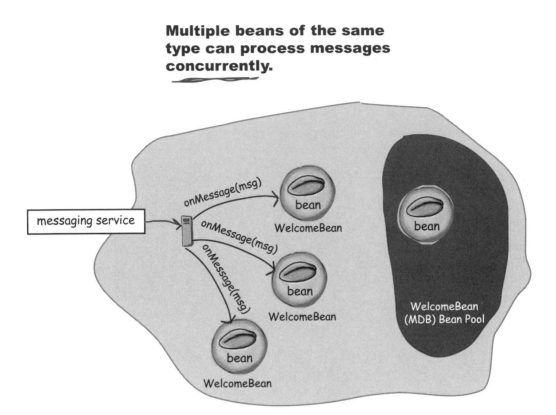

But the container will make sure that each bean is thread safe!

The lifecycle of message-driven beans looks just like stateless session beans

Message-driven bean

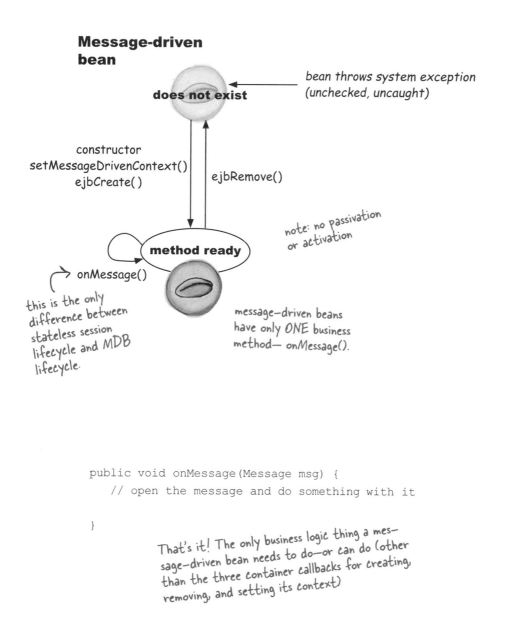

bean throws system exception
(unchecked, uncaught)

constructor
setMessageDrivenContext()
ejbCreate()

ejbRemove()

does not exist

method ready

onMessage()

note: no passivation or activation

this is the only difference between stateless session lifecycle and MDB lifecycle.

message-driven beans have only ONE business method— onMessage().

```
public void onMessage(Message msg) {
    // open the message and do something with it

}
```

That's it! The only business logic thing a message-driven bean needs to do—or can do (other than the three container callbacks for creating, removing, and setting its context)

Message-driven bean class

```
package headfirst;

import javax.ejb.*;          a new import:
import javax.jms.*;          the javax.jms package          TWO interfaces to implement!

public class WelcomeBean implements MessageDrivenBean, MessageListener {
```

javax.ejb.MessageDrivenBean (with the container callbacks) javax.jms.MessageListener (with the onMessage() callback method)

```
    private MessageDrivenContext context;
```

MessageDrivenContext extends EJBContext just like SessionContext and EntityContext

```
    public void ejbCreate() { }
```

you MUST have a single, no-arg ejbCreate()

```
    public void ejbRemove() { }
```

works just like stateless session beans... called when the Container wants to reduce the pool

```
    public void setMessageDrivenContext(MessageDrivenContext ctx) {
        context = ctx;
    }
```

just do the same thing you always do... save your context

```
    public void onMessage(Message msg) {
        // process the message
        try {

            if (msg instanceof TextMessage) {
              TextMessage message = (TextMessage) msg;

              System.out.println(message.getText());
            }
        } catch (JMSException ex) {
            ex.printStackTrace();
        }
    }
}
```

FINALLY! A real business method. This is the only method defined in the MessageListener interface.

TextMessage is-a Message, but it might have been another kind of message like BytesMessage, MapMessage, ObjectMessage or StreamMessage. So we test it with instanceof before the cast.

Yikes. A checked exception! It's from the getText() method.

Writing a message-driven bean: your job as Bean Provider

> This time, there's no client view, so I don't have to match anything from the home or component interfaces. They don't exist. Just like me.

You put THREE kinds of methods in the bean class:

(1) Bean Law: ejbCreate() method

Write a single, no-argument ejbCreate() method in the bean. It doesn't match anything or come from any interface. It's there because it MUST be.

```
<<interface>>
MessageListener

onMessage()
```

(2) MessageListener implementation: onMessage()

This is your business method. Your *only* business method.

```
<<interface>>
MessageDrivenBean

ejbRemove()
setMessageDrivenContext()
```

(3) MessageDrivenBean implementation: container callbacks

Implement both of the methods from the MessageDrivenBean interface, which your bean *must* implement in the official Java way (i.e. using the 'implements MessageDrivenBean' declaration either in your bean class or one of its superclasses)

Sharpen your pencil

Of the three types of methods you put in your bean, check off the ones the compiler cares about.

Compiler-checked?

- ☐ ejbCreate()
- ☐ onMessage()
- ☐ ejbRemove() and setMessageDrivenContext()

Rules for the message-driven bean class

(1) The class must implement *javax.ejb.MessageDrivenBean* and *javax.jms.MessageListener*.

```
public class WelcomeBean implements MessageDrivenBean, MessageListener {
```

(2) The class must be *public*, must not be *final*, and must not be *abstract*.

(3) The class must have a public **constructor** that takes no arguments. (Just like the other beans... so the Container can make a new instance.)

```
public WelcomeBean() { }
```

If you can, just let the compiler put in the default constructor. But if you do have one, be SURE it's no-arg, and don't put any code in it. Wait for ejbCreate()

(4) The class must have a no-arg **ejbCreate()** method. It must be *public*, not *final*, not *static*, with a void return type.

```
public void ejbCreate() { }
```

Put initialization code in here. By the time this method is called, you already have your context.

(5) The class must define the **onMessage()** method from the MessageListener interface. It must be *public*, not *final*, not *static*, with a void return type, and it takes a single argument of type javax.jms.Message.

```
public void onMessage(Message msg) { ... }
```

The REAL business method. Your logic goes here...

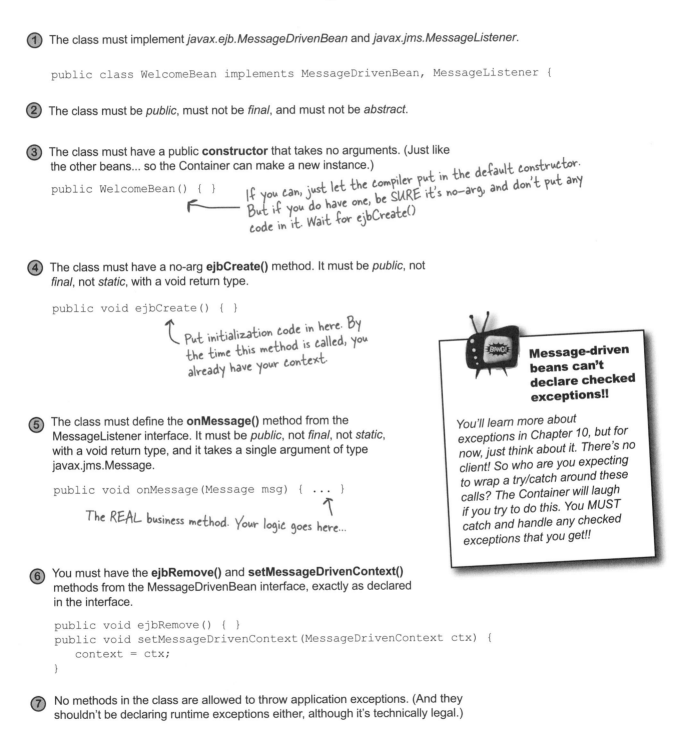

Message-driven beans can't declare checked exceptions!!

You'll learn more about exceptions in Chapter 10, but for now, just think about it. There's no client! So who are you expecting to wrap a try/catch around these calls? The Container will laugh if you try to do this. You MUST catch and handle any checked exceptions that you get!!

(6) You must have the **ejbRemove()** and **setMessageDrivenContext()** methods from the MessageDrivenBean interface, exactly as declared in the interface.

```
public void ejbRemove() { }
public void setMessageDrivenContext(MessageDrivenContext ctx) {
   context = ctx;
}
```

(7) No methods in the class are allowed to throw application exceptions. (And they shouldn't be declaring runtime exceptions either, although it's technically legal.)

Notice something missing from the code?
We never said what kind of messages we're listening for, or where they might be coming from.

You don't put anything in your code that indicates the JMS destination. You can probably guess when that happens... *deploy-time*.

But as a Bean Provider, you tell the Deployer whether you're looking for messages from a topic or queue. And for that, we'll use a new tag in the deployment descriptor, just for message-driven beans. At deploy-time, the Deployer will bind your bean to a specific Topic or Queue configured as a resource in the EJB server.

```
<message-driven-destination>

    <destination-type>javax.jms.Topic</destination-type>

</message-driven-destination>
```

You tell the Deployer if you're expecting messages from a Topic or a Queue

Complete DD for a message-driven bean

```
<enterprise-beans>

    <message-driven>

        <ejb-name>WelcomeNewCustomer</ejb-name>

        <home>headfirst.CustomerHome</home>

        <remote>headfirst.Customer</remote>


        <ejb-class>headfirst.WelcomeBean</ejb-class>

        <transaction-type>Container</transaction-type>

        <message-driven-destination>

            <destination-type>javax.jms.Topic</destination-type>

        </message-driven-destination>

    </message-driven>

</enterprise-beans>
```

There's no client view! No local view, no Remote view. No view at all. So you don't put in the tags for home and component interface.

(We'll look at an optional tag in a few pages)

Topics and Queues

Messaging comes in two flavors: topics and queues, although topics come in two subflavors—durable subscriptions and non-durable subscriptions.

Queues are like FIFO lists (although First-In-First-Out order isn't guaranteed). The producer sends a message that's intended for just a single consumer. Once somebody processes the message, that's it. An example might be an employee reimbursement system, where the employee sends his reimbursement request to the messaging service, and somebody in accounting will process the request. It doesn't need to go to anybody else at that point. If it turns out that the next step is to send it for management processing, the accounting department might send a message to a different destination—the ManagerApproval queue.

Topics use a publish and subscribe model, where a producer sends a message, and anyone who's listening as a consumer will get a copy of the message. Works just like a mailing list. If any one subscriber doesn't get the message, the producer doesn't care.

A topic subscriber can request a *durable subscription* if he wants to make sure that he sees all messages, including the ones that accumulated while he was offline, for example. That will almost always be your choice, because you'll want to get all the messages. Think about it...a non-durable topic subscription would be like you must be home at the time your magazine is delivered, os you simply won't see it.

Enterprise systems tend to use either queues or durable topic subscriptions. A non-durable topic subscription might be appropriate sometimes, but if I'm a message consumer it's really like saying, "I don't care much about whether I get these messages."

Queue: one to <u>one</u> (point-to-point)

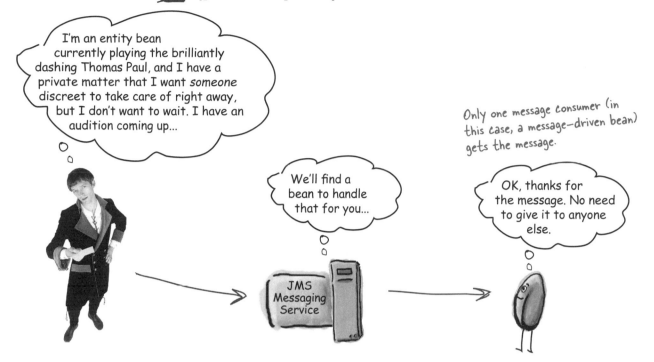

Topic: one to <u>many</u> (publish/subscribe)

there are no
Dumb Questions

Q: How does JMS fit into all this? And if I have a message-driven bean, where do I get the messaging service?

A: JMS 1.02 is the Java Messaging Service API that's required by EJB 2.0. That means your EJB container *must* have some kind of messaging service included, although many vendors can work with multiple messaging services as long as those services support the JMS API.

The JMS API works much like JDBC—you have a driver that knows how to take your standard JMS API calls, and translate them into something the underlying messaging system understands.

Q: Can I get messages from non-JMS messaging services?

A: Not right now, in EJB 2.0, but they (the infamous J2EE team) hope to add that capability... some day.

Q: Why doesn't the MessageDrivenBean just extend the MessageListener interface? That way you wouldn't have to implement both interfaces.

A: See your previous question. The J2EE team didn't want to lock all message-driven beans into being JMS listeners. One day, there might be many kinds of listener interfaces for different messaging types.

Q: Are messages guaranteed to come in order? Will I always get the first one first?

A: No!! You better not depend on it or Bad Things Might Happen. For example, you might get the "Cancel the Order" message before you get the "Place the Order" message. Design your system and code your bean on the assumption that message order is not strictly guaranteed.

Q: If it's a topic, does that mean *all* beans in a particular subscriber pool will get the message?

A: No! Remember, one bean can stand in for all the other beans. The Container will deliver the message to just ONE bean in the pool. *Unless...* no never mind.

Q: Unless *what*? Tell me!

A: OK, OK. But this isn't on the exam, so relax. Let's say your server is running as a clustered configuration, where you could have multiple instances of your server running. In that case, there is no guarantee about how the Container will represent itself to the messaging service.

The question becomes, does the messaging service see the whole cluster as ONE version of your application, no matter how many JVMs its running on, or does the messaging service see each cluster (with its own duplicated pool for each bean type) as a separate listener?

Only ONE bean per pool gets a copy of a topic message

If you have, say, the WelcomeBean subscribed to the NewCustomer topic, when a new message is published to that topic, the Container will choose *only one* bean from the WelcomeBean pool to get the message. Remember, the Container keeps a separate pool of beans for each home (and every deployed bean type gets its own home). The Container doesn't put all message-driven beans into one pool, even if they're subscribed to the same topics.

But if there are multiple bean types subscribed to that topic, one bean from *each* of those pools will also get the message. In this picture, both the WelcomeBean and the NewSalesBean are subscribers to the NewCustomer topic, so the Container selects one bean from each pool to get the message.

Only one bean per subscriber pool will get the message. NOT every bean in the pool!

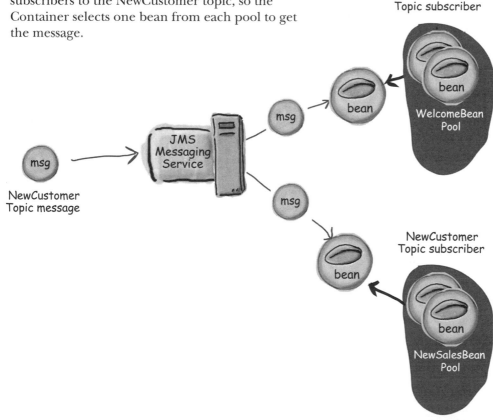

With a queue, only one bean gets the message. Period.

If you have a queue for messages requesting that a new customer be processed, only one bean from the pool associated with that queue will get the message. That's it.

Oh, and don't even think about asking what happens if you have more than one bean type (pool) associated with that queue.

But if you persist, we'll tell you that JMS doesn't define what happens when there is more than one consumer for a particular queue. That means there's no way to know how the messages might be distributed among the different queue consumers. Maybe the messaging service will just pick one at random. But maybe it won't. Maybe it'll just pick the first one in a properties file and send everything there. *So, just don't do it.*

Only one bean in the pool will get the message. NOT every bean in the pool!

ProcessCustomer
queue listener

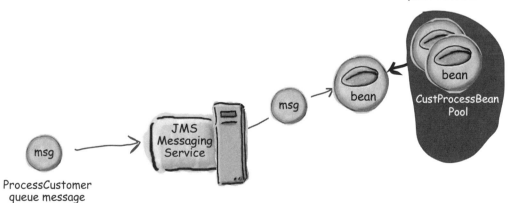

bean

CustProcessBean
Pool

msg

bean

JMS
Messaging
Service

msg

ProcessCustomer
queue message

MessageDrivenContext

The server makes message-driven beans virtually the same way in which it makes stateless session beans.

1. Call the bean's constructor (must be no-arg).

2. Call the bean's context setter.

3. Call the beans ejbCreate() method.

In fact, the first two steps are the same for *all* bean types. The context setter always comes immediately after the bean's constructor, and at some point before ejbCreate(). (And of course an entity bean might never get an ejbCreate() call, if there aren't any clients trying to insert new entities into the database.)

So, what can a message-driven bean do with its context? We think it's time for you to figure that out. We can guarantee there will be questions on the exam related to what a message-driven bean can and cannot do with its context. In fact, you'll find these questions scattered throughout the objectives, not just in the message-driven bean objectives (10.1 – 10.4). Questions from the transactions, exceptions, and security objectives might involve a message-driven bean and its context.

This is just our way of saying.. *do the damn exercise!*

You don't want to have to memorize this stuff, but if you just spend a few moments thinking about it, you'll figure it out.

The answers are on the next page, though, so don't turn until you're done.

Sharpen your pencil

Think about which methods a message-driven bean could call on its context.

From the list of methods in EJBContext, cross out those methods that do not make sense for a message-driven bean (and by "do not make sense" we mean "will cause a horrible runtime exception with devastating and potentially career-ending consequences").

Oh, and be prepared to defend your answers. Imagine us sitting right behind you, scarily, demanding justification for your choices.

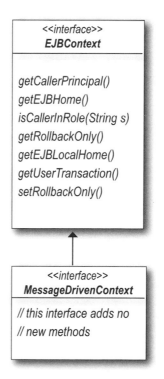

MessageDrivenContext

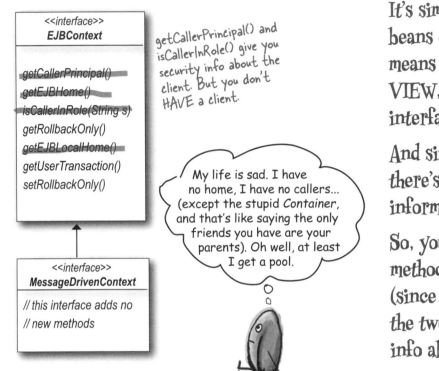

```
<<interface>>
EJBContext

getCallerPrincipal()
getEJBHome()
isCallerInRole(String s)
getRollbackOnly()
getEJBLocalHome()
getUserTransaction()
setRollbackOnly()
```

getCallerPrincipal() and isCallerInRole() give you security info about the client. But you don't HAVE a client.

```
<<interface>>
MessageDrivenContext

// this interface adds no
// new methods
```

My life is sad. I have no home, I have no callers... (except the stupid *Container*, and that's like saying the only friends you have are your parents). Oh well, at least I get a pool.

It's simple. Message-driven beans don't have <u>clients</u>. That means they don't have a client VIEW, so there's no home interface.

And since there's no client, there's no client security information.

So, you can't call the two methods for getting the home (since you HAVE no home), or the two methods for getting info about the caller's security.

there are no Dumb Questions

Q: **You keep saying that message-driven beans don't have clients. But SOMEBODY has to call the bean's methods, right? They don't call themselves...**

A: Technically, yes, the bean's methods are called. But we don't consider the Container to be a client. It's the boss, not the customer. So, in the Java sense, the Container is the bean's caller, but not a client. And as for getting security info, if the bean doesn't trust its own Container, you have waaaay bigger problems. We're talking one seriously paranoid bean.

What if something goes wrong?

Everything was going so well...

When suddenly...

Message acknowledgement

You don't want messages getting lost. If you have a crucial message on the queue, and the one bean who gets it can't commit—or worse, throws an exception and dies—what happens to your critical message?

That's the point of acknowledgement. The Container tells the messaging service (*not* the original producer) that the message was delivered and everything is fine.

But if later, while the consumer (the message-driven bean) is processing the message, a Bad Thing happens, the Container can tell the messaging service to put the message back in the queue.

How does the Container really know that something went wrong? Two ways, and it's your choice as a Bean Provider.

① **The transaction status**

Message acknowledgement is tied to whether the transaction commits or rolls back. If the transaction rolls back, the message goes back on the queue. You get this behavior for beans that use *container-managed transaction demarcation* (we'll cover transactions in the next chapter).

OR

② **The method completion**

Message acknowledgement is tied to whether the method completes successfully. If the method throws a runtime exception, the message goes back on the queue. You get this behavior for beans that use *bean-managed transaction demarcation.*

That's all well and good, but let's go back and see how our earlier scenario ended...

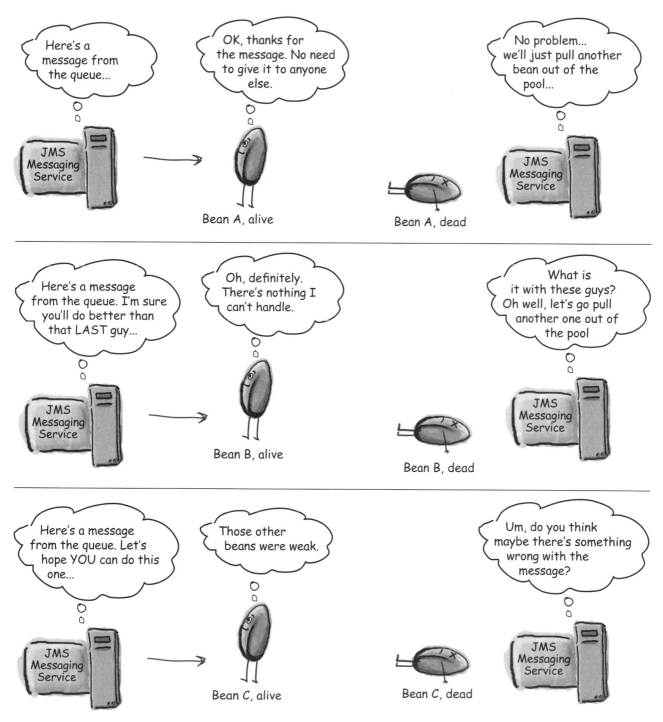

Off the path

Think about it.

If you want your message acknowledgement tied to the status of the transaction, use container-managed transactions (CMT). Most of the time, this will be your choice.

But if you want to decouple message-acknowledgement from the status of your transaction, your only choice is to use bean-managed transaction demarcation (BMT). With BMT, the Container looks only at whether your method completes. Method completes? Fine, the message acknowledgement stands. Runtime exception? Message goes back in the queue.

But what if you have a scenario where the bean can never commit, because of something inherently bad about the message? With CMT, that message will keep coming and coming and coming and... but not forever. Most messaging services let you configure how many times a particular message is resent before the service says, "This message looks like poison; let's send it to a Special Place (like a Bad Message queue) where it can't harm anyone". You really need to watch out for this, because there's nothing in the spec to help. You're reliant on your server vendor!

There is another possibility, though. With BMT, you could write your method in such a way that you rollback the method, but still finish the method. That way, the Container just goes whistling on its merry way thinking everything was fine. It has no idea that things went badly. In this scenario, you'd catch whatever exception comes up, rollback the transaction yourself (again, you'll learn how to do that very soon), and then end the method *looking* successful (at least to the Container).

Setting the acknowledgement mode

If you DO use BMT, you have two choices for how the Container sends an acknowledgement to the messaging service. The choices are:

`<acknowledge-mode>Auto-acknowledge</acknowledge-mode>`

OR

`<acknowledge-mode>Dups-ok-acknowledge</acknowledge-mode>`

This doesn't change the Container's behavior of whether it decides to do the acknowledgement—for a BMT bean it's always based on whether the method completes. The acknowledge mode is simply a way to tweak how the Container sends the acknowledgement.

With Dups-ok-acknowledge, you're telling the Container that you don't mind if it's kind of *slow* with the acknowledgement to the message service... that you don't *mind* if you get duplicate messages ("dups-ok"). This lets the Container take whatever time it wants to do the acknowledgement, and it might make the server more efficient, but at the risk of duplicate messages because the poor messaging service didn't get an acknowledgement quickly enough.

Fill-in the blanks with the code that must be inserted for the bean to be a legal message-driven bean class.

```
package headfirst;

import javax.ejb.*;
import javax.jms.*;

public class FooListenerBean _____ {

    private MessageDrivenContext context;



    public void _____


    public void _____


    public void setMessageDrivenContext(MessageDrivenContext ctx) {
        context = ctx;
    }

    public void _____

}
```

2 List two things a stateful session bean can call on its SessionContext, that a message-driven bean can never call on its MessageDrivenContext.

_____

_____

① Fill-in the blanks with the code that must be inserted for the bean to be a legal message-driven bean class.

```
package headfirst;

import javax.ejb.*;
import javax.jms.*;

public class FooListenerBean    implements MessageDrivenBean, MessageListener    {

    private MessageDrivenContext context;



    public void  ejbCreate() { }


    public void  ejbRemove() { }


    public void setMessageDrivenContext(MessageDrivenContext ctx) {
        context = ctx;
    }

    public void  onMessage(Message msg) { }

}
```

② List two things a stateful session bean can call on its SessionContext, that a message-driven bean can never call on its MessageDrivenContext.

call isCallerInRole()   (there's no client!)

call getEJBHome()   (there's no client view, so there's no home or component interface)

1 What's true about message-driven beans? (Choose all that apply.)

❏ A. A message-driven bean has a home interface but no component interface.

❏ B. A client never knows a message-driven bean's identity.

❏ C. A client sees a message-driven bean as a JavaMail message consumer.

❏ D. The lifetime of a message-driven bean is controlled by the container.

2 Which interfaces must be implemented in a message-driven bean class or in one of its superclasses? (Choose all that apply.)

❏ A. `javax.jms.Message`

❏ B. `javax.jms.MessageListener`

❏ C. `javax.jms.MessageConsumer`

❏ D. `javax.ejb.MessageDrivenBean`

❏ E. `javax.ejb.MessageDrivenContext`

3 Which list properly sequences the methods called in the lifecycle of a message-driven bean? (Choose all that apply.)

❏ A. `ejbCreate(), newInstance(), setMessageDrivenContext(), onMessage()`

❏ B. `onMessage(), newInstance(), ejbCreate(), setMessageDrivenContext()`

❏ C. `newInstance(), setMessageDrivenContext(), ejbCreate(), onMessage()`

❏ D. `newInstance(), ejbCreate(), setMessageDrivenContext(), onMessage()`

❏ E. `ejbCreate(), setMessageDrivenContext(), newInstance(), onMessage()`

4 Which are valid signature(s) for methods in a message-driven bean? (Choose all that apply.)

❑ A. `public void onMessage()`

❑ B. `public void ejbCreate()`

❑ C. `public static void onMessage()`

❑ D. `public void ejbCreate(javax.jms.Message m)`

❑ E. `public void onMessage(javax.jms.Message m)`

❑ F. `public void onMessage(javax.jms.Message m) throws java.rmi.RemoteException`

5 When is a message-driven bean able to access java:comp/env via JNDI?

❑ A. `ejbCreate()`

❑ B. `ejbRemove()`

❑ C. `setMessageDrivenContext()`

❑ D. None of the above

6 Which message-driven bean methods take an argument? (Choose all that apply.)

❑ A. `ejbCreate()`

❑ B. `ejbRemove()`

❑ C. `onMessage()`

❑ D. `setMessageDrivenContext()`

7 When is a message-driven bean able to access other enterprise beans?

❑ A. `ejbCreate()`

❑ B. `ejbRemove()`

❑ C. `onMessage()`

❑ D. `setMessageDrivenContext()`

❑ E. None of the above

8 What's true about Container support for message-driven beans? (Choose all that apply.)

❑ A. The Container must support the deployment of a message-driven bean as the consumer of a JavaMail queue.

❑ B. The Container is NOT required to support transaction scoping for message-driven beans.

❑ C. The Container guarantees first-in, first delivered message processing.

❑ D. The Container must ensure that the bean instances are non-reentrant.

9 When is a message-driven bean with BMT demarcation able to access resource managers?

❑ A. `ejbCreate()`

❑ B. `ejbRemove()`

❑ C. `onMessage()`

❑ D. `setMessageDrivenContext()`

❑ E. None of the above

10 What's true about message acknowledgment for message-driven beans? (Choose all that apply.)

❑ A. Message acknowledgement modes cannot be defined declaratively.

❑ B. The JMS API should be used for message acknowledgment.

❑ C. For BMT beans, the Container uses the acknowledge-mode deployment descriptor element.

❑ D. For CMT beans, the Container uses the acknowledge-mode deployment descriptor element.

11 What's true about the deployment descriptor for message-driven beans? (Choose all that apply.)

❑ A. The bean provider must guarantee that the bean is associated with a specific queue or topic.

❑ B. The deployment descriptor can indicate whether a bean is intended for a topic or a queue.

❑ C. It can indicate whether a Queue type bean should support durable subscription or not.

❑ D. It is appropriate to associate multiple beans with the same JMS queue.

Mock Exam Answers

(spec: 311–312)

1 What's true about message-driven beans? (Choose all that apply.)

❏ A. A message-driven bean has a home interface but no component interface. — *MDBs have NO client view*

☑ B. A client never knows a message-driven bean's identity.

❏ C. A client sees a message-driven bean as a JavaMail message consumer.

☑ D. The lifetime of a message-driven bean is controlled by the container.

(spec: 314–315)

2 Which interfaces must be implemented in a message-driven bean class or in one of its superclasses? (Choose all that apply.)

❏ A. `javax.jms.Message`

☑ B. `javax.jms.MessageListener` — *this is where the onMessage() method is defined*

❏ C. `javax.jms.MessageConsumer`

☑ D. `javax.ejb.MessageDrivenBean`

❏ E. `javax.ejb.MessageDrivenContext`

(spec: 319)

3 Which list properly sequences the methods called in the lifecycle of a message-driven bean? (Choose all that apply.)

❏ A. `ejbCreate()`, `newInstance()`, `setMessageDrivenContext()`, `onMessage()`

❏ B. `onMessage()`, `newInstance()`, `ejbCreate()`, `setMessageDrivenContext()`

☑ C. `newInstance()`, `setMessageDrivenContext()`, `ejbCreate()`, `onMessage()`

❏ D. `newInstance()`, `ejbCreate()`, `setMessageDrivenContext()`, `onMessage()`

❏ E. `ejbCreate()`, `setMessageDrivenContext()`, `newInstance()`, `onMessage()`

4 Which are valid signature(s) for methods in a message-driven bean? (Choose all that apply.) *(spec: 324)*

- ❑ A. `public void onMessage()`
- ☑ B. `public void ejbCreate()`
- ❑ C. `public static void onMessage()`
- ❑ D. `public void ejbCreate(javax.jms.Message m)`
- ☑ E. `public void onMessage(javax.jms.Message m)`
- ❑ F. `public void onMessage(javax.jms.Message m) throws java.rmi.RemoteException` — *you must never declare a RemoteException*

5 When is a message-driven bean able to access java:comp/env via JNDI? *(spec: 320)*

- ☑ A. `ejbCreate()`
- ☑ B. `ejbRemove()`
- ☑ C. `setMessageDrivenContext()`
- ❑ D. None of the above

6 Which message-driven bean methods take an argument? (Choose all that apply.) *(spec: 319, 324)*

- ❑ A. `ejbCreate()`
- ❑ B. `ejbRemove()`
- ☑ C. `onMessage()` — *takes a message*
- ☑ D. `setMessageDrivenContext()` — *takes a context*

7 When is a message-driven bean able to access other enterprise beans? *(spec: 320)*

- ❑ A. `ejbCreate()`
- ❑ B. `ejbRemove()`
- ☑ C. `onMessage()` — *only in a method with a 'meaningful transaction context'*
- ❑ D. `setMessageDrivenContext()`
- ❑ E. None of the above

8   What's true about Container support for message-driven beans? (Choose all *(spec: 325–326)* that apply.)

❏   A. The Container must support the deployment of a message-driven bean as the consumer of a JavaMail queue.

❏   B. The Container is NOT required to support transaction scoping for message-driven beans.

❏   C. The Container guarantees first-in, first delivered message processing.

☑   D. The Container must ensure that the bean instances are non-reentrant.

9   When is a message-driven bean with BMT demarcation able to access resource *(spec: 320)* managers?

❏   A. `ejbCreate()`

❏   B. `ejbRemove()`

☑   C. `onMessage()` — when there is a 'meaningful transaction context'

❏   D. `setMessageDrivenContext()`

❏   E. None of the above

10 What's true about message acknowledgment for message-driven beans? *(spec: 317)* (Choose all that apply.)

❏   A. Message acknowledgement modes cannot be defined declaratively.

❏   B. The JMS API should be used for message acknowledgment.

☑   C. For BMT beans, the Container uses the acknowledge-mode deployment descriptor element.   — can be Auto–acknowledge or Dups–ok–acknowledge

❏   D. For CMT beans, the Container uses the acknowledge-mode deployment descriptor element.

11 What's true about the deployment descriptor for message-driven beans? *(spec: 317)* (Choose all that apply.)

❏   A. The bean provider must guarantee that the bean is associated with a   — that's the deployer's job specific queue or topic.

☑   B. The deployment descriptor can indicate whether a bean is intended for a topic or a queue.

❏   C. It can indicate whether a Queue type bean should support durable   — durable subscriptions are just for topics! subscription or not.

❏   D. It is appropriate to associate multiple beans with the same JMS queue.

9 EJB transactions

The Atomic Age

It was a long transaction, but she finally committed. She had plenty of time to rollback, but I just kept catching all the exceptions, so it all worked out in the end.

Transactions protect you. With transactions, you can take a risk. You can try something BIG, knowing that if anything goes wrong along the way, you can just pretend the whole thing didn't happen. Everything goes back to the way it was *before*. The idea is simple—you either *commit* to *everything* in the transaction, or you *rollback*, so that nobody sees what you were trying (but failed) to do. Transactions in EJB are a thing of beauty— you can deploy a bean with customized transaction behavior *without* touching the bean's source code! But you can write transaction code, if you need to, so we'll learn that too.

Enterprise Javabeans Transactions

<table>
<tr><td>

Official:

11.1 Identify correct and incorrect statements or examples about EJB transactions, including bean-managed transaction demarcation, and container-managed transaction demarcation.

11.2 Identify correct and incorrect statements about the Application Assembler's responsibilities, including the use of deployment descriptor elements related to transactions, and the identification of the methods of a particular bean type for which a transaction attribute must be specified.

11.3 Given a list of transaction behaviors, match them with the appropriate transaction attribute.

11.4 Given a list of responsibilities, identify those which are the container's with respect to transactions, including the handling of getRollbackOnly, setRollbackOnly, getUserTransaction, SessionSynchronization callbacks, for both container and bean-managed transaction demarcation.

(Note: we cover the part of 11.4 that deals with SessionSynchronization in the Session Bean chapter.)

</td><td>

What it really means:

You need to know the rules, and implications of, bean-managed (BMT) vs. container-managed (CMT) transaction demarcation. For example, you must know that both message-driven and session beans can use CMT *or* BMT but entity beans can use only CMT. And message-driven beans and stateless session beans using BMT must end the transaction before the end of the method, but stateful session beans are allowed to keep a transaction open across multiple method invocations from a client. You need to know that propagation of transactions in BMT is a one-way street: a BMT transaction can propagate out with a bean's method calls (i.e. be used by the called method), but an existing transaction context can never be propagated into a BMT bean. In other words, a BMT bean will run only in transactions the bean itself has started.

You must be very clear about the effects of transaction attributes for CMT. For example, you must understand that message-driven beans can use only *two* of the six attributes (NotSupported and Required), because the others don't make sense for a message-driven bean (no calling transaction can ever be propagated into a message-driven bean because it is only the container that invokes the bean's onMessage() method. You also have to know the methods of each bean type (session, entity, or message-driven) for which transaction attributes must be specified. For example, an entity bean's create() method is transactional, but a session bean's create() method runs in "an unspecified transaction context." You must be able to specify transaction attributes in the deployment descriptor.

Finally, you need to know what your bean can count on from the container when it comes to transactions. For example, you must know that if you invoke setRollbackOnly on a bean's context, the container must **not** commit.

</td></tr>
</table>

An EJB transaction is an atomic unit of work.

A transaction means you've wrapped some work (statements, method calls, whole methods, access to a database, etc.) into a single unit in such a way that either everything succeeds, or everything reverts to its previous state.

In other words, you either __commit__ or __rollback__ the whole atomic unit.

Either it all works, or we just forget the whole thing ever happened.

Shopping cart checkout: a quintessential EJB transaction example.

Imagine you have an online shopping cart system. When it comes time to checkout, what needs to happen? At the very least:

- Have user **confirm** order
- Validate and debit user's **credit card**
- Remove purchased items from **inventory**
- Create and submit a shipping **order**

These must all happen as one unit— if ANY of this goes bad, ALL of it should rollback as though none of this ever happened...

You don't want to debit the inventory if the credit card isn't valid. And you don't want to submit a shipping order if the items aren't yet in stock. And you don't want any of it to happen if the user doesn't confirm the order! If any of these things go wrong, you want your transaction to end with a rollback, rather than a commit. Think of the horror you'd go through if you couldn't do a transaction rollback. Imagine that you went through the first three out of the four steps only to find the user doesn't confirm the order. You would have to go back and add money to the user's credit card, cancel the order, and put the items back in inventory.

Relax **You don't need to know about JTS, XA, or any other transaction APIs except javax.transaction.UserTransaction.**

You won't be tested on any of the lower-level transaction API details. For example, you don't need to know anything about HOW the server/container communicates with a transactional resource such as a database. And although EJB supports distributed transactions, you won't be asked about how it works. We know it's depressing that you won't get to show off your two-phase commit protocol prowess.

The ACID test

Is your transaction safe?

Five out of five experts (plus pretty much the entire rest of the industry) agree on four characteristics of a good, safe transaction. (This is not just an EJB thing, by the way—the ACID test goes back long before Java was a gleam in Gosling's eye.) To put your transactions through the ACID test, make sure the transaction is:

Atomic

Either it all works, or it all fails (and rolls back).

A transaction isn't atomic if it's possible for *some* of it to commit while other parts don't.

Consistent

Whether it works (commits) or fails (rolls back), the data should stay consistent with the business logic reality. You'd have real trouble if, say, you could take items out of inventory without actually submitting an order. You'd end up with items that exist in the *real* inventory (i.e. in a warehouse somewhere), but that don't show up in anybody's computer records.

Isolated

Let's say you have two different transactions running, potentially hitting the same database. You don't want the effect of one transaction to corrupt the state of another transaction. In other words, the transactions should be protected (*isolated*) from one another. Isolation is very similar to thread synchronization—you don't want one transaction reading some data (with the intention of acting on it) if that data is smack in the middle of another transaction that hasn't finished committing its own changes to the data.

Durable

Once a transaction commits, the changes made by that transaction must become permanent! Even if the server goes down, it must come back up and finish what it started to commit.

Distributed transactions: two-phase commit

Off the path

Most EJB containers support distributed transactions through a two-phase commit protocol. If you're a transaction manager (like a J2EE server), you might have multiple participants, including a database, another bean, and another server on the network. Once you've told everyone to commit, there's no good way to undo it, so before you give the signal to commit, you need to make *sure* that everyone can do what you're asking. As the transaction manager, your job is to find out if everyone is ready to perform (update the database, debit the account, etc.), and then, depending on the results, tell them all to do it (commit) or tell them all to forget it (rollback).

Phase ONE

Before I tell everyone to commit, I have to make sure that everybody is ready to do it.

are you ready?
good to go!

Transaction Participant

are you ready?
good to go!

Transaction Participant

are you ready?
good to go!

Transaction Manager

Transaction Participant

Transaction Participant

Phase TWO

It looks like everybody can do it, so now I tell them all to commit.

go for it!
no problem

Transaction Participant

go for it!
no problem

Transaction Participant

go for it!
no problem

Transaction Manager

Transaction Participant

Transaction Participant

How it works in EJB

Transactions can propagate through method calls

When a bean is running code in a transaction, and calls a method on another bean, three different scenarios are possible:

A) The called method runs *in the caller's transaction.*

B) The called method runs *without a transaction.*

C) The called method runs *within its own new transaction.*

(A) **The transaction started in the first method propagates to all other methods in the call stack. All called methods run within the same transaction. (In this book, we'll abbreviate "transaction" to "tx".)**

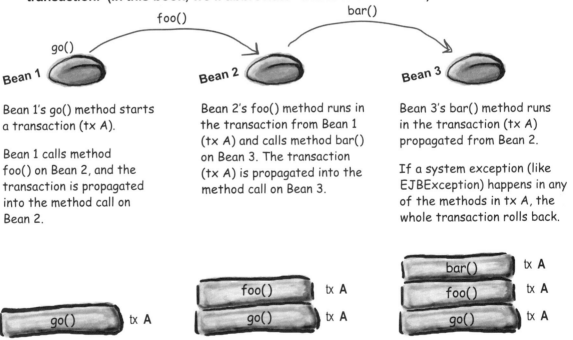

Bean 1's go() method starts a transaction (tx A).

Bean 1 calls method foo() on Bean 2, and the transaction is propagated into the method call on Bean 2.

Bean 2's foo() method runs in the transaction from Bean 1 (tx A) and calls method bar() on Bean 3. The transaction (tx A) is propagated into the method call on Bean 3.

Bean 3's bar() method runs in the transaction (tx A) propagated from Bean 2.

If a system exception (like EJBException) happens in any of the methods in tx A, the whole transaction rolls back.

So, what does it mean for multiple methods to run in the same transaction context? That depends on the bean type and what the beans do in their code. For example, imagine Bean A has a method with JDBC code that does an update to a database row. If any *other* method in the same transaction causes a rollback, Bean A's update won't commit, even if the database would have been more than happy to do it.

Some transactions <u>don't</u> propagate

The caller's transaction might be suspended

If a transactional bean method calls another method, the called method (whether it's in the same or a different bean) might not run in the same transaction. The called method, in that case, will run with either a brand new transaction, or with no transaction at all. (In a few minutes, we'll look at how the container decides whether to propagate the transaction, run without one, or start a new one.)

(B) **The first transaction is suspended and the second method runs *without* a transaction.**

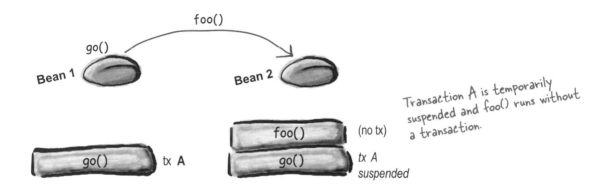

Transaction A is temporarily suspended and foo() runs without a transaction.

(C) **The first transaction is suspended and the second method runs within a *new* transaction.**

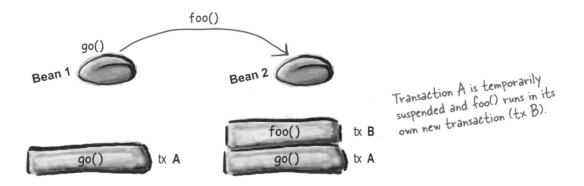

Transaction A is temporarily suspended and foo() runs in its own new transaction (tx B).

How do I make (or get) a transaction?
Two ways: code it or declare it

The container manages your transactions, but you have to tell it how. You can either put transaction code in your bean class, or you can put transaction declarations in the DD. By far, the most common approach is to use the DD, because it's simpler, supports bean reuse, and is the *only* way you can do transactions for entity beans. By putting transaction information in the DD instead of in code, you can deploy the same bean multiple times and get different transaction behavior each time without ever touching the code!

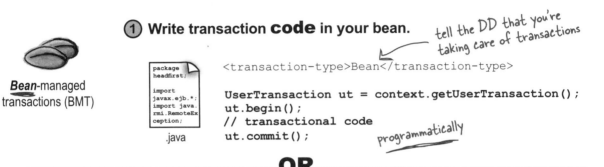

Bean-managed transactions (BMT)

① **Write transaction code in your bean.**

tell the DD that you're taking care of transactions

```
package headfirst;

import javax.ejb.*;
import java.rmi.RemoteException;
```
.java

```xml
<transaction-type>Bean</transaction-type>
```

```java
UserTransaction ut = context.getUserTransaction();
ut.begin();
// transactional code
ut.commit();
```
programmatically

─────────────────**OR**─────────────────

Container-managed transactions (CMT)

② **Declare transactions in the DD.**

```
<?xml version="1.0" encoding="UTF-8"?>

<!DOCTYPE ejb-jar PUBInc./
```
.xml

```xml
<transaction-type>Container</transaction-type>

<method>
    <ejb-name>MyBean</ejb-name>
    <method-name>bar</method-name>
</method>
<trans-attribute>Required</trans-attribute>
```
declaratively

You can't use BOTH in the same bean! You can't mix BMT and CMT in one bean.

You CAN have a combination of BMT and CMT beans in the same ejb-jar, but each bean must have only one transaction type. On the exam, if you see transaction code in a bean, make sure that if you see the DD for that bean, it says:
```xml
<transaction-type>Bean</transaction-type>
```

Transaction-related methods are in two interfaces

UserTransaction

begin()
commit()
getStatus()
rollback()
setRollbackOnly()
setTransactionTimeout()

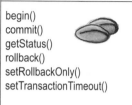

javax.transaction.UserTransaction

Everything in the UserTransaction interface is for beans using bean-managed transactions (BMT).

Beans with container-managed transactions (CMT) aren't allowed to call ANYTHING in this interface.

EJBContext

getUserTransaction()

getCallerPrincipal()
getEJBHome()
getEJBLocalHome()
isCallerInRole()

setRollbackOnly()
getRollbackOnly()

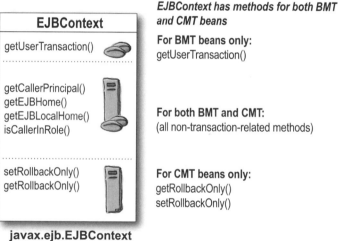

javax.ejb.EJBContext

EJBContext has methods for both BMT and CMT beans

For BMT beans only:
getUserTransaction()

For both BMT and CMT:
(all non-transaction-related methods)

For CMT beans only:
getRollbackOnly()
setRollbackOnly()

(Super class of SessionContext, EntityContext, and MessageDrivenContext)

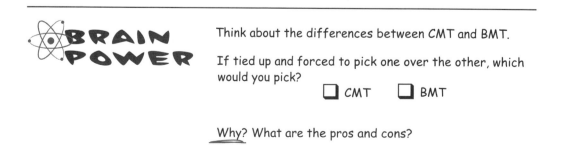

BRAIN POWER

Think about the differences between CMT and BMT.

If tied up and forced to pick one over the other, which would you pick?

☐ CMT   ☐ BMT

Why? What are the pros and cons?

Making a BMT transaction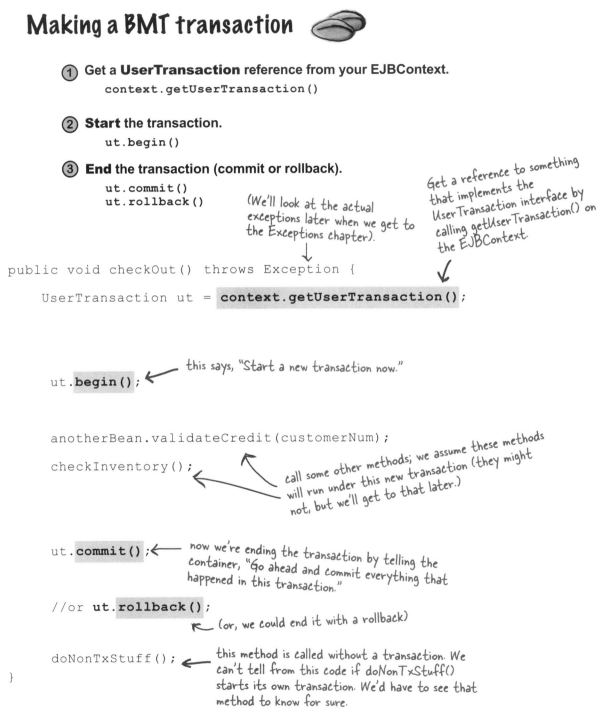

① Get a **UserTransaction** reference from your EJBContext.

```
context.getUserTransaction()
```

② **Start** the transaction.

```
ut.begin()
```

③ **End** the transaction (commit or rollback).

```
ut.commit()
ut.rollback()
```

(We'll look at the actual exceptions later when we get to the Exceptions chapter).

Get a reference to something that implements the UserTransaction interface by calling getUserTransaction() on the EJBContext.

```
public void checkOut() throws Exception {

    UserTransaction ut = context.getUserTransaction();
```

```
    ut.begin();
```
this says, "Start a new transaction now."

```
    anotherBean.validateCredit(customerNum);
    checkInventory();
```
call some other methods; we assume these methods will run under this new transaction (they might not, but we'll get to that later.)

```
    ut.commit();
```
now we're ending the transaction by telling the container, "Go ahead and commit everything that happened in this transaction."

```
    //or ut.rollback();
```
(or, we could end it with a rollback)

```
    doNonTxStuff();
}
```
this method is called without a transaction. We can't tell from this code if doNonTxStuff() starts its own transaction. We'd have to see that method to know for sure.

Call stack of the checkOut() method

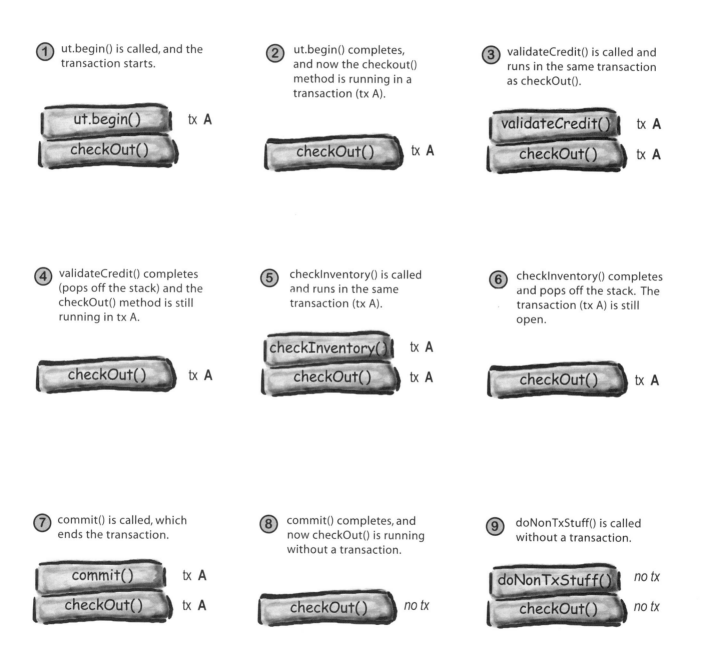

1 ut.begin() is called, and the transaction starts.

2 ut.begin() completes, and now the checkout() method is running in a transaction (tx A).

3 validateCredit() is called and runs in the same transaction as checkOut().

4 validateCredit() completes (pops off the stack) and the checkOut() method is still running in tx A.

5 checkInventory() is called and runs in the same transaction (tx A).

6 checkInventory() completes and pops off the stack. The transaction (tx A) is still open.

7 commit() is called, which ends the transaction.

8 commit() completes, and now checkOut() is running without a transaction.

9 doNonTxStuff() is called without a transaction.

Sharpen your pencil

Using this code listing, mark the matching call stack frames with a checkmark if that frame is currently in a transaction. We did one in the middle for you.

```
public void test() throws Exception {
    blue();
    UserTransaction ut = ctx.getUserTransaction();
    green();
    ut.begin();
    purple();
    ut.commit();
    red();
}

void blue() { green(); }
void green() { }
void purple() { red(); }
void red() { }
```

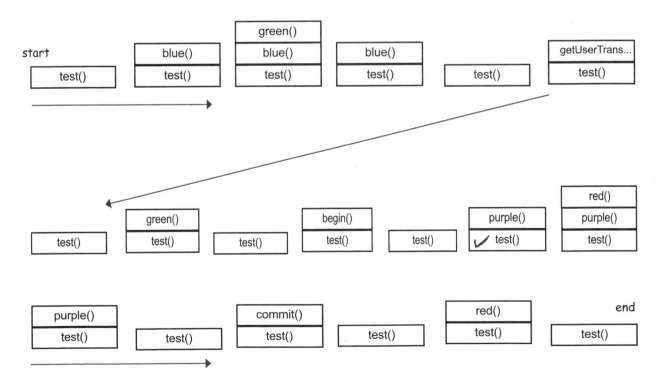

Things you must NOT do with BMT

(1) **A BMT bean must NOT start a transaction before ending the current transaction.**

```
public void go() {

    UserTransaction ut = context.getUserTransaction();

    ut.begin();

    doStuff();

    ut.begin();    ← NO! NO! NO! Can't start a transaction without
                      completing (through a commit or rollback) the
    // more           previous one. If you COULD do that, it would
                      mean you could have "nested transactions".
}
```

Imagine the implications of starting a new transaction before ending the current one. What might happen if you were allowed to do this?

> **Nested transactions are not allowed in EJB!**
> *You're expected to know what the term "nested transaction" means, and what it might look like in code.*

---

(2) **A BMT stateless session or message-driven bean must NOT complete a transactional method without ending the transaction.**

```
public void go() {

    UserTransaction ut = context.getUserTransaction();

    ut.begin();

    doMore();    ← This is a problem! We're ending the method
}                  without ending the transaction we started. In
                   other words, there's no commit() or rollback().
```

> **Only STATEFUL session beans can leave a transaction open at the end of a method.**

Why are stateful session beans allowed to end a method without ending the transaction?

For a stateful bean, can you think of a scenario where you might want to do this (leave the transaction open)?

What might go wrong if you do this?

BMT transactions are one way: they can propagate <u>out</u> to a CMT bean, but no other transaction can propagate <u>in</u> to a BMT bean

Both BMT and CMT bean transactions propagate into a CMT bean.

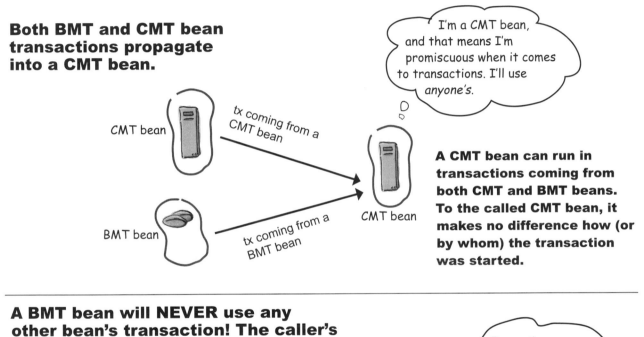

I'm a CMT bean, and that means I'm promiscuous when it comes to transactions. I'll use anyone's.

CMT bean

tx coming from a CMT bean

CMT bean

BMT bean

tx coming from a BMT bean

A CMT bean can run in transactions coming from both CMT and BMT beans. To the called CMT bean, it makes no difference how (or by whom) the transaction was started.

A BMT bean will NEVER use any other bean's transaction! The caller's transaction will be suspended.

Transactions are suspended when they get to a BMT bean!

I practice safe tx. The only transactions I run in are my own. If a caller's transaction comes in, I just say "suspend."

CMT bean

transactions coming from a CMT bean

BMT bean

transactions coming from a BMT bean

BMT bean

The <u>only</u> transaction a BMT bean will run in is one that the bean itself creates.

What does it mean to suspend a transaction?

If a transaction is in progress when a method on a BMT bean is called, the transaction is suspended. *Temporarily.* The transaction just sits there waiting for the BMT bean to complete its work. Work that's not part of the caller's original transaction. Once the BMT method finishes and is popped off the stack, the original transaction kicks back in, right where it left off.

Imagine this scenario: a CMT bean, bean one, is running a method foo() in a transaction (tx A) when it calls a method bar() on bean two (a BMT bean). Once bar() completes and pops off the stack, method foo() invokes another method, bcc(), but this time the called bean is another CMT bean (bean three).

When a transaction is suspended, it waits until it can pick up where it left off. But this means that the things that happen while the transaction is suspended are NOT part of the same atomic unit. In other words, the things that happen while the transaction is suspended won't be rolled back if the suspended transaction (after it comes back to life) fails to commit.

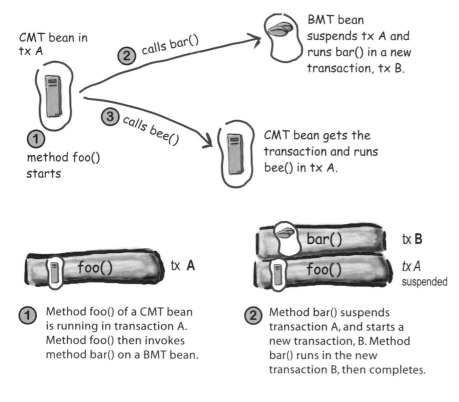

CMT bean in tx A

② calls bar()

BMT bean suspends tx A and runs bar() in a new transaction, tx B.

① method foo() starts

③ calls bee()

CMT bean gets the transaction and runs bee() in tx A.

foo()   tx **A**

bar()   tx **B**

foo()   *tx A* suspended

bee()   tx **A**

foo()   tx **A**

① Method foo() of a CMT bean is running in transaction A. Method foo() then invokes method bar() on a BMT bean.

② Method bar() suspends transaction A, and starts a new transaction, B. Method bar() runs in the new transaction B, then completes.

③ When method bar() completes, foo() resumes and picks up transaction A again. It then calls method bee() on bean three (a CMT bean). Method bee() runs in foo()'s existing transaction (A).

The UserTransaction interface

(javax.transaction.UserTransaction)

 Sharpen your pencil

The UserTransaction interface has six methods for
the things a BMT bean might want to do. Try to figure
out the method names, based on the description of
what you want to do. (The answers are at the bottom,
upside down, so don't look down there.)

(1) Begin a transaction

```
ut._____
```

(2) End a transaction

```
ut._____
// or
ut._____
```

(3) Mark a transaction for **rollback**

```
ut._____
```

(4) Find out the **status** of the transaction

```
ut._____
```

(5) Set the transaction **timeout**

```
ut._____
```

 **UserTransaction is
for BMT beans only!
A CMT bean is never
supposed to get (or try
to use) a reference to a
UserTransaction.**

**UserTransaction is NOT
for entity beans. Since
entity beans MUST
be CMT, if you see
UserTransaction code in
an entity bean, you know
the code's not legal.**

 Relax *There's nothing about transaction
timeout on the exam.*

*All transactions have some default timeout value,
but you can change that with:
setTransactionTimeout(anIntValue). As a bean developer,
you'll probably never use anything but the default timeout
value, so we don't test for it on the exam.*

1. begin(), 2. commit() or rollback(), 3. setRollbackOnly(),
4. getStatus(), 5. setTransactionTimeout()

setRollbackOnly()
The sound of a transaction's death

When a bean calls setRollbackOnly() it means that transaction is going down. Once you invoke setRollbackOnly(), *the transaction is doomed to never, ever commit.*

So, what does it mean to sentence a transaction to death? It means the transaction definitely won't commit. *Duh.* But it also means that any participant in the transaction (i.e. any bean) can check to see if the transaction is already marked for death.

Remember, a transaction started by a BMT bean might propagate to method calls that the BMT bean makes on CMT beans. A CMT bean in a BMT-started transaction might want to sentence the transaction to death, or at least *find out* whether it's already doomed.

In a CMT bean, setRollbackOnly() is how you tell the container that it *must not commit the transaction.* If you can figure out in your business logic that a transaction is going to end badly, call setRollbackOnly(). The container won't *end* the transaction at that point, but when it *does* end at its natural time, it definitely won't commit.

So, when *does* a transaction end? Assuming no System Exceptions are thrown, a transaction ends when the CMT method that started the transaction completes, or for a BMT bean, when the bean's code calls commit() or rollback().

> It's tragic.
>
> When you call the setRollbackOnly() method, you set a flag that can tell other beans that the transaction will end only one way... horribly.
>
> If you know, in your code, that things aren't going to work, call this method.
>
> If the transaction is going to die, it's probably for the best. It was meant to be. It's going to a better place.

Bean A
starts tx Z

a method in
Bean B is called,
and runs in tx Z

a method in
Bean C is called,
and runs in tx Z

Any bean in this transaction can call setRollbackOnly() to make sure transaction Z never commits.

If Bean B calls setRollbackOnly(), it won't matter what Bean C does -- the transactional code in Bean C will never be committed. Wouldn't it be nice if Bean C could find that out BEFORE Bean C does a bunch of work? We'll see that in a minute.

I'm still missing something here... if I'm using BMT, why would I call setRollbackOnly(), when I can just call rollback() and end it right there?

You might know HOW a BMT transaction should end *before* it's time to actually end it.

In your BMT code, you might have a single place at the end of the transactional code where you say either ut.commit() or ut.rollback(). That single place might be a simple *if* test:

```
if (thingsLookGood) {
    ut.commit();
 else {
    ut.rollback();
}
```

A typical example: at the end of the transaction, commit or rollback based on some conditions.

But if somewhere *earlier* in your code you can tell that the transaction is doomed, you should call setRollbackOnly():

```
if (thingsLookBad) {
    ut.setRollbackOnly();
}
```

This gives other transaction participants a signal (if they care to check) that the transaction is already doomed.

Even if *your* BMT code doesn't call setRollbackOnly(), some *other* code in the transaction could have, so you might want to find that out. (In just a few more pages from now, we'll learn how a bean can check whether anyone has marked a transaction for rollback.)

setRollbackOnly() lives in TWO interfaces

UserTransaction

begin()
commit()
getStatus()
rollback()
setRollbackOnly()
setTransactionTimeout()

Everything in UserTransaction is for BMT beans ONLY!

EJBContext

getCallerPrincipal()
getEJBHome()
getEJBLocalHome()
getRollbackOnly()
getUserTransaction()
isCallerInRole()
setRollbackOnly()

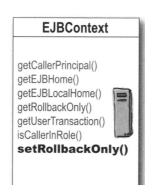

setRollbackOnly() in EJBContext is for CMT beans ONLY!

The methods in the UserTransaction interface are for BMT beans only; CMT beans can't use *anything* in UserTransaction.

The EJBContext interface, on the other hand, is for both BMT and CMT beans, *except for the two transaction methods.*

The setRollbackOnly() and getRollbackOnly() methods in EJBContext are off-limits to BMT beans.

Bottom line: BMT beans call setRollbackOnly() on a UserTransaction; CMT beans call setRollbackOnly() on an EJBContext.

A bean that calls setRollbackOnly() MUST be in a transaction!

You can call setRollbackOnly() from a BMT bean ONLY if you're inside a transaction. In other words, only within code that's between a ut.begin() and a ut.commit() or ut.rollback(). For a CMT bean, the method that calls setRollbackOnly() must have an appropriate transaction attribute (we'll get into that a few pages from now).

Be SURE you know the rules for BOTH of the setRollbackOnly() methods!

Be ready for the exam to test you on the use of setRollbackOnly() for both BMT and CMT beans.

EJBContext.setRollbackOnly()

UserTransaction.setRollbackOnly()

Remember, no single bean can ever use BOTH of these!

CMT beans can use **only** the **EJBContext**.setRollbackOnly()

BMT beans can use **only** the **UserTransaction**.setRollbackOnly()

Expect to see code examples where you'll need to figure out if the bean is BMT or CMT by looking at the code. And it won't be as obvious as a call to getUserTransaction(). If you see a call to EJBContext.setRollbackOnly(), for example, you know that this **must** be a CMT bean. So if that same bean later starts a UserTransaction, you know the code is illegal.

getRollbackOnly()
Because life's too short for a bean to waste time

Once a bean has called setRollbackOnly(), the transaction is sentenced to death. It will never commit. But the transaction might still have a long way to go, with plenty of other methods in other beans, and with lots of heavy code.

Imagine you're a bean. How would *you* feel if the transaction were already doomed before your methods were called, *but nobody told you?*

CMT beans call getRollbackOnly() to find out if the transaction they're in is already doomed. If the transaction is never going to commit, why should the bean waste time with lots of code?

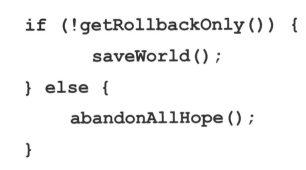

If you're a CMT bean, you can call getRollbackOnly() to find out if your transaction has already been sentenced to death. If it has, why bother doing any work?

```
if (!getRollbackOnly()) {
        saveWorld();
} else {
    abandonAllHope();
}
```

getRollbackOnly() is NOT for BMT beans! Only CMT beans can call getRollbackOnly()

BMT beans use getStatus() instead of getRollbackOnly()

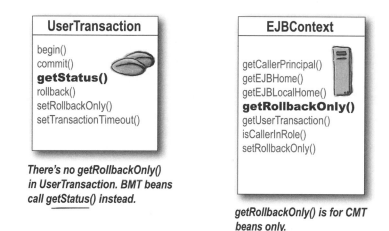

UserTransaction
begin()
commit()
getStatus()
rollback()
setRollbackOnly()
setTransactionTimeout()

There's no getRollbackOnly() in UserTransaction. BMT beans call getStatus() instead.

EJBContext
getCallerPrincipal()
getEJBHome()
getEJBLocalHome()
getRollbackOnly()
getUserTransaction()
isCallerInRole()
setRollbackOnly()

getRollbackOnly() is for CMT beans only.

The getRollbackOnly() method returns a boolean—true if the method has been marked for rollback, false if nobody's asked for a rollback. That's all a CMT bean can (and needs) to know about the transaction's status.

BMT beans, on the other hand, are more involved in controlling the transaction, and they might want to know a lot more. The getStatus() method in UserTransaction can tell you anything you'd ever want to know, and so much more, about how the transaction is doing.

> **Relax** **You don't need to memorize the status constants.**
>
> The getStatus() method returns an int representing a constant for things like: STATUS_ACTIVE, STATUS_COMMITTED, STATUS_COMMITTING, STATUS_THINKING_ABOUT_COMMITTING (just kidding on this one), STATUS_MARKED_ROLLBACK, STATUS_ROLLING_BACK, and our personal and most useful favorite, STATUS_UNKNOWN.
>
> These constants are defined in the javax.transaction.Status interface (which has no methods, just a pile of these status constants), and you might find them helpful if you're writing BMT code. But they're not on the exam. You DO need to know that the getStatus() method is in UserTransaction, and that it's the only way a BMT bean can find out if somebody called setRollbackOnly(), but that's it.

BMT can be a really BAD idea.
BMT hurts bean reuse

Off the path

Can you figure out why?

Think about what you learned on the last few pages, especially about transaction propagation (the whole one-way thing).

If you write a BMT bean, nobody else can ever include your bean in their transaction!

Your BMT bean puts up a big fat wall so calling transactions can't pass. Remember, a BMT bean will run only in the transactions the bean itself creates and starts. You defeat the whole point of a component model if you lock down the transaction demarcation inside the bean. Remember, the cool thing about a component model is that components can be mixed and combined in new ways to make new applications that the Bean Provider hadn't ever thought about. The purpose of the deployment descriptor is to give the application assembler a way to configure transactions specific to a particular application, *without touching the bean code!*

If it's so bad to use BMT, why is it there?

Because it lets you do a few things you simply cannot do with CMT. But most of the time, you won't need these things.

With BMT, you can reduce the scope of a transaction.

Using CMT, you cannot mark a transaction at anything smaller than a single method. You put in the deployment descriptor which transaction attribute (we're getting there) goes with which method. You can't specify a part of a method. But with BMT, you can start the transaction and end it at a smaller scope. This can improve performance because the longer a transaction lasts, the more likely you are to hurt your concurrency. But the tradeoff—hurting your reuse—is almost never worth it, and there are usually *much* better ways of increasing the performance...

With BMT, you can leave a stateful session bean transaction open across multiple invocations from the client.

With BMT, you can open a transaction (call ut.begin()) in one method, and end the method without ending the transaction. (A big no-no for message-driven or stateless session beans.) But this is almost always a really bad design idea, so it's probably never going to be a good reason for BMT.

With BMT, you separate transaction commit status from message acknowledgment. This might be a good reason for BMT.

We covered this in more detail in the MDB chapter, but the short version is: with CMT, message acknowledgment is sent only when (and if) the transaction commits. In some designs, you can end up with poison messages.

I manage your transactions by looking at what you put in the deployment descriptor for each method. If your method needs a transaction, I'll start one or add you to the caller's, depending on the attributes. I can even suspend a transaction if you need to run without one.

Container-managed transactions

Now that we've looked at the do-it-yourself way to demarcate transactions, you'll see how easy it is with CMT. So easy that you don't write anything transactional in your code except maybe an occasional call to EJBContext.setRollbackOnly() or EJBContext.getRollbackOnly().

With CMT, transactions are started and completed (with either a commit or rollback) by the container, based solely on the deployment descriptor. You (OK, technically the Application Assembler) mark some attributes in the deployment descriptor and that's it.

Almost.

Unless you understand exactly what the six transaction attributes are, and the implications of how different attributes interact at runtime, you won't have a clue about whether your bean is even going to be in a transaction. Or, how big the transaction will be. Or, whether you've created a dangerous situation that could blowup at runtime.

Fortunately, there are only six. And the rules for how the container behaves with each of those attributes is very clear and simple.

How attributes work

(1) Mark a method with one of six transaction attributes:

- Required
- RequiresNew
- Mandatory
- Supports
- NotSupported
- Never

FooBean	
setFoo()	*Required*
getFoo()	*Supports*
doBar()	*Required*
doBigThing()	*RequiresNew*

(2) When the method is called, the container uses the attribute to do one of five things:

- Run the method in the *caller's transaction.*

OR

- *Suspend* the caller's transaction and start a *new* transaction.

OR

- *Suspend* the caller's transaction and run the method *without* a transaction.

OR

- Throw an *exception* because the caller does *not* have a transaction.

OR

- Throw an *exception* because the caller *does* have a transaction.

```
void go() {
    aFooBean.setFoo();
}
```

Let's see... the go() method is already in a transaction when it calls setFoo(), and setFoo() has a Required tx attribute, so I will run setFoo() in the same transaction as go()

> As an Application Assembler, I have to know my attributes so that I can get the behavior I desire from my beans.

Know your attributes

How an attribute affects behavior depends on one thing:

Is the calling method in a transaction?

```
public void foo() {
    aBean.bar();
}
```

foo() is in a transaction (tx A) when it calls bar() on another bean. The bar() method is marked as Required.

① Method **foo()** is in a transaction (tx A).

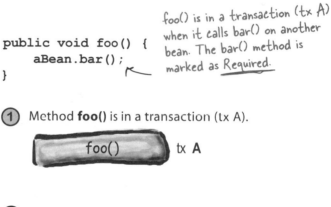

② Method **bar()** is marked with the *Required* transaction attribute.

```
<method>
    <ejb-name>MyBean</ejb-name>
    <method-name>bar</method-name>
</method>
<trans-attribute>Required</trans-attribute>
```

The bar() method runs in the same transaction as foo() because bar() is marked Required and foo() has a transaction. If foo() had NOT been in a transaction, the container would have started a new transaction for bar() to run in.

③ The **bar()** method runs in the caller's transaction (tx A).

Transaction attributes that require a transaction

Attribute for bar()	foo() transaction status	result

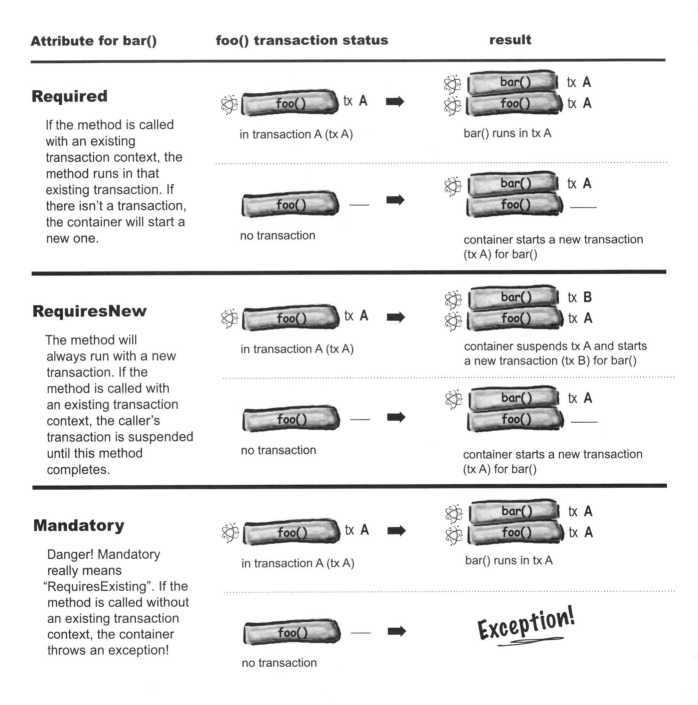

Required

If the method is called with an existing transaction context, the method runs in that existing transaction. If there isn't a transaction, the container will start a new one.

in transaction A (tx A)

bar() runs in tx A

no transaction

container starts a new transaction (tx A) for bar()

RequiresNew

The method will always run with a new transaction. If the method is called with an existing transaction context, the caller's transaction is suspended until this method completes.

in transaction A (tx A)

container suspends tx A and starts a new transaction (tx B) for bar()

no transaction

container starts a new transaction (tx A) for bar()

Mandatory

Danger! Mandatory really means "RequiresExisting". If the method is called without an existing transaction context, the container throws an exception!

in transaction A (tx A)

bar() runs in tx A

no transaction

Exception!

Transaction attributes that do not require a transaction

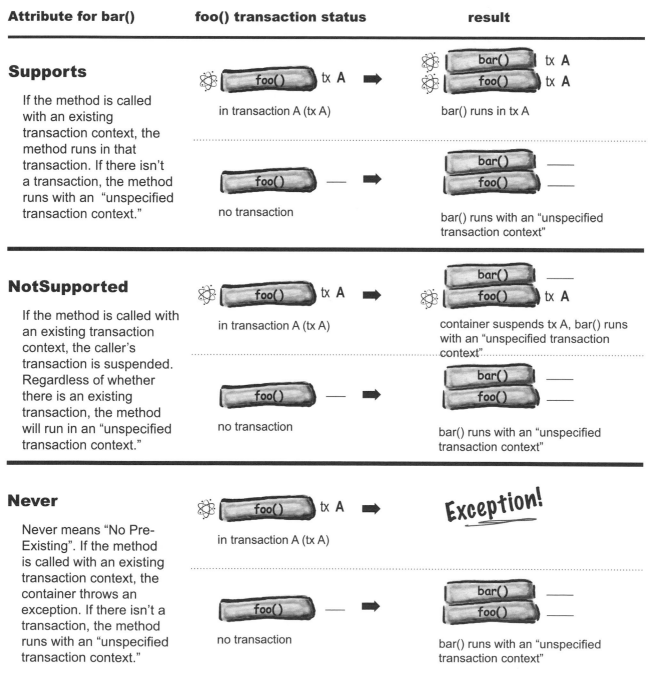

Attribute for bar()	foo() transaction status	result

Supports

If the method is called with an existing transaction context, the method runs in that transaction. If there isn't a transaction, the method runs with an "unspecified transaction context."

in transaction A (tx A)

bar() runs in tx A

no transaction

bar() runs with an "unspecified transaction context"

NotSupported

If the method is called with an existing transaction context, the caller's transaction is suspended. Regardless of whether there is an existing transaction, the method will run in an "unspecified transaction context."

in transaction A (tx A)

container suspends tx A, bar() runs with an "unspecified transaction context"

no transaction

bar() runs with an "unspecified transaction context"

Never

Never means "No Pre-Existing". If the method is called with an existing transaction context, the container throws an exception. If there isn't a transaction, the method runs with an "unspecified transaction context."

in transaction A (tx A)

Exception!

no transaction

bar() runs with an "unspecified transaction context"

Sharpen your pencil

Know your attributes

The exam expects you to figure out which combination of attributes can (or will) lead to a particular outcome. You might be asked to look at a sequence of methods, where the methods show which transaction they're running in, and you have to figure out which combination of transaction attributes could make that scenario possible. They might be formatted something like this...

(The answers are at the bottom of the next page.)

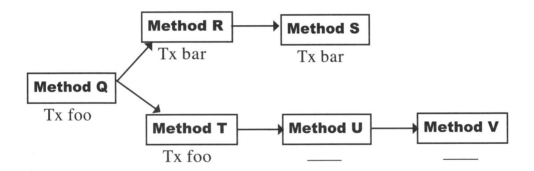

QUESTION: Which two combinations of attributes would make this possible?

1) R-Supports, S-Required, T-Mandatory, U-NotSupported, V-Never

2) R-RequiresNew, S-Required, T-Required, U-Never, V-NotSupported

3) R-RequiresNew, S-Supports, T-Supports, U-NotSupported, V-Supports

4) R-Requires, S-Mandatory, T-Mandatory, U-Supports, V-Never

5) R-RequiresNew, S-Required, T-Required, U-NotSupported, V-NotSupported

Sharpen your pencil

For the exam (and bean developer life in general) you have to know some REALLY important rules about transactions, and it will be much easier for you if you take the time now to figure some of this out for yourself. Understanding is much better than memorizing, and it's not like you don't have enough to memorize as it is. You'll find all of these questions answered over the next few pages, but you should *really* try to do this first.

(1) **Of the six transaction attributes, which one (or ones) must NOT be used by a bean that calls getRollbackOnly() or setRollbackOnly()?**

---

(2) **Which transaction attribute (or attributes) must NOT be used by a message-driven bean?**

(Hint: remember, a message-driven bean doesn't have a "client"; the container invokes the onMessage() method.)

---

(3) **Under what circumstances do you think the container should automatically roll back a transaction?**

If the bean gets a runtime exception?

If the bean throws an application exception? (e.g. InsufficientFundsException?)

---

(4) **Of the six transaction attributes, three of them can be dangerous, with one in particular being EXTREMELY risky. Keeping in mind that the Bean Provider is NOT the one who specifies the attributes for the bean's methods, which of the six is potentially the most dangerous?**

answer to the Attributes sharpen: three and five

These are the methods you <u>MUST</u> mark with an attribute (for a CMT bean)

Session beans

- **Business methods in the component interface**

- *NONE of the other methods the client sees in the component interface (from EJBObject or EJBLocalObject)*

- *NONE of the methods in the home interface, including those written by the Bean Provider as well as those from EJBHome or EJBLocalHome*

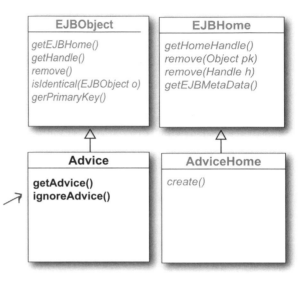

these are the only methods you have to mark in the deployment descriptor

---

Entity beans

- **Business methods in the component interface**

- *NONE of the other methods the client sees in the component interface (from EJBObject or EJBLocalObject) except* **remove()**

- ALL of the home interface *methods written by the Bean Provider, as well as the* **remove()** *methods from EJBHome or EJBLocalHome.*

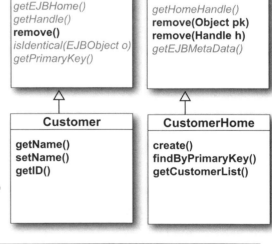

You have to mark more methods with an attribute when you use entity beans than you do with session beans..Remember, create() and remove() are a Big Deal to an entity (insert and delete!).

Message-driven beans

- **onMessage()**

A message-driven bean doesn't have any client interfaces.

onMessage()

Hmmmm.... what happens if I use "Supports"? How will I really know if there's a transaction? And what about NotSupported? Never? What about ejbCreate() and ejbRemove() for session beans? What happens if I quit my job and become a surfing instructor in Kauai?

"Unspecified Transaction Context"

The term "an unspecified transaction context" is the EJB spec's way of saying, "You have no clue. I (the container) can do whatever I want and you'll just have to deal!"

You must know, for the exam, the methods (and circumstances) that might be running in an "unspecified transaction context."

- Any CMT method marked **NotSupported**, **Never**, or **Supports**.
  NotSupported and Never are supposed to mean "no transaction", but in reality, the container can do whatever it wants. And with Supports, you never know *anyway* (which is why we think it's a really dumb attribute that nobody should ever use).

- **CMT session bean** methods **ejbCreate()** (any of them), **ejbRemove()**, **ejbPassivate()**, **ejbActivate().**
  The create and remove methods of a session bean are not considered part of a client's transaction (unlike the way it works with entity beans). And remember, activate and passivate will *never* be called if the session bean is in a transaction.

- **CMT message-driven bean** methods **ejbCreate()** and **ejbRemove().**
  Remember, for a message-driven bean, ejbCreate() and ejbRemove() are called by the container when it wants to add or remove beans from the pool. There's no calling client transaction, because a message-driven bean doesn't have a real client!

So, is there a transaction or not? Why is it "unspecified"? Why isn't it just "definitely *no* transaction"?

The spec lets the Container do whatever it wants. The spec suggests several options, including everything from executing without any transaction at all to merging multiple calls to a resource manager together into one transaction.

The point is... YOU DON'T KNOW!

The key point here is that you must NOT rely on any exact behavior from the container because you just don't know. As a bean developer, you'll probably never lose a moment's sleep over this. But you need to know what is and isn't guaranteed.

We think being a snowboard instructor is better than teaching surfing. Just as fun, but without all that neoprene. Or sharks.

Burn these in

These are all things you might be tested on. But remember, you won't be asked a simple true or false question, like, "The getRollbackOnly() method can be called from a method with a transaction attribute of NotSupported." (In which case the answer would be *false*, of course). No, you're likely to see something much more clever, like bean code plus the bean's deployment descriptor, and you have to decide if it all works together.

getRollbackOnly() MUST be called from a bean in a transaction!

You already know that getRollbackOnly() can be called only by CMT beans, and that the method exists only in EJBContext and NOT in UserTransaction. (Remember? BMT beans can call getStatus() on UserTransaction, but they can't call getRollbackOnly().)

But for getRollbackOnly() to work, the method must be in a transaction, which means you MUST use only:

* ***Requires***
* ***RequiresNew***
* ***Mandatory***

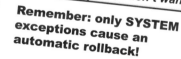

Message-driven beans can use only TWO attributes: *Requires* and *NotSupported.*

Think about it. A message-driven bean doesn't have a calling client! The container calls the on-Message() method, so it doesn't make any sense to use the other ones. RequiresNew? That's useless because there will never be a pre-existing transaction. Mandatory? That would blow up every time (by "blow up" we mean throw an exception) because Mandatory means "Requires Pre-Existing". Never? Well, that is always the case anyway, and Supports is silly too. You can say only two things for onMessage():
YES, I want to start a transaction (Required)
or
NO, I don't want a transaction (NotSupported)

Remember: only SYSTEM exceptions cause an automatic rollback!

We'll cover this in detail in the Exceptions chapter, but for now be aware that application exceptions do NOT automatically cause a rollback. An application exception is any checked exception that is declared on a bean interface, unless it's a RemoteException (RemoteException is in a special category).

Let's say you see some code on the exam that shows the bean throwing an application exception (say, a FinderException). Do NOT say that the transaction will be rolled back! If YOU (Bean Provider) decide in your logic that the situation is too bleak to allow the transaction to continue, then YOU must call setRollbackOnly(). The container does an automatic rollback ONLY for system exceptions (like EJBException or any other runtime exception).

Overheard at
THE TIKIBEAN LOUNGE

(We caught a BMT bean and a CMT bean arguing at the bar.)

BMT: You suck.

CMT: Oh, that's so *clever.* What a way with words. And what do you mean by that? And is it just me personally, or all CMT beans in general?

BMT: All of you. Weenies. You're not bean enough to handle your own transactions, so you leave it all up to the container. You're probably afraid of the garbage collector, too.

CMT: Weenie? Don't tell me you actually *believe* that *you're* managing your own transactions? The container is *always* in charge my friend. Same for you as it is for me.

BMT: That's not true! *I* start the transaction and *I* decide if—and when—to commit or rollback. Where's the container in all that? I mean, sure, the container has to *give* me the transaction, but after that, I'm in charge.

CMT: *No*, you're *not.*

BMT: *Yes*, I *am.*

CMT: All you're doing is demarcating the boundaries of the transaction. You get to say where it *starts* and *stops.* End of story.

BMT: Uh, you're forgetting that *I* have the power to rollback.

CMT: So do I.

BMT: *No*, you *don't.*

CMT: *Yes*, I *do.* What do you think setRollbackOnly() is for?

BMT: You can't call that. That's in the UserTransaction interface and that's off-limits to you CMT peasants.

CMT: I can't believe they let you be a bean. You *know* that EJB-Context has a setRollbackOnly() method just for CMT beans.

BMT: Oh. I forgot about that. But so what? You still aren't in control of your transaction boundaries.

CMT: But what does that matter? My methods are all marked with how I want transactions to be applied, so how is that different from controlling the boundaries of a transaction?

BMT: HELLO! Your transactions must be at *least* as long as a whole method! I can scope my transactions to something more granular than the whole darn method.

CMT: But why would you ever *want* to?

BMT: You really have to ask that. OK, let me break it down so that even *you* can understand: transactions hurt concurrency. That means they hurt performance and scalability. And that means—

CMT: [interrupting] Yeah, yeah I know all that. But without transactions, you can't even run your business.

BMT: Duh. I'm not talking about *not* using transactions. I'm talking about keeping them *as short as possible.* It's just like the difference between synchronizing an entire method versus making a synchronized block.

CMT: I'm not sure that really matters, but OK. No, wait, if your methods are that big, you probably have a bad OO design anyway. So if that's the only benefit to BMT...

BMT: It's not. I can do things you can't *ever* do.

CMT: For example?

BMT: Like open a transaction in one stateful bean method and close the transaction in some other method of that bean.

CMT: Oh, yeah, like *that's* not gonna kill your performance? Don't you know how much that hurts your scalability? That prevents your stateful beans from being passivated! You risk just leaving the transaction open, like, forever. And how are you gonna even guarantee that the method that starts the transaction will be called *before* the method that ends it? Geez, you could call commit() or rollback() before you ever said begin()!

BMT: Yeah but if someone *needs* to do that, BMT is the only way to do it.

CMT: Except almost nobody ever needs to do that! Or should. OK, yes, I'll agree that if in the unbelievably and incredibly unlikely event that a developer needs to do that, you're the only way.

But there's no other reason I can see to use BMT, especially since BMT defeats the whole reusable component thing. How arrogant can you be? You can *never* run in anybody else's transactions! Only your own. Talk about "doesn't play well with others..."

BMT: Well, OK, maybe I really am just for *special* occasions, but next time we'll have to talk about preventing poison message-driven bean messages. I'm the *only* one who can do *that.*

CMT: Yeah, well, we'll just have to see about that when we get to the MDB chapter. I'm outta here.

Marking transactions in the DD

All beans must say whether they're using bean- or container-managed transactions. For BMT beans, that's it for the DD.

But for CMT beans that's just the beginning.

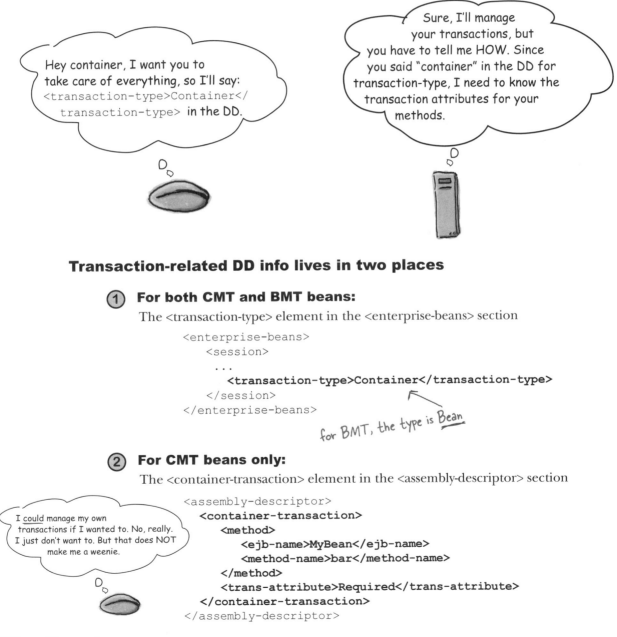

Hey container, I want you to take care of everything, so I'll say: `<transaction-type>Container</transaction-type>` in the DD.

Sure, I'll manage your transactions, but you have to tell me HOW. Since you said "container" in the DD for transaction-type, I need to know the transaction attributes for your methods.

Transaction-related DD info lives in two places

(1) For both CMT and BMT beans:

The <transaction-type> element in the <enterprise-beans> section

```
<enterprise-beans>
   <session>
   . . .
      <transaction-type>Container</transaction-type>
   </session>
</enterprise-beans>
```

for BMT, the type is Bean

(2) For CMT beans only:

The <container-transaction> element in the <assembly-descriptor> section

I *could* manage my own transactions if I wanted to. No, really. I just don't want to. But that does NOT make me a weenie.

```
<assembly-descriptor>
   <container-transaction>
      <method>
         <ejb-name>MyBean</ejb-name>
         <method-name>bar</method-name>
      </method>
      <trans-attribute>Required</trans-attribute>
   </container-transaction>
</assembly-descriptor>
```

DD example for CMT

In the <enterprise-beans> element

```
<enterprise-beans>

  <session>
    <display-name>AdviceBean</display-name>
    <ejb-name>AdviceBean</ejb-name>
    <home>headfirst.AdviceHome</home>
    <remote>headfirst.Advice</remote>
    <ejb-class>headfirst.AdviceBean</ejb-class>
    <session-type>Stateless</session-type>
    <transaction-type>Container</transaction-type>
    <security-identity>
      <use-caller-identity></use-caller-identity>
    </security-identity>
  </session>

</enterprise-beans>
```

← *for BMT you'd say (surprise!) "Bean" instead of "Container"*

In the <assembly-descriptor> element

```
<assembly-descriptor>
  <container-transaction>
    <method>
        <ejb-name>MyOtherBean</ejb-name>
        <method-name>foo</method-name>
    </method>
    <trans-attribute>RequiresNew</trans-attribute>
  </container-transaction>
</assembly-descriptor>
```

there are a few variations of the <method> element (we'll look at them on the next page)

You specify attributes by listing a specific attribute (RequiresNew, Supports, etc.) and putting in all of the methods that are supposed to have that attribute. You might *think* you're supposed to first specify a method and then give the attribute for that method (because that's how it looks in this example), but that's not how it works. It'll all make sense on the next page...

More DD examples for CMT

Option 1: Wildcard

Use a wildcard to say that all methods in the specified bean have the attribute in the <trans-attribute> tag.

```
<container-transaction>
    <method>
        <ejb-name>BigBean</ejb-name>
        <method-name> * </method-name>
    </method>
    <trans-attribute>RequiresNew</trans-attribute>
</container-transaction>
```

Specify a method by giving the bean name and the method name. But here, we use a wildcard (*) which means "ALL methods of BigBean have RequiresNew attribute."

Option 2: Individually-named methods

Specify each method of each CMT bean in the ejb-jar (unless you use the wildcard to indicate all methods of the specified bean class have the specified attribute).

```
<container-transaction>
    <method>
        <ejb-name>BigBean</ejb-name>
        <method-name>foo</method-name>
    </method>
    <method>
        <ejb-name>BigBean</ejb-name>
        <method-name>go</method-name>
    </method>
    <method>
        <ejb-name>BigBean</ejb-name>
        <method-name>bar</method-name>
    </method>
    <trans-attribute>RequiresNew</trans-attribute>
</container-transaction>
<container-transaction>
    <method>
        <ejb-name>BigBean</ejb-name>
        <method-name>doStuff</method-name>
    </method>
    <trans-attribute>Required</trans-attribute>
</container-transaction>
```

Here we have three different methods, in one bean, that all have the RequiresNew attribute.

This is a different transaction attribute -- Requires -- so here we list the method that uses Requires. Notice that we're naming the same bean we used in the previous <container-transaction> element.

Wait a minute-- are you telling me I can't have overloaded methods? I don't see any argument lists in there. If all I get to put in is the method name, I'm screwed.

Don't worry.

Chances are, your design will treat all versions of an overloaded method in the same way (for transactions). In the examples we've seen so far, a method name represents *all* overloaded versions of that method.

But just in case you do need to distinguish between different overloaded methods, there is a way to specify the arguments. The optional **<method-params>** tag looks like this:

```
<container-transaction>
    <method>
        <ejb-name>ShoppingBean</ejb-name>
        <method-name>addItem</method-name>
        <method-params>
          <method-param>java.lang.String</method-param>
          <method-param>int</method-param>
        </method-params>
    </method>
    <trans-attribute>RequiresNew</trans-attribute>
</container-transaction>
<container-transaction>
    <method>
        <ejb-name>ShoppingBean</ejb-name>
        <method-name>addItem</method-name>
        <method-params>
          <method-param>int</method-param>
        </method-params>
    </method>
    <trans-attribute>Requires</trans-attribute>
</container-transaction>
```

Here we have an overloaded method, addItem, where one version takes a String and an int, and the other takes only an int. The first one uses RequiresNew and the second version uses Required. So we have to specify WHICH overloaded version we're talking about in each section. The optional <method-params> and <method-param> tags give you a way to do that.

Yes you DO need to know the tags for transactions.

You're not expected to memorize every tag in the whole DD, but you DO need to know how to specify transaction attributes, including the way you can use the wildcard (*) to represent all the methods of a bean, and that there IS a way to give overloaded methods different transaction attributes.

Be sure you know that transaction attributes are NOT specified in the <enterprise-beans> part of the DD, but rather in the <assembly-descriptor> section. Think about why that makes sense... a Bean Provider has to say (in the DD) whether the bean is using BMT or CMT, but that's it. The app assembler will come along later and decide exactly how transactions should be handled for this particular deployment of the bean.

Transaction attributes are part of application assembly, NOT bean development.

That means the attributes are specified in the <u>assembly</u> part of the DD rather than in the <u>bean</u> part.

The only thing you say about transactions in the bean part is whether the bean is using Container- or Bean-managed transactions.

Q: **Can I combine the wildcard with specific method names? I mean, what happens if I want to have all the bean's methods, except one use RequiresNew, and just one method to use NotSupported?**

A: No problem. Using the wildcard is like saying, "All methods *not otherwise specified in the DD* should use this attribute." So go ahead and use the wildcard for the RequiresNew part of the DD, and when you get to the NotSupported attribute, give the method name.

```
<container-transaction>
   <method>
      <ejb-name>BigBean</ejb-name>
      <method-name> * </method-name>
   </method>
   <trans-attribute>RequiresNew</trans-attribute>
</container-transaction>
<container-transaction>
   <method>
      <ejb-name>BigBean</ejb-name>
      <method-name>useOldDatabase</method-name>
   </method>
   <trans-attribute>NotSupported</trans-attribute>
</container-transaction>
```

Sharpen your pencil

Which methods need transaction attributes?

This one is a combination of how much you remember, and how much you can think through what makes sense. Looking at the interfaces below, one for a session bean and one for an entity bean, figure out which methods MUST have transaction attributes when the bean is using CMT. Put a checkmark by it, circle it, run your highlighter through it. But don't try to simply remember what you've seen in this chapter... really think about it.

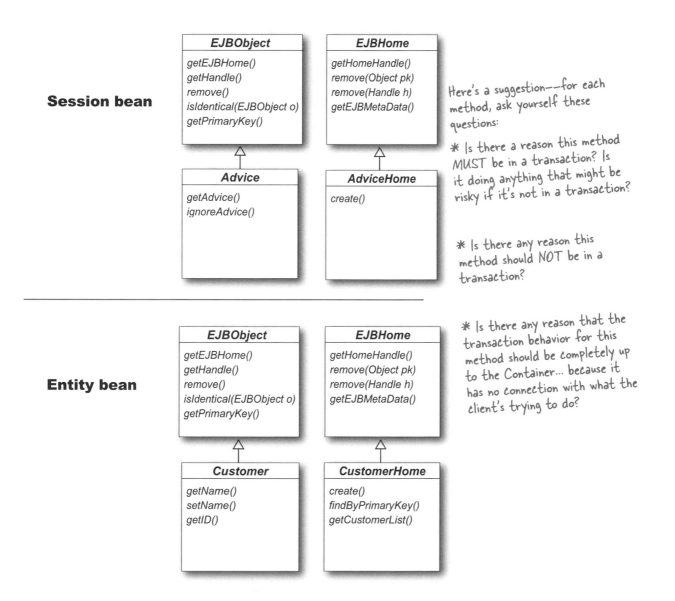

Session bean

EJBObject
getEJBHome()
getHandle()
remove()
isIdentical(EJBObject o)
getPrimaryKey()

EJBHome
getHomeHandle()
remove(Object pk)
remove(Handle h)
getEJBMetaData()

Advice
getAdvice()
ignoreAdvice()

AdviceHome
create()

Here's a suggestion—for each method, ask yourself these questions:

* Is there a reason this method MUST be in a transaction? Is it doing anything that might be risky if it's not in a transaction?

* Is there any reason this method should NOT be in a transaction?

* Is there any reason that the transaction behavior for this method should be completely up to the Container... because it has no connection with what the client's trying to do?

Entity bean

EJBObject
getEJBHome()
getHandle()
remove()
isIdentical(EJBObject o)
getPrimaryKey()

EJBHome
getHomeHandle()
remove(Object pk)
remove(Handle h)
getEJBMetaData()

Customer
getName()
setName()
getID()

CustomerHome
create()
findByPrimaryKey()
getCustomerList()

Summary of Bean-managed demarcation

Bean-managed (BMT)

- Used by stateless and stateful session beans.

- Used by message-driven beans.

- Must *NOT* be used by entity beans.

- Can be used to reduce the scope of a transaction, which can help performance.

- Can be used to keep a transaction open across multiple invocations to a stateful method bean.

- Can be used by a message-driven bean to acknowledge a method even though the transaction ends in a rollback.

- Message-driven beans must complete a transaction by the end of onMessage().

- Stateless session beans must complete a transaction by the end of the business method in which the transaction was started.

- The BMT bean must not start a transaction without first ending the previous transaction. (Remember, no nested transactions in EJB!)

- The BMT bean must *not* use the getRollbackOnly() and setRollbackOnly() methods of EJBContext.

- The BMT bean can call the setRollbackOnly() method on the UserTransaction.

- The bean gets a UserTransaction from the bean's EJBContext.

- Propagation of transactions in a BMT bean are one-way: a bean-started transaction can propagate *out to other beans*, but no transaction can ever be propagated *in* to a bean using BMT.

- The UserTransaction interface does NOT have a getRollbackOnly() method, but BMT beans can call getStatus() to find out if someone in the transaction has called setRollbackOnly().

- The getStatus() method returns an int representing a constant, one of which is STATUS_MARKED_ROLLBACK.

- Session beans using BMT must not implement SessionSynchronization.

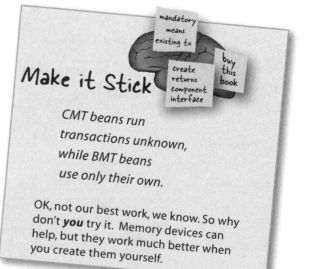

Make it Stick

mandatory means existing tx

create returns component interface

buy this book

CMT beans run transactions unknown, while BMT beans use only their own.

OK, not our best work, we know. So why don't **you** try it. Memory devices can help, but they work much better when you create them yourself.

Container-managed (CMT)

- Used by all bean types.

- Compulsory for entity beans.

- Transaction attributes are specified in the deployment descriptor.

- The six transaction attributes are: Required, RequiresNew, Supports, Mandatory, Never, Not Supported.

- Transactions can be propagated into and out of a CMT bean.

- The CMT bean must not attempt to use BMT, including getting a UserTransaction reference.

- The CMT bean must not use the setRollbackOnly method of UserTransaction. (Guess you could figure that out from the previous bullet point...)

- The CMT bean can use the getRollbackOnly and setRollbackOnly methods of EJBContext.

- CMT transactions cannot stay open across multiple method invocations from a stateful session client (BMT transactions can).

- CMT transactions are scoped at the method level. Either the whole method runs in a particular transaction context, or it doesn't.

- Calling setRollbackOnly on an EJBContext means the container must NOT commit the transaction.

- A CMT bean that calls setRollbackOnly() or getRollbackOnly() MUST have an attribute of Required, RequiresNew, or Mandatory.

- A CMT session bean must specify attributes for: all business methods in the component interface, none of the methods in the home, and none of the methods from EJBObject (or EJBLocalObject).

- All entity beans must specify attributes for: all business methods in the component interface, all the methods declared by the Bean Provider in the home interface, and any remove() method that the client can access (i.e. the ones defined in EJBHome, EJBLocalHome, or EJBObject and EJBLocalObject.

- You probably do not want to use Supports because you can't know for certain whether your bean is going to run in a transaction. If you've written calls to getRollbackOnly() or setRollbackOnly(), the bean can get an exception.

- A message-driven bean can use only two attributes: Required or NotSupported.

Entity beans have ejbLoad() to stay synchronized, even if the transaction rolls back.

①

setNewLimit()

Client calls methods on the bean, that change the bean's internal state.

bummer

② Bean has a problem and can't commit the transaction. But now that leaves the bean out of sync with the database. The bean's limit state is 420, but the limit in the database is 343, exactly where it was before the transaction began.

③ Container simply does a new load on the bean, to refresh it with the original data from the database.

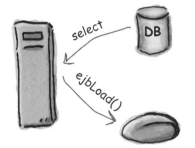

select

DB

ejbLoad()

Now everything is just like it was before. As if nothing ever happened...

④ Bean is happy, and now all of its persistent state matches the entity's data in the database.

Session Synchronization
because <u>session</u> beans don't have ejbLoad and ejbStore

The point is this:

An entity bean has ejbLoad() and ejbStore() to tell it when to synchronize with the database. If the transaction is about to commit, ejbStore() is called to give the bean one last chance to get it's persistent state in order, ready to be written to the database. And if the transaction does *not* commit, the bean just gets another ejbLoad() to return it to its original pre-transaction state, and everything is fine.

But a session bean doesn't have that luxury. No ejbLoad()or ejbStore() to tell it when it's time to synchronize itself with a database. But if your session bean implements SessionSynchronization, you *can* give a session bean three new container callbacks, that notify the bean of three more *special moments* in the bean's transactional life: when a transaction starts, when it's about to end, and when it's over.

SessionBean interface

(javax.ejb.SessionBean)

SessionSynchronization interface

(javax.ejb.SessionSynchronization)

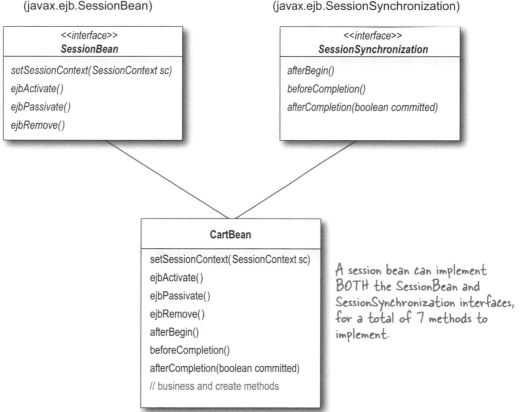

A session bean can implement BOTH the SessionBean and SessionSynchronization interfaces, for a total of 7 methods to implement.

SessionSynchronization "special moments"

	afterBegin()	beforeCompletion()	afterCompletion()
When it's called	At the beginning of a stateful bean's transaction, BEFORE the business method that's going to run in the transaction is called.	Just before the transaction ends, AFTER the business method completes.	After the transaction has ended either in a commit or rollback. The method passes a boolean argument to tell you whether the transaction committed.
Which entity bean method it's most like	ejbLoad()	ejbStore()	Nothing in the entity bean lifecycle corresponds to this. (Because there's no need.)
What to do when you're in it	Load in data from the database, knowing that the database resource is now part of the transaction, so you can cache the data in the bean for the rest of the transaction.	Last chance to update the database before the transaction commits, and the locks on the database are released.	Find out how the transaction went, and do whatever you have to do to stay synced with the database. For example, if you were caching newly-changed data in temporary variables, you can now assign the temporary values to your permanent state variables. Or if the transaction rolled back, you might have to reset some values with data from the database.
Bean things you *can* do while you're in it	Call methods on your SessionContext: get your home, get your EJB object, get caller security info, force the transaction to rollback, check the rollback status.\n\nAccess: your special JNDI context, resource managers, and other beans. *You're in a transaction, so it's all safe!*	*You're still in a transaction...* so you can do the same things you can do in afterBegin().	Call methods on your SessionContext: get your home, get your EJB object, get caller security info. You can't do any transaction-related things because *you're no longer in a transaction!* You can access ONLY your special JNDI context. It's not safe to access resource managers or other beans.

MORE special moments?

stateful CMT bean

Stateless session beans can't implement SessionSynchronization!

Only stateFUL session beans can implement SessionSynchronization, because stateless session bean's aren't allowed to maintain a transaction once a method has ended.

SessionSynchronization is for CMT beans ONLY!

*Does it make sense for a BMT bean to use SessionSynchronization? No. Remember, the point of SessionSynchronization is to give the bean three more "special moment" callback methods, so that the bean can find out **when** a transaction starts and ends, and also **how** it ends.*

But think about it... a BMT bean knows EXACTLY when a transaction starts and ends, because the bean is the one demarcating the transaction boundaries.

It's the bean that says when the transaction starts and ends!

Nobody can end that transaction except the bean that started it, so there aren't any surprises the bean needs to be "told" about.

there are no Dumb Questions

Q: If you want synchronization so badly, why not just use an entity bean?

A: Because your bean might represent a process, and not an entity. Not everything that involves database data is an entity! If your session bean represents a process, like a shopping session, but it still uses a database, you might want to wait until the transaction is complete before updating information in the database.

On the other hand, using a session bean as as a "poor-man's entity bean", *just for the sake of avoiding entity beans,* is silly. If you need an entity, make it an entity bean and get all the advantages the Container has to offer, like automatic synchronization with the persistent store. But if your bean is a process, but still needs to stay on top of how the transaction is going, you've got the option with SessionSynchronization (as long as it's a stateful, CMT bean.)

Pool Puzzle

Your *job* is to take code snippets from the pool and place them into the blank lines in the code. You will use each snippet **exactly once**.

Your *goal* is to make a method in a BMT bean that will create a total of five transactions. But wait, there's more! Exactly TWICE during this method, a transaction will be temporarily suspended. (We won't tell you whether it's the same transaction suspended twice, or two different transactions.) Any method with "cmt" in its name is from a CMT bean, and its transaction attribute is revealed in its name.

Assume that the variables "c" and "ut" have been properly initialized as instance variables.

Oh yeah, you must NOT throw any transaction related exceptions!

(Answers are on the next page, so don't look, unless you have absolutely no concern for the loss of self-esteem that you'll experience by going straight for the answers.)

```
void bmtMethodWithTransactions () {

    _____

    c.cmtRequiresNew();

    _____

    _____

    _____

    _____

    _____

    _____

    _____

    _____

    _____

    _____
}
```

Note: Each snippet from the pool can be used only once!

ut.begin();

c.cmtNever();

ut.commit();

c.cmtMandatory());

c.cmtSupports();

c.cmtMandatory);

c.cmtRequiresNew();

c.cmtRequired();

ut.begin();

ut.commit();

c.cmtNotSupported();

Pool Puzzle Solution

(Which of course you won't be looking at until you've completed the puzzle on the previous page.)

```
void bmtMethodWithTransactions () {
    ut.begin();                    tx 1
    c.cmtRequiresNew();            tx 2, suspend tx 1
    c.cmtMandatory();              tx 1 (tx 2 ended when the previous method completed)
    c.cmtRequiresNew();            tx 3, suspend tx 1 (that's the second and final transaction suspension.)
    ut.commit();                   now there's no tx
    c.cmtNotSupported();           still no tx
    c.cmtNever();                  still no tx
    c.cmtRequired();               tx 4
    ut.begin();                    tx 5 (tx 4 ended when the previous method completed)
    c.cmtSupports();               tx 5
    c.cmtMandatory();              tx 5
    ut.commit();                   Done
}
```

Mock Exam

1 Which are true about transactions in EJB 2.0? (Choose all that apply.)

- ❏ A. EJB containers must support both JTA and JTS.

- ❏ B. EJB 2.0 supports nested transactions.

- ❏ C. The **javax.transaction.UserTransaction** API allows you to set isolation levels.

- ❏ D. A bean instance can run multiple transactions in parallel.

- ❏ E. A message-driven bean instance must complete a transaction before the 'onMessage' method returns.

2 When using BMT demarcation, which of the following must commit a transaction before the method that initiated the transaction returns? (Choose all that apply.)

- ❏ A. message-driven beans

- ❏ B. stateful session beans

- ❏ C. stateless session beans

- ❏ D. none of the above

3 Which are true about container-managed transactions in EJB 2.0? (Choose all that apply.)

- ❏ A. Differentiating between overloaded methods is possible in the bean's deployment descriptor.

- ❏ B. Every business method in the bean class must have a transaction attribute.

- ❏ C. If an onMessage() method returns before committing a transaction the container will throw an exception.

- ❏ D. A message-driven bean with CMT demarcation must not invoke the EJBContext.getUserTransaction() method.

4 What's true when specifying transaction attributes in the deployment descriptor? (Choose all that apply.)

❏ A. For session beans, transaction attributes can be applied only to methods in the bean's component interface.

❏ B. The <method-name> tag can take a wild card.

❏ C. A single method can have multiple transaction attributes specified in the deployment descriptor.

❏ D. Transaction attributes must NOT be specified for methods in an entity bean's home interface.

5 Which transaction attributes can cause an in-progress transaction to be suspended? (Choose all that apply.)

❏ A. NotSupported

❏ B. Required

❏ C. Supports

❏ D. RequiresNew

❏ E. Mandatory

❏ F. Never

6 The use of which transaction attribute can cause a `javax.transaction.TransactionRequiredException` exception to be thrown?

❏ A. NotSupported

❏ B. Required

❏ C. Supports

❏ D. RequiresNew

❏ E. Mandatory

❏ F. Never

7 If a set of CMT bean methods has the following transaction attributes:

Method-1 = Supports

Method-2 = Required

Method-3 = NotSupported

Method-4 = RequiresNew

In the diagrams that follow, an arrow indicates that the method on the left calls the method on the right, and the "tx" number indicates a unique transaction. Which diagrams work with the transaction attributes listed above? (Choose all that apply.)

❏ A. M1 (Tx 1) –> M2 (No Tx) –> M3 (No Tx) –> M4 (Tx 2)

❏ B. M1 (No Tx) —> M2 (Tx 1)

       \\ \\——> M3 (Tx 1)

         \\——> M4 (Tx 2)

❏ C. M1 (No Tx) —> M2 (Tx 1) —> M3 (No Tx)

        \\——> M4 (Tx 2)

❏ D. M1 (Tx 1) –> M2 (Tx 1) –> M3 (Tx 1) –> M4 (Tx 2)

8 Which methods of a session bean, with container-managed transaction demarcation, run in an unspecified transaction context? (Choose all that apply.)

❏ A. `ejbActivate()`

❏ B. `ejbPassivate()`

❏ C. Business method marked `'NotSupported'`

❏ D. `ejbRemove()`

❏ E. Business method marked 'RequiresNew'

9 If a session bean's business method invokes `EJBContext.setRollbackOnly()`, which transaction attribute settings can cause the container to throw the `java.lang.IllegalStateException`? (Choose all that apply.)

❏ A. NotSupported

❏ B. Required

❏ C. Supports

❏ D. RequiresNew

❏ E. Mandatory

❏ F. Never

10 Which method can be called successfully by a bean using bean-managed transaction demarcation?

❏ A. `getUserTransaction()`

❏ B. `afterBegin()`

❏ C. `afterCompletion()`

❏ D. `getRollbackOnly()`

COFFEE CRAM

Mock Exam Answers

(spec: 340-341)

1 Which are true about transactions in EJB 2.0? (Choose all that apply.)

❏ A. EJB containers must support both JTA and JTS. *– just UserTransaction from JTA*

❏ B. EJB 2.0 supports nested transactions.

❏ C. The `javax.transaction.UserTransaction` API allows you to set isolation levels. *– No*

❏ D. A bean instance can run multiple transactions in parallel.

☑ E. A message-driven bean instance must complete a transaction before the 'onMessage' method returns. *– Yes!*

(spec: 340-341)

2 When using BMT demarcation, which of the following must commit a transaction before the method that initiated the transaction returns? (Choose all that apply.)

☑ A. message-driven beans

❏ B. stateful session beans

☑ C. stateless session beans

❏ D. none of the above

(spec: 353-356)

3 Which are true about container-managed transactions in EJB 2.0? (Choose all that apply.)

☑ A. Differentiating between overloaded methods is possible in the bean's deployment descriptor.

☑ B. Every business method in the bean class must have a transaction attribute.

❏ C. If an onMessage() method returns before committing a transaction the container will throw an exception. *– No*

☑ D. A message-driven bean with CMT demarcation must not invoke the EJBContext.getUserTransaction() method.

4 What's true when specifying transaction attributes in the deployment descriptor? (Choose all that apply.)   (spec: 351–354)

☑ A. For session beans, transaction attributes can be applied only to methods in the bean's component interface.

☑ B. The <method-name> tag can take a wild card.

❑ C. A single method can have multiple transaction attributes specified in the deployment descriptor.

❑ D. Transaction attributes must NOT be specified for methods in an entity bean's home interface. _– they must be specified_

5 Which transaction attributes can cause an in-progress transaction to be suspended? (Choose all that apply.)   (spec: 357–359)

☑ A. NotSupported

❑ B. Required

❑ C. Supports

☑ D. RequiresNew

❑ E. Mandatory

❑ F. Never

6 The use of which transaction attribute can cause a **javax.transaction.TransactionRequiredException** exception to be thrown?   (spec: 357–359)

❑ A. NotSupported

❑ B. Required

❑ C. Supports

❑ D. RequiresNew

☑ E. Mandatory

❑ F. Never

7 If a set of CMT bean methods has the following transaction attributes: (spec: 357-359)

Method-1 = Supports

Method-2 = Required

Method-3 = NotSupported

Method-4 = RequiresNew

In the diagrams that follow, an arrow indicates that the method on the left calls the method on the right, and the "tx" number indicates a unique transaction. Which diagrams work with the transaction attributes listed above? (Choose all that apply.)

❏ A. M1 (Tx 1) –> M2 (No Tx) –> M3 (No Tx) –> M4 (Tx 2)

❏ B. M1 (No Tx) —> M2 (Tx 1)

        \ \——> M3 (Tx 1)

          \——> M4 (Tx 2)

✔ C. M1 (No Tx) —> M2 (Tx 1) —> M3 (No Tx)

        \——> M4 (Tx 2)

❏ D. M1 (Tx 1) –> M2 (Tx 1) –> M3 (Tx 1) –> M4 (Tx 2)

---

8 Which methods of a session bean, with container-managed transaction demarcation, run in an unspecified transaction context? (Choose all that apply.)   (spec: 363-364, 376)

✔ A. `ejbActivate()`

✔ B. `ejbPassivate()`

✔ C. Business method marked `'NotSupported'`

✔ D. `ejbRemove()`

❏ E. Business method marked 'RequiresNew'

---

9 If a session bean's business method invokes `EJBContext.setRollbackOnly()`, which transaction attribute settings can cause the container to throw the `java.lang.IllegalStateException`? (Choose all that apply.)   (spec: 360-361)

✔ A. NotSupported

❏ B. Required

✔ C. Supports

❏ D. RequiresNew

❏ E. Mandatory

✔ F. Never

10 Which method can be called successfully by a bean using bean-managed *(spec: 361)*
transaction demarcation?

☑ A. **getUserTransaction()**

❏ B. **afterBegin()** } These are callbacks from

❏ C. **afterCompletion()** } SessionSynchronization

❏ D. **getRollbackOnly()** — this is for CMT beans only

10 exceptions in EJB

✳ *When beans go bad* ✳

> Everything was going so well... we had it all... a nice transaction, non-corrupt conversational state, a great group of references... and then something went horribly wrong, and now he's <sniff> gone forever. And all I have left is a log entry...

Expect the unexpected. Despite your best efforts, things can go wrong. Terribly, *tragically*, wrong. You need to protect yourself. Others depend on you. You can't let your entire program collapse, just because one bean in the family throws an exception. ***The application must go on.*** You can't *prevent* tragedy, but you can *prepare* for it. You need to know what is and is *not* recoverable, and *who* is responsible when a problem occurs. Should the Bean Provider tell the Container there's still hope? Should the Container tell the client to try again? Or should the Container cut its losses, kill the bean, and let the Sys Admin sort it out later...

Exceptions

Official:	*What it really means:*
12.1 Identify correct and incorrect statements or examples about exception handling in EJB.	You have to know that application exceptions are things the client expects, and might recover from, while system exceptions are for things the client can't recover from. You need to know the five standard EJB application exceptions, and all of the common system exceptions. You have to know exactly how the Container behaves when the bean throws an application exception vs. a system exception, and you have to know the difference between exceptions for local clients and exceptions for remote clients.
12.2 Given a list of responsibilities related to exceptions, identify those which are the Bean Provider's, and those which are the responsibility of the Container. Be prepared to recognize responsibilities for which neither the bean or Container are responsible.	You need to know that if the bean throws an application exception, the Container does not automatically rollback the transaction, and that the Container gives the exception to the client exactly as the bean threw it. With system exceptions, however, the Container always rolls back the transaction, and gives the exception to a remote client as a RemoteException, and to a local client as an EJBException. You'll need to know that if a bean wants to rollback a transaction, as part of an application exception, the bean must call setRollbackOnly(), since the rollback won't happen automatically. You need to know that the Container will log system exceptions but not application exceptions, and that the Container will kill any bean that raises a system exception.
12.3 & 12.4 Identify correct and incorrect statements or examples about application exceptions and system exceptions in entity beans, session beans, and message-driven beans. Given a particular method condition, identify the following: whether an exception will be thrown, the type of exception thrown, the Container's action, and the client's view.	If you're going to answer these questions correctly, you have to know bean details from previous chapters. For example, you have to know that a message-driven bean doesn't have a client view (i.e. client interfaces) so a message-driven bean can't declare or throw any application exceptions. And you have to know, for example, that a bean will get an IllegalStateException if it tries to call methods on its context from places where those operations aren't allowed.

What can go wrong?

① In the **Bean**

- The business logic in a method realizes that it cannot do its job because of a *problem the client expects*. For example, a banking bean can't do a balance transfer, because the 'transfer from' account doesn't have any money!

- The *bean catches a checked exception* while running business logic. For example, the bean fails to get a JDBC connection, or a JNDI lookup throws a NamingException to the bean. This is a problem that the *bean* expects, but the *client* doesn't.

- A method in the bean (or a method the bean calls) *throws a runtime exception* (like NullPointerException) that the bean doesn't catch, and the client doesn't *expect*.

② In the **Container**

- The Container can't complete an operation for which its responsible, such as updating the state of an entity bean in the database, that causes a problem the client *expects*.

- The Container catches a checked exception thrown by the bean, that the client *expects*.

- A Container catches a runtime exception thrown by the bean, or by some other object the Container interacts with. This is a problem that the client does *not* expect.

③ In the **RMI subsystem**, or some other part of the communication path between client and container.

- The EJB object throws a runtime exception before it communicates with the client about the result of a client's business method call to the bean.

- The RMI subsystem can't communicate with the client.

- The client stub throws a runtime exception, or a RemoteException while trying to send a method call, or receive a return value.

Remember, Java exceptions can be checked or unchecked

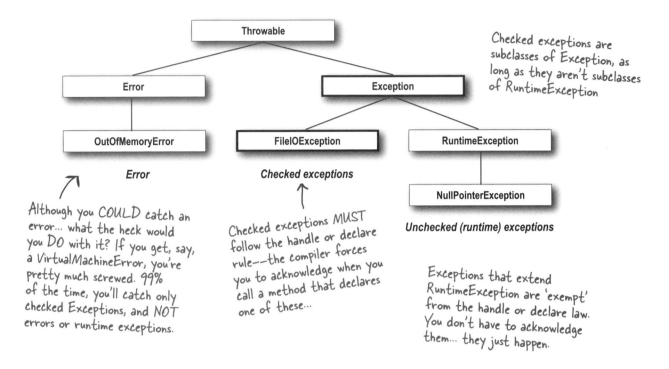

Throwable

Error

Exception

OutOfMemoryError

FileIOException

RuntimeException

NullPointerException

Error

Checked exceptions

Unchecked (runtime) exceptions

Checked exceptions are subclasses of Exception, as long as they aren't subclasses of RuntimeException

Although you COULD catch an error... what the heck would you DO with it? If you get, say, a VirtualMachineError, you're pretty much screwed. 99% of the time, you'll catch only checked Exceptions, and NOT errors or runtime exceptions.

Checked exceptions MUST follow the handle or declare rule—the compiler forces you to acknowledge when you call a method that declares one of these...

Exceptions that extend RuntimeException are 'exempt' from the handle or declare law. You don't have to acknowledge them... they just happen.

We know that you remember all of this, but just so we're all speaking the same language here—Java has both *checked* and *unchecked* exceptions. Checked as in *compiler-checked*. If you call a method that declares a throws clause with a checked exception, you *must* reassure the compiler that you know all about this potential problem, and you're ready to take the risk. It's the **handle or declare** rule. You either wrap the risky method call in a try/catch, or you declare that you, too, throw the exception.

Remember, declaring an exception means *ducking* it—letting someone else in the call stack deal with it. Declaring an exception is like saying, "I don't want to catch this exception, because I think someone else can do a better job of handling it (or someone else *should* be handling it).

If you handle an exception and exit the catch block, it should make no difference whether the exception occurred or not. If it does matter, then you aren't handling the exception correctly, and you probably should have ducked it instead.

Runtime exceptions are unchecked (they matter only at *runtime*, not *compile* time). You can declare them, catch them, and throw them in code any way that you like, but the compiler won't care. But if your code causes a runtime exception, the call stack/thread of execution you're running in dies. If that's the last non-daemon thread in your program, your whole program shuts down.

It's all about expectations...

Exception handling in EJB (or Java in general) centers on expectations. You *hope* that everything works correctly. You *hope* that you don't get a runtime exception. But you take risks. So you *expect* that some things *will* go wrong. The key is in knowing what those things *are*, and what you can do to *recover*.

Most of the time, the things that can go wrong are pretty obvious. You do a JNDI lookup, but the object isn't there. You try to connect to a naming service, and can't. You try to connect to the database and can't. You try to create a new entity bean, and the insert fails because you have a duplicate primary key. And for each of those, you can write a catch block that nows how to deal with the specific problem you have. Can't connect to the naming service? Maybe you have a second naming service to try. Can't connect to the database? Maybe you can try using a local cache for now, until you can re-establish your connection. Can't do the insert? Try again, using a different primary key.

When you provide a catch block for a risky method call, you're saying that you expect something *specific* might go wrong. Almost every exception for which you provide a catch block is an exception that you expect. So you might, for example, expect a NamingException or a FinderException or a CreateException.

Wrapping a risky method call in a try/catch tells the compiler (and your design) that you <u>expect</u> that certain things might go wrong.

You hope that everything works correctly, but you can't guarantee it, so you have a list of catch blocks, for things you expect MIGHT go wrong...

> Breathing in... I let go of my attachments. Breathing out... I let go of my expectations. Breathing in... I let go of my attachments. Breathing out... I let go of my expectation that my boss will give me the recognition I deserve. Breathing in... I let go of my need to back my SUV over my boss again and again and...

As it is in all of life, with exceptions, the key to happiness is to manage <u>expectations</u>.

Exception pathways

(1) Bean throws something the client <u>expects</u>

"Hey client, something you *expect* has happened"

"Tell client that something she *expects* has happened"

exception object

(2) Bean throws something the client does <u>NOT</u> expect

"Sorry client, but something *terrible* has happened"

"Tell client that something *terrible* has happened"

(3) Container throws something the client expects

"Hey client, something you expect has happened."

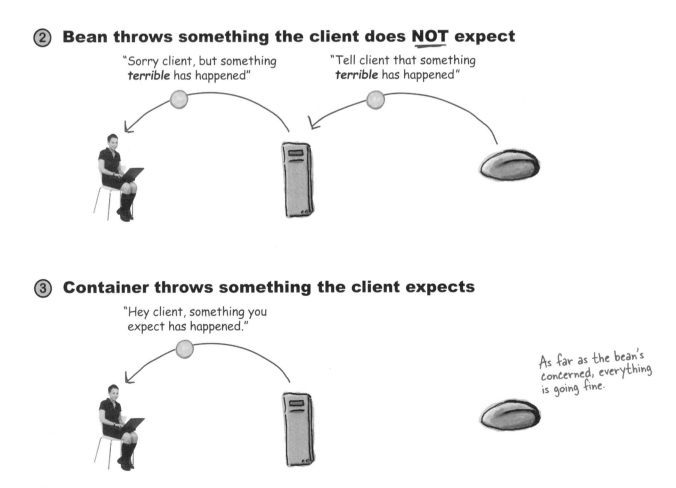

As far as the bean's concerned, everything is going fine.

(4) Container throws something the client does <u>NOT</u> expect

"Sorry client, but something ***terrible*** has happened"

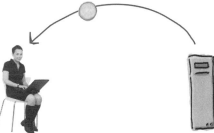

Bean doesn't directly cause the problem.

(5) The stub throws something the client expects

"Something you ***expect*** has happened"

Both the bean and the Container think everything is fine.

(6) The stub throws something the client does <u>NOT</u> expect

"Something ***terrible*** has happened"

no problems with the bean or the Container

In EJB, exceptions come in two flavors: application and system

Application exceptions are things the client *expects*, which means the client has to handle them one way or another. This means that application exceptions are declared in the interfaces exposed to the client, and the client uses a try/catch when she calls the method. Since the client can *catch* the expected exception, the client might be able to *recover* and keep going. Application exceptions include things like CreateException (maybe the client-supplied arguments weren't valid), or AccountBalanceException (perhaps the client can try a different account with the next call), or ObjectNotFoundException (that entity is no longer in the database). Application exceptions include all checked exceptions thrown by a bean or a Container, except java.rmi.RemoteException. Although RemoteException is checked, and the client catches it, as far as the client is concerned, whatever caused the RemoteException on the server was *unexpected*.

System exceptions are for things the client does *not* expect and/or can't recover from. This could be virtually any runtime exception that happens on the server (from the bean or the Container or any other object on the server), or even in the client's local stub object. System exceptions are things the client really can't recover from, either because they're not recoverable (like a failure in the database or a NullPointerException) or because the client doesn't have enough information to know what to do (like with a RemoteException which—even though it *is* a checked exception the client catches—tells the client only that something unexpectedly bad happened on the server.)

> Oh sh**! A system exception. Nothing I can do about it. There goes my stateful bean. I'll have to start over...

> Gotta love application exceptions... I can recover from this if I put in a different value for the argument to the create() method...

With an Application Exception, the Container will...

① send it back to the client **UNDERLINE** as it was thrown

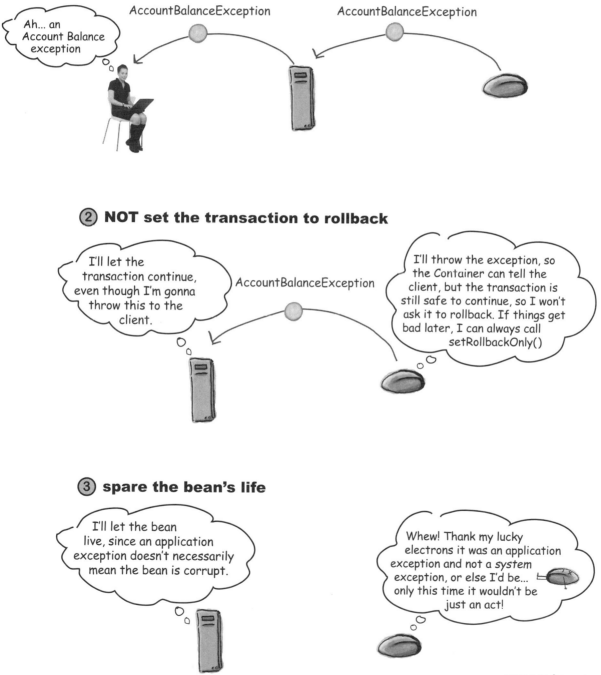

AccountBalanceException

AccountBalanceException

Ah... an Account Balance exception

② **NOT** set the transaction to rollback

I'll let the transaction continue, even though I'm gonna throw this to the client.

AccountBalanceException

I'll throw the exception, so the Container can tell the client, but the transaction is still safe to continue, so I won't ask it to rollback. If things get bad later, I can always call setRollbackOnly()

③ spare the bean's life

I'll let the bean live, since an application exception doesn't necessarily mean the bean is corrupt.

Whew! Thank my lucky electrons it was an application exception and not a system exception, or else I'd be... only this time it wouldn't be just an act!

With a System Exception, the Container will...

① **send it back to a Remote client as a <u>Remote</u>Exception, or to a local client as an <u>EJB</u>Exception**

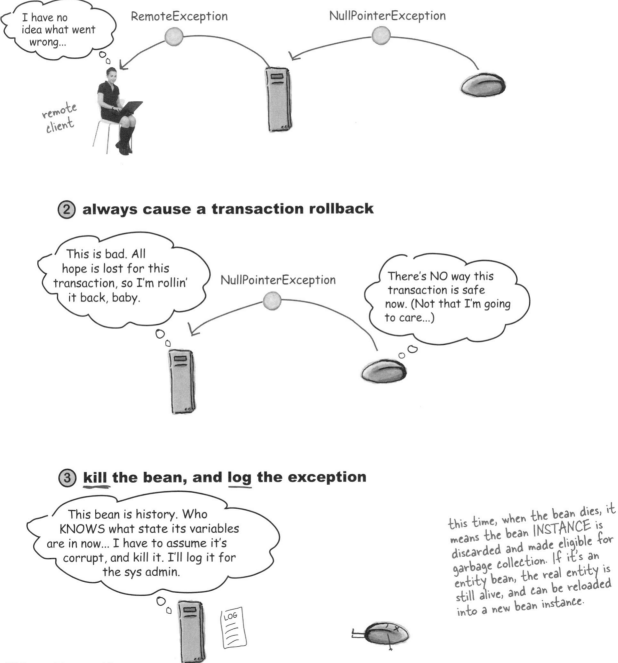

I have no idea what went wrong...

RemoteException

NullPointerException

remote client

② **always cause a transaction rollback**

This is bad. All hope is lost for this transaction, so I'm rollin' it back, baby.

NullPointerException

There's NO way this transaction is safe now. (Not that I'm going to care...)

③ **<u>kill</u> the bean, and <u>log</u> the exception**

This bean is history. Who KNOWS what state its variables are in now... I have to assume it's corrupt, and kill it. I'll log it for the sys admin.

LOG

this time, when the bean dies, it means the bean INSTANCE is discarded and made eligible for garbage collection. If it's an entity bean, the real entity is still alive, and can be reloaded into a new bean instance.

	Application Exceptions	**System Exceptions**
Client recovery	client can try to recover 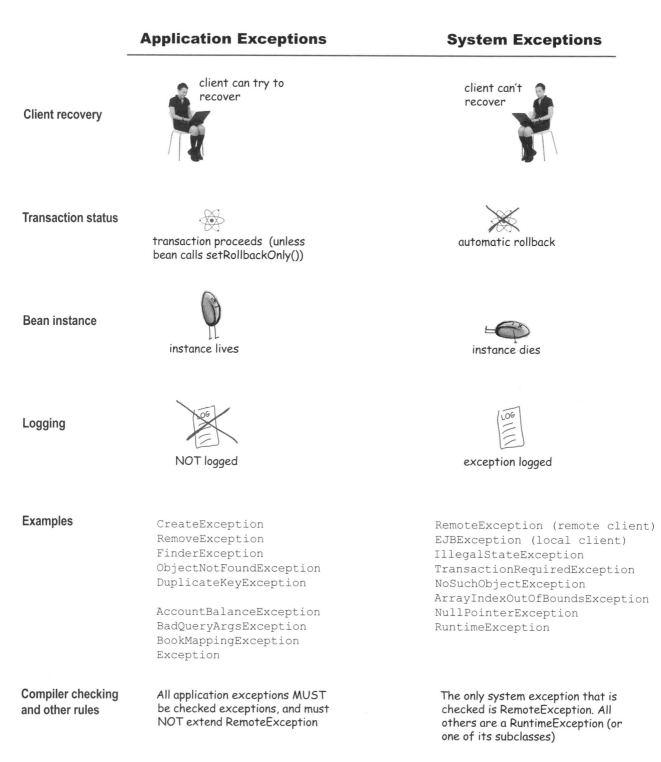	client can't recover
Transaction status	transaction proceeds (unless bean calls setRollbackOnly())	automatic rollback
Bean instance	instance lives	instance dies
Logging	NOT logged	exception logged
Examples	CreateException RemoveException FinderException ObjectNotFoundException DuplicateKeyException AccountBalanceException BadQueryArgsException BookMappingException Exception	RemoteException (remote client) EJBException (local client) IllegalStateException TransactionRequiredException NoSuchObjectException ArrayIndexOutOfBoundsException NullPointerException RuntimeException
Compiler checking and other rules	All application exceptions MUST be checked exceptions, and must NOT extend RemoteException	The only system exception that is checked is RemoteException. All others are a RuntimeException (or one of its subclasses)

That can't be right... if I throw an application exception, I think there's a darn good chance that I do NOT want the transaction to commit...

What, if anything, can you do if you know you want to throw an application exception to the client, but you do NOT want the transaction to commit?

Think about that for a moment.

We'll take a look at this scenario in a few pages.

Warning! RemoteException is <u>checked</u>, but not <u>expected</u>!

Normally when we think of expected vs. unexpected exceptions, we map it to checked vs. unchecked exceptions. A FileIOException is expected. A NullPointerException is not. Any direct subclass of Exception is expected. A subclass of RuntimeException is not. A checked exception must be handled. An unchecked exception usually won't be.

But there's one big exception to the whole exceptions and expectations thing—*java.rmi.RemoteException.*

RemoteException *is* a checked exception, of course, so the client is forced to acknowledge a RemoteException by handling it with a try/catch. But unlike the other checked exceptions a client sees in a bean's interface, RemoteException is still considered unexpected. OK, not *exactly* unexpected... but *unexpected.*

From the client's point of view, think of RemoteException a kind of runtime exception on the remote part of the application. Because that's often what it means. A NullPointerException on the server means a RemoteException to the client. A DivideByZeroException on the server means a RemoteException to the client. A ClassCastException on the server means a RemoteException to the client. Those are all unchecked exceptions on the server, but they propagate back to the client as a checked RemoteException. In other words, the *client* has to *expect* that the *server* can throw something *unexpected.*

Does this mean that every RemoteException on the client was originally triggered by a bean getting a runtime exception? No. A bean might, for example, catch a checked exception as part of its business logic, and then realize it can't recover. At that point, the bean turns what was originally a checked exception (from the bean's perspective) to an unchecked (system) exception by wrapping and rethrowing it as an *EJBException,* which ultimately shows up as a RemoteException on the remote client.

In fact, the client can get a RemoteException even *without* the server. A stub, for example, might throw a RemoteException because it can't even *reach* the server. The key here is to think of *application* exceptions as checked exceptions that the client must acknowledge *and might recover from,* and system exceptions as all *other* exceptions, including RemoteException (and its subclasses).

Application exceptions are always compiler-checked exceptions, except for RemoteException.

Think of RemoteException as "a runtime exception on the server", even though RemoteException is a checked exception to the client.

In other words, a remote client must EXPECT that the server can throw something UNEXPECTED.

A <u>Remote</u> entity bean home interface declares application exceptions and one system exception (RemoteException)

```
package headfirst;

import javax.ejb.*;
import java.rmi.RemoteException;
import java.util.Collection;

public interface CustomerHome extends EJBHome {

    public Customer create(String last, String first) throws CreateException, RemoteException;

    public Customer findByPrimaryKey(String key) throws FinderException, RemoteException;

    public Collection findByCity(String city) throws FinderException, RemoteException;
}
```

application exception ↓

system exception ↓

↑ *something the client expects, and can potentially recover from (an application exception)*

↑ *something unexpected happened on the server, so the client can't recover.*

A <u>local</u> entity bean home interface declares only application exceptions

```
package headfirst;

import javax.ejb.*;
import java.util.Collection;

public interface CustomerHomeLocal extends EJBLocalHome {

    public Customer create(String last, String first) throws CreateException;

    public Customer findByPrimaryKey(String key) throws FinderException;

    public Collection findByCity(String city) throws FinderException;
}
```

application exception ↓

↑ *application exception*

RemoteException goes to <u>remote</u> clients
EJBException goes to <u>local</u> clients

When something unexpected happens on the server, the Container tells the client by throwing either a ***RemoteException*** or an ***EJBException***.

RemoteException is for remote clients only, and even though it *is* a checked exception, it's telling the client that something *unexpected* happened. Something from which the client can't recover.

EJBException is for local clients only, and it's *unchecked*. In other words, EJBException is a subclass of RuntimeException. To the client, getting an EJBException isn't much different from getting, say, an ArrayIndexOutOfBoundsException. It means something unexpected went wrong, and there's nothing you can do to recover. The only difference is that the client does have to *catch* the RemoteException, but once he catches it, the client usually won't be able to tell what happened (at least not in any *recoverable* way).

When something unexpected happens on the server, a local client gets a RuntimeException (EJBException) but a remote client gets a compiler-checked RemoteException

Remote client

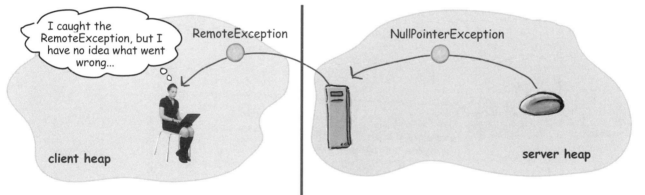

Local client

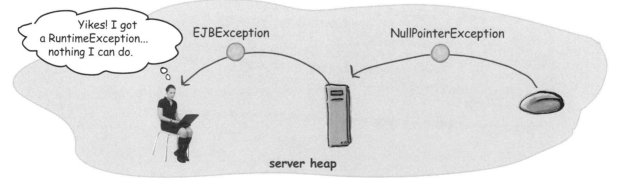

there are no
Dumb Questions

Q: In the picture, you show the client thinking, "I have no idea what happened" when she gets a RemoteException. But when I get a RemoteException in my shell terminal, it usually tells me what happened with a message like, "A NullPointerException occurred on the server" or something like that...

A: And at runtime that helps you *how*? Sure, it helps you a TON at development and testing time, but when your application is actually running, your client code probably isn't going to parse the stack trace. When we say that the client has no idea what happened, we mean that the client wasn't able to catch something specific— something *recoverable*.

Contrast that with something like CreateException, where the client can catch the exception, and from the catch block try the create again, possibly with different arguments.

It's tempting to think of application exceptions vs. system exceptions as simply checked vs. unchecked.

And in fact, from the client's perspective, the only system exceptions that are NOT unchecked (runtime) exceptions are RemoteExceptions. So for local clients, ALL system exceptions are unchecked exceptions (subclasses of RuntimeException) while all application exceptions are checked (subclasses of Exception, but not RuntimeException). For remote clients, all application exceptions are checked, but there is also one checked exception that's considered a system exception. From the client's point of view, you can think of RemoteException as being a wrapper for an unchecked runtime exception that happens on the server. (Although from the bean's point of view, the original exception might have been a checked exception... but one that the bean knew it couldn't recover from.)

Bean Provider's responsibilities

① If your business logic catches (or creates) an application exception, throw it to the Container as the application exception

In bean code, if you catch an application exception thrown by other code (or you create the exception as part of your business logic), throw it to the Container exactly as-is. For example, if your bean code gets a FinderException while trying to look up another bean (in other words, while calling a finder method on another bean's home interface), give the FinderException to the Container exactly as you got it. That means either declaring it (ducking it and letting it propagate back down the stack to the Container):

```java
public void someBusinessMethod() throws FinderException {
    CustomerHome home = null;
    try {
        InitialContext ic = new InitialContext();
        Object o = ic.lookup("Customers");
        home = (CustomerHome) PortableRemoteObject.narrow(o, CustomerHome.class);
    } catch(NamingException ne) {
        // deal with NamingException
    }
    try {
        Customer cust = home.findByPrimaryKey("42");
        // more stuff
    } catch(RemoteException re) {
        // deal with RemoteException
    }
}
```

if you intend to throw it, you have to declare it (just regular Java law)

We catch a NamingException and RemoteException, but NOT the FinderException, so the FinderException propagates back to the Container automatically

Or catching it and rethrowing it as-as:

```java
public void someOtherBusinessMethod() throws FinderException {
    CustomerHome home = null;
    try {
        InitialContext ic = new InitialContext();
        Object o = ic.lookup("Customers");
        home = (CustomerHome) PortableRemoteObject.narrow(o, CustomerHome.class);
    } catch(NamingException ne) {
        // deal with naming exception
    }
    try {
        Customer cust = home.findByPrimaryKey("42");
        // more stuff
    } catch(RemoteException re) {
        // deal with it
    } catch(FinderException fe) {
        if (! recoverable()) {
            throw fe;
        } else { //other stuff}
    }
}
```

still have to declare it, of course

We caught it, but if we can't recover, we rethrow it exactly as we got it

Bean Provider's responsibilities

(2) **If you catch an application exception, and find that you can't continue the transaction, call setRollbackOnly() before throwing the exception to the Container.**

Remember, the Container won't rollback a transaction just because there's an application exception. With an application exception, the Container assumes that the whole thing might be recoverable, and that the transaction can continue. Unless you find out, in your business logic, that committing would be a Really Bad Idea (it often *is*). What's your option? Force the Container to rollback the transaction using setRollbackOnly() on your EJBContext (for a CMT bean) or on your UserTransaction (for a BMT bean).

```
public void someOtherBusinessMethod() throws FinderException {
    CustomerHome home = null;
    try {
        InitialContext ic = new InitialContext();
        Object o = ic.lookup("Customers");
        home = (CustomerHome) PortableRemoteObject.narrow(o, CustomerHome.class);
    } catch(NamingException ne) {
        // deal with naming exception
    }
    try {
        Customer cust = home.findByPrimaryKey("42");
        // more stuff
    } catch(RemoteException re) {
        // deal with it
    } catch(FinderException fe) {
        if (! recoverable()) {
            context.setRollbackOnly();
            throw fe;
        } else { //other stuff}
    }
}
```

We caught it, but we know that we can't recover AND we can't let the transaction commit!!

Bean Provider's responsibilities

③ If your business logic catches an exception the client is <u>not</u> expecting (in other words, not declared in your client view) wrap it and rethrow it as an EJBException.

How much should the client know about your internal behavior? Little or nothing, right? For example, is it any of the client's business that you're using JDBC to get your work done? And that you might, as part of your business logic, catch an SQLException? Throwing an EJBException is the programmer's way of telling the Container, "I've lost control."

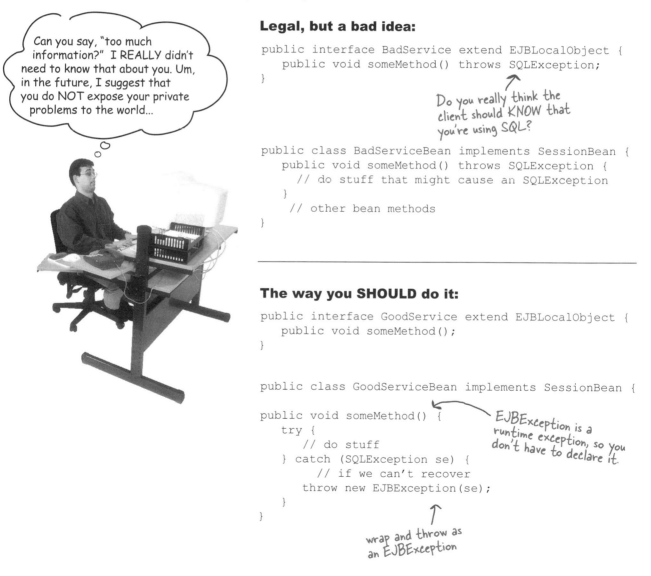

Can you say, "too much information?" I REALLY didn't need to know that about you. Um, in the future, I suggest that you do NOT expose your private problems to the world...

Legal, but a bad idea:

```
public interface BadService extend EJBLocalObject {
   public void someMethod() throws SQLException;
}
```

Do you really think the client should KNOW that you're using SQL?

```
public class BadServiceBean implements SessionBean {
   public void someMethod() throws SQLException {
     // do stuff that might cause an SQLException
   }
     // other bean methods
}
```

The way you SHOULD do it:

```
public interface GoodService extend EJBLocalObject {
   public void someMethod();
}


public class GoodServiceBean implements SessionBean {

public void someMethod() {
   try {
     // do stuff
   } catch (SQLException se) {
     // if we can't recover
     throw new EJBException(se);
   }
}
```

EJBException is a runtime exception, so you don't have to declare it.

wrap and throw as an EJBException

Bean Provider's responsibilities

④ If your business logic encounters a runtime exception, let it propagate to the Container. Don't try to catch it!

Just don't do it. Don't use a try/catch to catch, say, Exception. That would mean you'd catch everything, and the worst thing you can do is to *eat* runtime exceptions without letting them pass back up to the Container. If you do need to catch a runtime exception, but then find that you can't recover, you can simply throw it as-is. But whatever you do, don't do this:

```
public void dumbMethod() {
    try {
        //
    } catch (Exception ex) { }
}
```

Really stupid idea. Don't catch all Exceptions (or even worse -- all Throwables!) Catch only what you need for your business logic, and let the other runtime exceptions propagate back down the call stack to the Container.

⑤ If your business logic generates an application exception, you must have declared the exception in both your client interface AND your bean class.

Remember, just because you declare an exception in an interface doesn't mean you have to declare the exception in your implementation of the method. That's true regardless of whether you implement the method in the formal Java way (because your class says, "extends ThisInterface"). But if there's a chance that you'll throw an application exception, either because you have a try/catch in your code, or because your own business logic can create one, you must declare the exception in your bean class.

You have to declare it, if you might throw it.

```
public void withdraw(double d) throws AccountBalanceException {
    if ((balance - d) < 0) {
        throw new AccountBalanceException(overdrawnMsg);
    } else {
        balance -= d;
    }
}
```

```
public abstract void withdraw(double d) throws AccountBalanceException;
```

Bean Provider's responsibilities

⑥ If you create your own application exceptions, they must extend (directly or indirectly) Exception, but not RuntimeException or RemoteException

Although you're encouraged to use, or extend, the standard EJB exceptions (we'll get to those in a minute), when your design calls for your own custom exceptions, you must make them checked exceptions. That means they must extend java.lang.Exception (or one of its subclasses) as long as it does not extend java.lang.RuntimeException. The other restriction is that application exceptions must not extend java.rmi.RemoteException (directly or indirectly). Remember, an application exception is any checked exception declared in the client view, except RemoteException.

```java
public void withdraw(double d) throws AccountBalanceException {
    if ((balance - d) < 0) {
        throw new AccountBalanceException(overdrawnMsg);
    } else {balance -= d;}
}
}
class AccountBalanceException extends Exception {
    AccountBalanceException(String s) {
        super(s);
    }
}
```

there are no Dumb Questions

Q: I just realized something... the container callbacks declared in the SessionBean and EntityBean interfaces don't declare checked exceptions, right? So, doesn't this mean that you can't throw an application exception from, say, ejbActivate()?

A: That's right! You can throw only *unchecked* exceptions from a container callback that is not part of your client view. This is just plain old Java... *you can't throw a checked exception from a method that doesn't declare the exception*, and since those interfaces don't declare any checked exceptions that you can use, you're stuck with runtime exceptions. The only thing you should throw from one of the container callbacks of SessionBean, EntityBean, or MessageDrivenBean, is an EJBException.

Q: You said the interfaces don't declare any checked exceptions THAT YOU CAN USE. What does that mean? What's an example of a declared checked exception that you *can't* use?

A: If you go to the J2EE API (we'll wait, while you do that... still waiting... waiting... waiting), you can see that all of the methods declare a RemoteException! Yes, a Big Fat Checked exception. (They also declare EJBException, as a nice gesture, but not a requirement since EJBException is a subclass of RuntimeException). Does this mean you can throw a RemoteException yourself? Like, if you caught one while your bean is being a client to another bean, for example? NO! NO! A 1024 times NO!

In the days of steam-driven containers, the EJB 1.0 spec allowed *you* to throw RemoteExceptions, from your bean. Those days are over, and EJB 2.0 doesn"t allow it. So unless you're a poor soul tasked with legacy bean maintenance, you should avert your gaze when you look at the API docs, and pretend you never saw that RemoteException...

The Container's responsibilities

(1) If the bean throws an <u>application</u> exception, send it back to the client EXACTLY as it was thrown, and do NOT rollback the transaction.

If the bean throws a CreateException, send that exception to the client. If the bean throws a FinderException, send that exception to the client. If the bean throws an AccountBalanceException, send that exception to the client.

It makes no difference whether the exception is one of the standard EJB exceptions from the java.ejb package, or one that the Bean Provider defined.

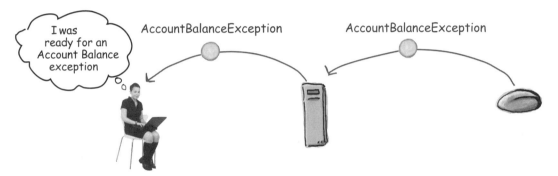

(2) If the bean throws a <u>system</u> exception (including EJBException or any runtime exception)

- Throw a **RemoteException** if the client is **Remote**
- Throw an **EJBException** if the client is **local**
- Log the exception
- Rollback the transaction
- Discard the bean instance (assume it's toast)

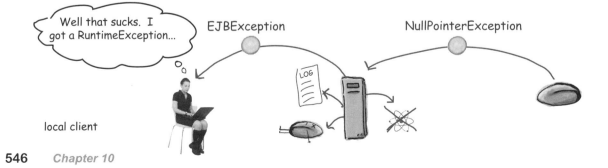

Think about the client for a moment. If the client gets a RemoteException, does the client know for certain that the business method completed?

Does the client know for certain that the transaction was rolled back?

Is there any way the client might be able to find out?
What if the client is another bean?

Relax *There's nothing on the exam about non-J2EE client strategies for coping with transaction failures.*

But as a developer, you need to think about what might happen on the client side, especially for situations in which you don't know whether a transaction succeeded. If your client is a bean, or another part of your J2EE application, you're in good shape. The J2EE client can usually find out the status of the transaction. But a non-J2EE client will need some other mechanism, or at least a way to guarantee that if he attempts the same transaction again, after it already succeeded (but he doesn't know), that the second (or any subsequent) attempt won't cause problems. When you have an operation that won't cause problems if attempted after its already succeeded, that means your operation is 'idempotent'. And though we really don't like the sound of that word, it might be critical to the integrity of your app.

From the list of possible options, select what you, as a Bean Provider, should do in each of the following scenarios. Assume that they all take place within a business method of a session bean.

Options (you may use an option more than once)

A. Throw an EJBException

B. Throw a RemoteException

C. Invoke setRollbackOnly()

D. Allow the exception to propagate (in other words, duck it).

Scenarios

You catch a checked exception in your ejbActivate method. The method is not in a transaction.

A DivideByZero exception occurs as your business logic is running. You do not have a try/catch for this.

You throw a CreateException from your ejbCreate() method, and you realize that you probably cannot safely complete your transaction.

You catch a checked exception in a business method, and realize that your bean is probably corrupt.

The five standard EJB application exceptions

The javax.ejb package has five standard application exceptions used by the EJB container, but you can use them as well, either directly or as superclasses to your own custom exceptions.

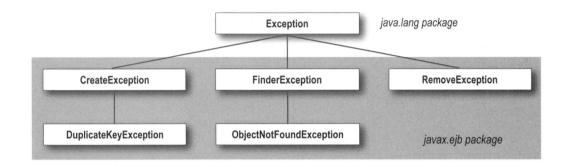

① CreateException

The Container throws this from, you guessed it, a create method, if something goes wrong during creation. This includes scenarios in which the bean code throws CreateException itself, while running a create method. (Although if the bean's gonna throw it, the bean's gotta declare it in the bean class, not just the home interface)

② DuplicateKeyException

The Container throws this to the client from an entity bean create method (see how it's a subclass of CreateException?) if the business logic related to the create asks the Container to insert a new entity using a primary key that has already been assigned to another entity.

③ FinderException

The Container throws this to the client from an entity bean's finder method, to tell the client that something went wrong during the finder. The bean might have thrown it (BMP beans only), but for CMP beans, only the Container can throw this method.

④ ObjectNotFoundException

The Container throws this to the client ONLY during single-entity finder methods, when there's no entity in the database matching the primary key parameter of the finder method.

⑤ RemoveException

The Container throws this to the client from a session or entity bean when something goes wrong in a remove method. But... the bean provider can throw this exception if, for example, he doesn't want to let clients remove entity beans.

The five standard application exceptions from the client's point of view

Two of the five are more specific—DuplicateKeyException and ObjectNotFoundException. If the client gets an ObjectNotFoundException, the client has more information than if he gets a more abstract FinderException. And if the client gets a DuplicateKeyException, he knows a lot more about what went wrong than if he gets a generic CreateException.

CreateException

The client does *not* know for certain whether the bean was actually created. The Container might have had a problem *after* the transaction committed.

DuplicateKeyException

If the client catches a DuplicateKeyException, she can be 100% certain that the bean was not created.

FinderException

The client does *not* know whether a matching entity (or entities, for multiple-entity finders) exists in the database. The Container might throw a FinderException because of something that went wrong before it was able to look in the datbase.

ObjectNotFoundException

If the client catches an ObjectNotFoundException, she can be 100% certain that there was no match for this primary key in the database. Remember, ObjectNotFoundException is for single-entity finders only, so a client will never get this for a multi-entity finder.

RemoveException

The client does *not* know for certain whether the bean was actually removed. The bean provider might simply have rejected the client's request, as in, "You can ask all day long, but there is no WAY that I'm going to remove that entity from the database." Or the entity might have been removed from the database, but then something else went wrong that triggered the RemoveException.

Stateless session bean clients will NEVER get a RemoveException!

If you see a scenario where the client gets a RemoveException, you can rule out stateless session beans. Think about it... a stateless session bean's removal is NEVER tied to a client, so there's nobody to give the exception to. You can throw a RemoveException from your ejbRemove() method, but the client will never see it if the bean is a stateless session bean.

The client might NOT get the most specific exception

Don't count on ALWAYS getting the most specific exception on the client. The Container might not, according to the spec, send the client a DuplicateKeyException even if that is the problem.
What does this mean to the client? If the client's code has a catch for both a CreateException and a DuplicateKeyException, the client can't be completely certain that if she catches a CreateException, the problem is NOT a duplicate key issue. This would be bad if, for example, the client code just kept trying to create(), sending in the same key thinking,"I didn't get a DuplicateKeyException, so I know THAT can't be the problem..." If you get a CreateException on the client, and NOT a DuplicateKeyException, you won't know for certain that the key is oK. It's up to the Container whether it gives you the more specific exception.

Q: **If a RemoveException makes no sense for a stateless session bean, why are you allowed to throw it (assuming you declare it on your bean's remove() method)?**

A: Remember, there's nothing in the bean class that can tell you whether the bean is definitely state*less*. You *can* tell if a bean is state*ful*, of course, because any bean with overloaded creates (or it's only create has args) must be stateful. But even if a session bean has only a single no-arg create method, you still don't know whether that bean is going to be marked stateless or stateful at deploytime.

This would all be different if there were a separate interface for StatelessSessionBean and StatefulSessionBean, that your bean had to implement (instead of just SessionBean), but that's not how it works.

Q: **If the Bean Provider doesn't want to let entity bean clients remove a bean, why does he have a remove method?**

A: Aren't you forgetting something obvious here? Where do the remove() methods *live*? How are they exposed to the client? That's right. In the client interfaces. Remember, there are three remove() methods available to a remote entity bean client (the no-arg in the EJBObject interface, and the remove that takes a key and the remove that takes a handle in the EJBHome interface). A local entity bean client has two remove methods—the one in EJBObject, and the one in the home that takes a primary key. So there's nothing you can do to hide the remove() methods from a client, but if you don't support it from your bean, throw a RemoveException from your bean's ejbRemove() method, and the Container won't go through with the remove. This is your way of telling the Container,"Don't do it!! I don't care what the client says, don't you dare go through with the remove!"

Common system exceptions

Besides the standard application exceptions for EJB, there are several important system exceptions. A few (including EJBException) are part of the J2EE API, but two of the most likely system exceptions in EJB include java.rmi.NoSuchObjectException and java.lang.IllegalStateException.

Local clients and beans will get these (unchecked)

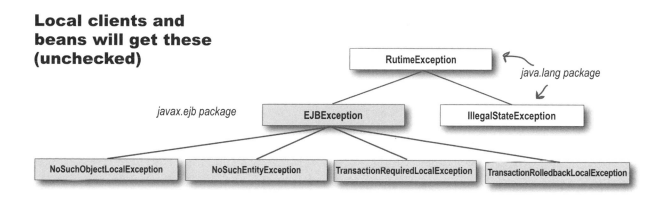

Only Remote clients will get these (checked)

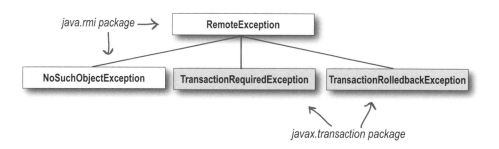

Common system exceptions

① IllegalStateException

The Container throws this to a bean if the bean calls a method on its context that isn't allowed at that time. For example, a session bean can't ask its context for a reference to its EJB object while in the setSessionContext() method. It's too early. A bean can also get an IllegalStateException if it calls a transaction method like setRollbackOnly() or getRollbackOnly(), when there's no transaction!

② EJBException

The *bean* throws this to tell the Container a system exception has occurred (which forces the Container to rollback the transaction, log the exception, kill the bean, and give a local client the EJBException and a remote client a RemoteException). But the Container can also throw this for a variety of other reasons we'll look at in a minute.

③ NoSuchObjectLocalException

This exception is kind of a local companion to java.rmi.NoSuchObjectException. The Container throws it to the client when the client invokes a method on a local home or component interface, but there's no underlying bean to support the object. This can happen, for example, if the bean has already been removed (either through a previous client call to remove(), or because the Container killed the bean due to an exception, stateful bean timeout, or to reduce the size of the pool).

④ NoSuchEntityException

You probably won't see or use this exception much, especially with CMP, but it's for you to throw from your bean code when you want to tell the Container that the entity you're trying to access is no longer in the database (perhaps because it was removed by an admin application).

⑤ TransactionRequiredLocalException / TransactionRequiredException

The Container throws this to the caller when the called method has a transaction attribute of mandatory, but there's no transaction context coming in with the call. In other words, it's mandatory that the caller invokes the method within an existing transaction, and if there isn't one, the appropriate TransactionRequired exception is thrown (depending on whether the client is local or remote)

⑥ TransactionRolledbackException / TransactionRolledbackLocalException

The Container throws this to the caller when the Container can't commit the transaction, and the caller invoked the method within an existing transaction context. But the Container will not throw this exception if the failure to commit is because the bean explicitly called the setRollbackOnly() method. In that case, the Container will rollback the transaction and pass the business method result back to the client (unless the bean also throws an application exception).

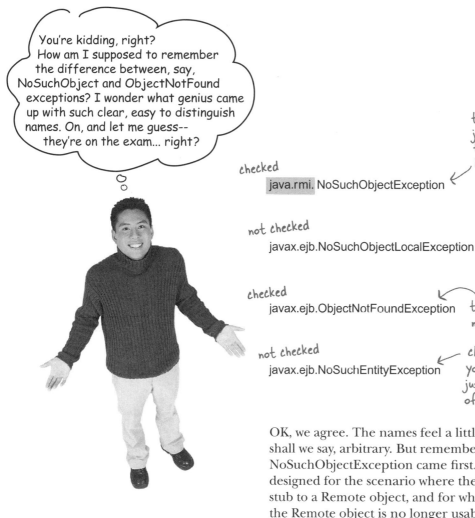

You're kidding, right?
How am I supposed to remember the difference between, say, NoSuchObject and ObjectNotFound exceptions? I wonder what genius came up with such clear, easy to distinguish names. On, and let me guess-- they're on the exam... right?

checked

java.rmi. NoSuchObjectException

the only one that's NOT in javax.ejb is in java.rmi. It means the client has a stub, but the Remote object is gone.

not checked

javax.ejb.NoSuchObjectLocalException

this was added to EJB when local interfaces came in version 2.0. It means the client has an invalid EJB object reference.

checked

javax.ejb.ObjectNotFoundException

this is ONLY for finder methods! (single-entity finders)

not checked

javax.ejb.NoSuchEntityException

clients will never see this, and you'll probably never use it... just don't confuse it with any of the others!

OK, we agree. The names feel a little, shall we say, arbitrary. But remember, the NoSuchObjectException came first. It was designed for the scenario where the client has a stub to a Remote object, and for whatever reason the Remote object is no longer usable. Might have been a server crash. Might be that the service itself has been undeployed. Doesn't matter. As far as the client's concerned, the phone has been disconnected over at the server side.

NoSuchObject*Local*Exception was added when local client views were added in EJB 2.0. The concept is slightly different, because the local client is using not a stub, but a real Java object reference. But from the client's perspective, it really doesn't matter whether it's local or Remote—a NoSuchObject<whatever> exception means you can't use your EJB object reference to get to a bean! You have to go back through the home and start over.

Are you sure you looked everywhere? And you still didn't **find** any record of Paul Wheaton?

I tried to **find** him, but an exotic dancer named Paul Wheaton was **Not Found** anywhere in the records. Maybe if we upgraded to a database that's in *color* I could actually get something done around here...

I'm sorry, but there's **No Such** person here. Yes, I realize that this is how you contacted him in the past. But trust me, honey. He's been **removed**. I put his body through the wood chipper not two days ago...

Object**NotFound**Exception is a **Finder**Exception

NoSuchObectException is when the client still has a stub to a Remote object, but the object has been **removed** (or is no longer valid for any other reason.)

NoSuchObject*Local*Exception is when the local client has a reference to an EJB object for a bean that's been **removed** (or is no longer valid for any other reason).

BULLET POINTS

- Exceptions in Java can be checked or unchecked. Checked exceptions extend java.lang.Exception, but not java.lang.RuntimeException

- Exceptions in EJB can be thrown from the bean to the Container, and from the Container to the bean.

- EJB exceptions come in two types: *application* and *system*.

- *Application* exceptions are checked exceptions that the client is expecting, and might be able to recover from. This includes all checked exceptions *except* java.rmi.RemoteException and its subclasses.

- *System* exceptions are all other exceptions, and include all runtime exceptions, plus RemoteException.

- For the client, a RemoteException can be treated as though a runtime exception (i.e. something unexpected) happened on the server.

- When the Container gets a system exception, it will rollback the transaction, log the exception, and throw away the bean.

- When the Container gets an application exception, it will send it to the client exactly as it was received. The transaction will not automatically rollback, and the bean's life will be spared.

- The Bean Provider should throw application exceptions to the Container as-is, so that the Container can pass them on to the client. If the bean's transaction is possibly corrupt, the Bean Provider should call setRollbackOnly() before throwing application exception, so that the Container will not commit the transaction.

- If the Bean Provider catches an exception from which the bean cannot recover, he should wrap and re-throw the exception as an EJBException (a runtime exception, so he didn't need to declare it).

- There are five standard EJB application exceptions: CreateException, DuplicateKeyException (extends CreateException), FinderException, ObjectNotFoundException (extends FinderException), and RemoveException

- Common system exceptions include EJBException, IllegalStateException, TransactionRequiredLocalException, and NoSuchObjectLocalException.

- ObjectNotFoundException is for when single-entity finder methods cannot find an entity in the persistent store, that matches the primary key argument to the finder method.

- NoSuchObjectException is an RMI exception for when a Remote client has a stub to a Remote object that's been removed, or is invalid for some other reason.

- NoSuchObjectLocalException is a runtime exception for when a local client has a reference to an EJB object that's no longer valid (most likely because the bean has already been removed).

Scenarios: what do you think happens?

Technically, this section is like a big stealth Sharpen Your Pencil exercise. Only we just told you, so maybe not so stealthy. Sure, we could just tell you everything one fact after another... but you'll have a much better chance at remembering it if you work it out for yourself. We summarize everything near the end of the chapter, but do NOT jump there now! Even if you're someone who never does the exercises, do this scenario walk-through. You'll think of us fondly when you're holding your lovely lapel pin that you get from passing the certification exam.

 A message-driven bean's onMessage() method catches an application exception. Can it re-throw the application exception to the Container?

(Hint: what does a Container usually do when it gets an application exception from a bean? Would the Container be able to do that in this scenario?)

2 A session bean using CMT has a method marked with the NotSupported transaction attribute. While the method is running, the bean calls setRollbackOnly() on its context. Will this cause an exception? What kind?

(Hint: think about what setRollbackOnly() does, and what state the bean has to be in.)

 A message-driven bean, in the onMessage() method, calls getCallerPrincipal(). What happens?

(Hint: what's getCallerPrincipal() used for? Does that make sense here?)

4 A session bean using CMT has a method marked with the Mandatory transaction attribute. The client calling the method is not in a transaction. What happens?

(Hint: Think about the names of the common system exceptions. Is there one that makes sense here?)

5 A bean realizes it can't commit a transaction, but it doesn't want the client to get an exception. What can the bean do?

 A bean wants the client to get an application exception, but the bean still wants the transaction to commit. What should the bean do?

 **Sharpen your pencil**

Match the scenarios with the exception(s) that might occur with that scenario. Don't turn the page!! The answers are just a page away.

Scenarios

A CMT bean calls context.getUserTransaction().

Client calls remove() on a bean that's already been removed.

Client calls remove() on a stateful bean that is still in an open transaction.

A session bean calls getPrimaryKey() on its context.

A CMT bean calls getRollbackOnly(), from a method marked NotSupported.

Client calls a method on a Remote CMT bean, and the method is marked Mandatory. The caller does not have a transaction context in place when the call comes in.

A message-driven bean calls isCallerInRole() on its context, from within the onMessage() method.

Client calls the home remove method on the LOCAL home interface of a session bean

A stateless session bean calls getCallerPrincipal() on its context, during the setSessionContext method.

Client Foo calls a method on a remote stateful bean, while that same bean is already executing a method for client Bar.

Client calls getPrimaryKey() on the local component interface of a session bean.

A message-driven bean catches a NamingException, from which it can't recover. Which exception (if any) can the bean throw to tell the Container?

A session bean wants the Container to know that the transaction should be rolled back and the bean should be killed.

Client calls findByPrimaryKey("23"), where there is no entity with a primary key of "23".

Although the bean is fine, the Container has a system exception it wants to throw to a local client.

Exceptions

IllegalStateException

EJBException

CreateException

RemoveException

ObjectNotFoundException

NoSuchObjectException

RemoteException

TransactionRequiredException

NotSupportedException

RuntimeException

NoSuchObjectLocalException

DuplicateKeyException

SystemException

NoSuchEntityException

Scenario Summary

Transaction Scenarios

A CMT bean calls context.getUserTransaction().

The bean gets an IllegalStateException. (Only BMT beans can get a UserTransaction)

Client calls remove() on a stateful bean that is still in an open transaction.

The client gets a RemoveException. You can't remove a stateful bean while its in a transaction. (Which is just one of a gazillion reasons why it's a Bad Idea to leave a transaction open across multiple client invocations. In other words, if you begin a BMT transaction in a method, you should end it in that method!)

A CMT bean calls getRollbackOnly(), from a method marked NotSupported.

The bean gets an IllegalStateException. You must be in a transaction when you call getRollbackOnly() or setRollbackOnly(). That means you can't call them within a method marked NotSupported, Never, or Supports (session and entity beans) or NotSupported (message-driven beans— remember, message-driven beans can't use Never or Supports, because they don't make sense given that transactions can never propagate into a message-driven bean.)

Client calls a method on a Remote CMT bean, and the method is marked Mandatory. The caller does not have a transaction context in place when the call comes in.

The client gets a TransactionRequiredException (a local client would get TransactionRequiredLocalException).

A session bean wants the Container to know that the transaction should be rolled back and the bean should be killed.

The bean should throw an EJBException. The Container takes over and does its normal Container thing for system exceptions—rollback the transaction, log the exception, kill the bean, and throw a RemoteException to a Remote client or the EJBException to a local client.

Scenario Summary

Client Scenarios

Client calls remove() on a bean that's already been removed.

You might be tempted to say RemoveException, but that's not it! Remember, remove() is just another method in the bean's interface, and if you call it on a removed bean, you'll get the same exception you'd see if you called any other business method on a removed bean—remote clients get RemoteException, and local clients get EJBException.

Client calls the home remove method on the LOCAL home interface of a session bean.

The client gets a RemoveException. Why? Because the only remove() method in a session bean's local home is the one that takes a primary key, and that can never work. Remote clients would also get a RemoveException.

Client Foo calls a method on a remote stateful bean, while that same bean is already executing a method for client Bar.

Client Foo gets a RemoteException (if client Foo had been local, he'd get an EJBException). A session bean handle only one client at a time!

Client calls getPrimaryKey() on the local component interface of a session bean.

This is just like the one where the client calls remove() on a local bean's home. The client gets an EJBException (if the client were remote, he'd get a RemoteException). The point is? Session beans don't have primary keys! Any method you call related to the primary key of a bean will fail if that bean is a session bean.

Client calls findByPrimaryKey("23"), where there is no entity with a primary key of "23".

The client gets an ObjectNotFoundException, a subclass of FinderException.

Although the bean is fine, the Container has a system exception it wants to throw to a local client.

The client gets an EJBException.

Scenario Summary

Bean Scenarios

A session bean calls getPrimaryKey() on its context.

The bean gets an IllegalStateException. You know why. Session beans and primary keys don't go together...

A message-driven bean calls isCallerInRole() on its context, from within the onMessage() method.

Think about it. Does a message-driven bean have a calling client (we don't really count the Container as a 'client', although it is calling the bean's methods). If there's no client, then WHOSE security information would the bean get? The bean gets an IllegalStateException just for being clueless enough to even try.

A stateless session bean calls getCallerPrincipal() on its context, during the setSessionContext method.

The bean gets an IllegalStateException, because setSessionContext() is too early in the bean's life to get client information. In fact, a stateless bean can get client security information ONLY while running a business method of the component interface. And even if the bean were stateFUL, it would still be too early for client information, although a stateful bean (but not stateless) could call getCallerPrincipal() and isCallerInRole() from within ejbCreate().

A message-driven bean catches a NamingException, from which it can't recover. Which exception (if any) can the bean throw to tell the Container?

The bean should throw an EJBException. Remember, message-driven beans don't have clients. They don't have client interfaces. So there's no place to declare application exceptions. That means your bean can't throw anything but system exceptions. The only exception the message-driven bean should ever throw is EJBException. It can never throw application exceptions, and it should let other system exceptions propagate to the Container.

Exercise

Fill this chart in to describe the differences between remote and local clients. You'll want to use this as a cheat sheet before the exam, so don't screw it up.

Some things might be the same for both remote and local clients, but we aren't telling.

	Remote clients	**Local clients**
How system exceptions in the bean are delivered to the client.		
The exception for when the client calls a method on a bean that's been removed.		
The exception for when the client calls a method marked Mandatory, without a transaction context in place.		
The exception for when the client starts a transaction, and the Container has to roll it back.		
The exception for when the client calls getPrimaryKey() on the component interface of a session bean.		
The exception for when the client calls a method in a session bean and the bean is already executing a method for another client.		
The exception for when the client calls a remove() method on a stateful session bean that's still in a transaction.		

Deja vu? Yes, you've seen this. Near the beginning of this chapter. Except it was all filled in. Now it's your turn. Bonus points if you use drawings along with your words.

Exercise

Application Exceptions	**System Exceptions**
Client recovery	
Transaction status	
Bean instance	
Logging	
Examples	
Compiler checking and other rules	

Mock Exam

1   What is true when an entity bean's client receives a javax.ejb.EJBException?
    (Choose all that apply.)

❏ A. The client must be remote.

❏ B. The client must be local.

❏ C. A client will never receive this exception.

❏ D. The client must handle or declare this exception.

❏ E. This exception can only occur if the client is in a transaction.

2   Which scenario will cause a java.rmi.NoSuchObjectException to be thrown?
    (Choose all that apply.)

❏ A. A remote client invokes a method on a stateful session bean which has
       been removed.

❏ B. A remote client invokes a method on an entity bean which has been
       removed.

❏ C. A remote client invokes a finder method with invalid arguments.

❏ D. The container invokes an ejbPassivate() method on a bean that is not
       ready to be serialized.

3   Which is a subclass of java.lang.RuntimeException? (Choose all that apply.)

❏ A. `javax.ejb.EJBException`

❏ B. `javax.ejb.RemoveException`

❏ C. `javax.ejb.CreateException`

❏ D. `javax.ejb.NoSuchEntityException`

❏ E. `java.rmi.RemoteException`

❏ F. `javax.ejb.ObjectNotFoundException`

❏ G. `java.rmi.NoSuchObjectException`

4 Which of the following are EJB 2.0 specification guidelines regarding system exceptions? (Choose all that apply.)

❏ A. Bean methods should catch RuntimeException exceptions.

❏ B. Bean methods should wrap unrecoverable checked exceptions in a `javax.ejb.EJBException` exception.

❏ C. For remote clients, bean methods should wrap unrecoverable checked exceptions in a `java.rmi.RemoteException`.

❏ D. If a CMT bean throws a system exception, the transaction will still commit unless the bean invokes `setRollbackOnly`.

5 If a business method of a CMT demarcated bean throws a system exception, in which case will the container always throw a `javax.transaction.TransactionRolledbackException`? (Choose all that apply.)

❏ A. If the method's transaction attribute is marked 'RequiresNew'.

❏ B. If the method's transaction attribute is marked 'Mandatory'.

❏ C. If the method's transaction attribute is marked 'Never'.

❏ D. If the method's transaction attribute is marked 'NotSupported'.

6 Which is a subclass of javax.ejb.FinderException? (Choose all that apply.)

❏ A. CreateException

❏ B. NoSuchEntityException

❏ C. RemoveException

❏ D. DuplicateKeyException

❏ E. ObjectNotFoundException

7 From which methods can MDBs with CMT demarcation throw application exceptions? (Choose all that apply.)

❏ A. `onMessage()`

❏ B. `ejbCreate()`

❏ C. `ejbRemove()`

❏ D. `getUserTransaction()`

❏ E. `setMessageDrivenContext()`

❏ F. none of the above

8 What's true for a local client that receives an exception from an EJB invocation? (Choose all that apply.)

❑ A. The exception might be from the java.rmi package.

❑ B. The exception might be an application exception.

❑ C. The exception might be a system exception.

❑ D. None of the above.

9 Which action(s) will the container take if a message-driven bean with BMT demarcation throws a system exception? (Choose all that apply.)

❑ A. Log the exception.

❑ B. Discard the instance.

❑ C. Mark the transaction for rollback.

❑ D. Commit the transaction unless the bean has invoked `setRollbackOnly()`.

❑ E. None of the above

10 From which types of beans can clients receive system exceptions? (Choose all that apply.)

❑ A. Session beans with CMT demarcation.

❑ B. Session beans with BMT demarcation.

❑ C. Message-driven beans with CMT demarcation.

❑ D. Message-driven beans with BMT demarcation.

❑ E. Entity beans with CMT demarcation.

COFFEE CRAM

Mock Exam Answers

—————————————————————————————————————— (spec: 374)

1 What is true when an entity bean's client receives a javax.ejb.EJBException? (Choose all that apply.)

❑ A. The client must be remote. — Remote clients get RemoteException

☑ B. The client must be local.

❑ C. A client will never receive this exception.

❑ D. The client must handle or declare this exception.

❑ E. This exception can only occur if the client is in a transaction.

—————————————————————————————————————— (spec: 374)

2 Which scenario will cause a java.rmi.NoSuchObjectException to be thrown? (Choose all that apply.)

☑ A. A remote client invokes a method on a stateful session bean which has been removed.

☑ B. A remote client invokes a method on an entity bean which has been removed.

❑ C. A remote client invokes a finder method with invalid arguments.

❑ D. The container invokes an ejbPassivate() method on a bean that is not ready to be serialized.

— client gets FinderException or ObjectNotFoundException (subclass of FinderException)

3 Which is a subclass of java.lang.RuntimeException? (Choose all that apply.)

☑ A. `javax.ejb.EJBException`

❑ B. `javax.ejb.RemoveException`

❑ C. `javax.ejb.CreateException`

☑ D. `javax.ejb.NoSuchEntityException`

❑ E. `java.rmi.RemoteException`

❑ F. `javax.ejb.ObjectNotFoundException`

❑ G. `java.rmi.NoSuchObjectException`

(API docs)

4 Which of the following are EJB 2.0 specification guidelines regarding system exceptions? (Choose all that apply.) (spec: 373-374)

❑ A. Bean methods should catch RuntimeException exceptions.

☑ B. Bean methods should wrap unrecoverable checked exceptions in a `javax.ejb.EJBException` exception.

❑ C. For remote clients, bean methods should wrap unrecoverable checked exceptions in a `java.rmi.RemoteException`. *No, the Container will do this*

❑ D. If a CMT bean throws a system exception, the transaction will still commit unless the bean invokes `setRollbackOnly`. *– system exceptions always cause a tx rollback*

5 If a business method of a CMT demarcated bean throws a system exception, in which case will the container always throw a `javax.transaction.TransactionRolledbackException`? (Choose all that apply.) (spec: 375-376)

❑ A. If the method's transaction attribute is marked 'RequiresNew'.

☑ B. If the method's transaction attribute is marked 'Mandatory'.

❑ C. If the method's transaction attribute is marked 'Never'.

❑ D. If the method's transaction attribute is marked 'NotSupported'.

The others are wrong because they indicate that the caller's tx was not the active tx when the exception occurred. There's no need to tell a caller (through an exception) unless it's the caller's transaction that is rolled back!

6 Which is a subclass of javax.ejb.FinderException? (Choose all that apply.) (spec: 263-264)

❑ A. CreateException

❑ B. NoSuchEntityException

❑ C. RemoveException

❑ D. DuplicateKeyException *– subclass of CreateException*

☑ E. ObjectNotFoundException

7 From which methods can MDBs with CMT demarcation throw application exceptions? (Choose all that apply.) (spec: 377)

❑ A. `onMessage()`

❑ B. `ejbCreate()`

❑ C. `ejbRemove()`

❑ D. `getUserTransaction()`

❑ E. `setMessageDrivenContext()`

☑ F. none of the above

– MDBs cannot declare / throw any application exceptions... who would catch them? there's no client.

8 What's true for a local client that receives an exception from an EJB invocation? (Choose all that apply.)

    ❏ A. The exception might be from the java.rmi package.

    ☑ B. The exception might be an application exception.

    ☑ C. The exception might be a system exception.

    ❏ D. None of the above.

(spec: 381–382)

9 Which action(s) will the container take if a message-driven bean with BMT demarcation throws a system exception? (Choose all that apply.)

    ☑ A. Log the exception.

    ☑ B. Discard the instance.

    ☑ C. Mark the transaction for rollback.

    ❏ D. Commit the transaction unless the bean has invoked
`setRollbackOnly()`.

    ❏ E. None of the above

(spec: 378)

10 From which types of beans can clients receive system exceptions? (Choose all that apply.)

    ☑ A. Session beans with CMT demarcation.

    ☑ B. Session beans with BMT demarcation.

    ❏ C. Message-driven beans with CMT demarcation.

    ❏ D. Message-driven beans with BMT demarcation. — *MDBs have no clients!*

    ☑ E. Entity beans with CMT demarcation.

(spec: 377)

11 security in EJB

Protect Your Secrets

... no way! You can't let Susie hear this. I better put some method permissions in my DD to stop her from calling! Let's put her in the 'crybaby' security role...

Keep your secrets. Security is about **authentication** and **authorization**. First, you have to prove your identity, and then we'll tell you what you're allowed to do. Security is easy in EJB, because you're only dealing with *authorization*. You decide *who* gets to call which *methods* on your beans. Except one problem... if you're a Bean Provider or App Assembler, you probably don't *know* who the users are going to be! So you make stuff up. You make up roles, like job titles, including Manager, Supervisor, Admin, etc. and when someone deploys your application in a real company, that Deployer maps between your made-up names (Manager) and *real* people who will use the app.

Security

Official:	*What it really means:*
14.1 Identify correct and incorrect statements about the EJB support for security management including security roles, security role references, and method permissions.	You have to know that you can do two kinds of security in EJB: programmatic and declarative. Declarative means your security is defined in the Deployment Descriptor. You need to know that security in EJB is mostly about declaring a set of abstract security roles, then declaring which methods each of those roles is allowed to call.
14.2 From a list of responsibilities, identify which belong to the Application Assembler, Bean Provider, Deployer, Container Provider, or System Administrator.	Pay close attention to this in the chapter. You need to think about the whole process in a component-based development way, to know who is responsible for what. You need to know that the Bean Provider usually won't have any security responsibilities, but that if he does use the isCallerInRole() method, then he must tell the App Assembler what name he hard-coded in as the argument to the isCallerInRole() method, by putting a security role reference in the DD. You must know that the App Assembler's job is to define security roles, method permissions, and role-links mapping from the programmer's made-up role references and the App Assembler's real security roles. Finally, you must know that the Deployer is responsible for mapping (in a vendor-specific way) between real users and groups and the App Assembler's abstract security roles, and that this is done using Container tools or property files.
14.3 & 14.4 Given a code listing, determine whether it is a legal and/or appropriate way to programmatically access a caller's security context. Given a security-related deployment descriptor tag, identify correct and incorrect statements and/or code related to that tag.	You have to know everything about the DD tags related to security, including that security role references, and role links, are in the <enterprise-bean> section, but security roles and method permissions are in the <application-assembly> part. You must know how the <security-identity> tag is used, and that message-driven beans must never <use-caller-identity>! You need to know that the two programmatic security methods are called on a session or entity bean's context.

Imagine you're writing a payroll application...

What can you do?

Who really is responsible for making the program secure? How does it happen? There's good news and bad news with EJB security.

① Security in EJB is <u>easy</u>. *It's about AUTHORIZATION.*

- Most of the time, *you don't put any security-related code into your bean classes.*

- In fact, the *Bean Provider does not even think about security*, except in very special cases we'll look at in the last part of this chapter.

- Security in EJB is about saying WHO can call WHAT. *You can restrict access for each individual method in your application, to only those individuals that are in a privileged 'role'* (Director, Payroll Admin, Payroll Assistant, etc.)

- The EJB part of the security—the part that specifies the roles, and the methods those roles can access—is done *declaratively*, *in the deployment descriptor,* using simple XML tags.

- At the EJB level, *it really is as simple as saying, "The setSalary() method can be accessed by ONLY Directors and Payroll Administrators."*

② Security in EJB is <u>abstract</u>. *It's NOT about AUTHENTICATION.*

- The EJB spec makes it very easy to define roles, and to assign roles to methods in order to control access to the methods. But *the spec says NOTHING about how the system will KNOW which real human beings belong to those roles.* Somewhere outside of the EJB deployment descriptor (and outside the specification) you still have to say that Jack O'Bryan is in the Director role (and probably other roles as well). Or say that all Payroll Managers in company XYZ are qualified to be in the role of what the application has labeled Payroll Admin.

- The spec also *does not define how a real human being can be authenticated* to the system. In other words, there's nothing in EJB about how you will know that, say, the person logging in as Jack O'Bryan really *is* Jack O'Bryan. This might happen in a variety of ways, although one typical option is to have clients authenticate through the web tier (they log in using a browser) of a J2EE-friendly web server.

- The security in the real operating environment—the company running the application—must have a security structure in place, and in a format that your specific EJB server can hook into. Or, at the very least, you need a server that lets you specifically configure a security realm. Even if it's nothing more than a list of names, passwords, and the 'roles' those names belong to, you still need *some* infrastructure outside of EJB.

How to do security in EJB

My job is easy. Most of the time, I don't even have to *think* about security when I'm writing a bean. And that's good, because my philosophy is "Security is hard... don't do it."

Bill the Bean Provider

My job is more involved. I decide which roles make sense in the application. For Bill's payroll beans (plus I added some of my own beans to make the complete app), I chose Payroll Admin, Payroll Assistant, and Payroll Director as the roles. Then I set up method permissions in the DD, to say which roles can call which methods.

Annie the Application Assembler

Annie can set up as many roles as she wants... but unless I map *real* people or groups into those roles, it won't matter, because NOBODY will be able to call those methods. I have to configure the server to use the real users and groups in our internal employee system, and I have to map between our groups and Annie's roles. So let's see... I'll make our Payroll Managers group map to what Annie called "Payroll Admin"...

Dick the Deployer

The **Application Assembler's** job: access control

The App Assembler knows the application. She knows what the methods do, and how they're supposed to be used. The App Assembler knows the abstract roles that make sense logically, for this application. For example, she knows that there's no need for a Marketing role in the payroll application. But she knows that there should be a least three levels of access for the app:

1. People who have full control and can both view and change an employee's payroll data.

2. People who can read everything and modify some things.

3. People who can read some things, but can't modify anything.

So her job is broken into two parts:

① Define the roles

- Figure out which roles makes sense in the application, and come up with names for these roles. Since the App Assembler might not be working in the real environment where the application will run, she's just *making up abstract names*. In other words, her names don't have to correspond to anything in the real world. For all we care, she could name the three roles Clown, Mime, and Juggler. As long as she can describe them well enough for the deployer to figure out which real people belong to those roles, it doesn't matter that the names are made up.

- In the deployment descriptor, define a **<security-role>** element for each role in the application.

- In the deployment descriptor, use the **<role-name>** element to define the made-up name for this role.

② Assign method permissions

- Figure out the methods from the client view to which each of the roles should have access. Remember, the client view includes not only the methods the Bean Provider declared in the home and component interface of the bean, but also the methods of the super interfaces EJBObject, EJBHome, or EJBLocalObject, and EJBLocalHome.

- In the deployment descriptor, define a **<method-permission>** element that lists one or more security roles and one or more methods.

- If she chooses, the App Assembler can can use the **<unchecked/>** element to indicate that a particular method doesn't require any authorization (in other words, *anybody* can call it).

- If she chooses, she can use the **<exclude-list>** element to define a list of methods that nobody can call, ever. In other words, no role will be able to call the methods on the exclude list.

there are no
Dumb Questions

Q: You mention an exclude-list. If nobody will be allowed to call the method, then why is the method there?

A: Remember, beans are reusable components, meant to be assembled in multiple applications. A method that makes sense in one application might not make sense in another. For example, a ProductInventory bean that represents products in a database might have methods for an inventory administrator to add products or change prices, etc., but a client catalog program using that same bean should never need to see anything but the *read-only* methods (i.e. just the *getters*).

Q: I would think that the person writing the beans would be the one who REALLY knows what the roles should be.

A: Remember, beans are reusable components. Yes, we just said that in the previous question, but it works here too. The Bean Provider should not know *exactly* how these beans are being used. If he gets too specific when he designs the code and writes the beans, then the beans probably won't work well outside the specific payroll application that he has in mind.

Only the Application Assembler knows for sure how the different pieces of the application related to one another, and which roles make sense. There is one small exception to this that we'll talk about later in the chapter, when we look at 'programmatic security'.

Sharpen your pencil

Look at the following applications, and try to come up with security roles that might make sense for these applications. Later, we'll figure out which methods each of the roles should be allowed to call.

1. An inventory system for an online store, keeps track of products sold and shipped, inventory levels, and prices.

2. An application for reserving and booking dude ranch vacations, through a travel agent.

3. A rule-based product recommendation system, that asks the user a series of questions, and then gives appropriate advice on which product the user should purchase.

4. An online match-making / personal ad service.

Defining the roles

The ‹security-role› element

Create the security roles in the <assembly-descriptor> part of the deployment descriptor. Remember, the deployment descriptor has two parts:

1. The <enterprise-beans> section that's created by the Bean Provider, and describes each bean in the application.

2. The <assembly-descriptor> part that's created by the App Assembler, and describes characteristics of the application as a whole, including the ways in which beans refer to one another, most security information, and transaction attributes.

```
<assembly-descriptor>

    <security-role>
        <role-name>Payroll Director</role-name>
    </security-role>

    <security-role>
        <role-name>Payroll Admin</role-name>
    </security-role>

    <security-role>
        <role-name>Payroll Assistant</role-name>
    </security-role>
    . . .
</assembly-descriptor>
```

the only element you must have in a
<security-role> element is <role-name>

Defining the roles... a better way

The <security-role> element with descriptions

Descriptions are optional elements for the
<security-role> element.
But think about it.

Think about the poor, overworked, underpaid
deployer (which in reality, is probably you
since chances are good that you're wearing all
three hats: Bean Provider, App Assembler, and
Deployer—and what the heck, probably some
Sys Admin in there too).

He's not a mind-reader.

What's the difference between Payroll Admin and Director? What was she thinking???

```
<assembly-descriptor>

    <security-role>
       <description>
            This role is for the employees who have the
            power to view and change all employee payroll
            information.
       </description>
       <role-name>Payroll Director</role-name>
    </security-role>

    <security-role>
       <description>
            This role is for the employees who have the
            power to view all employee information, and
            change some pieces
       </description>
       <role-name>Payroll Admin</role-name>
    </security-role>

    <security-role>
       <description>
            This role is for the employees who have the
            power to view all employee payroll
            information.
       </description>
       <role-name>Payroll Assistant</role-name>
    </security-role>
    ...
</assembly-descriptor>
```

descriptions make it MUCH easier for the deployer to map the made-up abstract roles to the REAL groups in the company where the application will run.

Defining the method permissions

The <method-permission> element

Everything in a bean's home and component interface is potentially callable by clients. Now that the App Assembler has defined the roles, she can define which methods each role is allowed to call. As she did with the security role definitions, she'll put the method permissions in the `<assembly-descriptor>` section of the deployment descriptor.

```
<assembly-descriptor>

    <method-permission>
        <role-name>Payroll Director</role-name>

        <method>
            <ejb-name>ChangePay</ejb-name>
            <method-name>*</method-name>
        </method>

        <method>
            <ejb-name>Employee</ejb-name>
            <method-name>*</method-name>
        </method>

    </method-permission>


    <method-permission>
        <role-name>Payroll Admin</role-name>

        <method>
            <ejb-name>ChangePay</ejb-name>
            <method-name>reimburse</method-name>
        </method>

        <method>
            <ejb-name>ChangePay</ejb-name>
            <method-name>giveBonus</method-name>
        </method>

        <method>
            <ejb-name>Employee</ejb-name>
            <method-name>getSalary</method-name>
        </method>
        . . .
    </method-permission>
    . . .
</assembly-descriptor>
```

A method permission starts with a role, and then says which methods in which beans this role is allowed to call

this method permission says, "A client in the role of 'Payroll Director' is allowed to call ALL methods in the ChangePay bean's client view (i.e. the home and component interfaces) and ALL methods in the Employee bean's client view.

this permission says "A client in the role of 'Payroll Admin' can call the reimburse and giveBonus methods of the ChangePay bean, and the getSalary method of the Employee bean.

Defining the method permissions

Three different ways to specify methods

You just saw two ways to specify a bean's method name: the wildcard (*) which means ALL methods in the bean, and the actual name of the method. But the name alone isn't always enough. We talked about this before—in the transactions chapter we faced the same problem when we had to specify transaction attributes. What happens if the method is overloaded?

Chances are, your design will treat all versions of an overloaded method in the same way. But there's an optional `<method-params>` element just in case you want, say, a particular security role to have permission for only *one* version of an overloaded method, but not the others.

① By wildcard (*) for ALL methods

```
<method>
    <ejb-name>WorldDomination</ejb-name>
    <method-name>*</method-name>
</method>
```

an asterisk (*) is the wildcard that means ALL methods in the bean's interfaces

② By name alone, for all methods with this name, regardless of arguments or whether they're in the home or component interface

```
<method>
    <ejb-name>WorldDomination</ejb-name>
    <method-name>takeOver</method-name>
</method>
```

this means that ALL overloaded methods named 'takeOver' will be accessible to the role.

③ By name and arguments, to distinguish between overloaded methods

```
<method>
    <ejb-name>WorldDomination</ejb-name>
    <method-name>takeOver</method-name>
    <method-params>
        <method-param>String</method-param>
    </method-params>
</method>
```

this specifies ONLY the takeOver method that takes a String, but no other overloaded versions.

Method permissions interact with one another as a <u>union</u>!

Method permissions do not relate to one another in the same way that transaction attributes do. With transaction attributes, using a wildcard says, "Every method in this bean will have this attribute unless I say otherwise, by naming a specific method in a different container-transaction tag." In other words, naming a specific method overrides the wildcard setting.

But with method permissions, using the wildcard says, "All methods in this bean can be accessed by this role." Nothing else you do in any other method permission will change that.

Transaction attributes

```
<container-transaction>
    <method>
        <ejb-name>BigBean</ejb-name>
        <method-name> * </method-name>
    </method>
    <trans-attribute>RequiresNew</trans-attribute>
</container-transaction>

<container-transaction>
    <method>
        <ejb-name>BigBean</ejb-name>
        <method-name>useOldDatabase</method-name>
    </method>
    <trans-attribute>NotSupported</trans-attribute>
</container-transaction>
```

This says that all methods in BigBean will use the RequiresNew attribute, EXCEPT the useOldDatabase method, which will use the NotSupported attribute.

The second <container-transaction> overrides the wildcard one, and takes the useOldDatabase method *out* of the *RequiresNew* list and moves it to the *NotSupported* list.

Method permissions

```
<method-permission>
    <role-name>Minion</role-name>

        <method>
          <ejb-name>WorldDomination</ejb-name>
          <method-name>*</method-name>
        </method>
</method-permission>

<method-permission>
    <role-name>Boss</role-name>

        <method>
          <ejb-name>WorldDomination</ejb-name>
          <method-name>learnPlan</method-name>
        </method>
</method-permission>
```

This says that the role Minion can access ALL methods of WorldDomination.

AND that the Boss role can access ONLY the learnPlan method of WorldDomination.

The second <method-permission> adds to the first.

Watch out for

Think of as standing in for a <role-name> in a method permission. But because of the way method permissions interact, if you have a method permission defined for a method using , it won't matter what other method permissions you set up for that method. One little and it means the method is free for anyone to call, regardless of their principal or security role!

Method permissions with

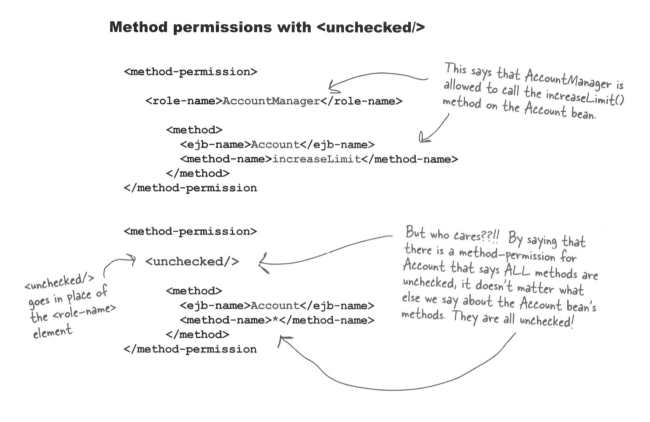

```
<method-permission>

    <role-name>AccountManager</role-name>

        <method>
          <ejb-name>Account</ejb-name>
          <method-name>increaseLimit</method-name>
        </method>
</method-permission>
```

This says that AccountManager is allowed to call the increaseLimit() method on the Account bean.

```
<method-permission>

    <unchecked/>

        <method>
          <ejb-name>Account</ejb-name>
          <method-name>*</method-name>
        </method>
</method-permission>
```

<unchecked/> goes in place of the <role-name> element

But who cares??!! By saying that there is a method-permission for Account that says ALL methods are unchecked, it doesn't matter what else we say about the Account bean's methods. They are all unchecked!

The <unchecked/> element overrides ALL other method permissions for a method.

Wait... I just thought of something else. Suppose I have the same method name in BOTH the home and component interface? And I want them to have different access controls?

How to deal with a bean that has two methods of the same name, but one is in the home interface and the other is in the component interface.

(Yes, we lied, there are actually *four* ways to describe a method: by wildcard (*), by name, by name and parameters, and by name and interface)

```
<method>
    <ejb-name>WorldDomination</ejb-name>
    <method-intf>Remote</method-intf>
    <method-name>takeOver</method-name>
</method>
```

The value of <method-intf> must be one of these four:

```
<method-intf>Remote</method-intf>
```

```
<method-intf>Home</method-intf>
```

```
<method-intf>Local</method-intf>
```

```
<method-intf>LocalHome</method-intf>
```

The `Deployer's` job: mapping actual humans to abstract roles

The App Assembler knows the *application*, but the Deployer knows the *operational environment*. We (and the spec) use the term *operational environment* as a fancy way of saying, *the business where the application is running*. Maybe the company bought the app off-the-shelf. Maybe they built it in-house. Doesn't matter. The Deployer *works* there. He knows the place. Most importantly, he knows how security is managed at the company (for example, the company might have all the employee names and passwords as part of an LDAP system). He's the best person to know how the abstract roles the App Assembler put in should map to real people and groups in his company.

He has two main jobs:

① Assigning the security domain and principal realm to the app

- The company where the app is running has real employees. Somehow, those employees have a way of authenticating themselves to a server, probably with a name and a password. The security information in the operational environment has to be configured into the server, in such a way that the server can tell *who* is actually calling the method.

This happens outside of the EJB specification! In other words, it's vendor-specific.

② Mapping users and/or groups to the abstract security roles

- The App Assembler made up the abstract security roles that best fit the payroll app. But those roles don't mean anything in the company where the app is going to run. The Deployer has to map between what Annie (the App Assembler) defined: Payroll Director, Payroll Admin, Payroll Assistant, to what *really* exists in the Deployer's company: Payroll Manager, Payroll Supervisor, HR Admin.

This, too, happens outside of the EJB specification, in a vendor-specific way.

> **Relax**
>
> **For the exam, you don't need to know HOW the Deployer does this, only that he MUST do these things.**
>
> Remember, the exam doesn't expect you to know about any vendor-specific functionality. But you DO have to know that it is the Deployer's responsibility to do this level of mapping between real humans and the App Assembler's abstract roles.

Note: the spec uses the term "logical security roles" to refer to what we're calling the "abstract security roles", but we like the term "abstract". Just know that "logical security roles" and "abstract security roles" mean the same thing.

Principals and Roles, Users and Groups

Dan Johnsson authenticates to the system (using his login name and password) and is now represented by an instance of type Principal. In a vendor-specific way, the Deployer has told the EJB application that Dan's Principal is associated with one or more roles. So whenever Dan, as the client, calls a method on one of the bean's client interfaces, his Principal (and the roles to which that Principal has been assigned) propagates with the call. That means every call on the (conceptual) call stack will see Dan's Principal as the caller.

In EJB
---

① Principal

abstract actor in the system (usually maps to a person)

The client, authenticated to the system, is represented by a java.security.Principal object. This Principal is an abstract representation of some *thing* associated with a name, but there's no guarantee that the Principal name matches the login name of the client. It all depends on how your system handles security authentication. And don't be too attached to thinking that a Principal is always a unique individual. Sometimes a Principal represents a larger group like, say, SysAdmin. The Principal is associated with one or more abstract security roles that the App Assembler defined. About the only useful thing a bean can do with a Principal object is get its name (aPrincipal.getName()), but that's risky, because you won't be able to know exactly what that name represents unless you know the exact environment in which the bean is running. Yuck.

Manager
KeyAccount
Customer
PayrollDirector
SwedishTeam
SwingDancers

② Role

In EJB, a security role is an abstract role defined by the App Assembler, and although it doesn't match anything in the real world, the Deployer will map real users and groups in the company where the application is running, to the abstract roles. For example, the "Employee" abstract role might map to the "Slaves" group in the Deployer's company.

In the operational environment
---

③ Users

Users are people in the real environment. Real users. Living, breathing, humans. They're represented in the real environment in some way, but of course in EJB we have no way of knowing in advance that, say, the company uses an LDAP server to hold the user security information. Typically, users are mapped to a log-in name and password, and that information is stored somewhere, and if you're lucky and make the right server decision, your EJB server can be configured directly to the system holding your security info. Pretty much the last thing you want to do is sit there and type 10,000 user names and passwords into your EJB server's property files, simply because your EJB server wasn't compatible with whatever your company is using to store user security information.

Customer
PayrollManager
Sweden
SalsaDancers

④ Groups

Typically, security information organizes users into one or more groups, often by department or location. The Deployer can often map directly from groups to abstract security roles, but he might also have to map individual users.

OK, I know I'm not supposed to be thinking about this when I write my code... but there's something bugging me. Looking at the deployment descriptor, it lets you say who can access which bean type. But you can't say which *instance* of that bean type.

I know what he's getting at, because I was thinking the same thing. What do I do if I want employees to be able to have access to some of their own data—but only their OWN data. How do I set individual entity-level control? Otherwise, I'd have to either block ALL employees from these methods, or let ALL employees have access to the methods that would work on ANY entity bean. How can I let the role of 'employee' call, say, getSalary() but only see his OWN salary?

Class-level vs. instance-level security

When <u>declarative</u> security is not enough, you might need <u>programmatic</u> security to restrict access to a specific <u>instance</u> of a bean.

So far, all the security we've looked at has been *declarative*...not hard-coded into the bean class. Declarative security is cool because it supports the whole idea of component-based development—you can customize the bean at deploy-time without touching the code. Company A might be using a bean in one application, and need a particular type of access control that's completely different from the way Company B is using that same bean. Or even two uses of the same bean in the same company might need different access control.

But declarative security is at the class-level. You specify which methods a particular role can call, but it means that role can call the method on ANY instance of the bean class. If you need instance-level security, you can't do it in the deployment descriptor. But you can do programmatic security, which of course you already know... you've seen the two security-related methods in SessionContext and EntityContext.

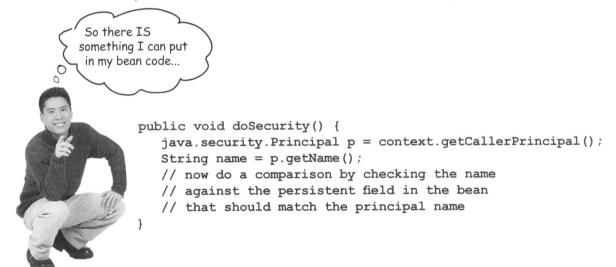

So there IS something I can put in my bean code...

```
public void doSecurity() {
    java.security.Principal p = context.getCallerPrincipal();
    String name = p.getName();
    // now do a comparison by checking the name
    // against the persistent field in the bean
    // that should match the principal name
}
```

But be careful! There is no guarantee that the name coming from the getName() method on the principal matches the user's log-in name. So you have to assume that as soon as you put programmatic security into your bean, you're drastically reducing it's reusability, and portability. And it means the Bean Provider might need to be more tightly-coupled to the operational environment than you'd normally want. Because the Bean Provider is making an assumption that the name coming from the getName() method will match a persistent field in the entity bean, and that might not be true in all environments, depending on how your system handles security.

Using programmatic security to custom-tailor a method

We just looked at getCallerPrincipal(), to see how you could find out exactly WHO the container believes is calling the method. But we can also use the isCallerInRole() method to test whether the principal (*whoever* it is and in this case we don't care) is a member of a specific *role* that we do care about. Imagine that you have a private pricing method, called by one of your business methods, that checks to see if this customer authenticated as a member of your special VIP customer group. If he is, you treat him differently than if he isn't. Maybe you give him a discount. Maybe you raise the price. Whatever your business logic tells you to do.

```
private void determinePrice() {

    if (context.isCallerInRole("VIPCustomer")) {
      // treat customer well
    } else {
      // treat him like the loser he is
    }
}
```

Besides the obvious problem with hard-coding security information (cuts down your reuse, increases the chances that things won't work in a portable way, etc.), there's another big problem—how the heck does the Bean Provider know in advance what roles the App Assembler is going to assign?

He doesn't. Or at least, he probably shouldn't. We know, we know. In reality, the Bean Provider and App Assembler are, if not the same person, closely related (professionally-speaking, of course). But we're still pushing for a component-based development model here, and at the very least, we want the App Assembler to take what the Bean Provider has done and somehow fit it into her own application. And that might mean integrating the bean with beans from other providers.

So now imagine this scenario: Annie the App Assembler is building a new app from four existing beans, two of which came from different providers. Providers who didn't work for the same company or know one another. *How could they have communicated in advance*, to know which roles Annie was going to choose for her application?

> With isCallerInRole(), you can use security information to tailor the way a method runs, depending on which role called the method.
>
> This is usually NOT a good way to handle security. To control access to a method, you're much better off using the method permissions to stop an unauthorized role from ever calling the method.
>
> But you can still USE the caller's role information to do other non-security things in your code.

The problem with isCallerInRole()...

the Bean Provider hard codes a role name, but how does he know what roles the App Assembler will use? And what if there's more than one Bean Provider?

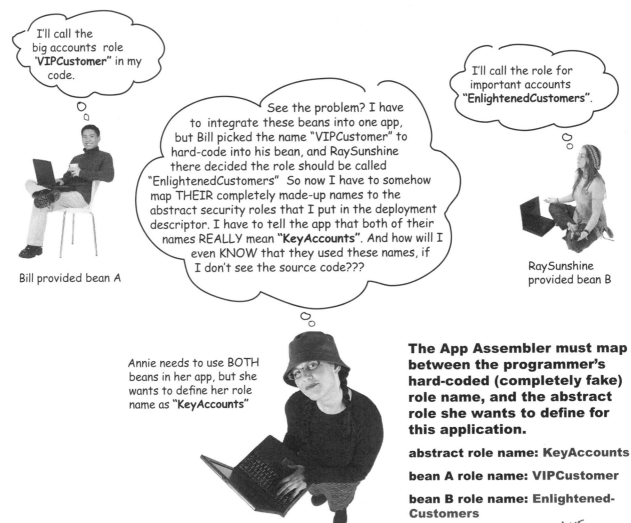

I'll call the big accounts role **'VIPCustomer'** in my code.

I'll call the role for important accounts **"EnlightenedCustomers"**.

See the problem? I have to integrate these beans into one app, but Bill picked the name "VIPCustomer" to hard-code into his bean, and RaySunshine there decided the role should be called "EnlightenedCustomers" So now I have to somehow map THEIR completely made-up names to the abstract security roles that I put in the deployment descriptor. I have to tell the app that both of their names REALLY mean **"KeyAccounts"**. And how will I even KNOW that they used these names, if I don't see the source code???

Bill provided bean A

RaySunshine provided bean B

Annie needs to use BOTH beans in her app, but she wants to define her role name as **"KeyAccounts"**

The App Assembler must map between the programmer's hard-coded (completely fake) role name, and the abstract role she wants to define for this application.

abstract role name: KeyAccounts

bean A role name: VIPCustomer

bean B role name: Enlightened-Customers

three different names for the SAME role!! Annie wants the deployer to map REAL customer groups to "KeyAccounts" and not those other two names, but those names are in code, and she can't touch the Java source code!

Map declarative security roles to the programmer's hard-coded (fake) roles

The App Assembler maps between security role *references* (hard-coded role names the programmer made up) and security *roles* (abstract role names she chose for this app) using the **<role-link>** element.

Bean Provider

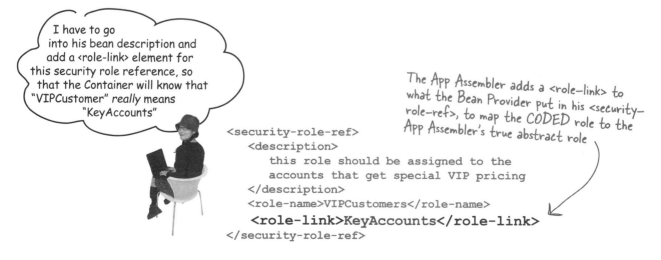

> Oh yeah... the App Assembler needs to know that I put a role name in my code. I'll make a security role **reference** in the DD I make for this bean...

The Bean Provider has to TELL the App Assembler what he did in code, by putting in a <security-role-ref> tag

```
<enterprise-beans>
    <session>
        <ejb-name>ShoppingCart</ejb-name>
        . . .
        <security-role-ref>
            <description>
                this role should be assigned to the
                accounts that get special VIP pricing
            </description>
            <role-name>VIPCustomer</role-name>
        </security-role-ref>
        . . .
    </session>
</enterprise-beans>
```

These names must MATCH. You don't put in the 'real' role name, you put in the one you used as the argument to isCallerInRole()

```
context.isCallerInRole("VIPCustomer")
```

App Assembler

> I have to go into his bean description and add a <role-link> element for this security role reference, so that the Container will know that "VIPCustomer" *really* means "KeyAccounts"

The App Assembler adds a <role-link> to what the Bean Provider put in his <security-role-ref>, to map the CODED role to the App Assembler's true abstract role

```
<security-role-ref>
    <description>
        this role should be assigned to the
        accounts that get special VIP pricing
    </description>
    <role-name>VIPCustomers</role-name>
    <role-link>KeyAccounts</role-link>
</security-role-ref>
```

The complete security mapping picture

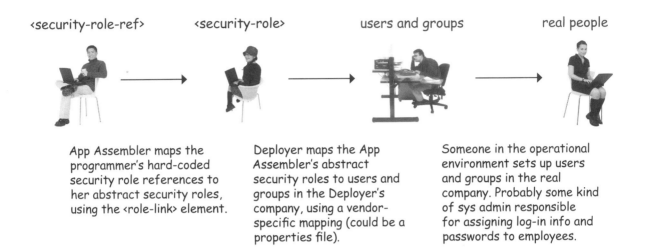

<security-role-ref>	<security-role>	users and groups	real people

App Assembler maps the programmer's hard-coded security role references to her abstract security roles, using the <role-link> element.

Deployer maps the App Assembler's abstract security roles to users and groups in the Deployer's company, using a vendor-specific mapping (could be a properties file).

Someone in the operational environment sets up users and groups in the real company. Probably some kind of sys admin responsible for assigning log-in info and passwords to employees.

Where and how the mapping happens

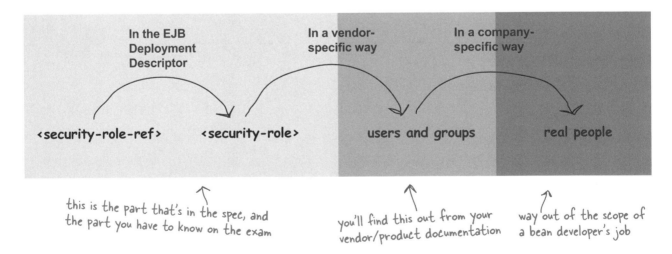

In the EJB Deployment Descriptor

In a vendor-specific way

In a company-specific way

<security-role-ref>   <security-role>   users and groups   real people

this is the part that's in the spec, and the part you have to know on the exam

you'll find this out from your vendor/product documentation

way out of the scope of a bean developer's job

Use <run-as> security identity to pretend someone <u>else</u> is calling...

When a client calls a method, the Container always knows the client's Principal, which includes the abstract security roles the Deployer assigned to that Principal. And remember, the caller's security context is propagated throughout the application as the client's original method goes about doing its work. Each method called in the conceptual call stack will get the security context along with the call.

But... let's say that you don't want the client's security context to keep propagating. Let's say that when the client calls Bean A, and Bean A in turn calls Bean B, you want Bean B to think that someone else is calling. In other words, what if you want Bean A to pretend to be someone else? That way, any bean that Bean A calls will think the Principal (and roles) of the caller is something other than the original client's.

Why would you do this? Bean B might have tighter access control. Perhaps Bean B won't allow outside clients to call its methods, so it doesn't have method permissions set up for any of the abstract roles mapped to clients users and groups. But perhaps you have a special role set-up just for other beans, and Bean B will take calls from other beans, as long as those beans are in that role.

Now whenever *I* call another bean in the application, that bean thinks I'm someone special. Someone cooler. Someone with power, who can really GO places. Someone a LOT more interesting than the *client* who called the business method that started all this...

When you want the bean to BE someone other than the calling client

```
<enterprise-beans>
   <session>
      <ejb-name>BeanA</ejb-name>
      ...
      <security-identity>
         <run-as>
            <role-name>SuperBean</role-name>
         </run-as>
      </security-identity>
      ...
   </session>
</enterprise-beans>
```

role-name must match a real abstract security-role set up by the App Assembler

Explicitly saying that you want the calling client's identity to be used

```
<enterprise-beans>
   <session>
      <ejb-name>BeanA</ejb-name>
      ...
      <security-identity>
         <use-caller-identity/>
      </security-identity>
      ...
   </session>
</enterprise-beans>
```

This is what you get by default, if you don't put in a <security-identity> element at all. So you don't have to say this, but you can.

Security context propagation with <run-as>

Client calls with a security context that says she's a member of the "customers" role.

Rather than propagate the client's security identity, Bean A takes on the role of 'SuperBean', then calls a method on Bean B.

Bean B doesn't know about the original client, and thinks the caller's security identity is 'SuperBean'. Unless Bean B has its OWN run-as identity, it will propagate 'SuperBean' with any calls Bean B makes on other beans.

Bean A

Still Bean A, but now running as '**SuperBean**'

Bean B

Client in the 'customers' role

Message-driven beans must NOT say <use-caller-identity/>!!

Which caller would that be? Message-driven beans don't HAVE a calling client! So watch out for a deployment descriptor that shows a message-driven bean with a security identity that says <use-caller-identity/>. However, message-driven beans CAN have a <run-as> identity. And while we're here, don't forget that a message-driven bean must never try to ask its MessageDrivenContext for the calling client's security identity. A <security-identity> doesn't specify who the bean thinks is calling IT, but rather who the bean pretends to be when it makes calls to OTHER beans.

Bean A's <security-identity> is not about who Bean A should see as its caller, but rather what Bean B will see when Bean A calls it.

In other words, <security-identity> is not about changing the incoming client identity, but about changing what the bean propagates as the outgoing identity, when the bean calls other beans.

(Like registering at a hotel under the name "Jennifer Lopez", when you're ACTUALLY "Simon Roberts"... and the hotel clerk can't tell. As far as he is concerned, you're J–Lo.)

Mock Exam

---

1 What's true about security for EJBs? (Choose all that apply.)

❏ A. All security policies must be expressed declaratively.

❏ B. The default security principal under which a method invocation is performed is that of the component's creator.

❏ C. Using EJBs, method permissions can be declared using EJB QL in the deployment descriptor.

❏ D. Security authorization can be bypassed on a method by method basis.

❏ E. Security authorization can be bypassed on an instance by instance basis.

---

2 What's true about methods that should run without being checked for authorization? (Choose all that apply.)

❏ A. They can be listed in the <exclude-list> element.

❏ B. They can be listed in the <unchecked> element.

❏ C. When the <unchecked> element is used, it should be placed where the <role-name> element normally occurs in the deployment descriptor.

❏ D. When a method permission relation specifies both <unchecked> and a security role, the container will use the security role.

---

3 Which role(s) should typically define the appropriate security policies for an application? (Choose all that apply.)

❏ A. bean provider

❏ B. application assembler

❏ C. deployer

❏ D. system administrator

❏ E. server provider

4 In which of the following methods can a stateful session bean invoke the `isCallerInRole` method in order to perform a security check? (Choose all that apply.)

❏ A. `ejbCreate()`

❏ B. `ejbActivate()`

❏ C. `ejbPassivate()`

❏ D. None of the above

5 Which are the bean provider's responsibilities when making an application secure? (Choose all that apply.)

❏ A. Assigning the security domain to the application.

❏ B. Authentication of principals.

❏ C. Mapping the principals used by the client to the principals defined for the bean.

❏ D. None of the above.

6 In which of the following methods can a CMP entity bean invoke the getCallerPrincipal() method in order to perform a security check? (Choose all that apply.)

❏ A. `ejbCreate()`

❏ B. `ejbActivate()`

❏ C. `ejbPassivate()`

❏ D. `ejbPostCreate()`

❏ E. Business methods

7 In which of the following methods can a BMP entity bean invoke the `getCallerPrincipal()` method in order to perform a security check? (Choose all that apply.)

❏ A. `ejbLoad()`

❏ B. `ejbStore()`

❏ C. `ejbPassivate()`

❏ D. `ejbPostCreate()`

❏ E. Business methods

8 When describing method permissions in the deployment descriptor for a specific bean, what's true? (Choose all that apply.)

   ❏ A. A wild-card character can refer to all of the bean's methods.

   ❏ B. Individual overloaded methods cannot be distinguished from each other.

   ❏ C. A method in the home interface cannot be distinguished from a method with the same name in the component interface.

   ❏ D. Individual methods can be referred to.

9 The **\<role-name\>** element can be used within what other security related deployment descriptor element(s)? (Choose all that apply.)

   ❏ A. **\<security-role\>**

   ❏ B. **\<run-as\>**

   ❏ C. **\<method-name\>**

   ❏ D. **\<exclude-list\>**

   ❏ E. **\<security-role-ref\>**

10 Which roles have what responsibilities when implementing security for EJB applications? (Choose all that apply.)

   ❏ A. The Application Assembler typically specifies when run-as identity should be used in an application.

   ❏ B. The Bean Provider maps security role references to security roles.

   ❏ C. The Bean Provider is typically responsible for assigning the security domain and principal realm to the application.

   ❏ D. The Deployer maps security role references to security roles.

11 Within the **\<security-role-ref\>** deployment descriptor element, which sub-elements are optional? (Choose all that apply.)

   ❏ A. **\<role-name\>**

   ❏ B. **\<role-link\>**

   ❏ C. **\<description\>**

   ❏ D. None of the above are optional

Mock Exam Answers

(spec: 434–435)

1 What's true about security for EJBs? (Choose all that apply.)

❏ A. All security policies must be expressed declaratively.

❏ B. The default security principal under which a method invocation is performed is that of the component's creator.

❏ C. Using EJBs, method permissions can be declared using EJB QL in the deployment descriptor.

☑ D. Security authorization can be bypassed on a method by method basis.

❏ E. Security authorization can be bypassed on an instance by instance basis.

(spec: 443)

2 What's true about methods that should run without being checked for authorization? (Choose all that apply.)

❏ A. They can be listed in the <exclude-list> element. – For methods that must NEVER be called

☑ B. They can be listed in the <unchecked> element.

☑ C. When the <unchecked> element is used, it should be placed where the <role-name> element normally occurs in the deployment descriptor.

❏ D. When a method permission relation specifies both <unchecked> and a security role, the container will use the security role.

(spec: 435–436)

3 Which role(s) should typically define the appropriate security policies for an application? (Choose all that apply.)

❏ A. bean provider

☑ B. application assembler

☑ C. deployer

❏ D. system administrator

❏ E. server provider

4 In which of the following methods can a stateful session bean invoke the *(spec: 80)*
isCallerInRole method in order to perform a security check? (Choose all
that apply.)

☑ A. ejbCreate()

☑ B. ejbActivate()

☑ C. ejbPassivate()

☐ D. None of the above

---

5 Which are the bean provider's responsibilities when making an application *(spec: 448-454)*
secure? (Choose all that apply.)

☐ A. Assigning the security domain to the application. Typically the Deployer's job

☐ B. Authentication of principals.

☐ C. Mapping the principals used by the client to the principals defined for
the bean.

☑ D. None of the above.

---

6 In which of the following methods can a CMP entity bean invoke the *(spec: 179-180)*
getCallerPrincipal() method in order to perform a security check? (Choose
all that apply.)

☑ A. ejbCreate()

☐ B. ejbActivate()   — who would the client be?

☐ C. ejbPassivate()

☑ D. ejbPostCreate()

☑ E. Business methods

---

7 In which of the following methods can a BMP entity bean invoke the *(spec: 257)*
getCallerPrincipal() method in order to perform a security check?
(Choose all that apply.)

☑ A. ejbLoad()

☑ B. ejbStore()

☐ C. ejbPassivate() — who would the client be?

☑ D. ejbPostCreate()

☑ E. Business methods

8 When describing method permissions in the deployment descriptor for a specific bean, what's true? (Choose all that apply.)

(spec: 444)

☑ A. A wild-card character can refer to all of the bean's methods.

☐ B. Individual overloaded methods cannot be distinguished from each other.

The <method-intf> element does this

☐ C. A method in the home interface cannot be distinguished from a method with the same name in the component interface.

☑ D. Individual methods can be referred to.

9 The **<role-name>** element can be used within what other security related deployment descriptor element(s)? (Choose all that apply.)

(spec: 444-447)

☑ A. **<security-role>**

☑ B. **<run-as>**

☐ C. **<method-name>**

☐ D. **<exclude-list>**

☑ E. **<security-role-ref>**

10 Which roles have what responsibilities when implementing security for EJB applications? (Choose all that apply.)

(spec: 446-449)

☑ A. The Application Assembler typically specifies when run-as identity should be used in an application.

☐ B. The Bean Provider maps security role references to security roles.

Usually defined by the Application assembler

☐ C. The Bean Provider is typically responsible for assigning the security domain and principal realm to the application.

☐ D. The Deployer maps security role references to security roles.

11 Within the **<security-role-ref>** deployment descriptor element, which sub-elements are optional? (Choose all that apply.)

(spec: 527)

☐ A. **<role-name>**

☑ B. **<role-link>** *Usually defined by the Application assembler*

☑ C. **<description>**

☐ D. None of the above are optional

12 a bean's environment

The Joy of Deployment

You worked hard on that bean. You coded, you compiled, you tested. About a hundred zillion times. The *last* thing you want to touch is already-tested source code, just because something simple changed in the deployment configuration. Maybe the name of the database is different. Maybe you hard-coded a tax-rate (remember—bean's can't access property files). And what if you don't even *have* the source code? Maybe you got it from Beans-r-Us, and they won't sell you the source (not on *your* budget, anyway). EJB supports bean reuse through the Deployment Descriptor and a bean's special *environment*.

A Bean's Environment

| *Official:* | *What it really means:* |

13.1 Identify correct and incorrect statements or examples about an enterprise bean's JNDI naming.

13.2 Identify correct and incorrect statements about the purpose and/or use of the deployment descriptor elements for environment entries, EJB references, resource manager connection factory references, including whether a given code listing is appropriate and correct with respect to a particular DD element.

13.3 Given a list of responsibilities, identify which belong to the Deployer, Bean Provider, App Assembler, Container, Sys Admin, or any combination.

1.2 Given a list of technology specifications, identify which are requirements for an EJB 2.0 container.

1.3 Identify correct and incorrect statements or examples about EJB programming restrictions.

1.4 Match EJB roles with the corresponding description of the role's responsibilities, where the description may include deployment descriptor information.

1.5 Given a list, identify which are requirements for an ejb-jar file.

You must know the ways in which a bean can be customized at deployment time, without changing source code. When a bean does a JNDI lookup using the bean's own special environment, you must know how the code relates to what's in the deployment descriptor, and a bunch of finicky details that mean the difference between a successful deployment or one that won't deploy. Or much worse... one that deploys but blows up sometime later, while its running.

You need to know what *is* and is *not* guaranteed by the EJB 2.0 specification. For example, an EJB 2.0 container is *not* required to support JXTA, JMX,Servlets or JSPs, but it *is* required to support JNDI, JMS, and JAXP. You need to know what EJB really gives you.

You also need to know what you can and cannot do in EJB, if you want to make a bean that is portable across all EJB 2.0-compliant containers. For example, you can't *listen* on a ServerSocket, but you *can* create a client Socket. You *can't* access the server's local file system, or make your own threads. But you *can* make your bean class extend another.

You need to know about the EJB roles (Bean Provider, Application Assembler, etc.) and who does what during development and deployment. Although you won't have many questions about this, it's an area the exam beta testers struggled with, so if we were you, we'd study this part carefully.

Finally, you must know what *is* and is *not* supposed to be in an ejb-jar file. For example, the home and component interface **must** be there (unless you're using a message-driven bean), but the stubs must **not** be there.

I just LOVE to change source code. That's why I have a high-paying job working in a respected IT company... cafeteria.

Raise your hand if you like changing your source code every time you need to change the way your bean behaves.

Of course you don't like going back to your source code just because, say, somebody changed the name of the database. You already know that you can change transaction attributes and security access just by tweaking the deployment descriptor. But wait... *there's more!*

Every EJB container gives your bean its own special environment, that your bean can use to look up four different things:

- **Environment Entries**
  These are deploy-time values (so you don't have to code in values like the current discount percentage or tax rate).

- **Resource Manager Connection Factories**
  You'll use these to get a connection to a database.

- **Enterprise Bean References**
  When one bean wants to look up another bean. You'll do this a lot! Most designs involve at least some level of bean-to-bean communication.

- **Resource Environment References**
  You'll use this to get a reference to something called "an administered object" from the server, like a JMS destination.

A bean's special place- java:comp/env

Your bean is entitled to a JNDI context all its own. A special
place that's just for your bean, where your bean can look things
up. It all starts with an InitialContext, but the java:comp/env
subcontext is where the bean begins navigating when he wants
to look something up.

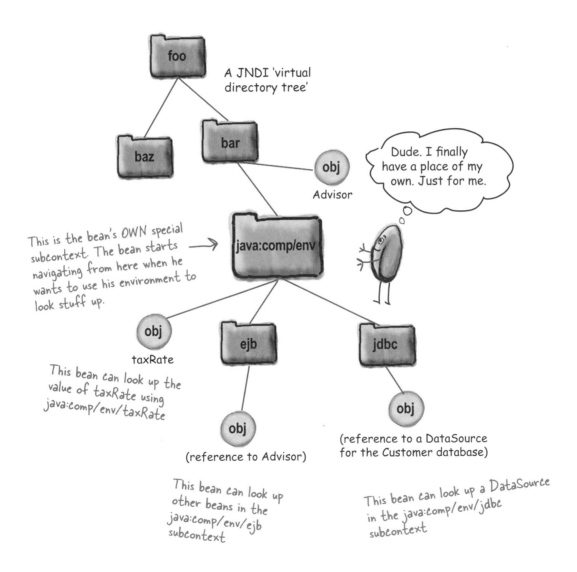

A JNDI 'virtual
directory tree'

Advisor

Dude. I finally
have a place of my
own. Just for me.

This is the bean's OWN special
subcontext. The bean starts
navigating from here when he
wants to use his environment to
look stuff up.

taxRate

This bean can look up the
value of taxRate using
java:comp/env/taxRate

(reference to Advisor)

(reference to a DataSource
for the Customer database)

This bean can look up
other beans in the
java:comp/env/ejb
subcontext

This bean can look up a DataSource
in the java:comp/env/jdbc
subcontext

But it's not per bean <u>instance</u>... It's per bean <u>home</u>

The scope of a bean's environment is for all beans from the same home. If you deployed a particular bean type into your server three times, each of the three deployments would have it's own unique home, so there'd be three different environments.

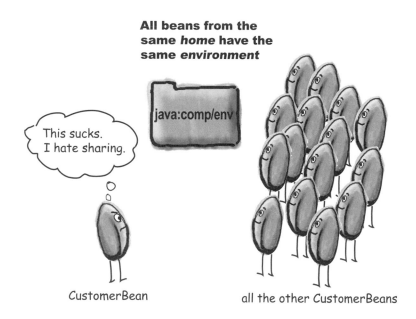

All beans from the same *home* have the same *environment*

This sucks. I hate sharing.

CustomerBean

all the other CustomerBeans

```
InitialContext ic = new InitialContext();
Double discount =  (Double) ic.lookup("java:comp/env/custDiscount");
```

This value will be the same no matter which instance of CustomerBean runs this code.

Environment subcontexts

java:comp/env/jdbc/CustomerDB

the private environment for this bean type

A subcontext we named 'jdbc' by convention (although 'jdbc' is not required, and we could have said java:comp/env/CustomerDB

The name of the 'thing' you're looking up (in this case, resource connection factory to the 'CustomerDB' database)

in a bean's business method:

```
InitialContext ic = new InitialContext();
DataSource ds =  (DataSource) ic.lookup("java:comp/env/jdbc/CustomerDB");
Connection conn = ds.getConnection();
```

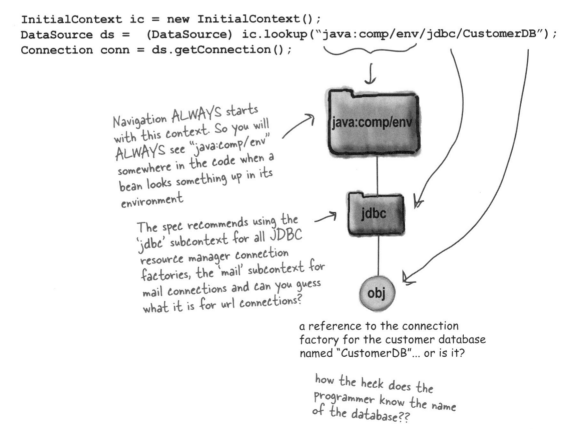

Navigation ALWAYS starts with this context. So you will ALWAYS see "java:comp/env" somewhere in the code when a bean looks something up in its environment

The spec recommends using the 'jdbc' subcontext for all JDBC resource manager connection factories, the 'mail' subcontext for mail connections and can you guess what it is for url connections?

a reference to the connection factory for the customer database named "CustomerDB"... or is it?

how the heck does the programmer know the name of the database??

> Deja vu... it's the same issue we had with security. I have to put SOMETHING in code, but I don't know the real name of the database. Hmmmm....

How can we deal with this? How does the programmer hard-code a lookup String like "java:comp/env/jdbc/CustomerDB" without knowing how the database was configured into the server?

(hint: how did we deal with it earlier when the Bean Provider used programmatic security with isCallerInRole("someRole")?)

It's simple...
if the programmer puts a made-up JNDI name in code, he has to <u>announce</u> that to the deployer in the DD.

The Deployer has *no* clue what the Bean Provider put in code, unless the Bean Provider:

A. Tells him.

B. Writes the names on a sticky note and sticks it on the Deployer's monitor or

C. Declares references in the Deployment Descriptor, complete with helpful descriptions that make it very clear what the Deployer is supposed to map to the programmer's made-up names.

The deployer gets really pissed off if you don't declare your JNDI lookup strings in the deployment descriptor. Ask me about the fight we had last month. Seriously. Ask me...

He better declare all his JNDI environment references in the DD, so I can map them to REAL names that only I know. And if he doesn't, I'll show him what three years of Pilates can do.

Declares the made-up JNDI names in the Deployment Descriptor, for the Deployer.

Maps the programmer's made-up/fake names to the REAL JNDI names under which the resources were deployed or configured into the server.

Environment entries: deploy-time constants

Imagine you're writing a simple checkout bean for an online shopping cart system. You don't know where that bean might end up. Even if you do, you know that things like tax rates and discount policies can change, even within the same company.

Environment entries let you write your code using a variable that you'll fill in at runtime using a JNDI lookup. Remember, the Bean Provider chooses the name, and it's up to the Deployer to fill in the value.

this is the part of the lookup that must go in the DD

in a bean's business method:

```
InitialContext ic = new InitialContext();
Double dbl =  (Double) ic.lookup("java:comp/env/smartCustomerDiscount");
customerDiscount = dbl.doubleValue();
// use the primitive double value to calculate the discount
```

in the Deployment Descriptor

You do NOT put the "java:comp/env/" part in the deployment descriptor. Ever! In the DD, you put ONLY the part that comes after the "java:comp/env/"

```
<entity>
    . . .
    <env-entry>
        <description>discount for smart customers</description>
        <env-entry-name>smartCustomerDiscount</env-entry-name>
        <env-entry-type>java.lang.Double</env-entry-type>
        <env-entry-value>0.05</env-entry-value>
    </env-entry>
    . . .
</entity>
```

The programmer made up this name

if you have any compassion at all, you'll put in a description for the poor Deployer.

the type must be either a String or a wrapper class

The value is optional for the Bean Provider, but he can use this element to supply a default. But the Deployer MUST ensure that there's a valid value before the bean is deployed.

Environment entries are different from the other customizations in that the Deployer doesn't map from the Bean Provider's name to some other real name. Environment entries don't exist until the Bean Provider says they do, by putting in the <env-entry>. As long as the <env-entry> has a value when its deployed, the environment entry will be created.

> **BANG!** **You can't change a value dynamically!**
>
> *Once a bean has been deployed, there is NO WAY to change the value of the environment variable! The only way to update the value a bean sees is to redeploy the bean with the new DD.*

there are no
Dumb Questions

Q: Why can't you just use Java property files instead of environment entries?

A: You're not allowed to use properties because you can't access the file system to read them in, and you don't have any control over system properties (for example, you have no way to set a property as a JVM command-line argument.)

Q: Why can't I have an environment entry that's shared among multiple beans in the same app? Or at least within the same ejb-jar?

A: Because... because you can't. There's simply no mechanism for sharing the bean's environment because that would defeat the whole purpose of the bean having his own private space. Having a bean's environment prevents what would be an extremely likely disaster: naming collisions between different beans! In other words, different beans deployed with environment entries (or other references) that use the same name.

If you have a shared resource or environment entry, you MUST configure it with each bean you deploy. This is NOT per Deployment Descriptor, but per every individual bean, regardless of where the bean lives.

**Environment entries must
be one of these types:**

- String
- Byte
- Short
- Integer
- Long
- Float
- Double
- Character
- Boolean

**Only Strings
and wrappers
are allowed for
environment
entries**

You MUST know the scope of an environment entry!

You're expected to know that environment entries are private and unique to each home. If you deploy an environment entry 'foo' with a value of 10, for the Customer bean, all instances of CustomerBean will get that same value when they do a lookup using java:comp/env/foo from a business method.

But your environment entry 'foo' does NOT cause a naming collision with any other BEAN type that's been deployed with the same environment entry name. *Customer bean's 'foo' is not the same as Advice bean's 'foo', even though the lookup strings are identical: ic.lookup("java:comp/env/foo") and even if both beans are in the same ejb-jar or enterprise archive (.ear).*

But we're not done yet... a single bean type must NOT be deployed with more than one 'thing' of the same name. So you can't call an environment entry 'foo' and a resource manager connection factory 'foo' in the Customer bean. As long as you use subcontexts, though, you're OK. Because 'jdbc/foo' is different from just 'foo' alone. So you CAN have both:
java:comp/env/foo
and
java:comp/env/jdbc/foo
but NOT two things named:

java:comp/env/foo, even if those two things are different resource types.

It's subcontexts all the way down

Remember, your java:comp/env space is just a subcontext. A special one, sure, but still a context. So you can save that in a Context variable, and save yourself from having to retype "java:comp.env" every frickin' time you want to look something up.

Saving your special environment context:

```
InitialContext ic = new InitialContext();
Context mySpecialPlace = (Context) ic.lookup("java:comp/env");
// now look something up on mySpecialPlace
Double dbl =  (Double) mySpecialPlace.lookup("smartCustomerDiscount");
```

java:comp/env

taxInfo

obj

taxRate

Using a subcontext

taxInfo is a subcontext, of the bean's environment

```
InitialContext ic = new InitialContext();
Context myTaxInfoCtx = (Context) ic.lookup("java:comp/env/taxInfo");
// now look something up on myTaxInfoCtx subcontext
Double dbl =  (Double) myTaxInfoCtx.lookup("taxRate");
```

taxRate is an object within the taxInfo subcontext

Note: you don't need to narrow anything coming out of JNDI lookups EXCEPT for stubs (Remote home interface references), so all you need is a plain old cast.

Creating a subcontext

A subcontext exists simply because you say it does. If you type "java:comp/env/foo/bar" into your lookup code, you've said, "There is a subcontext in my environment named "foo", and it contains the object "bar". As long as you use the same subcontext in the deployment descriptor when you deploy the bean, the subcontext will magically exist, just because you said it does. In other words, you don't have to go through a process of somehow creating a new JNDI context and naming it. Act like it's there, and it's there. Don't you wish everything worked that way?

In the DD for the environment entry name, anything followed by a slash automatically becomes a subcontext!

```
<env-entry-name>taxInfo/taxRate</env-entry-name>
```

putting "taxInfo/" before "taxRate" automatically creates the taxRate subcontext when this bean is deployed

Resource manager connection factories (think: *database*)

Any bean can use a database. In fact, even an entity bean with container-managed persistence can get a connection to a database, as long as its using that database for something other than managing its own persistence. The code is simple: look up a DataSource, and ask it for a Connection. Once you have a Connection, you can send JDBC statements to do your SQL. Although javax.sql.DataSource is by far the most commonly-used resource manager connection factory, you can have others including a mail or URL connection.

in a bean's business method:

```
InitialContext ic = new InitialContext();
DataSource ds =  (DataSource)ic.lookup("java:comp/env/jdbc/CustomerDB");
Connection conn = ds.getConnection();
// use the connection to do JDBC
```

this is the part of the lookup that must go in the DD

in the Deployment Descriptor

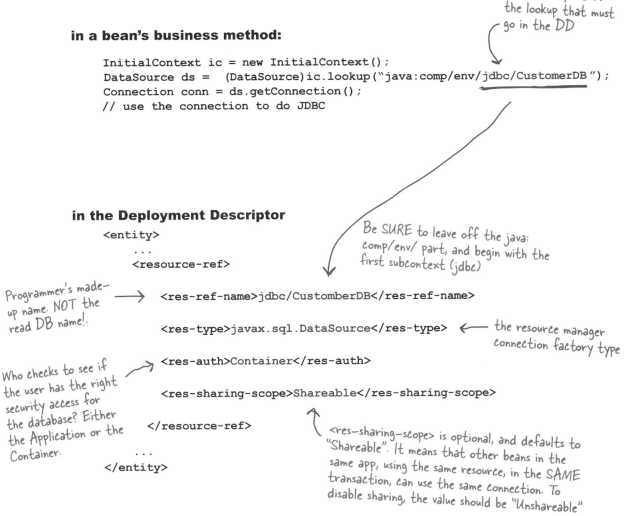

```
<entity>
    ...
    <resource-ref>

        <res-ref-name>jdbc/CustomberDB</res-ref-name>

        <res-type>javax.sql.DataSource</res-type>

        <res-auth>Container</res-auth>

        <res-sharing-scope>Shareable</res-sharing-scope>

    </resource-ref>
    ...
</entity>
```

Be SURE to leave off the java: comp/env/ part, and begin with the first subcontext (jdbc)

Programmer's made-up name. NOT the read DB name!.

the resource manager connection factory type

Who checks to see if the user has the right security access for the database? Either the Application or the Container.

<res-sharing-scope> is optional, and defaults to "Shareable". It means that other beans in the same app, using the same resource, in the SAME transaction, can use the same connection. To disable sharing, the value should be "Unshareable"

Resource manager connection factory types

You can't put arbitrary types into the DD. For the four standard resource manager connection factories (five, if you count JMS topics and queues as two different types), you must use one of the following:

(1) `<res-type>javax.sql.DataSource</res-type>`

(2) `<res-type>javax.jms.QueueConnectionFactory</res-type>`
`<res-type>javax.jms.TopicConnectionFactory</res-type>`

(3) `<res-type>javax.mail.Session</res-type>`

http://www.headfirst.com **(4)** `<res-type>java.net.URL</res-type>`

Although these four are the only types standard to EJB 2.0, you can use the Connector architecture if you need access to other resources, like legacy systems. Connectors are out of scope for this book (and the exam), so you can relax. But you do need to know it's out there, if you need it.

Resource authorization

Authentication to the EJB server itself is one thing, but chances are, the database has its own log-in scheme. A user might need a log-in name and password that is different from the one he uses to authenticate to the EJB server.
As a Bean Provider, you can choose between two ways to give the resource manager (such as a database) the user's log-in data.

(1) `<res-auth>Container</res-auth>`

Container authorization means the Deployer must configure the sign-on information for the resource manager. It's completely vendor and resource-specific, and might mean that the deployer has to map between the principals and roles used in EJB security to whatever the resource manager needs. At the simplest level, the Deployer might specify a name and password that'll let anybody in.

(2) `<res-auth>Application</res-auth>`

Application authorization means the programmer uses the overloaded version of getConnection() that takes a name and a password:

```
Connection conn = ds.getConnection(userName, password);
```

The complete resource mapping picture

fake JNDI name:

<resource-ref>**CustDB**</resource-ref>   actual JNDI name: **CustDatabase**   REAL database name: **CustomerData**

sys–admin

In code, the Bean Provider does a JNDI lookup on a DataSource (which he uses to get a database connection). He doesn't know the real JNDI name of the database (and he DEFINITELY doesn't know actual database name), so he makes one up. But he tells the deployer what he's done, by declaring a <resource-ref> element in the DD.

Deployer maps the Bean Provider's made-up <resource-ref> name to the actual JNDI name under which the DataSource is registered.

The Sys-Admin (or someone in the operational environment configures the database into the server, and gives it a JNDI name.

Where and how the mapping happens

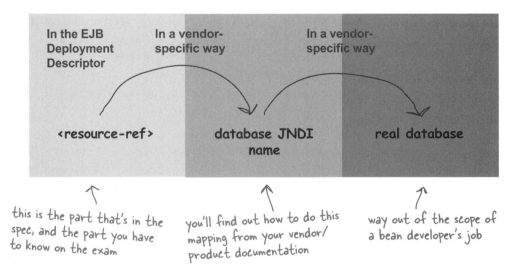

In the EJB Deployment Descriptor   **In a vendor-specific way**   **In a vendor-specific way**

<resource-ref>   database JNDI name   real database

this is the part that's in the spec, and the part you have to know on the exam

you'll find out how to do this mapping from your vendor/ product documentation

way out of the scope of a bean developer's job

EJB references
(when a bean wants another bean)

Beans who need other beans are the luckiest beans in the server. But
remember, beans have to go through the home interface just like everybody
else. If Bean A wants to do a JNDI lookup on Bean B's home, we've got the
same problem as always—what's Bean B's JNDI name? As a Bean Provider,
you're just making one up. At deploy time, the Deployer will map your
fake coded name to the real JNDI name matching a bean of the type you
specified in the DD.

*"ejb/AdviceGiver" must go in the
DD (without the quotes). Remember,
when coding you have no idea what
the REAL name will be...*

in a bean's business method:

```
InitialContext ic = new InitialContext();
Object o =  ic.lookup("java:comp/env/ejb/AdviceGiver");
AdviceHome home = (AdviceHome) PortableRemoteObject.narrow(o, AdviceHome.class);
Advice advisor = home.create();
// call methods on Advisor
```

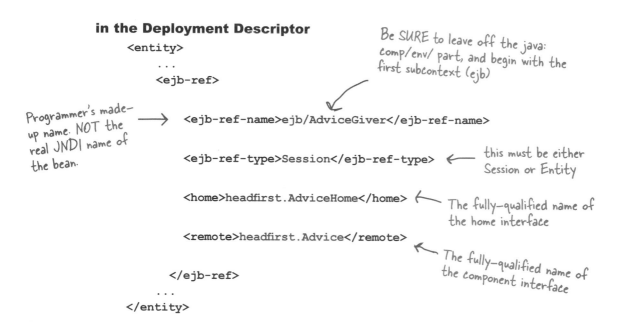

in the Deployment Descriptor

*Be SURE to leave off the java:
comp/env/ part, and begin with the
first subcontext (ejb)*

```
<entity>
    ...
    <ejb-ref>

        <ejb-ref-name>ejb/AdviceGiver</ejb-ref-name>

        <ejb-ref-type>Session</ejb-ref-type>

        <home>headfirst.AdviceHome</home>

        <remote>headfirst.Advice</remote>

    </ejb-ref>
    ...
</entity>
```

*Programmer's made-
up name. NOT the
real JNDI name of
the bean.*

*this must be either
Session or Entity*

*The fully-qualified name of
the home interface*

*The fully-qualified name of
the component interface*

EJB local references

Use the <ejb-local-ref> tag if you want to look up the bean's *local* home.

```
<ejb-local-ref>

    <ejb-ref-name>ejb/AdviceGiver</ejb-ref-name>

    <ejb-ref-type>Session</ejb-ref-type>

    <local-home>headfirst.AdviceHomeLocal</local-home>

    <local>headfirst.AdviceLocal</local>

</ejb-local-ref>
```

The sub-elements are different for the local interfaces: <local-home> instead of <home> and <local> instead of <remote>

there are no Dumb Questions

Q: I understand the element names for <home> and <local-home>. Makes sense. But what's up with <remote> and <local>? Shouldn't it be <component> and <local-component>?

A: You can run from your past, but you can't hide. Before EJB 2.0, there was no concept of local interfaces. So the client view was always called Home and Remote. Although even that was an inconsistent name scheme, since both the home and the business method interface were Remote (as in java.rmi.Remote). But once local interfaces came on the scene, things got a bit more complicated. "Let's see... we can name the local home "local-home" and then we'll name the local remote "local-remote". See the problem? So with EJB 2.0, we stopped calling the business interface "the *remote* interface" and started calling it "the *component* interface". And now we call them "local component interfaces" and "remote component interfaces".

Q: Um, you still didn't answer my question. How come the tag still says "remote" for the remote component interface and "local" for the local component interface?

A: Because of the past. Backward compatibility and all that. In EJB 1.1, the <ejb-ref> tags said <home> and <remote>, so they still do. The naming scheme is basically this: "The component interface is either *local* or *remote*. If the tag doesn't explicitly say "home", then you're talking about the component interface. These quirky little inconsistencies are just part of EJB's *charm*.

<res-ref-type> must NOT be a message-driven bean!

The <res-ref-type> element can be either "Session" or "Entity". That's it. How could anyone, let alone a bean, lookup a message-driven bean? Remember, message-driven beans don't have clients! They don't have homes! There's no interface to look up in JNDI. So don't be tricked...

You do NOT specify the bean type in <ejb-ref>

But is is SO tempting to think that you should. You put in ONLY the home and component interface types for the bean, but not the bean class. Why not the bean type? Think about the flexibility this gives you. Think about how tightly-coupled the Bean Provider and Deployer would need to be if the Bean Provider had to know the exact class type of the bean!

Using <ejb-link> with EJB references

If the Application Assembler sees that one bean's EJB reference it to another bean in the same application, she should use the <ejb-link> to link the <ejb-ref> to *another bean specified in the deployment descriptor*. Think of <ejb-link> as a kind of "jump to this label" thing, where the value of the link matches the value of an <ejb-name> element somewhere else.

Somewhere in the DD

```
<entity>
    ...
    <ejb-ref>
        <ejb-ref-name>ejb/AdviceGiver</ejb-ref-name>
        <ejb-ref-type>Session</ejb-ref-type>
        <home>headfirst.AdviceHome</home>
        <remote>headfirst.Advice</remote>
        <ejb-link>AdviceEJB</ejb-link>
    </ejb-ref>
    ...
</entity>
```

The <ejb-link> MUST match the value of an <ejb-name> for some other bean in this DD (or another DD in the same J2EE app).

Somewhere *else* in the DD

```
<session>
    <ejb-name>AdviceEJB</ejb-name>
    ...
</session>
```

Remember, <ejb-name> is just a label in the DD, for other parts of the DD to refer to. It's not the real BEAN class name or anything (unless you happen to make your ejb-name the same as the bean class).

<ejb-link> values MUST match the value of some OTHER bean's <ejb-name>

And remember: <ejb-name> is nothing more than a label in the DD. It doesn't have to match the class name, interface name, JNDI name, or anything else. It's just the label in the DD for a particular bean.

Nobody but your co-workers will care if you name your beans after, say, your pets.

<ejb-name> must be unique within a single DD (which means a single ejb-jar), but not within a single J2EE app.

But this does NOT mean all beans in the same J2EE app must have unique <ejb-name> values. A single .ear can have multiple ejb-jar files, with one DD per ejb-jar, and each of the DD's in the app can have the same <ejb-name>. Ah.... but THEN there's a problem with <ejb-link>, which looks in the entire app, not just the current DD, for a matching <ejb-name>. Not to worry. If you DO have two DD's in the app with identical <ejb-name> entries, use the alternate <ejb-link> syntax to add the path to the ejb-jar where this link's matching <ejb-name> lives. The path (followed by "#") is relative to the current DD's jar.

<ejb-link>../custServices/advice.jar#AdviceEJB</ejb-link>

Resource environment references
(think: *JMS destinations*)

As a Bean Provider, you can look up two different kinds of resource-related things in JNDI: a resource manager connection factory reference, and a reference to something known as an *administered object*. The main difference is that a resource environment reference is to a *thing you want*, not the factory that gives you a *connection* to the thing you want. In other words, the administered object *is* the destination, whereas a resource manager connection factory reference is just the first step in getting what you really want (a *connection*).

But today, just do a mental search and replace in your mind so that everywhere you see resource environment reference, you substitute JMS destination. Because that's pretty much all you'll use it for now. Yes, they could have called it "JMS destination reference", but that would be too limiting for the future. Not to mention too clear, unambiguous, and meaningful to have any value whatsoever as a cognitive challenge.

in a bean's business method:

```
InitialContext ic = new InitialContext();
Object o =  ic.lookup("java:comp/env/jms/NewCustomerQueue");
javax.jms.Queue custQ = (javax.jms.Queue) o;
// use the custQ
```

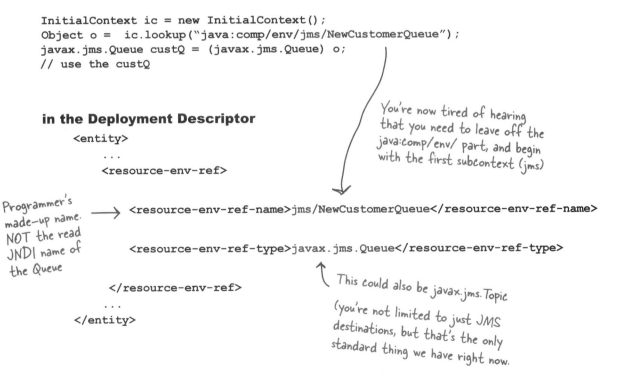

in the Deployment Descriptor

```
<entity>
    . . .
    <resource-env-ref>

        <resource-env-ref-name>jms/NewCustomerQueue</resource-env-ref-name>

        <resource-env-ref-type>javax.jms.Queue</resource-env-ref-type>

    </resource-env-ref>
    . . .
</entity>
```

You're now tired of hearing that you need to leave off the java:comp/env/ part, and begin with the first subcontext (jms)

Programmer's made-up name. NOT the read JNDI name of the Queue

This could also be javax.jms.Topic (you're not limited to just JMS destinations, but that's the only standard thing we have right now.

Bean Provider and Application Assembler
responsibility for the Deployment Descriptor

Don't worry about memorizing all of these now! It will make more sense as we get farther into the topics. For now, it's OK for you to have just an overall concept of what each is responsible for.

Bill puts in mostly things that are related to the code in the bean classes

Annie puts in mostly things about how two or more beans are related to one another in the application, and sometimes she customizes the bean info for a particular application.

Bean Provider

- bean name
- fully-qualified name of bean class and home and component interfaces
- bean type (session, entity, etc.)
- re-entrancy (for entity beans only)
- state management for session beans (stateless or stateful)
- transaction demarcation type (bean or container)
- entity bean persistence management (bean or container)
- primary key class
- for CMP, abstract schema name, CMP fields, CMR relationships, finder and select queries.
- resource manager connection factory *references*
- environment entry declarations
- EJB references (local and remote)
- security role *references*
- for message-driven beans: destination, message selector, and acknowledgement mode.

Application Assembler

Modifications to Bean Provider information:

- values of environment entries
- description fields (change or create)
- relationship name modifications
- message-driven bean message selector (may restrict, but not replace)

Application Assembly information (all optional):

- binding enterprise bean references (i.e. linking one bean to another in the same ejb-jar or J2EE app)
- security roles (the recommended roles for clients of the beans.)
- method permissions: a relationship between security roles and methods of the home and component interface of the bean
- linking security role *references* to security *roles*
- security identity type: *caller* or *run-as*
- transaction attributes for methods of a CMT bean

Deployer responsibility for the Deployment Descriptor

Deployer

Modifications to Bean Provider information:

- ensure legal values for all environment entries

Other tasks related to the deployment descriptor. All are done in a vendor-specific tool and NOT a part of the ejb-jar deployment descriptor:

SECURITY

- assign of the security domain and principal realm to the app
- assign principals and/or groups to security roles, but NOT the security role *references*.
- principal delegation for inter-component calls (i.e. configuring the run-as principal).

RESOURCE MANAGER CONNECTION FACTORIES

- binding of resource manager connection factory references to an actual resource manager connection factory in the operational environment
- configuration sign-on info for container-authorized resource access.

EJB REFERENCES

- ensure that all EJB references are bound to the homes of beans that exist in the operational environment
- ensure that the target bean is type-compatible with the types declared in the EJB reference.

RESOURCE ENVIRONMENT REFERENCES (JMS topic or queue)

- ensure that all declared resource references are bound to objects that exist in the operational environment, and ensure that the target object is type-compatible with the declared type

The Deployer does things using vendor-specific tools

*You might see a question about the deployer and things related to the deployment descriptor and think: "The deployer isn't supposed to touch things in the DD, so this can't be his job." But... the deployer **does** have a lot of responsibilities **related** to things in the DD, so look carefully at the description of the task.*

*For example, who maps security **roles** to security role **references**? The App Assembler. Who maps **principals** to security **roles**? The Deployer.*

Remembering who does what

Think about it... how can I possibly know the names of things in the server where this bean might run? I write code without knowing where the beans will end up! So I have to code in guesses about security role names or the JNDI name of another bean my bean is using.

Bean Provider

I'm the only one who really knows how the server is configured and what JNDI names everything has. And I'm the only one who knows about the security domain in this company. But I don't know what's in the code, so I'm counting on the Bean Provider to tell me (via the deployment descriptor) about his 'made-up' names so I can map those fake names to real names in the server.

Deployer

I have to integrate two or more beans (possibly from different vendors). So if Bean A uses the made-up security reference "Employee" and Bean B has code using the made-up security reference "Minions", I have to map them both to a single security role, "Slaves". The Bean Provider declares the made-up name in the DD. That's how he tells me what he's done in the code.

Application Assembler

Now let's look at the bean's runtime environment

We're almost done with the bean's world. Now that we've seen the bean'sspecial JNDI environment, we still have a few more little details on the bean's runtime environment. Each of these is covered by the exam objectives, so don't fall asleep now. We're almost done!

- **Guaranteed APIs**
  You must which APIs are and are not guaranteed to be part of every EJB 2.0 container. For example, JMS is supported, JXTA is not.

- **Guaranteed services**
  You must know what is and is not guaranteed to be supported by every EJB 2.0 container. For example, transaction support is guaranteed, load-balancing is not.

- **Structure of the ejb-jar**
  Maybe this isn't really a runtime environment thing, but we didn't have another good place to stick it, and you have to know it. So here it is, just in case you don't remember what we covered waaaaay back in chapter 1. For example, you must know that the an ejb-jar does not have a manifest, but MUST have a META-INF directory, and that directory MUST hold the deployment descriptor. Which, oh yes, MUST be named "ejb-jar.xml".

- **Programming restrictions**
  If you want your bean to be portable to / compatible with any EJB 2.0-compliant container, you must not do any of the things on the list, even if your vendor allows it (which the vendor may do *unintentionally*).
  And it's not just for portability, but for *safety*. If you try to manage your own threads, for example, you're stepping on the Container's toes, and who knows what kind of mess you'll end up with. You do not want to mess with the Container's job.
  Just because your Container permits it, doesn't make it right. And for the exam, you must know what's restricted in the spec.
  If the exam asks if something is possible, and it's one of the explicitly-restricted things in the spec, you must say NO, even if your vendor lets you do it. As far as the exam is concerned, if you can't do it and remain portable, *you can't do it.*

Which APIs does EJB 2.0 guarantee?

Supported APIs

- Java 2 Standard Edition, v 1.3 (**J2SE**)

- **JNDI** API 1.2

- **JTA** 1.01 extension (the `UserTransaction` interface only)

- **JDBC** 2.0 extension

- **JMS** 1.02 extension

- **JavaMail** 1.1, sending mail only

- **JAXP** 1.0

J2SE support is Java 1.3, NOT 1.4!

Just because an API is in the J2SE standard library for version 1.4, does not mean that API is guaranteed for EJB! The EJB spec requires only J2SE version 1.3, so if you write a bean that relies on something in J2SE 1.4, your bean is not guaranteed to be portable across any EJB 2.0 container.

That means, for example, that the Java Cryptography Extension (JCE) APIs are not guaranteed to be supported by EJB 2.0, even though they are now part of the J2SE platform as of version 1.4.

Relax **You don't have to memorize all of the exact version numbers**

The exam isn't going to trick you on something as trivial as remember whether JavaMail is 1.1 or 1.2, or whether the JTA extension is 1.01 or 1.03. The only numbers you really need to know (besides the 2.0 in EJB 2.0!) are the JDBC 2.0 extension, and that only version 1.3 (not necessarily 1.4) of J2SE is guaranteed.

Sharpen your pencil

Without looking it up, write down what each of these APIs do. If you don't know, take a good guess based on what you know about EJB.

We'll start you off by giving you the most difficult one.

J2SE	_____
JNDI	_____
JTA	_____
JDBC	_____
JMS	_____
JavaMail	*sending mail* _____
JAXP	_____

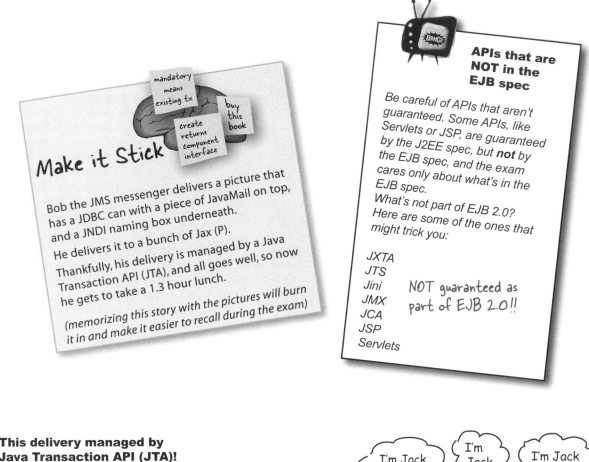

Make it Stick

mandatory means existing tx

create returns component interface

buy this book

Bob the JMS messenger delivers a picture that has a JDBC can with a piece of JavaMail on top, and a JNDI naming box underneath.

He delivers it to a bunch of Jax (P).

Thankfully, his delivery is managed by a Java Transaction API (JTA), and all goes well, so now he gets to take a 1.3 hour lunch.

(memorizing this story with the pictures will burn it in and make it easier to recall during the exam)

APIs that are NOT in the EJB spec

Be careful of APIs that aren't guaranteed. Some APIs, like Servlets or JSP, are guaranteed by the J2EE spec, but **not** by the EJB spec, and the exam cares only about what's in the EJB spec.

What's not part of EJB 2.0? Here are some of the ones that might trick you:

JXTA
JTS
Jini   NOT guaranteed as
JMX   part of EJB 2.0!!
JCA
JSP
Servlets

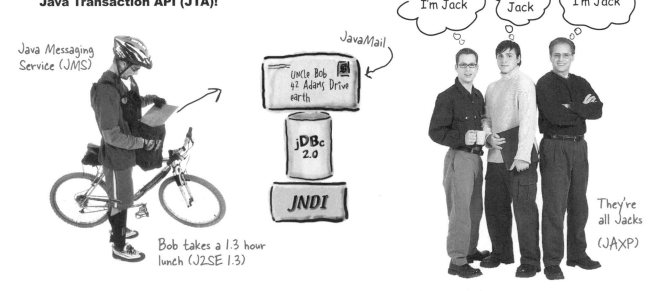

This delivery managed by Java Transaction API (JTA)!

Java Messaging Service (JMS)

JavaMail

Uncle Bob
42 Adams Drive
earth

jDBc 2.0

JNDI

Bob takes a 1.3 hour lunch (J2SE 1.3)

I'm Jack

I'm Jack

I'm Jack

They're all Jacks

(JAXP)

Some of the key, guaranteed services and behavior:

- Distributed **transactions**

- **Thread-safety**

- Container-managed **persistence** for entity beans

- A **security domain** and one principal realm (multiple realms is not guaranteed)

- **Enforce client access** security policies specified by the deployment descriptor and other deployment tools

- Implementation of the **java:comp/env** environment naming context provided to the bean

- **Generation of classes** that implement the home and component interfaces, and stub classes for remote objects.

- **Implementation of the** resource manager connection factory classes for resources configured with the server.

Some things sound good but aren't guaranteed!

Everybody talks about their clustered, load-balanced, fault-tolerant system. Oh yeah, with fail-over, lazy-loading of entity data, and in-memory data caching.

Although most J2EE vendors provide one or more of these capabilities, they aren't guaranteed in the spec!!

Be sure you know the difference between what is guaranteed and what is not. Look in the spec, under the sections titled "Container Provider responsibility"

> I used to think clustering, fail-over, and load balancing were part of the spec. But they aren't. If I need those features, I have to find a vendor that supports them. Many do...but don't be fooled into thinking this is part of the EJB spec.

> It's always about *your* needs...

What MUST be in an ejb-jar?

beans

JAR 1

ejb-jar

deployment descriptor

ejb-jar.xml

Structure of an ejb-jar

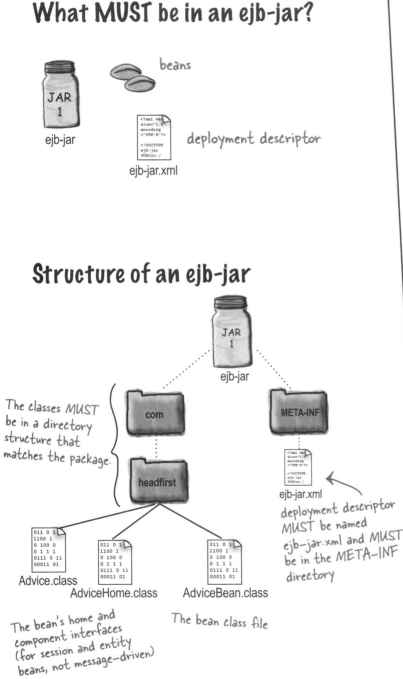

The classes MUST be in a directory structure that matches the package.

JAR 1

ejb-jar

com

META-INF

headfirst

ejb-jar.xml

deployment descriptor MUST be named ejb-jar.xml and MUST be in the META-INF directory

Advice.class

AdviceHome.class

AdviceBean.class

The bean's home and component interfaces (for session and entity beans, not message-driven)

The bean class file

Programming restrictions

What to avoid in EJB if you want to guarantee your bean can be deployed on ANY EJB 2.0-compliant server

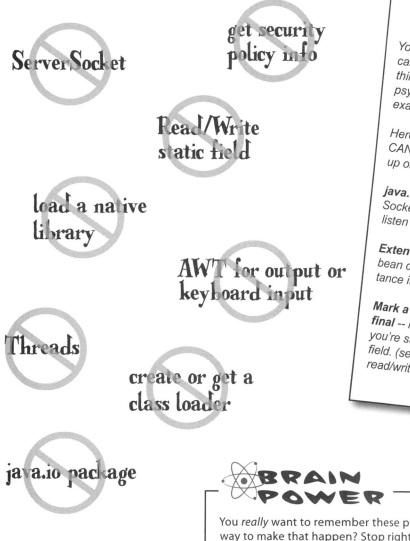

ServerSocket

get security policy info

Read/Write static field

load a native library

AWT for output or keyboard input

Threads

create or get a class loader

java.io package

Don't be fooled by things that only SEEM bad, but aren't

You're expected to know what you can and can't do in EJB 2.0. If you think about it too much, you can psych yourself into thinking (on the exam) that anything could be bad.

Here are a few things that you CAN do in EJB, that might trip you up on the exam:

java.net.Socket -- plain old client Sockets are fine. You just can't listen on a ServerSocket.

Extend another class from your bean class -- normal java inheritance is OK for a bean class.

Mark a bean field static and final -- in fact, that's the only way you're supposed to mark a static field. (see the restriction about no read/write static fields.)

BRAIN POWER

You *really* want to remember these programming restrictions. The best way to make that happen? Stop right now and think about each of these restricted things, and come up with one or more reasons for why the restriction exists. When you're done, turn to page 494 in the EJB 2.0 spec, where these restrictions (and others) are described.

Memorize THIS

Exercise

(1) Looking at the picture below, see if you can tell the story, putting in the API's where they belong. We did one for you.

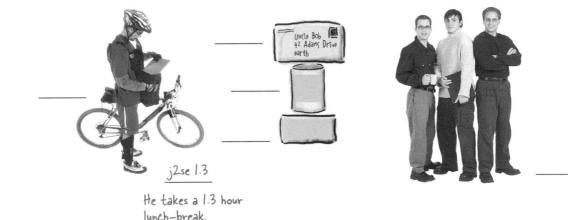

_____

UNCLE BOB
42 Adams Drive
earth

_____

_____

_____

j2se 1.3

He takes a 1.3 hour
lunch-break.

---

(2) Using the pieces below (and ONLY the pieces below) reassemble them into their correct configuration (drawing lines as needed). Draw your finished structure in the space at the right, and write the correct names on the directories, and name the .xml file. The bean is in the *com.headfirst* package.

Draw the structure of the JAR file here:

↓

JAR 1

ejb-jar

011 0 1
1100 1
0 100 0
0 111 1
0111 0 11
00011 01

Advice.class

011 0 1
1100 1
0 100 0
0 111 1
0111 0 11
00011 01

AdviceBean.class

011 0 1
1100 1
0 100 0
0 111 1
0111 0 11
00011 01

AdviceHome.class

<?xml ver
sion="1.0
encoding
="UTF-8"?>

<!DOCTYPE
ejb-jar
PUBInc./

_____.xml

Mock Exam

---

1 Which APIs are guaranteed to be supported by EJB 2.0 containers? (Choose all that apply.)

❏ A. JAXP

❏ B. JNDI

❏ C. JXTA

❏ D. JDBC

❏ E. JMS

---

2 What's true about an enterprise bean's environment? (Choose all that apply.)

❏ A. Environment entries can be unique for instances of the same enterprise bean type.

❏ B. Within a single EJB 2.0 container, an EJB can have multiple sets of environment entries.

❏ C. An EJB's environment entry's values can be modified by the EJB at runtime.

❏ D. Environment entry values may be primitives or wrapper types.

---

3 Which APIs are guaranteed to be supported by EJB 2.0 containers? (Choose all that apply.)

❏ A. J2SE 1.3

❏ B. JAXB 1.0

❏ C. JAXR 1.0

❏ D. JAXP 1.0

4 Given a bean named 'Customer', and an environment entry named 'lastName', which code fragment(s) inside of the bean class would return the value of the environment entry? (Choose all that apply.)

❏ A. `Context c = new SessionContext();`
   `Context e = (Context) c.lookup("java:comp/env");`
   `String name = (String) e.lookup("lastName");`

❏ B. `Context c = new InitialContext();`
   `Context e = (Context) c.lookup("java:comp/env/`
   `Customer");`
   `String name = (String) e.lookup("lastName");`

❏ C. `Context e = new Lookup("java:comp/env");`
   `Context c = new InitialContext(e);`
   `String name = (String) c.lookup("lastName");`

❏ D. `Context c = new InitialContext("Customer");`
   `Context e = (Context) c.lookup("java:comp/env");`
   `String name = (String) e.lookup("lastName");`

❏ E. `Context c = new InitialContext();`
   `Context e = (Context) c.lookup("java:comp/env");`
   `String name = (String) e.lookup("lastName");`

5 When programming a session bean class which technique(s) should always be avoided to ensure bean portability across all EJB 2.0 containers? (Choose all that apply.)

❏ A. Using the `java.net.Socket` class.

❏ B. Using inner classes.

❏ C. Using the 'final' modifier for fields.

❏ D. Passing 'this' as an argument.

6 Which of the following are valid data types in a **<env-entry-type>** element in a bean's deployment descriptor? (Choose all that apply.)

❑ A. **byte**

❑ B. **short**

❑ C. **ArrayList**

❑ D. **java.lang.Boolean**

❑ E. **java.lang.Character**

7 When programming EJBs which declaration(s) should be avoided to ensure bean portability across all EJB 2.0 containers? (Choose all that apply.)

❑ A. **final int x;**

❑ B. **static int x;**

❑ C. **final static int x;**

❑ D. **final transient int x;**

8 Who is typically responsible for specifying finder and select queries in the bean's deployment descriptor?

❑ A. The bean provider.

❑ B. The application assembler.

❑ C. The deployer.

❑ D. The system administrator.

❑ E. The server provider.

9 Which deployment descriptor element(s) would be used when obtaining a JDBC connection? (Choose all that apply.)

❑ A. **<ejb-ref>**

❑ B. **<ejb-link>**

❑ C. **<role-name>**

❑ D. **<env-entry>**

❑ E. **<resource-ref>**

10 Who will typically merge multiple ejb-jar files into a single ejb-jar file.

❏ A. The bean provider.

❏ B. The application assembler.

❏ C. The deployer.

❏ D. The system administrator.

❏ E. The server provider.

11 Which deployment descriptor element(s) would be used by a bean provider to locate the home interfaces of other EJBs? (Choose all that apply.)

❏ A. `<ejb-ref>`

❏ B. `<res-type>`

❏ C. `<env-entry>`

❏ D. `<role-name>`

❏ E. `<resource-ref>`

12 Which are bean provider responsibilities concerning resource manager connection factory references? (Choose all that apply.)

❏ A. Configure resource managers in the EJB server.

❏ B. Configure sign-on information for the resource manager.

❏ C. Assign such a reference to the deployment descriptor.

❏ D. Creating a symbolic link to JNDI.

13 The ejb-jar file is considered to be part of the contract between which pairs? (Choose all that apply.)

❏ A. bean provider and system administrator

❏ B. bean provider and application assembler

❏ C. application assembler and deployer

❏ D. application assembler and system administrator

❏ E. deployer and system administrator

14 Which class files must be included, either directly or by reference, in every ejb-jar file? (Choose all that apply.)

❏ A. The enterprise bean class.

❏ B. The stub class for the EJBObject interface.

❏ C. The enterprise bean's super classes.

❏ D. Any J2SE classes used as arguments or return types.

15 Which role is typically responsible for declaring the resource connection factory references in the deployment descriptor?

❏ A. bean provider

❏ B. application assembler

❏ C. deployer

❏ D. container provider

❏ E. system administrator

16 What's true about a legal ejb-jar file? (Choose all that apply.)

❏ A. It must contain both a home interface and a component interface.

❏ B. The deployment descriptor is mandatory.

❏ C. It must contain any J2EE classes used by the bean.

❏ D. The enterprise bean class is optional.

17 Which role would typically set up resource manager sign-on information?

❏ A. bean provider

❏ B. application assembler

❏ C. deployer

❏ D. container provider

❏ E. system administrator

Mock Exam Answers

---

1 Which APIs are guaranteed to be supported by EJB 2.0 containers? (Choose all that apply.)   *(spec: 493)*

- ☑ A. JAXP
- ☑ B. JNDI
- ☐ C. JXTA
- ☑ D. JDBC
- ☑ E. JMS

---

2 What's true about an enterprise bean's environment? (Choose all that apply.)   *(spec: 410-412)*

- ☐ A. Environment entries can be unique for instances of the same enterprise bean type.
- ☑ B. Within a single EJB 2.0 container, an EJB can have multiple sets of environment entries.
- ☐ C. An EJB's environment entry's values can be modified by the EJB at runtime.
- ☐ D. Environment entry values may be primitives or wrapper types. — Only Strings and Wrappers

---

3 Which APIs are guaranteed to be supported by EJB 2.0 containers? (Choose all that apply.)   *(spec: 496-497)*

- ☑ A. J2SE 1.3
- ☐ B. JAXB 1.0
- ☐ C. JAXR 1.0
- ☑ D. JAXP 1.0

4 Given a bean named 'Customer', and an environment entry named 'lastName',   (spec: 411-412)
which code fragment(s) inside of the bean class would return the value of the
environment entry? (Choose all that apply.)

❏ A. `Context c = new SessionContext();`   — SessionContext is not the same as JNDI Context

   `Context e = (Context) c.lookup("java:comp/env");`

   `String name = (String) e.lookup("lastName");`

❏ B. `Context c = new InitialContext();`

   `Context e = (Context) c.lookup("java:comp/env/`
   `Customer");`

   `String name = (String) e.lookup("lastName");`

❏ C. `Context e = new Lookup("java:comp/env");`

   `Context c = new InitialContext(e);`

   `String name = (String) c.lookup("lastName");`

❏ D. `Context c = new InitialContext("Customer");` — no argument here

   `Context e = (Context) c.lookup("java:comp/env");`

   `String name = (String) e.lookup("lastName");`

☑ E. `Context c = new InitialContext();`

   `Context e = (Context) c.lookup("java:comp/env");`

   `String name = (String) e.lookup("lastName");`

5 When programming a session bean class which technique(s) should always be   (spec: 494-495)
avoided to ensure bean portability across all EJB 2.0 containers? (Choose all
that apply.)

❏ A. Using the **java.net.Socket** class. — client Sockets are OK,
                                             just not a ServerSocket

❏ B. Using inner classes.

❏ C. Using the 'final' modifier for fields.

☑ D. Passing 'this' as an argument.

6 Which of the following are valid data types in a **<env-entry-type>** element in a bean's deployment descriptor? (Choose all that apply.)   *(spec: 413)*

- ❏ A. **byte**
- ❏ B. **short**
- ❏ C. **ArrayList**
- ☑ D. **java.lang.Boolean**   *– only Wrappers and Strings are supported*
- ☑ E. **java.lang.Character**

7 When programming EJBs which declaration(s) should be avoided to ensure bean portability across all EJB 2.0 containers? (Choose all that apply.)   *(spec: 494)*

- ❏ A. **final int x;**
- ☑ B. **static int x;**   *– statics should also be final*
- ❏ C. **final static int x;**
- ❏ D. **final transient int x;**

8 Who is typically responsible for specifying finder and select queries in the bean's deployment descriptor?   *(spec: 456–457)*

- ☑ A. The bean provider.
- ❏ B. The application assembler.
- ❏ C. The deployer.
- ❏ D. The system administrator.
- ❏ E. The server provider.

9 Which deployment descriptor element(s) would be used when obtaining a JDBC connection? (Choose all that apply.)   *(spec: 424)*

- ❏ A. **<ejb-ref>**
- ❏ B. **<ejb-link>**
- ❏ C. **<role-name>**
- ❏ D. **<env-entry>**
- ☑ E. **<resource-ref>**

10 Who will typically merge multiple ejb-jar files into a single ejb-jar file.   (spec: 458)

- ❏ A. The bean provider.
- ☑ B. The application assembler.
- ❏ C. The deployer.
- ❏ D. The system administrator.
- ❏ E. The server provider.

11 Which deployment descriptor element(s) would be used by a bean provider to locate the home interfaces of other EJBs? (Choose all that apply.)   (spec: 416)

- ☑ A. `<ejb-ref>`
- ❏ B. `<res-type>`
- ❏ C. `<env-entry>`
- ❏ D. `<role-name>`
- ❏ E. `<resource-ref>`

12 Which are bean provider responsibilities concerning resource manager connection factory references? (Choose all that apply.)   (spec: 421)

- ❏ A. Configure resource managers in the EJB server.
- ❏ B. Configure sign-on information for the resource manager.
- ☑ C. Assign such a reference to the deployment descriptor.
- ❏ D. Creating a symbolic link to JNDI.

13 The ejb-jar file is considered to be part of the contract between which pairs?   (spec: 487)
(Choose all that apply.)

- ❏ A. bean provider and system administrator
- ☑ B. bean provider and application assembler
- ☑ C. application assembler and deployer
- ❏ D. application assembler and system administrator
- ❏ E. deployer and system administrator

14 Which class files must be included, either directly or by reference, in every ejb-jar file? (Choose all that apply.)   (spec: 488)

- ☑ A. The enterprise bean class.
- ❏ B. The stub class for the EJBObject interface.
- ☑ C. The enterprise bean's super classes.
- ❏ D. Any J2SE classes used as arguments or return types. — It'll already be there, baby!

15 Which role is typically responsible for declaring the resource connection factory references in the deployment descriptor?   (spec: 423)

- ☑ A. bean provider
- ❏ B. application assembler
- ❏ C. deployer
- ❏ D. container provider
- ❏ E. system administrator

16 What's true about a legal ejb-jar file? (Choose all that apply.)   (spec: 488)

- ❏ A. It must contain both a home interface and a component interface. — If it holds only MDBs, there won't be a home or component interface.
- ☑ B. The deployment descriptor is mandatory.
- ❏ C. It must contain any J2EE classes used by the bean.
- ❏ D. The enterprise bean class is optional.

17 Which role would typically set up resource manager sign-on information?   (spec: 422)

- ❏ A. bean provider
- ❏ B. application assembler
- ☑ C. deployer
- ❏ D. container provider
- ❏ E. system administrator

Appendix A:
Final Mock Exam

Do NOT try to take this exam until you believe you're ready for the real thing. If you take it too soon, then when you finally come back to it you'll already have some memory of the questions, and it could give you an artificially high score. We really do want you to pass the *first* time. (Unless there were some way to convince you that you need to buy a fresh copy of this book each time you retake the exam...)

To help defeat the "I remember this question" problem, we've made this exam just a little *harder* than the real exam, by *not* telling you how many answers are correct for each of our questions. Our questions and answers are virtually identical to the tone, style, difficulty, and topics of the real exam, but by not telling you how many answers to choose, you can't automatically eliminate any of the answers. It's cruel of us, really, and we wish we could tell you that it hurts us more than it hurts you to have to take the exam this way. (But be grateful—until a few years ago, Sun's real Java exams *were* written this way, where most questions ended with "Choose all that apply.")

Most exam candidates have said that our mock exams *are* a little more difficult than the real SCBCD, but that their scores on our exam and on the real one were very close. This mock exam is a perfect way to see if you're ready, but only if you:

1) Give yourself no more than two hours to complete it, just like the real exam.

2) Don't look anywhere else in the book while you're taking the exam!

3) Don't take it over and over again. By the fourth time, you might be getting 98% and yet still not be able to pass the real exam, simply because you were memorizing our exact questions and answers.

4) Wait until *after* you finish the exam to consume large quantities of alcohol or other mind-altering substances (Ben and Jerry's™ Fudge Brownie, Red Bull™, Frosted Flakes™ cereal to name a few of the more deadly ones).

Master Mock Exam

1 Which are benefits of EJB 2.0? (Choose all that apply.)

❑ A. MDBs survive server crashes.

❑ B. Representations of a single entity can be shared among multiple clients.

❑ C. Support for nested transactions.

❑ D. Dynamic service discovery.

❑ E. Declarative isolation level settings.

2 Which methods are directly invoked by the client? (Choose all that apply.)

❑ A. `ejbPassivate()`

❑ B. business methods

❑ C. `setSessionContext()`

❑ D. `newInstance()`

❑ E. `create()`

3 Which method(s) can be found in the EJBHome interface? (Choose all that apply.)

❑ A. remove(Handle handle)

❑ B. remove(Object primaryKey)

❑ C. getHandle()

❑ D. none of the above

4 Which method(s) can be run by a CMP bean in the pooled state? (Choose all that apply.)

❏ A. `ejbLoad()`

❏ B. `ejbFind()`

❏ C. `ejbStore()`

❏ D. `ejbCreate()`

❏ E. Business method

❏ F. `ejbHome()`

5 What's true about message-driven beans? (Choose all that apply.)

❏ A. All calls to a message-driven bean instance must be serialized.

❏ B. The container guarantees that messages will be processed in the order in which they are received.

❏ C. The bean's `ejbCreate()` method must take a single argument of type `javax.jms.Message`.

❏ D. The bean provider uses the deployment descriptor to indicate whether instances of the bean class are intended for topics or queues.

6 What's true about an enterprise bean's environment? (Choose all that apply.)

❏ A. Before a bean can access its environment entries, the bean must first obtain the naming context using a `SessionContext` object.

❏ B. Only the bean provider can set an environment entry value.

❏ C. A bean's environment entries can be stored only in `'java:comp/env'` or one of its subcontexts.

❏ D. Every environment entry lookup in a bean's code must have a matching `<env-entry>` element in the bean's deployment descriptor.

7 What's true about security roles in EJBs? (Choose all that apply.)

❏ A. Security roles are defined in the deployment descriptor using <security-role> elements.

❏ B. Security roles are scoped to the instance level

❏ C. Many methods can be mapped to a single security role.

❏ D. A method can appear in only one security role.

8   An EJB 2.0 container must support at least a subset of which APIs? (Choose all that apply.)

- ❏ A. JTA 1.0.1
- ❏ B. JDBC 2.0
- ❏ C. JMS 1.0.2
- ❏ D. JAX-RCP 1.0

9   Which statements concerning stateless session beans are true? (Choose all that apply.)

- ❏ A. They can use bean-managed transaction demarcation.
- ❏ B. They must have one no-argument create method.
- ❏ C. A single instance can support concurrent calls.
- ❏ D. They must extend javax.ejb.SessionBean

10   What capability exists in ONLY ONE of the two (but not both)?

     - an entity object's remote component interface

     - an entity object's local component interface

(Choose all that apply.)

- ❏ A. Removing the object.
- ❏ B. Obtaining the object's handle.
- ❏ C. Invoking business methods.
- ❏ D. Obtaining the object's primary key.

11   When creating a CMP entity bean, which method(s) are optional? (Choose all that apply.)

- ❏ A. `ejbLoad()`
- ❏ B. `ejbCreate()`
- ❏ C. `ejbRemove()`
- ❏ D. `ejbSelect()`
- ❏ E. `ejbPassivate()`
- ❏ F. `setEntityContext()`

12 Which method(s) can be called on a bean in the pooled state? (Choose all that apply.)

❑ A. `ejbFind()`

❑ B. `ejbLoad()`

❑ C. `ejbStore()`

❑ D. `ejbSelect()`

❑ E. `ejbPassivate()`

13 What's true about the lifecycle of a message-driven bean? (Choose all that apply.)

❑ A. When the the **onMessage** method completes, the container will typically call ejbRemove.

❑ B. The on**Message()** method can throw application exceptions.

❑ C. Message-driven beans can run only with CMT demarcation.

❑ D. The **getRollbackOnly()** method can be called only from the onMessage method.

14 Which statement(s) concerning message-driven bean classes are true? (Choose all that apply.)

❑ A. They must implement, directly or indirectly, **javax.jms.Message**.

❑ B. They must have a public constructor that takes a single argument of type **javax.jms.Message**.

❑ C. Implementing the **finalize()** method is allowed.

❑ D. Implementing the **ejbCreate()** method is optional.

❑ E. The class must not be declared 'final'.

15 Within the deployment descriptor's **<ejb-local-ref>** element, which elements are optional? (Choose all that apply.)

❑ A. **<local>**

❑ B. **<ejb-link>**

❑ C. **<local-home>**

❑ D. **<description>**

❑ E. **<ejb-ref-name>**

❑ F. **<ejb-ref-type>**

16 What's true about resource manager connection factories? (Choose all that apply.)

❏ The **<res-sharing-scope>** deployment descriptor element is used to indicate whether connections to a resource manager are shareable across multiple EJBs in an application.

❏ B. The **<res-sharing-scope>** deployment descriptor element contains the **<resource-ref>** element.

❏ C. All of a bean's resource manager connection factory references are declared in a single **<resource-ref>** element, using **<res-ref-name>** elements to distinguish them.

❏ D. By default, connections to a given resource manager are shareable across multiple beans in an application.

17 What's true about security roles referenced from an EJB's code? (Choose all that apply.)

❏ A. In the deployment descriptor, such references are contained in the **<security-role-ref>** element.

❏ B. The **<security-role>** element includes the **<security-role-ref>** element.

❏ C. Within the **<security-role-ref>** element, the **<role-name>** element's value is the same as the argument for the bean's invocation of the **isCallerInRole** method.

❏ D. The **<role-link>** element is used to link two **<security-role-ref>** elements.

18 What's true about the client's view of security? (Choose all that apply.)

❏ A. A transactional client cannot change its principal association within a transaction.

❏ B. A session bean's client cannot change its principal association for the duration of the communication with the session object.

❏ C. Transactional requests within a single transaction cannot arrive from multiple clients.

❏ D. None of the above.

19 When programming an entity bean class which technique(s) should be AVOIDED to ensure bean portability across all EJB 2.0 containers? (Choose all that apply.)

❏ A. Changing a thread's priority.

❏ B. Using the reflection API.

❏ C. Using wrapper classes.

❏ D. Using static nested classes.

20 When programming a message-driven bean class which technique(s) should be avoided to ensure bean portability across all EJB 2.0 containers? (Choose all that apply.)

❏ A. Using Swing APIs for a GUI.

❏ B. Using the 'transient' modifier.

❏ C. Using native libraries.

❏ D. Reading file descriptors..

21 What is required of the container when it passivates a stateful session bean?

❏ A. The bean's instance state will always undergo Java programming language Serialization.

❏ B. It must save all of the bean's instance field state regardless of the fields' modifiers.

❏ C. It must save any references to the bean's SessionContext object.

❏ D. It must save all non-null transient variables.

22 Which capabilities are defined in the **javax.ejb.EJBLocalObject** interface? (Choose all that apply.)?

❏ A. Remove an entity object.

❏ B. Obtain an entity object's primary key.

❏ C. Obtain a local home interface for the entity object.

❏ D. Obtain a remote component interface for the entity object.

❏ E. Expose the methods of the **javax.ejb.EntityBean** interface to the client.

23 What's true about ejbSelect methods? (Choose all that apply.)

❏ A. They can be exposed to the client.

❏ B. They can return only EJBObjects or EJBLocalObjects.

❏ C. They can be invoked only by a bean in the ready state.

❏ D. They must be associated with a query element in the deployment descriptor.

---

24 Which methods can NEVER be successfully invoked from a message-driven bean? (Choose all that apply.)

❏ A. `isCallerInRole()`

❏ B. `getEJBHome()`

❏ C. `getRollbackOnly()`

❏ D. `setRollbackOnly()`

❏ E. `getCallerPrincipal()`

---

25 Which role is typically responsible for adding <ejb-link> elements to an EJB's deployment descriptor?

❏ A. bean provider

❏ B. application assembler

❏ C. deployer

❏ D. container provider

❏ E. system administrator

---

26 In which of the following methods can a stateless session bean invoke the `isCallerInRole()` method in order to perform a security check? (Choose all that apply.)

❏ A. `ejbCreate()`

❏ B. `ejbRemove()`

❏ C. `setSessionContext()`

❏ D. None of the above

27 Which two are typically responsible for creating ejb-jar files? (Choose two.)

❑ A. The bean provider.

❑ B. The application assembler.

❑ C. The deployer.

❑ D. The system administrator.

28 Which of the following stateless session bean container callback method(s) takes an argument? (Choose all that apply.)

❑ A. **ejbRemove**

❑ B. **ejbCreate**

❑ C. **ejbCreate**

❑ D. **ejbPassivate**

❑ E. **setSessionContext**

29 Which of these can never be called on a SessionContext interface? (Choose all that apply.)

❑ A. **getEJBHome()**

❑ B. **getEJBObject()**

❑ C. **getEJBTransaction()**

❑ D. **isCallerInRole()**

❑ E. **getUserTransaction()**

30 What's true about an entity bean's remote component interface? (Choose all that apply.)

❑ A. If a client attempts to invoke a method on an entity that does not exist, a **java.rmi.NoSuchRemoteObjectException** will be thrown.

❑ B. It must extend **javax.ejb.EJBHome**

❑ C. Its methods must declare **java.rmi.RemoteException**

❑ D. It defines a **remove(Handle handle)** method.

31 Which are true about finder methods in an entity bean's local home interface? (Choose all that apply.)

- ❏ A. They can have any legal Java name.
- ❏ B. They must all declare `javax.ejb.FinderException`.
- ❏ C. They can optionally declare `java.rmi.RemoteException.`
- ❏ D. The **findByPrimaryKey** method can be overloaded.
- ❏ E. The **findByPrimaryKey** method's return type must be the bean's local component interface.
- ❏ F. A method called "findXXX" must have the bean's local component interface as its declared return type.

32 Which are true for a message-driven bean? (Choose all that apply.)

- ❏ A. The Deployer uses the deployment descriptor to determine whether a bean is intended for a Queue or a Topic.
- ❏ B. The class must be declared final.
- ❏ C. The class must define one **ejbRemove**() method.
- ❏ D. The class can have overloaded **ejbCreate()** methods.
- ❏ E. The class must define a no-argument onMessage method.

33 Given the following subset of a deployment descriptor:

```
<entity>
 <ejb-name>Payroll</ejb-name>
 <security-role-ref>
      <role-name>clerk</role-name>
  </security-role-ref>
</entity>
```

Which code snippet(s) makes a legal security check? (Choose all that apply.)

- ❏ A. `context.isCallerInRole("Payroll");`
- ❏ B. `context.isCallerInRole("clerk");`
- ❏ C. `context.isCallerInRole("Payroll.clerk");`
- ❏ D. `context.isCallerInRole("Payroll/clerk");`

34 Which are valid local home interfaces for a stateful session bean? (Choose all that apply.)

❑ A. `public interface TestBean implements`
`javax.ejb.EJBLocalHome {`

`void create() throws CreateException;`

`}`

❑ B. `public interface TestBean extends`
`javax.ejb.EJBLocalHome {`

`TestBeanLocal ejbCreate() throws CreateException;`

`}`

❑ C. `public interface TestBean extends`
`javax.ejb.EJBLocalHome {`

`TestBeanLocal create() throws CreateException;`

`}`

❑ D. `public interface TestBean extends`
`javax.ejb.EJBLocalHome {`

`TestBeanLocal create() throws CreateException,`
`RemoteException;`

`}`

❑ E. `public interface TestBean extends`
`javax.ejb.EJBLocalHome {`

`TestBeanLocal create() throws LocalException;`

`}`

35 Which methods can be called by a bean provider? (Choose all that apply.)

❑ A. `remove()`

❑ B. `ejbCreate()`

❑ C. `afterBegin()`

❑ D. `getCallerPrincipal()`

❑ E. `ejbPassivate()`

36 Who will typically specify whether a bean is re-entrant in the bean's deployment descriptor?

- ❑ A. The bean provider.
- ❑ B. The application assembler.
- ❑ C. The deployer.
- ❑ D. The system administrator.

37 Which statements about stateful and stateless session beans are true?
(Choose all that apply.)

- ❑ A. Only stateful session beans support transactions.
- ❑ B. Only stateful session beans can be passivated.
- ❑ C. Only stateful session beans have a `setSessionContext` method.
- ❑ D. Both stateful and stateless session beans can support overloaded `ejbCreate` methods.
- ❑ E. Both stateful and stateless session beans can implement the `javax.ejb.SessionSynchronization` interface.
- ❑ F. Both stateful and stateless session beans can have instance variable state.

38 Which must be included in every ejb-jar file? (Choose all that apply.)

- ❑ A. The stub for the EJBHome interface, either directly or by reference.
- ❑ B. The JAR Manifest file.
- ❑ C. A deployment descriptor.
- ❑ D. The JNDI context.
- ❑ E. The EJB's home interface, either directly or by reference.

39 Which method(s) are declared in the javax.ejb.EJBHome interface? (Choose all that apply.)

- ❑ A. `create()`
- ❑ B. `lookup()`
- ❑ C. `getHandle()`
- ❑ D. `getHomeHandle()`
- ❑ E. `setSessionContext()`

40 How many javax.ejb.EJBLocalHome interface methods can be called without an exception, from a session bean client?

❏ A. 0

❏ B. 1

❏ C. 2

❏ D. 3

❏ E. 4

41 Which of the following, if called, always have the same transaction context as a session bean's business methods? (Choose all that apply.)

❏ A. constructor

❏ B. `setSessionContext()`

❏ C. `afterBegin()`

❏ D. `afterCompletion()`

❏ E. `beforeCompletion()`

42 Given a stateful session bean with container-managed transaction demarcation, from which methods can you access another bean? (Choose all that apply.)

❏ A. `setSessionContext()`

❏ B. `ejbCreate()`

❏ C. `afterBegin()`

❏ D. `beforeCompletion()`

❏ E. `afterCompletion()`

43 Which deployment descriptor element(s) can optionally specify cascade-delete functionality? (Choose all that apply.)

❏ A. `<ejb-relation>`

❏ B. `<abstract-schema-name>`

❏ C. `<ejb-relationship-role>`

❏ D. `<relationship-role-source>`

44 What's true about cascade-delete? (Choose all that apply.)

❏ A. It is declared in the `ejbRemove()` method.

❏ B. When a cascade-delete enabled bean is deleted, it causes all of the beans with relationships to it to be automatically deleted too.

❏ C. It can be specified for one-to-one, one-to-many, or many-to-many relationships.

❏ D. A cascade-delete enabled bean is automatically removed when any "multiplicity of one" bean with which it is related is removed.

45 Which method(s) from the EntityContext interface can be invoked, regardless of transaction context? (Choose all that apply.)

❏ A. `getEJBHome()`

❏ B. `getEJBObject()`

❏ C. `setRollbackOnly()`

❏ D. `getRollbackOnly()`

46 What's true about an entity bean's primary key? (Choose all that apply.)

❏ A. Primary key fields must be cmp-fields.

❏ B. Setter methods for fields associated with a primary key must not be exposed through a client view.

❏ C. If two entity objects have the same home and the same primary key, they are considered identical.

❏ D. The `getPrimaryKey()` method can be invoked on references to only remote home interfaces, not local home interfaces.

47 Which interface(s) are used by the bean provider to perform BMT demarcation? (Choose all that apply.)

❏ A. `javax.transaction.Transaction`

❏ B. `javax.transaction.UserTransaction`

❏ C. `javax.transaction.Synchronization`

❏ D. `javax.transaction.TransactionManager`

48 Which of the following are legal EJB QL queries? (Choose all that apply.)

❏ A. SELECT c

FROM Customer c

❏ B. SELECT (OBJECT) c.name

FROM Customer c

❏ C. SELECT OBJECT c

WHERE Customer c

❏ D. SELECT OBJECT (c)

FROM Customer c

❏ E. SELECT c.name

FROM Customer c

49 Which are true about transactions in EJB 2.0? (Choose all that apply.)

❏ A. Only one database can be updated within a single transaction.

❏ B. Entity beans with BMT demarcation must use the setStatus method instead of the **setRollbackOnly** method.

❏ C. Entity beans with BMT demarcation must use the getStatus method instead of the **getRollbackOnly** method.

❏ D. BMT demarcation should be used when beans access resource managers that do not support transactions.

❏ E. The 'SessionSynchronization' interface can be used only by stateful session beans.

50 To ensure bean portability, which transaction attributes should be used on the business methods in the component interface of an entity bean using CMP? (Choose all that apply.)

❏ A. NotSupported

❏ B. Required

❏ C. Supports

❏ D. RequiresNew

❏ E. Mandatory

❏ F. Never

51 Which of the following exceptions would cause a bean to be discarded by the container? (Choose all that apply.)

❑ A. `javax.ejb.ObjectNotFoundException`

❑ B. `javax.ejb.CreateException`

❑ C. `javax.ejb.NoSuchEntityException`

❑ D. `javax.ejb.FinderException`

❑ E. `javax.ejb.RemoveException`

52 In which cases should the container log an exception thrown by a business method of a CMT demarcated bean? (Choose all that apply.)

❑ A. If the method runs with an unspecified transaction context and throws a system exception.

❑ B. If the method runs with an unspecified transaction context and throws an application exception.

❑ C. If the method runs with a RequiresNew context and throws a system exception.

❑ D. If the method runs with a Required context and throws a system exception.

❑ E. If the method runs with a RequiresNew context and throws an application exception.

❑ F. If the method runs with a Required context and throws an application exception.

53 Which session bean component interface method(s) can be called successfully, by a local client? (Choose all that apply.)

❑ A. `remove()`

❑ B. `getHandle()`

❑ C. `isIdentical()`

❑ D. `getEJBHome()`

54 In what scenario(s) can a bean's business method call the **isCallerInRole()** method of the SessionContext interface? (Choose all that apply.)

❏ A. A stateful session bean with container-managed transaction demarcation.

❏ B. A stateless session bean with container-managed transaction demarcation.

❏ C. A stateful session bean with bean-managed transaction demarcation.

❏ D. A stateless session bean with bean-managed transaction demarcation.

❏ E. None of the above.

55 When creating an entity bean using container-managed persistence, which can be accessed through the bean's remote component interface? (Choose all that apply.)

❏ A. Accessor methods for the relationship fields.

❏ B. The local interface of the entity bean.

❏ C. The bean's business methods.

❏ D. The collection classes used for container-managed relationships.

❏ E. Accessor methods for the persistent fields.

56 Given the container-managed, one-to-one, bidirectional relationship:

Foo   <--->   Bar

And the object relations:

f1   <--->   b1

f2   <--->   b2

Which boolean expression will be true after the following code runs:

b2.setFoo(b1.getFoo());

(Choose all that apply.)

❏ A. **f1.getBar() == null**

❏ B. **b2.getFoo() == null**

❏ C. **f2.getBar() == null**

❏ D. none of the above

57 What's true about an entity bean's identity? (Choose all that apply.)

❏ A. If two entity object references are compared using the == operator, the container provider is not required to produce consistent results.

❏ B. If two entity object references are compared using the **equals()** method, the container will return true if the two entity objects have the same primary key.

❏ C. If two entity object references are compared using the **isIdentical()** method, the container will return true if the two entity objects have the same primary key, and are from the same home.

❏ D. None of the above statements are true.

58 Given CMP beans CustomerBean, OrderBean, and LineItemsBean with the following relationships:

CustomerBean (1) <—> OrderBean (n)

OrderBean (1) <—> LineItemsBean (n)

Which will return a set of customers that have orders? (Choose all that apply.)

❏ A. SELECT Customer
FROM Order

❏ B. SELECT DISTINCT Customer
FROM Order

❏ C. SELECT o.custnum
FROM Order o, Customer c
WHERE c.custnum = o.custnum

❏ D. SELECT OBJECT (c)
FROM Customer c, Order o
WHERE c.custnum = o.custnum

❏ E. SELECT DISTINCT OBJECT (c)
FROM Customer c, Order o
WHERE c.custnum = o.custnum

59 Given:

```
Method-1 (Tx-1) -->  Method-2 (Tx-1) ---> Method-3 (Tx-1)
                \-->  Method-4 (Tx-2)
```

If the calling method is on the left side of an arrow, and the called method on the right, which set of transaction attributes will support the transaction scope specified? (Choose all that apply.)

❏ A. **M1 = Never**
   M2 = Supports
   M3 = Required
   M4 = RequiresNew

❏ B. **M1 = Required**
   M2 = Supports
   M3 = Mandatory
   M4 = RequiresNew

❏ C. **M1 = RequiresNew**
   M2 = RequiresNew
   M3 = Supports
   M4 = RequiresNew

❏ D. **M1 = Required**
   M2 = Mandatory
   M3 = Supports
   M4 = Supports

---

60 Given the EJB QL expression:

p.discount NOT BETWEEN 10 AND 15

Which expression is equivalent?

❏ A. **p.discount < 10 OR p.discount > 15**

❏ B. **p.discount <= 10 OR p.discount > 15**

❏ C. **p.discount < 10 OR p.discount >= 15**

❏ D. **p.discount <= 10 OR p.discount >= 15**

61 When a business method in an entity bean calls the **getRollbackOnly()** method, which transaction attribute settings could cause the container to throw an exception? (Choose all that apply.)

❏ A. NotSupported

❏ B. Required

❏ C. Supports

❏ D. RequiresNew

❏ E. Mandatory

❏ F. Never

62 Which of the following is performed by the container if a message-driven bean does not complete its transaction before the end of the onMessage() method? (Choose all that apply.)

❏ A. Log an application error.

❏ B. Roll back the started transaction.

❏ C. Discard the instance of the bean.

❏ D. Throw an exception.

63 From which class(es) can application exceptions extend? (Choose all that apply.)

❏ A. **java.lang.Exception**

❏ B. **java.lang.RuntimeException**

❏ C. **java.rmi.RemoteException**

❏ D. **javax.ejb.CreateException**

64 What's true about application exceptions? (Choose all that apply.)

❏ A. They are intended to be handled by the system administrator.

❏ B. They should report system level problems.

❏ C. They cause automatic marking of transactions for rollback.

❏ D. They must not extend **java.lang.RuntimeException**

❏ E. They may extend **java.rmi.RemoteException**

65 Which cases can cause a session bean instance to be destroyed without the container calling **ejbRemove()**? (Choose all that apply.)

❏ A. A transaction is rolled back on a stateful session bean with container-managed transaction demarcation.

❏ B. A system exception is thrown from a business method.

❏ C. An inactive client is timed out while the bean is in a passivated state.

❏ D. The client invokes the remove method while the bean is in a transaction.

66 Which deployment descriptor element(s) are used to specify a Collection interface? (Choose all that apply.)

❏ A. **<ejb-name>**

❏ B. **<cmr-field>**

❏ C. **<ejb-relation>**

❏ D. **<cmr-field-type>**

❏ E. **<abstract-schema-name>**

67 If a bean catches a checked exception, from which it cannot recover, what should it do? (Choose all that apply.)

❏ A. If the client is remote, throw a **java.rmi.RemoteException.**

❏ B. Print a stack trace.

❏ C. Regardless of the client, throw a **javax.ejb.EJBException**.

❏ D. Regardless of the client, propagate the same exception to the container.

68 Which are requirements for a CMP entity bean class? (Choose all that apply.)

❏ A. All **ejbSelect()** methods must be declared as abstract..

❏ B. The class must NOT define an **ejbCreate** method.

❏ C. The **ejbPostCreate** methods are implemented by the container.

❏ D. Helper methods must NOT be implemented in the bean class.

❏ E. Methods starting with '**ejbFind**' must not be implemented.

69 Which are valid deployment descriptor segment(s) to define a cmr-field? (Choose all that apply.)

❏ A. `<ejb-relationship-role>`

```
<!-- assume mandatory ejb-relationship-role elements
inserted here -->
    <cmr-field>
        <cmr-field-type>java.util.Collection</cmr-field-type>
    </cmr-field>
</ejb-relationship-role>
```

❏ B. `<ejb-relationship-role>`

```
<!-- assume mandatory ejb-relationship-role elements
inserted here -->
    <cmr-field>
        <cmr-field-name>lineItems</cmr-field-name>
        <cmr-field-type>java.util.Collection</cmr-field-type>
    </cmr-field>
<ejb-relationship-role>
```

❏ C. `<relationship-role-source>`

```
<!-- assume mandatory relationship-role-source ele-
ments inserted here -->
    <cmr-field>
        <cmr-field-type>java.util.Collection</cmr-field-type>
    </cmr-field>
</relationship-role-source>
```

❏ D. `<relationship-role-source>`

```
<!-- assume mandatory relationship-role-source ele-
ments inserted here -->
    <cmr-field>
        <cmr-field-name>lineItems</cmr-field-name>
        <cmr-field-type>java.util.Collection</cmr-field-type>
    </cmr-field>
</relationship-role-source>
```

70 What's true about a remote client's view of exceptions received from an entity bean? (Choose all that apply.)

❏ A. If the container marks a transaction for rollback, the container will always issue a **javax.transaction.TransactionRolledbackException** exception.

❏ B. If the client receives a **javax.transaction.TransactionRolledBackEx ception**, the container guarantees that that transaction will never commit.

❏ C. A **javax.transaction.TransactionRequiredException** exception, informs the client that the bean needed to be called within the context of a transaction.

❏ D. If the container discovers that a requested bean no longer exists, it will always throw the **javax.ejb.NoSuchObjectEntityException**.

Master Mock Exam Answers

(spec: 108)

1 Which are benefits of EJB 2.0? (Choose all that apply.)

☐ A. MDBs survive server crashes.

☑ B. Representations of a single entity can be shared among multiple clients.

☐ C. Support for nested transactions.

☐ D. Dynamic service discovery. — That's a Jini thing

☐ E. Declarative isolation level settings.

2 Which methods are directly invoked by the client? (Choose all that apply.)

☐ A. `ejbPassivate()` — invoked by the Container

☑ B. business methods

☐ C. `setSessionContext()`

☐ D. `newInstance()` — invoked by the Container

☑ E. `create()`

3 Which method(s) can be found in the EJBHome interface? (Choose all that apply.) (API docs)

☑ A. remove(Handle handle)

☑ B. remove(Object primaryKey)

☐ C. getHandle() — this is in EJBObject

☐ D. none of the above

4 Which method(s) can be run by a CMP bean in the pooled state? (Choose all that apply.) *(spec: 168)*

- ❑ A. `ejbLoad()`
- ☑ B. `ejbFind()` — The bean doesn't leave the pool for home and finder methods
- ❑ C. `ejbStore()`
- ❑ D. `ejbCreate()`
- ❑ E. Business method
- ☑ F. `ejbHome()`

5 What's true about message-driven beans? (Choose all that apply.) *(spec: 314, 316, 324)*

- ☑ A. All calls to a message-driven bean instance must be serialized.
- ❑ B. The container guarantees that messages will be processed in the order in which they are received.
- ❑ C. The bean's `ejbCreate()` method must take a single argument of type `javax.jms.Message`. — must have a no-arg create, onMessage takes the message as its argument
- ☑ D. The bean provider uses the deployment descriptor to indicate whether instances of the bean class are intended for topics or queues.

6 What's true about an enterprise bean's environment? (Choose all that apply.) *(spec: 412-413)*

- ❑ A. Before a bean can access its environment entries, the bean must first obtain the naming context using a `SessionContext` object.
- ❑ B. Only the bean provider can set an environment entry value. — typically set by the Deployer or Application Assembler
- ☑ C. A bean's environment entries can be stored only in `'java:comp/env'` or one of its subcontexts. — don't confuse a JNDI context and an EJBContext (like SessionContext)
- ☑ D. Every environment entry lookup in a bean's code must have a matching `<env-entry>` element in the bean's deployment descriptor. — otherwise the code would have nothing to look up!

7 What's true about security roles in EJBs? (Choose all that apply.) *(spec: 440-443)*

- ☑ A. Security roles are defined in the deployment descriptor using <security-role> elements.
- ❑ B. Security roles are scoped to the instance level
- ☑ C. Many methods can be mapped to a single security role.
- ❑ D. A method can appear in only one security role.

---

8 An EJB 2.0 container must support at least a subset of which APIs? (Choose all *(spec: 493-493)* that apply.)

☑ A. JTA 1.0.1

☑ B. JDBC 2.0

☑ C. JMS 1.0.2

❏ D. JAX-RCP 1.0

---

9 Which statements concerning stateless session beans are true? (Choose all that *(spec: 95)* apply.)

☑ A. They can use bean-managed transaction demarcation.

☑ B. They must have one no-argument create method.

❏ C. A single instance can support concurrent calls.

❏ D. They must extend javax.ejb.SessionBean – <u>implements</u> :)

---

10 What capability exists in ONLY ONE of the two (but not both)?

- an entity object's remote component interface

- an entity object's local component interface

(Choose all that apply.)

❏ A. Removing the object.

☑ B. Obtaining the object's handle.   *not for local interfaces*

❏ C. Invoking business methods.

❏ D. Obtaining the object's primary key.

---

11 When creating a CMP entity bean, which method(s) are optional? (Choose all *(spec: 171-174)* that apply.)

❏ A. `ejbLoad()`

☑ B. `ejbCreate()` *– you don't have to allow clients to insert new entities*

❏ C. `ejbRemove()`

☑ D. `ejbSelect()`

❏ E. `ejbPassivate()`

❏ F. `setEntityContext()`

12 Which method(s) can be called on a bean in the pooled state? (Choose all that apply.)   *(spec: 168)*

☑ A. `ejbFind()`

☐ B. `ejbLoad()`

☐ C. `ejbStore()`

☑ D. `ejbSelect()`

☐ E. `ejbPassivate()`

finder and select methods aren't specific to one entity

13 What's true about the lifecycle of a message-driven bean? (Choose all that apply.)   *(spec: 318-320)*

☐ A. When the the **onMessage** method completes, the container will typically call ejbRemove.   *— bean just goes back to the pool*

☐ B. The **onMessage()** method can throw application exceptions.   *— to whom ?*

☐ C. Message-driven beans can run only with CMT demarcation.

☑ D. The **getRollbackOnly()** method can be called only from the onMessage method.

14 Which statement(s) concerning message-driven bean classes are true?   *(spec: 323)* (Choose all that apply.)

☐ A. They must implement, directly or indirectly, **javax.jms.Message**.   *— it's MessageListener*

☐ B. They must have a public constructor that takes a single argument of type **javax.jms.Message**.

☐ C. Implementing the **finalize()** method is allowed.   *—No! not in any bean*

☐ D. Implementing the **ejbCreate()** method is optional.

☑ E. The class must not be declared 'final'.   *— the Container might want to deploy a subclass of your bean*

15 Within the deployment descriptor's **<ejb-local-ref>** element, which elements are optional? (Choose all that apply.)   *(spec: 466)*

☐ A. `<local>`

☑ B. `<ejb-link>`

☐ C. `<local-home>`

☑ D. `<description>`

☐ E. `<ejb-ref-name>`

☐ F. `<ejb-ref-type>`

16 What's true about resource manager connection factories? (Choose all that apply.) *(spec: 423, 481)*

☑ The **<res-sharing-scope>** deployment descriptor element is used to indicate whether connections to a resource manager are shareable across multiple EJBs in an application.

❏ B. The **<res-sharing-scope>** deployment descriptor element contains the **<resource-ref>** element. — *backwards*

❏ C. All of a bean's resource manager connection factory references are declared in a single **<resource-ref>** element, using **<res-ref-name>** elements to distinguish them. — *each must be individually specified with a <resource-ref>*

☑ D. By default, connections to a given resource manager are shareable across multiple beans in an application.

17 What's true about security roles referenced from an EJB's code? (Choose all that apply.) *(spec: 439–441, 446)*

☑ A. In the deployment descriptor, such references are contained in the **<security-role-ref>** element.

❏ B. The **<security-role>** element includes the **<security-role-ref>** element.

☑ C. Within the **<security-role-ref>** element, the **<role-name>** element's value is the same as the argument for the bean's invocation of the **isCallerInRole** method. — *this is NOT the same as a real <security-role> role name*

❏ D. The **<role-link>** element is used to link two **<security-role-ref>** elements. — *no, it links a <security-role-ref> to a <security-role>*

18 What's true about the client's view of security? (Choose all that apply.) *(spec: 450)*

☑ A. A transactional client cannot change its principal association within a transaction.

☑ B. A session bean's client cannot change its principal association for the duration of the communication with the session object.

❏ C. Transactional requests within a single transaction cannot arrive from multiple clients.

❏ D. None of the above.

19 When programming an entity bean class which technique(s) should be AVOIDED to ensure bean portability across all EJB 2.0 containers? (Choose all that apply.)

(spec: 494–495)

☑ A. Changing a thread's priority.

☑ B. Using the reflection API.

☐ C. Using wrapper classes.

☐ D. Using static nested classes.

20 When programming a message-driven bean class which technique(s) should be avoided to ensure bean portability across all EJB 2.0 containers? (Choose all that apply.)

(spec: 494–495)

☑ A. Using Swing APIs for a GUI.

☐ B. Using the 'transient' modifier.

☑ C. Using native libraries.

☑ D. Reading file descriptors..

21 What is required of the container when it passivates a stateful session bean?

(spec: 71)

☐ A. The bean's instance state will always undergo Java programming language Serialization. *– it might be something similar*

☐ B. It must save all of the bean's instance field state regardless of the fields' modifiers.

☑ C. It must save any references to the bean's SessionContext object.

☐ D. It must save all non-null transient variables. *– no, it won't save transient variables, but it might not reset them to default values...*

22 Which capabilities are defined in the **javax.ejb.EJBLocalObject** interface? (Choose all that apply.)?

☑ A. Remove an entity object.

☑ B. Obtain an entity object's primary key.

☑ C. Obtain a local home interface for the entity object.

☐ D. Obtain a remote component interface for the entity object.

☐ E. Expose the methods of the **javax.ejb.EntityBean** interface to the client.

23 What's true about ejbSelect methods? (Choose all that apply.)   (spec: 183)

❏ A. They can be exposed to the client.

❏ B. They can return only EJBObjects or EJBLocalObjects. – They can return almost anything

❏ C. They can be invoked only by a bean in the ready state. – No, they're good for home biz methods

☑ D. They must be associated with a query element in the deployment descriptor.

---

24 Which methods can NEVER be successfully invoked from a message-driven bean? (Choose all that apply.)   (spec: 320-321)

☑ A. `isCallerInRole()`

☑ B. `getEJBHome()`

❏ C. `getRollbackOnly()`

❏ D. `setRollbackOnly()`

☑ E. `getCallerPrincipal()`

MDBs have no client view, so they have no home or client security information

---

25 Which role is typically responsible for adding <ejb-link> elements to an EJB's deployment descriptor?   (spec: 418)

❏ A. bean provider

☑ B. application assembler – linking one bean that refers to another

❏ C. deployer

❏ D. container provider

❏ E. system administrator

---

26 In which of the following methods can a stateless session bean invoke the `isCallerInRole()` method in order to perform a security check? (Choose all that apply.)   (spec: 90)

❏ A. `ejbCreate()`

❏ B. `ejbRemove()`

❏ C. `setSessionContext()`

☑ D. None of the above

– isCallerInRole() can be called from business methods only

27 Which two are typically responsible for creating ejb-jar files? (Choose two.)   (spec: 487)

- ☑ A. The bean provider.
- ☑ B. The application assembler.
- ☐ C. The deployer.
- ☐ D. The system administrator.

28 Which of the following stateless session bean container callback method(s) takes an argument? (Choose all that apply.)   (spec: 77)

- ☐ A. `ejbRemove`
- ☐ B. `ejbCreate`
- ☐ C. `ejbCreate`
- ☐ D. `ejbPassivate`
- ☑ E. `setSessionContext` — *takes a SessionContext object*

29 Which of these can never be called on a SessionContext interface? (Choose all that apply.)   (spec: 74)

- ☐ A. `getEJBHome()`
- ☐ B. `getEJBObject()`
- ☑ C. `getEJBTransaction()` — *no such method :)*
- ☐ D. `isCallerInRole()`
- ☐ E. `getUserTransaction()`

30 What's true about an entity bean's remote component interface? (Choose all that apply.)   (spec: 190)

- ☐ A. If a client attempts to invoke a method on an entity that does not exist, a `java.rmi.NoSuchRemoteObjectException` will be thrown. — *it's NoSuchObjectException*
- ☐ B. It must extend `javax.ejb.EJBHome` — *it's EJBObject*
- ☑ C. Its methods must declare `java.rmi.RemoteException`
- ☐ D. It defines a `remove(Handle handle)` method. — *This is only in the home*

31   Which are true about finder methods in an entity bean's local home interface? (Choose all that apply.)

(spec: 196)

- ❏ A. They can have any legal Java name. – must start with "find"
- ☑ B. They must all declare `javax.ejb.FinderException`.
- ❏ C. They can optionally declare `java.rmi.RemoteException`. – not in a local interface!
- ❏ D. The **findByPrimaryKey** method can be overloaded.
- ☑ E. The **findByPrimaryKey** method's return type must be the bean's local component interface.
- ❏ F. A method called "findXXX" must have the bean's local component interface as its declared return type. – it could also be a Collection

32   Which are true for a message-driven bean? (Choose all that apply.)

(spec: 324–325, 317)

- ☑ A. The Deployer uses the deployment descriptor to determine whether a bean is intended for a Queue or a Topic.
- ❏ B. The class must be declared final.
- ☑ C. The class must define one **ejbRemove**() method.
- ❏ D. The class can have overloaded **ejbCreate()** methods. – there's no client
- ❏ E. The class must define a no-argument onMessage method. – onMessage takes a message

33   Given the following subset of a deployment descriptor:

```
<entity>
  <ejb-name>Payroll</ejb-name>
  <security-role-ref>
        <role-name>clerk</role-name>
   </security-role-ref>
</entity>
```

(spec: 440)

Which code snippet(s) makes a legal security check? (Choose all that apply.)

- ❏ A. `context.isCallerInRole("Payroll");`
- ☑ B. `context.isCallerInRole("clerk");`
- ❏ C. `context.isCallerInRole("Payroll.clerk");`
- ❏ D. `context.isCallerInRole("Payroll/clerk");`

34 Which are valid local home interfaces for a stateful session bean? (Choose all that apply.) *(spec: 98)*

❏ A. `public interface TestBean implements`
   `javax.ejb.EJBLocalHome {`

`void create() throws CreateException;`

   `}`

❏ B. `public interface TestBean extends`
   `javax.ejb.EJBLocalHome {`

`TestBeanLocal ejbCreate() throws CreateException;`

   `}`

☑ C. `public interface TestBean extends`
   `javax.ejb.EJBLocalHome {`

        `TestBeanLocal create() throws CreateException;`

   `}`

❏ D. `public interface TestBean extends`
   `javax.ejb.EJBLocalHome {`

`TestBeanLocal create() throws CreateException,`
   `RemoteException;`

   `}`

❏ E. `public interface TestBean extends`
   `javax.ejb.EJBLocalHome {`

`TestBeanLocal create() throws LocalException;`

   `}`

Must:
  – throw CreateException
  – return local interface type
  – start with "create"
  – NOT throw RemoteException

35 Which methods can be called by a bean provider? (Choose all that apply.)

☑ A. `remove()` – *the callback is ejbRemove*

❏ B. `ejbCreate()`

❏ C. `afterBegin()`

☑ D. `getCallerPrincipal()`

❏ E. `ejbPassivate()`

The others are Container callbacks

36 Who will typically specify whether a bean is re-entrant in the bean's deployment descriptor?

(spec: 457)

- ☑ A. The bean provider.
- ❏ B. The application assembler.
- ❏ C. The deployer.
- ❏ D. The system administrator.

37 Which statements about stateful and stateless session beans are true?

(Choose all that apply.)

- ❏ A. Only stateful session beans support transactions.
- ☑ B. Only stateful session beans can be passivated.
- ❏ C. Only stateful session beans have a '**setSessionContext**' method.
- ❏ D. Both stateful and stateless session beans can support overloaded '**ejbCreate**' methods. *— stateless must have a single, no-arg ejbCreate*
- ❏ E. Both stateful and stateless session beans can implement the *— only stateful* **javax.ejb.SessionSynchronization** interface.
- ☑ F. Both stateful and stateless session beans can have instance variable state. *— stateless can have state, just not client-specific state*

38 Which must be included in every ejb-jar file? (Choose all that apply.) *(spec: 488-490)*

- ❏ A. The stub for the EJBHome interface, either directly or by reference.
- ❏ B. The JAR Manifest file. *— not needed as of EJB 2.0*
- ☑ C. A deployment descriptor. *— This is the Container's job*
- ❏ D. The JNDI context.
- ☑ E. The EJB's home interface, either directly or by reference.

39 Which method(s) are declared in the javax.ejb.EJBHome interface? (Choose all that apply.) *(API docs)*

- ❏ A. **create()**
- ❏ B. **lookup()**
- ❏ C. **getHandle()**
- ☑ D. **getHomeHandle()**
- ❏ E. **setSessionContext()**

40 How many javax.ejb.EJBLocalHome interface methods can be called without an exception, from a session bean client?   *(spec: 60)*

☑ A. 0

❏ B. 1   *The only method in EJBLocalHome is remove that takes a primary key*

❏ C. 2

❏ D. 3

❏ E. 4

41 Which of the following, if called, always have the same transaction context as a session bean's business methods? (Choose all that apply.)   *(spec: 76)*

❏ A. constructor

❏ B. `setSessionContext()`

☑ C. `afterBegin()`

❏ D. `afterCompletion()` — *transaction is over*

☑ E. `beforeCompletion()`

42 Given a stateful session bean with container-managed transaction demarcation, from which methods can you access another bean? (Choose all that apply.)   *(spec: 80)*

❏ A. `setSessionContext()`

☑ B. `ejbCreate()`

☑ C. `afterBegin()`   *setSessionContext and afterCompletion have NO meaningful tx context*

☑ D. `beforeCompletion()`

❏ E. `afterCompletion()`

43 Which deployment descriptor element(s) can optionally specify cascade-delete functionality? (Choose all that apply.)   *(spec: 468)*

❏ A. `<ejb-relation>`

❏ B. `<abstract-schema-name>`

☑ C. `<ejb-relationship-role>`

❏ D. `<relationship-role-source>`

44 What's true about cascade-delete? (Choose all that apply.)   *(spec: 133)*

   ❏ A. It is declared in the **ejbRemove()** method.

   ❏ B. When a cascade-delete enabled bean is deleted, it causes all of the   *– cascade-delete says "delete* beans with relationships to it to be automatically deleted too.   *ME if my partner is removed"*

   ❏ C. It can be specified for one-to-one, one-to-many, or many-to-many rela*not for many-to-many* tionships.

   ☑ D. A cascade-delete enabled bean is automatically removed when any "multiplicity of one" bean with which it is related is removed.

---

45 Which method(s) from the EntityContext interface can be invoked, regardless   *(spec: 180)* of transaction context? (Choose all that apply.)

   ☑ A. **getEJBHome()**

   ☑ B. **getEJBObject()**

   ❏ C. **setRollbackOnly()**

   ❏ D. **getRollbackOnly()**

---

46 What's true about an entity bean's primary key? (Choose all that apply.)   *(spec: 120, 130)*

   ☑ A. Primary key fields must be cmp-fields.

   ☑ B. Setter methods for fields associated with a primary key must not be exposed through a client view.

   ☑ C. If two entity objects have the same home and the same primary key, they are considered identical.

   ❏ D. The **getPrimaryKey()** method can be invoked on references to only remote home interfaces, not local home interfaces.

---

47 Which interface(s) are used by the bean provider to perform BMT demarca-   *(spec: 332)* tion? (Choose all that apply.)

   ❏ A. **javax.transaction.Transaction**

   ☑ B. **javax.transaction.UserTransaction**

   ❏ C. **javax.transaction.Synchronization**

   ❏ D. **javax.transaction.TransactionManager**

48 Which of the following are legal EJB QL queries? (Choose all that apply.) *(spec: 236)*

❏ A. SELECT c   *—needs Object (c) or a path*

FROM Customer c

❏ B. SELECT (OBJECT) c.name   *— Just all wrong! must be OBJECT(c) or*

FROM Customer c   *c.name (see answers D and E)*

❏ C. SELECT OBJECT c   *— must have a FROM, and (c)*

WHERE Customer c

☑ D. SELECT OBJECT (c)

FROM Customer c

☑ E. SELECT c.name

FROM Customer c

49 Which are true about transactions in EJB 2.0? (Choose all that apply.) *(spec: 339, 348)*

❏ A. Only one database can be updated within a single transaction.   *— This would eliminate a key EJB 2.0 feature of distributed transactions*

❏ B. Beans with BMT demarcation must use the setStatus method instead of the **setRollbackOnly** method.

☑ C. Beans with BMT demarcation must use the getStatus method instead of the **getRollbackOnly** method.

❏ D. BMT demarcation should be used when beans access resource managers that do not support transactions.   *— use CMT with "NotSupported"*

☑ E. The 'SessionSynchronization' interface can be used only by stateful session beans.

50 To ensure bean portability, which transaction attributes should be used on the business methods in the component interface of an entity bean using CMP? (Choose all that apply.)   *(spec: 352)*

❏ A. NotSupported

☑ B. Required

❏ C. Supports

☑ D. RequiresNew

☑ E. Mandatory

❏ F. Never

51 Which of the following exceptions would cause a bean to be discarded by the container? (Choose all that apply.)

(spec: 372–374)

- ❏ A. `javax.ejb.ObjectNotFoundException`
- ❏ B. `javax.ejb.CreateException`
- ☑ C. `javax.ejb.NoSuchEntityException`
- ❏ D. `javax.ejb.FinderException`
- ❏ E. `javax.ejb.RemoveException`

The others are recoverable application exceptions

52 In which cases should the container log an exception thrown by a business method of a CMT demarcated bean? (Choose all that apply.)

(spec: 376)

- ☑ A. If the method runs with an unspecified transaction context and throws a system exception.
- ❏ B. If the method runs with an unspecified transaction context and throws an application exception.
- ☑ C. If the method runs with a RequiresNew context and throws a system exception.
- ☑ D. If the method runs with a Required context and throws a system exception.
- ❏ E. If the method runs with a RequiresNew context and throws an application exception.
- ❏ F. If the method runs with a Required context and throws an application exception.

– system exceptions are always logged

53 Which session bean component interface method(s) can be called successfully, by a local client? (Choose all that apply.)

- ☑ A. `remove()`
- ❏ B. `getHandle()` *– local client views don't have handles*
- ☑ C. `isIdentical()`
- ❏ D. `getEJBHome()` *– should be getEJBLocalHome()*

54 In what scenario(s) can a bean's business method call the **isCallerInRole()** method of the SessionContext interface? (Choose all that apply.)

Transaction demarcation doesn't matter here

- ☑ A. A stateful session bean with container-managed transaction demarcation.
- ☑ B. A stateless session bean with container-managed transaction demarcation.
- ☑ C. A stateful session bean with bean-managed transaction demarcation.
- ☑ D. A stateless session bean with bean-managed transaction demarcation.
- ☐ E. None of the above.

(spec: 130)

55 When creating an entity bean using container-managed persistence, which can be accessed through the bean's remote component interface? (Choose all that apply.)

- ☐ A. Accessor methods for the relationship fields.
- ☐ B. The local interface of the entity bean.
- ☑ C. The bean's business methods.
- ☐ D. The collection classes used for container-managed relationships.
- ☑ E. Accessor methods for the persistent fields. *— legal, just not a good idea...*

(spec: 138)

56 Given the container-managed, one-to-one, bidirectional relationship:

```
Foo   <--->  Bar
```

And the object relations:

```
f1  <--->  b1
f2  <--->  b2
```

Which boolean expression will be true after the following code runs:

```
b2.setFoo(b1.getFoo());
```

(Choose all that apply.)

When b2 took b1's Foo, he replaced his own foo2 with foo1. So now, foo2 has no bar.

- ☐ A. **f1.getBar() == null**
- ☐ B. **b2.getFoo() == null**
- ☑ C. **f2.getBar() == null**
- ☐ D. none of the above

57 What's true about an entity bean's identity? (Choose all that apply.)   *(spec: 121)*

✓ ☑ A. If two entity object references are compared using the == operator, the
container provider is not required to produce consistent results.

☐ B. If two entity object references are compared using the **equals()**
method, the container will return true if the two entity objects have the
same primary key.   *— not guaranteed*

✓ ☑ C. If two entity object references are compared using the **isIdentical()**
method, the container will return true if the two entity objects have the
same primary key, and are from the same home.

☐ D. None of the above statements are true.

58 Given CMP beans CustomerBean, OrderBean, and LineItemsBean with the   *(spec: 232)*
following relationships:

CustomerBean (1) <—> OrderBean (n)

OrderBean (1) <—> LineItemsBean (n)

Which will return a **set** of customers that have orders? (Choose all that apply.)

☐ A. SELECT Customer   *— need OBJECT or path*
FROM Order

☐ B. SELECT DISTINCT Customer   *— need OBJECT or path*
FROM Order

☐ C. SELECT o.custnum
FROM Order o, Customer c   *— not a Customer type*
WHERE c.custnum = o.custnum

☐ D. SELECT OBJECT (c)   *— doesn't guarantee you won't*
FROM Customer c, Order o   *get duplicates*
WHERE c.custnum = o.custnum

✓ ☑ E. SELECT DISTINCT OBJECT (c)
FROM Customer c, Order o
WHERE c.custnum = o.custnum

59 Given:

(spec: 357–359)

```
Method-1 (Tx-1) -->  Method-2 (Tx-1) ---> Method-3 (Tx-1)
                \-->  Method-4 (Tx-2)
```

If the calling method is on the left side of an arrow, and the called method on the right, which set of transaction attributes will support the transaction scope specified? (Choose all that apply.)

❑ A. **M1 = Never**
    M2 = Supports
    M3 = Required
    M4 = RequiresNew

— Never means... NEVER. Method I could not be in a transaction if its transaction attribute was Never

☑ B. **M1 = Required**
    M2 = Supports
    M3 = Mandatory
    M4 = RequiresNew

❑ C. **M1 = RequiresNew**
    M2 = RequiresNew
    M3 = Supports
    M4 = RequiresNew

— method 2 is running in method I's transaction, but if it had RequiresNew, it would be a new transaction

❑ D. **M1 = Required**
    M2 = Mandatory
    M3 = Supports
    M4 = Supports

— method 4 starts a new transaction, so it obviously does not have Supports as an attribute

---

(spec: 229)

60 Given the EJB QL expression:

p.discount NOT BETWEEN 10 AND 15 — 10 and 15 are EXCLUDED

Which expression is equivalent?

☑ A. **p.discount < 10 OR p.discount > 15**

❑ B. **p.discount <= 10 OR p.discount > 15**

❑ C. **p.discount < 10 OR p.discount >= 15**

❑ D. **p.discount <= 10 OR p.discount >= 15**

61 When a business method in an entity bean calls the **getRollbackOnly()** *(spec: 361)* method, which transaction attribute settings could cause the container to throw an exception? (Choose all that apply.)

- ☑ A. NotSupported
- ☐ B. Required
- ☑ C. Supports — *because there might not be one*
- ☐ D. RequiresNew
- ☐ E. Mandatory
- ☑ F. Never

---

62 Which of the following is performed by the container if a message-driven bean *(spec: 356)* does not complete its transaction before the end of the onMessage() method? (Choose all that apply.)

- ☑ A. Log an application error.
- ☑ B. Roll back the started transaction.
- ☑ C. Discard the instance of the bean.
- ☐ D. Throw an exception. — *to whom?*

---

63 From which class(es) can application exceptions extend? (Choose all that ap- *(spec: 373)* ply.)

- ☑ A. `java.lang.Exception`
- ☐ B. `java.lang.RuntimeException` — *they must be checked*
- ☐ C. `java.rmi.RemoteException` — *you just can't do this, even though it IS a checked exception... it's Bean Law*
- ☑ D. `javax.ejb.CreateException`

---

64 What's true about application exceptions? (Choose all that apply.)   *(spec: 372–373)*

- ☐ A. They are intended to be handled by the system administrator.
- ☐ B. They should report system level problems.   *They are intended to be handled by the client*
- ☐ C. They cause automatic marking of transactions for rollback.
- ☑ D. They must not extend `java.lang.RuntimeException`
- ☐ E. They may extend `java.rmi.RemoteException` — *NO*

65 Which cases can cause a session bean instance to be destroyed without the container calling **ejbRemove()**? (Choose all that apply.) *(spec: 79)*

   ❏ A. A transaction is rolled back on a stateful session bean with container-managed transaction demarcation.

   ✓ B. A system exception is thrown from a business method.

   ✓ C. An inactive client is timed out while the bean is in a passivated state.

   ❏ D. The client invokes the remove method while the bean is in a transaction.   — *client gets exception, bean survives*

66 Which deployment descriptor element(s) are used to specify a Collection interface? (Choose all that apply.) *(spec: 462)*

   ❏ A. **<ejb-name>**

   ❏ B. **<cmr-field>**

   ❏ C. **<ejb-relation>**

   ✓ D. **<cmr-field-type>**   — *for "many" multiplicity, to indicate Set or Collection*

   ❏ E. **<abstract-schema-name>**

67 If a bean catches a checked exception, from which it cannot recover, what should it do? (Choose all that apply.) *(spec: 373)*

   ❏ A. If the client is remote, throw a **java.rmi.RemoteException**. — *a bean must NEVER throw RemoteException. Only the Container can do it.*

   ❏ B. Print a stack trace.

   ✓ C. Regardless of the client, throw a **javax.ejb.EJBException**.

   ❏ D. Regardless of the client, propagate the same exception to the container.

68 Which are requirements for a CMP entity bean class? (Choose all that apply.) *(spec: 190–191)*

   ✓ A. All **ejbSelect()** methods must be declared as abstract..

   ❏ B. The class must NOT define an **ejbCreate** method.

   ❏ C. The **ejbPostCreate** methods are implemented by the container.

   ❏ D. Helper methods must NOT be implemented in the bean class.

   ✓ E. Methods starting with '**ejbFind**' must not be implemented.

69 Which are valid deployment descriptor segment(s) to define a cmr-field? (Choose all that apply.)

(spec: 162, 463)

☐ A.

```
<ejb-relationship-role>

    <!-- assume mandatory ejb-relationship-role elements
    inserted here -->

        <cmr-field>

            <cmr-field-type>java.util.Collection</cmr-field-type>

        </cmr-field>

</ejb-relationship-role>
```

—missing field name

☑ B.

```
<ejb-relationship-role>

    <!-- assume mandatory ejb-relationship-role elements
    inserted here -->

        <cmr-field>

            <cmr-field-name>lineItems</cmr-field-name>

            <cmr-field-type>java.util.Collection</cmr-field-type>

        </cmr-field>

    <ejb-relationship-role>
```

☐ C.

```
<relationship-role-source>

    <!-- assume mandatory relationship-role-source ele-
    ments inserted here -->

        <cmr-field>

            <cmr-field-type>java.util.Collection</cmr-field-type>

        </cmr-field>

</relationship-role-source>
```

— missing name, and in role source, as opposed to role

☐ D.

```
<relationship-role-source>

    <!-- assume mandatory relationship-role-source ele-
    ments inserted here -->

        <cmr-field>

            <cmr-field-name>lineItems</cmr-field-name>

            <cmr-field-type>java.util.Collection</cmr-field-type>

        </cmr-field>

</relationship-role-source>
```

—can't be in a role source

70 What's true about a remote client's view of exceptions received from an entity bean? (Choose all that apply.)

(spec: 383)

❏ A. If the container marks a transaction for rollback, the container will always issue a **javax.transaction.TransactionRolledbackExce ption** exception.

— only if the caller's transaction was rolled back (as opposed to suspended)

☑ B. If the client receives a **javax.transaction.TransactionRolled BackException**, the container guarantees that that transaction will never commit.

☑ C. A **javax.transaction.TransactionRequiredException** exception, informs the client that the bean needed to be called within the context of a transaction.

— happens with the Mandatory tx attribute

❏ D. If the container discovers that a requested bean no longer exists, it will always throw the **javax.ejb.NoSuchObjectEntityException**.

— java.rmi.NoSuchObjectException

This isn't goodbye

**Bring your brain over to
wickedlysmart.com**

**And don't forget to write and tell us
when you pass the exam!**

Ikickedbutt@wickedlysmart.com
We'll have a drink in your honor.

Don't you know there's more on the wickedlysmart.com website? You'll find some code, some more mock exam questions, and maybe even our favorite martini recipe.
And if you're going to take the exam be sure to drop by javaranch.com and spend some time in the SCBCD study forum. Folks there are just so damn friendly it'll make you want to throw up.

Cover Rough Drafts for the series

It was a tough decision.
Before we finally settled on:

...we kicked around
a lot of promising
candidates...

1 We were thinking this might play up the whole hands-on approach... what do you think? —K & B

well since it's brain-based, why don't we emphasize the HEAD and call it Head First? —marketing

2 Hey, is this what you had in mind by "emphasize the Head?" —K & B

[um, no. —marketing]

4 Yes I KNOW this one is more festive, but what the #%^@! does it mean? PLEASE leave this to the professionals. —marketing

3 Wasn't this the one we agreed on last week? —K & B

Index

Symbols

C

F

G

H

I

N

O

P

Q

R

S

T

V

W

U

Interface summary

javax.ejb.EJBContext

getCallerPrincipal()
getEJBHome()
getEJBLocalHome()
getRollbackOnly()
getUserTransaction()
isCallerInRole(String role)
setRollbackOnly()

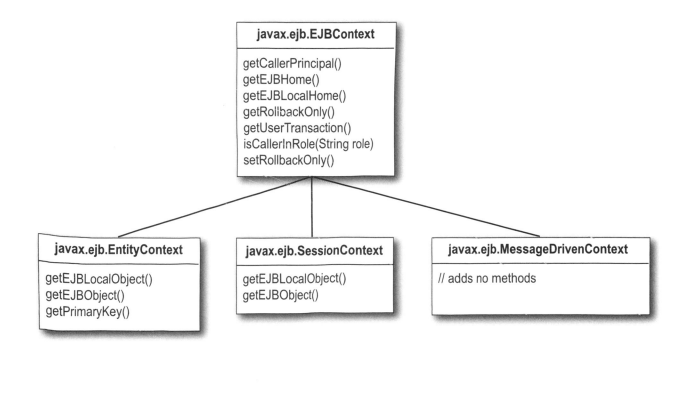

javax.ejb.EntityContext

getEJBLocalObject()
getEJBObject()
getPrimaryKey()

javax.ejb.SessionContext

getEJBLocalObject()
getEJBObject()

javax.ejb.MessageDrivenContext

// adds no methods

java.rmi.Remote

// no methods declared

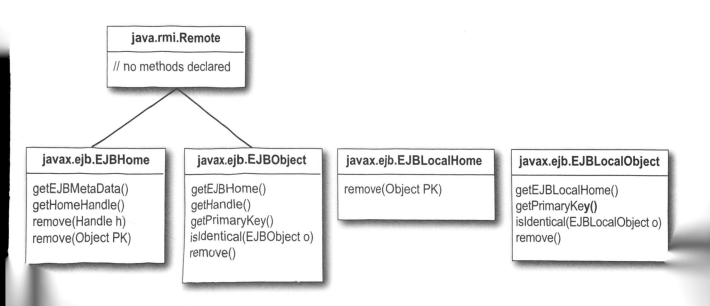

javax.ejb.EJBHome

getEJBMetaData()
getHomeHandle()
remove(Handle h)
remove(Object PK)

javax.ejb.EJBObject

getEJBHome()
getHandle()
getPrimaryKey()
isIdentical(EJBObject o)
remove()

javax.ejb.EJBLocalHome

remove(Object PK)

javax.ejb.EJBLocalObject

getEJBLocalHome()
getPrimaryKey()
isIdentical(EJBLocalObject o)
remove()

Interface summary

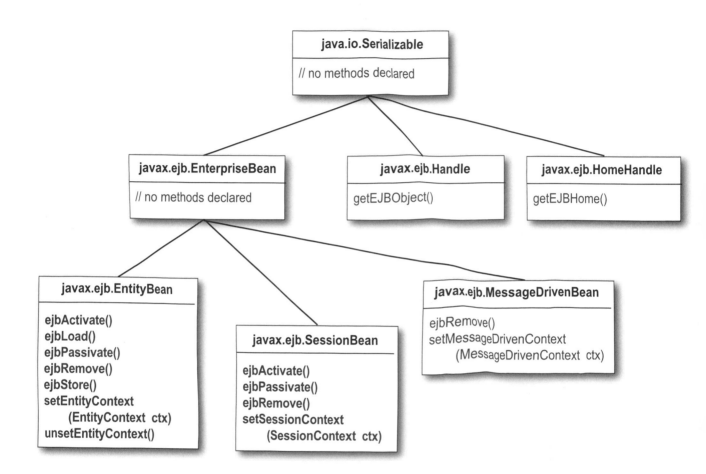

Interface summary

javax.ejb.SessionSynchronization
afterBegin() afterCompletion(boolean committed) beforeCompletion()

javax.transaction.UserTransaction
begin() commit() getStatus() rollback() setRollbackOnly() setTransactionTimeout(int seconds)

javax.jms.MessageListener
onMessage(Message message)

setTransactionTimeout() is not on the exam...
it lets you tune the elapsed time before the
Container decided the transaction has timed
out, and automatically rolls it back.

Related Titles Available from O'Reilly

Java

Ant: The Definitive Guide
Eclipse: A Java Developer's Guide
Enterprise JavaBeans, *3rd Edition*
Hardcore Java
Head First Servlets & JSP
J2EE Design Patterns
Java and SOAP
Java & XML Data Binding
Java & XML
Java Cookbook
Java Data Objects
Java Database Best Practices
Java Enterprise Best Practices
Java Enterprise in a Nutshell, *2nd Edition*
Java Examples in a Nutshell, *3rd Edition*
Java Extreme Programming Cookbook
Java in a Nutshell, *4th Edition*
Java Management Extensions
Java Message Service
Java Network Programming, *2nd Edition*
Java NIO
Java Performance Tuning, *2nd Edition*
Java RMI
Java Security, *2nd Edition*
Java ServerPages, *2nd Edition*
Java Serlet & JSP Cookbook
Java Servlet Programming, *2nd Edition*
Java Swing, *2nd Edition*
Java Web Services in a Nutshell
Learning Java, *2nd Edition*
Mac OS X for Java Geeks
NetBeans: The Definitive Guide
Programming Jakarta Struts
Tomcat: The Definitive Guide
WebLogic: The Definitive Guide

O'REILLY®

Our books are available at most retail and online bookstores.
To order direct: 1-800-998-9938 • *order@oreilly.com* • *www.oreilly.com*
Online editions of most O'Reilly titles are available by subscription at *safari.oreilly.com*

Keep in touch with O'Reilly

1. Download examples from our books

To find example files for a book, go to:

www.oreilly.com/catalog

select the book, and follow the "Examples" link.

2. Register your O'Reilly books

Register your book at *register.oreilly.com*

Why register your books?
Once you've registered your O'Reilly books you can:

- Win O'Reilly books, T-shirts or discount coupons in our monthly drawing.
- Get special offers available only to registered O'Reilly customers.
- Get catalogs announcing new books (US and UK only).
- Get email notification of new editions of the O'Reilly books you own.

3. Join our email lists

Sign up to get topic-specific email announcements of new books and conferences, special offers, and O'Reilly Network technology newsletters at:

elists.oreilly.com

It's easy to customize your free elists subscription so you'll get exactly the O'Reilly news you want.

4. Get the latest news, tips, and tools

www.oreilly.com

- "Top 100 Sites on the Web"—PC Magazine
- CIO Magazine's Web Business 50 Awards

Our web site contains a library of comprehensive product information (including book excerpts and tables of contents), downloadable software, background articles, interviews with technology leaders, links to relevant sites, book cover art, and more.

5. Work for O'Reilly

Check out our web site for current employment opportunities:

jobs.oreilly.com

6. Contact us

O'Reilly & Associates, Inc.
1005 Gravenstein Hwy North
Sebastopol, CA 95472 USA

TEL: 707-827-7000 or 800-998-9938
(6am to 5pm PST)

FAX: 707-829-0104

order@oreilly.com
For answers to problems regarding your order or our products. To place a book order online, visit:

www.oreilly.com/order_new

catalog@oreilly.com
To request a copy of our latest catalog.

booktech@oreilly.com
For book content technical questions or corrections.

corporate@oreilly.com
For educational, library, government, and corporate sales.

proposals@oreilly.com
To submit new book proposals to our editors and product managers.

international@oreilly.com
For information about our international distributors or translation queries. For a list of our distributors outside of North America check out:

international.oreilly.com/distributors.html

adoption@oreilly.com
For information about academic use of O'Reilly books, visit:

academic.oreilly.com